An Encyclopedia
of the History of
Classical Archaeology

An Encyclopedia
of the History
# of Classical Archaeology

Edited by
Nancy Thomson de Grummond

L–Z

GREENWOOD PRESS
Westport, Connecticut

Library of Congress Cataloging-in-Publication Data

An encyclopedia of the history of classical archaeology / edited by
   Nancy Thomson de Grummond.
        p.   cm.
     Includes bibliographical references and index.
     ISBN 0–313–22066–2 (alk. paper : set). — ISBN 0–313–30204–9
   (alk. paper : A–K). —ISBN 0–313–30205–7 (alk. paper : L–Z)
        1. Classical antiquities—Encyclopedias.   2. Art, Classical—
   Encyclopedias.   3. Architecture, Classical—Encyclopedias.
   4. Excavations (Archaeology)—Mediterranean Region—Encyclopedias.
   5. Archaeology and history—Mediterranean Region—Encyclopedias.
   I. De Grummond, Nancy Thomson.
   DE5.E5   1996
   938'.003—dc20   94–29838

British Library Cataloguing in Publication Data is available.

Library of Congress Catalog Card Number: 94–29838
ISBN: 0–313–22066–2 (set)
         0–313–30204–9 (A–K)
         0–313–30205–7 (L–Z)

First published in 1996

Greenwood Press, 88 Post Road West, Westport, CT 06881
An imprint of Greenwood Publishing Group, Inc.

Printed in the United States of America

The paper used in this book complies with the
Permanent Paper Standard issued by the National
Information Standards Organization (Z39.48–1984).

10   9   8   7   6   5   4   3   2   1

In memory of
Louise Ponder Thomson (1913–1994)
and
Alfred Valerie Thomson (1913–1993)

Contents

Preface

> I entered upon it, as one does on a country newly discovered; without any paths made and generally much embarrassed. Had any work of this kind been published . . . I certainly could have made this much more perfect, with extremely less pains; whereas all I can beg for it now is, that the difficulty of making one's way almost everywhere, may be duly considered; and that the many imperfections and errors which that must occasion, may meet with the indulgence that the case deserves.
>
> —J. Spence, Introduction to *Polymetis* (1747)

Since this is the first time an encyclopedia of the history of classical archaeology has been prepared, it is appropriate to begin by describing the scope and methodology of the work. It is necessary to explain first what is understood by "classical archaeology." The expression is used here to mean basically the study of the visual remains of the ancient classical lands, Greece and Italy. Greek and Roman material is central; but also included here are the prehistoric or proto-historical cultures of the Bronze Age Aegean and of the Etruscans, which have a relationship of continuity and overlapping with the succeeding cultures in Greece and Italy, respectively, and the study of which is often inseparable from the historical Greek and Roman periods. Also included are manifestations of these cultures outside Italy and Greece proper; in France, for example, Roman arches, amphitheaters and aqueducts that were known, reused, admired and studied are of significance for the history of the study of classical remains. Greek temples and sites in Asia Minor were noted from the fifteenth century, and the story of their systematic recovery and study in the nineteenth century constitutes an important chapter in the history of archaeology. But other related archaeological spheres—Egyptian, Near Eastern, Phoenician, Celtic, Scythian, and New World—are referred to only in passing, for to treat these fully would have meant to write a very different book.

As for the word "archaeology," some today apply the term only to the rigorously systematic and scientific aspects of the discipline that have grown up in connection with purposeful excavation in the field. A book like Glyn Daniel's *A Short History of Archaeology* (1981) is based on the idea that archaeology is properly the science of excavating and interpreting excavated evidence and that it reaches its greatest purity when the study is completely prehistoric; inscriptions and literary traditions are considered far less relevant for the discipline. Advocates of this approach have given little attention to those who studied antiquities prior to the advent of scientific fieldwork. Bruce Trigger's recent work, *A History of Archaeological Thought* (1989), shows an awareness of scholarly study of classical remains prior to the nineteenth century but allots a quite small amount of space to early classical archaeologists. For a just survey, one must go back more than one hundred years to the work of C. B. Stark, *Systematik und Geschichte der Archäologie der Kunst* (1880), approximately half of which is devoted to archaeology of the fifteenth to eighteenth centuries.

In this encyclopedia the Middle Ages, Renaissance and seventeenth and eighteenth centuries are treated as periods to be taken seriously for their archaeological study of the visual remains of antiquity. This approach constitutes one of the principal ways in which the work differs from the studies of Daniel, Trigger and others who have, in recent years, written on the history of archaeology. Included here are the biographies of travelers, collectors, artists and scholars whose activities made a difference in knowledge of the sites and monuments in their own day and in the history of archaeological scholarship. Scholars such as Peiresc and Bellori were on the cutting edge of research on antiquities in the seventeenth century and were passionately committed to the exchange of knowledge; we still follow some of their basic methodology and even conclusions. Travelers of the fifteenth century such as Buondelmonti and Ciriaco of Ancona made valuable records of the status of sites and monuments in their day and thus enlarge our own view. Artists like Alberti and Vasari reported on antiquities excavated in their time (Alberti himself attempted an underwater excavation at Nemi), and their reports help us to recover the context of artifacts and monuments under study today.

In addition, here the reader will find entries on famous monuments as seen, changed and interpreted through time; obvious inclusions are the Parthenon, the Mausoleum of Halikarnassos, the Colosseum and the Pantheon, which were visited and studied during the Renaissance and later (for some monuments there are continuous records from the Middle Ages). There are entries on major works of art, such as the *Laocoon* group, the Farnese *Herakles* and the Aldobrandini *Wedding,* which were excavated during the Renaissance and seventeenth century (albeit with an intent and by techniques that are considered very limited today), as well as works that were known throughout the Middle Ages and later, such as the Capitoline *Wolf.* Studying the "biographies" of these works, we understand how they came to be the way they are today and are better able to conjecture what they were like originally. The different restorations of the missing parts of the *Laocoon* group, which make a critical difference in our interpretation of its style and subject matter, can be traced from the sixteenth century. The seventeenth-century report that the Portland Vase was discovered in a sarcophagus is of great interest for our understanding of the usage and meaning of this unusual artifact. Besides such major monuments, many others are included; clearly, not every building or statue or artifact that has been studied through the centuries can have an entry of its own, though a quite large number of works are at least mentioned (the index may be consulted to locate those that do not have an entry). In selecting sites, monuments and statuary for individual entries, an attempt has been made to choose the items that have had a strong impact on classical studies and that have a rich historical past. These are often works that have, or have had, an important place also in the history of art or architecture; for this, perhaps the encyclopedia may be criticized, since New Archaeology in the twentieth century believes that the discipline should not be concerned with the beauty of excavated materials. To this the answer is that in reconstructing antiquity, the basic task of archaeology, it is appropriate to try to see with the eyes of the ancients, who cared a great deal about the beauty of their monuments. In this sense, those who practiced the Old Archaeology were much closer to understanding antiquity than are some scholars today.

Other considerations in selection of materials and viewpoints are listed by the following categories.

ARTISTS

Art historians may consult this work for information about the study and imitation of antiquity by artists of the Renaissance and later periods. Since the number of artists who worked within the "classical tradition" is vast (Michael Greenhalgh has surveyed them in *The Classical Tradition in Art,* 1978), it is impossible to include them all; an attempt has been made to determine which artists should have priority, with the operative criterion that the artist should demonstrate some concrete evidence of study of the visual remains of classical antiquity. Thus, artists who did sketchbooks and created a repertory of illustrations of such material, even though they may be minor figures in the history of art, are certainly appropriate subjects for entries. For artists who simply show a style that has an "antique" feeling, it is sometimes difficult, if not impossible, to determine how they contributed to archaeological knowledge in their time. With great reluctance the decision was made to eliminate certain key artists of the Renaissance who left no drawing or written record of the study of specific antiquities and whose painted or sculptured works reveal relatively little data about antiquities visible in this period.

SCHOLARS

The omission most regretted relates to humanist scholars and philologists who were powerfully influential in their time but whose scholarly output reveals little

or no involvement with archaeological material. Those who collected manuscripts and studied and wrote ancient history are borderline cases and are normally excluded if there is little or no evidence of serious study of at least
inscriptions and/or coins for their own sakes. The decision was made to omit
paleography as well as papyrology, disciplines that are more properly the sphere
of philologists. It is not that this encyclopedia intends to promote categorization,
only that from a practical point of view, some things must be omitted, and since
histories of classical scholarship have normally given heavy emphasis to research on texts and literary criticism (e.g., J. E. Sandys, *A History of Classical
Scholarship,* 3rd ed., 1958; Ulrich von Wilamowitz-Moellendorff, *A History of
Classical Scholarship,* 1982), information may be sought there rather than in
these pages.

Scholars living today, however significant their place in the history of archaeological scholarship, have not been included.

SITES

It has been especially difficult to explain to potential readers and contributors
what the encyclopedia would do in regard to sites. Those who were asked to
write about sites thought immediately of the *Princeton Encyclopedia of Classical
Sites* and wanted to know what more needed to be done. The present reference
work differs from the *Princeton Encyclopedia,* above all, in its attempt to give
fuller coverage to the history of the study of sites. Dates when excavations took
place, who directed the work, what results were obtained and what conclusions
were drawn, what significance the finds had for the development of scholars'
understanding of the site and the culture represented—these are the matters that
were recommended to the contributors. In a way, the sites have "biographies"
like those of artists, travelers and scholars, including information about what
happened at the site in antiquity and what happened to it in later periods, as
well as an evaluation of its contribution to our archaeological knowledge.

The selection of sites has been extremely difficult. Again, the number of
possibilities is enormous, as demonstrated by the *Princeton Encyclopedia* itself.
Further, each site seems important to the person who digs it or studies it. Emphasis was given to those sites that have a longer or more prominent history of
visitation and excavation and to those that seem to have generated important
changes in archaeological thinking. Some attempt has been made to take into
account geographical distribution and, by including sites in areas outside Greece
and Italy, to give some idea of the development of classical archaeology in other
countries.

ABOUT THE BOOK

A word is in order about the history of this encyclopedia of the history of
archaeology. The idea to do the work was not my own; when first invited to be

a coeditor, I replied that I would love to look up things in such a work but was unable to commit to such a large undertaking. When approached a second time, my resolve weakened, and my enthusiasm for the project was so strong that I agreed to serve as coeditor as well as coauthor of a certain percentage of the articles, especially those that had to do with my own area of Etruscan studies and with the development of classical archaeology in the seventeenth century, a subject that had been part of my dissertation. With the help of an advisory board (see Acknowledgments, later in Preface), a master list was drawn up (it had 748 entries), and a list of some fifty potential contributors was compiled. Editorial and authorial duties were divided and invitations sent out.

Then the entries began to come in, and a remarkable phenomenon developed. Authors had been asked to supply suggestions for cross-references in the encyclopedia, and almost every entry submitted listed one or more cross-references that did not appear on the master list. The master list thus began to expand, and more contributors were invited. At this point my coeditor withdrew, and I determined to continue the work; on two occasions I sought a new coeditor, inviting colleagues whom I considered ideal for the job. They were not so rash as I had been, and no collaborator was secured.

Today, some fifteen years later, the list of entries numbers 1,125, and the number of contributors 171. My editors at Greenwood, urging practicality, have nevertheless graciously acquiesced as the work expanded well beyond what they had envisioned. In the final months of completing the manuscript, I continued to discover entries that should be on the list, and no doubt reviewers will likewise note (I hope without being overly indignant) that omissions have occurred. A limit had to be drawn, however arbitrary it might seem, and thus some entries of potential importance have been omitted. Others that might seem in retrospect of lesser significance were contributed early and would have been excluded unfairly.

Other matters became evident as entries were completed and compared. Each individual contributor had his or her own style of presenting the information requested. As editor, I recommended a rewrite if a contributor had not included enough of the appropriate historical material, and I requested condensation when too much purely descriptive material was given. But, on the whole, it seemed desirable to let each scholar have some latitude in self-expression and to avoid an excessively standardized or sterilized form for entries.

Thus, normally each entry begins with a brief identifying phrase and ends with a bibliography of approximately four items. But there is considerable variation among entries, depending, first of all, on whether the subject is a site or monument, scholar or traveler, or yet another kind of entry in which a topic is the focus (e.g., underwater archaeology), and depending further on the way in which the author organized the material. All entries have some kind of historical content, but this is often combined with descriptive material that helps to identify or explain the subject, with opinions of archaeologists of the past and present and with references to achievements in archaeological scholarship. These do not necessarily follow a standard order or predetermined balance from entry to entry.

The bibliographies were intended to serve several purposes. They often show what sources an author used, though they are not meant to substitute for footnotes to an entry, and they also show which sources the author recommends for further study. Works that are especially rich in illustration are marked by a + mark before the listing of the author and title of the book. An attempt was made to keep these bibliographies short (about two to four items), but contributors were concerned lest they might prove insufficient, and in some cases, for longer entries on weighty topics, I have allowed an increase. In addition, as press time drew nearer, many authors kindly updated entries that had been written in the early years, and they were allowed to insert new and important bibliography. On the whole, whenever bibliographies were trimmed, I have been partial to listings that are recent, that themselves contain abundant, up-to-date bibliography, that are well illustrated and that are in the English language.

Within entries, an asterisk is used before a name or topic to indicate a cross-reference to a separate entry. The asterisk would be redundant for "Rome" and "Athens" and is therefore omitted.

Articles that are unsigned were written by the editor. No articles, signed or unsigned, were written after 1994, and many entries were completed considerably before that date. In some articles the bibliographies do include items published in 1995 or forthcoming. Under no circumstances are contributors of the articles to be held accountable for the timeliness of their scholarship; the editor alone is responsible in this matter.

For whom was *An Encyclopedia of the History of Classical Archaeology* written? A broad spectrum of users of this reference tool is envisioned. Obviously, it is meant for readers of the English language; thus, quotations from other languages are regularly translated into English, and archaeological terms that are derived from other languages, especially Latin and Greek, have been replaced with equivalent English terms when possible or have been "translated" in the text.

It is hoped that the encyclopedia will be of use to students and researchers in a variety of fields, especially archaeology, classics, history, topography, art history and architectural history. The history of archaeology is a discipline that is comparatively new; some of its results have only recently become more available and mostly remain to be integrated into various other areas of scholarship. A fine example of what may be accomplished lies in R. T. Ridley's work *The Eagle and the Spade: The Archaeology of Rome During the Napoleonic Era, 1809–1814* (1992), a detailed study of Napoleon's effect on the monuments of the city of Rome, a work of the utmost significance for those studying the programs of Napoleon and, more specifically, the political uses to which he put archaeological research. Equally fascinating is the analysis of exploitation of archaeological projects and Roman revival architecture by Mussolini and Hitler, published recently by A. Scobie, *Hitler's State Architecture, The Impact of Classical Antiquity* (1990). Another recent work on the history of archaeology in the city of Rome is the richly illustrated survey by Claude Moiatti, *The Search for Ancient Rome* (1993). For Greece, the companion volume in the same series is *The Search for Ancient Greece* by Roland and Françoise Etienne (1990).

Another area that has recently received attention is the history of the discovery, collecting and study of Greek and Roman sculpture. The information is critical for art historians of the Renaissance and Baroque, and they are the ones who have made the most significant contributions in assembling the data and in integrating them into a context. The *Census of Works of Antique Art Known in the Renaissance,* conducted for many years by Phyllis Bober and Ruth Rubinstein at the Warburg Institute of the University of London and the Institute of Fine Arts at New York University, has reached fruition in their rich volume of *Renaissance Artists and Antique Sculpture: A Handbook of Sources* (1986). Similar material, with a different interpretive approach, may be found in the now-classic catalog of F. Haskell and N. Penny, *Taste and the Antique: The Lure of Classical Sculpture, 1500–1900* (1981). Their aim is to reveal significant aspects of the history of taste over the span of some four centuries by cataloging the ancient sculptures that were most popular and most influential. In citing information about the find spots of famous sculptures and in quoting opinions of critics and scholars about these pieces, Haskell and Penny have created a fabric often interwoven with archaeological scholarship and immensely useful for those who wish to understand a piece of sculpture through its "biography." Not many scholars working on Greek and Roman sculpture today concern themselves with this kind of background. A rare exception is Brunilde Ridgway, who has published searching studies of Greek sculpture from the Archaic to the Hellenistic, in which she frequently takes into account the history of study of a particular work of art. Her review of this history, not only in the Renaissance but also, or especially, in nineteenth-century scholarship, has led to a healthy deconstruction of the edifice of attributions to Pheidias, Polykleitos, Skopas, Lysippos and others made by German scholars of the last century. Retracing their steps, she has made far-reaching conclusions.

Curators and researchers in museums have been in position to contribute much to the history of archaeology in their study of object proveniences; it is hoped that entries in the encyclopedia can serve as ready reference for this kind of information and that the bibliographies will provide access to fuller detail than could be incorporated gracefully into the brief format adopted for the entries.

It is hoped, above all, that the encyclopedia will be useful to teachers and students of classical archaeology. New textbooks in Greek and Roman art by John Pedley (*Greek Art and Archaeology,* 1992) and by Andrew and Nancy Ramage (*Roman Art,* 1995) include some discussion and illustrations that will give students a taste of the material that is waiting to be studied. But, on the whole, very little of the information on the history of archaeology found in this encyclopedia is regularly included in the classroom; students of classical archaeology are given little exposure to the roots of the discipline. An exception is the case of Heinrich Schliemann, whose name is known to most students; unfortunately, what seems to continue to fascinate is the idea that he had a unique dream of proving the truth of the poems of Homer and that he fulfilled it with an uncanny ability to locate archaeological sites. He continues to be lionized as a great archaeologist, in spite of the books and articles by William Calder and David Traill that dispel the myths promoted by Schliemann about himself and his own importance. In these pages one may consult the entry on Frank Calvert, who actually ascertained the location of Troy and suggested it to Schliemann, and the entry on Troy itself, where it is noted that many travelers had believed in the truth of the Homeric poems long before Schliemann. In the eighteenth century Dawkins had visited the Troad, Homer in hand, and had even invented a form of ethnoarchaeology, studying the modern inhabitants of the area in order to understand Homeric society. It is hoped that such entries can help to sift out the facts of the history of archaeology. No doubt much that is reported in this encyclopedia will, and rightly should be, subject to scrutiny and revision, as more archaeologists join in the study of our fascinating past. Most of all it is hoped that the mere existence of this work will create awareness of the long tradition of this discipline and the richness of the perspective gained by reviewing the discovery and study of specific monuments and sites as well as general trends in the history of archaeological scholarship.

ACKNOWLEDGMENTS

There are very many whom I wish to thank. First are the kind colleagues who consented to act as advisers in the earliest stage of the encyclopedia, in planning the master list and in suggesting the names of potential contributors for the various entries. Though they must certainly not be held responsible for the final shape of this volume, I wish to acknowledge the many wonderful suggestions made by Phyllis Pray Bober, Larissa Bonfante, William M. Calder III, Philipp Fehl, David Ridgway and Homer A. Thompson. My sincere thanks for similar advising at a later date goes to Elizabeth McGraw, Marjon van der Meulen and Ruth Rubinstein, who generously shared their rich knowledge of Renaissance and Baroque scholarship, and to Katherine Geffcken, who consulted on several crucial points. Brunilde S. Ridgway characteristically gave up her own time to help other authors, reading many entries and making valuable suggestions for entries on Greek sculpture. Larissa Bonfante, as usual, helped with every bibliographical question I asked her, as well as many that I did not. Francesca Ridgway (related to David but not Brunilde) gave much welcome advice on Etruscan entries. L. Richardson, jr, provided unfailing support, moral as well as scholarly, in regard to Roman archaeology, especially topography; Ronald Ridley willingly shared the burden of entries on Rome and its archaeologists. William Calder III poured forth information from his fund of knowledge of German archaeological scholarship. Jack Davis and Philip Betancourt made helpful suggestions for Bronze Age Aegean archaeology, and so did Robert Koehl, who also advised generally on potential authors for other entries on Greek archaeology. No one helped me or cheered me more than Judith Binder, unless it was Norma and Bernard Goldman, faithful correspondents who kept me laughing and believing that the encyclopedia would surely be finished one day. Elfriede R. Knauer energized me with her own total commitment to quality in scholarship. I was inspired by Phyllis Lehmann, with her rare ability to move skillfully and easily back and forth between antiquity and Renaissance.

Many of these colleagues also wrote multiple entries for the encyclopedia. I am so very grateful to them for that and to others who valiantly wrote entry after entry in their special areas, sometimes in several areas. I will restrict my mention of names to those who wrote seven or more: James Anderson, Barbara Barletta, Clifford Brown, John Camp, Mortimer Chambers, Glenys Davies, W. W. de Grummond, Ann Gunter, A. Trevor Hodge, Peter Holliday, Fred S. and Diana E. E. Kleiner, Carol Mattusch, Emeline Hill Richardson, David Thompson, David A. Traill, and Shellie Williams.

Finally, I wish to express my gratitude to those who aided in the construction of this book, whether retyping manuscripts, filing, Xeroxing, editing, searching bibliography, confirming references, corresponding, indexing, or helping in some other way. I think of Deborah Halsted at the beginning and Melissa Moss, Dara Helser and Diane Kampert at the end, of Claudette Gatlin all along. I wish to thank Sharon Loucks Wichmann, who provided an enormous boost in the middle years of the project, with her varied talents as author, editor, secretary. I was delighted when Joann McDaniel agreed to prepare the Select Bibliography for the History of Classical Archaeology and wish to record now my warm appreciation for her work on this assignment. I thank Rochelle Marrinan, who transformed my working habits by providing computer support, and Elizabeth de Grummond, who did a wonderful job on the cross-references, thereby also getting training for the day when she will edit the second edition of the encyclopedia. I thank Patty Grandy for effective prayer for the completion of the work, and, I am grateful to Louise Thomson for the kind of support that only a mother can give.

I reserve a special place to thank my editor at Greenwood, Cynthia Harris. In all the years she has been associated with the project, she has truly never said a discouraging word and always seemed to have an unquestioning faith that the book would be delivered. For this steadfast confidence and her genuine enthusiasm, which kept me going on, I wish to express my deep gratitude.

The entire undertaking has provided a great lesson in humility for me. On the one hand, I have never learned so much on any other project I have attempted; on the other, I have not failed so much in learning at any other time in my life. The scope of the subject is so large that even today I am not sure of its limits. For many years, I have kept the book from the hands of the publishers, haunted by the specters of reviewers, feeling ashamed to let it go with the many omissions I knew of or simply suspected, feeling the need to check and check again the hundreds of entries completed, and often noting with horror the errors that existed. In effect, I have spent much of my ''free'' time for the last quarter of my life on this manuscript. I often felt deeply moved as I reviewed the history of archaeological scholarship and the lives of its practitioners. With Joseph Spence, I trembled over the reception of an untried publication; his fears turned out to be quite well founded, in light of the fury with which Lessing later attacked him. With John Leland, who was assigned in 1533 to do a survey of antiquities throughout the realm of England, I agonized that the enormous amount of material would never be gathered together and properly arranged for publication. His torment over the work was so intense that he was forced to give it up; it is reported that his antiquarian research overtaxed his brain and that the insane scholar had to be turned over to his brother for safekeeping. A fairly well-known case of scholarly overwork in modern times is that of Rostovtzeff, who suffered a mental collapse after the completion of *The Social and Economic History of the Hellenistic World* (1941). Others were able to endure unimaginable deprivation and pressure as they devoted their lives to the tasks they had assumed. I was inspired by Tommaso Fazello (d. 1570), who, to further his studies of ancient Sicily, cut back on the amount of time he wasted eating, so that he had only one meal a day; by Janus Gruter (d. 1627), who always stood upright and vigilant while he worked; by Bernard Montfaucon (1741), who, for the last forty-six years of his life, normally spent thirteen hours a day studying or writing. Again and again I was reminded of the humanity of the archaeologists of the past, of their failures and successes, and was compelled to continue the quest to publish this work about their work. In the end it was for them—and, of course, for the contributors who have waited so patiently for their entries to appear—that I was able to finish the encyclopedia.

—Nancy Thomson de Grummond

Bibliographical Abbreviations

AA	*Archäologischer Anzeiger*
AAA	*Athens Annals of Archaeology*
ActaArch	*Acta Archaeologica* [Copenhagen]
Aerial Atlas of Crete	*The Aerial Atlas of Ancient Crete*, ed. J. W. Myers—E. E. Myers—G. Cadogan (Berkeley, 1992)
AfrIt	*Africa Italiana*
AIRF	*Acta Instituti Romani Finlandiae*
AJA	*American Journal of Archaeology*
AJP	*American Journal of Philology*
AM	*Mitteilungen des Deutschen Archäologischen Instituts, Athenische Abteilung*
AnatSt	*Anatolian Studies. Journal of the British Institute of Archaeology at Ankara.*
ANRW	*Aufstieg und Niedergang der römischen Welt*
AnnInst	*Annales Institutorum*
AntK	*Antike Kunst*
AntP	*Antike Plastik*
Archäologenbildnisse	*Archäologenbildnisse, Porträts und Kurzbiographien von klassischen Archäologen deutscher Sprache*, ed. R. Lullies—W. Schiering (Mainz am Rhein, 1988)
ArchCl	*Archeologia Classica*
ArchDelt	*Archaiologikon Deltion*
ArchEph	*Archaiologike Ephemeris*
ArchEspArq	*Archivo Español de Arqueologia*

ArchEspArt	*Archivo Español de Arte*
ArchJ	*Archaeological Journal*
ArtB	*Art Bulletin*
ArchRep	*Archaeological Reports*
ASAtene	*Annuario della Scuola Archeologica di Atene e delle Missioni italiane in Oriente*
AttiMGrecia	*Atti e Memorie della Società Magna Grecia*
BABesch	*Bulletin Antieke Beschaving*
BCH	*Bulletin de Correspondance Hellénique*
BdA	*Bollettino d'Arte*
Beazley—Ashmole	J. D. Beazley—B. Ashmole, *Greek Sculpture and Painting to the End of the Hellenistic Period* (London, 1966)
Berve—Gruben	H. Berve—G. Gruben, *Greek Temples, Theaters and Shrines* (New York, 1963)
BICS	*Bulletin of the Institute of Classical Studies,* University of London
Bieber	M. Bieber, *The Sculpture of the Hellenistic Age,* rev. ed. (New York, 1961)
BIM	*Boletin de Information Municipal,* Valencia
BiogJahr	*Biographisches Jahrbuch und Deutscher Nekrolog*
Bober—Rubinstein	P. P. Bober—R. Rubinstein, *Renaissance Artists and Antique Sculpture: A Handbook of Sources* (London, 1986)
BMon	*Bulletin Monumental*
BMMA	*Bulletin of the Metropolitan Museum of Art*
Briggs—Calder	*Classical Scholarship: A Biographical Encyclopedia,* ed. W. W. Briggs—W. M. Calder III (New York, 1990)
BSA	British School at Athens, *Annual*
BU	*Biographie Universelle*
BullCom	*Bulletino della Commissione Archeologica Comunale di Roma*
BurlMag	*Burlington Magazine*
CIG	*Corpus Inscriptionum Graecarum*
CIL	*Corpus Inscriptionum Latinarum*
Coarelli	F. Coarelli, *Guida Archaeologica di Roma,* 2nd ed. (Rome, 1975)
CR	*Classical Review*

CRAI	*Comptes Rendus de l'Académie des Inscriptions et Belles Lettres*
CVA	*Corpus Vasorum Antiquorum*
DAB	*Dictionary of American Biography*
DBF	*Dictionaire de Biographie Française*
DBI	*Dizionario Biografico degli Italiani*
DialAr	*Dialoghi di Archeologia*
DNB	*Dictionary of National Biography*
DOP	*Dumbarton Oaks Papers*
EAA	*Enciclopedia dell'Arte Antica, Classica e Orientale*
EC	*Enciclopedia Cattolica*
EI	*Enciclopedia Italiana*
EPRO	*Études preliminaires aux religions orientales dans l'empire romain*
EWA	*Encyclopedia of World Art*
FGrHist	F. Jacoby, *Fragmente der griechischen Historiker* (Berlin, 1923–)
GBA	*Gazette des Beaux-arts*
GGA	*Göttingische gelehrte Anzeiger*
Gnomon	*Gnomon*
GRBS	*Greek, Roman and Byzantine Studies*
Greenhalgh, *Survival*	M. Greenhalgh, *The Survival of Roman Antiquities in the Middle Ages* (London, 1989)
Haskell—Penny	F. Haskell—N. Penny, *Taste and the Antique: The Lure of Classical Sculpture, 1500–1900* (New Haven, CT, 1981)
Helbig	W. Helbig, *Führer durch die öffentlichen Sammlungen klassischer Altertümer in Rom,* 4th ed., ed. H. Speier, 1–4 (Tübingen, 1963–72)
IJNA	*International Journal of Nautical Archaeology and Underwater Exploration*
ILN	*Illustrated London News*
IstForsch	*Istanbuler Forschungen*
IstMitt	*Mitteilungen des Deutschen Archäologischen Instituts,* Abteilung Istanbul
JdI	*Jahrbuch des Deutschen Archäologischen Instituts*
JEA	*Journal of Egyptian Archaeology*
JHS	*Journal of Hellenic Studies*
JRS	*The Journal of Roman Studies*

JSAH	*Journal of the Society of Architectural Historians*
JWAG	*Journal of the Walters Art Gallery*
JWarb	*Journal of the Warburg and Courtauld Institutes*
Kleiner, *Roman Sculpture*	Diana E. E. Kleiner, *Roman Sculpture* (New Haven, CT, 1992)
Klio	*Klio.* Beiträge zur alten Geschichte
Lanciani, *Destruction*	R. Lanciani, *The Destruction of Ancient Rome* (London, 1899; repr. New York, 1980)
Lanciani, *Storia degli scavi*	R. Lanciani, *Storia degli scavi di Roma e notizie intorno le collezioni romane di antichità,* 1–4 (Rome, 1902–12; "Edizione integrale," ed. L. M. Campeggi, Rome, 1989–92).
LIMC	*Lexicon Iconographicum Mythologiae Classicae* (Zürich, 1974–)
Ling, *Roman Painting*	R. Ling, *Roman Painting* (Cambridge, 1991)
Lullies—Hirmer	R. Lullies—M. Hirmer, *Greek Sculpture,* rev. ed., tr. M. Bullock (New York, 1960)
MA	*Le Moyen âge*
MAAR	*Memoirs of the American Academy in Rome*
Meded	*Mededeelingen van het Nederl. Historisch Instituut te Rome*
MEFRA	*Mélanges de l'École Française de Rome, Antiquité*
MelRome	*Mélanges d'Archéologie et d'Histoire de l'Ecole française de Rome*
MemLinc	*Memorie. Atti della Accademia Nazionale dei Lincei, Classe di scienze morali, storiche e filologiche*
MGH	*Monumenta Germaniae Historica*
Michaelis	A. Michaelis, *A Century of Archaeological Discovery,* tr. B. Kahnweiler (London, 1908)
MittFlor	*Mitteilungen des Kunsthistorischen Instituts in Florenz*
MJb	*Münchener Jahrbuch der bildenden Kunst*
MonAnt	*Monumenti Antichi*
MonPiot	*Monuments et Mémoires. Fondation E. Piot*
MonPitt	*Monumenti della pittura antica scoperti in Italia*
MSNAF	*Memoires de la Societé Nationale des Antiquaires de France*
Nash	E. Nash, *A Pictorial Dictionary of Ancient Rome,* rev. ed., 1–2 (London, 1968)
NBG	*Nouvelle Biographie Generale*
NCAB	*National Cyclopaedia of American Biography*

NDB	*Neue Deutsche Biographie*
Pastor, *History of the Popes*	L. von Pastor, *History of the Popes* 1–40 (London, 1938–)
NSc	*Notizie degli Scavi di Antichità*
OpAth	*Opuscula Atheniensia*
OpRom	*Opuscula Romana*
PBSR	*Papers of the British School at Rome*
PECS	*Princeton Encyclopedia of Classical Sites,* ed. R. Stillwell (Princeton, NJ, 1976)
Pfeiffer	R. Pfeiffer, *History of Classical Scholarship from 1300 to 1850* (Oxford, 1976)
Platner—Ashby	S. B. Platner—T. Ashby, *A Topographical Dictionary of Ancient Rome* (London, 1929)
Pliny, *NH*	Pliny the Elder, *Natural History*
Pollitt, *Hellenistic Age*	J. J. Pollitt, *Art in the Hellenistic Age* (Cambridge, 1986)
Porträtarchiv	*Der Archäologe: Graphische Bildnisse aus dem Porträtarchiv Diepenbroick,* catalog of exhibition (Münster, 1983)
PP	*La Parola del Passato*
ProcBrAc	*Proceedings of the British Academy*
RA	*Revue Archéologique*
RACrist	*Rivista di Archeologia Cristiana*
RBN	*Revue Belge de Numismatique*
RE	*Real-Encyclopädie der Altertumswissenschaft,* ed. A Pauly—G. Wissowa
RendPontAcc	Atti della Pontificia Accademia Romana di Archeologia, Rendiconti
RepKunstW	*Repertorium für Kunstwissenschaft*
RhM	*Rheinisches Museum für Philogie*
Richardson, *New Topographical Dictionary*	L. Richardson, jr, *A New Topographical Dictionary of Ancient Rome* (Baltimore, 1992)
Richter, *Sculpture and Sculptors*	G.M.A. Richter, *The Sculpture and Sculptors of the Greeks,* 4th ed. (New Haven, CT, 1984)
Ridgway, *Hellenistic Sculpture* I	B. S. Ridgway, *Hellenistic Sculpture,* 1, *The Styles of ca. 331–200* B.C. (Madison, WI, 1990)
Ridgway, *Fifth Century Styles*	B. Ridgway, *Fifth Century Styles in Greek Sculpture* (Princeton, NJ, 1981)
Ridley, *Eagle and the Spade*	R. T. Ridley, *The Eagle and the Spade: The Archaeology of Rome During the Napoleonic Era, 1809–1814* (Cambridge, 1992)

RM	*Mitteilungen des Deutschen Archäologischen Instituts, Römische Abteilung*
RQ	Renaissance Quarterly
Sheard	W. S. Sheard, *Antiquity in the Renaissance,* catalog of exhibition (Northampton, MA, 1978–79)
StEtr	Studi Etruschi
Steingräber	S. Steingräber, *Città e necropoli dell'Etruria* (Rome, 1981)
Stewart, *Greek Sculpture*	A. Stewart, *Greek Sculpture: An Exploration* (New Haven, CT, 1990)
Stoneman, *Land of Lost Gods*	R. Stoneman, *Land of Lost Gods, The Search for Classical Greece* (London, 1987)
StRom	*Studi Romani*
TAD	*Turk Arkeoloji Dergisi*
TAPS	*Transactions of the American Philosophical Society*
Thieme-Becker	*Allgemeines Kunstlerlexikon,* ed. U. Thieme—F. Becker
Travlos	J. Travlos, *Pictorial Dictionary of Ancient Athens* (New York, 1971)
Tsigakou, *Rediscovery*	F.-M. Tsigakou, *The Rediscovery of Greece: Travellers and Painters of the Romantic Era* (New Rochelle, NY, 1981)
Valentini—Zucchetti	R. Valentini—G. Zucchetti, *Codice topografico della città di Roma,* 1–4 (Rome, 1940–53)
Weiss, *RDCA*	R. Weiss, *The Renaissance Discovery of Classical Antiquity,* 2nd ed. (Oxford, 1988)
ZfK	*Zeitschrift für Kunstgeschichte*

An Encyclopedia
of the History of
Classical Archaeology

L

LABYRINTH OF GORTYN. Ancient stone quarry west of *Gortyn on *Crete.

The "Labyrinth" is located on the south side of a hill detached from the massif of Psiloriti, thirty-five minutes' walk west-northwest of Ampelouzos Kainourgiou, at an altitude of 400m. Galleries extended 400m into the hill, in a great figure eight whose levels, detours and culs-de-sac gave travelers the impression of a maze of many miles. The quarry provided yellowish limestone for the buildings of Gortyn, especially the sixth century church of Hagios Titos.

The quarry was identified as a labyrinth continuously from A.D. 404 until the nineteenth century. The eleventh-century history by George Cedrenus connected the labyrinth with Gortyn, the Minotaur and Theseus.

Nearly everyone who visited Crete, at least from the fifteenth century on, toured the "Labyrinth." The earliest explorer was the Italian C. *Buondelmonti (1416). G. Barzizza attests visits by Venetian magistrates that date to 1422 at the latest. In the sixteenth century the Frenchman P. Belon (1553) first put forth the idea that the "Labyrinth" was nothing but a quarry, an idea accepted before its time by a Polish traveler of the same century, Prince Radziwill (1584). English travelers from the sixteenth to the eighteenth centuries (F. Moryson, 1596; W. Lithgow, 1610; G. Sandys, 1611; B. Randolph, 1680; R. Pococke, 1739) considered the "Labyrinth" a necessary stop in their tour of Cretan antiquities, and G. Sandys followed Belon and Radziwill in pronouncing it a quarry.

The French traveler and scholar J. de Tournefort (1700) maintained that the galleries were the fabled labyrinth and noted graffiti dating back to 1444. The French traveler M. Savary (1788) recorded graffiti from the fourteenth century, exactly the time when Italian humanists had become interested in classical antiquity. It was not until the nineteenth century that the identity of the "Labyrinth" as a stone quarry was established by the German F. Sieber (1817) and the Englishman T. Spratt (1865). The quarry has been dated to Roman times by the French archaeologist P. Faure (1964).

In 1942 the German army sheltered its vehicles in the quarry and used it for a munitions depot. Since many postwar visitors have been killed by abandoned explosives, this ancient quarry is now closed.

BIBLIOGRAPHY

A. M. Woodward, "The Gortyn Labyrinth and Its Visitors in the Fifteenth Century," *BSA* 44 (1949), 324–25; M. Guarducci, "Hoi Archaioterioi Episkeptai tou 'Labyrinthou' tes Gortynos," *Kretika Chronika* 4 (1950), 527–28; M. Guarducci, *Inscriptiones Creticae,* 4 (Rome, 1950), 13–14; B. Rutkowski, "Les antiquités crétoises dans la relation d'un voyageur Polonais du XVIe siècle," *BCH* 62 (1968), 85–96; P. Warren, "16th, 17th and 18th Century British Travellers in Crete," *Kretika Chronika* 24 (1972), 65–92.

MARTHA W. BALDWIN BOWSKY

LAFRÉRY (LAFRERI, LAFRERIUS, LAUFRERIUS), ANTOINE (ANTONIO; ca. 1512–77). French-Italian engraver, cartographer and publisher.

Born at Salins in France, Lafréry was active in Rome by 1544 as a publisher of engravings. He collaborated with the book dealer Antonio Salamanca beginning in 1553 in issuing separate plates of Rome and its antiquities that could be combined in an album according to the buyer's selection. In 1573, Lafréry created a catalog of the 107 plates he had issued in thirty years, all in categories. Soon afterward he had *Du Pérac produce a frontispiece that could be sold as a cover for the albums, with the title *Speculum romanae magnificentiae* (the "Mirror of Roman Magnificence," not the "Mirror of Marvelous Rome," as it has been translated). Listed on his repertory are numerous monuments of ancient Rome, sometimes in actual state and sometimes in reconstruction (e.g., the *Colosseum, the *Pantheon), sculptures (the *Capitoline *Wolf,* the *Laocoon, the *Marforio,* the *Pasquino, the *Nile and *Tiber* river gods, the *Spinario*), as well as contemporary art and architecture (the tomb of Julius II by *Michelangelo, St. Peter's, the Capitoline Hill, the Palazzo Farnese), with the whole prefaced by three maps of Rome. His selection of skilled and imaginative artists like *Ligorio and Du Pérac to design his plates (though sometimes he picked up prints that had been issued earlier, e.g., by Enea *Vico) and his use of standardized sizes for related illustrations were significant factors in the popularity of his prints.

After Lafréry's death, the *Speculum* was inherited by Étienne and especially Claude Duchet (d. 1586), who expanded the number of prints available while maintaining "in print" many Lafréry plates. In the seventeenth, eighteenth and nineteenth centuries, many collectors selected prints by other artists to include in their *Speculum* albums, so that sometimes a volume might contain hundreds of prints and go far beyond the size and scope of Lafréry's original *Speculum.*

Lafréry is also noted for his contribution to geography through his creation of maps on a large scale and of views and plans of various cities. Around 1570 he published a collection of maps keyed to the ancient geography of Ptolemy,

Tavole moderne di geografia raccolte e messe secondo l'ordine di Tolomeo, with a frontispiece featuring an image of Atlas holding up the world on his shoulders, based on the Farnese statue of *Atlas* (now *Museo Nazionale, Naples). The emblem of Atlas was picked up by later compilers of collections of maps, giving rise to the name of "Atlas" for such a publication of maps.

BIBLIOGRAPHY
C. Hülsen, "Das Speculum romanae magnificentiae des Antonio Lafreri," in *Collectanea variae doctrinae L. S. Olschki* (Munich, 1921), 121–70; B. Lowry, "Notes on the Speculum romanae magnificentiae and Related Publications," *ArtB* 34 (1952), 46–50; L. R. McGinniss, with H. Mitchell, *Catalogue of the Earl of Crawford's "Speculum romanae magnificentiae" Now in the Avery Architectural Library, Columbia University* (New York, 1976); +*Mirror of Marvelous Rome–16th Century Engravings,* catalog of exhibition, State University of New York, Binghamton (Binghamton, 1979); Bober—Rubinstein, 461.

LAMB, WINIFRED (1894–1963). English archaeologist.

Honorary keeper until 1958 of the Greek and Roman Department in the *Fitzwilliam Museum, Cambridge University, Winifred Lamb published *Greek and Roman Bronzes* in 1929; it was still unrivaled as a basic text at the time of her death. Associated with A.J.B. Wace's *Mycenae excavations since 1920, she acquired a personal reputation as a prehistorian with her masterly Bronze Age *Excavations at Thermi in Lesbos* (1936), corresponding to Troy I. Her subsequent investigation at Kusura near Afyonkarahisar (*Archaeologia,* 1936) achieved the first step toward cross-dating between the prehistoric Aegean and *Anatolia—where Lamb was the first woman archaeologist.

BIBLIOGRAPHY
S. Lloyd, *Early Anatolia* (Harmondsworth, 1956); R. D. B[arnett], "Winifred Lamb," *BSA Annual Report 1962–63,* 16–18.

DAVID RIDGWAY

LANCIANI, RODOLFO (1847–1929). Italian archaeologist, expert on the topography of Rome and the history of archaeology in the city.

Lanciani brought scientific methods to the excavations of Rome in the late nineteenth century and was for nearly fifty years a master teacher of the topography of the ancient city. He took a degree in engineering but from the start was an avid enthusiast of classical studies and thus directed his technical training to studying the history of the monuments of Rome. In 1867 he was assigned the survey work of the *Portus Traiani, and the resulting monograph, published in the following year, established an initial reputation for the young engineer that resulted in his appointment as secretary of the Commissione Archeologica Comunale founded in 1872. During the years that ensued, intense building activity in Rome, especially in eastern portions of the city, brought to light abundant remains of the ancient city, and Lanciani's publication of these new discoveries was prolific. He was elected to the *Accademia dei Lincei as a corresponding member in 1876 and in 1879 was awarded the academy's Premio

Reale for his annotated edition of the commentaries of Frontinus; he was elevated to full membership in 1885. In 1882, a chair had been created for him at the University of Rome, where he served as professor of Roman topography until 1927. Lanciani's subsequent research resulted in his publication of the *Forma Urbis Romae,* a detailed plan of Rome in forty-six sheets (scale 1:1,000) documenting the entire monumental history of the city, including all the ancient remains either still in existence or known, with bibliographies. This plan was the first and greatest foundation for modern studies of ancient Roman topography.

In 1902 Lanciani started to publish, from research of archival material, his *Storia degli scavi di Roma,* a systematic history of the excavations of Rome beginning in the Middle Ages. While originally he planned five volumes, covering the period to 1879, only four actually were published, documenting excavations from the eleventh century to 3 March 1605. The Commissione Lanciani, under the auspices of the Istituto Nazionale di Archeologia and the editorship of L. M. Campeggi, has undertaken to reprint *Storia degli scavi* in seven volumes, with the addition of some 1,200 illustrations (plans, drawings, photographs) and with the sections previously unpublished on the period 1605–1879.

Lanciani knew English perfectly and published in that language a number of very well received books that even today are required reading for any student of the ancient city. He was made a senator of Rome in 1911.

BIBLIOGRAPHY

R. Lanciani, *Forma Urbis Romae* (Milan, 1893–1901; repr. Rome, 1988); idem, *Ancient Rome in the Light of Recent Discoveries* (Boston, 1894); idem, *The Ruins and Excavations of Ancient Rome* (Boston, 1897); idem, *Storia degli scavi di Roma e notizie intorno le collezioni romane di antichità* (Rome, 1902–12; repr. Bologna, 1975, with preface by F. Castagnoli).

DAVID L. THOMPSON

LANGLOTZ, ERNST (1895–1978). German art historian and archaeologist; specialist in Greek art of the sixth and fifth centuries B.C.

Born in Ronneburg (Thuringia) as the son of a weaver, Langlotz studied classical archaeology, philology and art history at Leipzig and Munich. Under F. *Studniczka he learned the positivist approach and was influenced by the theories on stylistic analysis of H. Wölfflin.

After travels to Italy and Greece (in Athens his encounter with E. *Buschor was meaningful), he was lecturer (*Privatdozent*) at Würzburg and conservator of the Martin von Wagner Museum. His catalog, *Griechische Vasen in Würzburg* (1932), is one manifestation of a long-lasting interest in Greek vase painting.

Called to the university of Frankfurt am Main in 1941, Langlotz served there as professor (*Ordinarius*) until 1963 and simultaneously as director of the Akademisches Kunstmuseums in Bonn.

The formal qualities of Greek art, especially sculpture, always absorbed him.

He felt that stylistic change and the spirit of an age (Zeitgeist) were made manifest in the depiction of the human body. Accordingly, he specialized in Greek sculpture of the sixth and fifth centuries B.C., where these principles are most clearly articulated. He published the *korai* from the *Akropolis (*korai and *kouroi*) in a comprehensive section of *Die archaischen Marmorbildwerke der Akropolis* (ed. H. Schrader, 1939). Another important contribution was his recognition of many copies of lost works by classical masters and reconstruction of them in casts. Langlotz is remembered, too, for his authoritative works on the art of the western Greeks in Southern Italy and Sicily (e.g., *The Art of Magna Graecia*, 1965, with M. Hirmer). Near the end of his life he extended his horizons still further, with a volume on the art of northeastern Greece (*Studien zur nordostgriechischen Kunst*, 1975).

BIBLIOGRAPHY

H. Dittmers Herdejürgen, "Langlotz, Ernst," *NDB* 13 (1982), 607–8; A. H. Borbein, in *Archäologenbildnisse*, 268–69.

LANZI, LUIGI (1732–1810). Italian archaeologist, philologist, art historian and curator.

Lanzi's contributions, especially to the fields of philology and archaeology, led the nineteenth-century German philologist Wilhelm Corssen to acclaim him as "the father of ancient Italian studies."

Lanzi was born in 1732 at Treia and was educated as a Jesuit priest. Following the papal suppression of the Jesuit order in 1773, he was first appointed to the office of antiquities assistant at the galleries of Florence, and then in 1776 he became the curator at the museum, where he published a guide to the collections, *Guida alla Galleria di Firenze* (Florence, 1782). He became a scholar on the subjects of Italian painting and Etruscan antiquities and language. Through his principal work in the field of art history, *Storia pittorica dell'Italia* (Bassano, 1795–96), in which he concentrated on schools of style rather than on "lives" of the artists, he came to be regarded as the founder of modern Italian art history.

In the field of classical archaeology, Lanzi's greatest achievement was his *Saggio di lingua etrusca e di altre antiche d'Italia* (Rome, 1789), which was a summary of current knowledge on the Etruscans, including not just their language but also their history, art and customs. Earlier writers on ancient languages had assumed that Etruscan, along with all other languages, was derived from Hebrew. The object of Lanzi's *Saggio di lingua etrusca* was to prove that Etruscan was related to the languages of the neighboring peoples of Italy—the Greeks, Umbrians, Oscans and Romans. His theory, though it was cautiously stated, met with abuse from later writers on the Etruscan language. The philologist Corssen, however, whose own work (*Ueber die Sprache der Etrusker*) was also attacked, defended Lanzi's scholarship and praised his services to philology.

Lanzi's astute, critical judgment also guided him to produce a work on the so-called Etruscan vases (*Dei Vasi antichi dipinti volgarmente chiamati etruschi*, 1806), of which he rightly perceived their Greek origin. By pointing out that these vases were inscribed with Greek characters, not Etruscan ones, Lanzi was able to refute one of the many errors deeply rooted in *Etruscheria, the "Etruscomania" of his time. He also intended to illustrate all of antiquity from the existing monuments and literature, but he never (understandably so) accomplished the task. This project had grown out of his study of the antiquities added at that time to the Florentine collections from the Villa Medici. His observations on ancient sculpture and its styles were published as an appendix to *Saggio di lingua etrusca*. Lanzi organized a collection of Etruscan antiquities in Florence, which later grew into the collection now displayed at the Florence Archaeological Museum.

In addition to his other contributions in the field of classical antiquity, Lanzi also published an edition of Hesiod's *Works and Days*. He died on 31 March 1810 and was buried in the church of Santa Croce at Florence, next to Michelangelo.

BIBLIOGRAPHY

U. Segrè, *Luigi Lanzi e le sue opere* (Assisi, 1904); B. Nogara, *L'Abate Luigi Lanzi e l'opera sua negli studî etruscologici e di storia d'arte* (Rome, 1910); G. Natali, "Il Varrone del secolo XVIII," in *Idee, costumi, uomini del Settecento* (Turin, 1926). G. Natali, s.v. "Luigi Lanzi," *EI* 20 (1933), 515; M. Pallottino, "Luigi Lanzi fondatore degli studi di storia, storia della civiltà e storia dell'arte etrusca," *StEtr* 29 (1961), 27–38; M. Cristofani, *Luigi Lanzi antiquario* (Florence, 1982).

CHERYL L. SOWDER

LAOCOON. Renowned marble sculpture group representing the Trojan priest who, with his two sons, was destroyed by sea serpents after he had warned the Trojans against the wooden horse; attributed by Pliny to Hagesandros, Polydoros and Athenodoros of Rhodes and described as an ornament of the palace of the emperor Titus (*NH.* 36.37).

The *Laocoon* was discovered on 14 January 1506 on the property of Felice de' Freddi near S. Maria Maggiore in Rome. This land was in the area between the *Baths of Trajan and the water reservoir known as the "Sette Sale." Francesco da Sangallo, the son of Pope *Julius II's architect Giuliano da *Sangallo, described in 1567 how his father and *Michelangelo had been summoned to inspect the newly discovered sculpture and how his father had instantly identified the group as that celebrated by Pliny. Julius II competed successfully with prominent collectors of the day (including Cardinal Galeotto della Rovere and Federico II Gonzaga (*Gonzaga family) to acquire the *Laocoon*. It was taken to the Belvedere (*Vatican Museums) and by June 1506 was installed in a niche in the courtyard. There it remained until it was ceded to the French in 1797; *Napoleon triumphantly displayed it in Paris, installing it at the Musée Central des Arts when it was inaugurated in 1800. By the end of February 1816 the *Laocoon* had been returned to the Belvedere courtyard.

On discovery, the right arms of Laocoon and his younger son were missing from the shoulder; the fingers were missing from the right hand of the elder son. The sons were probably restored in marble by 1523, but these restorations were amended by A. Cornacchini (1725–27). The position of Laocoon's right arm varies in early copies and prints. In *Bandinelli's copy of 1523, the arm is flexed; by the eighteenth century, antique gems were adduced in support of this interpretation. A roughed-out marble version with Laocoon's arm in a bent position was attributed in the eighteenth century to Michelangelo. A terracotta arm, almost fully extended, was attached to the statue by Giovanni *Montorsoli (1532–33); a sixteenth-century replacement of the Montorsoli arm was often attributed to *Bernini. All restorations were detached before the group was removed to France; in Paris they were replaced by after-casts from a late seventeenth-century cast of a model whose arms were supposed to be by *Girardon. On the group's return to Rome, Cornacchini's marble restorations were fitted once more to the sons, and a stucco arm, different in minor respects from the terracotta one, was fitted to Laocoon. In 1905, Laocoon's original right arm (completely flexed) was found in a dealer's shop in Rome by L. Pollak, but it was not attached to the statue until 1957–60, when Magi supervised a complete restoration of the *Laocoon* group.

Pliny had specifically stated that the group was carved from a single block of marble. However, disparities in the type of marble and some joins were noted in the sixteenth century (e.g., by Fulvio *Orsini, Pirro *Ligorio and Cesare Trivulzio, who cited Michelangelo and *Giulio Romano). *Montfaucon, *Richardson, Falconet and *Winckelmann contributed to this heated discussion. Winckelmann maintained that the joins could have been so fine as to escape notice, and thus Pliny's reputation, rather than that of the statue, was called into question.

The group has been admired for the brilliant rendering of the muscles and for the variety of expression in the figures. Indeed, the exact nature of Laocoon's pathos became the issue of lengthy debate in reference to Vergil's description of the death of the Trojan priest in the *Aeneid*. This controversy usually concerned the proper limits of the literary and visual arts and included *Lessing's celebrated essay (1766), with further contributions by Schiller, Herder, *Goethe and Hirt.

Further debate centered on whether or not the sculpture was inspired by the passage in the *Aeneid*. If it was a work contemporaneous with Vergil or later, it could not have been produced during that earlier epoch so highly esteemed by the philhellenes of the late eighteenth century. Some countered that Vergil had been inspired by the sculpture or even by an earlier, lost literary source. Winckelmann held that the statue's perfection proved a dating to the period of Alexander the Great. Having rejected the idea that art declined after Alexander, Éméric-David and E. Q. *Visconti placed the group in the Early Imperial period.

In recent years evidence has emerged to suggest that the *Laocoon* is a reconstruction by the artists named by Pliny, now believed to have been working in the first century A.C. (At *Sperlonga a group of sculptures in a Baroque style like that of the *Laocoon* has been excavated, along with an inscription naming the three Rhodian sculptors; it seems to date to the first century A.C.) Von Blanckenhagen suggests that their model was of Pergamene origin and involved only the father and younger son. It is therefore interesting to note that reservations about the pose and proportions of the elder son already had been expressed in the sixteenth and eighteenth centuries.

BIBLIOGRAPHY

+M. Bieber, *Laocoon: The Influence of the Group Since Its Rediscovery* (New York, 1942); +F. Magi, "Il ripristino del Laocoonte," *Atti della Pontificia Accademia Romana di Archeologia* ser. 3, 9 (1960), 5–59; W. Fuchs, in Helbig, I, 162–66; +P. H. von Blanckenhagen, "Laokoon, Sperlonga und Vergil," *AA* 3 (1969), 256–75; Sheard, nos. 60–62; Haskell—Penny, 243–47; G. P. Warden, "The Domus Aurea Reconsidered," *JSAH* 40 (1981), 271–78, esp. 277 and n. 40; +B. Andreae, *Laokoon und die Grundung Roms* (Mainz am Rhein, 1988).

PETER HOLLIDAY

LAPIS NIGER. A pavement of "black stone" in a small portion of the oldest Roman meeting place, the Comitium.

The name is told to us by Festus (Lindsay, p. 184), who says that it marked a deadly spot the Romans associated with the tomb of Romulus or another legendary king. The phrase *lapis niger* is sometimes mistakenly applied to a truncated stone marker (*cippus*) inscribed with very old Latin and set up in the Comitium apparently ca. 560 B.C. at the level of Pavement II. The pavement of black stone covered the marker and its ambit, perhaps ca. 80 B.C. (Pavement VI), and was doubtless chosen to preserve in concealment a sacred site whose purpose had long since become unclear. The area and its buried marker were first excavated by G. Boni in 1899 and 1900. The history of the study of the monument has been fraught with controversy.

The marker's partially surviving text contains key words whose certain meanings are "accursed," "king," "herald," "team of draft animals," "trip" (or "procession"), "just." Along with independent testimony, the text suggests that the Roman king or priest-king both sacrificed and had public assemblies on or near the site. Palmer argues for the site as originally a sacred grove clearing, which he believes is a word (*lucus*) met on the marker and, further, argues for a date of the inscription in the early Republic as legislation touching the priest-king. Gantz, taking his lead from the entry in Festus, argues for the site as a shrine of some hero (*heroon*), which he dates to ca. 570, the beginning (for him) of the Etruscan kingship at Rome. Coarelli, in contrast, subjects both the archaeological and literary evidence to a thoroughly new review and identifies the site as an Archaic shrine of the god Vulcan (Volcanal) and the text of the marker as a *lex sacra* concerning the king's sacred and political functions in the Comitium.

BIBLIOGRAPHY

G. Boni, *NSc* (1899), 151–58; (1900), 312–40; R.E.A. Palmer, *The King and the Comitium, A Study of Rome's Oldest Public Document*, Historia, Einzelschriften 11 (Wiesbaden, 1969); T. N. Gantz, "*Lapis Niger:* The Tomb of Romulus," *La Parola del*

Passato 29 (1974), 350–61; F. Coarelli, "Il Comizio dalle origini alla fine della repubblica, Cronologia e topografia," *La Parola del Passato* 32 (1977), 166–238.

ROBERT E. A. PALMER

LARGO ARGENTINA, AREA SACRA, Rome. A row of temples, possibly all dedications of victorious generals, in the southern *Campus Martius in Rome.

The complex was discovered in 1926, when street widening between Via Arenula and Corso Vittorio Emanuele led to the demolition of the church of S. Nicola a'Cesarini. The church was known to be built over the northernmost temple, a Republican structure of great interest, and to have remains of a round temple next to it, but two farther to the south were now discovered, and it was decided to preserve the area as an archaeological park. Excavation was under the direction of G. Marchetti-Longhi, who published much but left much still to be published. There may be more temples continuing the row to the south also.

The oldest temple is probably the northernmost (A), which began as a small shrine, having a façade with four columns on a high platform of Grotta Oscura tufa above an altar court raised four steps above the surrounding ground. Its date is almost certainly third century B.C. Temple C has a similar altar court, but the temple is much larger, with a façade of four widely spaced columns and colonnades down the sides. It is only a little younger than Temple A, which was subsequently enlarged to balance C, as a peripteral temple with six columns on the façade. This must have occurred in the second century B.C. Temple B, a circular peripteral temple, is very likely Lutatius Catulus's temple of Fortuna Huiusce Diei of ca. 101 B.C. Temple D seems to have had no columns, although it is the largest, a rectangular temple with a deep pronaos. The present building dates from the paving of the whole area with tufa in the first century B.C., but the temple platform has not been emptied and explored.

A portico of slender Ionic columns runs along the north side of Temple A, and an arcade with an engaged order runs along most, perhaps all, of the east side of the area, leaving a deep apron in front of the temples. The identity of the divinities worshiped here has been much debated. No complete study of the area and the finds is yet available, but it is regarded as one of the signal archaeological discoveries under *Fascism.

BIBLIOGRAPHY

G. Marchetti-Longhi, in *BullCom* 60 (1932), 253–346; 61 (1933), 164–94; 64 (1936), 83–139; 76 (1956), 45–118; 82 (1970–71), 7–62; F. Coarelli et al., *L'Area sacra di largo Argentina* (Rome, 1981).

L. RICHARDSON, JR

LARNACA. See KITION.

LATERAN. Roman family name preserved as a place designation in San Giovanni in Laterano, first church built by Constantine and Rome's Cathedral.

Throughout the Middle Ages the grandeur of Christian Rome and papal legitimacy were proclaimed by the Lateran's collection of ancient bronze statuary, especially the Etruscan she-wolf (*lupa mater romanorum;* *Capitoline *Wolf*) and the equestrian statue of **Marcus Aurelius,* identified as Constantine (*caballus Constantini*). Pope Innocent II (1130–38) brought the porphyry sarcophagus of Hadrian from the *Castel Sant'Angelo to serve as his tomb; Anastasius IV (1153–54) chose the porphyry sarcophagus of Saint Helena for his. In 1347 *Cola di Rienzo, "tribune" of the people, consecrated himself in a ritual bath using the ancient tub located in the Lateran baptistery believed to have been employed in Constantine's baptism; with the ancient bronze plaque, the *Lex de imperio vespasiani* (CIL VI, 930), he demonstrated how the Roman Senate and people commanded ultimate power.

All the Lateran's imperial trophies were transferred to the Campidoglio during the Renaissance, beginning with *Sixtus IV's 1471 donation of the Lupa, **Spinario,* *Capitoline *Camillus,* colossal head, hand and globe (fragments of a statue of *Constantine or *Constantius II); donations continued, by Paul III in 1538 with the *Marcus Aurelius,* followed by Gregory XIII in 1574 with the *Lex de imperio.* In 1587 *Sixtus V transferred to the Lateran the largest of Rome's *obelisks, from the *Circus Maximus, as a symbol of the Church's triumph. In 1595 three lead pipes inscribed with the names of the Lateran family were discovered near the church (*CIL* XV, 7536); they were preserved by Fulvio *Orsini, canon of the Lateran. Four bronze columns of Imperial date, first recorded in the church in the eleventh century and said to have come from the Temple of Jerusalem, were employed ca. 1600 to form the colossal aedicula of the Altar of the Sacrament commissioned by Pope Clement VIII.

BIBLIOGRAPHY
P. Lauer, *Le Palais de Latran, Étude historique et archéologique* (Paris, 1911); R. Krautheimer et al., *Corpus basilicarum christianarum Romae,* 1–5 (Rome, 1937–77), 1–92; I. Herklotz, "Der Campus Lateranensis im Mittelalter," *Römisches Jahrbuch für Kunstgeschichte* 22 (1985), 1–43; P. Liverani, "Le proprietà private nell'area lateranense fino all'età di Costantino," *MEFRA* 100 (1988), 891–915; Jack Freiberg, *The Lateran in 1600: Christian Concord in Counter-Reformation Rome* (Cambridge, 1995).

JACK FREIBERG

LAUREION. Greek mining district in Attika that provided Athens with a major source of its wealth in the sixth to fourth centuries B.C.

Rich deposits of silver were exploited in the area of southeast Attika from the Early Bronze Age into modern times, paying for many of the ships used at Salamis and fueling Athenian recovery in the fourth century. The actual mineral rights were owned by the state and were let out on contract by the *poletai,* whose accounts on stone have been found in the Athenian *Agora. The mining district itself is honeycombed underground with adits, galleries and ventilation shafts that were studied in the nineteenth century by Ardaillon (1890s) and that extend over an area measuring some 14 km north-south and 3 km east-west. On the surface are dozens of washeries used to refine the ore, huge cisterns to provide the necessary water and dining quarters for the large slave population that worked the mines. Smelting furnaces, which produced noxious fumes, were removed and set along the coast, in positions easy for the import of firewood and the transport of the metal, both silver and lead. Considerable work was done in the 1970s at these various surface installations by the Belgians (Mussche) at Thorikos, the British (Jones) at Agrileza, the *Greek Archaeological Service (Kakovoyannis) in various places and the Politechnic University at Souresa (Conophagos).

BIBLIOGRAPHY

E. Ardaillon, *Les Mines de Laurion dans l'Antiquité* (Paris, 1897); R. J. Hopper, "The Laurion Mines: A Reconsideration," *BSA* 63 (1968), 293–326; C. Conophagos, *Le Laurium antique* (Athens, 1980).

JOHN McK. CAMP II

LAVINIUM (PRATICA DI MARE). Site of a major Italian sanctuary, associated with the Roman hero Aeneas, in use from the Archaic period (sixth century B.C.).

Discovered near the modern town of Pratica di Mare, Lavinium stood at milestone 18 of the ancient Via Laurentina, 28km south of Rome and 4km from the sea. The tradition, followed by Vergil, Livy, Dionysios of Halikarnassos and others, that the town was founded by Aeneas and named after his wife Lavinia, can be traced back at least to Timaios (fl. ca. 300 B.C.), who says that the Penates of Troy were preserved there. Lavinium was a cult center, not only of the Penates but of Vesta, Indiges, Aeneas, Venus Frutis, Juturna, the Dioscuri and others.

The site of Lavinium was already recognized in the sixteenth century by Pirro *Ligorio, and finds occurred there sporadically, especially in the nineteenth century. In 1900 *Lanciani hypothesized the location of the sanctuary, but not until 1955 did Ferdinando Castagnoli and Lucos Cozza begin their excavations that were to lead to the final identification of the site. From 1963, the work at Lavinium was sponsored by the Istituto di Topografia Antica of the University of Rome.

Bronze Age and Early Iron Age settlement has been traced on the acropolis, but the most important finds are thirteen altars of local tufa, dating from the mid-sixth (#13) to the second centuries B.C. (#8, overlying a sixth-century altar), found in a sanctuary several hundred meters south of the town. The fourth-century Heroon nearby, built over a seventh-century tomb, was referred to by Dionysios as the tomb of Aeneas and is accepted by many scholars as such.

To the east of the altars, a second sanctuary was investigated by Castagnoli in 1960 (another campaign in 1977 was sponsored by the Istituto di Topografia Antica), uncovering a votive deposit with remarkable terracotta statues of approximately life size or even larger, as well as many smaller votive offerings, the whole dating from the late seventh to the early third centuries B.C.

BIBLIOGRAPHY
G. K. Galinsky, *Aeneas, Sicily and Rome* (Princeton, NJ, 1969); F. Castagnoli, s.v. "Lavinium," *PECS,* 491–92; C. F. Giuliani in *Enea nel Lazio: Archeologia e mito* (Rome, 1981), 162–77.

W. W. DE GRUMMOND

LEAKE, WILLIAM MARTIN (1777–1860). English soldier, traveler, numismatist and topographer.

From an affluent family, Leake was commissioned in the Royal Regiment of Artillery, serving from 1794 to 1815, retiring with the rank of lieutenant colonel. In 1799 he was sent on a mission with the Turkish army, and for three years he was able to explore widely in Asia Minor, Syria and Egypt. His next tour was in Greece, where from 1805 to 1807 he made surveys of northern and southern Greece and, before returning home, persuaded Ali Pasha to work for reconciliation between England and Turkey. His final visit to Greece lasted a year, 1809–10, when Leake not only supported Ali against the French with military supplies but also made further travels in Epiros and Thessaly. Leake left England one more time, briefly in 1815, on a mission with the Swiss army.

His distinguished military career over, Leake turned to the detailed journals that he had made on all his excursions; these, together with his collections, particularly of coins, were to fill his remaining forty years. His first major publication appeared in 1821, *The Topography of Athens;* then followed, to name the most significant works, *Journal of a Tour in Asia Minor* in 1824, *Travels in the Morea* in 1830 and *Travels in Northern Greece* in 1835, all classic studies still important today. In the year before his death, Leake at the age of seventy-nine published *A Supplement to Numismata Hellenica,* and he notes that his purpose in writing has always been to tell modern Greeks something of the geography of the country they have inherited and of the monuments that contain no small part of their past history. Few have succeeded so well in their intentions; as a topographer of classical Greece, Leake has no peers. He deserves a place alongside Pausanias.

BIBLIOGRAPHY
J. H. Marsden, *A Brief Memoir of the Life and Writings of the Late Lieutenant Colonel William Martin Leake* (London, 1864); W. W. Wroth, "Leake, William Martin," *DNB* 11 (repr. 1949–50), 764–65; G. Savvides, "Approaches to William Martin Leake" (in Greek) *Epoches* 43 (November 1966), 480–500.

C.W.J. ELIOT

LEAR, EDWARD (1812–88). English painter of landscape and topography and traveler; writer of nonsense verse and limericks.

Lear, one of the youngest of twenty-one children, was raised by his sister Ann and led a solitary life, mainly abroad. He traveled to the Continent in 1837 to spend some eight years touring, sketching and painting in Italy. (His *Views in Rome and Its Environs* was published in 1841; *Illustrated Excursions in Italy* appeared in two volumes in 1846.) Lear visited Greece in 1848–49 and resided in Korfu (*Korkyra) in 1855–58 and 1861–64. He published his impressions in his illustrated *Journal of a Landscape Painter in Greece and Albania* (London, 1851) and *Views in the Seven Ionian Islands* (London, 1863). Lear also traveled to Palestine, Syria, Egypt, India and Ceylon. At the end of his life he resided in San Remo.

During his years in Greece, Lear made over 2,000 drawings of local views and subjects. His many pen and watercolor sketches show great topographical accuracy and a moving sensitivity. Though classical ruins were not his central interest, he has left some striking depictions of them, recording them in a period when Greece was not yet overrun by tourists or defiled by pollution. His ecstasy at their appearance is almost religious: "[T]he Acropolis . . . is quite beyond my expectations . . . poor old scrubby Rome sinks into nothing by the side of such beautiful magnificence. . . .I wish you could see the temple of the Parthenon . . . by sunset. . . . Most of the columns being rusty with age the whole mass becomes like gold & ivory."

Many of Lear's drawings are today in Athens in the *Benaki Museum, the Gennadius Library (J. *Gennadius) and the Museum of the City of Athens and at Harvard University.

BIBLIOGRAPHY

+P. Hofer, *Edward Lear as a Landscape Draughtsman* (Cambridge, MA, 1967); Tsigakou, *Rediscovery of Greece*, esp. 199a–b; V. Noakes, *Edward Lear, The Life of a Wanderer* (London, 1985); R. Eisner, *Travelers in an Antique Land, The History and Literature of Travel to Greece* (Ann Arbor, 1991), 155–67.

LE BRUN (LEBRUN), CHARLES (1619–90).

French artist who essentially created *le style Louis XIV* and gave the age of *Louis XIV its classical character.

Best known for his decorative painting at Versailles and other palaces, Le Brun was a founding member of the Royal Academy of Painting and Sculpture (1648) and served as its chancellor (1663), rector (1668) and director (1683). During his tenure the *French Academy in Rome was founded (1666) to serve as the backbone of education in classical antiquity for French artists.

Trained by F. Perrier and S. Vouet, Le Brun took advantage of the opportunity to study antique art when he accompanied *Poussin to Rome in 1642. Prepared to leave after only a few months, Le Brun was encouraged to stay longer by his protector Chancellor Pierre Séguier. In works produced in Rome and after his return to Paris in 1646, Le Brun demonstrated his direct knowledge of archaeological details. His Roman sketchbook served as reference for monuments he had seen and was used by others as well (including *Montfaucon, who drew from it for illustrations in his *L'Antiquité expliquée,* 1719 and 1724).

His numerous ambitious projects of decoration (Apollo Gallery of the Louvre, 1661 ff.; Gallery of Hercules at the Hôtel Lambert, ca. 1658–1661; decorations at Versailles, 1674–84; etc.) epitomize the French Baroque and at the same time reflect the way the classical past permeated contemporary art and thought. Le

Brun specialized in coordinating an ensemble of colored marbles, stucco, gilding and painting filled with classical allusions, in a system that ultimately took its inspiration from ancient Roman imperial remains, such as the *Domus Aurea.

Le Brun's major easel paintings included five canvases with the classical theme of the history of Alexander the Great (1661–ca. 1668; the *Louvre and Versailles). Evidence of his abiding respect for the canons and subjects of ancient art is provided by the portrait of Le Brun presented to the Royal Academy by Largillière (1686), where the director is shown with small copies of the *Belvedere *Antinous* and the *Borghese *Gladiator* beside his easel.

Major exhibitions of Le Brun's works were held at Versailles in 1963 and at the Louvre in 1985–86.

BIBLIOGRAPHY

J. Guillet de Saint-Georges, "Mémoires historiques des ouvrages de Charles Le Brun," *Mémoires inédits sur la vie et les ouvrages des membres de l'Académie Royale de Peinture et Sculpture* (Paris, 1854), I, 1–72; +D. Posner, "Charles Le Brun's 'Triumphs of Alexander,' " *ArtB* 41 (1959), 237–48; +J. Thuillier—J. Montagu, *Charles Le Brun, 1619–1690: peintre et dessinateur* (Versailles, 1963); +A. Chatelet—J. Thuillier, *French Painting from Le Nain to Fragonard* (Geneva, 1964).

JOYCE M. DAVIS

LEFKANDI. Greek site located on the west coast of the island of Euboia, between *Eretria and *Chalkis; its Iron Age cemeteries have provided some of the earliest evidence of wealth in post-Mycenaean Greece.

Excavations by the *British School at Athens in collaboration with the *Greek Archaeological Service were first carried out from 1964 to 1970. Finds from the Iron Age cemeteries showed a chronological range of ca. 1100–825 B.C. and grave offerings that grew increasingly rich. On the hillock known as Toumba were found the burials that indicated the greatest prosperity, with gold jewelry, Near Eastern imports and Attic vases.

In 1980, bulldozing took place at Toumba as the result of plans by the owner to build there. The following year a joint Greek-British team, under M. Popham, L. H. Sackett and E. Touloupa, investigated a building that had been partially demolished by the bulldozing and uncovered the remains of its stone foundation and mud-brick walls, indicating a structure ca. 47m long and 10m wide with an apsidal end and flanking porticoes. Dating to about the middle of the tenth century B.C., the structure provides some of the earliest known evidence for Hellenic Greek architecture.

Within the structure was found a pit with the burial of a wealthy female, whose inhumed body was adorned with gold discs on the breasts as well as other gold or gilt ornaments; an iron knife lay beside the head. Adjacent was a bronze amphora covered with a bronze bowl and containing some remarkably well preserved decorated cloth, next to which were an iron sword, spearhead and whetstone. In a nearby pit were discovered the skeletons of horses that accompanied the dead. The excavators interpreted the complex as the cremation

Photograph of *Karl Lehmann-Hartleben*. (Deutsches Archäologisches Institut, Berlin.)

burial of a hero, with his consort and horses, and the imposing building as a heroon in honor of the warrior buried there. The structure was not in use for long but was soon partially dismantled and filled in with rubble, earth and mud bricks in which were mixed some 26,000 potsherds dating to the Middle Protogeometric period. The results at Lefkandi, with evidence of wealth, trade and imposing architecture at a very early date, have led to a reevaluation of the period once known as the ''Dark Age'' in Greece.

BIBLIOGRAPHY

L. H. Sackett—M. R. Popham, "Lefkandi, A Euboean Town of the Bronze Age and the Early Iron Age," *Archaeology* 25 (1972), 8–19; +M. Popham—E. Touloupa—L. H. Sackett, "The Hero of Lefkandi," *Antiquity* 56 (1982), 169–74; M. R. Popham—L. H. Sackett—P. G. Themelis, eds., *Lefkandi* 1, *The Iron Age* (London, 1979–80); R.W.V. Catling—I. S. Lemos, *Lefkandi* 2, *The Protogeometric Building at Toumba*, pt. 1, *The Pottery*, ed. M. R. Popham—P. G. Calligas—L. H. Sackett (London, 1990).

LE GALLUZZE. See ''TEMPLE OF MINERVA MEDICA.''

LEHMANN (-HARTLEBEN), KARL (1894–1960). Archaeologist, art historian, classicist; director of excavations at *Samothrace, 1938–60.

Karl Lehmann was born in Rostock, Germany, of culturally eminent parents and studied at Tübingen (under Noack), Munich (under Wölfflin) and Göttingen. After serving in the Red Cross and as interpreter to the Turkish navy in Istanbul (1914–18), he received the Ph.D. at Berlin under *Wilamowitz-Moellendorff. He taught first at Berlin and later (after serving as assistant director of the *German Archaeological Institute in Rome) at Heidelberg and Münster, as professor of archaeology and director of the archaeological museum (1929–33). Brought up as a Lutheran but of Jewish descent, he left Nazi Germany in 1933. After two years of independent work in Italy, he was called to the Institute of Fine Arts, New York University, where he founded and directed the Archaeological Research Fund and its excavations in Samothrace until his death.

Broadly trained, especially in archaeology, classics, ancient history and philosophy and the history of art, he was a brilliant teacher and prolific scholar. Among his most influential publications were *Die Trajanssaüle* (1926), ''The Dome of Heaven,'' in the *Art Bulletin* (1945), *Thomas Jefferson, American Humanist* (1947) and the *Guides,* reports, and his volumes in *Samothrace* (Bollingen Series, 60). His honors included Knight Commander of the Royal Greek Order of the Phoenix and honorary citizen of Samothrace (1951).

BIBLIOGRAPHY
P. H. von Blanckenhagen, ''Necrology,'' *AJA* 65 (1961), 307–8; *Essays in Memory of Karl Lehmann,* Institute of Fine Arts, New York University (New York, 1964), v–viii; D. Fleming—B. Bailyn, *The Intellectual Migration, Europe and America, 1930–1960* (Cambridge, MA, 1969), 580–81; W. McGuire, *Bollingen, An Adventure in Collecting the Past* (Princeton, NJ, 1982), 241–47.

                                        PHYLLIS WILLIAMS LEHMANN

LELAND (LEYLAND), JOHN (1506?–52). English antiquary.

Born and reared in London, John Leland studied at Christ's College, Cambridge (B.A., 1522) and All Souls' College, Oxford. He completed his education in Paris, where he met G. *Budé and from which he returned as a finished scholar in both Greek and Latin.

In 1533, Henry VIII named Leland as ''king's antiquary,'' an office held by no one before and no one since. He was directed to make a search for English antiquities in libraries, monasteries and colleges throughout the realm. His antiquarian tour of England and Wales seems to have occupied him from about 1534 to 1543, during which time he claims that he visited every body of water, every mountain and valley, every city, castle, monastery and college in the kingdom. He investigated and described Roman, Saxon and Danish remains, and he examined numerous coins and inscriptions; his principal interest was topography, and he gave much attention to place-names and genealogies.

Leland's results were to be published in a great work, *History and Antiquities of This Nation,* which, however, never saw the light. His mass of miscellaneous notes was left to be consulted by succeeding generations of antiquaries.

Leland conceived numerous schemes for publications and assembled copious notes but rarely succeeded in bringing forth results. In the end, his antiquarian research overtaxed his mind, and he was declared insane. In 1550 he was turned

Portrait of *Charles Lenormant*, lithograph by A. Lemoine after P. Delaroche, from *Panthéon des illustrations françaises au XIXe siècle* 8 (1865–69). (Westfälisches Landesmuseum für Kunst und Kulturgeschichte, Münster, Porträtarchiv Diepenbroick. Photo: R. Wakonigg.)

over to his brother John for safekeeping, and he died, without recovering his reason, in 1552. Most of Leland's manuscripts, including five volumes of *Collectanea* that contain his notes on antiquities, were deposited in 1632 in the Bodleian Library, Oxford.

BIBLIOGRAPHY

S. Lee, "Leland, John," *DNB* 11 (1950), 892–96; L. T. Smith, ed., *The Itinerary of John Leland* (Carbondale, 1964); S. Piggott, *Ruins in a Landscape, Essays in Antiquarianism* (Edinburgh, 1976), 10–12.

LENORMANT, CHARLES (1802–59). French archaeologist and numismatist; Egyptologist.

Born in Paris, Charles Lenormant first studied law, then developed an interest in archaeology during a trip to Italy. In 1828, he participated in the expedition of Champollion to Egypt. Returning to Paris, he served as librarian and keeper of antiquities at the Bibliothèque Nationale and then as professor of archaeology at the Collège Français.

In 1844 Lenormant founded the *Revue Archéologique,* still one of the foremost French periodicals on archaeology. He was one of the editors/authors of the twenty-volume *Trésor de numismatique et de glyptique* (Paris, 1834–58) and published studies on Egyptian antiquities, Greek royal coinage and Roman imperial iconography.

Late in his life, Lenormant journeyed to Greece, where he undertook excavations at *Eleusis and was the first to identify the Varvakeion statuette of Athena (excavated in Athens in 1859) as a replica of the *Athena Parthenos of Pheidias.

He died in Athens and was buried on the hill of Kolonos, next to Karl Otfried *Müller. His famous son, François *Lenormant, followed in his footsteps in many ways.

BIBLIOGRAPHY

Stark, 11, 286, 297, 298, etc.; Michaelis, 136, 309; *Porträtarchiv,* no. 164.

LENORMANT, FRANÇOIS (1837–83). French Assyriologist, classicist and numismatist.

Son of the Orientalist Charles *Lenormant, François traveled widely in the Mediterranean and Near East. After serving as sublibrarian in the Institut de France, he succeeded C. E. *Beulé in the chair of archaeology at the Bibliothèque Nationale in 1874. With Baron J. J. de Witte, he founded the *Gazette archéologique* in 1875. He made significant contributions to the early understanding of Akkadian and was the first to publish an Akkadian grammar. An early supporter of *Schliemann, Lenormant recognized twenty years before *Dörpfeld that Troy II was far too early to be Homer's Troy. His comprehensive numismatic work, *La Monnaie dans l'antiquité,* three volumes (1878–79), is still useful.

Lenormant was also a successful popularizer. His *Manuel d'histoire ancienne de l'Orient* (1868 and 1881–87) helped awaken popular interest in the ancient civilizations of the Near East. Among other important books were his *Études accadiennes* (1873–74) and *La Grande Grèce* (1881–83). Though most of his scholarly work was of the highest caliber, Lenormant's reputation was ruined when he was revealed in 1882–83 as a forger of manuscripts, inscriptions and antiquities. Shortly after articles exposing him began to appear, he died at the age of forty-six.

BIBLIOGRAPHY

J. J. de Witte, *Notice sur François Lenormant* (Brussels, 1887); H. Trevor-Roper, *Hermit of Peking* (Harmondsworth, 1979), 371; G. Furlani—S. L. Cesano, s.v. "Lenormant, François," *EI* 20 (1933), 847; "Lenormant, François," *Grand Dictionnaire Universel du XIXe Siècle* 10 (1873), 363.

DAVID A. TRAILL

LEO X (GIOVANNI DE' MEDICI; 1475–1521). Renaissance pope (1513–21) from the *Medici family; art collector and patron.

Born in Florence as the second son of Lorenzo de' Medici (Il Magnifico), Giovanni de' Medici was early destined for the clergy, becoming cardinal at the earliest possible date (1492) and transferring to Rome. He soon gathered around himself a circle of artists and writers, opened to scholars his rich library and began to commission works of art. In 1505 he purchased a palace on the Monte

Mario (later called the Palazzo Madama), where he began to assemble a collection of marbles, among which was a statue of *Bacchus.*

Elevated to the papacy in 1513 as the successor to *Julius II, Leo X took advantage of his situation to secure positions of power for his relatives, sometimes resorting to warfare that drained the papal treasuries and deceitful acts of diplomacy that led to the execution of enemies. Leo X sought to make Rome the cultural center of the world and, in so doing, attracted to his court and employ a brilliant array of intellectuals and artists. *Bembo and *Colocci served as his secretaries, and *Raphael served as his commissioner of antiquities (*Commissario delle Antichità). He engaged Paolo Giovio as master of the University of Rome and patronized the poet Sannazaro, the historian Guicciardini and the humanist Trissino. The printer Jacopo Mazzochi, encouraged by Leo, published books on classical antiquity such as the *Illustrium imagines* of Andrea *Fulvio (1517) and an album of Roman inscriptions by *Albertini, the first such (1521). Baldassare Castiglione published his dialogue on the perfect courtier, *Il Cortegiano,* in the Rome of Leo X and became a central figure in the cultural life of the city.

In the Vatican, Leo continued the decoration of the papal apartments, partly completed by Raphael and his followers under Julius II; he also commissioned the adornment of the Vatican Logge with the "Bible of Raphael" and the decorations of *grottesche* by Giovanni da *Udine. In regard to antiquities, Leo X is remembered as having little interest in the Belvedere collection begun by Julius II, though he did add to it the *Nile* river god in 1513 and acquired for the Vatican the *Kneeling Persian.* It was one of a group of statues (reported as five or seven in number) excavated together in Rome by 1514/15 and later referred to as the *Horatii and Curiatii* (others were sent to the Palazzo Medici and later went to Naples).

Above all, Leo is known for having created the job of commissioner of antiquities for Raphael, so that the artist might oversee the recovery of ancient materials to be used in the building of St. Peter's (1515). Leo X was the addressee of a famous but problematic letter ostensibly written by Raphael but widely believed to be composed with the help of Castiglione (date unknown). The letter laments the terrible destruction of antiquities in the city, some of which could evidently be blamed on Leo himself, though the pope had spoken strongly in favor of the preservation of carved inscriptions. The letter also reveals that Raphael had been asked by the pope to create a map of ancient Rome, a project that he left incomplete at his death in 1520. In this undertaking the artist is thought to have been aided by several scholars who were at the court of Leo X, including Marco Fabio Calvo of Ravenna (who made a translation of Vitruvius for Raphael), the topographer Andrea Fulvio and the architectural theorist Fra *Giocondo. Calvo's own archaeological map of Rome as it appeared at the time of Pliny may be the end result of this project of Raphael and Leo X.

BIBLIOGRAPHY
Pastor, *History of the Popes,* VIII, esp. 242–49, 373–76; F. Castagnoli, "Raphael and Ancient Rome," in *The Complete Work of Raphael* (New York, 1969), 569–84; Bober—Rubinstein, 179, 477; +Lanciani, *Storia degli scavi* 1 (1989), 211–70.

LEONTINOI (LENTINI). Greek colony in *Sicily.

Leontinoi was established by Chalkidian Greeks from Sicilian Naxos about 728 B.C. following expulsion of the Sikels (Thucydides 6. 3, 3). At the beginning of the fifth century it was conquered by Hippokrates of *Gela (Herodotos 7. 154) but regained its autonomy after 466 B.C. The city was reconquered by *Syracuse in 422 B.C. and thereafter enjoyed only brief periods of freedom. The Romans took control of Leontinoi in 215 B.C.

Later destructions overwhelmed the ancient monuments of Leontinoi, with the exception of some tracts of fortifications. The site was firmly identified on the basis of Polybios's topographical description (7. 6) by the nineteenth century (Schubring, 1874). Sporadic finds were reported from the settlement, and numerous tombs were opened by chance or for plunder. Only at the end of the century did systematic excavations begin in Sikel and Greek necropoleis under P. *Orsi. Material recovered dated the Greek tombs from the late seventh to fourth centuries B.C. In 1930 Orsi explored the southern part of San Mauro Hill (site of earliest occupation at Leontinoi) and excavated segments of the fortification wall. Investigations were briefly resumed in 1940 under Griffo, who opened more tombs and traced a continuation of the fortifications on Metapiccola Hill. Rizza initiated a series of campaigns between 1950 and 1955 in order to firmly establish the topography of the city. He concentrated on tracing the line and development of fortifications but also brought to light additional tombs (fourth–second centuries), as well as sanctuary and habitation remains. Some brief campaigns have been carried out since then.

BIBLIOGRAPHY
P. Orsi, "Scavi di Leontini-Lentini," *AttiMGrecia* (1930), 7–39; D. Adamesteanu, "Lentini-scavo nell'area sacra delle città di Leontini," *NSc* 10 (1956), 402–14; G. Rizza, "Stipe votiva sul colle di Metapiccola a Leontini," *BdA* 48 (1963), 342–47.

BARBARA A. BARLETTA

LEPTIS (LEPCIS) MAGNA. Punic and Roman city in the region of Tripolitania in North Africa, on the Mediterranean coast of modern-day Libya.

Founded as a Punic settlement no later than 500 B.C., Leptis became a major port and trading center under the Roman Empire. As the birthplace of Septimius Severus (reigned A.D. 193–211), it received special privileges and monuments from the emperor. The city then declined, suffering successively from floods, invasion by the Vandals (ca. A.D. 455) and conquest by Justinian (A.D. 533). Finally, with the coming of the Arabs (A.D. 643), urban life ended; the harbor silted up, and the sands drifted over the abandoned city.

The remains of the city are extensive. The Old Forum near the harbor assumed its form at the time of Augustus, through the patronage of a local, Annobal Tapapius Rufus, named in an inscription in both Latin and Punic. Adjoining the forum are numerous temples, including one of Augustus and Roma that held colossal statues of Augustus, Livia, Tiberius and other Julio-Claudians (now in the Museum at Tripoli). Annobal Tapapius Rufus also donated the magnificent limestone theater (A.D. 1–2) with a shrine of Augusta Ceres at the top of the seating area. Under Hadrian in the second century A.C., huge baths were built, among the largest in the Roman world. Most important are the buildings gracing the city through the patronage of Septimius Severus. Besides the famous four-sided *Arch of Septimius Severus, there was a large new forum with a temple in honor of the Severan family, a basilica near the forum and new installations in the harbor. A long, colonnaded street (366m) led from the harbor to the town.

Leptis became known as a source for building materials by the sixteenth century, when some forty-eight columns were hauled away to be used in a mosque at the oasis of Tagiura. In the next century, the remains of the site were described by Arab and European travelers. Claude Lemaire, the French consul at Tripoli (1686 ff.) excavated in the Leptis area for building materials, which he then shipped to France. Several columns of green breccia were used in the altar of the church of St. Germain des Prés in Paris, and some Leptis marble may be found in the pulpit at Rouen cathedral, as well as in the palace at Versailles (*Louis XIV). Study of the remains also began at this time, but not until the early nineteenth century were a detailed survey and overall plan of the city produced, by Captain H. W. Smith; he sent off sculptures, columns and inscriptions to London, and these were later transferred to Windsor Castle.

In 1910–11, the Italian Archaeological Mission under F. *Halbherr began to work at Leptis, and interest in the site continued as the Italians occupied Libya (1911) and appointed a superintendent of antiquities there, Salvatore Aurigemma (1913–19). Systematic excavation of the city took place under Pietro Romanelli (1920–22), Renato Bartoccini (1923–28) and Giacomo Guidi (1928–36). Restoration of the theater was directed by Giacomo Caputo. In 1927 the publication *Africa Italiana* was founded to report on Italian work at Leptis and other sites, with a report on the Arch of Septimius Severus appearing in the first volume. After World War II, the *British School at Rome under J. B. *Ward-Perkins did a detailed topographic survey and published inscriptions from Leptis, *Sabratha and Tripoli.

BIBLIOGRAPHY

R. Bianchi Bandinelli—E. Vergara Caffarelli—G. Caputo, *The Buried City, Excavations at Leptis Magna* (New York, 1966); J. B. Ward-Perkins, s.v., ''Leptis Magna,'' *PECS*, 499–500; G. Caputo, *Il Teatro augusteo di Leptis Magna: Scavo e restauro (1937–51)* (Rome, 1987).

LERICI, CARLO MAURILIO (1890–1981). Italian leader in the development of geophysical prospection in archaeology.

An aeronautical pioneer and steel industrialist, Ing. Lerici revealed the scope of his cultural interests by founding the Istituto Italiano di Cultura in Stockholm (1941) and later (from 1954 in Rome) promoting the development and application to archaeological research of geophysical prospecting methods. He was an innovator in this field in Italy; his team, the Fondazione Lerici Prospezioni Archeologiche, achieved its most conspicuous successes at *Cerveteri, *Tarquinia and *Sybaris (besides *Metapontion, Croton, etc.). The Fondazione Lerici continues to promote wider knowledge of scientific techniques among archaeologists through annual courses (since 1963) and publication of the journal *Prospezioni Archeologiche* (since 1966).

BIBLIOGRAPHY
C. M. Lerici, *Una grande avventura dell'archeologia moderna* (Milan, 1965); Idem, "Nuove applicazioni della scienza e della tecnica alla ricerca archeologica," *RA* (1970), 97–116; *Scritti di archeologia ed arte in onore di C. M. Lerici* (Stockholm, 1970); *Gli Etruschi e Cerveteri: La prospezione archeologica nell'attività della Fondazione Lerici,* catalog of exhibition (Milan, 1980).

F. R. SERRA RIDGWAY

LERNA. Prehistoric settlement at Myloi on the Gulf of Argos in Greece, excavated 1952–58 for the *American School of Classical Studies at Athens, by J. L. *Caskey, then director; an especially long and clear stratigraphic sequence has made Lerna the major type site in the southern mainland of Greece for the Early and Middle Bronze ages; extensive Neolithic remains are also notable.

During part of the Early Bronze Age, a small settlement was guarded by an impressive towered fortification of casemate design. The "House of the Tiles" (so-called from thousands of terracotta and schist roofing slabs) contained clay sealings (stamped with elaborate patterns) that had been used to secure pots, baskets and chests. It and similar structures at Lerna and elsewhere were probably elite residences and administrative centers.

Caskey in 1960 reasoned that the destruction of the "House of the Tiles" by fire and the apparent veneration of its ruins might reflect the arrival of the first Greek speakers, thus revising the thesis of J. B. Haley and C. W. *Blegen (1928): such local calamities at the end of the Early Bronze Age belong to a widespread horizon of devastations, followed by abandonment of settlements and the introduction of new types of artifacts (e.g., gray burnished "Minyan" pottery and apsidal houses). Plentiful finds from the Middle Bronze Age document early interaction between *Crete and the Greek mainland, while two shaft graves are roughly contemporary with those at *Mycenae. Human, faunal and botanical remains, though ignored by most excavators, were given due attention by J. L. Angel (1954, 1957), N.-G. Gejvall (1958) and M. Hopf (1959), respectively.

BIBLIOGRAPHY
J. L. Caskey, "The Early Helladic Period in the Argolid," *Hesperia* 29 (1960), 285–303; +*Lerna* 1–2 (Princeton, NJ, 1969, 1971), +J. L. Caskey, *Lerna in the Argolid*

(Athens, 1977); +M. H. Wiencke, "Change in Early Helladic II," *AJA* 93 (1989), 495–509.

JACK L. DAVIS

LEROY (LE ROY), JULIEN-DAVID (1728–1803). French architect.

A native of Paris, Leroy won the first prize for architecture to study at the *French Academy in Rome and set off to pursue his studies in Italy and Greece. At the French Academy (1754) he was regarded as something of a troublemaker, and he soon departed for Athens. There he learned of the plan of *Stuart and *Revett to produce a work on the antiquities of Athens and determined to up-stage them, by publishing a similar work quickly and cheaply. Upon his return to Paris in 1758, he issued his *Les Ruines des plus beaux monuments de la Grèce,* the work thus appearing several years before the first volume of *Antiquities of Athens* (1762). Stuart and Revett furiously condemned Leroy as a pirate and criticized his many mistakes. Nevertheless, with the book and with his teaching in Paris, he had no small influence on the development of a taste for things Greek, especially in France.

Leroy was a remarkable pioneer in the study of ancient ships and maritime activity. On the basis of ancient models, he constructed a ship, which he called a *naupotame,* that was capable of going on rivers and seas. Leroy succeeded in setting the ship to sail, but when he tried to organize a public subscription to build an entire fleet of *naupotames,* support did not materialize. His knowledge of ancient ships was disseminated in *Marine des anciens peuples expliquée* (1777).

BIBLIOGRAPHY

"Leroy, Julien-David," *Grand Dictionnaire Universel du XIXe siècle,* 10 (1873), 399; D. Constantine, *Early Greek Travellers and the Hellenic Ideal* (Cambridge, 1984), 158, 198, 200, 211.

LESSING, GOTTHOLD EPHRAIM (1729–81). German author and critic.

With his early schooling in Greek and Latin (Latin School at Kamenz, St. Afra's at Meissen) began a lifelong concern with classical antiquity. At Leipzig Lessing studied with J. A. Ernesti and especially with J. F. Christ (professor of poetry and archaeology; teacher of J. J. *Winckelmann), although his official subjects were theology, medicine, journalism, poetry and drama. Winckelmann had in his epoch-making *Gedanken . . .* of 1756 characterized Greek art as em-bodying "noble simplicity and calm grandeur" and applied this to poetry as well as to the visual arts. Lessing objected to this new version of *ut pictura poesis* and developed over the next ten years his astutely argued differentiation between the arts, that is, his famous *Laokoon: oder über die Grenzen der Mal-erei und Poesie* (1766). Lessing's method was inductive, though not purely empiricistic. He sought the universal in the particular. This method was to de-termine his *Briefe antiquarischen* [archaeological] *Inhalts* (1768/69), containing a sharp, lengthy polemic against C. A. Klotz, who had criticized the *Laokoon* in an archaeological treatise on gems (1768). Also noteworthy is Lessing's treatise on the representation of death in antiquity, *Wie die Alten den Tod gebildet: Eine Untersuchung* (illustrated) of 1769, written in a milder mood, though again against Klotz, maintaining that the ancients depicted death nontragically, for example, as an attractive youth with a lowered torch.

While his role in archaeology is minor, Lessing's intellectual vigor, lucidity and unrelenting search for truth engendered new ideas among his own and future generations in this field as well as in his other fields of endeavor.

BIBLIOGRAPHY

K. Lachmann—F. Muncker, eds., *Sämtliche Schriften,* 3rd ed. (Leipzig, 1886–1924; reprint Berlin, 1968); D. Reich, ed. with introd. and comment, *Laokoon . . .* (Oxford, 1965); E. H. Gombrich, *Lessing, ProcBrAc* 13 (London, 1957); W. Jens, "Lessing und die Antike," in *Text und Kontext* 6 (1978); K. S. Guthke, *Gotthold Ephraim Lessing,* 3rd ed. (Stuttgart, 1979).

                                                                    ULRICH K. GOLDSMITH

LETO, GIULIO POMPONIO (1428–97). Italian humanist and antiquarian.

Pomponio Leto's life before the age of forty is obscure by his deliberate choice. Born in Diano in Southern Italy, possibly the illegitimate son of Count Giovanni Sanseverino, he studied the classics in Rome with Lorenzo Valla and Pietro Odi of Montopoli. By 1468 he had held a chair for two or three years at the University of Rome and had gathered around himself the group of students and curial humanists known as the Roman Academy.

Leto and his academy burst into prominence in 1468 with their arrest and imprisonment at the hands of Pope *Paul II on charges of sedition, sodomy and paganism. The pope's actions originated in his attempt to reform the curial staff; he feared the academy because he regarded it, accurately, as the nucleus of his chief opposition to such reforms. Though the pope succeeded in purging the Vatican bureaucracy, he failed to squelch the stubborn, vociferous academicians and their laurel-crowned, toga-clad rituals. Though confined in the *Castel Sant' Angelo and tortured intermittently, Leto and his learned companions were eventually released, finding favor under the papacy of Pope Paul's successor, *Sixtus IV. Leto returned to his chair at the university and remained there until his death.

Though he also composed works on grammar and philology, Leto's most conspicuous achievements as a scholar were entirely rooted in his devotion to Rome, both the idea of the Eternal City and the physical reality of its archaeological past. His study of the Roman rustic writers induced him to try his hand at ancient methods of agriculture. He began to revise the text of the *Scriptores Historiae Augustae,* a Late Antique compendium of emperors' lives, though neither the *Scriptores* nor Leto is notable for devotion to historical accuracy in any modern sense. The same distinctly fifteenth-century sensibility shows in his reworked version of the *Catalogue of the Fourteen Regions of Rome;* the basic text derives from late antiquity, probably from Constantinian times, and consists of a census of the buildings in each of Rome's administrative districts. Much altered and interpolated before Leto's time, the *Catalogue* was subjected at his hands to further alterations and interpolations. Nonetheless, it served as the basis for the researches of the next generation of antiquarians in Rome. Even more informative are the *Excerpta,* the notes, recorded by a student, to a guided tour that Leto offered a visiting dignitary sometime after 1484.

In his garden on the Quirinal, Leto also collected and recorded (and may have forged) inscriptions. Yet his greatest contribution to the study of ancient Rome may have been the enthusiasm he inspired in two generations of scholars, including one of Rome's few women humanists, his daughter, Nigella Laeta. In effect, the Roman Academy served to impose professional standards of Latinity on the curial staff as it stimulated that profoundly physical consciousness of the ancient city that so distinguishes the art and architecture of the Roman High Renaissance.

BIBLIOGRAPHY
V. Zabughin, *Giulio Pomponio Leto: Saggio Critico* (Rome, 1909–Grottaferrata, 1910); Valentine—Zucchetti, I, 63–257.

INGRID ROWLAND

LEVI, DORO (1898–1991). Italian archaeologist, a leader of the second generation of Italian archaeologists in the Aegean area, following *Halbherr, *Pernier and others.

Although he was involved in the study of Etruscan Italy and the Syro-Palestinian area (e.g., his study of the *Antioch mosaics, 1947), his research centered on the Aegean, with publications on Athens, *Kos, Lemnos and Tinos; he initiated excavations at Iasos (1960). His main focus, however, was *Crete; he published the Archaic bronzes from Axos (1931) and investigated Archaic Arkades (1929), which also led to his general study of Greek pottery from Crete (1945). But above all, he investigated prehistoric Minoan remains of the *Phaistos area, beginning with his study of the sealings from *Hagia Triadha and Kato *Zakros (1926), eventually to be followed by those he discovered at Phaistos (1958). The latter emerged as the result of his initiative to excavate the remains of the Middle Minoan or first palace there, much of which lay below the earlier excavator's dump. The massive architectural remains can serve as guides to Middle Minoan (MM) palatial architecture, and the often-beautiful pottery is basic to any study of MM ceramics.

Levi's productive scholarly career and his administrative acumen and devotion to archaeology as longtime director (1947–77) of the *Italian School of Archaeology in Athens were celebrated on his seventy-fifth birthday with a double volume published in Catania.

BIBLIOGRAPHY
Antichità Cretesi, Studi in onore di Doro Levi, 1–2, University of Catania, *Cronache di archeologia* 12 (1973), with bib. to 1973, xi-xix, and 13 (1974); D. Levi, *Festòs e la*

civiltà minoica (Rome, 1976–88); C. Laviosa, "Doro Levi, 1898–1991," *AJA* 97(1993), 165–66.

JOSEPH W. SHAW

LEYLAND, JOHN. See LELAND, JOHN.

LIEVEN, VAN DER BEKE. See TORRENTIUS, LAEVINUS.

LIGORIO (LIGORIUS), PIRRO (ca. 1513–83). Italian painter, architect, cartographer and antiquarian.

Pirro Ligorio was born in Naples ca. 1513 and died in 1583 in Ferrara. We know almost nothing of his formative years. He is documented in Rome in 1542, working as a façade painter, but had apparently arrived ca. 1534. By 1543 Ligorio was intimate with scholars of the *Farnese family circle and was already collecting information on Roman antiquities. His painting earned him nomination to the Virtuosi al Pantheon in 1548, but from 1549 he turned more to architecture and secured employment as *antiquario* with the cardinals of Carpi and Ferrara. For the latter, Ippolito d'Este (*Este family), Ligorio collected antique statuary, and in 1550, when the cardinal began work on a villa at *Tivoli, he conducted the expropriation of land and antiquities for the project. The cardinal financed Ligorio's excavations at nearby *Hadrian's Villa, which continued sporadically until 1568, yielding significant finds (of which Ligorio wrote in detail) but dispersing and destroying evidence in the process.

Ligorio's growing archaeological knowledge was revealed, with its idiosyncratic aspects clearly visible, in his maps of Rome (1552, 1553) and his *Libro delle antichità di Roma* (1553), which dealt with ancient circuses, theaters, amphitheaters and contentious topographical problems. In the 1550s Ligorio drew reconstructions of the *Circus Maximus, Circus Flaminius, Castra Praetoria, the port of *Ostia, the Aviary of Varro, the *Baths of Diocletian and the *Theater of Marcellus. These survive only in engravings by Antoine *Lafréry. Between 1557 and 1563 Ligorio also published maps of Naples, France, Belgium, Hungary, Spain, Greece and Friuli, but only that of Greece incorporated new historical research.

Appointed architect of the Vatican by Paul IV in 1558, Ligorio began work on his finest building, completed under Pius IV, the Casino in the Belvedere (*Vatican Museums) garden. He gave this an allegorical decorative scheme that included scores of Roman sculptures on the façade, which he personally collected and identified. Ligorio was made an honorary citizen of Rome in December 1560. In 1561 he published his large archaeological map of twelve sheets, reconstructing ancient Rome. He drew plans for the rebuilding of the aqueduct known as Acqua Vergine, transformed *Bramante's exedra of the Belvedere along the lines of the *Stadium of Domitian on the Palatine and added an open-air theater decorated by classical portraits. After *Michelangelo's death in 1564,

Ligorio was made architect of St. Peter's but did not last beyond June 1567 in that role.

The Cardinal of Ferrara reemployed Ligorio on the Villa d'Este. He designed the gardens and their learnedly classicizing fountains and returned to Hadrian's Villa for further excavations. By the spring of 1569, he had moved to Ferrara as *antiquario* to Duke Alfonso II d'Este. There he had various responsibilities, including temporary *lector* at the university, designer of earthquake-resistant architecture, engineer of hydraulics and fortifications and collector of classical portraits and statuary for the duke's library and museum, which he designed. Ligorio also provided Girolamo Mercuriale with drawings of ancient gymnastic exercises for the second edition of his *De arte gymnastica* of 1573. He died in the duke's service in 1583.

From ca. 1540 until his death Ligorio busied himself writing on multifarious aspects of classical antiquity. His *Libro* of 1553 published just a fragment of this material, and the more than forty surviving volumes of his antiquarian manuscripts are only part of his vast compendium. Ligorio assembled two enormous encyclopedias encompassing classical and late-antique civilization. The first, planned to contain fifty books, exists in twenty-five books in ten volumes of manuscripts. It contains studies, often richly illustrated, on Greek and Roman coins and medals, Roman dress, iconography of the gods and goddesses, weights, measures and vases, Latin and Greek inscriptions of Rome and Italy, names and iconography of rivers and springs and ancient burial customs, especially those of Rome. This recension was completed ca. 1566 and was used soon after by *Panvinio and F. *Orsini and in the seventeenth century by Holstenius and the copyists of Cassiano dal *Pozzo.

The second encyclopedia, which had a wider influence, was completed in twenty-three books in Ferrara and is now bound in eighteen volumes. It is alphabetical, and the contents differ somewhat from those of the earlier recension. There is, for example, new work on ancient ships and on *grottesche.* Written in the same years are studies on Roman portraits, abbreviations in classical inscriptions, Roman magistrates and priests, cities on coins and carved gems.

The distinctive tenor of Ligorio's erudition arises from his artistic sensibility. His studies recorded the visual evidence of antiquity, objects he could claim to have seen excavated, to have discovered himself or to have inspected in private collections. Whereas most artists drew antique remains for adaptation in pictorial, sculptural or architectural work, Ligorio illustrated his learned dissertations to offer a complete survey of customs of the ancient world.

His manuscripts, however, must be used with extreme caution. Ligorio's passion for imaginatively reconstructing antiquity, coupled with imperfect knowledge of classical languages, led him to transform a very personal vision of the ancient world into what passes for sound archaeological scholarship. While his textual documentation is remarkably thorough, his use of inscriptions is suspect. His volumes on ancient coins have only lately been carefully studied, but an aura of suspicion surrounds them, too. Ligorio's reconstructions of Roman buildings have received more sympathetic appraisal in recent years, as have his drawings of classical statuary. His topographical research is less reliable than that of *Marliani but more fully documented with archaeological evidence.

Ligorio was a precious witness to the Renaissance destruction of ancient Rome. While *Aldrovandi (1550) describes many Roman collections that received excavated antiquities, Ligorio provides find spots and archaeological contexts, as well as collectors and vendors. Generalizations about the value of Ligorio's studies are risky. In some cases modern archaeology has vindicated his opinions, for example, on the arch bearing the *Fasti* in the Roman Forum and the ruins at Anguillara. But in many instances he perhaps forged evidence or at least was overly enthusiastic in dealing with fragmentary remains.

BIBLIOGRAPHY

D. R. Coffin, *Pirro Ligorio and the Villa d'Este,* Ph.D. diss., Princeton University, 1954; E. Mandowsky—C. Mitchell, *Pirro Ligorio's Roman Antiquities* (London, 1963); E. Salza Prina Ricotti, "Villa Adriana in Pirro Ligorio e Francesco Contini," *MemLinc* 17 (1973–74), 3–47; M. L. Madonna, "L'enciclopedia del mondo antico di Pirro Ligorio," in *I° Congresso Nazionale di Storia dell'Arte, Roma 1978* (Rome, 1980), 257–71; G. Vagenheim, "Les inscriptions ligoriennes, Notes sur la tradition manuscrite," *Italia Medioevale e Umanistica* 30 (1987), 199–309; R. Gaston, ed., *Pirro Ligorio Artist and Antiquarian, The Harvard University Center for Italian Renaissance Studies* 10 (Milan, 1988); +B. Palma Venetucci, ed., *Pirro Ligorio e le erme tiburtine; Le Erme tiburtine e gli scavi del Settecento,* 1–2 (Rome, 1992); P. Jacks, *The Antiquarian and the Myth of Antiquity* (Cambridge, 1995), 214ff.

ROBERT W. GASTON

LINEAR A and B. Related systems of syllabic-ideographic writing used, respectively, by the Minoans (ca. 1800–1450 B.C.) and *Mycenaeans (ca. 1450–1200 B.C.) primarily to record economic information on clay documents of various shapes.

Linear A is found painted on the interiors of two clay cups from *Knossos and incised on other objects like stone libation vessels, gold and silver pins, miniature gold double axes, a gold ring, clay storage vessels and even wall plaster. Besides inscriptions on clay tablets, labels and sealings, Linear B is only found painted on distinctive transport vessels known as stirrup jars and on the outside of a few clay cups. The language represented by Linear A remains unknown, despite many misguided attempts and self-proclaimed decipherments. Linear B was deciphered by Michael *Ventris in 1952 as an early form of Greek having special affinities with the later Arcado-Cypriote dialect and exhibiting forms, specialized vocabulary and proper names, like Achilles and Hector, found in the Homeric epics. The Linear B tablets are a major source of information, albeit often indirect and tentative, about Mycenaean religion, economy and society. The richer typological variety and wider geographical distribution of Linear A documents help to define the spread of Minoan culture and its regional economic interests. In 1956 the Comité international permanent des études mycéniennes was established by the United Nations Educational, Scientific, and Cultural Organization (UNESCO), which still unites scholars interested in the linear scripts and provides guidelines for research.

The existence and close relationship of Linear A and B and a third system called Cretan hieroglyphic or pictographic, which overlaps with Linear A, were recognized by Sir Arthur *Evans as a result of his investigations on the island of *Crete in the 1890s and his excavation of the major Minoan and later Mycenaean center Knossos beginning in 1900. He called the two scripts *linear* because their signs are composed of linear or curvilinear strokes; *A* and *B* because the Minoan system preceded and inspired the Mycenaean, as is proved by the significant number of phonetic signs (ca. 80% of Linear B syllabograms) and basic ideographic commodity signs (WHEAT, FIGS, WINE, OLIVES, OLIVE OIL) shared by the two scripts.

The first three decades of Minoan archaeology were also a period of sensational epigraphical finds. Linear A documents were unearthed by Evans's contemporaries at all the chief Minoan palace, town and villa sites: *Hogarth at Kato *Zakro, *Halbherr and Paribeni at *Hagia Triadha, Hazzidakis at Tylissos, *Hawes at *Gournia, Bosanquet at *Palaikastro and *Pernier at *Phaistos, where the earliest proto-Linear A material was found. Meanwhile, Evans himself uncovered at Knossos the largest group of Linear B texts (nearly 3,400) from any single site, and Chapouthier published in 1930 a few Linear A and many hieroglyphic inscriptions from *Malia.

Major discoveries of Mycenaean Linear B texts from the Greek mainland followed later, forcing a revision, long championed by Alan J. B. *Wace and Carl W. *Blegen, of Evans's Cretocentric interpretations of Aegean prehistory and scripts: 1,112 from Blegen's excavation at *Pylos in 1939 and 1952–63; 73 excavated by Wace and others at *Mycenae, mainly from buildings outside the citadel, from 1952 onward; 43 tablets and, in 1982, 55 inscribed sealings from separate plots at *Thebes (plus several hundred tablets and fragments discovered by Aravantinos in 1993–94), complementing Keramopoullos's discovery in 1921 of over 50 inscribed stirrup jars; 24 mostly fragmentary texts from the German excavations at *Tiryns; and, from 1964 onward, a growing number of inscribed stirrup jar fragments and even three classifiable Linear B tablets from the Greek-Swedish excavations at Khania (ancient Kydonia) in western Crete.

In the last decade, photographic corpus volumes of all Linear A inscriptions and of one-third of the Knossos Linear B material have appeared. These have led to important reassessments of the development of writing and its role in Minoan and Mycenaean societies and economies. Prominent centers for research with Aegean scripts have been established in Rome (the Istituto per gli Studi Micenei ed Egeo-Anatolici) and Austin, TX (the Program in Aegean Scripts and Prehistory).

BIBLIOGRAPHY
M. Ventris—J. Chadwick, *Documents in Mycenaean Greek,* 2nd ed. (Cambridge, 1973); Y. Duhoux, ''Mycénien et écriture grecque,'' in *Linear B: A 1984 Survey,* A. Morpurgo

Davies—Y. Duhoux, eds., (*BCILL* 26, Louvain, 1985); +J.-P. Olivier, "Cretan Writing in the Second Millennium B.C.," *World Archaeology* 17:3 (1986), 377–89; T. G. Palaima, "The Development of the Mycenaean Writing System," in J.-P. Olivier—T. G. Palaima, eds., *Texts, Tablets and Scribes: Studies in Mycenaean Epigraphy and Economy Offered to Emmett L. Bennett, Jr.*, Suplementos a *MINOS* 10 (Salamanca, 1988).

THOMAS G. PALAIMA

LININGTON, RICHARD EDGAR (1936–84). British pioneer in the archaeological application of geophysical survey techniques.

Long active in archaeology, Linington reached *Sybaris in 1961 with a University of Pennsylvania magnetic survey team. He was associated thenceforward with the *Lerici Foundation in Rome, joining the permanent staff in 1966, becoming director in 1970 and coediting *Prospezioni Archeologiche* (1966–74). In Italy, he conducted the foundation's successful geophysical campaigns at *Metapontion, *Croton, and Camarina and in Etruria, where he also took a leading part in the Lerici excavations at *Cerveteri and *Tarquinia. His accurate geophysical prediction in 1962 of the position and configuration of the then-elusive second temple at *Pyrgi signaled the coming of age of geophysical techniques in Italian archaeology.

BIBLIOGRAPHY

R. E. Linington, "Esplorazione geofisica a Pyrgi, giugno-luglio 1962," *ArchCl* 15 (1963), 256–61; idem, "Techniques Used in Archaeological Field Surveys," *Philosophical Transactions, Royal Society of London* 269 (1970), 89–108; +*Gli Etruschi e Cerveteri: Catalogo della Mostra* (Milan, 1980), 13–55.

DAVID RIDGWAY

LION GATE. Monumental stone entrance to the acropolis at *Mycenae.

Constructed in the fourteenth century B.C., this megalithic structure was built of ashlar masonry using a hard local limestone. The portal is surmounted by a large triangular relief that depicts a central column heraldically flanked by two felines. Their heads, presumably made separately of stone or bronze, have been lost. This work of the Bronze Age is considered the earliest known monumental stone sculpture in Greece.

Pausanias was the first to describe the gate (2.16.5), noting that it was topped with two "lions" and claiming that it was built by the same "Cyclopes" who had labored at Tiryns. For the next 1,600 years the existence of the gate was not recorded. *Ciriaco of Ancona unfortunately mistook the classical fort at Katsingri for Mycenae, and *Chandler intended to go there but missed the site entirely. Between 1800 and 1806, *Clarke, *Dodwell and *Gell all described the gate, and both Dodwell and Gell published drawings of it. Gell was the first to notice that the creatures should more properly be called lionesses or panthers; Clarke observed that the triangle is an *alto-relievo* and additionally speculated that the column may have had a religious significance. *Leake (1846) corrected earlier erroneous reports that the relief was made of the same stone used for the columns of the *Treasury of Atreus. He also drew attention to the military aspects of the ground plan used in constructing the gate. *Adler (1865) initiated an iconographical debate and noted that the column bears similarities to those found in Lycian tombs.

On 7 August 1876, *Schliemann began his excavation of Mycenae, and the Lion Gate took on a new importance. Pointing to the descriptions of Pausanias, Schliemann was sure that the Lion Gate was a part of that wall within which would be found the grave of Agamemnon. The gate and its environs were therefore the first areas excavated. Schliemann brought to light the gate's enormous threshold and theorized about the ruts and furrows found in that stone. He interpreted the column as representing Apollo Agyeus, the "Guardian of the Gate," and the lions as being indicative of a Phrygian cult brought to Mycenae by its founder, Pelops.

BIBLIOGRAPHY

F. Adler, "Das Relief vom Lowenthore zu Mykenae," *Archäologische Zeitung* (January 1865), 1–13; A.J.B. Wace, *Mycenae: An Archaeological History and Guide* (Princeton, NJ, 1949); E. Vermeule, *Greece in the Bronze Age* (Chicago, 1964), 214–15; J. G. Frazer, *Pausanias's Description of Greece* 3 (London, 1965).

STEPHEN C. LAW

LIPPI, FILIPPINO (FILIPPO DI FILIPPO LIPPI; 1457–1504). Italian painter.

The mature works of the Florentine artist Filippino Lippi abound in motifs derived from ancient art, but the painter did not exhibit this interest before he left Florence for Rome in 1489. Here he made accurate drawings after monuments, including the newly discovered Golden House of Nero (*Domus Aurea), and he depicted the *Marcus Aurelius* Equestrian Statue, on Sixtus IV's base, in the Carafa Chapel in Santa Maria sopra Minerva.

Returning to Florence, Filippino helped introduce these ancient treasures there. Benvenuto *Cellini studied his sketchbooks, and Giorgio *Vasari described him as "the first to bring to light grotesques. . . . he never executed a single work in which he did not avail himself of Roman antiquities." This exaggerated praise applies best to the Strozzi Chapel in Santa Maria Novella, Florence (1487–1502), filled with ancient trophies, armor, statues and fantastic buildings. Music-making figures on the altar wall derive from a *Muse* sarcophagus (Vienna) and a *Hermaphrodite* gem (Florence), once owned by the *Medici family. Filippino invariably transformed his sources and, unlike most contemporaries, often captured their spirit. His study of *grottesche in the Golden House led to innumerable imaginative variations; the stucco decoration there inspired the vault of Carafa's burial chamber. The confusing illusionism and emphasis on ornamentation in the Strozzi Chapel may reveal the painter's study of (lost) ancient murals. This hypothesis could also explain the striking similarity between Filippino's drawings of the *Death of Laocoon,* executed for a fresco at Poggio a Caiano (1493), and the famous sculpture of *Laocoon, discovered after Filippino's death.

BIBLIOGRAPHY

J. R. Sale, *The Strozzi Chapel by Filippino Lippi in Santa Maria Novella* (New York, 1979); T. M. Thomas, *Classical Reliefs and Statues in Later Quattrocento Religious Paintings*, Ph.D. diss., University of California at Berkeley, 1980; G. Geiger, *Filippino Lippi's Carafa Chapel: Renaissance Art in Rome* (Kirksville, MO, 1986); J. Nelson, "Filippino Lippi at the Medici Villa of Poggio a Caiano," in *Florentine Drawing at the Time of Lorenzo the Magnificent*, ed. E. Cropper (Bologna, 1994), 159–74.

JONATHAN NELSON

LIPPOLD, GEORG (1885–1954). German archaeologist; specialist in ancient sculpture and painting and in carved gems of antiquity and modern times.

Lippold was born in Mainz and studied in Munich and Berlin (1903–7). One of the last students of A. *Furtwängler, he was strongly marked by the personality of his teacher, for whom he wrote a study on ancient shields, published in a volume in memory of Furtwängler as "Griechische Schilde" (1909).

After working as a volunteer at the Römisch-Germanischen Zentralmuseum in Mainz (1908) and at the Martin von Wagner Museum in Würzburg (1910–11), he was called to Erlangen as lecturer. In 1925 he was made professor (*Ordinarius*) at Erlangen, a role he kept until his retirement in 1953. He died in 1954 after a traffic accident. Lippold openly voiced his opposition, beginning in 1933, to the policies of the National Socialist Party of Hitler.

Among Lippold's most important publications were his *Kopien und umbildungen griechischer Statuen* (1923), long a standard treatment of the many questions regarding copyism of Greek sculpture; *Griechische Plastik* in the *Handbuch der Archäologie*, 3.1 (1950), a clear and concise outline of the history of Greek sculpture as it was perceived at that time on the basis of literary sources, originals and copies; and his corpus of cameos and gems, *Gemmen und Kameen des Altertums und die Neuzeit* (Stuttgart, 1923).

Lippold inherited and was distinguished continuator of some of the grandest German archaeological projects. He picked up the cataloging of the *Vatican Museums from *Amelung, producing *Die Skulpturen des Vatikanischen Museums*, volumes 3.1 (1936) and 3.2 (1956). He also served as editor of *Brunn's *Denkmäler griechischer und römischer Sculptur* (published by the Bruckmann Press in Munich) and of *Arndt's *Griechische und römische Porträts* (also Bruckmann); he wrote many articles on painters and sculptors for Pauly-Wissowa's *Realencyclopädie* and the *Allgemeines Kunstlerlexikon* of Thieme and Becker.

BIBLIOGRAPHY

M. Bieber, "Georg Lippold," *AJA* 59 (1955), 63–64; R. Lullies, in *Archäologenbildnisse*, 228–29.

LIPSIUS, JUSTUS (1547–1606). Flemish humanist and classicist, one of the most influential of the great sixteenth-century scholars.

After studying at Louvain, Lipsius lived for a period in Italy (1568–70), where he came to admire the style of the Latin writers of the Silver Age and mastered the Italian antiquarian tradition. Throughout his long career as a professor at Lutheran Jena (1572–74), Calvinist Leiden (1579–91) and Catholic Louvain (1592–1606), he pursued both fields of study faithfully. Lipsius's editions of Tacitus (1574) and Seneca (1605) seemed definitive; his writings made their loose, nonperiodic style immensely fashionable in Northern Europe. Such masters of vernacular prose as Michel de Montaigne and Francis Bacon found the new tools they employed in Lipsius.

At the same time and even more important, Lipsius transplanted to Northern Europe the mature techniques Italian scholars had applied to the study of ancient material remains and social institutions. A stream of large books, profusely illustrated, reconstructed the various forms of the cross, the arms and armor of gladiators and the amphitheater. An edition of the corpus of inscriptions that Martinus *Smetius had gathered in Italy and elsewhere (1588) became the standard epigraphical compendium for a generation. A path-breaking interpretation of Polybius, the *De militia romana libri V* (1595), was the first serious effort to reconstruct all aspects of the Roman military order. It served as the blueprint for the military revolution that Lipsius's pupil Maurice of Nassau and his successors brought about in the seventeenth century and inspired a long series of related works by Lipsius's professional successors for the next century and more. Lipsius was not so original as his friend and rival Joseph *Scaliger; but his scholarship had an enormous impact on European life and thought. Among his students were the *Rubens brothers, Philip and Peter Paul.

BIBLIOGRAPHY

J. L. Saunders, *Justus Lipsius* (New York, 1955); M. W. Croll, *Style, Rhetoric and Rhythm* (Princeton, NJ, 1966); G. Oestreich, *Neostoicism and the Early Modern State* (Cambridge, 1982).

ANTHONY GRAFTON

LOEB, JAMES (1867–1933). American banker trained as a classicist; benefactor of archaeology and philology.

Born in New York of a wealthy German-Jewish banking family, Loeb graduated in classics from Harvard College in 1888, formed by John Williams White and Charles Eliot *Norton. American anti-Semitism prevented an academic career. After fourteen unhappy years in banking, Loeb retired to self-imposed exile in Bavaria as private scholar and benefactor of American and German classics. He translated into English four French philological studies by Decharme, Croiset, Legrand and Couat.

His more enduring contributions were five philanthropic ones. Trustee of the *American School of Classical Studies (ASCS) in Athens (1909–30), he established the Charles Eliot Norton Fellowship at Harvard for study at the school. He endowed the Charles Eliot Norton Lectureship for the *Archaeological Institute of America. He bequeathed his personal collection of Greek antiquities to the Munich Museum. At his death he left $5 million to the ASCS, which enabled it to purchase the *Agora, Athens, for excavation. In 1912 with the advice of *Wilamowitz, he established his greatest legacy, the Loeb Classical Library, now nearing 500 volumes. Its profits support the Harvard Classical Department. Munich and Cambridge granted Loeb honorary degrees. A modest, lonely, generous man, he was the greatest benefactor American classics ever knew.

BIBLIOGRAPHY

"James Loeb," in *The National Cyclopedia of American Biography* 100 (New York, 1930), 73–74; F. S. Warburg, *Reminiscences of a Long Life* (New York, 1956); W. M. Calder III, "Ulrich von Wilamowitz-Moellendorff to James Loeb: Two Unpublished Letters," *Illinois Classical Studies* 2 (1977), 315–32; F. W. Hamdorf, *James Loeb: Mäzen von Beruf* (Munich, 1983).

WILLIAM M. CALDER III

LOESCHCKE, GEORG (1852–1915). German archaeologist, specializing in ancient pottery; beloved teacher of a number of distinguished archaeologists of the early twentieth century.

Born in Penig/Sachsen in 1852, Loeschcke was lured to archaeology by J. *Overbeck at Leipzig (1871–73), where he was a fellow student of A. *Furtwängler. Studying next at Bonn with R. *Kekulé and others, he solidified his interest and training and laid the foundations for his research on ceramics.

In 1877, on a travel stipend from the *German Archaeological Institute, he set off for Italy and Greece. He was drawn to the unpublished vases and sherds from *Schliemann's excavations at *Mycenae and, with masterly studies of this allegedly insignificant material, was able to lay out a chronological framework for Mycenaean studies (*Mykenische Thongefäße,* 1879; *Mykenische Vasen,* 1886). He also made major contributions to the study of early Greek pottery, analyzing the groups excavated at *Naukratis into imports from *Miletos, *Samos and *Mytilene.

Called to Dorpat in 1879 as professor of philology and archaeology, Loeschcke remained for nearly a decade before accepting the post of first secretary for the *German Archaeological Institute in Athens (1887–89). He was then summoned to Bonn to succeed his teacher Kekulé. In the ensuing, highly productive period in his life, he taught, among others, M. *Bieber, H. Dragendorff, P. *Jacobsthal, G. *Karo, T. Leslie *Shear, F. *Weege. He involved his students in his own research on the Roman *limes,* in particular, the phases of fortifications and the relevance of ceramics for historical questions.

When Kekulé died at Berlin, again Loeschcke was summoned to succeed him (1912), but he served there only briefly before his own death in 1915.

BIBLIOGRAPHY

W. R. Megow, in *Archäologenbildnisse,* 106–7.

LOMBARD, LAMBERT (1505/6–66). Flemish painter, architect and collector from Liège.

Lombard was taught by Jan *Gossaert and Jan van *Scorel, both great admirers of antiquity. Hired by the bishop of Liège, Erard de la Marck, he spent a year in Rome (1537–38) as part of the suite of the English cardinal and leading humanist Reginald Pole.

Influenced by Baccio *Bandinelli, on his return to Liège, Lombard founded the first art academy in the Low Countries, in which erudition was stressed. Learned in numismatics, he included among his numerous pupils Hubert *Goltzius, the author of the most important essays of the sixteenth century on Greek and Roman coins. Frans *Floris, Willem Key and Domenicus Lampsonius attended his academy.

His vision of antiquity, as described by his biographer Lampsonius, is dominated by a veneration for the works of the ancient artists whose rules, or *grammatica,* he tries to reconstruct. In a letter to *Vasari, he mentions the *Belvedere Apollo, the *Laocoon,* and the *Quirinal *Horse Tamers* among antique sculptures, and he asks the Italian artist to write an essay on the calculation of proportions in ancient artists' work.

Lombard's 600 drawings and eighty engravings show his artist-scholar's interest in classical authors, ancient history and religion, mythography, numismatics, glyptics, hieroglyphics and emblematics. His remarkable curiosity about all forms of art stimulated him to copy Gallo-Roman and medieval works as well. His works reflect the development of humanism in the Low Countries and its impact on the artists of that time.

BIBLIOGRAPHY

J. Helbig, "Lambert Lombard, peintre et architecte," *Bull. des Commissions Royales d'Art et d'Archéologie* (1892), 331–440; N. Dacos, *Les Peintres belges à Rome au XVIe siècle* (1964); E. H. Kemp, *Lambert Lombard als Zeichner,* diss., Munster, 1970; +G. Denhaene, *Les Dessins de Lambert Lombard dans l'album d'Arenberg,* diss., Brussels, 1983.

G. DENHAENE

LONDON (LONDINIUM). The largest town and capital city of Roman Britain.

Located at a low point on the Thames River where it could control traffic going up the river as well as across it, the site may have been visited by Caesar (54 B.C.) and by Claudius's general Aulus Plautius, during the Roman conquest of Britain in A.D. 43. It was a merchants' center by A.D. 60, when the settlement suffered burning during the rebellion of Boudicca (cf. Tacitus, *Annales* 14.32–33). The quarters of the governor of the province may have been there in the first century A.C. and certainly were there by the second century, along with a large forum and basilica and an important fort on the outskirts of the city. Other significant remains excavated in the city include public baths (later first century) and a temple to Mithras (second century) with (originally) well-preserved timber; the latter is perhaps the most impressive example of the preservation of organic materials from Roman London, a common occurrence along the Thames and the Walbrook stream that ran through the city. There are also traces of an extensive city wall (early third century), furnishing the most visible remains of the Roman city in London today. Little is known of the city after Honorius disclaimed Roman responsibility for its protection in A.D. 410, although a Roman-style house with hypocaust system in Lower Thames Street seems to have been in use still in the fifth century.

The exploration of Roman London began in the seventeenth century, at the time of the rebuilding of the city after the Great Fire of 1666. When Sir Christopher Wren was rebuilding St. Paul's Cathedral, he uncovered Roman kilns and pottery, of which drawings were made by the pharmacist John Conyers. *Stukely published a plan of Roman London in 1722, many parts of which were fanciful. (E.g., he invented a temple of Diana on the site of St. Paul's.) But great strides were to be made in the study of the topography of the city in the course of the nineteenth century. Charles Knight published a plan of Roman London in 1841 that showed a total of only 19 discoveries, but by 1909 a detailed account of the city, published in the *Victoria County History,* was to include nearly 300 Roman discoveries.

The leading figure in this heroic period was Charles Roach Smith, the "father of London archaeology," who fought a running battle with the Corporation of London in an effort to get corporation officials to take proper care of local antiquities and to create a museum. Roach Smith himself assembled a large collection of the antiquities that were ignored by the corporation itself, but ironically, he was arrested for receiving stolen property. Soon after his retirement in 1855, the contents of his large collection were purchased not by the city but by the *British Museum; not until 1868 did the corporation create a public museum, associated with the Guildhall Library, to receive the city's antiquities, which were emerging at a spectacular rate. The public was keenly interested; when a splendid mosaic with geometric patterning turned up in Queen Victoria Street in 1869 (the Bucklersbury Mosaic), more than 50,000 people visited the site within the first three days of discovery.

The Corporation of London still ignored the need for official supervision of the many sites accidentally discovered during the construction of offices, streets and sewers, and the story of archaeology in London in the twentieth century is a rather dreary tale of the apathy of the corporation and the frustration of concerned individuals who lacked the authority to act. Mortimer *Wheeler, as director of the London Museum, took the lead in encouraging professional research and establishing official posts. After World War II and the bombing of one-third of the historic city of London, an extensive area lay open to be investigated and recorded. The Roman and Medieval London Excavation Council was founded, and excavations were directed by William Grimes, the director of the London Museum succeeding Wheeler. He discovered the military fort and explored the walls of the Roman city and unearthed the remarkable temple of Mithras, within which was buried a cache of rare marble sculptures. Through the 1960s, the burden of excavation was shouldered by dedicated volunteers, coordinated mainly by Peter Marsden. Finally, in 1973, the corporation established the Department of Urban Archaeology, which has come to operate with an annual budget of over £.25 million and with a staff of about sixty. A new display of Roman material in the Museum of London (a merger of the old Guildhall Museum and the London Museum) is at once an excellent guide to the ancient city and an enlightening introduction to Roman daily life.

BIBLIOGRAPHY

S. S. Frere, s.v. "Londinium," *PECS*, 524–25; P. Marsden, *Roman London* (London, 1980), 187–205; J. Hall—R. Merrifield, *Roman London* (London, 1986), 46–47.

LOUIS XIV (1638–1715). King of France (1643–1715).

Louis XIV has lent his name to the French classical age. In his own lifetime, very conscious efforts were made to link the Sun King with the great rulers of classical antiquity (Alexander, Augustus), and ancient models permeated court art and ceremonial. The emulation of ancient literary models during this reign brought French culture into rivalry with antiquity, leading to the Quarrel of the Ancients and the Moderns in the 1680s and 1690s.

As a collector, Louis XIV was able to add to the royal collection some stellar pieces from the collections of Cardinals Richelieu and Mazarin (the seated porphyry *Minerva,* running *Atalanta,* seated Roman matron designated as Agrippina or Poppaea, etc.). Displayed in the Tuileries Palace, they were among the works proudly shown to Gianlorenzo *Bernini during his trip to Paris in 1665. Between 1669 and 1679 the finest statues and busts in the royal holdings were engraved by Claude Mellan, and the guardian of the collection, André Félibien, wrote a commentary. His text was reprinted in several of his books on royal artistic enterprises, and the plates and text eventually formed one volume of the vast *Cabinet du Roi* (1727).

The founding of the *French Academy in Rome in 1666 resulted in a flurry of collecting by the directors, who shipped many cases of sculpture and precious marbles to Paris. This culminated in the acquisition of the statues of "*Germanicus*" and the "*Cincinnatus*" in 1685. Alarmed by the wholesale export of antiquities, Pope Innocent XI passed a law to curtail this activity by the next year. The directors of the academy continued to follow closely antiquarian studies in Rome, sending to France the latest engravings after antiquities by Pietro Santi *Bartoli and commissioning copies of manuscripts for the royal library (e.g., Flaminio *Vacca's account of sixteenth-century archaeological finds in Rome).

Missions to the Orient were undertaken by scholars and diplomats with orders to acquire ancient coins, carved gems and manuscripts; the lost books of Livy were high on the list of *desideranda*. The French ambassador to Constantinople, the Marquis de *Nointel, collected inscriptions in Asia Minor and Greece and was able to make drawings of the *Parthenon sculptures before the disastrous explosion of 1687. Sculpture was sought after but difficult to obtain, however, a French agent was able to procure a statue of a woman in Tripoli, and three statues were brought from a Dutch merchant in Smyrna for the royal collection.

It was also possible to buy marble columns from *Leptis Magna, and their arrival in Paris was the occasion for a description of the ancient site in the March 1694 edition of the *Mercure Galant.*

After the court took up its official residence at Versailles in 1682, the most highly regarded antiquities were used to embellish that palace. The niches in the Hall of Mirrors contained the *Artemis* of Versailles, *Bacchus* of Versailles, *Venus* of Arles (a gift from that city, which was heavily restored by *Girardon) and others. The *Jupiter* of Versailles, a colossal figure once at the Villa Medici and later belonging to Cardinal *Perrenot de Granvelle, was given to Louis XIV by his descendants in 1683; restored as a herm, it was placed in the gardens of Versailles. A large Hellenistic group of a Silenos abducted by a marine centaur was given to the king in 1712 by Prince Alessandro Albani (*Albani family); it became the central motif of a fountain on the landing of the Ambassadors' Staircase. All of these works are now in the *Louvre.

A few ancient statues still stand in the gardens of Versailles, along with the many copies of ancient works made by *pensionnaires* at the French Academy in Rome. Their peregrinations in the royal gardens of Versailles and the pleasure palace of Marly have been traced, thanks to inventories and guidebooks.

BIBLIOGRAPHY
R. Cagnat, ''Les ruines de Leptis Magna à la fin du XVIIe siècle,'' *MSNAF* 10 (1901), 63–78; H. Omont, *Missions archéologiques françaises en Orient aux XVIIe et XVIIIe siècles* (Paris, 1902); C. Pinatel, *Les Statues antiques des jardins de Versailles* (Paris, 1963); E. Kantorowicz, ''Oriens Augusti—Lever du Roi,'' *DOP* 17 (1963), 119–77.

BETSY ROSASCO

LOUVRE MUSEUM (MUSÉE NATIONAL DU LOUVRE), Paris. World-renowned museum, whose superlative holdings include an important collection of Greek, Roman and Etruscan antiquities.

Opened as a public museum in 1793, the Louvre and its collections have a history that considerably predates that event. The building itself, beginning between ca. 1190 and 1204 as the fortress of the king of France, Philip II Augustus, was transformed into a Gothic castle by Charles V (1364–80). Under Francis I (1515–47) this royal residence in Paris received a Renaissance façade on its west wing, and later in the century, the architects of *Louis XIV (1643–1715) subsumed what was left of the medieval Louvre into a magnificent French Baroque palace of the classical style, best revealed at its main entrance façade on the east.

The Louvre was already used for the display of antiquities on a modest scale during the reigns of Francis I and Henry IV (1589–1610). While the former chose to display his bronze casts of ancient sculpture and most of his antiques at Fontainebleau, the latter created a special room at the Louvre, the Salle des Antiques, the centerpiece of which was the *Diane à la biche* (*Artemis of Versailles). Louis XIV amassed a considerable collection, drawing from his predecessors and from the collections of the cardinals Mazarin (e.g., a *Dancing*

Satyr) and Richelieu (e.g., the *Amazon* attributed to Polykleitos); the *Venus* of Arles was a gift to the crown in 1651. Louis soon moved the antiquities to his new residence at Versailles (1682 and following), where they remained until after the French Revolution. Along with established favorites, he showed his new acquisitions (1685/6), the *"Germanicus"* (*Marcellus*) and the *"Cincinnatus"* (*Hermes*). The Salle des Caryatides in the Louvre was still used to contain reserve pieces, and it kept this character as a repository from 1692 to the end of the eighteenth century.

In the seventeenth century the French had begun to take an interest in collecting antiquities in Greece. The marbles of the Marquis de *Nointel, ambassador to Constantinople, were temporarily deposited in the Louvre in 1722 and later became a permanent part of the collection.

In 1793 came the opening at the Louvre of the Museum Central des Arts, which displayed, however, very few classical antiquities. The royal marbles remained under seizure at Versailles or on the grounds of the Louvre and the Tuileries gardens. The first important antiquity to be acquired was a segment of the *Parthenon frieze (1798), appropriated from the collection of the Comte de *Choiseul-Gouffier. With *Napoleon's victories in Italy came the plundering of the great Italian collections—the *Vatican, especially—to create the Musée Napoleon in 1803. Magnificent works like the *Laocoon* and the *Belvedere *Apollo* made the trip, destined to return home in 1816 after the fall of Napoleon. The *Albani family collection had been requisitioned, and later, when it proved too costly to send it back, a large portion of it was bought at auction for France. The *Borghese family collection was actually purchased in 1808, but at the buyer's price; later, some 106 pieces remained in France, including the *Borghese *Hermaphrodite,* the *Borghese *Gladiator* and a celebrated portrait of *Homer.* The *Tiber* from the Vatican remained permanently in exile when the Belvedere sculptures were returned to Rome.

Under the directorship of Vivant Denon and the curatorship of E. Q. *Visconti, the Musée des Antiques of the Louvre was reorganized; it was almost totally devoted to marbles. Smaller antiquities from the royal collections, such as the *Gemma Tiberiana and other gems and coins, had been placed in the Cabinet des Médailles (Bibliothèque Nationale). This tendency was reinforced with the acquisition of the *Venus de Milo* (*Aphrodite* of Melos) in 1821 and of the *Piombino *Apollo,* bought for 16,000 francs in 1834.

A new approach to acquisition came into being during the reign of Charles X (1824–30), with the encouragement of scientific missions, exploration and excavations in the classical lands. The *Expedition scientifique de Morée (1829) brought back metopes from the *Temple of Zeus at *Olympia. In 1863 from *Samothrace came the *Winged Victory,* which was to become the antiquity most representative of the glory of the Louvre, with its dramatic placement on the staircase of the Pavillon Daru. The *Hera* of Cheramyes from Samos was acquired in 1875, and the head of a horseman found on the *Akropolis in Athens

(1877) came to the Louvre with the Rampin collection in 1896. (The torso of the Rampin *Horseman,* discovered in 1886, remains in the Akropolis Museum.)

The most sensational single event in the acquisition of antiquities for the Louvre was the purchase in Rome of the collection of the disgraced financier the Marchese *Campana. For 4,364,000 francs, Napoleon III purchased 3,400 painted vases, 1,600 terracottas (cf. *Campana Reliefs), 600 bronzes (including a fine collection of Etruscan mirrors), 300 marble sculptures, a thousand pieces of jewelry and hundreds of inscriptions. The whole collection was shown temporarily in the Musée Napoleon III (1862) and then moved into the Louvre in 1863. Many of the antiquities had been excavated at Etruscan sites, which yielded prodigious amounts of *Greek vases, the result being that the Louvre took its place as the museum with the richest collection of Greek ceramics in the world. Among the Etruscan works the prize piece was the "Sarcophagus of the *Married Couple*" from *Cerveteri. An important fragment of the procession scene from the north side of the *Ara Pacis, which had been so restored that it was mistaken for a *Sacrifice by Antoninus Pius,* was part of the Campana sale; it remains in the Louvre today, one of the few pieces from the altar that were not integrated into its reconstruction in Rome. Also from the Campana collections are a number of Roman portraits, which along with items from the Borghese and Albani collections account for the majority of more than 300 Roman portraits in the Louvre.

The overcrowded department of antiquities continued to receive new materials, such as the collections of Greek terracotta figures from Tanagra, where secret excavations had begun in 1870 (gift of P. Gaudin), and from Myrina, excavated in 1880–82 by S. Reinach and E. Pottier. A highly important group of Roman antiquities was the silver treasure from *Boscoreale, donated in 1895 by the Rothschild family, who also contributed marbles excavated at *Didyma (fragments of columns from the temple of Apollo) and *Miletos.

In the twentieth century the most important acquisitions in the department of Greek, Etruscan and Roman antiquities was the fine set of Late Antique mosaics from *Antioch, acquired by the Louvre during World War II. The relatively stable collection underwent reorganization from 1934 to 1949 under the curation of J. *Charbonneaux and again in 1975 and the following years. The goals of the museum have been oriented toward conservation and enhancement of the existing collection, as seen in a complete revision of the Etruscan rooms, with the newly restored "Sarcophagus of the *Married Couple*" as its centerpiece (1980). Galleries on the ground floor and first floors have been generally refurbished to have more sober backgrounds and sharper lighting, using artificial means instead of sparse daylight.

BIBLIOGRAPHY

E. Coche de la Ferté, s.v. "Parigi," *EAA* 5 (1963), 955–56; F. Villard, "La réorganization du département des antiquités grecques et romaines au Musée du Louvre," *RA* 1 (1980), 190–92; K. de Kersauson, *Musée du Louvre, Catalogue des portraits romains,* 1, *Por-*

traits de la République et d'epoque Julio-Claudienne (Paris, 1986); +A. Pasquier, *The Louvre: Greek, Etruscan and Roman Antiquities* (London, 1991).

LUDOVISI ARES (MARS). Roman marble copy, slightly over lifesize (1.56m), of the god Ares, based on a lost Greek original of the fourth century B.C.

The god is shown beardless, with tousled hair, and nearly nude. He is in a seated position with his legs loosely spread apart and both hands resting upon his proper left knee. The contrapposto effect of the arms across the body combines with a turning figure of Eros at the god's feet to provide viewing interest from various angles. The approach is typical of the work of Lysippos, to whom the work was attributed by F. P. Johnson and others. Some scholars have seen it as a work closely related to Skopas (A. Stewart) or a second-century sculptor working in a neo-Attic style (B. Palma). B. Ridgway recommends suspension of judgment in attribution but supports a date for the original of ca. 320 B.C.

The *Ares* was found, according to P. S. *Bartoli, near the Palazzo Santa Croce in Rome; it was in the *Ludovisi family collection by 1622, identified as a figure of Adonis. *Bernini was paid sixty scudi for restoration, particularly of the head of the Eros and the pommel of the sword. Soon afterward, the statue was referred to as a seated gladiator, an interpretation that recurred in the eighteenth century. Doubts persist about the identity; Achilles has recently been suggested.

The statue was displayed in the Palazzo Grande of the Ludovisi from 1633 until the early years of the nineteenth century. For a while it was then shown in a casino on the estate, and between 1885 and 1890 it was moved to a new palace of the Ludovisi descendants on the Via Veneto. The family sold most of its collection to the Italian state in 1901, and the Ludovisi *Ares,* along with the other antiquities, was transferred to the Museo Nazionale delle *Terme, where it remains today.

BIBLIOGRAPHY

Bieber, 41; Haskell—Penny, 260–61; +B. Palma, *Museo Nazionale Romane, Le Sculture,* I, 4: *I Marmi Ludovisi: Storia della collezione,* ed. A. Giuliano (Rome, 1983), 22; I, 5; *I Marmi Ludovisi nel Museo Nazionale Romano* (Rome, 1983), 115–21; Ridgway, *Hellenistic Sculpture,* I, 84–87.

LUDOVISI BATTLE SARCOPHAGUS. Colossal marble Roman sarcophagus (length 2.73m), with traces of polychrome and a binder for gilding preserved, dating to the third century A.C.; upon it is represented in masterly fashion a battle between Romans and Goths, with a jumble of figures in a balanced composition.

The sarcophagus was discovered in Rome in 1621 in the Bernusconi *vigna* in front of Porta S. Lorenzo. It was acquired by Cardinal Ludovisi (*Ludovisi family) for 120 scudi and was set up in the garden of the Villa Ludovisi under an aediculum supported by four columns of gray granite. It stood there until 1890, when it was transferred to the Museo Ludovisi. In 1901, it came into the possession of the state, along with the Ludovisi collection of antiquities, and is today in the Museo Nazionale delle *Terme, Rome. The Late Antique style of the sarcophagus does not seem to have appealed to artists of the seventeenth and eighteenth centuries, but Pompeo Batoni (1708–87) has left a handsome three-part drawing in which the figures are made more naturalistic.

The sarcophagus depicts a general on horseback in the very center of the composition, with his right arm flung wide in a gesture that seems to dominate the action. He wears a thin beard, and the forehead is marked with the X that was the seal of a follower of Mithras, and behind his head emerges the serpent of the god.

Although all authorities agree on a third-century date, there has been much debate over the identity of the general. The problem is exacerbated by the fact that the head seems small for the body and thus may be recut. The earliest recorded identification of the individual, in a Ludovisi inventory of 1633, refers to him as the emperor Volusianus. R. Venuti (1766) ascribed the work to the period of Alexander Severus, an argument later taken up by E. *Braun (1854), who thought the battle might be the defeat of Artaxerxes by Alexander in A.D. 232. *Platner believed the general was Septimius Severus, while E. *Strong identified him as Claudius Gothicus. Various other identifications have been proposed in the twentieth century, some arguing that the figure is not an emperor (e.g., H. von Heintze: Hostilianus, son of Decius). Many now support a date in the reign of Gallienus.

BIBLIOGRAPHY
L. de Lachenal in *Museo Nazionale Romano, Le Sculture,* I, 5, *I Marmi Lodovisi nel Museo Nazionale Romano,* ed. A. Giuliano (Rome, 1983), 56–67.

LUDOVISI FAMILY. Noble Italian family, known for its great collection of antiquities, today largely in the Museo Nazionale delle *Terme, Rome.

The Ludovisi family, originating in Bologna, reached the heights of power and wealth in Rome when ALESSANDRO LUDOVISI (1554–1623) became pope in 1621, with the name of Gregory XV. His nephew, LUDOVICO LU-DOVISI (1595–1632), became cardinal the following year. Well known as a patron of Guercino, *Domenichino and Guido Reni and as the founder of the church of Sant'Ignazio, Cardinal Ludovico established an imposing presence in Rome as he began to build a new villa between the Porta Pinciana and the Porta Salaria. He collected ancient marbles with such vigor that by the time of his death he had amassed some 380 sculptures (inventoried 1633), which were disposed about the Palazzo Grande, the Casino and the Galleria of the villa, as well as among the fountains and gardens.

Some of the sculptures were likely unearthed on the villa grounds, which were in antiquity the site of the *Gardens of Sallust. This provenance is often suggested for the *Dying Trumpeter and the *Ludovisi Gaul, since both were

Statue of *Pomona*, formerly in the Ludovisi collection, drawing by J. Riepenhausen, ca. 1840. (Deutsches Archäologisches Institut, Rome. Inst. Neg. 85.4228.)

in the villa by 1623, but there is no firm evidence for this, as the cardinal secured items from many sources in the early years. He had also acquired the Villa Altemps at Frascati in 1621, and from there he transferred nineteen portraits (including twelve heads of *Emperors*) and fifteen other sculptures. In these early years he had the services of Ippolito Buzzi as a restorer; later restorations were done by *Algardi and *Bernini.

In 1622 the cardinal acquired the *Ludovisi Battle Sarcophagus (excavated outside Porta San Lorenzo) and the *Ludovisi *Ares* (excavated near the Palazzo Santa Croce) and made the important purchase of some one hundred items from the *Cesi family collection; these included *Apollo and Daphne, Boy Strangling a Goose*, *Crouching Venus* and *Sleeping Cupid*, as well as the famous basalt head of *Scipio Africanus* and the head of the Ludovisi *Juno*. He also acquired a number of pieces from the *Cesarini family collection, among which were "three philosophers," probably **Sokrates, Diogenes* and *Epikouros*. Many donations were made to Cardinal Ludovisi by clients seeking favor with the family. In this way he acquired marbles from the collections of Achille Mattei, Paolo Capranica and Muzio Mattei. From the *Medici family came the *Reclining Satyr*, now among several pieces on the grounds of the U.S. Embassy in Rome.

The cardinal's spendthrift nephew GIAMBATTISTA, assuming the title of Prince of Piombino in 1665, was disposed to sell the antiquities belonging to himself and his sisters (IPPOLITA, LAVINIA and OLIMPIA). Among the buyers were Queen *Christina of Sweden and Ferdinand II, Grand Duke of Tuscany, who purchased a *Hermaphrodite* (now in the *Uffizi) claimed to rival the *Borghese *Hermaphrodite*.

In the nineteenth century, the still quite considerable collection was installed in a casino on the estate of the Prince of Piombino. Between 1885 and 1890, the collection was moved to the family's new palazzo on the Via Veneto; acquisition of antiquities continued, as the *Ludovisi Throne was discovered on the grounds of the old villa in 1887. Finally, in 1901, the bulk of the Ludovisi collection was sold to the Italian government.

BIBLIOGRAPHY

T. Schreiber, *Die Antiken Bildwerke der Villa Ludovisi in Rome* (Leipzig, 1880); R. Paribeni, *Le Terme di Diocleziano e il Museo Nazionale Romano*, 2nd ed. (Rome, 1932); G. Felici, *Villa Ludovisi in Roma* (Rome, 1952); B. Palma, *Museo Nazionale Romano, Le Sculture*, I.4, *I Marmi Ludovisi: Storia della collezione*, ed. A. Giuliano (Rome, 1983).

                                        MARJON VAN DER MEULEN

LUDOVISI GAUL KILLING HIMSELF AND HIS WIFE (PAETUS AND ARRIA; SEXTUS MARIUS AND HIS DAUGHTER, etc.). Pair of figures made from Asiatic marble, over lifesize, representing a Gaul (height 2.11m) plunging a sword into his neck, as he holds by the arm the collapsing figure of a female.

The figures are usually considered copies of lost bronze Hellenistic originals that once adorned a victory monument of Attalos I of Pergamon after victories over the Gauls (233 B.C.; 228–223 B.C.). Much of the right arm of the Gaul and much of the left arm of his wife are restored, and there are numerous minor restorations to both figures.

The group is closely associated with the famous *Dying Trumpeter* in the Capitoline Museum and perhaps was discovered at the same time. The place and date of discovery are unknown, but the pair is first listed in an inventory of the *Ludovisi family collection in 1623 as "Marius Killing Himself and His Daughter." The story alluded to (Dio Cassius 58.22; Tacitus, *Annals* 6.19) is that of Sextus Marius, who sought to protect his daughter from the lust of Tiberius. A far more popular and longer-lasting interpretation was that the pair represented the well-known suicide of Arria, who tried to convince her husband, taken in a conspiracy, that he should commit suicide. "It doesn't hurt, Paetus" (*Paete, non dolet;* Martial 1.13), she declared, as she killed herself. Various stories of dual deaths were adduced before E. Q. *Visconti identified the pair, with their coarse features and thick hair, as defeated Gauls; he connected them with the *Dying Trumpeter* and suggested that the statues once adorned a monument erected in Rome to commemorate defeat of the Gauls by Julius Caesar or Germans by Germanicus.

F. Coarelli has recently circled back to the idea that these statues were erected in Rome, calling them copies made at Pergamon of Attalid statues, brought to Rome to commemorate the victories of Caesar (46–44 B.C.). He argued that the suicidal Gaul and his wife actually stood over the *Trumpeter,* on the same base, creating a radial arrangement. B. Palma and B. Ridgway approved the idea of a Roman date, but not the reconstruction. Ridgway went so far as to suggest that the work is a Roman original and not Hellenistic at all.

From the time of its first display in the Palazzo Grande of the Villa Ludovisi in 1633, the group of the Gaul and his wife was one of the most famous of all sculptures to be seen in Rome. It was often anthologized, copied and imitated, for example by N. *Poussin, in the powerful Roman soldier in the foreground of his *Rape of the Sabines* (Metropolitan Museum of Art, New York, 1634) and by P. P. *Rubens in his *Government of the Queen* for the Maria de' Medici series (*Louvre, Paris, 1622–25). The group remained there until the nineteenth century (while the *Trumpeter* found its way to the Capitoline Museum), moved briefly to a casino on the Ludovisi property and then transferred to a new palace of the family on the Via Veneto. In 1901, it was purchased with the other Ludovisi marbles by the Italian state and is kept today in the Museo Nazionale delle *Terme, Rome.

BIBLIOGRAPHY

Haskell—Penny, 282–84; B. S. Ridgway, "The Gauls in Sculpture," *ArchNews* 11 (1982), 97–98; +B. Palma, *Museo Nazionale Romana, Le Sculture,* I, 4, *I Marmi Ludovisi: Storia della collezione,* ed. A. Giuliano, (Rome, 1983), 19; idem, in I, 5, *I Marmi Ludovisi nel Museo Nazionale Romano,* ed. A. Giuliano (Rome, 1983), 146–52.

LUDOVISI MARS. See LUDOVISI ARES.

LUDOVISI "THRONE." Greek monument consisting of a block of Parian marble (max. height 1.07m) with relief carving on three sides, dating ca. 460 B.C. and probably made in Southern Italy or Sicily.

The work was found in Rome in 1887 in the gardens of the Villa Ludovisi (*Ludovisi family), where the *Gardens of Sallust lay in antiquity and where numerous sculptures had been discovered from the seventeenth century onward. The piece was acquired by the Museo Nazionale delle *Terme in 1901, when the descendants of the Ludovisi sold the bulk of the long-established collection to the Italian government.

Known for over one hundred years, the piece has retained its high status and continues to be admired for the beauty of its carving. But the history of scholarship on the Ludovisi "Throne" is marked by controversy and uncertainty. The function of the monument is simply not understood; E. *Petersen originally suggested that it was a throne for a religious image (hence the popular name), while others have proposed that it was somehow part of an altar. Various suggestions have also been made for the subject of the principal relief on the front of the throne, which represents a female figure being lifted up by two female attendants. The beautiful interlocking composition may show Aphrodite rising from the sea; other candidates are Persephone rising from the earth, Ge, Rhea, Hera. The sides of the "throne" are also elusive: each shows a seated female figure, one naked and playing the pipes, the other wrapped in a mantle and putting incense over a burner.

Answers to these questions are sometimes sought by looking at a "counterpart" in the *Museum of Fine Arts, Boston, which is of similar shape and size but is also a highly problematic work. Of unknown provenance, the work appeared in Rome in 1894 and was acquired by E. P. *Warren in 1896 (on display in Boston in 1908). It, too, has a puzzling iconography (the front relief perhaps shows Thanatos weighing the destiny of Achilles and Memnon). Irregularities of the style and composition have led many to think that the piece is a learned forgery of the nineteenth century, inspired by the Ludovisi "Throne"; it has been analyzed, however, as having the same kind of marble as the "Throne" and showing similar conditions of weathering. On these grounds, B. Ashmole accepted the Boston counterpart as authentic. M. Guarducci has recently condemned the work anew, saying that it was made for W. *Helbig, whose association with other forgeries has been observed (*Praenestine Fibula).

BIBLIOGRAPHY
G. Becatti, s.v. "Trono di Boston," *EAA* 3 (1966), 1019–20; E. Paribeni, s.v. "Trono Ludovisi," *EAA* 3 (1966), 1020–22; Ridgway, *Severe Style*, 50, 55; A. Andrén, *Deeds and Misdeeds in Classical Art and Antiquities* (Goterna, 1986), 75–78; M. Guarducci, "Il cosidetto trono di Boston," *BdA* 43 (1987), 49–62; +Stewart, *Greek Sculpture*, 149.

LUDWIG I (1786–1868). King of Bavaria (1825–48); distinguished connoisseur and patron of the arts.

Well known as an enthusiastic and discriminating art collector (perhaps the most important of the period in Germany), Ludwig pressed the arts into state service and used classical motifs for expressing new social and political ideas.

Sponsoring the revival of classicism in Munich, he guided the city's period of greatest cultural growth and development. His city building plan, developed along classical prototypes, contributed greatly to Munich's present character. Also bearing witness to his initiative and taste are the unprecedented art treasures filling his monumental works of architecture. Ludwig's long-aspired goal, to make Munich into the "Athens of the Isar," is reflected in the construction of the Königsplatz complex. Comprising three neoclassical structures—the *Glyptothek, the Staatliche *Antikensammlung and the Propylea—it was envisioned by him as a permanent home for his collected Greek and Roman antiquities. His collection, acquired at immense cost, thus forms the nucleus of Munich's most famous museums. His vase collection was especially renowned for its quality and included works from all periods of Greek art. (Many pieces were destroyed during World War II.) Martin von *Wagner, art agent, commissioned to arrange the vase collection exhibit, recommended that its display room in the recently constructed Neue Pinakothek be decorated with copies of wall paintings from the Etruscan tombs in which many of the vases had been discovered (see Carlo *Ruspi).

"Die Vereinigten Sammlungen Ludwigs" contain treasures of various kinds and periods, dating from the third millennium B.C. through the tenth century A.C., and were enhanced through extensive acquisitions from collections and excavations in Italy and Sicily. His art agents obtained outstanding objects from the Panittera collection; the Candelori brothers' excavations of Etruscan tombs near *Vulci; estate of the Prince of *Canino (Lucien Bonaparte) and the Lipona collection (of Caroline Murat, former Queen of Naples, later Countess Lipona). The most remarkable pieces in his sculpture collection are the Archaic pedimental decorations from the Temple of Aphaia at *Aigina, which were discovered in 1811 and bought in 1815. Ludwig had them removed to Rome for restoration by his longtime friend, the sculptor *Thorvaldsen, before putting them on display in Munich.

Ludwig also showed great interest in numismatics and played a large part in building up Bavaria's classical coin collection, the origins of which date to the reign of Duke *Albrecht V in the sixteenth century.

BIBLIOGRAPHY

K. Bosl, *Zur Geschichte der Bayern* (Darmstadt, 1965); H. Bauer, *The Alte Pinakothek—Munich* (New York, 1969); W. Mittlemeier, *Die Neue Pinakothek in München, 1843–1854* (Munich, 1977); K. Vierneisel—G. Leinz, eds., *Glyptothek München 1830–1980: Jubiläumsausstellung zur Entstehungs- und Baugeschichte* (Munich, 1980).

INGEBORG A. SCHWEIGER

LUGLI, GIUSEPPE (1890–1967). Italian archaeologist; professor of Roman topography at the University of Rome and founder of the Istituto di Topografia Antica.

A pupil of *Lanciani, Lugli devoted himself first to the study of the topography and architecture of the villas near Rome, especially the imperial retreats, but his interests extended to every aspect of the archaeology of the region, and he was one of the first contributors to the *Forma Italiae* (1926–28). Later he focused on Rome itself and produced *I Monumenti antichi di Roma e suburbio* (1930–40) and *Roma antica, il centro monumentale* (1946–47), as well as scores of papers. His interest in the field continued throughout his life and is represented by his posthumous *Itinerario di Roma antica* (1975), but his crowning achievements were his monumental study of Roman construction, *La Tecnica ediliza romana* (1957), and his organization and work on the sources for the topography of Rome, *Fontes ad topographiam veteris urbis Romae pertinentes* (1952–62), the latter unfortunately never completed.

L. RICHARDSON, JR

LUSIERI, GIOVANNI BATTISTA (1751–1821). Italian painter, known as the assistant of Lord *Elgin in procuring marbles from the *Parthenon in Athens.

Lusieri was working as a court painter to the King of Naples when Sir William *Hamilton recommended him to *Elgin (1799) as an artist who might make accurate drawings of antiquities in Greece. Lusieri became the leader of a team that was equipped to make drawings and casts of antiquities but that, in effect, spent more time in excavating and the physical labor of dismantling the desired sculptures from the Parthenon (1801–4). Lusieri's role necessitated a constant investment of time and energy in diplomatic negotiations and intrigues with the Turkish authorities in Athens. He also was constantly maneuvering to elude the schemes of the French artist *Fauvel, who had earlier managed to secure a metope and a slab of the Parthenon frieze and send them off to France and longed to take away more of the marbles for *Napoleon's museum in Paris.

Lusieri's years of negotiations culminated in the final shipment, in 1811, of the Parthenon marbles he had collected. He journeyed part of the way to London with them (they arrived in 1812) and then returned to Athens, where he continued to petition Elgin for employment. Elgin had found him useful for the difficult job of collecting sculptures for him but was now unwilling to retain him simply as an artist, especially as Lusieri had proved slow in completing drawings and paintings that had been commissioned. In 1819, Elgin made a clear statement of Lusieri's release. The artist stayed on in Athens and continued to entreat Elgin, up until his death in 1821, but also dawdled endlessly and failed to complete many works. A portfolio of his art, assembled over a twenty-year period, was all lost in a shipwreck in 1828. The only completed drawing Elgin ever received was a view of the *Monument of Philopappos, today in the possession of the Elgin family.

BIBLIOGRAPHY

W. St. Clair, *Lord Elgin and the Marbles* (London, 1967); Tsigakou, *Rediscovery of Greece* 24, 191a; B. F. Cook, *The Elgin Marbles* (Cambridge, 1984), 53, 55–56, 58–61; C. Hitchens, *The Elgin Marbles: Should They Be Returned to Greece?* (London, 1987), 39–49.

Portrait of the *Duc de Luynes*, Rome, Deutsches Archäologisches Institut (German Archaeological Institute). (Deutsches Archäologisches Institut, Rome. Inst. Neg. 76.648.)

LUYNES, HONORÉ-THÉODORIC-PAUL-JOSEPH D'ALBERT, DUC DE (1802–67). French statesman, archaeologist and numismatist; a founder of the *Instituto di Corrispondenza Archeologica.

Born in Paris, the Duc de Luynes visited Italy at an early age. In 1828, he investigated ancient temple remains at *Metapontion with the architect F. J. Debacq and published the results as *Métaponte* (1833). In Rome he formed a close friendship with E. *Gerhard and the members of his circle who were interested in establishing an international archaeological association. Luynes provided financing and general support from the French for the Instituto di Corrispondenza Archeologica, officially founded in 1829. (In spite of the efforts of Luynes, the French dropped out in 1848.)

Luynes visited other lands (Egypt, 1840; Near East, 1864; he was an early visitor to Petra) and provided generous financial support for research other than his own in Egypt and Tunisia. The duke's other publications pertain especially to numismatics—Persian, Phoenician, Cypriot and Greek—and painted vases (*Description de quelques vases peints, étrusques, italiotes, siciliennes et grecs,* 1840).

Sometimes referred to as the "French Arundel," the Duc de Luynes was an ardent collector of manuscripts, vases, gems, coins, bronzes. He gathered his treasures at his castle at Dampierre, where the setting was enhanced by paintings of *Ingres, Flandrin and others. But from 1855 he began to donate items to the state; many objects are today in the *Louvre and the Cabinet des Médailles, Paris (some 7,000 Greek coins).

BIBLIOGRAPHY
"Luynes, Honoré-Théodoric-Paul-Joseph-d'Albert," *NBG* 32 (1860), cols. 361–63; Stark, 300–301; Michaelis, 48, 61, 76, 277, 281; *Porträtarchiv*, no. 165.

LYONS (LYON; LUGDUNUM). City in France, the capital of Roman Gaul.

Founded in 43 B.C. by Caesar's lieutenant, L. Munatius Plancus, Lugdunum was located on the heights of Fourvière (Forum Vetus) overlooking the confluence of the Saône and the Rhône. Much of the Roman city, including some 300m of the principal east-west street (*decumanus*), has been uncovered. Among the chief antiquities is the theater (108m in diameter after a Hadrianic extension to increase its capacity to 10,500 seats). Beside it is an odeion (ca. A.D. 160). The Amphitheater of the Three Gauls lies apart from the rest, on a spit of land formed by the confluence of the two rivers, known as Condate. It is dated to A.D. 19 by its dedicatory inscription, found down a well in 1958.

Lugdunum was served by four *aqueducts, famous for the nine siphons they contain; there are remains to the southwest of the city, notably, at Beaunant, Chaponost and Soucieu. The Musée de la civilisation gallo-romaine, a modern concrete structure of revolutionary (and efficient) design on the Fourvière hillside overlooking the site, houses a large mosaic illustrating races in the circus and "la table claudienne," a fine bronze plaque discovered by Bellièvre in 1527 and identified by him as containing the text of a speech to the Roman Senate (A.D. 48) delivered by the emperor Claudius, a native of Lugdunum.

In the sixteenth century Lyons became one of the leading literary and artistic centers in France. Numismatic research flourished, and publications by G. du Choul, G. Rouille and G. Symeoni achieved international fame. The papers of *Peiresc record numerous collectors in the city in the early seventeenth century. Its most noteworthy scholar was Jacob *Spon, whose *Recherche des antiquités de la ville de Lyon* (1673) launched provincial Roman studies.

BIBLIOGRAPHY
E. Babelon, *Traité des monnaies grecques et romaines* (Paris, 1901), 95, 102, 116, 130, 147; G. de Montauzan, *Les Aqueducs antiques de Lyon* (Paris, 1908); A. Audin, *Essai sur la topographie de Lugdunum,* 3rd ed. (Lyons, 1964); S. Walker, ed., *Récentes recherches en archéologie gallo-romaine et paléochrétienne sur Lyon et sa région,* BAR International Ser. 108 (Oxford, 1981).

A. TREVOR HODGE

M

MABUSE. See GOSSAERT, JAN.

MADERNO (MADERNA), CARLO (1556–1629). Italian architect, leading figure of the Early Baroque style in Rome.

Born near Milan, Maderno was in Rome by 1576, employed by his uncle Domenico *Fontana. As Fontana became famous for his erection of the Vatican obelisk (*obelisks), Maderno's fortunes also rose, and he played a key role in setting up other obelisks for Pope *Sixtus V at the *Lateran, S. Maria Maggiore and the Piazza del Popolo (1588–89).

Maderno soon succeeded Fontana at the Vatican and, as Rome's leading architect, inherited not only Fontana's former commissions but also those of Francesco da Volterra and Giacomo della Porta. His productive career, often involving the completion of projects begun by others or the designing of buildings that he left unfinished at his death, was crowned by his completion of the nave and façade of St. Peter's. Another of Maderno's proudest achievements was the moving in 1614 of a colossal monolithic column from the ruins of the *Basilica of Maxentius to the piazza in front of S. Maria Maggiore. The great fluted column of green *cipollino* (height 14.30m) was the only remaining column of eight in the basilica. On behalf of Pope Paul V (1605–21) and before an admiring crowd, Maderno moved and reerected the column by methods similar to those used by Fontana for the erection of the Vatican obelisk. On top of the column was placed a bronze statue of the Madonna weighing 14,000 pounds, made from bronze taken from melted-down cannon from *Castel Sant'Angelo.

In 1625 Pope Urban VIII (1623–44) undertook to refortify Castel Sant'Angelo, and for the making of new artillery he removed the bronze beams from the porch of the *Pantheon (the church of S. Maria Rotonda). The following year he began to build new campanili for the church, and two towers were erected flanking the central pediment. The towers, much despised and sometimes referred to as the "ass's ears of the Pantheon," have been attributed to Maderno (although more popularly to *Bernini).

The only building of significance designed by Maderno and actually finished by him is the *Palazzo Mattei, created for Asdrubale Mattei (*Mattei family) to house the family's collection of antiquities. Completed in 1618, the palace featured a courtyard sumptuously decorated with ancient and modern reliefs and busts, for which Maderno is presumed to have designed the frames and even the general iconographic arrangement. Other rooms of the palace also contain original ancient reliefs from sarcophagi and other monuments set in the walls, as well as niches designed for the display of sculpture in the round. During excavations for the foundation of the palace (1599), remains of antique structures were discovered, which are now thought to be part of the theater of Balbus (identified at the time as the Circus Flaminius).

BIBLIOGRAPHY

+H. Hibbard, *Carlo Maderno and Roman Architecture, 1580–1630* (University Park, PA, 1971); T. Magnuson, *Rome in the Age of Bernini* 1–2 (Stockholm, 1982–86).

MAFFEI, FRANCESCO SCIPIONE, Marchese (1675–1755). Italian writer, archaeologist and collector; specialist in local antiquities at *Verona and in Etruscan studies.

Born at Verona, Scipione Maffei at an early age developed an interest in poetry, art and the theater. In 1711 he was in Turin, where he helped with the organization of the art collection of Carl Emanuel of Savoy and investigated the royal library for worthwhile manuscripts. Returning to Verona, he began to prepare a detailed history of his native city, which soon appeared as *Verona illustrata* (1731–32).

Maffei traveled to southern France in 1732, where he became thoroughly familiar with the Roman antiquities of Provence and took an especial interest in the theaters and amphitheaters, which provided significant comparisons with the theater in Verona. The fruit of these studies was his *Galliae antiquitates selectae* (Paris, 1733). Other travels followed to Paris, where he became a member of the Académie des inscriptions, to Oxford and to London. On his return trip to Verona, he also visited Holland and Germany.

Maffei was passionately interested in the early history of Italy and was constantly on the alert for information about Etruscan antiquities and inscriptions. He was a true pioneer of the systematic study of the Etruscans, involved in the subject before Filippo *Buonarroti brought forth his edition of T. *Dempster's *De Etruria regali;* indeed, he waited eagerly for the work to appear and reviewed it in the journal of which he was a founder, the *Giornale dei Letterati.* As a member of the *Accademia Etrusca, Maffei kept abreast of all developments in the field and became embroiled in controversies over the origin of the Etruscans and the nature of the Etruscan alphabet. He incurred the fierce enmity of A. F. *Gori, who went so far as to accuse Maffei of plagiarism. His principal publi-

LONDON BRITISH MUSEUM   THE WARBURG INSTITUTE

LONDON BRITISH MUSEUM   THE WARBURG INSTITUTE

Portrait of *F. Scipione
Maffei* (obverse), Aca-
demia Philarmonica (re-
verse), bronze medal,
1755. London, British
Museum. (The Warburg
Institute, University of
London.)

cation in this arena was his *Trattato sopra la nazione etrusca e sopra gl'itali primitivi* (1739).

Whenever he received news of the discovery or availability of Etruscan antiquities, Maffei was drawn to investigate and was constantly seeking to acquire items for display in Verona. As early as 1719, he dreamed of a public museum for the city, and at his own expense he diligently collected antiquities toward that end. His collection can be reconstructed in part; he owned Etruscan urns from *Chiusi, *Volterra and *Perugia, as well as objects with paleovenetic inscriptions from around Padua. His antiquities were given to the city of Verona and form part of the modern Museo Lapidario Maffeiano at Verona. Maffei had an abiding interest in epigraphy, publishing his ideas on the famed bronze tablets from *Gubbio and carefully and correctly copying the extant inscriptions from around Verona. (The latter were published in *Museum Veronense*, 1749).

BIBLIOGRAPHY
Stark, 109, 118; *Il Museo Maffeiano riaperto al pubblico* (Verona, 1982); M. Cristofani, *La Scoperta degli etruschi, Archeologia e antiquaria nel '700* (Rome, 1983); *Porträtarchiv*, no. 55.

MAFFEI FAMILY. Family of collectors settled in Rome, with branches in Volterra and Verona, during the Renaissance.

BENEDETTO MAFFEI (d. 1494) first bought the family house in the Rione Pigna, near the Arco di Ciambella, behind the *Pantheon. His son ACHILLE (d. 1510) brought together a collection comprising twenty-one inscriptions and several famous statues. Among these was a male *Dead Niobid,* described as being in the collection ca. 1500 by "Prospetto Milanese"; later it was drawn by *Aspertini, who adapted the pose for the body of a decapitated saint in his *Burial of Sts. Valerian and Tiburtius* (Bologna). It was also imitated by *Raphael and *Giulio Romano for a hanging figure in the *Fire in the Borgo* (Vatican, Stanze). By 1589, the piece had been acquired by Mario Bevilacqua in Verona, and in 1811 it went to Bavaria, eventually to be placed in the Munich *Glyptothek. Another major sculpture was the *"*Cleopatra*," which was acquired from ANGELO MAFFEI by *Julius II in 1512 and taken to the Belvedere court (*Vatican Museums). There was also a relief of the visit of Dionysos to the poet Ikarios (cf. *Sassi family).

When van *Heemskerck visited the collection and drew the courtyard in the 1530s, the assemblage of sculptures was impressive, as is also obvious from *Aldrovandi's records made in 1550. During the lifetime of BERNARDINO (d. 1553), it contained a large number of portrait heads and busts, including a head of *Laocoon. *Orsini used six of the portraits for his *Imagines* (1570) and also used a coin in the collection as a basis for his identification of the famous *Pseudo-*Seneca* portrait type. Finally, mention should be made of ACHILLE II (d. 1568), an ardent antiquarian and close friend of *Pighius and *Ligorio.

BIBLIOGRAPHY
+A. Michaelis, "Römische Skizzenbücher Marten van Heemskercks," *JdI* 6 (1891), 133–35; Lanciani, *Storia degli scavi* I (1902), 109–11; III (1907), 162; +A. Schmitt,

"Römische Antikensammlungen im Spiegel eines Musterbuchs der Renaissance," *MJb* 21 (1970), 114–15; +Bober—Rubinstein, 476.

MARJON VAN DER MEULEN

MAFFEI, PAOLO ALESSANDRO (1653–1716). Italian scholar, known for his publications on ancient sculpture and gems.

Born at Volterra to a noble family, P. A. Maffei was sent to Rome, where he eventually obtained the command of a company of papal guards. In his free time he pursued the study of antiquity and kept up a rich correspondence for many years with learned men of Italy and France. Exceedingly modest, he long resisted the urgings of his friends to publish his own scholarship. His first publication came at the age of fifty-one, when he produced the commentary for a great album of ancient and modern sculptures, *Raccolta di statue antiche e moderne,* published in Rome in 1704 by Domenico de Rossi.

The sumptuous volume, providing a canonical guide to the ancient sculpture that shaped taste in the early eighteenth century, included 163 plates, arranged by location of the statuary; works were drawn mainly from the Belvedere statue court in the *Vatican, the *Capitoline and the private collections of the *Borghese family, *Farnese family, *Ludovisi family and *Medici family. The work also included four treatises by Maffei—on a tomb discovered near the Via Ostia, on the *Baths of Titus and on marbles from the *Albani family collection. A second important publication was his edition of *Gemme antiche figurate* (4 vols., 1707–9), also published by de Rossi, a revised and expanded version of the corpus of ancient gems published earlier by L. *Agostini. Containing over 400 images in actual size of portraits, deities, myths and symbols on gems, the work was used heavily by *Stosch, among others, and was generally well received among students of glyptics.

BIBLIOGRAPHY

Weiss, "Maffei (Paolo Alessandro)," *BU* 34 (1827), 271; Haskell—Penny, esp. 23–24; Zazoff, *Gemmensammler und Gemmenforscher,* 38–40.

MAGNESIA-ON-THE-MAEANDER (MAGNESIA AD MAEANDRUM). Ionian Greek city located on a tributary of the Maeander River, ca. 20km southeast of *Ephesos.

The city was founded by Aiolians in the seventh century B.C. and subsequently was taken over by Gyges of Lydia (685–652 B.C.) and assaulted by the Kimmerians. It later fell to the Persians, from whom Thibron of Sparta captured it (440 B.C.). He transferred Magnesia to a new site, at a place where a sanctuary of Artemis Leukophryene had been established.

The earlier location of Magnesia is unknown, but the new location was finally identified by W. M. *Leake in 1800. He drew the plan of the temple of Artemis, a structure dated to the second century B.C. and designed by the famed Hellenistic architect Hermogenes (mentioned by Vitruvius 3.2.6). Excavations were undertaken at the site in 1842 by Charles *Texier, resulting in the retrieval of many portions of the Amazon frieze and architectural decoration that adorned the temple (now in the *Louvre). In 1890, the *German Archaeological Institute initiated excavations at the site under K. *Humann, and these were continued until 1893 by the *Berlin Museum. Other parts of the Amazon frieze were deposited in the archaeological museum in Istanbul, and architectural fragments went to Berlin. A number of other components of Magnesia were discovered (agora, Roman gymnasium, theater, inscriptions), but these have all been reburied by the annual inundations of the river.

BIBLIOGRAPHY
O. Kern, *Die Inschriften von Magnesia am Mäander* (1900); C. Humann, *Magnesia am Maeander* (1904); G. E. Bean, s.v. "Magnesia ad Maeandrum," *PECS,* 544; A. Yaylali, *Der Fries der Artemisions von Magnesia am Mäander* (Tübingen, 1976), 9–11.

MAGOFFIN, RALPH VAN DEMAN (1874–1942). American archaeologist.

Born in Rice County, Kansas, to the sister of Esther Boise *Van Deman, Ralph Magoffin studied at the University of Michigan and Johns Hopkins University (Ph.D., 1908) and at the American Academy in Rome (1907–8). He served in the U.S. army during the war with Spain and in World War I and held academic positions at Johns Hopkins (1908–23) and New York University (1923–39).

Magoffin was president of the *Archaeological Institute of America (1921–31) and author of *A Study of the Topography and the Municipal History of Praeneste* (1908) and *The Quinquennales* (1913), as well as popular books on archaeology, *Magic Spades* (1923) and *The Lure and Lore of Archaeology* (1930). He died in 1942 at Columbia, South Carolina.

BIBLIOGRAPHY
S. B. Luce, "Ralph Van Deman Magoffin," *AJA* 46 (1942), 412–13.

LARISSA BONFANTE

MAHDIA. Location on the coast of Tunisia near which the wreck of an ancient ship or barge was discovered in 1907.

The wreck, discovered by sponge divers in ca. 40m of water at a distance of 4.8km from the shore, was laden with a cargo of about sixty-five marble columns as well as bases and capitals, most of which remain today in the water. The barge itself has been estimated to have been about 40m long and about 10m wide. That it originally sailed from Athens is suggested by the presence of Attic marbles and Athenian inscriptions. A. Merlin and L. Poinssot, who first published the finds from the wreck, dated it to the period after the plundering of Athens by Sulla (86 B.C.). W. Fuchs has disputed this dating and argued for an earlier period, the second half of the second century B.C.

A number of bronzes were found in the cargo, including a bronze herm signed by Boethos of Kalchedon and an associated bronze lifesize *Eros* or *Agon,* perhaps by the same artist, as well as some smaller bronzes (the grotesque dwarf dancers are among the best known) and fragments of marble kraters of the same type as the *Borghese Vase. These are now to be seen in the Musée du Bardo, Tunis.

BIBLIOGRAPHY

Bieber, 97, 104, 145; W. Fuchs, *Der Schiffsfund von Mahdia* (Tübingen, 1963); G. B. Bass, s.v. "Shipwrecks," *PECS, 833.*

MAISON CARRÉE, Nîmes. Roman temple, dedicated to Gaius and Lucius Caesar in the years A.D. 2–5.

Measuring about 15m × 32m, the temple combines Italic and Greek elements; it is set on a high podium and features a deep porch and cella wall even with the edge of the podium, as in Etruscan temples. But it also has a lofty roof and the Greek Corinthian order, used on pseudoperipteral columns going around the cella. It is regarded by many as one of the best-preserved examples of temple architecture under Augustus.

Its history prior to the ninth century is unknown, though it may have served as a church for the Early Christians, and its preservation by the fifth-century Visigoths implies that they found it useful in some capacity. At King Odo's death (898), the Maison Carrée was in the royal domain and was used for judicial assemblies; it later passed into private hands. In 1015, when it was left by the canon Pons to his nephew, its interior was still intact. Its steps were soon removed, and a chapel was built in its entranceway. Not long after, the counts of Toulouse made it the city hall; it retained this function until the sixteenth century and the epithet *Le Capitole* even longer.

The earliest author to refer to the building was Sebastiano *Serlio; the first known to call it the Maison Carrée was J. Poldo d'Albenas (1560). The city hall was divided into compartments at each of three different levels, and windows were pierced. Again private property, the building was rented out in the later sixteenth century and was used as a stable for two or three generations, when several alterations and mutilations occurred. In 1670 the Maison Carrée was sold to the Augustinian convent of Nîmes. The Augustinians, authorized by *Louis XIV, built their church inside the Maison Carrée and their monastery close by; badly needed repairs and restorations were carried out skillfully by the architect Gabriel Dardalhion. In 1674 digging for buried treasure inside the building threatened its foundations and had to be stopped by city magistrates. The Augustinian church remained intact through the restorations of Jean-François Séguier (1778–81) but was removed by the engineer Grangent during the restorations of 1816–22.

Excavation in 1821–33 first brought to light the plan of the architectural complex dominated by the Maison Carrée, which, from the center of its south (short) side, overlooked a space about 70m × 140m that stood 1.1m lower than the porticoes that embraced it. Grain had been stored in the Maison Carrée during the French Revolution; it was later used to house the Préfecture du Gard; then, it was used as archives. In 1823 it became a museum, which it has remained. Further restorations were carried out in 1954–56. Famous visitors who have written about the building include Thomas *Jefferson, *Dumas père, Stendhal and Prosper Mérimée. Among modern buildings influenced by its design are the State Capitol of Virginia and La Madeleine in Paris.

BIBLIOGRAPHY

J. C. Balty, *Études sur la Maison Carrée de Nimes,* Collection Latomus 47 (Brussels, 1960); R. Amy—P. Gros, *La Maison Carrée de Nîmes,* Gallia suppl. 38 (Paris, 1979).

W. W. DE GRUMMOND

MAIURI, AMEDEO (1886–1963). Italian archaeologist.

Maiuri was born at Ceprano in the Hernican valley and died at *Naples. He began his career as a philologist and epigrapher, then studied archaeology in Crete, excavating first at *Gortyn. After a brief period as inspector at the museum in Naples, he was appointed director of the archaeological services at *Rhodes, where he remained for ten years, 1914–24, excavating at Ialysos and organizing the museum of Rhodes.

Maiuri was appointed superintendent of antiquities for Campania in 1924 and remained such until 1961. During that time he excavated at numerous sites, beginning with *Pompeii and *Capri. For the celebration of the bimillennium of Vergil's birth, he directed work in the Campi Flegrei, especially at *Cumae but also at *Baiae, Puteoli and Misenum. In 1927 he was responsible for the reopening of excavations at *Herculaneum, which continued under his direction to 1958. For some years parts of southern Latium and Lucania were under his superintendency, and he directed excavations at *Paestum and Velia.

At Pompeii Maiuri took special interest in the pre-Roman history of the city, concentrating first on the fortifications and then conducting the first stratigraphic excavations in the city, especially in the vicinity of the forum. After the war he was responsible for the removal of the enormous dumps left by his predecessors around the edge of the site and the excavation of a vast zone in Regiones I and II, as well as the discovery of a new necropolis outside the Porta di Nocera.

From 1942 to 1962 he was professor of archaeology at the University of Naples. Throughout his life he wrote constantly and voluminously; Romanelli catalogs 401 works of scholarship and 323 of journalism. His most important works are *La Villa dei Misteri,* two volumes (Rome, 1931); *La Casa del Menandro e il suo tesoro di argenteria,* two volumes (Rome, 1933); *L'Ultima fase edilizia di Pompei* (Rome, 1942); *La Peinture romaine* (Geneva, 1953); *Ercolano: i nuovi scavi (1927–1958),* two volumes (Rome, 1958); *Alla ricerca di Pompei preromana* (Naples, 1973).

BIBLIOGRAPHY

P. Romanelli, *Amedeo Maiuri, 1886–1963* (Cava dei Tirreni, 1968).

L. RICHARDSON, JR

MALIA (MALLIA). Site on the northern coast of *Crete, location of a Bronze Age Minoan palace.

The site of Malia was first excavated in 1915 and 1919 by J. Hazzidakis, who recognized immediately that the ruins were those of a Minoan palace. He also found portions of the ancient town, as well as tombs by the sea. In 1922, the rights of excavation were transferred to a team from the *French School at Athens, led by F. Chapouthier, J. *Charbonneaux and others. The French school has since conducted a number of campaigns at Malia through the twentieth century.

The palace, third in size behind the Minoan palaces at *Knossos and *Phaistos, has a style that is independent of central Crete, showing fewer outside influences and having few luxury features. It has the typical large central court running north-south as an organizing element around which rooms are arranged in a somewhat irregular plan; an unusual feature is the square open pit in the middle of the court, probably of ritual usage. The palace has an earlier phase ("Old Palace," Early Minoan III–Middle Minoan II) and a later phase ("New Palace," Middle Minoan III–Late Minoan I). The later plan, which differs markedly from the earlier, is basically what is visible today.

One of the most famous artifacts excavated by the French at Malia is the striking gold "Bee Pendant," discovered by P. Demargne in 1945, featuring two bees or wasps facing each other from opposite sides of a fruit or honeycomb (dated ca. 1700 B.C.; now in the *Herakleion Museum). It was found in the royal cemetery known as Chrysolakkos, the "Gold Hole," which had been subject to plunder by local tomb robbers beginning in the 1880s. The so-called Aegina Treasure, made up of stone beads, gold ornaments and a gold cup, acquired by the *British Museum in 1892, was once thought to have come from the same cemetery.

BIBLIOGRAPHY

R. A. Higgins, *The Aegina Treasure: An Archaeological Mystery* (London, 1979); +O. Pelon, *Le Palais de Mallia,* vol. 5, École française d'Athènes, *Études Crétoises* 25 (Paris, 1980); J. W. Graham, *The Palaces of Crete,* rev. ed. (Princeton, NJ, 1987); +O. Pelon et al., in *Aerial Atlas of Ancient Crete,* 175–85.

MANSFELD (MANSFELDT), PETER ERNEST VON (1517–1604). General and governor of Luxembourg and other provinces of the Netherlands; collector of antiquities in that region.

Biographical reference volumes generally neglect this loyalist general of Charles V and Philip II in favor of an illegitimate son, Graf Ernest II of Thirty Years' War fame. Having fought with the emperor from Tunis in 1535 to St. Dizier, Count Mansfeld's honors in 1545 commenced with his appointment as governor of the province of Luxembourg (then the largest of the Pays-Bas) and county of Namur, as well as election to the Order of the Golden Fleece at its next session (January 1546). At one time supreme military commander and governor stationed in Brussels (1572–76), he shared direction of the Catholic campaigns in the Netherlands with Alessandro Farnese, becoming on the death of the latter (1592) coadministrator with de Fuentes of all the Belgian provinces (1592–98).

From 1563, outside Luxembourg in the suburb of Clausen, Mansfeld established a palace and gardens with hunting *parc* that were the marvel of his age, as ambitious in scale and program as at the Italian villas of sixteenth-century princes of the Church like Cardinals *Cesi, *Farnese, Rodolfo Pio da *Carpi or Ippolito II d'*Este. If he could not hope to match the quality of their classical sculptures or the wealth of ancient objects displayed in their private studies, nevertheless, he made good use of local resources. In a region particularly rich in Gallo-Roman votive and funerary sculptures (he attempted to transport the *Igel monument!), Mansfeld assembled an impressive array of inscriptions and reliefs from Metz, *Trier and other sites, including—conspicuously—Arlon. At the latter (ancient *Orolaunum*), his command of French troops demolishing medieval bastions in 1558 allowed him to acquire works that had been used as building material; among resurrected blocks was a fragment considered precious because it was taken as part of the *Ara Lunae* thought to have given Arlon its name.

Following Mansfeld's death, the antiquities were dispersed locally, and few are to be found today. Quantities of contemporary sculptures and paintings—for the most part, portraits and views of famous battles of the Cinquecento—had been willed to Philip III; many entered the collection of the Pardo in Madrid in 1608/9, and a good number turn up in a 1634 inventory of the Alcazar Palace.

BIBLIOGRAPHY

+J.-G. Wiltheim, *Mansfeldici apud Luxemburgenses Palatij epitoma priscis romanorum marmoribus intertexta,* in MS Brussels, Bibliothèque Royale, inv. 7146, fols. 179 verso–245 verso; +A. Kemp, "Pierre-Ernest de Mansfeld et le palais de Clausen," *Les Cahiers luxembourgeois,* XI, 1 (1934), 99–112; J. Massarette, *La Vie martiale et fastueuse de P.E. de Mansfeld* (Paris, 1930); E. Espérandieu, *Recueil général des bas-reliefs, statues et bustes de la Gaule romaine,* 5 (Paris, 1913), 212–14, 301–29.

PHYLLIS PRAY BOBER

MANSIONARIO, GIOVANNI (MATOCIIS, GIOVANNI DE; d. 1337). Italian humanist, historian and antiquarian.

Giovanni de Matociis—whose more popular name Mansionario ("sacristan") derives from his position as such at the cathedral of Verona from 1311 on—is known today, in part, for his still-unpublished history of the Roman emperors from Augustus to Charlemagne. The *Historia imperialis,* on which the author was already at work by the second decade of the fourteenth century, may well have been planned to have an even broader scope. In this massive compilation, in the words of Roberto Weiss, the author "gave full scope to his humanist and antiquarian leanings."

The text of the *Historia* survives in only three incomplete manuscripts, one of which—now in the Vatican Library—has been identified as the author's own. Particularly remarkable about the *Historia,* according to Rino Avesani, are the author's antiquarian tastes: "Mansionario paid careful attention to epigraphical evidence, and to the visual, concrete aspect of monuments generally." One example is his concern for clarifying precisely where games such as those celebrated by the emperor Balbinus would have been held. Not only did he provide a full verbal description of a Roman circus, but he even sketched a diagram of one in the margin of his text. Giovanni also used his margins for portraits of several of the emperors whose careers he described, copied possibly from coins. What is particularly significant about his sketches, despite the fact that medieval precedents for such drawings do exist, is that he copied them on account of their antiquity and with some understanding of what they originally meant. They were not used as an artist's models, in other words, or otherwise removed from their original historical context. This same sensitivity to anachronism later enabled Giovanni at last to establish that there had been two Plinys instead of one, as had long been commonly believed.

An important key to Giovanni's accomplishments as an early antiquarian and a humanist lay in his position as the Veronese cathedral's mansionary. Like the *Chronicon* of his contemporary *Benzo d'Alessandria, Giovanni's works benefited greatly from his access to the cathedral's library, a rich repository of both classical and medieval texts.

BIBLIOGRAPHY

R. Sabbadini, *Le Scoperte dei codici latini e greci ne' secoli XIV e XV, Nuove ricerche col riassunto filologico dei due volumi,* ed. E. Garin, 1–2. (Florence, 1967); R. Avesani, "Il preumanesimo veronese," in *Storia della cultura veneta* (Vicenza, 1976), II, 111–41; Weiss, *RDCA* 22–24, 37.

ANDREW P. McCORMICK

MANTEGNA, ANDREA (ANDREA DE VICENTIA; 1431/2–1506).

Italian painter and engraver; collector of antique art and major continuator of the classical tradition; important figure in the court at Mantua.

Mantegna's early exposure to the classical past began when he was adopted by the artist *Squarcione, a collector of antiquities and casts of ancient sculptures. As a student in Squarcione's workshop in Padua for six years, the young Mantegna learned through endless copying from Squarcione's collection. His early knowledge of monuments from antiquity were not from travel but from his association with many other artists, including Squarcione, *Donatello, Jacopo Bellini (*Bellini family) and Leon Battista *Alberti. Mantegna himself eagerly collected statues and busts, including one of the empress *Faustina* that was sold to Isabella d'*Este and may be seen today in the Ducal Palace, Mantua.

Although Mantegna was born in Vicenza, he signed a number of his works "Patavinus." The bond he felt for Padua went beyond his relationship with Squarcione. Padua, as a city where the humanist movement flourished, provided an environment that fostered enthusiasm for antiquity, and its reputation attracted many scholars and pupils. Mantegna's acceptance into this circle clearly augmented the artist's knowledge of classical studies. It also offered him an introduction to the master Florentine sculptor Donatello. Mantegna undoubtedly learned many lessons through Donatello's contemporary interpretations of ancient sculpture at S. Antonio. He also had access to Donatello's notebooks, which were filled with drawings and sketches from his travels. Mantegna's frescoes at the church of the Eremitani in Padua (ca. 1455) serve to illustrate the extent of his assimilation and comprehension of classical art. His use of a full range of classical vocabulary in these frescoes, from the costumes of the soldiers, to architectural elements such as the triumphal arch, barrel vaults and medallions, indicates the strength of this vocabulary as well as his conscious efforts toward authenticity.

Over the next decade, Mantegna's reputation grew as an artist schooled in the art of the ancients. His paintings attracted the attention of Lodovico Gonzaga (*Gonzaga family), who appointed Mantegna as court painter in 1460. The humanist court at Mantua was an active center for the study of classical art and archaeology, and it provided the perfect environment for Mantegna's continuing interest in the art and life of ancient Greece and Rome. Lodovico respected Mantegna's background, which secured his entrance into the famous Gonzaga court. He permitted Mantegna to take part in the reenactment of ancient plays held at court. In 1464, the artist accompanied *Marcanova and other scholars on an antiquarian expedition to Lake Garda. The group inspected the ancient remains and playacted in ancient costumes among the ruins. Mantegna also functioned as a consultant to the duke when Lodovico traveled to Porretta to view and possibly purchase a collection of ancient gems and bronzes. Through his connections at court, Mantegna had the opportunity to meet Alberti and to use Lodovico's extensive library. Within the Gonzaga collection, Plutarch's *Lives* and Flavio *Biondo's *Roma Triumphans* (Book X) probably were sources of influence for Mantegna's masterpiece, the *Triumph of Caesar* (ca. 1485), whose all'antica subject was depicted in the manner of a classical frieze. The engraving *Battle of the Sea Gods* (ca. 1475) inspired many contemporary artists, most notably *Dürer. As in the *Triumph of Caesar,* the subject is classical in spirit, and Mantegna drew much from ancient sources, such as the *Felix Gem.

From 1488 to 1490, Mantegna was called to Rome by invitation of Pope Innocent VIII to paint the pope's private chapel in the Belvedere. Historians often argue that Rome was a disappointment for Mantegna. His extensive knowledge of the ancient city and his familiarity with its art had been obtained indirectly through his teacher, Squarcione, and his father-in-law, Jacopo Bellini, whose sketchbooks contained important drawings from Bellini's travels to Tuscany and Rome. Nonetheless, the influence of Mantegna's journey to Rome is apparent from his surviving sketches of the *Spinario and the *Quirinal *Horse Tamers.*

Mantegna spent his final years painting for the court of Isabella d'Este. Isabella, herself a major collector of ancient art, was impressed by the artist, who shared her enthusiasm for the antique. For Isabella, he painted fashionable scenes of mythological subjects, such as the so-called *Parnassus,* which drew from many antique sources; the Muses, for example, were depicted on the basis of a drawing by *Ciriaco of Ancona (1444), taken from an Archaic frieze of

Dancers seen on *Samothrace. Beyond his death in 1506, Mantegna's approach to antiquity made lasting impressions upon many other artists, including Giovanni Bellini, Albrecht Dürer and Nicholas *Poussin.

BIBLIOGRAPHY

+G. Fiocco, *Paintings by Mantegna* (New York, 1963); G. Paccagnini, ed., *Andrea Mantegna,* catalog of exhibition (Venice, 1961); +P.W. Lehmann, "The Sources and Meaning of Mantegna's *Parnassus,*" in *Samothracian Reflections, Aspects of the Revival of the Antique* (Princeton, NJ, 1973), 59–178; A. Martindale, *The Triumphs of Caesar* (London, 1979); Sheard, nos. 4–14; E. Pogány-Balás, *The Influence of Rome's Antique Monumental Sculptures on the Great Masters of the Renaissance* (Budapest, 1980).

CHERYL SUMNER

MARATHON. Coastal plain in Attica, Greece; site of the great battle in 490 B.C. in which the Greeks turned back the Persians, ca. 40km northeast of Athens.

The most conspicuous monument of Marathon is the mound, originally 12m high, identified with the Soros erected after the battle to contain the burials of the 192 Athenians who perished fighting. W. M. *Leake, visiting the site in 1806, reported finding at the base of the mound flint tools, which he interpreted as arrowheads used by the Persians. The site appealed to the Romantic imagination during this period, when the Greeks were seeking their liberation from modern invaders, and inspired the famous verses of *Byron, penned in 1819: "The mountains look on Marathon—And Marathon looks on the sea; And musing there an hour alone I dream'd that Greece might still be free; For standing on the Persians' grave, I could not deem myself a slave" (*Don Juan,* Canto 3, 11.701–706).

G. Finlay, writing in 1839, noted that the Soros had been ripped up by speculators in antiquities. In 1870, *Schliemann excavated the mound to a depth of 1m and reached the remarkable conclusion that it was a cenotaph dating to the ninth century B.C. and had nothing to do with the Battle of Marathon. Proper excavation of the feature by G. Staes for the French Archaeological Society in 1890 uncovered a thin pavement strewn with ashes, bones and funeral vases appropriate for a date in the early fifth century B.C. and confirmed the identity of the mound as the tomb of the Athenians.

BIBLIOGRAPHY

+W. K. Pritchett, *Marathon* (Berkeley, 1960); E. Vanderpool, "A Monument to the Battle of Marathon," *Hesperia,* (1966), 93–106.

MARATHON BOY. Lifesize Greek bronze statue of a youth, with inset eyes and copper nipples, found in the net of fishermen in the Bay of Marathon in 1925 (*National Archaeological Museum, Athens; height 1.24m); no further information was retrieved about the context of the find.

The statue represents an adolescent with a gracefully curved body, weight on the right foot, left leg trailing. The tongued fillet the youth wears may identify him as an athlete. His left hand is raised palm up with a bronze pin in it for attachment of some object. The right hand is raised and extended to the side, thumb and forefinger together. The action and the nature of the now-missing attributes have been much debated. One suggestion is that he held on his left palm a box from which he pulled a fillet. Because of its grace, exaggerated thrust of the hip and set of the head, the work is usually considered an original by Praxiteles or one of his followers (third quarter of the fourth century B.C.). The stance and gesture recall the type of the *Apollo Sauroktonos*.

BIBLIOGRAPHY

K. A. Rhomaios, "Ho Ephebos tou Marathonos," *Deltion* 9 (1924–25), 145–87; R. Carpenter, *Greek Sculpture* (Chicago, 1960), 171, 175; Lullies—Hirmer, 93.

CAROL MATTUSCH

MARBLE PLAN. See FORMA URBIS ROMAE.

MARCANOVA, GIOVANNI (ca. 1410–67). Italian humanist and antiquarian.

A native Venetian, Marcanova studied at the university at Padua, where he took his degree in arts and medicine in 1440. After teaching at the university in Padua, Marcanova moved to Bologna to teach in 1452. In 1467 he returned from Bologna to Padua, where he died the same year.

Marcanova belonged to a circle of Paduan humanists that included *Felice Feliciano and the painter Andrea *Mantegna. Their distinctively Paduan view of antiquity was idealistic, intense and slightly fantastical, yet founded upon archaeological observation and reading of the ancient authors. It is vividly illustrated by Felice Feliciano's *Jubilatio* (1464), which describes an excursion to Lake Garda by Felice, Mantegna, Samuele da Tradate and Marcanova to copy Roman inscriptions.

These inscriptions survive in Marcanova's sylloge of inscriptions. This corpus largely comprises transcriptions from the epigraphic collections of *Ciriaco of Ancona and *Poggio Bracciolini, together with some inscriptions copied from the antique originals by Marcanova himself. The inscriptions are primarily in Latin; the Greek inscriptions from Ciriaco's travels of 1435–37 are accompanied by Latin translations.

The most complete surviving manuscript of Marcanova's sylloge is in the Biblioteca Estense in Modena. Dated 1465, it is dedicated to Malatesta Novello of Cesena. The hand has been identified as Felice Feliciano's. Besides the inscriptions, the manuscript contains sketches of various monuments and eighteen full-page reconstructions of ancient Rome. A less complete, slightly earlier (1457–60) sylloge of Marcanova exists in Bern, and there are fifteenth-century copies from the Modena manuscript in the Bibliothèque Nationale, Paris, and the Princeton University library (the Garrett Manuscript).

Marcanova wrote an antiquarian treatise, now lost, entitled *De dignitatibus romanorum triumphorum et rebus bellorum.* He read the ancient authors and owned a library that was very extensive for his day, consisting of nearly 600 manuscripts.

Marcus Aurelius Equestrian Statue, depicted at the Lateran, Rome, drawing from G. Marcanova, *Collectio antiquitatum*, 1465. Modena, Biblioteca Estense. (Deutsches Archäologisches Institut, Rome. Inst. Neg. 1287. With permission of the Ministero per i Beni Culturali e Ambientali.)

BIBLIOGRAPHY
G. Tiraboschi, *Storia della letteratura italiana* VI, 1 (Milan, 1824), 306–9; +H. van
Mater Dennis, "The Garrett Manuscript of Marcanova," *MAAR* 6 (1927), 113–26; E.
W. Bodnar, *Cyriacus of Ancona and Athens* (Brussels, 1960), 98–101.

CHRISTINE SPERLING

MARCO DA RAVENNA. See DENTE, MARCO.

MARCUS AURELIUS EQUESTRIAN STATUE. Over-lifesize statue of the
emperor Marcus Aurelius (A.D. 121–80) on the *Capitoline Hill in Rome; the
only bronze equestrian monument from antiquity to have always been visible
and to survive virtually intact.

The statue was first mentioned in A.D. 966 as *Caballus Constantini,* "Constantine's Horse," standing north of the "Constantinian Basilica," an old designation of San Giovanni in Laterano. Until its removal to the Capitol at the
behest of *Paul III in 1538, it was alternatively claimed as a symbol of secular
or pontifical authority.

Its original placement and purpose are not known. Since both the emperor's
family home and the barracks of the mounted imperial escort lay on the Caelian,
one can surmise that the statue commemorated Marcus's connection with the
hill. Various dates and occasions for its possible removal from other locations
in the city have been suggested. Intentional optical distortions in the modeling
prove that the statue was not meant to be seen frontally but somewhat from the
left and that it must have been mounted on a base not higher than the one
created for it by *Michelangelo on the Capitol.

The cavalier is referred to in medieval sources and first pictured on fourteenth-
century maps of Rome, in pilgrims' guides and "world histories." Exposed and
vulnerable as it was, it suffered many vicissitudes, documented by precious
drawings of the first half of the fifteenth century. Repairs and relocations can
be ascertained (*Paul II in 1466, *Sixtus IV in 1473–74). The first to establish
its true identity was Platina (d. 1481), who was helped by comparisons with
datable coin portraits of Marcus. Filippino *Lippi includes the statue in his view
of the *Lateran of 1489 in S. Maria sopra Minerva; a *Heemskerck pen-and-
ink drawing (1532–35) also places it there. As the hub of the newly designed
Capitoline area (Capitoline Hill), the statue was moved in January 1538, though
the surrounding palaces were not completed before the seventeenth century.
Placed on Michelangelo's pedestal, the sculpture became part of a program to
restore to the Capitoline Hill its ancient dignity as the venerable center of Roman
national and religious life.

The effect of the statue on the history of Western art cannot be overestimated.
A distinguished series of equestrian figures of the Renaissance and Baroque
periods derives from it, including the painted "monuments" by Paolo Uccello
(*Sir John Hawkwood,* Florence, S. M. del Fiore) and Andrea del *Castagno
(*Niccolo da Tolentino,* Florence, S. M. del Fiore) as well as the compelling

Marcus Aurelius Equestrian Statue, depicted at the Lateran, Rome, drawing by M. van Heemskerck, Berlin, Kupferstichkabinett. (© Bildarchiv Preussischer Kulturbesitz, Berlin, 1994. Photo: J. P. Anders 79 D 2a.)

bronzes of *Gattamelata* (Padua) by *Donatello and *Colleoni* by Verrocchio. *Bernini was also following the antique tradition in his creation of the equestrian statue of *Constantine* (Vatican), as was Falconet in his *Peter the Great* (St. Petersburg).

The rider was briefly studied and repaired in 1912. Gravely endangered by environmental hazards, it was again removed from its pedestal to undergo thorough restoration in 1981. It was returned in 1990 and housed in a climatized room in the Museo Capitolino (*Capitoline Museums). The decision whether to mount it again on its socle in the center of the piazza or to keep it in a controlled environment was pending, until 1995, when work on a replica to be mounted on Michelangelo's socle was initiated.

A number of fresh insights have resulted from the repair that also concern the statue's date. While the emperor's features were thought to represent a contamination of two out of four portrait types created during his career (namely, types III and IV produced between 160/1 and 169 and at an unknown date after 169, respectively), it now appears that the face is an autonomous variant of type III. To pinpoint a date, a renewed study of the evidence provided by coins—primarily those featuring the emperor on horseback—and by the literary sources has been undertaken. A number of scholars now favor A.D. 176, the occasion being a triumph over the Marcomanni and Sarmati, although the fact that the emperor does not wear *ornamenta triumphalia* speaks against it. The mount's curious saddle blanket, known from Achaemenid and later Eastern monuments, offers a clue. It must refer to an important event in the Orient. Though Marcus himself had not fought in the Parthian War of 162–66, he went to the East to establish peace with the Parthian Vologaeses III and his client kings after the downfall of the usurper Avidius Cassius in 176. Since the Parthians were considered the new Persians, that must have been the occasion for the erection of the monument, and coins of 177 support this conclusion. His garb and gesture signal peace, and the saddle blanket indicates the eastern locale.

It has been suggested that the statue may be posthumous (that is, after A.D. 180) and part of a twin monument of the emperor and his son and coregent Commodus. The latter accompanied his father to the East and is commemorated, on horseback in the attitude of Marcus Aurelius's statue, on a coin of A.D. 180.

BIBLIOGRAPHY

Bober—Rubinstein, 206–8; A. Melucco Vaccaro—A. Sommella Mura, eds., *Marco Aurelio, Storia di un monumento e del suo restauro* (Rome, 1989); J. Bergemann, *Römische Reiterstatuen, Ehrendenkmäler im öffentlichen Bereich* (Mainz, 1990); C. Parisi Presicce, *Il Marco Aurelio in Campidoglio* (Milan, 1990); E. R. Knauer, "*Multa egit cum regibus et pacem confirmavit,* The Date of the Equestrian Statue of Marcus Aurelius," *RM* 97 (1990), 227–306; idem, " Bruchstück einer bronzenen Satteldecke in Bonn," *Bonner Jahrbücher* 192 (1992 [1993]), 241–60.

E. R. KNAUER

MARCUS AURELIUS PANELS. Three marble reliefs depicting scenes from the ceremonial life of the Antonine emperor Marcus Aurelius (A.D. 161–80); historically, a fourth, Hadrianic, relief has been associated with the others.

An inscription of 1515 records that Pope Leo X transferred the three Antonine reliefs from the Church of S. Martina in the Forum to the Capitol. By 1536 they had been fitted into one of the walls of the courtyard, and by 1572 they had been placed in their present position on a stair landing in the Palazzo dei Conservatori, set from left to right in chronological order of the scenes represented: *Clementia* (sometimes called the *Submission of the Germans*), *Triumph* and *Sacrifice*. In 1573 the Conservators bought the Hadrianic panel representing an *Adventus (Arrival);* this relief had been built into the wall of a house in Piazza Sciarra and was also installed in the stairway of the Palazzo dei Conservatori. The four panels were traditionally engraved and reproduced as a set.

The ninth-century *Einsiedeln Itinerary records an inscription dated A.D. 176 honoring Marcus Aurelius for his victories over the Germans and Sarmatians. It locates the inscription "in Capitolio"; presumably, the inscription comes from the same monument, an arch listed in the *Mirabilia* as *arcus panis aurei in Capitolio*. It is probable that the three Antonine panels came from an arch spanning the Clivus Argentarius between the end of the Via Lata and the entrance to the Forum (near S. Martina), which was still standing during the Middle Ages.

Toward the end of the nineteenth century *Helbig first established that the *Adventus* relief was unrelated to the other three panels. Subsequently, the head of Marcus Aurelius, which had been fitted onto the figure of the emperor in that relief (perhaps during the restorations of 1595 by Ruggiero Bescapè), was replaced with one of Hadrian in accordance with current scholarly opinion.

At the turn of the century, the eight reworked panels set into the attic of the *Arch of Constantine were associated with Marcus Aurelius; scholarship during this century has focused on their relationship with the three Conservatori panels. E. *Petersen and W. *Helbig believed all eleven panels belonged to one triumphal arch. J. Sieveking and G. *Rodenwaldt discerned stylistic differences between the two sets and attributed them to two different arches. Nevertheless, M. *Pallottino and H. *Kähler argue that the distinction is in the styles of individual artists working on a single series, not chronological.

In 1938 M. Wegner proved definitively that the Conservatori panels celebrated a triumph of A.D. 176. I. S. Ryberg analyzes the way Antonine reliefs illusionistically address the spectator and attributes the reworked panels on the Arch of Constantine to a separate series. Nevertheless, the cumulative circumstantial evidence is not conclusive. Simon still catalogs the three Conservatori panels as almost certainly forming part of a single set that included the eight reworked reliefs; E. Angelicoussis argues that this set of eleven decorated a *quadrifrons* arch dedicated to Marcus and Commodus. It is agreed that the Hadrianic *Adventus* relief displayed with the Conservatori panels does not belong with either group.

BIBLIOGRAPHY
E. Simon, in Helbig, II, 255–63; +I. S. Ryberg, *Panel Reliefs of Marcus Aurelius* (New York, 1967); +Haskell—Penny, 255–57; +E. Angelicoussis, "The Panel Reliefs of Marcus Aurelius," *RM* 91 (1984), 141–205; Kleiner, *Roman Sculpture*, 288–95.

PETER HOLLIDAY

Marforio and *Pasquino*, engraving by G. Bonasone, 1547. London, British Museum. (The Warburg Institute, University of London.)

MARFORIO (TIBERIS, MARS, NAR FLUVIUS, OCEANUS). Colossal Roman statue of a river god, dated to the first century A.C.

The god is represented as nude, with drapery over his crossed legs, reclining on a stone-strewn base, with his beard resting heavily on his chest. The hands and attributes of the original statue are lacking. It was visible throughout the Middle Ages in the *Forum Romanum alongside S. Martina, as drawn by *Heemskerck in 1532–35. In 1588 *Sixtus V moved it to the Campidoglio; Ruggiero Bescapè restored it as *Oceanus*, installing it in 1595 with a new base, shell-shaped fountain basin and sea creatures, in the niche of Giacomo della Porta's aedicula in the north wall of the piazza, as engraved by Nicolaus van Aelst in 1600. By 1654 the fountain of Marforio became the focal point, as it is today, of the courtyard of the present museum on that site (*Capitoline Museums).

The statue was first identified as the Tiber in the *Einsiedeln Itinerary of ca. 800, on the basis of a Late Antique source, but the twelfth-century *Mirabilia* called it Mars, and soon it became popularly known as "Marforio" (*Mars fori*). Andrea *Fulvio in his *Antiquitates urbis* (Rome, 1527) was the first Renaissance guidebook writer to identify the *Marforio* as a river god (*Nar Fluvius*), rigorously comparing it with other representations of the type. In 1588 the original fountain base was found in the Forum, with the inscription MARE IN FORO ("Oceanus in the Forum"), which inspired Bescapè's restoration.

In the sixteenth century, *Marforio,* like **Pasquino,* was one of Rome's *statue parlanti* ("speaking statues"), to which were attributed verse dialogues satirizing Roman authorities. Bonasone's engraving of 1547 shows Pasquino boating past *Marforio,* leaving his wall in the Forum posted with *pasquinades.* Another engraving published by *Lafréry in 1550 of *Marfuori* on his bed of stones includes a poem affectionately characterizing him as an ancient citizen of few but candid words.

The *Marforio,* like other antique colossi, served Renaissance and Baroque sculpture as a model of scale, and the type and pose were adapted in river-god fountains that began to abound in the Late Renaissance.

BIBLIOGRAPHY

E. Rossi, "Marforio in Campidoglio," *Roma* 5 (1928), 337–46; +L. Du Jardin, "Del simulacro tiberino di Marforio e delle statue affini," *MemAccPont,* ser. 3, 3 (1932), 35–80; Bober—Rubinstein, 99–101.

RUTH RUBINSTEIN

MARGOTTA, IL. See SANGALLO, FRANCESCO DA.

MARIETTE, PIERRE-JEAN (1694–1774). French connoisseur and collector, art historian and scholar of ancient glyptics.

Born into a Parisian family of engravers and art collectors, Mariette received a solid education that developed his natural bent for art appreciation. In 1716 he began a lifelong friendship with the well-known *amateur* and antiquarian the Count de *Caylus. Mariette senior sent Pierre-Jean on a prolonged artistic and commercial journey through Germany and the Low Countries, starting in 1717. His reputation as connoisseur was already well established, and he was asked to catalog the vast art collection of Prince Eugene of Savoy in Vienna. Mariette next proceeded to the principal art centers of Italy, making productive contacts in the art world at every point. Thereafter he maintained a broad and active correspondence with artists, scholars and *amateurs* throughout Europe.

Back in Paris in 1720, Mariette began a lasting friendship with the art enthusiast Pierre Crozat, whose large collection of paintings and engraved gemstones Mariette cataloged in 1741. He inherited his father's prosperous art print business in 1742 but sold it in 1750 in order to devote himself entirely to research and collecting. In 1752 he purchased a senior government function, which he kept for life.

Mariette was named member of the Academy of Drawing of Florence in 1733, associate member of the Royal Academy of Painting and Sculpture in 1750 and honorary member in 1757. His keenest interest was reserved for engravings and glyptography, but his expert knowledge far exceeded these subjects. His advice on matters of art was eagerly sought in all quarters. At his death his magnificent collection was sold at auctions in 1775.

Mariette's most important publications (all in Paris) were *Recueil des pierres gravées antiques* (1732–37); *Description sommaire des dessins des grands maistres . . . du cabinet de feu M. Crozat* (1741) *Description sommaire des pierres gravées du cabinet de feu M. Crozat* (1741); and his important treatise on engraved gems, *Traité des pierres gravées* (1750), which stands at the beginning of many modern bibliographies on ancient glyptics.

BIBLIOGRAPHY
Michaud, "Pierre-Jean Mariette," *BU* 26 (1823), 649–50; Hoefer, "Mariette (Pierre-Jean)," *NBG* 33 (1865), cols. 742–46; F. Viatte, "Mariette, biographie" and "Bibliographie," in Musée du Louvre, *Le Cabinet d'un grand amateur, P. J. Mariette, 1694–1774* (Paris, 1967), esp. 25–31, 34–38; P. Zazoff—H. Zazoff, *Gemmensammler und Gemmenforscher* (Munich, 1983), esp. 127–28.

J. S. TASSIE

MARINATOS, SPYRIDON N. (1901–74). Greek archaeologist.

Marinatos served as professor at Athens University (1939–68) and inspector-general of antiquities (1937–39, 1955–58 and 1967–74). After studies of philology and archaeology in Athens, he became ephor of antiquities in Herakleion at the age of twenty. *Crete, especially of the Bronze Age, was to remain his principal field of activity until 1937, with important excavations at *Amnisos, Sklavokampos, Vorou, Tylissos, Arkalochori, Dreros and others. In one of his numerous articles (*Antiquity* 13, 1939) Marinatos formulated the theory that the decline of Minoan Crete in the fifteenth century B.C. was due to the volcanic eruption of *Thera. After many years of fieldwork on the mainland, especially in Messenia and at Thermopylae (and later at *Marathon), he started excavations at Akrotiri in 1967 in order to prove his 1939 theory and uncovered "a Bronze Age Pompeii," destroyed, he conjectured, ca. 1500 B.C. by the eruption. The results were quickly published in *Excavations at Thera* 1–7 (1967–76). He died in an accident while excavating at Akrotiri.

BIBLIOGRAPHY
+S. Jakovidis, *Gnomon* 47 (1975), 635–38; G. S. Korres, *Demosievmata Sp. N. Marinatou* (Athens, 1979), with bib.

ROBIN HÄGG

MARLIANI, BARTOLOMEO (ca. 1488–1566). Italian antiquarian and topographer.

Marliani was born at Robbio near Vercelli (not in Milan), but little is known of his life, which seems to have been passed mainly in Rome. He was a well-known figure there, always dressed in black, with a gold chain around his neck (presumably the decoration of the Cavaliere di S. Pietro). He is called *Patricius* on the title page of his *Annales.*

Marliani lived a simple life, without servants, at Torre Sanguigna and mixed much with local tradespeople. He was famous for his alms to the poor and established a fund in 1565 to provide dowries for poor girls. He died on 25 July 1566 and was buried in S. Agostino (but his epitaph does not survive).

Friend of popes and cardinals, he devoted himself to surveying Rome's classical monuments and said that he knew the distances between parts of the city better than anyone else. He lived on the income from his books and some dealing in antiquities. *Lanciani says that had he given more information about contemporary excavations and monuments since destroyed, he would have been the leading antiquarian of the sixteenth century.

Marliani produced two main works. Few works had such currency as his *Antiquae urbis Romae topographia,* published in 1534 (2nd ed., much expanded, 1544; Basel ed., 1538; Lyons ed., edited by Rabelais, 1534; Italian tr. 1622; English version appended to Philemon Holland's tr. of Livy, as *A Summary Touching the Topography of Rome*). The work, written concisely, is noteworthy for its lack of dogmatism: he preferred to list variant opinions, seldom giving a personal preference. He frequently uses inscriptions to illustrate a point. There is no criticism of any ancient legend; rather, these are given at length (e.g., the reason for banning women from the rites of Hercules). Marliani will not argue over the location of the House of Decius, because there is nothing in the ancient sources (4.22), but he is sure that Marcellus was buried in the *Mausoleum of Augustus (5.7) and not at Porta del Popolo. Although he names no contemporary antiquarians, many recent excavations are briefly noted: the burial of the Vestals near the Palatine (1.15), the *Basilica Aemilia (3.7), the temple of Neptune on the Quirinal (4.23) and Pompey's temple of Venus (5.10). Marliani follows many of the standard identifications of his time: the *Temple of Saturn in the Forum is called that of Concord; that of the Dioscuri he calls Jupiter Stator; Saturn he places in S. Adriano; the *Basilica of Maxentius is the temple of Peace. On the other hand, he has the *Temple of Jupiter Optimus Maximus on the correct side of the Capitol, Apollo on the Palatine toward the Circus Maximus, the Basilica Aemilia next to S. Adriano and the *Baths of Trajan not on the Aventine but the Esquiline.

His other major work is the *Annales consulum, dictatorum, censorumque romanorum,* 1560, the first edition of the newly discovered "Capitoline Fasti" (143 pages), which was dedicated to Pius III. The preface explains that the *fasti* will fill many gaps in Roman history and that Marliani has endeavored therefore to fill any gaps in the *fasti.* He concentrates on the names and the chronology but gives notes on new magistracies and major events (such as the sack of Rome by the Gauls). Again, he does not criticize the credibility of the sources.

BIBLIOGRAPHY

A. Bertolotti, *Artisti subalpini* (1884), 51 f.; Lanciani, *Storia degli scavi,* II, 240–45.

R. T. RIDLEY

MARMOR PARIUM. A chronicle of Greek history inscribed on a marble slab (estimated size, ca. 6'7" × 2'3") and originally set up on *Paros.

Two fragments (A, B) are preserved. A was first discovered and acquired for *Peiresc, whose agent was arrested by the Turks; William Petty acquired the piece in 1627 at Smyrna for the Earl of *Arundel. John Selden edited its 93-line text in 1628; but lines 1–45 were lost in the English civil war, and for this part we must rely on Selden's not always accurate transcript. What remains of A is in the *Ashmolean Museum, Oxford. B, containing lines 101–32, was found in 1897 on Paros and is in a museum there. Careful textual studies by J.A.R. Munro and *Hiller von Gärtringen led to the standard edition by F. Jacoby (Das Marmor Parium, 1904; FGrHist, 239).

The compiler says that he collected his material "from sources of all kinds," probably including Athenian local histories and a universal history based on Ephoros. He gives the interval between each event and 264/3, when he presumably worked (e.g., "From the time when Xerxes bridged the Hellespont [480/79], there are 217 years; the Athenian archon was Kalliades"), but not all his dates are right. He began with "1581," when Kekrops supposedly ruled Athens; his earlier events are widely separated, but from 313 to 299/8, when B breaks off, there is an entry for each year. The compiler's selection of political events is capricious; he shows keen interest in religious history and the careers of Athenian writers.

BIBLIOGRAPHY

F. Jacoby, "Ueber das Marmor Parium," RhM New Series F 59 (1904), 63–107; R. Laqueur, "Marmor Parium," RE 14 (1930), 1885–97.

MORTIMER CHAMBERS

MARSEILLES (MASSALIA; MASSILIA). City in southern France, originally founded around 600 B.C. by Greeks from Phokaia.

The city was the first and greatest of the string of colonies that hellenized this coast from southern Spain to the borders of Etruria, and it coined extensively, mostly in small denominations for trade via the Rhône valley with inland Gaul; normal types are the head of Artemis and a lion. The ancient city was on the promontory north of the Vieux Port, which itself was the ancient harbor (the Lakydon). Some remains of the quay and warehouses of the north shore are preserved in situ in the Musée des Docks Romains (anchors, amphorae, sounding leads and other marine relics), but the east end of the harbor projected farther inland than today to form the "Corne du Port." Since 1967 (previously, excavation in Marseilles had been, at the best, only sporadic), this area has been excavated to form the main archaeological site and laid out as parkland ("Le Jardin des Vestiges"). It includes a long length of quay, the Hellenistic city gate and a section of wall 200m long ("Mur de Crinas") and a freshwater reservoir. A new museum overlooks the site. Elsewhere in the city are minor traces of a Roman theater and a large Archaic Ionic temple. Marseilles is also a prominent center for *underwater archaeology.

BIBLIOGRAPHY

M. Clerc, Massalia, Histoire de Marseille dans l'Antiquité des origines à la fin de l'Empire romain d'Occident, 1–2 (Marseilles, 1927–29); M. Euzennat—F. Salviat, "Les

Fouilles de Marseille (Mars-Avril 1968)," *CRAI* (1968), 145–59; M. Clavel-Leveque, *Marseille grecque, La dynamique d'un impérialisme marchand* (Marseilles, 1977); M. Euzennat, "Ancient Marseille in the Light of Recent Excavations," *AJA* 84 (1980), 133–40.

A. TREVOR HODGE

MARTHA, JULES (1853–1932). French archaeologist; historian of Greek and Roman art.

Born at Strasbourg, Martha was named a member of the *French School at Athens in 1876. In Greece he toured the Peloponnese and visited *Rhodes and other islands of the Aegean. He published the terracotta statuettes of the Archaeological Society of Athens (*Catalogue des figurines en terre cuite du Musée de la Société archéologique d'Athènes,* 1880) and a dissertation on Athenian priests (1882).

Martha subsequently taught Latin literature at Montpellier, Dijon, Lyons, the École normale and the Sorbonne. He occupied himself increasingly with the art of Italy, producing the manual *Archéologie étrusque et romaine* (1884) and eventually his monumental volume on Etruscan art, *L'Art étrusque* (Paris, 1889). For many years the well-illustrated compendium was regarded as a fundamental contribution to the field.

Martha died in Paris, honorary professor at the Sorbonne, at the age of seventy-nine.

BIBLIOGRAPHY

A. Neppi Modona, "Jules Martha," *StEtr* 6(1932), 420–21; *AJA* 37 (1933), 118.

MARTINO POLLAIUOLO, FRANCESCO MAURIZIO DI. See FRANCESCO DI GIORGIO MARTINI.

MARZABOTTO (MISANO). Site near *Bologna, known for its Etruscan city, dating from the sixth century B.C. to the fourth century B.C.

The Etruscan remains include cemeteries; a town laid out with a grid plan within which may be recognized streets, drains, houses, workshops and wells; and a sacred area on the height northwest of the city (Misanello), featuring altars and temples. Marzabotto is still the only Etruscan city for which the layout is known both in general and in particular.

The city was taken over by the Gallic Boii in the fourth century B.C. and soon afterward ceased to exist. At some unknown date a landslide caused the collapse of the south part of the inhabited area along the river Reno.

Remains of the city were first noted in the sixteenth century by Leandro *Alberti; formal excavation began only in 1862–63 with the work of *Gozzadini, who believed, however, that the entire site was a necropolis. *Brizio (1888–89) was the first to identify the essential elements of the town plan and was also the author of the first guide to the excavations and the Etruscan museum at the site. Work was interrupted for a long period until after World War II. In 1947,

P. E. Arias directed repairs from damage done during the war and reconstructed the museum, which had been destroyed in 1944 along with huge amounts of material from the site. New discoveries were made during subsequent excavations conducted at Marzabotto regularly from 1950 to 1975, by Arias, G. A. Mansuelli and G. V. Gentili.

BIBLIOGRAPHY
G. A. Mansuelli, s.v. "Misano," *PECS*, 584; idem, *Guida alla città etrusca e al Museo di Marzabotto* (Bologna, 1982), 131–32; G. Sassatelli, "Bologna e Marzabotto: Storia di un problema," *Studi sulla città antica, L'Emilia-Romagna* (Rome, 1982), 65–127.

MASSALIA. See MARSEILLES.

MASTAI-FERRETTI, GIOVANNI MARIA. See PIUS IX.

MASTRILLI, FELICE MARIA, Marchese (ca. 1694–1755?). Italian nobleman, collector of *Greek vases and other antiquities.

Little is known of the life of the Marchese Felice Maria Mastrilli. As an antiquarian active in the area of *Naples, he maintained contacts with scholars such as P. M. Paciaudi and A. F. *Gori, and vases from his collection were published by G. B. Passeri in his *Picturae etruscorum in vasculis* (1766–75). Displayed in the Palazzo di San Nicandro in Naples, Mastrilli's museum (referred to as the Museo Mastrilliano) was inspected by *Winckelmann, O. Bayardi and numerous visitors to the Naples area. The collection included portrait sculpture, bronzes, reliefs, cameos, gems and an important assemblage of some 400 vases, partly excavated on property of the Mastrilli family at *Nola. These were displayed in an innovative manner, with many of the vases installed on brackets projecting from the walls, rather than on shelves that would conceal parts of the vases.

The collection of vases can be studied through an anonymous illustrated manuscript in the Resource Collections of the Getty Center for the History of Art and the Humanities (Santa Monica), entitled *Spiega de'vasi antichi*. The manuscript, assembled ca. 1755, contains several hundred ink and watercolor drawings of vases, including Attic, Corinthian and South Italian examples. It constitutes one of the earliest attempts to systematize the study of Greek vase painting, organizing the material by theme and function and including Greek inscriptions, which were of considerable interest to Mastrilli. Many of the Attic vases from Mastrilli's collection were later sold to Sir William *Hamilton and are identifiable today in the *British Museum.

BIBLIOGRAPHY
C. L. Lyons, "The Museo Mastrilli and the Culture of Collecting in Naples, 1700–1755," *Journal of the History of Collections* 4.1 (1992), 1–26.

MATOCIIS, GIOVANNI. See MANSIONARIO, GIOVANNI.

MATTEI FAMILY. Family well known in Rome from the Renaissance to the eighteenth century for its antiquities collection.

There were several branches of the family. BATTISTA JACOPO MATTEI, living in Trastevere in the fifteenth century, had a collection of thirty-four Roman inscriptions, many of a sacred character, noted by Fra *Giocondo. Later, CIRIACO MATTEI (1545–1614) and his brother ASDRUBALE (1556–1638) each amassed a splendid collection. Ciriaco, a Roman senator, constructed a villa on the Monte Celio (1580s), into which he brought a large number of statues, busts, vases, sepulchral monuments and sarcophagi. These were displayed in a loggia along the façade, inside the mansion and in his garden and circus. The entire collection was inventoried at the death of Ciriaco, whose will stipulated that the collection was to pass to his firstborn male descendant and was not to be sold or divided. Thus, it stayed together for nearly two centuries.

Among Ciriaco's marbles were an inscribed bust of *Cicero* published in 1598 by T. Galle; two standing male nude statues identified in woodcuts by G. Franzini as *Aurelius* and *Augustus;* a well-known *Muse* sarcophagus, acquired from S. Paolo fuori le Mura, now in the *Terme Museum; a highly praised statue of *Ceres,* now recognized as a Greek original of the Hellenistic period; a *Pudicitia* (or ''*Livia*''); and an *Amazon* of a fifth-century type, perhaps created by Pheidias, that has been identified as one of the wounded Amazons made for the famous contest at Ephesos (Pliny *NH* 34.53). All three of the latter are now in the *Vatican. Ciriaco opened up his collection to visitors of good reputation, though, in fact, few artists seem to have made drawings in this out-of-the-way location. P. P. *Rubens did visit there, and his work shows his knowledge of several sculptures in the Mattei collection (drawings of figures from the *Muse* sarcophagus, as well as of the famous Mattei *Eagle;* inspiration from the *Pudicitia* in his *Holy Women at the Sepulcher,* Pasadena, and influence from the Mattei relief of the *Drunken Hercules* on Rubens's depiction of the same theme in Dresden).

When Ciriaco's son, GIOVANNI BATTISTA, died in 1631, the villa and its treasures were bequeathed to Ciriaco's brother, ASDRUBALE, who already had his own collection. Carlo *Maderno had built a new palace (*Palazzo Mattei di Giove) for Asdrubale near S. Caterina de' Funari and the Largo Argentina; there he displayed his collections, including many portraits (e.g., *Julius Caesar, Octavian, Caligula, Nero, Claudius, Domitian, Caracalla*), as well as statues of *Ceres, Jupiter, Aesculapius* and others. He installed some reliefs in the stairwell, cortile and façade (many are known from dal *Pozzo drawings) and placed the emperor portraits in niches, where they still may be seen in the Palazzo Mattei.

Both collections were drawn in 1740 by FRANCESCO MATTEI and were engraved and published by R. Venuti and J. C. Amaduzzi (*Vetera monumenta quae in Hortis Caelimontanis et in Aedibus Matthaeiorum adservantur,* Rome, 1777–79).

In the late eighteenth century, *Clement XIV annulled Ciriaco's stipulation and purchased for the *Vatican collection forty-five of the finest sculptures in that collection from the insolvent heir GIUSEPPE MATTEI. Giuseppe also sold off some of Ciriaco's treasures to English collections (Ince Blundell Hall has thirteen statues, ten busts and fifty-one sarcophagi) and some of Asdrubale's pieces as well.

BIBLIOGRAPHY
Lanciani, *Storia degli scavi* I (1902), 111–12; I (1989), 145; III (1907), 83–100; G. Panofsky-Soergel, "Zur Geschichte des Palazzo Mattei di Giove," *Römisches Jahrbuch für Kunstgeschichte* 11 (1967–68), 111–87; Haskell—Penny, 181–82, 300–301; L. Guerrini, *Palazzo Mattei di Giove, Le Antichità* (Rome, 1982); Bober—Rubinstein, 477.

MARJON VAN DER MEULEN

MATTINGLY, HAROLD (1884–1964). British numismatist.

Mattingly was the most prolific and influential scholar ever to write on Roman coins. After studying in Cambridge and Berlin he entered the *British Museum in 1910 and was assistant keeper of coins and medals from 1912 to 1946. Among his most lasting contributions are the volumes of *Roman Imperial Coinage* (1923 ff.), which he edited with E. A. Sydenham and which have now fallen to others; the individual volumes represent prologomena to corresponding ones of the much more detailed *Coins of the Roman Empire in the British Museum,* five of whose six volumes (1923–50) Mattingly prepared.

Mattingly was among the first scholars to recognize that the date of the denarius supported by the ancient texts could not be right, and his landmark 1933 paper (written with E.S.G. Robinson) started a revolution that ended only in 1961 with the confirmation of a "middle" chronology that Mattingly himself never embraced. He wrote on every aspect of Roman numismatics but always kept in mind the general reader, for whom several popular studies were written. His *Roman Coins* (2nd ed., London, 1960) is still in many ways the best introduction to the subject.

BIBLIOGRAPHY
H. Mattingly, *Coins of the Roman Empire in the British Museum,* 1–5 (London, 1923–50); H.S.A. Copinger, "Bibliography of Harold Mattingly's Works, 1910–1955," in *Essays in Roman Coinage Presented to Harold Mattingly,* ed. R.A.G. Carson—C.H.V. Sutherland (Oxford, 1956); R.A.G. Carlson, "Harold Mattingly," *ProcBrAc* 50 (1964), 331–40; idem, "Harold Mattingly 1884–1964," *Numismatic Chronicle,* ser. 7, 5 (1965), 239–54.

WILLIAM E. METCALF

MATZ, FRIEDRICH (1890–1974). German archaeologist.

Matz served as professor at the universities of Münster and Marburg (1934–58). In developing the principles of the *Strukturforschung* in the study of ancient art, from the Egyptian and Creto-Mycenaean to the late Roman, Matz became as influential as A. *Riegl and H. Wölfflin had been for art history in general. His first epoch-making book, *Die Frühkretischen Siegel* (1928), was followed by numerous others, as well as articles and reviews, especially in the field of Aegean art and culture but also on early Greek art (*Die Geometrische und die* *früharchaische Form,* 1950). He founded and edited the corpus of Minoan and Mycenaean seals *(Corpus der minoischen und mykenischen Siegel)* and *Archaeologia Homerica.* His second main field was Roman art; he became editor of *Die Römischen Sarkophagreliefs* and undertook himself the publication of the sarcophagi with Bacchic motifs (4 vols., 1968–75).

He was the nephew of the elder Friedrich Matz (1843–74), whose own work on Roman sarcophagi and English collections was cut short by an early death.
BIBLIOGRAPHY
Verzeichnis der Schriften von Friedrich Matz, bib. (Berlin, 1970); F. Matz, *Archäologische Erinnerungen aus sechs Jahrzehnten (1910–1970)* (Marburg, 1974); +B. Andreae, *Gnomon* 47 (1975), 524–28.

ROBIN HÄGG

MAU, AUGUST (1840–1909). German art historian and archaeologist.

August Mau made major contributions to our understanding of the development of the styles of Pompeian wall painting and to our vision of the life of the city as a whole. He journeyed to Italy in 1872, and the following year began to study *Pompeii. *Mommsen asked him to publish a wax tablet from the house of the Pompeian banker L. Caecilus Iucundus, but Mau's real interests lay in the understanding of how the styles of Pompeian painting developed. In 1882, he published his *Geschichte der dekorativen Wandmalerei in Pompeii,* in which he made his influential formulation of the four Pompeian styles of wall decoration.

In 1900 he published his general picture of Pompeii, at once guidebook and vision of the city and its life, *Pompeji in Leben und Kunst,* which developed out of a handbook written with others. In its many editions and translations into other languages (e.g., into English, by F. *Kelsey, 1900), it remains indispensable. All during these years, he published his careful and often definitive descriptions of many Pompeian houses in the *Mitteilungen* of the *German Archaeological Institute at Rome, where he was librarian.
BIBLIOGRAPHY
F. Studniczka, *RM* 23 (1908), 269–74; *Porträtarchiv,* nos. 78–79.

E. C. KOPFF

MAUSOLEUM OF AUGUSTUS, Rome. Tomb built by Augustus for himself and his family in the Campus Martius in 28 B.C.

The tomb is a large, circular building, ca. 87m in diameter, a series of concrete ring walls surrounding a relatively small burial chamber. By the early Middle Ages the ruins had become a mound known as the Hill of Augustus, formed, according to one tradition, by the peoples of the empire bringing gloves full of their native soil to Rome. Its identity as a tomb of the emperors, however, was not forgotten, and the funerary inscription of Nerva is quoted in the *Mirabilia,* the first of many inscriptions from the mausoleum to be recorded.

The site was used as a stronghold of the Colonna family. The original fortress

Photograph of *August
Mau*. (Deutsches Ar-
chäologisches Institut,
Rome. Inst. Neg.
63.1141.)

was destroyed in 1167, but the site was refortified in 1241 and continued in
Colonna hands for most of the thirteenth and fourteenth centuries. In the fifteenth
century it was covered in vineyards, and in 1546 it was acquired by Francesco
Soderini, who created a garden-museum in the inner part of the mausoleum.
These centuries saw the gradual spoliation of the fabric. In 1780 a wooden
bullring was built in the ruins, and this was followed by a succession of theaters
and, finally, a large concert hall, which continued in use until May 1936. The
mausoleum was excavated and restored between 1926 and 1938.

The earliest archaeological interest in the site was in the early sixteenth century, when *Peruzzi produced detailed drawings and measurements. Antonio da
*Sangallo (the younger) and Gianbattista da Sangallo also studied the remains.
Later engravers, whose understanding of the site was hampered by the Soderini
gardens and theatrical buildings, published plans of varying degrees of accuracy;

Mausoleum of Augustus, Rome, reconstruction by É. Du Pérac, engraving published by A. Lafréry, *Speculum romanae magnificentiae* (1575).

for example, those of Bufalini, reproduced by *Bartoli, are reasonably accurate, whereas *Piranesi's are less so. Various fanciful reconstructions of the mausoleum were also made, including versions with twelve entrances or rising through four or five tiers. Excavation has revealed the basic structure of the building, but some details still remain unresolved. Recent controversy has centered on whether it was inspired by Etruscan tumuli or mausoleums of the Hellenistic Greek world.

BIBLIOGRAPHY
R. A. Cordingley—I. A. Richmond, "The Mausoleum of Augustus," *PBSR* 10 (1927), 23–35; +Nash, II, 38–43; Richardson, *New Topographical Dictionary,* 247–49.

GLENYS DAVIES

MAUSOLEUM OF HADRIAN. See CASTEL SANT'ANGELO.

MAUSOLEUM (MAUSSOLLEION) OF HALIKARNASSOS. The burial monument of Mausolos of Karia, one of the seven wonders of the ancient world.

Mausolos, nominally the satrap of Karia under the Persian Empire, ruled as a virtually independent dynast from 362 until his death in 353 B.C. His wife/sister Artemisia oversaw the construction of the tomb at *Halikarnassos that Mausolos himself had planned. The structure continued an Anatolian tradition of architectural tombs evident in such monuments as the Nereid tomb in *Xanthos but exceeded them in size and decoration, to the extent that Mausolos's name survives in the modern word for an elaborately built tomb.

Pliny (*NH* 36.30–31) gives a fairly detailed description of the monument. It had a high, rectangular base surmounted by a peristyle, and above this was a pyramid with a marble quadriga on the top. The architects were Satyros and Pytheos (Vitruvius, *De arch.* 7 *Praef.* 12–13). The sculptural decoration on it was done by several of the best-known artists of the fourth century B.C., including Skopas, Bryaxis, Leochares and Timotheos. Artemisia died two years after her husband while the tomb was still unfinished, but supposedly the artists were so proud of their work that they completed it as a monument to their own skill. In fact, the Mausoleum was probably never completed.

The Mausoleum was apparently destroyed by an earthquake during the Middle Ages. Between 1494 and 1522 the Knights Hospitallers, while searching for stone to repair their fortress on a peninsula in the harbor of Halikarnassos (modern Bodrum), the Castle of St. Peter, discovered the Mausoleum and incorporated many of its blocks into the castle. Fra Sabba da *Castiglione visited the site before 1508 and conceived the idea of moving the remains of the Mausoleum to Mantua for Isabella d'*Este, but nothing ever came of the plan. He did, however, collect pieces of sculpture from the monument and sent these to her. In 1522 the Hospitallers evidently uncovered the burial chamber of Mausolos and some of its grave gifts, but these were abandoned and later stolen.

Thereafter, there was little interest in the Mausoleum until the mid-nineteenth century, when Stratford Canning brought several of its sculptured slabs to the

*British Museum. This led to the first archaeological investigation in Halikarnassos, by Charles *Newton, 1856–65. Newton identified the original site of the Mausoleum, a hill overlooking the harbor of Bodrum, and uncovered other fragments of sculpture. The extant material from the Mausoleum, which now included a frieze depicting an Amazonomachy, a relief of centaurs, several pieces of freestanding sculpture and well-preserved, over-lifesize portrait statues, thought by many to be of Mausolos and Artemisia, prompted several modern attempts at reconstructing the Mausoleum, although none are entirely satisfactory. Important new information was furnished by a Danish expedition to Halikarnassos under Kristian Jeppeson, 1966–77, which excavated the entire precinct of the Mausoleum. This expedition uncovered Mausolos's burial site, in a chamber under the Mausoleum, and evidence for animal sacrifices and valuable funerary gifts. Additional sculptural and architectural fragments were also found, which should enable a more accurate reconstruction of the Mausoleum to be prepared.

BIBLIOGRAPHY

+C. T. Newton, *A History of Discoveries at Halicarnassus, Cnidus, and Branchidae* (London, 1863); K. Jeppesen, "Zur Gründung und Baugeschichte des Maussolleions von Halikarnassos," *IstMitt* 27–28 (1977–78), 169–211; K. Jeppesen et al., *The Maussolleion at Halikarnassos: Reports of the Danish Archaeological Expedition to Bodrum* 1 (Aarhus, 1981); 2 (Aarhus, 1986).

LYNN E. ROLLER

MEDICI FAMILY. Italy's greatest noble family, centered in Florence; their grand collections of classical antiquities assembled in a period of over three centuries are now mainly in the *Uffizi, the *Florence Archaeological Museum and the *Museo Nazionale, Naples.

COSIMO IL VECCHIO (1389–1464), a powerful banker and the founder of the Medici fortunes, had the architect Michelozzo construct the Palazzo Medici (later Riccardi) in Florence in the 1440s, and it became the seat of the family collections of art. Cosimo himself, known for his interests in the fine arts and classical literature as well as business and politics, acquired the first Medici antiquities, precious gems and coins that were also convertible wealth of use to the financier. *Ghiberti made a mounting for one of these gems showing *Apollo and Marsyas* (also known as the "Seal of Nero," now in Naples). *Vasari reported that Cosimo owned a *Marsyas* (restored by Verrocchio) and a *Venus*. His son, PIERO IL GOTTOSO (1419–69) undoubtedly took an intellectual pleasure in these objects, as testified by Antonio Filarete in his well-known description of the arthritic scholar in his study (ca. 1463). Piero studied the effigies of emperors on coins and lingered lovingly over the precious stones, some of them engraved, and mused on their powers.

But the Medici collections assumed a greater size, variety of content and humanistic orientation under Piero's son LORENZO IL MAGNIFICO (1448–92). The "magnificent" Renaissance prince, who held power in Florence from

1469 until his death in 1492, was known for a wide variety of cultural activities; one of the most significant poets of the fifteenth century, he was keenly interested in the arts and patronized *Botticelli, Filippino Lippi and *Ghirlandaio. He encouraged associations for the study of literature and art and attracted to his court philosophers and poets, including Marsilio Ficino, Pico della Mirandola and Poliziano. At his villas in Careggi, Fiesole and Poggio a Caiano, he gathered with his circle of friends, often referred to as the ''Platonic Academy.'' In the garden of San Marco, Florence, Lorenzo sponsored a school for sculpture attended by *Michelangelo.

Some of Lorenzo's most prestigious antiquities were gifts. In 1471, Pope *Sixtus IV, who would later be his mortal enemy, gave Lorenzo two antique marble heads of *Augustus* and *Agrippa*. Also during this trip to Rome, Lorenzo may have received the incomparable sardonyx vase later known as the Tazza Farnese (*Farnese Cup; now in Naples) and a number of other intaglios and cameos that had belonged to *Paul II, the predecessor of Sixtus. Many of these he inscribed with his name LAV.R.MED [sic], and they may easily be identified today. Most of Lorenzo's gems are to be seen today in Naples, though others ended up in Paris, London, St. Petersburg, The Hague and Florence.

In the Florence Archaeological Museum is a bronze *Head of a Horse* that belonged to Lorenzo and may have once been placed in the garden of the Palazzo Medici-Riccardi. Its influence is seen in the painting of an equestrian monument to Niccolo da Tolentino by Andrea del Castagno in the Duomo in Florence (1455–56). In 1471 Lorenzo gave a similar bronze *Head of a Horse,* perhaps also antique, to Diomede Carafa of Naples, where it remains today. Lorenzo owned another valuable bronze, a head of *Jupiter* given to him by the Sienese in 1492. At the same time they bestowed a terracotta urn covered with an inscribed tile, attesting a provenance of the tomb of Porsenna. While it is unlikely that the materials came from that famous (lost) monument, they very probably were indeed Etruscan. The item provides an early piece of evidence for the Medici's regard for their Tuscan heritage. Lorenzo also owned ancient vases from Greece, and from Vasari's grandfather he received Italian vases from Arezzo (*Arretine ware).

After the death of Lorenzo came a period of exile from Florence for the Medici (until 1512), but their fortunes rose again with the election of Lorenzo's son GIOVANNI DE' MEDICI (1475–1521) as Pope *LEO X in 1513. He had acquired a palazzo on Monte Mario in Rome, where his family accumulated a collection of marbles. PIERO DE' MEDICI (1472–1503), the brother of Leo X, left his widow, Alfonsina Orsini, to inhabit the palace; she soon acquired an impressive group of dead or dying barbarians, including an *Amazon,* a *Gaul* and a *Persian,* identified then as the *Horatii* and *Curiatii.* By the 1530s this collection included a group of *Harmodios and Aristogeiton,* a seated *Jupiter,* a *Crouching Venus,* as well as altars and herms. In 1537, the palace became the home of Margaret of Austria, daughter of the emperor Charles V and wife of the assassinated ALESSANDRO DE' MEDICI (1510–37), great-nephew of the pope. The palace became known as the Palazzo Madama in reference to her, and there she kept for a brief time the collection of Medici gems that had remained safe through decades of political turmoil for the Medici and dispersion of many antiquities from the old collection. Upon her marriage to Ottavio Farnese the following year, the gems (including the Farnese Cup and the "Seal of Nero") and the marbles of Palazzo Madama passed into the *Farnese family collections and thence to Naples in the eighteenth century.

COSIMO I DE' MEDICI (IL GRANDE; 1519–74), descended from the brother of Cosimo il Vecchio, assumed power in Florence upon the death of Alessandro in 1537. Elected head of the republic of Florence, he held the title of duke and eventually was elevated to the status of grand duke by Pope Pius V in 1569; most of Tuscany was now under Medici control. Cosimo was married in 1539 to Eleonora of Toledo, and the pair took a great interest in their residences and collections. Cosimo transferred the Medici household to the Palazzo Vecchio (Palazzo della Signoria) in the heart of Florence; Eleonora purchased the Pitti Palace, located beyond the Arno River, and it was expanded according to designs by Ammanati. Vasari constructed the Uffizi (1560) as an office building that would be part of a connection between the Palazzo Vecchio and the Palazzo Pitti, and in these three Medici buildings Cosimo and his successors were to distribute their Florentine collections.

Practically nothing remained of the Medici collections of the fifteenth century, and Cosimo began to collect anew. With a great interest in the Etruscan past of Tuscany, Cosimo styled himself *Magnus Dux Etruriae* (Grand Duke of Etruria) and undoubtedly was delighted when he was able to acquire the magnificent bronze *Chimaera* discovered at Arezzo in 1553 and the *Arringatore* in 1566, both of which had authentic Etruscan inscriptions to ensure their pedigree. A great part of the rest of the collection was due to gifts and purchases made in Rome between 1560 and 1586 by Cosimo and his two sons FRANCESCO I (1541–87) and FERDINANDO I (1549–1609). Many of the marbles were originally destined to adorn the Pitti. In 1568 Vasari records ten sculptures in the niches in the Sala Principale of the Pitti and others round about, including a *Pomona,* the Belvedere *Mercury (Hermes),* the Wild Boar (*Il Porcellino*) and two *Molossian Hounds.* Other sculptures soon arrived and were set up at the Pitti in 1569, including twenty-six statues that had been stripped from the Belvedere and seventeen portraits, as well as a group of the *Dying Ajax* (cf. *Pasquino*), found at the *Mausoleum of Augustus. Because of periodic rearrangements of the collections in ensuing years, it becomes impractical hereafter to note the changing locations of the individual Medici marbles.

Cosimo's later life was tragic, for his wife, two sons and two daughters all died within a few years of each other (1557–62), and he decided to turn over the governing of the duchy to Francesco (1564), though he retained his own ducal status. At his death in 1574 the family collections were divided between Palazzo Vecchio and Palazzo Pitti.

As Francesco took over in Florence, Ferdinando began his career as a young cardinal in Rome in 1564, though he did not immediately settle there. In 1576 he purchased the villa of Cardinal Ricci on the Pincio Hill and thus developed the sixth and final Medici residence connected with an important collection of classical antiquities. Again sculpture was the desired commodity, and Francesco was able to acquire items for the new Villa Medici by purchase, donation and excavation. Among his acquisitions were portions of the former Capranica—della *Valle and *Cesi collections, the *Arrotino, the *Medici Vase, the *Medici Venus, the Wrestlers and the *Niobe Group. In 1598, when the villa was inventoried, over 450 pieces of sculpture were counted in what was clearly one of Rome's most magnificent collections.

In Florence, Francesco turned his attention to a new systematization of the holdings there, and the story of the Medici collections now is the same as that of the Uffizi Gallery. Francesco began to create galleries in the top floor for the display of marbles, and he hired Buontalenti to design the fabled octagonal room known as the Tribuna, which was not used, however, for the display of sculpture until many years later. When Francesco died in 1587, Ferdinando returned to Florence to succeed his brother as grand duke, leaving the sculpture collection at the Villa Medici intact.

There were relatively few major changes in the Medici collections in Florence in the seventeenth century. FERDINANDO II (1610–70) obtained the bronze *"Idolino" from Urbino through marriage (1630) and a group of busts and the Celestial Venus from Bologna (1657; restored by *Algardi). Cardinal LEOPOLDO DE' MEDICI (1617–75), an eager connoisseur of coins and small antiquities, was acquainted in Rome with the dealer Ottavio Falconieri, Leonardo *Agostini and Queen *Christina of Sweden. He secured a Hermaphrodite and thirteen busts from the *Ludovisi family collection. Under COSIMO III (1639–1723) and after the death of Leopoldo came the movement of some of the most celebrated marbles from the Villa Medici to Florence. The Arrotino, the Wrestlers and the Medici Venus were now placed in the Tribuna (1688).

Most of the rest of the marbles of the Villa Medici would not come to Florence until the years 1778–87, well after the death of the last of the Medici, GIAN GASTONE, in 1737 and the cession of Tuscany, and the Medici collections, to the house of Lorraine (Lorena). Inventories of 1704 and 1753 record around 500 Medici antiquities and an enormous collection of coins accumulated through the centuries. The Museum Florentinum of Francisco *Gori included a volume of the most treasured statues of gods and men in the Medici collection, Statuae antiquae deorum et virorum illustrium (1734). (See also *collecting [after 1500].)

BIBLIOGRAPHY
E. Müntz, Les Collections des Médicis au 15e siècle (Paris, 1888); idem, "Les Collections d'antiques formées par les Médicis au XVIe siècle," Memoires de l'Institut National de France (Académie des Inscriptions et Belles-Lettres 35.2 (1896), 85–168; +M. Cagiano de Azevedo, Le Antichità di Villa Medici (Rome, 1951); E. H. Gombrich, "The Early Medici as Patrons of Art," in Norm and Form, Studies in the Art of the Renaissance

(London, 1966), 35–37; G. M. Andres, *The Villa Medici in Rome* 1–2 (New York, 1976); E. L. Goldberg, *Patterns in Late Medici Art Patronage* (Princeton, NJ, 1983); +F. M. Tuena, *Il Tesoro dei Medici, collezionismo a Firenze dal Quattrocento al Seicento* (Florence, 1987); P. Ponza, ed., *Statue del Tesoro Mediceo* (Milan, 1991); F. Ames-Lewis, ed., *Cosimo 'Il Vecchio' de' Medici, 1389–1464* (Oxford, 1992).

MEDICI VASE. Great marble vessel (1.73m high) in the shape of a krater or mixing bowl for wine, closely resembling the *Borghese Vase and, like it, a product of neo-Attic art of the first century B.C.

The vessel shows a mixture of Hellenistic and classicizing motifs, featuring luxuriant acanthus leaves at the base of the bowl and a sculptured relief of two warriors flanking a statue (restored as Artemis, but possibly Apollo), with a figure at its base (restored as a suppliant, but possibly the Pythia, Apollo's prophetess). The other side of the vase features three males—a youth, a mature man and a veiled elderly man.

The vessel is first mentioned in the 1598 inventory of the Villa Medici in Rome, and it may have already been in the *Medici family collection thirty years earlier. In 1656, Stefano della Bella created a handsome etching of the vase, showing an aristocratic youth, probably his pupil, (later) Cosimo III de' Medici, engaged in drawing the object. The vase was moved to Florence in 1780, soon afterward to be displayed in the *Uffizi, where it has remained (except for three years in Palermo, 1800–3, to escape the plunder of *Napoleon) until the present day.

Discussions about the iconography have been vitiated by the early restoration of the vase to show Iphigenia before the altar of Artemis at Aulis. From the sixteenth to the nineteenth centuries, the two warriors were regularly interpreted as Greek heroes at the sacrifice of Iphigenia and the veiled old man as Agamemnon. *Amelung pointed out the intervention of the restorer, calling for a reevaluation of the subject matter. Like the famous *Portland Vase, which is nearly contemporary and features a heroic theme, the Medici object remains an object of debate.

The vessel was itself famed for centuries, and numerous copies were made, both full-sized and reduced, often as a pendant to the Borghese Vase, in marble, bronze, alabaster, biscuit and cast iron. Along with the Borghese piece, it remains of interest to archaeologists, for the two vessels are regarded as high-quality examples of the neo-Attic trend in art.

BIBLIOGRAPHY

W. Amelung, *Führer durch die Antiken in Florenz* (Munich, 1897), 79–80; G. A. Mansuelli, *Galleria degli Uffizi: Le sculture* (Rome, 1958–61), I, 189–92; Bieber, 185; Haskell—Penny, 316.

MEDICI VENUS. Nearly lifesize marble statue of Venus (Aphrodite).

Like its counterpart, the *Capitoline *Venus,* with which it is often compared, the Medici goddess is shown nude, with her hands placed modestly in front of

her body. The statue is a copy, perhaps of a bronze original of the third century
B.C., which was itself created in imitation of the *Knidian *Aphrodite* of Praxiteles. The Medici *Venus* is sometimes attributed to the sons of Praxiteles
(though there is a signature of Kleomenes of Athens on the base).

The find spot of the *Venus* is unknown, and there is no certain evidence of
its existence in the *Medici family collection until it was published by *Perrier
in 1638 as one of the most beautiful statues in Rome. In 1677, it was moved
from the Villa Medici to Florence, where it was placed in the Tribuna of the
*Uffizi (no later than 1688). The statue was much restored, including arms that
were completely remade at this time by Ercole Ferrata. Ardently coveted by the
French for the museum of *Napoleon, the Medici *Venus* was sent to Palermo
to escape predation but was yielded by the Neapolitan court. In 1803 it was on
display in Paris, remaining until 1815, at which time it was returned to Florence
for good.

The statue enjoyed a glorious reputation, but Innocent XI allowed its removal
from Rome because he feared that it stimulated lewd behavior. During the eighteenth and early nineteenth centuries especially, the Venus had many admirers
or even worshipers. Luca Giordano made copies of it from every possible angle,
and *Spence is said to have visited it a hundred times. *Byron described it in
five stanzas of *Childe Harold,* and in Florence, it even appeared in a ballet,
boldly represented by the prima donna as ''living'' and ''warm'' (in 1814, while
the statue was still in Paris). It was copied over and over in marble (four times
for *Louis XIV alone), in bronze (yet another copy for Louis, as well as for
others), in lead and in alabaster.

The statue was not totally without critics: *Winckelmann disliked its deep
navel and objected to the numerous restorations, while the writer Smollett
thought that its features lacked beauty; others complained about individual parts
of its body (the fingers, the arms, the feet) in a manner typical of eighteenth-
century criticism. During this period, too, German archaeologists began to argue
that the statue was but a copy.

In the twentieth century, the Medici *Venus* still sometimes receives lavish
praise, though it is studied as a copy rather than an original. Bieber's enthusiastic
description could have been written in the eighteenth century: ''The beautiful
head looks almost coquettishly to the side. . . . The features are sweet and soft.''
The purchase by the Metropolitan Museum, New York (1952) of a replica with
the head well preserved seems to have raised, rather than lowered, the stock of
the Medici statue. M. Robertson, though less generous than Bieber, still rates
the Medici *Venus* as closer to the Knidia than the rival Capitoline statue.

BIBLIOGRAPHY
C. Alexander, ''A Statue of Aphrodite,'' *BMMA* (1952–53), 241–51; Bieber, 20; Robertson, 548–50; Haskell—Penny, 325–28; Ridgway, *Hellenistic Sculpture* I, 354–55.

MEGARA HYBLAEA. Greek colony in *Sicily.

Megara Hyblaea was settled by Megarian Greeks on territory given them by the Sikel king Hyblon. Its foundation date is controversial: Thucydides (6.4.2) indicates ca. 728 B.C., while from Diodorus (13.59.4) and Eusebius we calculate ca. 750 B.C. Modern excavators of the site prefer the earlier date.

The city established a colony at *Selinus one hundred years after its own foundation. About 483 B.C., Megara Hyblaea was destroyed by Gelon of *Syracuse (Thucydides 6.4.2 Herodotus 7.156) and abandoned. It was refounded under Timoleon ca. 340 B.C. but destroyed again by the Romans ca. 313 B.C. (Livy 24.35). A small settlement continued to exist until the sixth century A.C.

The earliest excavations at Megara Hyblaea may have been carried out by *Frederick II in the thirteenth century. T. *Fazello (*De rebus siculis*) visited the ruins in the sixteenth century. Systematic excavation began in 1879, with additional campaigns later in the century. This work concentrated on tombs and topography. Further exploration was conducted by *Orsi between 1917 and 1921 in a sanctuary and along a segment of the city wall. In 1949 continuous excavations began by the French under G. Vallet and F. Villard. These investigations centered on the northern plateau and included public and residential areas as well as necropoleis. At the same time, work continued on a sporadic basis by the Italian authorities. Final publication of the site is not yet completed.

BIBLIOGRAPHY

F. S. Cavallari—P. Orsi, "Megara Hyblaea, storia, topografia, necropoli e anathemata," *MonAnt* 1 (1892), 689–950; G. V. Gentili, "Megara Hyblaea," *NSc* 8 (1954), 80–113, 390–402; G. Vallet et al., *Megara Hyblaea* 1 (Rome, 1976), 2 (Paris, 1964), 4 (Paris, 1966).

BARBARA A. BARLETTA

MELEAGER, Vatican. Over-lifesize marble statue of Meleager, now in the Vatican; Roman copy of a fourth-century B.C. original usually attributed to Skopas; the unpreserved left hand may have held a spear; chlamys, dog and boar's head are probably copyist's additions.

Discovered in Rome before 1546, the statue was in a private collection until it was bought by Pope *Clement XIV (1770). By 1792, it was installed in the Museo Pio-Clementino. The piece was removed to France under the terms of the Treaty of Tolentino, displayed in the Musée Central des Arts (1800–15) and returned to the Vatican by 1816. Until the eighteenth century, the *Meleager* was considered among the most beautiful statues in Rome and was coveted by many collectors, including *Arundel, Cardinal Chigi and *Louis XIV. But in later centuries, its style and execution were criticized (*Winckelmann declared it a copy), and the statue's reputation declined. Numerous versions of the *Meleager* are known today.

BIBLIOGRAPHY

Bieber, 24–25; S. Lattimore, "Meleager: New Replicas, Old Problems," *OpRom* 9 (1973), 157–66; +Haskell—Penny, 263–65.

ANN M. NICGORSKI

MELOS. Island of the Cycladic group, source of volcanic products, particularly obsidian (exploited already in the Mesolithic).

Chance finds (including the *Venus* de Milo) had, by the time of J. T. Bent, turned the "vale of Klima into the Eldorado of collectors." R. C. Bosanquet, D. Mackenzie, C. Smith and others were encouraged to conduct systematic excavations in 1896–99 at the site of classical Melos and at Phylakopi, the major Bronze Age settlement. The well-known *Flying Fish* fresco (*National Archaeological Museum, Athens) was found in 1896 in a house at Phylakopi. In 1974–77, supplemental explorations directed by C. Renfrew uncovered a new Mycenaean shrine at Phylakopi (with plentiful cult paraphernalia). Both British projects investigated the entire island, promoting the development of regional studies.

Phylakopi was a fortified peninsular town, dominated in the early phases of the Late Bronze Age by a literate bureaucracy based in a "mansion" and in Mycenaean times by a megaron-style "palace." There were exchanges with Crete from ca. 2000–1450 B.C. and local imitation of Minoan styles. By classical times, the focus of settlement had shifted southwest to a site on the Great Bay; extensive remains of the ancient polis were mapped by the Admiralty Survey ship *Volage* (1848) and include fortifications, a theater (cleared in 1836 by *Ludwig I of Bavaria and drawn by the *Expédition scientifique de Morée*), a stadium and Christian catacombs (visited by *Leake in 1806). The post-Bronze Age art of Melos—for example, gems, vases and relief plaques—has been studied by *Conze (1867), Boardman (1963), *Jacobsthal (1931) and Zaphiropoulou (1981), among others.

BIBLIOGRAPHY
+T. D. Atkinson et al., *Excavations at Phylakopi in Melos* (London, 1904); +C. Renfrew—M. Wagstaff, eds., *An Island Polity: The Archaeology of Exploitation in Melos* (Cambridge, 1982); +C. Renfrew, *The Archaeology of Cult: The Sanctuary at Phylakopi* (London, 1985); +R. Torrence, *Production and Exchange of Stone Tools: Prehistoric Obsidian in the Aegean* (Cambridge, 1986).

JACK L. DAVIS

MENANDER, portraits of. Images of the great Greek dramatist (342/1–293/89 B.C.), acknowledged as the leading writer of New Comedy.

A portrait of Menander was erected in his native Athens in the *Theater of Dionysos, created by the sculptors Timarchos and Kephisodotos (sons of Praxiteles), perhaps around the beginning of the third century B.C. The portrait was identified by F. *Studnizcka (first suggested, 1895) in a famous Hellenistic image now known in more than sixty-three replicas, the finest versions of which are located in the *Museum of Fine Arts, Boston, and the Seminario Patriarcale, Venice.

The bust shows a beardless individual, aged about fifty, with a sensitive face marked by furrows in the brow and crow's feet at the eyes. It is usually suggested that the man represented shows signs of physical suffering, a feature that fits with the rather delicate constitution of Menander. The hair has a characteristic pattern repeated in all the copies, in which it is combed forward on the right and backward on the left.

Studnizcka identified the famous type as Menander on the basis of a drawing by Theodore Gallaeus of an inscribed bust of Menander in Fulvio *Orsini's collection, though opponents argued that the plump face in the Gallaeus drawing is not a fully convincing comparison. Recently, a small bronze head of the type, inscribed with the name *(M)enandros,* was acquired by the Getty Museum, Malibu (1973). B. Ashmole argued that the bust (unfortunately unprovenanced) clinched the case for Menander.

A rival theory was proposed by J. F. Crome (1935), that the extremely popular individual represented in the numerous busts, themselves dating to the period of the Roman Empire, was the Roman epic poet Vergil of Mantua, who died at the age of fifty-one and who also suffered from ill health. Accordingly, the sculpture type would date some 300 years later. No convincing inscribed image of Vergil may be invoked, but R. *Carpenter noted that the hairstyle does not agree with the Gallaeus portrait, where the hair is combed forward on both sides, but is precisely that worn at the time of Vergil. Many argued that if this is not a portrait of Vergil, then there is no recognized sculpture of the illustrious poet. V. Poulsen countered (1959) by proposing that a dour, realistic Republican head in Copenhagen is actually the portrait of Vergil.

Though ancient copies of the controversial Menander–Vergil head were known during the Renaissance, there is no evidence on how the individual was identified at that time. Renaissance versions survive (e.g., in the Walters Art Gallery, Baltimore), associated with the ambient of Mantua.

BIBLIOGRAPHY

F. Studniczka, "Das Bildnis Menanders," *Neue Jahrbucher für das Klassische Altertums* 41 (1918), 1–31; J. F. Crome, "Das Bildnis Vergils," *Reale Accademia Virgiliana di Mantova, Atti e Memorie,* N. S. 24 (1935); +G. M. A. Richter, *Portraits of the Greeks* (Phaidon, 1965), II, 229–34; B. Ashmole, "Menander: An Inscribed Bust," *AJA* 17 (1973), 61; Sheard, no. 69.

MENGS, ANTON RAPHAEL (1728–79). German painter, antiquarian and critic of ancient art.

Mengs is known mainly as a painter who played an important role in the genesis of late eighteenth century neoclassicism, but his contribution to archaeological studies was far more radical than his often insipidly classicizing pictures would lead one to suppose. Mengs was the first to take the modern view that almost all the traditional masterpieces of ancient sculpture in Rome betrayed inadequacies of execution that marked them as copies or imitations rather than original Greek creations: "[T]he statues we possess are either not by the best artists of antiquity, or are copies after them."

The son of a minor pastel and enamel painter, Mengs was appointed first painter to the Saxon court in Dresden in 1751. A year later he settled in Rome, where in 1756 he met *Winckelmann. The two men worked together on a series of descriptions of the most famous sculptures in the *Vatican Belvedere, which, though never published, proved an important stimulus for their later involvement with ancient art. Mengs's first publication, *Gedanken über die Schönheit* ... (1762), already projected an unusually purist conception of the Greek ideal, realized in its full perfection only in a tiny handful of the most celebrated ancient sculptures. By 1761, when he had completed his famous *Parnassus* in the Villa Albani (cf. *Albani family) and had accepted a post as painter to the Spanish court in Madrid, Mengs had become an avid and adventurous collector of ancient art, building up a remarkable collection of the then newly fashionable Greek vases from Southern Italy (part of which entered the Vatican in 1773) and also one of the period's most extensive private collections of casts after antique sculptures (the remnants divided between Madrid and Dresden).

After Winckelmann's death Mengs developed his more novel ideas on ancient sculpture during two periods he spent in Italy on leave from the Spanish court in 1769–73 and 1777–79. At this point he was clearly considered something of an expert on ancient art: In 1769–70 he was consulted by Grand Duke Leopold of Tuscany about the reorganization of the famous *Medici collection of antiquities, and in 1779 he was sent for comment a scholarly dissertation on the *Niobe* Group (Uffizi) by the director of Pisa University, Angiolo Fabroni. In response to the latter, at the very end of his career, Mengs formulated his theory (first published posthumously in his *Opere,* Parma, 1780) of Graeco-Roman copies. The *Niobe* Group, he argued, far from being an early Greek masterpiece, as Winckelmann and Fabroni had claimed, was "a copy done from better originals, executed by artists of varying talent"; he went on to refute the commonly held assumption that other particularly famous pieces were Greek masterpieces of the best period, showing, for example, how the *Belvedere *Apollo* could be only a late work because it was of Italian marble and lacked the fleshiness and softness of surface one would expect of the best Greek sculpture. Three decades before the famous controversy over the *Elgin marbles, Mengs made the point that only the odd exceptional piece, such as the *Belvedere Torso or *Borghese *Gladiator* (the only works among the traditional masterpieces, except the *Laocoon and *Barberini *Faun,* still considered fine enough possibly to be originals rather than copies), might give some idea of "il vero" (or vitality, as the Romantics would have said) that distinguished pure Greek art.

The idea that many known antique sculptures were copies and that none of the early masterpieces of Greek sculpture celebrated by the writers of antiquity were likely to be found among the surviving sculptures in Italy had been mooted before; a quite unusual passage in the French edition (1728) of Jonathan Richardson's *Account of Statues* ... *in Italy* indeed anticipated many of Mengs's ideas. But these were only isolated instances that were not seen, as were Mengs's theories later on, to pose a threat to the status of the traditional masterpieces. Without a consistent historical perspective on ancient Greek art of the kind first elaborated by Winckelmann, it did not make sense to distinguish in any systematic way between a largely hypothetical pure Greek ideal and the Graeco-Roman copies that had survived. When Mengs set about making this "modern" distinction, expeditions were already being launched on a large scale to seek authentic examples of early Greek art.

Of some interest, too, was Mengs's analysis of ancient painting in a letter to Antonio Ponz, first published in Spanish in 1776. In opposition to most contemporary opinion, he argued that the absence of modern compositional devices in ancient paintings, far from being a fault, was part of a considered aesthetic that set a premium on the perfect rendering of each separate form. Mengs himself produced a highly successful pastiche of an ancient Roman painting, a *Jupiter and Ganymede* (Rome, Galleria Nazionale d'Arte Antica), which Winckelmann celebrated as a fine antique that put the paintings discovered so far at *Herculaneum in the shade.

BIBLIOGRAPHY

+S. Röttgen, "Storia di un falso: il Ganimede di Mengs," *Arte Illustrata* 54 (1973), 256–70; +A. D. Potts, "Greek Sculpture and Roman Copies I: Anton Raphael Mengs and the Eighteenth Century," *JWarb* 43 (1980), 150–73; +S. Röttgen, "Zum Antikenbesitz des Anton Raphael Mengs und zur Geschichte und Wirkung seiner Abguss- und Formensammlung," in *Antikensammlungen im 18. Jahrhundert,* ed. H. Beck et al. (Berlin, 1981), 129–48.

ALEX POTTS

MÉRIDA (AUGUSTA EMERITA). Site of the best-preserved and most important Roman city in Spain.

Founded in 25 B.C. as Colonia Emerita Augusta, it served as the capital of Lusitania. Excavations began in the early 1900s under the direction of José Ramon Mélida and have uncovered extensive remains of Roman, Visigothic and Arab date.

Spectacular monuments of the Roman period are visible. They include two reservoirs with dams, two aqueducts, two bridges, a circus, a theater, an amphitheater, an arch of Trajan and a temple of Mars (remains of which were incorporated into the Church of Sta. Eulalia, patron saint of the city, martyred in A.D. 303/4). A temple "of Diana," probably really of Augustus and Roma, was preserved from the sixteenth century as part of the house of the Conde de los Corbos. A seventeenth-century monument to Sta. Eulalia features the saint on a lofty columnlike pedestal actually made of three Roman altars stacked one on top of another.

At Mérida there have also been excavated Roman houses containing wall paintings and mosaics and a necropolis. The majority of artifacts recovered— including pottery, metal objects, glass, more than 200 inscriptions, and over seventy pieces of sculpture—are exhibited in the spacious new Museo Nacional de Arte in Mérida. Some objects are also displayed in the Museo Arqueológico Nacional in Madrid.

BIBLIOGRAPHY
A. Floriano, "Excavaciones en Mérida," *ArchEspArq* 17 (1944), 151–86; P. Mac-Kendrick, *The Iberian Stones Speak* (New York, 1969), 129–43; *Actas del Simposio Internacional Commemorativo del Bimilenario de Mérida* (1975); M.M.V. Guitan, *La Ciudad de Mérida* (Leon, 1987).

MARY ANN EAVERLY

METAPONTION (METAPONTO). Greek city in Southern Italy.

The history of Greek settlements in the area of Metapontion begins with a precolonial trading post (perhaps a successor to a Bronze Age settlement closer to Heraclea, at Termitito) at Incoronata, with remains of dwellings and local and imported pottery from the mid-eighth century B.C. The colony itself, founded by Achaeans ca. 650 B.C., was equipped with a city wall, streets on a grid plan, an early sixth-century B.C. *ekklesiasterion* or assembly hall, replaced by a fourth-century B.C. theater, and an extramural temple to Hera. The city flourished during the sixth and fourth centuries B.C. but continued to exist on a smaller scale with a *castrum* plan in the Roman period.

The development of the territory outside the city proper has been traced since the 1960s through the pioneering work of Dinu Adamesteanu and international teams of excavators. With the aid of aerial photography, surveys and extensive excavations, hundreds of farm sites have been located, as well as rural sanctuaries and burial grounds that suggest a system of individual farms, a local production of terracottas and pottery and communal gathering places for the worship of the rural deities, often located in connection with springs.

BIBLIOGRAPHY
+D. Adamesteanu, *La Basilicata antica* (Cava dei Tirreni, 1974); +D. Adamesteanu—D. Mertens—F. D'Andria, "Metaponto I," *NSc* 29 (1975), suppl.; +J. C. Carter, "Metapontum—Land, Wealth and Population," *Greek Colonists and Native Populations*, ed. J.-P. Descoeudres (Oxford, 1990), 405–41; E. Greco, *Magna Grecia* (Bari, 1980), 99–160; +J. C. Carter, "Agricoltura e pastorizia in Magna Grecia (tra Bradano e Basento)," *Magna Grecia,* ed. G. Pugliese Carratelli (Milan, 1987), 173–212; G. Nenci—G. Vallet, eds., *Bibliografia topografica della colonizzazione greca in Italia e nelle Isole Tirreniche* 10 (Pisa 1992), 65–112.

INGRID E. M. EDLUND

METROPOLITAN MUSEUM OF ART, New York. Major American museum, containing a rich and varied collection of classical antiquities.

Chartered in 1870, the Metropolitan Museum of Art had several locations in New York City from the time of its official opening in 1872 before settling in its present location at Fifth Avenue and 82nd Street (1880). From the beginning, classical antiquities were a high priority for the museum. The first gift received was a fine Roman sarcophagus of the Garland type, found at Tarsus and offered to the museum by Abdo Debbas, U.S. vice-consul there. When General Luigi Palma di *Cesnola served as U.S. consul to *Cyprus, he amassed a staggering collection of some 35,000 Cypriot antiquities, of which more than 10,000 were purchased for the Metropolitan. Of these, approximately half were placed on display, to create an exhibition of the finest stone sculpture, sarcophagi, pottery and glass as well as bronze, gold and silver pieces dating from prehistoric through Roman times. J. L. Myres published *A Handbook of the Cesnola Collection of Antiquities from Cyprus* (1914). The remaining parts of the Cesnola collection were sold as ''duplicates'' to other collections in the United States in 1928.

Cesnola became director of the Metropolitan (1874–1904), but relatively few other antiquities were acquired during this period. The most significant purchases were an Etruscan chariot from Monteleone di Spoleto (1903) and Roman frescoes from *Boscoreale and Boscotrecase (also 1903); donations included bronzes and glass given by Henry G. Marquand (1897) and engraved gems presented by John Taylor Johnston (1881).

J. Pierpont Morgan became president of the Metropolitan (1905–12), and in 1909 the Department of Greek and Roman Art was formally established. By means of bequests, occasional gifts and loans and, above all, annual purchases from the Rogers and Fletcher Funds, the museum assembled a premier collection. With John Marshall (d. 1928) as agent and Edward Robinson (d. 1931) as curator, scholar and then director of the museum, the Metropolitan laid the foundations for one of the world's finest collections of early Greek sculpture and Greek pottery. Representing the Classical period was a superb white-ground Attic cosmetic jar (pyxis) painted with the *Judgment of Paris* (acquired 1907). A grand Geometric Dipylon Vase was purchased in 1914, and J. P. Morgan donated fine Geometric bronzes (1917). Hellenistic Greek art was not neglected (the *Old Market Woman* was bought in 1909), nor was Roman art; Marshall bought Roman sarcophagi, such as one with the theme of *Muses and Sirens* (1910; the work had been known since the time of Cassiano dal *Pozzo) and others with *Endymion* (1920) and *Meleager* (1920). The museum was reorganized in this period to create a sequence of historical periods, as opposed to the former scheme in which like materials were grouped together.

Gisela M. A. *Richter, who had come to help catalog Greek vases at the museum in 1906, was the succeeding chief curator of Greek and Roman art (1925–48); with her advice, further major acquisitions were made, such as the great Attic *Kouros* (1932; *korai and *kouroi*) and the *Wounded Amazon* of a type attributed to Kresilas (gift of John D. Rockefeller, Jr., 1932). She concentrated on publishing the collection and turned out a number of books: *Handbook of the Classical Collection* (enlarged ed., 1930); *Handbook of the Etruscan Collection* (1940; Etruscan antiquities, previously displayed with Greek art, now received their own rooms); *Roman Portraits* (1948); *Catalogue of Engraved Gems, Greek, Etruscan and Roman* (1956).

In the ensuing years, the Metropolitan was criticized sharply in the wake of two sensational cases of purchasing antiquities. The first had to do with a group of terracotta warriors, purchased by John Marshall (1915, 1916 and 1921), alleged to be Etruscan Archaic masterpieces. The sculptures arrived in fragments and were finally assembled and displayed to the public in 1933. Richter published a monograph on the statues with full stylistic analysis and dating criteria, *Etruscan Terracotta Warriors in the Metropolitan Museum of Art* (1937). Objections to the authenticity of the pieces began immediately with Massimo Pallottino in Italy (1937) and reached their conclusion with the investigations of Richter and Dietrich von Bothmer (curator from 1959) and the confession by Alfredo Adolfo Fioravanti of Rome (1961) that he had participated in the construction of the statues; he produced a missing thumb he had kept from one of the warriors as proof of his authorship. Von Bothmer and J. V. Noble made known the results in *An Inquiry into the Forgery of the Etruscan Terracotta Warriors in the Metropolitan Museum of Art* (1961).

Von Bothmer himself was subjected to withering criticism in the following decade, when the Metropolitan paid, at his recommendation, $1 million for a single Greek vase, a wine-mixing bowl (krater) decorated with the *Death of Sarpedon,* signed by the well-known Archaic vase painter Euphronios. The shaky provenance of the vase, bought in 1972 and said to have lain in fragments in the family cabinet of Dikran Sarrafian in Beirut since 1920, led many to suspect that the piece had been recently plundered from an archaeological site in Italy, perhaps *Cerveteri. Von Bothmer and museum director Thomas Hoving defended their purchase, but they continued to be fiercely attacked by field archaeologists, who objected that the outrageously inflated sum paid for a vase that was probably stolen would only encourage the ravaging of other sites. Hoving admitted later (1993) that the fragments attested in the collection of Sarrafian may have belonged to another pot entirely.

The Roman paintings acquired by the Metropolitan in 1903 received proper study much later. Phyllis Lehmann produced a full monograph on the villa of P. Fannius Synistor, *Roman Wall Paintings from Boscoreale in the Metropolitan Museum of Art* (1953), and Peter von Blanckenhagen published a monograph on what was called the "Villa of Agrippa Postumus" in *The Augustan Villa at Boscotrecase* (with Christine Alexander, 2nd., rev. ed. 1990). The latter also received attention in a new display and publications by M. L. Anderson. Important acquisitions came by bequest from Walter C. Baker (bronzes, including the *Baker Dancer,* 1971, 1972) and by donation from Norbert Schimmel (102 Greek, Roman and Egyptian antiquities, 1989). The Etruscan chariot from Monteleone was thoroughly researched by Adriana Emiliozzi, with a new reconstruction proposed in accordance with her findings (1991).

BIBLIOGRAPHY
W. E. Howe, *A History of the Metropolitan Museum of Art* 1 (New York, 1913) and 2 (New York, 1946); J. L. Hess, *The Grand Acquisitors* (Boston, 1974); +A. M. McCann, *Roman Sarcophagi in the Metropolitan Museum of Art* (New York, 1978); +M. L. Anderson, *Pompeian Frescoes in the Metropolitan Museum of Art, MMA Bulletin* 45.3 (1987–88).

MEYER, EDUARD (1855–1930). German classicist and historian.

Born in Hamburg, Meyer added several ancient Near Eastern languages to his superb training in Greek and Latin. His masterpiece is his *Geschichte des Altertums* (5 vols., 1884–1902, later expanded). This massive history of antiquity from Egypt through Persian and Greek civilization ends at 350 B.C. It is based on documents studied in their original languages and on all relevant archaeological evidence. It far surpasses in scope the contemporary histories of *Busolt and *Beloch. Though himself antidemocratic in politics, Meyer saw Greek culture as the center of ancient history. He wrote many other works on various phases of antiquity and was professor in Berlin, 1902–23.

BIBLIOGRAPHY

H. Marohl, *Eduard Meyer, Bibliographie* (Stuttgart, 1941), with autobio. sketch by Meyer; K. Christ, *Von Gibbon zu Rostovtzeff* (Darmstadt, 1972), 286–333; W. M. Calder III—A. Demandt, eds., *Eduard Meyer: Leben und Leistung eines Universalhistorikers,* Mnemosyne Suppl. 112 (1990).

MORTIMER CHAMBERS

MEYER, ERNST (1898–1975). Swiss historian and topographer.

A pupil of Kahrstedt in Göttingen, Meyer was professor of ancient history in Zurich, 1927–68 and a scholar of extraordinary range. His first field of interest was the archaeology and topography of Greece. His many travels in Greece led to *Peloponnesische Wanderungen* (1939) and more than 200 articles on topography for Pauly-Wissowa; after the war he wrote *Neue peloponnesische Wanderungen* (1957), in which he identified and mapped the site of Typaneai in the western Peloponnese. He also published widely on the archaeology and history of Switzerland as a Roman province: *Die Römische Schweiz* (1941), *Die Schweiz im Altertum* (1946). His main theoretical work is his *Römischer Staat und Staatsgedanke* (1948; 3rd ed., 1964), an analytical description of the Roman constitution and a well-documented summary of Roman history. Finally, he surveyed the political systems of antiquity, including the ancient Near East, in *Einführung in die antike Staatskunde* (1968).

BIBLIOGRAPHY

F. G. Maier, *Gnomon* 48 (1976), 635–37.

MORTIMER CHAMBERS

MICALI, GIUSEPPE (1769–1844). Italian historian and archaeologist, specialist in the pre-Roman peoples of Italy.

Born in Livorno, Micali traveled about Europe as a youth, particularly to France and Germany. Returning to Livorno, he devoted himself to the study of Italy before the Romans, publishing his ideas in the four-volume *L'Italia avanti il dominio de' romani* (Florence, 1810), which included a folio atlas of sixty-seven plates of non-Roman antiquities. The work went through several editions and a French translation and was well received in many circles. (The Accademia della Crusca awarded Micali a prize for it.) Many Italians were drawn to the thesis that there had been a native Italy that somehow was suppressed by the

Romans and that the origins of Italian civilization should not be sought in Egypt or the Near East but in Italy itself.

Some criticized Micali as excessively schematic in his theories and as somehow old-fashioned in his regression to the *Etruscheria* of the eighteenth century. Nevertheless, his work, with its excellent plates, became a treasured classic. His *Storia degli antichi popoli italiani* (Florence, 1832), in three volumes with an album of monuments, was also a standard work. Containing unique illustrations by *Stackelberg, it served long as a principal reference work on Etruscan painting. The Micali Painter, one of the most prolific artists in black-figure vase painting, was named for Micali because he was the first to publish vases by this painter.

BIBLIOGRAPHY

F. Louvet, "Micali, Joseph," *NBG* 35 (1861), cols. 313–14; A. Neppi Modona, "Micali, Giuseppe," *EI* 23 (1934), 156; M. Cristofani, "Micali, L'Etruria e gli inglesi," in *Un Artista etrusco e il suo mondo, il pittore di Micali,* catalog of exhibition (Rome, 1988), 44–47; *Les Étrusques et l'Europe* (Paris, 1992), 322, 333, 337, etc.

MICHAELIS, ADOLF THEODOR FRIEDRICH (1835–1910). German archaeologist, known for his publications on museography and the history of archaeology.

Michaelis was born in Kiel and early came to an interest in the antique through his uncle, Otto *Jahn. In 1853 he began the study of classical philology and archaeology at Leipzig. Besides Jahn, he had as teachers J. *Overbeck at Leipzig and then E. *Gerhard, A. *Böckh and E. *Curtius at Berlin.

In 1857 Michaelis went to Rome, where he quickly made contacts with scholars at the *German Archaeological Institute. Provided with a travel stipend (1859–60), he visited Greece with his close friend A. *Conze. Returning to Germany, he was called to teach at Greifswald (1862) and Tübingen (1865). In 1872 he accepted the chair for archaeology at the newly established University of Strassburg, a post he held until his death in 1910.

Michaelis's most enduring work in his monumental catalog of sculptures in English private collections, published in English, *Ancient Marbles in Great Britain* (1882); immensely useful and informative is his *Die Archäologischen Entdeckungen des 19. Jahrhunderts* (1906; Eng. tr. of 2nd ed., *A Century of Archaeological Discoveries,* 1908). In the preface to the English translation, Michaelis quoted Sir Charles *Newton as an endorsement for his work: "It is from Germany that I always sought that sound and thorough information on every branch of archaeological and philological study, which no other country has produced in this generation."

BIBLIOGRAPHY

H. Dohl, in *Archäologenbildnisse,* 61–62.

MICHELANGELO BUONARROTI (1475–1564). Italian sculptor, painter and architect.

Michelangelo's keen interest in antiquity is attested not only by his surviving works of art but also in the accounts given by his contemporary biographers, Ascanio Condivi and Giorgio Vasari; in his schema of the history of modern art, the latter casts him as the "hero" of the "third manner" (High Renaissance)—an artist who not only equaled but surpassed the ancients. Throughout his life, Michelangelo was concerned with creating, in both painting and sculpture, monumental "animate" figures in heroic movement. To this end, he studied earlier Florentine Renaissance artists (Giotto, Masaccio, *Donatello), his contemporary Leonardo da Vinci and the surviving sculpture of antiquity, especially Hellenistic. What C. De Tolnay has stressed for the artist's late style might be generalized to all Michelangelo's art—that his approach to antiquity was less one of "archaeological quotation" than "creative assimilation" of the classical canon into his own figural repertoire.

Michelangelo entered the Florentine workshop of the painter Domenico *Ghirlandaio in 1488. Though his interests in ancient art may have been stimulated there (Ghirlandaio is said to have made drawings after the antique), it was in 1489–90 that the artist received a proper introduction to the study of antiquities. In those years, he became part of a circle of artists, headed by Bertoldo di Giovanni, who were allowed to study and copy Lorenzo de' Medici's rich collection of ancient marble sculpture, gems, cameos and small bronzes, housed in the garden of San Marco (*Medici family). In this environment, he was also exposed to humanist theories of literary imitation, especially those of Angelo Poliziano, who stressed the assimilation of varied ancient models in creating one's own style.

Michelangelo is recorded as making his first copies of ancient works during the 1490s (Condivi and Vasari tell of the head of an aged *Faun* that especially impressed Lorenzo), and he is also reported to have sculptured a *Sleeping Cupid* (now lost; probably based on a Greek statue of the same subject in the Medici collections), sold as an antique original to Cardinal Raffaele Riario in Rome. The one great surviving example of his *all'antica* work before his first Roman sojourn is a relief of the *Battle of the Centaurs* (Galleria Buonarroti, Florence), which demonstrates his familiarity with the compositional type of Antonine battle sarcophagi, in its dynamic entanglement of muscular figures.

In 1496, Michelangelo traveled to Rome, where he had the opportunity to study other collections of antiquities, for example, Riario's in the Cancelleria Palace, that of Cardinal Giuliano della Rovere (*Julius II), which included the *Belvedere Apollo,* and the sculpture "museum" established by *Sixtus IV on the Capitoline (*Capitoline Museums). During this first Roman sojourn, he produced, among other works, a lifesize *Bacchus and Infant Satyr* (1496–97; Bargello, Florence). The group shows an interest in multiple points of view, perhaps growing out of the fifteenth-century tradition of Florentine freestanding sculpture, but in its subject and treatment it is purely antique. The general type is derived from ancient models (e.g., the *Bacchus and Satyr;* Museo Chiaramonti,

Sculpture court of the Galli collection, with *Bacchus* by Michelangelo surrounded by antiquities, drawing by M. van Heemskerck, Berlin, Kupferstichkabinett. (© Bildarchiv Preussischer Kulturbesitz, Berlin, 1994. Photo: J. P. Anders, 79 D 2.)

Vatican), and the modeling and proportional system seem to reflect Hadrianic sculpture (compare the Farnese *Antinous;* *Museo Nazionale, Naples).

Upon the artist's return to Florence in 1501, his work takes on a new monumentality, while his interest in the depiction of various kinds of movement (e.g., the so-called *figura serpentinata*) is intensified as a result of his experience of Roman antiquities, as well as through his study of the works of Leonardo da Vinci (who also returned to that city in 1501). This monumentality is seen most dramatically in the colossal marble *David* (1501–4; Accademia, Florence). The pose derives generally from a Hercules on a sarcophagus now in the Museo delle *Terme in Rome, although the surface treatment (e.g., the deep cutting) may result from careful study of the colossal *Quirinal *Horse Tamers* in Rome.

In 1504–5 Michelangelo was commissioned to paint the over-lifesize *Battle of Cascina* in the Florentine Council Hall. The fresco was never executed, but the cartoon (now lost; known primarily through Aristotile da Sangallo's grisaille copy of the central section; Norfolk, Holkham Hall) was celebrated for its depiction of a densely packed group of muscular nudes in elaborately varied twisting poses. In this sense, it was a monumental variant of his earlier *Battle of the Centaurs* and a presage of the much later *Last Judgment* (1534–41; Sistine Chapel, Vatican). The *Belvedere *Torso,* the Quirinal figures and an ancient gem showing a figure pulling on his hose have all been identified as ancient sources for the work. It has also been suggested that the artist reworked the figures in the cartoon after 1506, the year in which he witnessed the momentous discovery of the *Laocoon* group in Rome.

In the monuments of his maturity (both Florentine and Roman), Michelangelo's figure canon underwent changes, but his exploration of the human body was still largely guided by meditation on the great statuary of antiquity. The pronounced twist of the Belvedere *Torso,* for instance, was the basis for figures as diverse as the Adam of the Sistine Ceiling (1508–12; Sistine Chapel, Vatican), the figure of *Day* in the Medici Chapel (1519–33; San Lorenzo, Florence) and the St. Bartholomew of the *Last Judgment.* The so-called *Pasquino* in Rome was similarly the stimulus for his unfinished *St. Matthew* (1504–8; Accademia, Florence) as well as the *Rebellious Slave* (ca. 1514; Louvre, Paris), executed for the Tomb of Julius II, and the complex pose of the *Crouching Venus* gave him a model for his Mary of the *Last Judgment.* Throughout his maturity, he also continued to produce antique subjects using antique models; the *Brutus* of 1539–40 (Bargello, Florence), for instance, is based upon Roman busts of Caracalla.

Michelangelo's architecture also demonstrates familiarity with classical models (e.g., the *bucrania* and garlands in the Medici Chapel; or its trapezoidal windows, based on those of the temple of Vesta in *Tivoli), and he is said to have been quite knowledgeable about the text of Vitruvius. The incorporation of various motifs—a wolf-skin headdress, for example—in drawings, paintings and sculpture suggests the artist was also familiar with examples of Etruscan art. Ancient painting may have also provided some stimulus to him; in a preliminary schema for the Sistine Ceiling, he considered using a compartmentalized framework of the type found in the *Domus Aurea. One must finally mention such projects as the design of a base for the *Marcus Aurelius Equestrian Statue in Rome and the various restorations of antiquities (e.g., the Vatican Tiber; *Nile and Tiber) that he is said to have executed.

BIBLIOGRAPHY

+C. de Tolnay, Michelangelo, 1–5. (Princeton, NJ, 1943–60); +H. Hibbard, Michelangelo, 2nd ed. (Cambridge, MA, 1985); +Michelangelo e l'arte classica, catalog of exhibition (Florence, 1987).

ANDREA BOLLAND

MICHIEL, MARCANTONIO ("ANONIMO MORELLIANO"; 1484–1552). Venetian humanist and diarist.

Born at Venice of a noble family, Marcantonio Michiel is known to have traveled to Florence, Rome and Naples (1518–20), returning to serve as senator of the Venetian republic (1525–32). He kept travel notes and diaries and planned a major historical account of the figurative arts in Italy, but most of his labors went unpublished.

In 1800, the Abate Don Jacopo Morelli discovered a manuscript in the Biblioteca Marciana in Venice in which were recorded the works of art, both ancient and modern, to be seen in various churches, private collections and public places in Padua, Cremona, Milan, Bergamo and Venice. For some time scholars drew no conclusions about the author of the notes and referred to him only as the Anonimo Morelliano; the authorship of Michiel is now generally accepted.

The manuscript is a significant document of the number and kind of antiquities to be found in Venice and the surrounding region in the early sixteenth century. Most of the citations refer to private collections, the most valuable for archaeology being the list of antiquities owned by Pietro *Bembo at Padua. From Venice, there are descriptions of the sizable collections of Antonio Foscarini, Gabrieli Vendramino (who owned sculptures brought from *Rhodes) and Andrea di Odoni (who was portrayed with his antiquities by Lorenzo Lotto; 1527, Royal Collection, Hampton Court). In Pavia, the author records the *Regisole, and in Milan he notes the location of various ancient monuments, including a temple of Mars, a theater and amphitheaters. All in all, a wide range of antiquities is noted, including marble statues, reliefs, bronze statuettes, coins, gems, books (Bembo's *Vatican Vergil) and, surprisingly frequently, earthen vases (i.e., ancient pottery).

BIBLIOGRAPHY

G. C. Williamson, ed., The Anonimo, Notes on Pictures and Works of Art Made by the Anonymous Writer in the Sixteenth Century, tr. P. Mussi (1903; repr. New York, 1969).

MILETOS. City in Ionia (western Asia Minor) on the Maeander River, ca. 180km south of modern Izmir.

Greek tradition held that Miletos was initially settled by Cretans; at Troy the city fought under Carian leadership as Trojan allies. In the Archaic period Miletos was an important and prosperous Ionian harbor settlement, founding some ninety colonies in the Hellespont, sea of Marmara and Black Sea. It also gained fame as an intellectual center, numbering among its citizens the philosopher Thales and the town planner Hippodamos. Miletos led the Ionian revolt against Persian rule in 499 B.C., in retaliation for which it was destroyed in 494 B.C. following a battle off the island of Lade. The city surrendered to Alexander in 334 B.C. and subsequently came under Seleucid rule. It was incorporated into the Roman province of Asia in 129 B.C. Miletos was closely associated with the sanctuary of Apollo at *Didyma to the south, to which it was linked by a processional way.

Excavations have been conducted by a series of German expeditions beginning in 1899 under T. *Wiegand and currently in progress. The earliest settlement at Miletos dates to ca. 1600 B.C., representing Minoan, then Mycenaean occupation. By Archaic times the city was already laid out in the grid arrangement associated with Hippodamos. Important sanctuaries that continued to be rebuilt in Classical and Hellenistic times, such as the temples of Athena and Dionysos, were first constructed in the seventh–sixth centuries B.C.

Miletos was rebuilt after the destruction of 494 B.C. and expanded in Hellenistic times. Major monuments of the latter period include the agoras, bouleuterion, gymnasium, stadium and temple of Apollo Delphinios. In Roman times the theater was considerably enlarged and rebuilt. From this period also date the well-preserved Baths of Faustina, an extensive complex that adjoined a stadium and palaestra. One of the most spectacular results of the German campaigns was the removal of the sumptuous Roman gate of the South Market (second century A.C.) to Berlin, where it is one of the showpieces of the *Pergamon Museum.

To late antiquity and Byzantine times, respectively, belong the Serapeion (third century A.C.) and the Byzantine basilica of St. Michael and Bishop's Palace, built ca. A.D. 600 above the sanctuary of Dionysos.

BIBLIOGRAPHY
*T. Wiegand, ed., *Milet, Ergebnisse der Ausgrabungen und Untersuchungen seit dem Jahre 1899*, 1–18 (Berlin, 1906–73); +G. Kleiner, *Die Ruinen von Milet* (Berlin, 1968); +idem, *Das Römische Milet, Bilder aus der griechischen Stadt in römischer Zeit* (Frankfurt, 1969); +V. M. Strocka, *Das Markttor von Milet* (Berlin, 1981); W. Muller-Wiener, ed., *Milet 1899–1990, Ergebnisse, Probleme und Perspective einer Ausgrabung, IstMitt,* Beiheft 31 (1986).

                                                              ANN C. GUNTER

MILVIAN BRIDGE (PONS MULVIUS or MILVIUS). The northernmost and oldest surviving of ancient Rome's bridges across the Tiber River.

As the most important cross-water entry into the city, the Milvian Bridge has had an especially colorful history. The Pons Mulvius (from no later than the fourth century A.C.: Milvius) may have been constructed at the time when the Via Flaminia was built, 220 B.C., to provide access from Rome northward. Alternatively and since no Mulvius is recorded as a censor of the third century

B.C., it may have been built more than a century earlier for access to Etruscan *Veii, conquered by Rome in 396 B.C. In either case, its existence in 207 B.C., during the Second Punic War, is attested by Livy (27.51.2). Certainly wooden, it was superseded by a stone replacement contracted in 109 B.C. by the censor M. Aemilius Scaurus.

The bridge has been subjected to numerous repairs, due, in part, to flooding of the Tiber—a constant source of damage since it was first constructed—and, in part, to regular man-made destruction in time of war. Its strategic military importance was demonstrated plainly in the battle fought here by Constantine and Maxentius in A.D. 312. Damage during the Middle Ages was repaired by the Comune di Roma in 1152. After 1335, wood gangways replaced the stone arches (by then destroyed) at either end; these were replaced or refurbished often (five repairs are recorded between 1429 and 1584) until a full restoration in stone was undertaken by G. *Valadier in 1805. The bridge's new, small north-ernmost arch was blown up—and the bridge as a whole dismantled, to the arches and pylons—during Garibaldi's defense of the city in 1849. Temporary repairs were made shortly thereafter, and a total restoration was carried out in 1871. In spite of its checkered history, however, the core of today's Milvian Bridge remains original.

BIBLIOGRAPHY
J. Le Gall, *Le Tibre: Fleuve de Rome dans l'antiquité* (Paris, 1953), 86–91; C. D'Onofrio, *Il Tevere* (Rome, 1980), 166–97.

DAVID L. THOMPSON

MINNESOTA MESSENIA EXPEDITION. Innovative interdisciplinary project to explore the regional archaeology of Messenia in Southwest Greece.

Under the leadership of William A. McDonald, classical archaeologist from the University of Minnesota, the Minnesota Messenia Expedition was carried out from 1959 to 1968. Embracing a wide variety of research specialties with seventeen participating experts, the project focused originally on illuminating the regional context of *Pylos and was especially directed toward an understanding of the environment of Messenia in the Late Bronze Age (ca. 1600–1100 B.C.). In the tradition of the *Expédition scientifique de Morée,* the Minnesota project studied geology, metallurgy, geography, botany and zoology, as well as philology, history, social anthropology and other special areas, with appropriate attention given to surveying and mapping. The investigation of prehistoric and historic periods ultimately ranged from the Neolithic to modern times. The results were published in a volume edited by McDonald and geologist George R. Rapp, Jr., *The Minnesota Messenia Expedition, Reconstructing a Bronze Age Regional Environment* (Minneapolis, 1972).

From the regional survey the team moved to excavation of a specific site, Nichoria, discovered by McDonald in 1959 and excavated from 1969 to 1975 (including study seasons). The final report presents the results pertaining to Bronze Age, Dark Age and Byzantine occupation, retaining the interdisciplinary approach but putting some emphasis on the traditional pursuits of pottery analysis and architectural reconstruction.

BIBLIOGRAPHY

Excavations at Nichoria in Southwest Greece, 1, *Site Environs and Techniques,* ed. G. Rapp, Jr.—S. E. Aschenbrenner; 2, *The Bronze Age Occupation,* ed. W. A. McDonald—N. C. Wilkie; 3, *Dark Age and Byzantine Occupation,* ed. W. A. McDonald—W. D. E. Coulson—J. Rosser (Minneapolis, 1978, 1992, 1983); N. C. Wilkie—W. D. E. Coulson, eds., *Contributions to Aegean Archaeology, Studies in Honor of William A. McDonald* (Minneapolis, 1985), xiii–xx.

MIRABILIA URBIS ROMAE (ca. 1140).

MIRABILIA URBIS ROMAE (ca. 1140). An account of the antiquities of Rome, identified by Fabre and Duchesne as part of the "Polyptych" of papal lore and ceremony compiled between 1140 and 1143 by Benedict, canon of St. Peter's, at the behest of Cardinal Guido de Castello.

This traditionally accepted attribution has been questioned by Schimmelpfennig, though he did not disprove it. The *Mirabilia* is dated by internal evidence to before 1143, and its topographical indications correspond closely to those in the papal *Ordo* certainly compiled by Benedict at that time. An edition with excellent topographical annotations has been published by Valentini and Zucchetti.

The *Mirabilia urbis Romae* has three major parts: cc. 1–10, a list of monuments by categories (gates, palaces, etc.); cc. 11–12, 14–16, 18, legends about particular monuments; cc. 19–31, an itinerary. Part I is a kind of inventory, based on official documents including the fourth-century *Curiosum urbis,* revised and expanded with personal observation. Part II collects tales that reveal the portentous origins or latent Christian meaning of conspicuous monuments and sites; for example, the steeds of the *Quirinal *Horse Tamers* represent worldly power, and they are riderless to signify that "a most powerful king will come and mount on them, that is upon the power of the princes of this world" (c. 12); the *Pantheon was dedicated to Cybele, *mater deorum,* foreshadowing its rededication by Pope Boniface to Mary, *mater omnium sanctorum* (c. 16). Part III, the itinerary, follows a walkable path around the city, proceeding from the Vatican and ending again in Trastevere. It describes the ancient, not the present, Rome, for example: "[O]n the Esquiline hill was the temple of Marius, which now is called *Cimbrum* . . . where S. Maria Maggiore is, was a temple of Cybele. Where S. Pietro in Vincoli is, was a temple of Venus" (c. 28). The purpose is to record "for the memory of future generations, how beautiful were [the ancient buildings], in gold and silver, bronze and ivory and more precious stones" (c. 32). The itinerary is an imaginative reconstruction based on empirical and archival research, using the evidence of "the oldest annals and our own eyes . . . and . . . what we heard from the ancients" (c. 32). The author's written sources included Ovid's *Fasti* and the *passiones* of the saints (cc. 8, 21, 24).

The importance of the *Mirabilia urbis Romae* is threefold: first, although it is not always certain which buildings stood and which were hypothetical, it is

an excellent source for the topography and toponymy of medieval Rome. Second, it gives evidence of the origins and character of the much-discussed twelfth-century interest in Roman antiquities. Unlike Magister *Gregorius, the author of the *Mirabilia* was not a humanist. His audience likewise was not confined to learned classicists but included simple pilgrims, citizens and local bureaucrats. The *Mirabilia* was among the official documents of the papal curia (witness its inclusion in the *Liber censuum* of 1192), but it also was copied with a diversity of texts for other users (e.g., the *Graphia aureae urbis,* ca. 1155; Cambrai, Bibl. munic. 554 [with the letters of Ivo of Chartres]; Vat. lat. 3973 [with the Chronicle of Romuald of Salerno]). The third importance of the *Mirabilia* is as the source of a tradition of Roman guidebooks. Translated into Italian in the thirteenth century (Valentini and Zucchetti, III, 111–136), it was copied repeatedly, with variations, for the next 200 years (*guidebooks to Rome [to 1500]).
BIBLIOGRAPHY
P. Fabre—L. Duchesne, *Le Liber censuum de l'eglise romaine* 1 (Paris, 1910), 1–4, 32–35, 97–104, 262–83; R. Valentini—G. Zucchetti, III, 3–65; M. Adriani, "Paganesimo e cristianesimo nei *Mirabilia urbis Romae,*" *Studi Romani* 8 (1960), 535–52; B. Schimmelpfennig, *Die Zeremonienbücher der römischen Kurie im Mittelalter* (Tübingen 1973), 4–16.

                                                                                    DALE KINNEY

MISANO. See MARZABOTTO.

MITHRAEUM OF SAN CLEMENTE, Rome. Ritual building for the worship of the god Mithras dating to the early third century A.C., lying underneath the church of San Clemente, ca. 400m from the *Colosseum in Rome.

The Basilica of San Clemente preserves at least four superposed levels of pagan and Christian monuments. The lowest, ca. 19m below ground level, comprises the remains of an unidentified structure (perhaps a warehouse), evidently destroyed in the Neronian fire (A.D. 64) and later filled in to serve as foundations for subsequent construction. Adjacent to this structure was built a private house in the late first century A.C., in the courtyard of which there came to be erected, in the late second or early third century, a shrine dedicated to the mystery cult of Mithras.

The Mithraic complex, discovered in 1869, had three known components: a dining room (*triclinium*) fitted with benches and containing a marble altar carved with Mithraic scenes, probably the setting for ritual banquets; a vestibule with graceful floral and geometric stucco decorations; and a hall with seven niches, perhaps for instructional purposes, corresponding to the levels an initiate passed before admittance to the central mysteries of the cult.

By A.D. 384, a church had been built next to the Mithraeum, evidently in the belief that the residence of the saint (martyred in A.D. 97) was preserved in the first-century house. Sometime after the prohibition of Mithraism in 395, the Christian structure was extended by construction of an apse over the former

Mithraic shrine. The fourth-century basilica remained in use until filled in during the twelfth century, when construction of the current church began. Its underlying levels were gradually forgotten.

Major excavations were undertaken first by Father Joseph Mullooly (1857–70) and then by Father Louis Nolan (1912–14). Due to seeping water, it was not possible for many years to excavate the Mithraeum properly. In 1912–14, a tunnel was built to divert the water to a large sewer near the Colosseum, thus facilitating exploration in the various components of the site.

BIBLIOGRAPHY

J. Mullooly, *St. Clement Pope and Martyr and His Basilica in Rome,* 2nd ed. (Rome, 1873); L. Nolan, *The Basilica of St. Clement's in Rome* (Rome, 1934); F. Guidobaldi, *Il Complesso archeologico di San Clemente: Risultati degli scavi più recenti e riesame dei resti architettonici* (Rome, 1978); +Nash, I, 353–56; II, 74–78; F. Guidobaldi, *San Clemente: Gli Edifici romani, la basilica paleocristiana e le fasi altomedievali* (Rome, 1992).

DAVID L. THOMPSON

MOCHLOS. Bronze Age Aegean site, located on the north coast of *Crete at the eastern edge of the Bay of Mirabello.

Like *Gournia and several neighboring sites in eastern Crete, Mochlos was occupied from the Early Bronze Age until the destructions that occurred in the Late Minoan (LM) IB period. It was reoccupied in LM III and then again in the Late Hellenistic and Early Byzantine periods. It was particularly important in two periods, the Prepalatial and LM IB. In the Prepalatial period, Mochlos was a rich and well-populated center engaged in many of the activities that were promoting the rise of civilization in Crete. In the LM IB period, it flourished again as a second-order administrative center controlling the resources of the adjacent coastal plain on Crete. A layer of volcanic tephra found in 1989 beneath the LM IB settlement disproved once and for all the theory that the eruption of the volcano on Santorini (*Thera) destroyed Minoan civilization.

The site was excavated in 1908 by Richard *Seager under the auspices of the *American School of Classical Studies in Athens. In the 1970s cleaning and survey work were carried out on the site, and in 1989 excavations resumed under the direction of Jeffrey Soles for the American School and Costis Davaras for the *Greek Archaeological Service.

BIBLIOGRAPHY

R. Seager, *Explorations on the Island of Mochlos* (Boston, 1912); J. Soles, *Prepalatial Cemeteries at Mochlos and Gournia, Hesperia* Suppl. 24 (Princeton, NJ, 1992); J. Soles—C. Davaras, ''Excavations at Mochlos, 1989,'' *Hesperia* 61 (1992), 413–45; +*Aerial Atlas of Crete* 186–93; J. Soles—C. Davaras, ''Excavations at Mochlos, 1990–1991,'' *Hesperia,* 63 (1994), 391–436.

JEFFREY S. SOLES

MOMMSEN, THEODOR (1817–1903). Renowned German historian of ancient Rome and greatest Latin epigraphist.

Portrait of *Theodor Mommsen*, steel engraving by L. Jacoby, 1862. (Westfälisches Landesmuseum für Kunst und Kulturgeschichte, Münster, Porträtarchiv Diepenbroick. Photo: R. Wakonigg.)

After six years of study at Kiel (1838–44), where he specialized in law and Latin epigraphy and became Doctor Iuris, Mommsen used two grants to travel in France and (mostly) Italy (1844–47). He did two stints of teaching at a girls' private school in Altona, then professed successively civil law at Leipzig (which dismissed him in 1851 for his political views and activities in the revolutionary movements of 1848–49), Roman law at Zurich, then at Breslau and finally went to Berlin (1858), where he professed ancient history (1861–1903). From 1850 on, his enormous output (Zangemeister/Jacobs's bibliography lists 1,513 items) was divided between Roman history and Latin inscriptions. His major works in history were his *Römische Geschichte,* volumes 1–3, 5 (1854–56, 1885—vol. 4, on the empire, never appeared—vol. 5 being on the provinces) and the *Römisches Staatsrecht* (Roman Public Law), three volumes (1871–87, partly in a 3rd ed.), supplemented by many other works on Roman chronology, coinage, criminal law, ancient South Italian dialects and so on, and by editions of later historians and legal sources. After editing the Latin inscriptions of the kingdom of Naples (1852) and those of Switzerland (1854), he succeeded after many years of frustration in founding the *Corpus Inscriptionum Latinarum (CIL,* 1862–) and was its most productive editor. He touched nothing that he did not adorn, and his *Roman History,* marked by passion and a deep sense of politics, won him the Nobel Prize in literature, 1902. But the codicil of his will (1899), published 1948, reveals him as disappointed in his career despite its outer success: "Ich habe in meinem Leben trotz meiner äusseren Erfolge nicht das Rechte erreicht" (In my life, despite my outer success, I have not attained what was right for me).

His personal appearance was strikingly recorded by Mark Twain, who referred to Mommsen's "long hair and Emersonian face" as seen at a banquet in Berlin. A grandson, Theodor Ernst Mommsen (1905–58), professed medieval history at Princeton, then at Cornell.

BIBLIOGRAPHY

G. Highet, *The Classical Tradition* (New York, 1949), 474–77; +L. Wickert, *Theodor Mommsen, Eine Biographie*, 1–4 (Frankfurt am Main, 1959–80); A. Demandt, "Theodor Mommsen," in Briggs—Calder, 285–309.

†ARTHUR E. GORDON

MONTEFELTRE (MONTEFELTRO), FEDERIGO DA (1422–82). Duke of Urbino, captain of mercenaries, promoter of art and humanistic and classical studies.

A bastard son of the house of Montefeltre, count of Urbino in the province of Marche, Federigo was educated in the famous "school for princes" run by Vittorino da Feltre; a condottiere of rising fame with an eye for modern warfare, he unexpectedly succeeded to the realm in 1444. In Urbino he developed a government of justice and security based on philosophy, soon considered a model. Owing to his continued successful military career, which brought him considerable wealth and high awards (for instance, the English Order of the Garter), Federigo was raised to a duke by Pope *Sixtus IV in 1474.

The flow of cash from Italian princes helped turn Urbino into a center for art, education and humanism. The very center of learning was the ducal library, established and managed without regard to expenses and containing manuscripts in Latin, Greek and Hebrew. Numerous scribes were employed at other libraries, keeping Urbino informed of acquisitions, new treatises and so on. The library served the group of philologists and antiquarians connected with the ducal court, and Federigo promoted studies and translations of ancient authors, mythology and ancient history and collected classical antiquities, too. In the planning of the famous palace (by L. Laurana), in the decorational schemes and names of rooms, mythology and ancient history were given a central place. Classical motifs and iconography based on ancient sculpture were used in the adornment of the palace and to illuminate the virtues of the duke and his wife, Battista Sforza, in the celebrated portraits and triumphal paintings of the pair made by Piero della Francesca (Uffizi, Florence).

The spirit and activities of Federigo's court were re-created by Baldassare Castiglione in his *Il Cortegiano*. The work actually was written to refer to Federigo's cultivated but unsoldierly son Guidobaldo, who lost the realm to the upstart papal Borgia dynasty in 1502. The library and art collections were looted and dispersed, but the major part was secured by the Vatican library.

BIBLIOGRAPHY
J. Dennistoun, *Memoirs of the Duke of Urbino* (London, 1851); G. Santi, *Federigo da Montefeltre, Duca di Urbino,* ed. H. Holtzinger (Stuttgart, 1893); W. Bombe, *Die Kunst am Hofe Federigos von Urbino* (Leipzig, 1914).

CHRISTOFFER H. ERICSSON

MONTELIUS, OSCAR (1843–1921). Swedish archaeologist.

Montelius was much influenced by the ideas of Darwin and the Danish scholars C. J. *Thomsen and J. J. Worsaae, who introduced the principles of relative chronology within archaeology and who proposed the division of prehistory into Stone Age, Bronze Age and Iron Age. Montelius's pioneering contribution was to apply these theories to Scandinavian, as well as to Mediterranean, archaeology and, as director of the Museum of National Antiquities in Stockholm, to develop a strong tradition of archaeological research in Sweden. Through excavations in different parts of Sweden, he determined the importance of stratigraphic analysis, from which he established a sequence of subdivisions within the Stone Age and the Bronze Age, based on a detailed classification of the finds.

Although the validity of the Three-Age system developed by Montelius has been questioned in recent years, archaeologists continue to recognize his role in establishing systems of typological analysis. Of his almost 400 published writings, the fundamental work on Scandinavian archaeology, *The Civilization of Sweden in Heathen Times* (first published in Swedish in 1873), and the presentation of material from Italy, *La Civilisation primitive en Italy* (1895–1910), have remained invaluable research tools.

BIBLIOGRAPHY
+B. Salin, "Minnesteckning över Oscar Montelius," *Kungl. Vitterhets Historie och Antikvitets Akademiens Handlingar* 34, III F., part 1:2 (Stockholm, 1922); G. Daniel, *The Origins and Growth of Archaeology* (New York, 1967), 86, 112–13; +E. W. Wetter et al., *Med kungen på Acquarossa* (Malmö, 1972), 13, 27.

INGRID E. M. EDLUND

MONTFAUCON, BERNARD DE (1655–1741). French Benedictine monk, compiler of monumental scholarly works on Greek paleography, classical archaeology and other subjects.

Born at the chateau of Soulage (Languedoc), the young Montfaucon served for two years in the army before entering the Benedictine order of Saint-Maur at Toulouse in 1675. His early travels included a three-year stay in Italy (1698–1701), described in his *Diarium italicum* (1702), which includes a full survey of the topography of Rome. He was to spend the rest of his life at the abbey of Saint-Germain-des-Prés and there produce the numerous ambitious folio volumes that made him one of the most influential of all Benedictine scholars. At the age of eighty-five he noted that the key to his great learning and productivity lay in the fact that for the last forty-six years of his life he regularly spent thirteen or fourteen hours a day writing or studying.

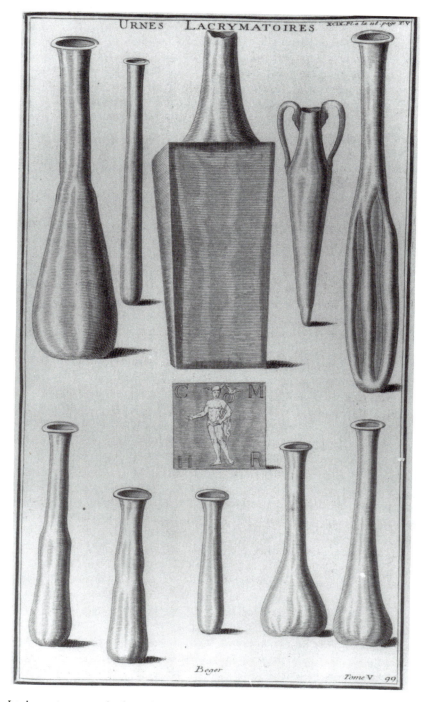

Lachrymatory vessels, from B. de Montfaucon, *L'Antiquité expliquée et represen-*
tée en figures 5 (1719–24). (The Warburg Institute, University of London.)

The range of Montfaucon's learning was wide, embracing the Greek fathers, Greek paleography, French civil and ecclesiastical archaeology and classical antiquities. His enduring place in the history of scholarship is secured, above all, by his *Palaeographia graeca* (1708), which laid the foundation for Greek paleography as a new science, and his *L'Antiquité expliquée et representée en figures,* issued in ten folio volumes with a five-volume supplement (1719–24). An English translation was promptly issued (1721–22).

L'Antiquité expliquée contains some 1,200 plates with around 40,000 figures, illustrating statues, reliefs, coins, gems, buildings, ground plans, utensils, mosaics, bronze statuettes, lamps, armor and other antiquities. Some of the illustrations were culled by Montfaucon from previous publications, but many were previously unpublished. In general, the illustrations in *L'Antiquité expliquée* have been much criticized. On occasion he reproduced the same object twice, not realizing that two authors had illustrated it very differently. In addition, many of the drawings he ordered himself were not made carefully.

For twenty-six years he gathered material for the work, not only in Rome and elsewhere in Italy but in many private collections in France and from his various correspondents. He utilized unpublished manuscripts of *Peiresc as well as many of the best books of the late seventeenth and early eighteenth centuries. Among his preferred authorities were *Spon, *Beger, S. *Maffei, *Boissart and de la *Chausse.

Montfaucon's mission in preparing his corpus was, first of all, to provide a context for reading ancient authors, particularly the Greek fathers. He noted that many passages were easily understood if only the appropriate antiquities were known. A further purpose was to present a kind of course on antiquities that could be completed in two years. He lamented the proliferation of publications, many of them too specialized, and expressed the hope that *L'Antiquité expliquée* would provide a concise, yet comprehensive survey for those who wished to be educated regarding antiquities.

The work is organized by the Benedictine monk so that it begins with the gods, recounting their myths and noting their attributes, with appropriate illustrations. His treatment is noteworthy for its rejection of the viewpoint that the pagan gods should be appreciated for their symbolic or allegorical significance, an attitude seen in the earlier publications of *Cartari, *Alciati and various French authors of the seventeenth century. The second major segment of the corpus deals generally with religion, while the third features every aspect of daily life—clothing, houses, vessels, games, marriage, theaters, amphitheaters, the Seven Wonders of the World. Section 4 covers military antiquities, and Section 5 has to do with death and burial as well as customs of punishment. Each segment takes up two volumes of the original publication, while the supplement provides five more volumes that follow the same sequence.

The antiquities included are not only Greek and Roman but also Egyptian, Arabic, Persian, Scythian, German, Gallic and Carthaginian. Chronologically, Montfaucon does not go beyond ca. A.D. 450. Though there had been earlier ambitious and encyclopedic works in archaeology—the *Thesauri* of *Graevius and J. Gronovius (*Gronovius family), the "Paper Museum" of Cassiano dal *Pozzo—they lacked the cultural range and unified concept of *L'Antiquité expliquée*.

BIBLIOGRAPHY

B. Haureau, "Montfaucon, Bernard de," *NBG* 36 (1861), cols. 223–29; Stark, 111, 143–46; Sandys, II, 385–89; *Porträtarchiv,* no. 51; J. Y. Boriaud, "Bernard de Montfaucon, *L'Antiquité expliquée et representée en figures,*" in *L'Antiquité gréco-romaine vue par le siècle des lumières,* ed. R. Chevallier (Tours, 1987), 13–22.

"MONUMENTAL PHILOLOGY."

Term used by *Wilamowitz to describe the archaeological interests of Otto *Jahn.

Wilamowitz meant "the bringing together of the literary sources with the monuments for the elucidation of both" (Schindler). This differs from art history because there is no interest in the artifact *as such*. Thus, Eduard *Gerhard would dismiss a vase or bronze with "It's only beautiful" and, therefore, unimportant. Jahn influenced early Wilamowitz and Carl *Robert (*Bild und Lied*). The tradition persists in Schefold, *Wort und Bild* (Basel, 1975). *Kekulé rejected Jahn to stress the beauty of the object. His archaeology became art history in *Winckelmann's sense but to which was added "the science of ancient monuments."

The term is occasionally employed to mean the use of philological method in archaeological research, for example, the re-creation of a lost Greek bronze on the basis of later copies and testimonia.

BIBLIOGRAPHY

W. Schindler, "Archäologie: Wilamowitz' Interdisziplinäre Konzeption," in *Wilamowitz nach 50 Jahren,* ed. W. M. Calder III—H. Flashar (Darmstadt, 1985), 244–45.

WILLIAM M. CALDER III

MONUMENT OF LYSIKRATES, Athens.

The only more or less fully preserved Greek choregic monument of the many that lined Pausanias's Street of Tripods on the eastern side of the *Akropolis in Athens.

An inscription on the architrave indicates that it was built by a certain Lysikrates in 335/4 B.C. in honor of his victory as *choregos* for a boys' chorus; the whole ornate marble building supported the prize tripod, which stood on the roof. The building takes the form of a circular monument on a tall, square base and consists of six Corinthian columns, supporting an architrave and sculptured frieze, with the spaces between them filled in with curved slabs of marble. The building is significant as one of the earliest uses of the Corinthian order and is the only Athenian Corinthian monument with a sculptured frieze.

The monument was popularly known well into the nineteenth century as the "Lantern of Demosthenes" or the "Lantern of Diogenes," the former name recorded as early as 1460. However, it was *Spon who first correctly identified its use in his publication of 1676. In 1669 the monument was built into a Capuchin monastery, and the hollow interior was used variously as a chamber,

Monument of Lysikrates, prior to its separation from the Capuchin Monastery, Athens, engraving from J. Stuart–N. Revett, *The Antiquities of Athens* 1 (1762).

library or study, as can be seen in the drawings by *Stuart and *Revett in 1751 and by *Dodwell in 1805. At least one source from 1851 records that *Byron used the little building as a study and that his name could be seen scratched on one of the panels. The monastery was destroyed in the Greek War of Independence, but the monument survived and was consolidated, preserved and restored by French archaeologists beginning in 1845. The work was completed in 1892.

BIBLIOGRAPHY

J. Stuart—N. Revett, *The Antiquities of Athens* 1 (London, 1762), 27–36; +L. Matton—R. Matton, *Athènes et ses monuments* (Athens, 1963), 141–44; H. Bauer, "Lysikrates-denkmal, Baubestand und Rekonstruktion," *AM* 92 (1977), 197–227. Travlos, 348–51.

WILLIAM R. BIERS

MONUMENT OF PHILOPAPPOS, Athens. Monumental Roman tomb erected on the Mouseion Hill, ca. A.D. 114–16, in honor of Caius Julius Antiochus Epiphanes Philopappos, grandson of Antiochus IV of Commagene, Roman suffect consul of A.D. 109 and Athenian archon.

The tomb housed a portrait of Philopappos and his sarcophagus. The façade faces the *Akropolis and is carved with a scene representing Philopappos in his consular procession. Three niches contained the seated portrait statues of Philopappos, Antiochus IV and Seleukos Nikator (the last now lost).

The tomb was described by Pausanias in the second century A.C. and was first sketched in 1436 by *Ciriaco of Ancona. His drawing, with some alterations, is preserved in an early sixteenth-century copy by Giuliano da *Sangallo. During the Renaissance, the tomb was described by other Italian travelers, including the Venetian Anonymous. Seventeenth-century visitors who sketched the tomb include Jacob *Spon and George *Wheler. During a siege of the Akropolis in 1687, the monument was struck by a Turkish projectile, which, however, did little damage.

The first meticulous scale drawings and a hypothetical reconstruction of the monument were prepared by *Stuart and *Revett (1794). In the nineteenth century the Mouseion Hill was visited by Lord *Byron and John Cam *Hobhouse, and an almost photographic record of the tomb was painted by G. B. *Lusieri.

In 1898, Andreas Skias excavated the area around the monument, and Nicholas Balanos consolidated the remains and restored portions of the façade. In 1947, Santangelo published the first major study of the monument and attempted to reconstruct the tomb. New evidence for the original form of the tomb was also uncovered in the 1940s by the excavations of Homer Thompson and John Travlos. The results of those excavations and a new reconstruction were published by Kleiner in 1983.

BIBLIOGRAPHY

J. Stuart—N. Revett, *The Antiquities of Athens* 3 (London, 1794), 35–39; +M. Santangelo, "Il monumento di C. Julius Antiochos Philopappos in Atene," *ASAtene* N.S. 3–5 (1941–43) [1947], 153–253; Travlos, 462–65; +D. E. E. Kleiner, *The Monument of Philopappos in Athens, Archaeologica* 30 (Rome, 1983); idem, "Athens Under the Romans: The Patronage of Emperors and Kings," *Rome and the Provinces: Studies in the Transformation of Art and Architecture in the Mediterranean World,* ed. C. B. Mc-Clendon (New Haven, CT, 1986), 8–20; idem, *Roman Sculpture,* 533–35.

DIANA E. E. KLEINER

MONUMENT OF THE JULII, St-Rémy. Monumental three-story Roman cenotaph, consisting of a socle with four great relief panels, a *quadrifrons* arch and a *monopteros,* erected ca. 30–20 B.C. just outside Glanum (*Glanon) by three sons of Caius Julius, a Romanized Gaul, in honor of their *parentes,* probably the father and the grandfather, whose (now headless) portrait statues are housed in the *monopteros.*

One of the best preserved monuments of the classical world, it is, together with the neighboring *Arch at St-Rémy, the emblem of St-Rémy-de-Provence. In the Middle Ages it had already given its name to the chapel of Saint-Pierre-de-Mausole (*ecclesia Sancti Petri ad Mausoleum,* 1080) and to the monastery of Saint-Paul-de-Mausole (*Sancti Pauli Mausolei,* 1117). The monument is first recorded in its own right in a 1521 manuscript of Andréas *Alciatus and was extensively described in verse by Pierre Rivarel in 1609. The monument is treated frequently in the antiquarian literature of the seventeenth, eighteenth and early nineteenth centuries and was a popular subject for drawings, prints and paintings (e.g., by Jean-Honoré Fragonard in 1760 and Hubert *Robert in 1787). The great relief panels have figured prominently in discussions by *Wickhoff, Sieveking, *Bianchi Bandinelli and many others of the "pictorial" nature of Roman relief sculpture.

BIBLIOGRAPHY

+H. Rolland, *Le Mausolée de Glanum, Gallia* suppl. 21 (Paris, 1969); F. S. Kleiner, "Artists in the Roman World, An Itinerant Workshop in Augustan Gaul," *MEFRA* 89 (1977), 661–96; idem, "The Glanum Cenotaph Reliefs, Greek or Roman?" *BonnJbb* 180 (1980), 105–26; P. Gros, "Note sur deux reliefs des 'Antiques' de Glanum," *Revue Archéologique de Narbonnaise* 14 (1981), 159–72.

FRED S. KLEINER

MONUMENTUM ANCYRANUM. The ruined temple of Roma and Augustus in Ankara, capital of Turkey (ancient Ancyra, capital of Roman Galatia), which is inscribed on the exterior with a copy of the *Res Gestae* ("Things Accomplished") of Augustus, along with a Greek version.

The Latin text was rediscovered by A. G. Busbee, and its rediscovery made known in the West by the Jesuit Andreas Schott in 1555, but the reading of the complete Greek version had to wait until the nineteenth century and the destruction of the house walls that had partly concealed it, by a team from the *French School in Athens, led by G. Perrot. Access to the inscriptions is restricted, the temple now belonging to the adjoining mosque. The Latin is a copy, with a few slips, of the inscription ordered by Augustus to be cut on bronze tablets after his death (19 August A.D. 14), to be set up in front of his *Mausoleum in Rome

(Suet. *Aug.* 101.1 and 4). (The original bronzes no longer exist.) It is one of the longest Latin inscriptions extant.

BIBLIOGRAPHY

T. Mommsen, ed., *Res Gestae Divi Augusti,* 2nd ed. (Berlin, 1883, repr. Aalen, 1970); D. Krencker—M. Schede, *Der Tempel in Ankara* (Berlin, 1936); E. Akurgal, *Ancient Civilizations and Ruins of Turkey,* 2nd ed., tr. J. Whybrow—M. Emre (Istanbul, 1970), 284–87; A. E. Gordon, *Illustrated Introduction to Latin Epigraphy* (Berkeley, 1983), inscr. no. 34.

†ARTHUR E. GORDON

MORGANTINA (SERRA ORLANDO). Greek city of central *Sicily.

Originally a settlement of native Sikels, Morgantina had become a Greek city with an orthogonal ground plan by the fifth century B.C. The agora reached its zenith in the third century B.C., when Morgantina served as an outpost of Hieron II of *Syracuse (269–215 B.C.). Two granaries flanking the agora testify to the role of Morgantina as a center in a grain-producing area; also present are stoas and a theater. The agora was on two levels, with a monumental stairway in the shape of a segment of a hexagon joining the two areas (third century B.C.). In 212 B.C., Morgantina was devastated in connection with the sack of Syracuse by Marcellus, and it never fully recovered. Habitation did continue, as indicated by the presence of kilns of the Late Hellenistic period in the agora, which now was used for the manufacture of tiles and pottery.

Excavations at the site of Serra Orlando were begun by Princeton University in 1955 under the direction of R. *Stillwell and E. Sjøqvist, with emphasis on the agora area. On the basis of coins, Serra Orlando was identified as Morgantina by K. *Erim. The excavation was continued by H. A. Allen of the University of Illinois. After a pause of nine years, work was resumed in 1980 under the direction of Malcolm Bell III of the University of Virginia. His efforts gave priority to the need to publish material from the early years, resulting in volumes on the terracottas (by Bell), the coins (T. V. Buttrey and others) and the late Hellenistic kilns (N. Cuomo di Caprio). In 1984 the Morgantina Museum was opened in the town of Aidone, not far from the site.

BIBLIOGRAPHY

R. Stillwell, s.v. ''Morgantina,'' *PECS,* 594–95; *Morgantina Studies* 1–4 (Princeton, NJ, 1981–93); S. Raffiotta, *Morgantina, la storia e i resti di un'antica città di Sicilia* (Palermo, 1985); +M. Bell III, ''Excavations at Morgantina, 1980–85: Preliminary Report XII,'' *AJA* 92 (1988), 313–42.

MOROSINI, FRANCESCO (1618–94). Venetian sea captain and statesman; archaeologists inevitably associate him with the ruin of the *Parthenon in Athens.

From the age of eighteen to seventy-eight, Morosini was constantly at sea, campaigning especially in Greece against the Turkish domination. In 1645 he participated in the capture of the island of *Melos, and in 1654 he seized *Aigina, which remained Venetian until 1718. In 1685–87 he reconquered the Peloponnese, receiving the honorific name "Peloponnesiaco"; it remained under Venice until 1715.

Morosini captured Athens in 1687, holding it for a year. But on 26 September 1687, a German officer in his force fired a mortar at the Parthenon, which the Turks were using as a powder magazine. The explosion blew off the roof, destroyed much of the interior and hurled down some fourteen columns. Morosini added to the damage by trying to remove some statues from the west pediment; these fell and were shattered.

Morosini was elected doge of Venice in 1688 and is commemorated by a "Morosini Fountain" in Herakleion, *Crete.

BIBLIOGRAPHY

Z. Morosini, *Francesco Morosini Peloponnesiaco* (Venice, 1845); L. Damerini, *Francesco Morosini* (Milan, 1932); A. Sacconi, *L'Avventura archeologica di Francesco Morosini ad Atene (1687–1688)* (Rome, 1991).

MORTIMER CHAMBERS

MUFFEL, NICOLAUS (dates unknown). German noble from Nuremberg; visitor to Rome in the fifteenth century.

Little is known of the life of Nicolaus Muffel. He has left an account of the city of Rome ("Beschreibung der Stadt Rom") made as a result of his trip to the city in 1452 to celebrate the coronation of Frederick III as Holy Roman Emperor. According to R. Valentini and G. Zucchetti the description is unsophisticated for its time, lacking in the humanistic spirit that had begun to permeate the accounts of Rome by Italians and even of foreigners like John *Capgrave.

Muffel has the interests of a pilgrim, detailing the number of indulgences available at various sites, and he has the credulity as well, since he is ready to believe such tales as that of the popess Johanna, who supposedly betrayed her identity as a woman by giving birth on the streets of Rome. The *Belvedere *Pigna* is said to have been carried by demons from Troy to Constantinople and from Constantinople to Rome; nevertheless, Muffel does speak of the beauty of the cast bronze of the pinecone, and its attendant peacocks are duly admired. The *Colosseum is described well, with references to its three orders, except that he repeats the fantastic medieval legend that over the place hung a great mirror, in which were reflected all the affairs of the world. Several antiquarian details are unique to Muffel's account: the *Pantheon is the temple of Diana and of a deity called Pantheon, a god of the sea; one of the Tiber bridges is referred to as the Lightning Bridge, because an emperor was struck by lightning there.

Muffel quotes few authors from antiquity—only Pliny the Elder, Vergil and the Acts of the Apostles. To his credit, he used the *De varietate fortunae* of *Poggio Bracciolini, incorporating some of its more reliable material on the topography of Rome.

BIBLIOGRAPHY
Valentini—Zucchetti, IV, 354–73; Weiss, *RDCA,* 75–76.

MÜLLER, KARL OTFRIED (1797–1840). German classicist with important publications in philology, archaeology, mythology, history, art history; major figure in classical scholarship in the nineteenth century.

Born at Brieg (Silesia), a pastor's son, Müller studied at Breslau, where Niebuhr's *Roman History* won him for classics, and at Berlin under Schleiermacher, Buttmann and especially *Böckh, who taught him a comprehensive approach to antiquity and whose greatest student he became. In his epoch-making dissertation on *Aigina from antiquity to the Frankish period (1817), he had already perfected his method of exploiting every sort of evidence to reconstruct antiquity in its totality. In 1819, at age twenty-two, Müller succeeded *Welcker at Göttingen as associate professor (*Extraordinarius*) for philology and archaeology. He lectured on archaeology, mythology, history of religion, comparative grammar of Greek and Latin and, once, modern art history. A flood of great books ensued, for example: *Orchomenos und die Minyer* (1820); *Die Dorier* (1824); *Mythologie* (1825); *De Phidiae vita et operibus* (1827) on the *Elgin marbles; *Die Etrusker* (1828); *Handbuch der Archäologie der Kunst* (1830), translated into French and English and still exemplary for coverage and exactitude; Aischylos, *Eumenides* (1835), which inaugurated the study of *scenic antiquities; *Antiquitates Antiochenae* (1839), where Müller reconstructed from literary sources the topography of Antioch so accurately that the book served as guide to the Princeton excavators a century later. His editions of Varro, *De lingua Latina* and Festus grew from his Etruscan interests. His *History of Greek Literature to Alexander* appeared posthumously. In 1839 he visited Italy and Greece and fell mortally ill at *Delphi while transcribing inscriptions. He died in Athens, attended by his student Ernst *Curtius, and was buried at Colonus.

In breadth of competence only *Mommsen and *Wilamowitz compare. His books remain models of historical research based on all available evidence (literary, archaeological, epigraphical, numismatic) and anticipate modern masterpieces like Oldfather's *Lokris,* Downey's *Antioch* and Fraser's *Alexandria.* Unlike Böckh, he urged autopsy of monuments. He was the first great German classicist to visit England, and his important works were early translated. His preference for history by "tribes" innocently influenced later irresponsible racist theory. His *Dorians* and *Etruscans* were used by Nazi ideologists to argue Nordic superiority and anti-Semitism. A dedicated, restless, brilliant fanatic, in two decades—by books, not students—Müller permanently changed European classical scholarship.

BIBLIOGRAPHY
S. Reiter, *Carl Otfried Müller: Briefe aus einem Gelehrtenleben 1797–1840,* 1–2. (Berlin, 1950); K. Hillebrand, "Otfried Müller und die historische Schule der deutschen Philologie," *Unbekannte Essays,* ed. H. Uhde-Bernays (Bern, 1955), 184–241; P. Janni, "Ro-

manticismo e mito della 'Doricità': Karl Otfried Müller,'' *Studi Germaniei* NS 6.3 (1968), 13–43; W. Unte, "Karl Otfried Müller,'' *Schlesien* 25 (1980), 9–21; A. Momigliano et al., "Seminario su K. O. Müller,'' *Annali della Scuola Normale Superiore di Pisa, Classe di Lettere e Filosofia* 3, 14 (1984), 893–1226; H. Döhl in *Archäologenbildnisse*, 23–24; W. Unte, "Karl Otfried Müller,'' in Briggs-Calder, 310–20.

WILLIAM M. CALDER III

MURLO. Italian village south of Siena; on the Poggio Civitate nearby are the remains of an early Etruscan site, not known from written sources, in the territory later dominated by *Chiusi.

Excavations started in 1966 by an American team from Bryn Mawr College have so far revealed a long building with terracotta decorations of early type, destroyed by fire at the end of the seventh century B.C. and covered by a larger complex surrounding a square porticoed yard, dated ca. 590 to 525 B.C.—after which date the site appears totally abandoned. The rich terracotta decoration includes a large number of akroterial seated statues; the small finds include gemstones, bronze figurines, carved ivories and Greek pottery of rare fabrics, which seem to give weight to the excavators' identification of the site as a (possibly federal) religious-political center; this interpretation is challenged by those scholars who prefer to see it as the "palace" or residence of a local aristocrat.

BIBLIOGRAPHY

K. M. Phillips, Jr.,—E. Nielsen, *AJA* 1967 onward; *NSc* (1976), 113–47 and (1983, pub. 1986), 5–24; +*Poggio Civitate (Murlo, Siena), The Archaic Sanctuary,* catalog of exhibition (Florence, 1970); K. M. Phillips, Jr., *In the Hills of Tuscany* (Philadelphia, 1993).

F. R. SERRA RIDGWAY

MUSÉE NATIONAL DU LOUVRE. See LOUVRE MUSEUM.

MUSEO ARQUEOLÓGICO NACIONAL, Madrid. Spain's national archaeological museum.

Founded in 1867 by Isabella II to consolidate archaeological and numismatic material previously housed in three separate locations (La Bibliotec National, La Escuela Superior de Diplomáticos and El Gabinete de Historia Natural), the museum contains an unparalleled collection of Iberian art and artifacts, ranging in date from prehistoric to the Baroque, as well as extensive Greek, Cypriot, Etruscan, Roman, North African, Egyptian and Near Eastern finds.

The core of the non-Iberian collection was formed through the efforts of Expedición Cientifica della Fragata "Arapiles,'' mounted in 1871, which journeyed to Greece, Malta, Syria and Egypt, and by the acquisition of the collection of the Marques de Salamanca (Greek ceramics) in 1874. The original Bibliotec National contained objects from *Pompeii and *Herculaneum collected by Charles III. In recent years the museum has been active in Jordan and North

Africa. Spanish excavations, especially that of P. Savirón in Cerro de los Santos (1875), have supplemented the Iberian collection.

Among the museum's most important holdings are the *Dama de Baja* and the *Dama de Elche* (Iberian style sculpture), an alabaster female statuette from Galera (Punic), the Madrid Puteal (a neo-Attic circular base depicting the *Birth of Athena*) and the Lex Malacitana (a bronze Roman colony charter). The extensive prehistoric exhibits include a facsimile of the Altamira caves. The museum publishes a bulletin (Boletin del Museo Arqueológico Nacional) and a monograph series (Monografías del Museo Arqueológico Nacional).

BIBLIOGRAPHY

J. R. Melida, *CVA Espagne Madrid: Musée Archeólogique National,* fasc. 1 (1930); fasc. 2 (1935); *Guía del Museo Arqueológico Nacional,* 2nd ed. (Madrid, 1965); A. M. Romanillo, ed., *5 Años de Adquisiciónes del Museo Arqueológico Nacional: 1982–1987* (Madrid, 1988).

MARY AɴN EAVERLY

MUSEO BARRACCO, Rome. Museum of antiquities, the only nineteenth-century private collection in Rome that survives intact.

The museum contains the collection of some 350 pieces of sculpture and other antiquities, assembled by Baron Giovanni Barracco (1829–1913) with the assistance of Wolfgang *Helbig and others.

In 1904, Barracco presented his collection to the Comune of Rome, together with funds for the construction of a museum, a neoclassical building known as the Museo di Scultura Antica. The first curator was Ludwig Pollak (1868–1943). The original museum was demolished in 1938, and the collection was moved to its present location, the small Renaissance palace known as the Farnesina dei Baullari. The palace was built for Bishop Thomas Le Roy in 1523. Expropriated by the Comune in 1885, it was restored by Enrico Gui in 1898–1904. During the restoration, excavations revealed the remains of a Roman building, perhaps part of a shopping precinct of the fourth century A.C., which are preserved in situ in the basement. The palace, now known as the Museo Barracco, was opened to the public in 1948.

Barracco formed his collection with the intention of assembling examples of sculpture from all the ancient civilizations of the Mediterranean region and western Asia: Egyptian, Assyrian, Greek, Cypriot, Etruscan and Roman. Where there were gaps, he acquired casts. Among the most famous pieces are a marble head of *Marsyas* (from a copy of the group of *Athena and Marsyas* by Myron), a head of *Perikles* in Pentelic marble (after the statue on the Athenian *Akropolis attributed to Kresilas) and the head of a child, possibly Nero.

BIBLIOGRAPHY

G. Barracco—W. Helbig, *La Collection Barracco* (Munich, 1893); G. Barracco—L. Pollak, *Catalogo del Museo di Scultura Antica* (Rome, 1928); C. Pietrangeli, "Il Museo Barracco riordinato," *Bollettino d'Arte* (1949), 76–80; idem, "Il Museo Barracco nella

'Farnesina ai Baullari','' *Capitolium* (1949), 137–43; Comune di Roma and Assessorato alla Cultura, *Il "Nuovo" Museo Barracco* (Rome, 1982).

DAVID WHITEHOUSE

MUSEO DEL FORO. See ANTIQUARIO FORENSE.

MUSEO DELLA CIVILTÀ ROMANA, Rome. Museum of Roman civilization, containing scaled replicas of artworks, buildings and other objects exemplifying Roman culture and civilization.

The plaster reproductions were gathered from throughout Europe and shown in Rome at the 1911 Mostra Archeologica and the 1937 Mostra Augustea della Romanità. In 1955 these exhibits were united and housed in a new structure at EUR (Esposizione Universale di Roma), the quarter on the south side of Rome designed in the 1930s as the site of a huge international exposition. The replicas are grouped into over fifty categories including construction, furnishings, communications, industry and religion. Other exhibits are organized chronologically, providing a unique opportunity to compare contemporary projects from far-flung locations. The museum's showpiece is a large, impressive gesso model of Constantinian Rome by Italo Gismondi.

BIBLIOGRAPHY

A. M. Colini—G. Q. Giglioli, *Il Museo della Civiltà Romana* (Rome, 1955); +*Museo della Civiltà Romana* (Colombo, 1958); M. Burri Rossi, *Museo della Civiltà Romana* (Rome, 1976).

DIANE FAVRO

MUSEO DELLE TERME. See TERME MUSEUM.

MUSEO NAZIONALE DI NAPOLI (NATIONAL MUSEUM, Naples). Major Italian archaeological museum, containing the former collection of the *Farnese family and finds from *Pompeii, *Herculaneum and other sites on the Bay of Naples.

The building that eventually housed the Museo Nazionale di Napoli was begun in 1585 as a barracks for the royal cavalry, but by 1616 it had been transformed into a palace to serve the university of Naples. The façade was adorned with ancient statuary in niches, some of it discovered at *Cumae in 1606, and sculptures were also displayed inside the palace. This Palazzo dei Studi, a grand university building in its time, was superseded by a new palace in 1777, and the idea arose at the court of the *Bourbon family to use the old structure (now called the Palazzo dei Vecchi Studi) as a museum.

King Ferdinand IV of Naples carried forward the plan to display Bourbon treasures, first moving the Farnese collections to Naples and then gradually consolidating them in the Palazzo dei Vecchi Studi, along with finds from the Bourbon excavations at Pompeii and Herculaneum (1787–1800). In the succeeding years, while Naples was under the rule of the French (1806–16), Joachim Murat and especially his queen, Caroline, took a keen interest in both the excavations and the collections. Joachim purchased the collection of Camillo Borgia from Velletri, containing an original Greek marble grave stele as well as Egyptian antiquities ranging from Old Kingdom to Roman times. (These did not arrive, however, until 1817.) Caroline gathered vases and other objects from excavations in Naples for her "Museo Palatino" and also had antiquities from the Bourbon collections transferred there. But the Murats were unable to take their treasures along when they were expelled from Naples in 1816, and their objects were transferred to the revived Bourbon museum.

With the return of Ferdinand (now as Ferdinand I, King of the Two Sicilies), the old Palazzo dei Vecchi Studi was renamed the Real Museo Borbonico, and it received much of the rest of the Bourbon holdings. In the 1830s it was enriched with Greek vases from Nola and from Etruria (Canino, *Chiusi, *Vulci) and the last of the Farnese sculptures; the *Farnese *Bull* was moved to the museum to join the famed *Farnese *Hercules, Flora* and *Atlas*. To the numismatic collections from the Farnese cabinet and the excavations at Pompeii and Herculaneum were added the collections of Marchese Forcella of Sicily, of Baron Genua del Vasto from the province of Chieti, of Marchese Arditi and of Cavaliere Poli. In 1830 was discovered at Pompeii the *Dancing Faun,* immediately transferred to the Museo, and the following year, in the House of the Faun, was discovered the famous *Alexander* Mosaic, which was not moved until 1843.

In 1848, under the short-lived constitutional Bourbon regime, a commission of noted Neapolitan archaeologists (S. Ruggiero, C. S. Minervini, G. *Fiorelli) was created to study the improvement of displays and security at the museum. With the unification of Italy came the new (and present) name for the collection, the Museo Nazionale di Napoli. Garibaldi named as honorary director of the museum Alexander *Dumas père, who had served him well in military campaigns. The latter is remembered for the fact that he opened up to the public the "giardino segreto" of erotic paintings from Pompeii, but on the whole he was not popular with the Neapolitans. He was succeeded in 1863 by the much-admired Giuseppe Fiorelli, who carried forward a new scientific and systematic arrangement of the collections. A three-dimensional model of the excavations at Pompeii was put on display in the museum, charting the progress of the excavations up to 1879. In 1865 there arrived a number of vases of Italiote manufacture from Apulia and Lucania and coins from Magna Graecia and Sicily, all from the collection of Marchese Santangelo, who had been a friend of Ferdinand II. Giulio De Petra, who served as director from 1875 to 1900, is remembered most for his failure to secure some highly important antiquities from the area, the frescoes and treasury from *Boscoreale and the terracotta tile from Capua with one of the longest Etruscan inscriptions (Berlin).

Successive directors were Paolo *Orsi (1900–1901), Ettore Pais (1901–4), Vittorio Spinazzola (1910–24) and Amedeo *Maiuri (1924–61). They saw the museum through struggles over the arrangement of the collections and through two world wars. Pais was criticized for his manner of rearranging the collection, too frequently moving objects about and thus causing them damage. In addition, he placed together objects of mixed date and typology. Rearrangements continued as more and more space became available for the museum; the Biblioteca Nazionale (in which were kept the ancient papyri from the *Villa of the Papyri) was removed to the Palazzo Reale (1927) and the gallery of paintings of the Renaissance and later was moved to the palace at Capodimonte (1957). Repairs to the building and the construction of a new wing, mostly between 1927 and 1937, created yet more usable space for the immense archaeological collections.

Maiuri's courage and dedication carried the antiquities through World War II, when he made the difficult decision in 1943 to move some sixty cases of sculptures and other objects out of the dangerous zone of Naples. His choice of the monastery of Montecassino as a haven turned out to be too optimistic, but miraculously the antiquities were moved out by the Germans before the devastating bombing of 1944, to the *Vatican Museums. All but a few cases were returned to Naples in 1945 under the escort of Alfonso De Franciscis (later to be named director of the museum). The museum was reopened promptly, with the other cases, including one with the objects of gold, restored by the Germans in 1947. Some of the most precious antiquities, such as the carved sardonyx *Farnese Cup and the cameo glass Blue Vase from Pompeii, had been sealed inside a wall of the museum. (The secret operation was performed in the dead of night by Maiuri and a few trusted assistants.) These were also restored to display.

Some of the sculptures were damaged during the movements from place to place, notably, some bronzes that had been in the Bourbon collections, such as the *Hermes Seated and the "Dancers" from the Villa of the Papyri. These had not held up well because they had been clumsily restored in earlier times, and the occasion now arose to do new restorations of such pieces.

There exist entire categories of materials for archaeological research that are better studied today at the Museo Nazionale than at almost any other place in the world. The picture gallery of works excavated and removed from walls at Pompeii, Herculaneum, Stabiae and Boscoreale is a unique collection of ancient painting. The holdings in erotic art from some of these sites (the so-called Pornographic Collection) include some 250 items—statuary, wall paintings, mosaics and household objects. The coins and gems, amassed over many centuries, are of exceptional value, as are the numerous painted vases of South Italian, Attic Greek and Etruscan fabrication. The sculptures in marble and especially bronze, excavated at Rome and on the Bay of Naples, provide important evidence both for lost Greek originals and for Roman taste at the time of the early Roman Empire. Finally, the well-preserved organic materials from Pompeii and Herculaneum provide a remarkable corpus of Roman food, including carbonized loaves of bread, eggshells, nuts, dates.

BIBLIOGRAPHY

A. Ruesch, *Guida illustrata del Museo Nazionale di Napoli,* pt. 1, *Antichità,* 2nd ed. (Naples, 1911); A. De Franciscis, *Il Museo Nazionale di Napoli* (Naples, 1963); J. B. Ward-Perkins—A. Claridge, *Pompeii, A.D. 79* (Boston, 1978); +U. Pannuti, *Catalogo della collezione glittica del Museo Nazionale di Napoli* (Rome, 1983); +*Le Collezioni del Museo Nazionale di Napoli* (Rome, 1989).

MUSEO NAZIONALE DI VILLA GIULIA. See VILLA GIULIA.

MUSEO NAZIONALE ROMANO. See TERME MUSEUM.

MUSEUM OF FINE ARTS, Boston. Major American museum with one of the most extensive collections of classical antiquities in the United States.

Striving to maintain high standards of quality and to encompass all aspects of Greek, Roman and Etruscan art, the museum has acquired numerous antiquities over a period of more than one hundred years. Such exceptional pieces as the Mantiklos *Apollo* and the Hadrianic portrait of *Augustus* exemplify the museum's merit. The sixth, fifth and fourth centuries B.C. are well represented in the collection, with special strength in Attic black- and red-figured vases (by Exekias, the Niobid Painter and others). Also of note are the museum's collection of Etruscan bronzes, including statuettes, *cistae* (cosmetic boxes) and mirrors, and the Warren collection of ancient coins, gems and cameos. As of 1991 the museum had over 20,000 objects in its classical collection. Almost every aspect of the material culture of Greece, Rome and Etruria is represented.

The Museum of Fine Arts was founded on 4 February 1870 by the Massachusetts state legislature because of a need to expand resources for Boston's growing interest in the visual arts; the new museum succeeded the Boston Atheneum as the principal site for the collection and exhibition of art in Boston. From the outset the museum displayed an intense dedication to the collection of antiquities. The first public exhibition (1872) was of a collection of Cypriot artifacts from the *Cesnola collection, the first classical antiquities purchased by the museum. In 1884, the two great Etruscan stone sarcophagi from *Vulci were lent to the museum, and soon afterward the two pieces were purchased for permanent display. Also in 1884, there came to the museum a gift from the *Archaeological Institute of America of a collection of antiquities excavated at *Assos, one of the largest single donations ever made to the museum. Edward Robinson, who had participated in these excavations, became the first curator of the Department of Classical Antiquities (later Department of Classical Art) when it was established in 1887.

From 1890 to 1910, the classical department experienced its "golden age," made possible through the generosity and acumen of such Bostonians as Catherine Page Perkins, Francis Bartlett and Edward Perry *Warren. Bartlett donated $100,000 in 1900 for the sole purpose of buying classical antiquities for the

Museum of Fine Arts. The responsibility of finding and buying the antiquities fell on the shoulders of Warren. From 1895 to 1904, the museum's holdings of ancient art were increased by 4,096 pieces, including over 1,300 Greek coins, ninety-six stone sculptures and many terracottas and bronzes.

In 1907 a new era was ushered in when Arthur Fairbanks was elected as both director of the museum and curator of the Department of Classical Art. His assistant was chosen in the following year: Lacey D. Caskey, who was then named Fairbanks's successor in the department in 1911, keeping the position of curator until his death in 1944. One of the most important acquisitions during these years was the ''Boston Relief'' or ''Boston Counterpart'' (1908), considered to be a companion piece to the more famous *Ludovisi ''Throne.'' Also in 1908 the museum quietly acquired the E. P. Warren collection of erotic art, but it was not officially accessioned until the 1950s.

During the era between the two world wars, a number of classical scholars contributed their expertise toward the study of the collection, and major publications appeared. Between 1922 and 1931, Caskey published *The Geometry of Greek Vases, Catalogue of Greek and Roman Sculpture* and *Attic Vase Paintings in the Museum of Fine Arts.* Fairbanks and George H. Chase published works on the museum's collection of Attic vase painting and Etruscan vases.

After Caskey's death, Chase served as acting curator until his own death in 1952. On 1 October 1957, Cornelius C. Vermeule III was chosen to head the classical department. He worked to procure select objects that reflect every aspect of ancient Greece and Rome. Among these were a gold votive double ax (ca. 1500 B.C.) featuring an inscription in Minoan Linear A (*Linear A and B); an Etruscan leopard from Vulci (ca. 560 B.C.); and a portrait of *Sokrates.*

Making headlines for the Museum of Fine Arts in 1963 was the theft by a mental patient of an exquisite fourth-century Greek gold earring showing *Nike Driving a Chariot* (acquired 1898). The culprit confessed that he had buried the piece in a soup can in the Fenway near Muddy River, and shortly after, in the spring of 1964, the piece was recovered in a Boston University archaeological practicum directed by Emily Vermeule. One of the students, Florence Wolsky, performed the unprecedented excavation of the gold Nike in the soup can, and the piece was triumphantly returned to the museum.

In 1970, the museum celebrated its centennial. In the summer of that year, members of the classical department were invited to do fieldwork at *Salamis and Nicosia as guests of the director of the Department of Antiquities, Republic of Cyprus. From 1971 to 1973, a joint expedition of Harvard University and the Museum of Fine Arts led by E. Vermeule excavated the Bronze Age site of Tomba tou Skourou. Although the acquisition of antiquities is increasingly associated with the plundering of archaeological sites, the museum has continued to acquire new pieces and to fulfill the wishes of Edward Perry Warren for Boston to have a substantial, high-quality and accessible collection of Graeco-Roman antiquities.

BIBLIOGRAPHY

W. M. Whitehill, *The Museum of Fine Arts, Boston: A Centennial History* (Cambridge, 1970); +M. B. Comstock—C. Vermeule, *Greek, Etruscan and Roman Bronzes in the Museum of Fine Arts, Boston* (Boston, 1971); +G. Chase, *Greek, Etruscan and Roman Art, The Classical Collections of the Museum of Fine Arts, Boston* (Boston, 1972); +M. B. Comstock—C. Vermeule, *Sculpture in Stone: The Greek, Roman and Etruscan Collections of the Museum of Fine Arts, Boston* (Boston, 1976).

J. K. WASANO

MUSEUMS. The concept of the museum as an institution open to the public, as opposed to a private collection (*collecting [to 1500] and *collecting [after 1500]), begins in Italy in the later fifteenth century. Originally referring to a place for learning (literally, a "place of the Muses"), the word *museum* came to be applied to a collection of items set on display in such a way that viewers might take pleasure and learn from the presentation.

The first such museum was the collection of ancient sculpture given to the city of Rome by *Sixtus IV in 1471. Four famous bronzes of historical and aesthetic significance—the *Capitoline *Wolf,* the *Spinario,* the head of *Constantius II* and the *Capitoline *Camillus*—were brought from their outdoor setting at the papal palace of the Lateran and set up in the governmental seat of the Palace of the Conservators on the Capitoline Hill for the general public to admire. This was the beginning of what would be called the Musei Capitolini (*Capitoline Museums). The didactic quality of the display was enhanced by the addition of a number of other sculptures, especially portraits of historical figures—the colossal marble head of *Constantine* (1486), the *Marcus Aurelius* Equestrian Statue (1538), the *Capitoline *Brutus.* The collection served to inspire patriotism and at the same time must have been quite exciting to behold.

If the Capitoline collection placed emphasis on instruction, the museum created in the Belvedere courtyard at the *Vatican brought delight. In the "Antiquario," as it was called, choice marble statuary—the *Belvedere *Apollo,* the *Laocoon,* the *"Cleopatra" and others—gratified the viewer with their narrative content, expression of emotion and artistic composition, as well as their way of presenting the human body (the *Belvedere *Torso* was most important for this). The pieces were disposed in a lovely garden setting, with orange trees and fountains, inviting meditation. In its history, there were periods when access to the Belvedere was limited. While the Capitoline collection was owned by the city, the Belvedere belonged to the Church, whose policies did not always leave the display open to the public.

Another type of museum was developed in the sixteenth century, in Italy and also north of the Alps, that sometimes had little or nothing to do with classical antiquity, in the *Wunderkammer,* or chamber of marvels, which emphasized natural science and had an intensely educational purpose. Professor *Aldrovandi's collection at Bologna, his *Musaeum,* contained a wide variety of items from the natural world (*naturalia*) as well as objects made by man (*artificialia*), which were set up in drawers around a room. An alphabetical index was used to organize the hundreds of items, which ranged from sculptures and paintings to animals, fossils and rocks. A similar approach may be seen in other collections of the second half of the sixteenth century—of Antonio Giganti, also at Bologna, Michele Mercati in Rome, Francesco Calceolari in Verona and Ferrante Imperato in Naples. North of the Alps the collections of the imperial naturalist buff Rudolf II (*Hapsburg family) and the Danish professor Olaus Worm (1588–1654) provide examples. Engravings of the collections of Calceolari and Imperato depict the museum space, with objects neatly arranged in cupboards and display cases along the walls of a well-lit room. Stuffed or dried animals often perch atop the cabinets or hang suspended from the ceiling.

The museum of Aldrovandi was bequeathed to the Senate of Bologna (1603), and in 1617 it was set up in six rooms in the Palazzo Pubblico, with its own curator. While the private cabinets of the sixteenth century had been opened freely to appropriate visitors, this was the first example of such a collection institutionally maintained. A close successor was the collection of the *Tradescants, father and son, located at Lambeth on the outskirts of London. "The Ark," as it was called, contained classical antiquities among its *artificialia* and a wide range of botanical, zoological and geological specimens and was opened to the public at a small charge. The *Musaeum Tradescantium,* which was published in 1656, came into the care of an institution, the *Ashmolean Museum of the University of Oxford, in 1683. The tradition of this type of museum was continued by General *Pitt-Rivers in his own nineteenth-century collections, opened to the public even before he donated them to Oxford in 1882. The Pitt-Rivers Museum is the best example surviving today of this important kind of museum, which not only first made the word *museum* applicable but also had a profound impact on educational concepts and display techniques.

A gallery type of museum was developed in Florence in the sixteenth century, in the spaces of the office building known as Gli *Uffizi, erected by *Vasari for Cosimo I (*Medici family). The long corridors on the upper floors of the Uffizi were converted to art galleries by Francesco I in 1588, so that large antiquities (statues and busts) could be contemplated in a lesiurely indoor stroll. A similar effect was obtained in the Antiquarium of Vespasiano Gonzaga (*Gonzaga family), built in 1580–84 at Sabbioneta, near Mantua, and in the Hall of Antiquities of the Munich Residenz of *Albrecht V of Bavaria. As collections grew larger and larger, the hall or gallery-type museum became the prevailing mode and may be seen, for example, in the extensions of the Belvedere at the Vatican, in the Museo Pio-Clementino created under *Clement XIV (1769–74) and *Pius VI (1775–99). The garden-type museum that had been seen in the Belvedere continued to be used for private collections, such as in the Villa Medici of Ferdinando de' Medici (1576).

In the late eighteenth and early nineteenth centuries arrived the true "Museum Age," in which great institutional collections were consolidated. In these years the museums of Europe became the great collectors of antiquities by virtue of their organization and staffing, their available space and their resources to mount an expedition or make a purchase. Enormous extensions of the Vatican and Capitoline were paralleled by the founding of the *British Museum in 1753. From the beginning, conceived as a universal museum, it became important for its classical holdings as it built on the nucleus of antiquities of Sir Hans *Sloane, acquiring the Greek vases of Sir William *Hamilton (1772), the collection of Charles *Townley (d. 1805) and the *Parthenon marbles of Lord *Elgin (1816). The foundations for the Antikensammlung in *Berlin were laid in 1830, and in the same year the *Glyptothek in Munich opened with a spectacular display of Greek art, including the sculptured pediments from *Aigina, all from the collection of *Ludwig I of Bavaria. Spain created its *Museo Arqueológico Nacional at Madrid in 1867, so that newly excavated antiquities could be seen as well as the established collections in the *Prado, exhibited since 1839. After Italy was unified in 1870, new national collections were begun at the *Florence Archaeological Museum (Etruscan antiquities) and at the *Terme Museum in Rome (Greek and Roman antiquities). The long-existing collection of superb antiquities amassed by the *Bourbon family in Naples became the *Museo Nazionale di Napoli.

The *Louvre, founded as a public museum in 1793, came into its own during the Napoleonic period, when the emperor displayed in the vast spaces of the building the incomparable array of ancient sculptures he had selected from the greatest collections of Italy. After these were returned in 1816, the French aspired to a permanent collection of this magnitude and, with the purchase of the *Campana collection in 1861, made a great step in this direction.

America began to present public exhibitions of classical antiquities with the chartering of the *Metropolitan Museum of Art in 1870. Its early acquisitions came from material excavated on *Cyprus by Luigi Palma di *Cesnola and subsequently sold to the museum. The *Museum of Fine Arts in Boston was also founded in 1870, while the *Royal Ontario Museum in Toronto came into being in 1912.

The Elgin marbles and Aigina sculptures had come from Greece before it was freed from the Turks, but with the formation of the Greek *National Archaeological Museum in 1834 and the enforcement of a decree of 1827 against the export of antiquities (cf. *Greek Archaeological Service), Greece was no longer legal territory for acquisition of antiquities. Major monuments still lay in Turkey, and thus a large proportion of the *Great Altar of Pergamon could be moved to Berlin in 1878–79 (*Pergamon Museum), along with the market gate from *Miletos. The great funerary monument from *Trysa was transported through engineering feats to the *Kunsthistorisches Museum in Vienna (1883).

In spite of antiquities laws, some museums still managed to export major items from Italy (e.g., the frescoes from *Boscoreale in the Metropolitan), but more and more acquisitions came to be made through purchase from old established private collections or through individual donations and purchases of smaller antiquities by contemporary collectors. The personal collection of Henry

*Walters became the Walters Art Gallery in Baltimore (1909). A proliferation of smaller museums took place in many European countries, as individual towns wished to provide an educational experience for their citizens. In Greece, local museums were regularly associated with prominent sites, as at *Olympia, *Delphi, *Corinth, the *Akropolis Museum in Athens, the *Agora in Athens. In Italy, the tendency to deposit newly excavated materials in the large and easily accessible collections of the big cities is balanced somewhat by the use of local museums, especially at Etruscan and South Italian sites.

The museums displaying classical antiquities in the twentieth century are numerous and worldwide, and the vast data concerning their activity cannot be easily summarized. Modern displays still exploit the gallery space, while cabinets and cupboards along the walls have been replaced by glass-enclosed cases, effectively lit and often freestanding to allow the viewer to circulate all around the antiquities. The question of organization of collections is not simple. On one hand, some archaeological museums are disposed topographically (e.g., the *Villa Giulia, Florence Archaeological Museum, local museums associated with archaeological sites in various countries), while others are arranged by culture with a chronological progression, a system that came into being in the nineteenth century, when art-historical research made such sequences possible (British Museum, Metropolitan). A few museums still attempt to keep together traditional collections that can still be studied as examples of collecting tastes or museology of past times (e.g., the Medici marbles in the Uffizi, the *Museo Barracco). Within any of these frameworks, like materials may be grouped together (e.g., Greek vases, small bronzes). Most show a certain amount of compromise in the use of topographical, cultural, chronological and material schemes and, in addition, may go beyond such policies simply to give special emphasis to one or more outstanding works of art.

As the acquisition of antiquities has become increasingly enmeshed in illegality, museums have turned their focus to other missions, such as conservation and preservation of the existing collections and public education. An especially significant international development is the practice of lending antiquities for exhibitions. Such loan exhibitions may spotlight a particular museum's holdings by transporting them to another locale or provide an occasion for the study of a particular theme or historical context. Often symposia are scheduled in connection with such shows, and appropriate catalogs and records of the proceedings are published to inform the public and to advance the course of scholarship. Supporting large staffs that would have been unthinkable in previous centuries but that nevertheless are insufficient to meet the public's demands, modern institutions contend with the problems posed by ever-increasing attendance and lack of space and available resources.

BIBLIOGRAPHY
+G. Bazin, *The Museum Age* (New York, 1967); O. Impey—A. MacGregor, eds., *The Origins of Museums, the Cabinet of Curiosities in Sixteenth- and Seventeenth-Century*

Europe (Oxford, 1985); E. Hooper-Greenhill, *Museums and the Shaping of Knowledge* (London, 1992).

MYCENAE. Major site of mainland Greece during the Bronze Age, with a palace and citadel reputed to have belonged to Agamemnon and with a number of royal burials, some within the citadel and some without; the culture of the *Mycenaeans takes its name from the site.

The location of Mycenae has never been in doubt. Ever since Pausanias and for more than a thousand years before him, visitors have admired the famous *Lion Gate. Careful observations on the visible ruins were made by *Leake and the *Expédition scientifique de Morée. These formed the basis for the excellent account of the site in Murray's *Handbook* (1854), which *Schliemann used as a guide when he visited Mycenae in 1868. In *Ithaque, le Péloponnèse et Troie* (1869), Schliemann made the original suggestion, which was later to have such far-reaching consequences, that the heroic tombs referred to by Pausanias (2.16) were located within, rather than outside, the existing citadel walls. In February 1874, without obtaining permission, he sank thirty-four shafts at Mycenae to determine the most promising spots to excavate before he was stopped by the authorities.

On 7 August 1876, with the requisite permission in hand, Schliemann embarked on what was to be the most spectacular fifteen weeks of excavation in the history of Aegean archaeology. He concentrated on three areas: the "Treasury of Clytemnestra," the Lion Gate and what proved to be Grave Circle A and its immediate surroundings. He employed usually from fifty to one hundred workers and was supervised by P. Stamatakis, whose attempts to restrain Schliemann's eagerness led to frequent and heated altercations with both Schliemann and his wife, Sophia.

Schliemann soon uncovered the circular wall enclosing the grave circle and the sculpted tombstones within it, but not until he began opening the five shaft graves themselves in mid-November did he come upon substantial finds of gold and silver. The enormous quantity and range of gold objects (belts, breastplates, buttons, crowns, cups, cutouts, diadems, discs, earrings, goblets, greave ornaments, masks, necklace pieces, scabbard bosses, seal rings, vases and other vessels, etc.) electrified the world. The discovery of a skeleton with the remains of a face, which Schliemann said resembled his own mental image of Agamemnon, under a gold mask (*not* the mask now called the "Mask of Agamemnon"), formed the dramatic climax of the excavations. Then, to the surprise of the archaeological community, Schliemann abruptly closed the excavations and returned to Athens on 4 December.

While working south of the grave circle on plans for the excavation report in January 1877, Schliemann's engineer, Drosinos, discovered the "Golden Treasure," apparently the goods from a disturbed shaft grave. Later in the same year Stamatakis uncovered the sixth shaft grave within the grave circle. *Tsountas excavated at Mycenae from 1884 to 1902, discovering the megaron on the summit of the acropolis, the subterranean passage leading to the cistern and a number of chamber and tholos tombs. His *Mycenaean Age* (1897) was a major work of synthesis. In a series of three campaigns (1920–23, 1939, 1950–57), Alan J. B. *Wace brought far greater precision to most aspects of our knowledge of Mycenae. In particular, progress was made in understanding the burial customs and in determining the sequence of pottery, and a chronology for the tholos tombs was established. After his death in 1957, his work was continued to 1969 by his wife, Helen Wace, his daughter, Elizabeth French, and Lord William Taylour.

The chance discovery of Grave Circle B in 1951 led to the excavation (1952–55) under J. Papademitriou and G. *Mylonas of twenty-four graves, of which fourteen were shaft graves. The earliest (ca. 1650 B.C.) are somewhat earlier than those of Circle A (1600–1500 B.C.), while the later ones overlap with the earliest of Circle A. The gold finds include cups, headbands, a ''garter,'' a fine sword-hilt cover and an electrum mask. Among other finds, the most notable is an elegant rock crystal bowl in the shape of a duck.

The *richest* graves of Circle B are comparable in wealth to the *poorest* in Circle A. The extraordinary wealth of Shaft Graves III, IV and V, which together account for 13.4kg of the 14kg of gold found in Shaft Graves I–VI, has never been satisfactorily explained. The increasing evidence of Schliemann's often unscrupulous behavior has recently led to the suggestion that he may have salted the richest shaft graves with purchases from local villagers and perhaps even with faked duplicates.

BIBLIOGRAPHY

H. Schliemann, *Mycenae* (London, 1878); A. Wace, *Mycenae* (Princeton, NJ, 1949; rep. New York, 1964); G. Mylonas, *Mycenae Rich in Gold* (Athens, 1983); W. M. Calder III—D. A. Traill, eds., *Myth, Scandal and History: The Heinrich Schliemann Controversy and a First Edition of the Mycenaean Diary* (Detroit, 1986); D. A Traill, *Schliemann of Troy: Treasure and Deceit* (London, 1995), 141–75 and passim.

DAVID A. TRAILL

MYCENAEANS. The inhabitants of mainland Greece during the period ca. 1650–1200 B.C.

The name derives from the type site *Mycenae, still the most spectacular of all the excavated Mycenaean palatial centers in terms of its fortifications, its topographical situation, its outlying buildings and the richness and architectural sophistication of its associated shaft grave and tholos burials. The excavation of Mycenae, especially of the artistically exquisite, often imported, burial goods in five of the six shaft graves of Grave Circle A, by Heinrich *Schliemann beginning in August 1876 had the stunning impact, upon scholars and general public alike, of bringing to life a lost Homeric civilization. No less a figure than William Gladstone in his preface to Schliemann's *Mycenae* (1878) describes his own reaction as ''strangely bewildered admiration, combined with a preponderance of sceptical . . . tendencies.'' Yet he ultimately declares his cautious ''belief that this eminent explorer has exposed to the light of day, after 3000 years, the memorials and remains of Agamemnon and his companions in the Return from Troy.'' Schliemann's own firm conviction that archaeological remains from a heroic age could be identified and interpreted by reference to Greek tradition, from Homer and the Attic tragedians to the traveler Pausanias (second century A.C.), was equally well rewarded during major seasons at *Troy (1870–73, 1878–79, 1882, 1890) and *Tiryns (1884–85) and in three short campaigns clearing the tholos tomb at *Orchomenos (1880–86). Only on the eroded ridges of *Ithaka did he fail, as have even modern scientific excavations, to find significant traces of what he would have considered the palace, town or resting places of Odysseus and his family, servants, subjects or rivals.

Although many of Schliemann's methods and interpretations are now considered naive and unacceptable, if not—when viewed by a fiercely critical school of history of scholarship—purposefully corrupt and deceitful, the genuine spirit behind them led to the discovery of all the major features of Mycenaean civilization; and it inspired further archaeological research that continued to use, until the present era of ''new archaeology,'' heroic or romantic names for sites and buildings—for example, the Palace of Nestor at *Pylos, Ephyraean goblets, the House of the Oil Merchant at Mycenae—as a conventional means of maintaining the humanistic tradition of Mycenaean prehistory.

From 1886 to 1888 Christos *Tsountas directed Greek excavations of the acropolis of Mycenae, revealing the palace, a monumental stairway and ramp leading to it and an elaborately constructed underground reservoir within the Cyclopean defense walls of the citadel. The palace had a distinctive central megaron, already identified by *Dörpfeld, working with Schliemann at Tiryns, as the canonical Mycenaean form. In *Mycenae and Mycenaean Civilization* (1893), Tsountas analyzed the other features that defined, as they still do, a relatively uniform Mycenaean culture throughout the Greek mainland. In addition to eight tholos tombs at Mycenae, thirteen others were known from such widely separated locations as Dimini in Thessaly, Orchomenos in Boeotia, Menidi and Thorikos in Attika, Kampos in Messenia and *Vapheio in Laconia. Besides the massive Cyclopean fortifications at Mycenae and Tiryns, those at Gla in Boeotia had been studied in the early 1890s, and Schliemann thought he had found remnants of some in Ithaka. Tsountas probed this material evidence to try to understand the culture itself, ''known to [him] as Mycenaean,'' its origin, history and chronology relative to Egyptian history, the society described by Homer and the Iron Age in which Homer lived long after the Dorian migration. Thus, he defined as chronological limits for the Mycenaeans those to which we still roughly adhere: the sixteenth to the twelfth centuries B.C.

During the twentieth century the questions of the origin, nature, spread and disappearance of Mycenaean civilization have been addressed through continuing archaeological research and, since 1952, through study of nearly 5,000 clay accounting documents, written in a script called Linear B (*Linear A and Linear B), discovered at all the major centers of the Mycenaean *floruit* (1400–1200 B.C.).

For the first quarter of the century, the Mycenaeans were viewed almost universally as poor, semibarbarous neighbors and colonial products of Minoan culture. The magnificent civilization discovered by Sir Arthur *Evans on the island of *Crete dominated the Aegean archaeological record and seemed to confirm Thucydides' allusion to a Minoan thalassocracy in pre-Homeric times. The Minoans influenced many aspects of culture during the formative stages of Mycenaean civilization (1700–1400 B.C.): palace architecture, wall painting, seal carving, work in precious metals, even the discovery and use of writing. Gustav Glotz in his synthesis *La Civilisation égéenne* (1923) explained that "from 1700 onwards Cretan civilization poured [into Hellas] in a mighty flood." He spoke of the Cretans' immigrating into the region of Mycenae and Tiryns and "making the natives accept the blessings of a superior civilization." The Mycenaeans excelled as stolid warriors, in the manufacture of armor and weapons, in the construction of defensive fortifications. And so they inevitably overwhelmed the Minoans, destroying the Palace of Minos at *Knossos about 1400 B.C.

Challenges to this view came from Alan J. B. *Wace and Carl *Blegen, who championed a substantial indigenous element in the development of Mycenaean civilization. They cooperated in Blegen's excavation of the site of Korakou in the territory of Corinth in 1915–16. Their careful study of the typological development of mainland or, as they called it, Helladic pottery afforded the Mycenaeans a fuller measure of independence. Blegen's publications of *Korakou* in 1921 and of his work at the mound of Zygouries nearer to Mycenae in 1928 outlined the transition from Middle to Late Helladic (or Mycenaean) culture and the chronologically limited Minoan *influence,* as opposed to *domination,* in the sixteenth and fifteenth centuries.

A further breakthrough came with the excavation of the Palace of Nestor at *Pylos, the major Mycenaean palace center of southwestern Greece, by Blegen in 1939 and 1952–65. Although unfortified, the palace exhibited all other typical Mycenaean features of architectural planning and execution: a megaron surrounded by workshops and storerooms, half-timbering, fresco decoration with an intentional iconographical program. Pylos also yielded in the first season of excavation 636 Linear B clay tablets that proved beyond doubt that the Mycenaeans of the mainland were not illiterate provincials. The decipherment of Linear B in 1952 proved that the Mycenaeans were Greek speakers. Tablets from *Thebes, Mycenae and Tiryns have since taken their places, along with the fuller collections from Pylos and Knossos, in providing a picture of the Mycenaeans that physical remains alone could not provide. The widespread, although narrowly applied, use of the writing system emphasized again the essential homogeneity underlying the regional variations within Mycenaean civilization.

Interpretation of the tablets led scholars to a dramatically expanded view of the Mycenaeans, confirmed in many details by the archaeological record. Each kingdom seems to have had a ruler called a *wa-na-ka* (cf. Homeric *wanax*). There were military leaders known as *ra-wa-ke-ta* (cf. Homeric *laos*) and important administrative officials known as *e-qe-ta* ("followers"). Religious texts reveal the names of major Greek divinities (Artemis, Athena, Hera, Zeus and Poseidon) alongside minor, even non-Greek deities. The kingdom of Pylos was broken down into administrative districts with provincial centers, by which important industries were closely controlled: flax and wool production, perfumed oil manufacture, bronzeworking, agriculture, even logging. It seems likely that modified versions of this setup prevailed in other Mycenaean territories, including Mycenaean Crete. The terms for hundreds of specialized crafts, trades, religious and secular offices have been recognized, giving an impression of highly bureaucratized and centralized social, political and economic systems, grown particularly intensive during the final period from which the tablets come (1350–1200 B.C.).

Two areas of research on the Mycenaeans in the last twenty years deserve mention. Intensive interdisciplinary regional archaeological surveys, like the *Minnesota Messenia Expedition (and its successor, the Pylos Regional Archaeological Project in the 1990s) with its affiliated excavation of the important provincial center of *Nichoria (Mycenaean ti-mi-to-a-ke-e) and the Nemea Valley Archaeological Project with its excavation of the Helladic settlement at Tsoungiza, have enabled us to see better the development of the Mycenaean palatial systems and their impact over time on resources and settlements within their specific territories. Likewise, work by numerous archaeologists has defined the stages and varying degrees of Mycenaean contact with, and expansion into, the Cyclades, the Anatolian coast, Cyprus and the Levant, Crete, Italy and Northern Europe. Many theories have been proposed for the sudden destruction of the Mycenaean palace centers ca. 1200 B.C.: earthquake (K. Kilian and S. Jakovidis), internal popular revolution (J. T. Hooker and J. Chadwick), warfare among the major palace centers, foreign invasion by the Dorians (Blegen, Stubbings) or by Sea Peoples (G. A. Lehmann), collapse of the intricate international Aegean-Near Eastern economy, exhaustion of natural resources, drought and so on. No one theory has yet prevailed, nor is one likely to explain so complicated a set of circumstances, but here we are in the enviable position, thanks to Schliemann and his successors, of trying to make sense of too much, rather than precious little, data.

BIBLIOGRAPHY

J. T. Hooker, Mycenaean Greece (London, 1976); +A. Morpurgo Davies—Y. Duhoux, eds., Linear B: A 1984 Survey, BCILL 26 (Louvain, 1985); K. Kilian, "Mycenaeans Up to Date, Trends and Changes in Recent Research," in Problems in Greek Prehistory, +E. B. French—K. A. Wardle, eds. (Bristol, 1988), 115–52; +W. A. McDonald, Progress into the Past, ed. C. Thomas, 2nd ed. (Bloomington, IN, 1990).

THOMAS G. PALAIMA

MYLONAS, GEORGE EMMANUEL (1898–1988). Greek American archaeologist; specialist in Bronze Age Greece.

Mylonas was born in Ionian Greek Smyrna (now Izmir, Turkey) and educated in Athens. Serving in the Greek army in World War I, he was taken prisoner by the Turks but survived through the help of American friends.

Employed at the *American School of Classical Studies in Athens, Mylonas at the same time wrote his dissertation on *The Neolithic Period in Greece,* for which he received his Ph.D. at the University of Athens (1927). The following year he received his doctorate in America as well, at the Johns Hopkins University in Baltimore. He settled there, becoming a naturalized citizen. He then held teaching posts at the University of Chicago, the University of Illinois and Washington University at St. Louis, where he remained from 1933 to 1969.

In the 1920s and 1930s, Mylonas participated in a number of American excavations (*Corinth, *Nemea, Aghiorghitika, *Olynthos) and Greek ones (*Eleusis, *Mycenae). He then directed excavations at various sites, being especially remembered for his work at Eleusis (1952–57) and Mycenae, where he guided the systematic investigation of the site from 1958 onward.

A prolific writer, Mylonas published numerous volumes on Mycenae, Eleusis and other sites and contributed frequently to various journals. Among his best-known volumes are *Mycenae and the Mycenaean Age* (Princeton, NJ, 1966) and *Eleusis and the Eleusinian Mysteries* (Princeton, NJ, 1961).

Many honors came to George Mylonas, including the Gold Medal for Distinguished Archaeological Achievement bestowed on him by the *Archaeological Institute of America (AIA) in 1970. He served as president of the AIA from 1956 to 1960. At the time of his death at the age of eighty-nine, Mylonas was serving as secretary of the *Greek Archaeological Society, a post he had held for twenty years. He was buried, according to his wish, at Mycenae.

BIBLIOGRAPHY
New York Times Biographical Service, May 1988, 491; S. Iakovidis, "George Emmanuel Mylonas, 1898–1988," *AJA* 93 (1989), 235–37.

MYRES, SIR JOHN LINTON (1869–1954). English ancient historian.

Myres was Wykeham Professor of Ancient History, Oxford University, 1910–39. Youthful travel in classical lands introduced Myres to *Cyprus and to Arthur *Evans, whose *Scripta Minoa* II—crucial to the decipherment of Linear B—he edited in 1952. His catalogs of the Cyprus Museum (1899) and of the Cesnola Collection in the *Metropolitan Museum, New York (1914), set new standards. On a wider front, Myres's approach to early civilization combined physical anthropology, archaeology, geography, geology, history and comparative philology. Myres founded no school; the small *Dawn of History* (1911) and the large *Who Were the Greeks?* (1930) broadened the interpretative horizons of Greek history and influenced Gordon Childe.

BIBLIOGRAPHY
J. L. Myres, *Geographical History in Greek Lands* (Oxford, 1953, with bib.); T. J. Dunbabin, "Sir John Myres 1869–1954," *ProcBrAc* 41 (1955), 349–65; J. N. L. Myres, *Commander J. L. Myres, R.N.V.R.: The Blackbeard of the Aegean* (London, 1980).

DAVID RIDGWAY

MYRMILLO. See DYING TRUMPETER.

N

NANNI, GIOVANNI. See ANNIO DA VITERBO.

NAPLES (NEAPOLIS). Greek colony on the Bay of Naples northwest of Vesuvius, probably an offshoot of *Cumae, with perhaps an intermediate foundation on Pizzofalcone (Parthenope? later perhaps Palai[o]polis), but there is no proof.

The heart of the modern city preserves many traces of the plan of the ancient one with a grid of orthogonal streets and long, narrow blocks on a low height with little in the way of natural defenses. Three main streets, the middle one now represented by Via dei Tribunali, divided the city into broad, equal strips, while numerous cross streets subdivided these. The whole was surrounded by a fortification following an irregular line with blunt angles of which only poor remains survive, part believed to be of the fifth century (under the Ospedale degli Incurabili), part of the fourth century (in Piazza Bellini).

Various buildings of antiquity survive, sometimes built into modern buildings. Around the Roman forum are the temples of the Dioscuri (S. Paolo Maggiore) and Ceres (S. Gregorio Armeno), a basilica or macellum (S. Lorenzo Maggiore), the curia (S. Antonio a S. Lorenzo) and a large theater. Baths have been identified at the eastern edge of the site, but there is no plan. Burials have been found at various points, notably on Via Nicotera behind Pizzofalcone.

Naples flourished and was proud of its Greek traditions. It did not fall under Samnite domination, nor to Pyrrhus or Hannibal. It seems to have maintained its Greek magistracies, phratries, gymnasia and quinquennial games through the Roman period. It was a *municipium* at the time of Cicero and became a *colonia* by the time of Nero, but was always a favorite resort of rich Romans, who referred to a trip to the Bay of Naples as *peregrinatio* or ''going abroad.'' Vergil seems to have lived much of his life there and was buried there. Although

Triumphal procession of works of art for Napoleon, Paris, 1798, vase painting by
A. Béranger after a design by A.J.E. Valois, Sèvres, Musée National de la Céramique.
(© R.M.N., Paris.)

remains of antiquity within the city are meager and disappointing, and excavations can be carried out only on a very limited scale, the vicinity of Naples,
especially the coast between Naples and Puteoli, is very rich in remains of villas,
many of which have been explored. The Castel dell'Ovo is widely believed to
be the site of a villa of Lucullus.

BIBLIOGRAPHY

+M. Napoli, *Napoli greco-romana* (Naples, 1959); S. De Caro—A. Greco, *Campania*
(Bari, 1981), 18–35; +E. Pozzi et al., *Napoli antica*, catalog of exhibition (Naples, 1985).

L. RICHARDSON, JR

NAPOLEON BONAPARTE (1769–1821). French general and emperor.

Napoleon declared war on the Papal States in 1797. By the Peace of Tolentino
(19 February), one hundred major antiquities and works of art and 500 of the
most precious manuscripts in the *Vatican were surrendered and taken to Paris.

A French army under General Berthier occupied Rome on 10 February 1798,
proclaimed a republic and deposed *Pius VI. The republic was overthrown on
30 September 1799, and the new pope, *Pius VII, came to Rome in July 1800.
A new vigor in archaeological excavation is attributable to the need to make
good the losses of Tolentino and to the appointment of a new commissioner of
antiquities, Carlo *Fea.

Rome was, however, hemmed in by French conquests in the peninsula beginning in 1800, and on 2 February 1808 the French again occupied Rome, this time under General Miollis, a cultured Vergilian and friend of antiquity. A Consulta was established to rule Rome, in which the "minister of culture" was de Gerando. In November 1809 arrived the prefect, Camille de Tournon, called "Camillo Capitolino" for his devotion to the classical past. The main Roman assistants of the French archaeological work were Fea, who continued as commissioner; Antonio *Canova, president of the Academy of St. Luke; and the two architects, Guiseppe *Valadier and Giuseppe *Camporese.

By decree of 21 June 1809, the Consulta set up a commission to inspect and preserve the monuments, but it seems to have done little. The Consulta also passed new regulations forbidding export of antiquities or unauthorized excavation. Further, stricter regulations were enacted on 9 July 1810, when a new commission for the monuments of some fourteen members, made up of architects, antiquarians and artists, was established under Tournon. For the first time, an expert commission was to oversee the classical monuments.

Six ateliers were planned: the *Forum Boarium, the Capitol end of the *Forum Romanum, the *Temple of Antoninus and Faustina, the *Colosseum, the *Domus Aurea and the Arch of Janus, all under Valadier and Camporese as architect-directors. The workforce was the unemployed poor, paid about 1 franc per cubic meter of earth removed as well as a midday soup. Work began on 12 November. By December, 800 men, women and boys were employed. The resulting clearances in the Forum and around the Capitol and Colosseum were illuminated on 25 March 1811 to celebrate the birth of Napoleon's son, a most original political use of archaeology.

In July 1811 Tournon went to Paris for his wedding and also had an interview with Napoleon. The result was a dramatic increase in tempo with the establishment of a "Commission for Embellishments" by imperial decree of 27 July, with a budget of 1 million francs per year to be divided among many public and archaeological works. In the latter category were, notably, the "Garden of the Capitol," the Forum of Trajan and the *Pantheon. Work was carried out by the same workers at the same rate as the earlier commission and commenced on 28 September. It was beset by continual crises over money, which had to cover not only the labor but also the very expensive demolitions, and by constant misunderstanding by the Paris bureaucracy.

Alongside the various commissions labored the Academy of St. Luke under Canova, which by imperial decree of 6 November 1810 was assigned 75,000 francs to see to all repairs of the classical monuments, a pitiful sum that did not cover even the enormous work of the Colosseum. By another decree of the same date, Martial Daru, commissioner of the Crown, was granted 200,000 francs to undertake excavations to find works of art for the imperial museums.

The *Basilica of Maxentius was cleared down to the paving, and the three remaining vaults were restored in 1812; this was the major undertaking of the whole program, employing 300–400 workers and removing 57,000m³ of earth.

The Colosseum was full of rubbish to a depth of 3–4m, and the fabric threatened ruin on all sides; the galleries were cleared, and a road was built around the periphery. The academy carried out many repairs, and the arena was excavated (1811–12); work was done by both the Commission for Embellishments and the Crown. A systematic clearance was undertaken in the Domus Aurea, mainly by the Crown (1811–13), revealing many new paintings. In the Forum Boarium both the *Temple of "Vesta" (1810) and the temple of "Fortune" (1811) were cleared. In the Forum Romanum, most of the modern buildings were demolished, and it was planned to excavate the whole area down to the ancient level. The French found the *Column of Trajan in a small pit; when they left, 6,000m² of the Basilica and Forum had been laid bare by the demolitions (costing 82,000 francs) by the Commission for Embellishments and excavations by the Crown (1811–14), and Valadier had designed a new square. The portico of the Temple of Antoninus and Faustina was cleared down to the Via Sacra (1811); those of the Dioscuri (1810), Saturn (1810–11), and Venus and Rome (1813) were cleared to their foundations, revealing the plan of this last temple for the first time. The three remaining columns of the *Temple of Vespasian were brilliantly rebuilt from the foundations by Camporese for the academy (1811–12), and the whole slope below the Capitol was cleared. The Commission for Embellishments alone spent 570,000 francs for the "Garden of the Capitol" and 182,000 francs on the Forum of Trajan.

Following the Russian campaign and the defeat at Leipzig on 18 October 1813, French control of Rome became increasingly precarious. The city was occupied by the traitor Joachim Murat on 19 January 1814, and the administration departed, although Miollis held out in Castel Sant'Angelo until 10 March. Pius VII returned on 24 May. Following the fall of Napoleon, the plunder of Tolentino was returned to Rome through the diplomacy of Canova.

The archaeological undertakings of the Napoleonic regime were, in large part, politically motivated: to win the affection of the alienated Romans by public amenities and to provide employment for the poor after the senseless suppression of the convents in April 1810. These projects also cleared almost every classical monument of Rome for the first time from the debris of centuries and initiated the modern era of Roman archaeology.

BIBLIOGRAPHY

+F. Boyer, *Le Monde des arts* (Paris, 1969); +A. Lapadula, *Roma e la sua regione nell'epoca napoleonica* (Rome, 1969); +M. Jonsson, *La Cura dei monumenti* (Stockholm, 1986); +*Ridley, Eagle and the Spade*.

R. T. RIDLEY

NARDINI, FAMIANO (?–1661). Italian antiquarian and topographer.

Little is known of the life of Nardini. He is generally said to have been Florentine by birth, but an alternative account is that he was born at Capranica di Sutri. He died in Rome and was buried in S. Nicola in Arcioni; no epitaph survives, and the church was demolished in 1906.

Nardini's *Roma antica* was published posthumously in 1661 (2nd ed., 1704; 3rd, 1771; 4th, ed. A. *Nibby, 1818–20). A Latin translation was included in *Graevius's *Thesaurus,* volume 4. The book is one of the largest of its time on Rome, 546 pages of small print. Nardini's innovation is that, after the standard introduction on the walls, gates and hills, he organized his description of the city according to the fourteen regions, using their boundaries as fundamental and instructive topographical markers. He gave full quotations of classical sources. He knew many things others did not, for example, the correct positions of the *Basilica Aemilia and the *Basilica Julia. On the other hand, the *Temple of Saturn he called Fortuna, and the *Temple of Vespasian he, like his contemporaries, named Jupiter Tonans. To solve the famous problem of the temples of Vespasian and of Concord facing the statue of Domitian, he imagined them in line with the *Arch of Septimius Severus at the foot of the Capitol. He made the *Forum Boarium very narrow; it did not extend to the Tiber so could not include the round temple (so-called *Temple of Vesta). He followed the then-current orientation of the *Forum Romanum toward the Tiber.

Jean Mabillon complimented Nardini on his knowledge of the regions, while Raffaele *Fabretti praised his judgment and modesty. *Montfaucon characterized him as "praised by men who are themselves praised," and recognized his enormous reading but criticized him for being eager to be controversial. Nibby stated, in the preface to his edition, that none of Nardini's contemporaries were so exact on topography. He is certainly not given the credit he deserves and is often unjustly criticized.

BIBLIOGRAPHY
Stark, 86, 275; Sandys, II, 279.

R. T. RIDLEY

NAR FLUVIUS. See MARFORIO.

NASH, ERNEST (1898–1974). Photographer and expert on the ancient ruins of Rome.

German-born, Nash served in World War I, studied at Berlin (Hermann Dessau was one teacher), practiced law in Potsdam, then emigrated to Rome; from there in 1939 he moved to the United States, where he dropped his original name, "Ernst Nathan," practiced as a professional photographer and began writing about Rome. Returning to Rome in 1951, he became acquainted with all its ancient ruins and wrote, among other things, his greatest work, the two-volume *Pictorial Dictionary of Ancient Rome* (to illustrate *Platner and *Ashby, *A Topographical Dictionary of Ancient Rome,* 1929), which appeared in both German and English versions (2nd ed., 1968). He also founded the Fototeca Unione, housed at the *American Academy in Rome. Thrice married, he is buried in Rome.

BIBLIOGRAPHY
K. Einaudi, M. Guarducci and B. Nash, personal communications, 1982.

†ARTHUR E. GORDON

NATIONAL ARCHAEOLOGICAL MUSEUM (ETHNIKON ARCHAIO-LOGIKON MOUSEION), Athens. Central museum and repository of art and archaeological finds from ancient Greece, with the most comprehensive collection of original Greek sculpture and vases; among the museum's fifty-two galleries are the renowned Mycenaean Hall and Thera Exhibition.

The National Museum, originally called the Central Archaeological Museum, was founded by a royal decree (13 November 1834) stating that the Theseum (i.e., the *Hephaisteion) was to be the location for the collection of Greek antiquities whose core was the sculptural remains gathered by the ephor of antiquities, Kyriakos Pittakis (1798–1863). With the addition of several private collections and the advent of the *Greek Archaeological Society (1837), a larger and more versatile museum was needed. The construction of this new museum was inaugurated 3 October 1866 in the presence of King George I at its current location on Patission Street.

The liberation of Greece from the Turks (1821–30) stirred the country's philhellenic spirit and a voracious desire for the retrieval and preservation of its native antiquities. This spirit, although constantly blunted by political and economic upheavals, was the catalyst for the construction of the panhellenic museum. In recent years, however, the museum, due to size impediments, has been forced to limit its new acquisitions to objects from Athens and finds of extraordinary importance from other sites.

The history of the collection is quite complex and is intricately tied to the political situation of Greece and the generosity of various patrons. The first museum was established in 1829 in an orphanage on the island of Aigina, where the first capital of the Greek states was located. The first exhibit (September 1829) consisted of several reliefs and a few statues, obtained from private donors and excavations around Greece, especially from the Cyclades, Megara and Salamis.

The person behind the foundation of the museum was a native Rhodian, Ioannis Kapodistrias (1776–1831), who believed that only through reestablishing its own cultural background could Greece liberate itself from the shadow of Turkish domination. Thus, the acquisition of Greek antiquities became not only a cultural statement but also a political movement. By the time of his assassination in 1831, Kapodistrias had so expanded the collection of artifacts, including now glassware, pottery and coins, that sculptures and reliefs were moved into a nearby church.

With the arrival of King Otho into Greece, the fervor for Greek antiquities increased, and a decision was passed to move the capital and the Central Museum to the historical seat of power, Athens. At this time (1833), Kyriakos Pittakis was made ephor of antiquities in Athens and merged Aigina's collection with his own, which was stored in the Theseum, to form the city's first museum. Pittakis is regarded as the first Greek archaeologist and was influential in the establishment of the *Greek Archaeological Service (1833) and the Greek Archaeological Society (1837). The finds from his excavations on the *Akropolis

(1838) and throughout Athens became the core of both the National and *Akropolis museums.

Among the first finds of the Archaeological Society incorporated into the Theseum collection were the Stele of Aristion and the *Marathon Boy. By 1836, the Theseum had become so congested that sculptures were also stored in the Library of Hadrian and the *Tower of the Winds. The Archaeological Society also began to house its finds separately at first in the University of Athens (1858), but later in the Varvakeion (1865) and the Polytechneion (1877). Prior to its merging with the state collection in 1893, the society's exhibit was the city's only real museum open to the public.

The National Archaeological Museum, as it now stands, was principally the design of the German architect Ludwig Lange, who was commissioned to build a central museum in the neoclassical style to house the expanding collection. Through the financial generosity of Eleni Tositsa and Demetrios Bernardakis, the project was partially completed in 1881. A catalog of that year records over 2,682 sculptures, including the famous *Hermes* of Andros (1833). A new wing was constructed in 1925–39, but before the building could be finished and the remainder of the society's finds properly transferred and displayed, World War II forced the dismantling of the exhibits and the burial of the finds. After the war, despite severe economic problems, the National Museum was reassembled in remarkable time under the aegis of the museum director, Christos Karouzos, and American assistants.

Acquisitions have, in general, come from site excavations such as H. *Schliemann's excavation of Grave Circle A at *Mycenae (1876), from which the museum acquired most of its Mycenaean collection, including the so-called Mask of Agamemnon. Other pieces, however, such as the Cape *Artemision God (1926–28), have been added to the collection singly. After World War II, local site museums, such as at *Olympia, *Delphi and *Argos, have become extremely important, since the National Museum has been forced to limit acquisitions to finds in the environs of Athens and exhibits needing special care, like the frescoes from *Thera. Donations from private benefactors have always played a large role in the expansion of the museum. The Hélène Stathatos Collection (1957) of ancient and Byzantine objects has a prominent place, especially among the museum's holdings of gold jewelry.

The National Archaeological Museum, with its emphasis on chronological and topographical displays, can be regarded as a ''working museum'' or ''research laboratory'' as much as an art gallery. The exhibits juxtapose masterpieces with works of poorer quality or preservation in order to present a realistic guide to Greek antiquities. Its sculptural and vase collections are unparalleled, and its association with the Epigraphical and Numismatic museums is a great asset.

BIBLIOGRAPHY

+S. Karouzou, *National Archaeological Museum: Collection of Sculpture* (Athens, 1968); +S. Karouzou, *National Archeological Museum: Illustrated Guide* (Athens,

1990); +A. Kokkou, *E Merimna gia tis archaiotetes sten ellada kai ta prota mouseia* (Athens, 1977).

ANNE J. LYONS

NATIONALMUSEET, COPENHAGEN. See COPENHAGEN, NATIONAL MUSEUM.

NATIONAL MUSEUM, COPENHAGEN. See COPENHAGEN, NATIONAL MUSEUM.

NATIONAL MUSEUM, NAPLES. See MUSEO NAZIONALE DI NAPOLI.

NATIONAL MUSEUM OF ANTIQUITIES, Leiden. See RIJKSMUSEUM VAN OUDHEDEN.

NAUKRATIS. Greek colony in Egypt, situated in the western Nile delta at the village of Kom Ge'if, 83km southeast of Alexandria.

Herodotos (2.97) states that Pharaoh Amasis gave Naukratis to the Greeks as a commercial center and that for a long time it was the only Greek port in Egypt. The early excavations were by W.M. Flinders Petrie in 1884–85, E. A. Gardner in 1886 and D. *Hogarth in 1899 and 1903. These brought to light the remains of five sancturaries of the seventh–sixth centuries B.C. In the south, Petrie discovered a large, open-air inner citadel, his "great temenos." Recent work, between 1977 and 1983, has been conducted by Coulson and Leonard. The early excavations are now under water, but two mounds still exist. The first, the south mound, is located inside the area of the "great temenos." Here excavations have yielded nothing pre-Ptolemaic and have confirmed Hogarth's claim that the "great temenos" never existed and that Petrie's massive walls were merely an aggregate of house remains. A second mound to the east, Kom Hadid, also yielded Ptolemaic material. A survey of the fields surrounding the south mound produced pottery from Late Classical times through the early seventh century A.C. The city was destroyed in the Arab invasions of A.D. 641.
BIBLIOGRAPHY
W. M. F. Petrie, *Naukratis* 1 (London, 1886); E. A. Gardner, *Naukratis* 2 (London, 1888); +D. G. Hogarth, "Excavations at Naukratis," *BSA* 5 (1898–99), 26–97; +W. D. E. Coulson—A. Leonard, Jr., *Cities of the Delta, Naukratis* 1 (Malibu, 1981).

WILLIAM D. E. COULSON

NAXOS. The first Greek settlement in Sicily.

Naxos was founded in 734/3 B.C., according to tradition (Thucydides 6.3). The site had been inhabited in the Neolithic and Bronze ages, and Sikels lived there until the arrival of the Greeks. During the Archaic period Naxos founded a colony called Kallipolis (Strabo 6.2.6), of which the location is unknown. Both cities were conquered by Hippokrates during the early fifth century, and the inhabitants of Naxos were moved to *Leontinoi (Diod. 11.49). The Naxians returned after 461 B.C., but the city was destroyed a second time in 403 B.C. by Dionysios of *Syracuse, and the territory was handed over to Sikels (Diod. 14.15.3). In 358 B.C. the surviving Naxians were again resettled, this time at the nearby site of Tauromenion (*Taormina).

The presence of ancient remains allowed the initial recognition of the site by T. *Fazello (*De rebus siculis* I, 2–3) in the sixteenth century. A thorough topography was provided by P. Rizzo (1894). Systematic excavations began in 1953 under G. V. Gentili and lasted three seasons. Gentili confirmed the identification of the site and the existence of a prehistoric level below. He uncovered large tracts of the city wall, as well as some private and public buildings, and located a temple, recognized as that of Aphrodite. Investigations were continued by P. Pelagatti in 1961. She discerned two phases of the city plan, corresponding to the two historical periods of Naxos. In the temenos of Aphrodite, Temple B was thoroughly uncovered, and an earlier building, A, was found below; the precinct walls were defined, and the chronological development of the enclosure was determined.

BIBLIOGRAPHY

P. Rizzo, *Naxos siceliota* (Catania, 1894); G. V. Gentili, "Naxos alla luce dei primi scavi," *BdA* 41 (1956), 326–33; P. Pelagatti, "Naxos II: Ricerche topografiche e scavi 1965–70," *BdA* 57 (1972), 211–19.

BARBARA A. BARLETTA

NEAPOLIS. See NAPLES.

NEMAUSUS. See NIMES.

NEMEA. Greek site, one of the four Panhellenic centers of classical times.

Nemea has been known by the three standing columns of the temple of Zeus since at least 1766, when it was visited by R. *Chandler and N. *Revett. For the next 150 years attention at Nemea focused on this monument, which was sketched by visitors, notably by the Baron Otto von *Stackelberg (1813), whose drawing was frequently copied. W. *Leake (1806) correctly located the stadium.

A small excavation was carried out in 1884 by the *French School at Athens, and R. Vallois (1912–13) made important observations about the temple. From 1924 to 1927 the *American School of Classical Studies undertook excavations led by C. W. *Blegen, who discovered prehistoric remains on the Tsoungiza hill and, south of the temple, an Early Christian Basilica and parts of three classical structures, including a bath. B. H. *Hill studied the temple during the 1930s.

In 1962 and 1964 C. K. Williams continued the work of Hill on the temple, which was then published, and excavated a kiln that had produced the tiles for the temple. Since 1973, S. G. Miller has defined the limits of the sanctuary of Zeus and its history, provided information about the predecessor of the temple, uncovered a candidate for the temenos of Opheltes and revealed the stadium, including the vaulted entrance tunnel of ca. 320 B.C. The years 1980–82 saw a detailed architectural study by F. A. Cooper that enabled the start of physical reconstruction of the temple of Zeus in 1984. That year also saw the beginning of systematic excavation in the prehistoric settlements of Tsoungiza by J. R. Wright.

BIBLIOGRAPHY

B. H. Hill, *The Temple of Zeus at Nemea* (Princeton, NJ, 1966); S. G. Miller, et al., *Nemea, A Guide to the Site and Museum* (Berkeley, CA, 1990); D. E. Birge—L. H. Kraynak—S. G. Miller, *Nemea 1: Topographical and Architectural Studies: The Sacred Square, the Xenon, and the Bath* (Berkeley, CA, 1992).

S. G. MILLER

NEMI. A small crater lake called by the poets the "Mirror of Diana" (*speculum Dianae*) in the Alban Hills within the territory of Aricia (Ariccia).

On the northeast side of the lake lay the *nemus aricinum*, a very ancient grove sacred to Diana in association with Egeria and Virbius on a natural shelf improved by terracing of the first century B.C. to make a large, rectangular platform. The temple, not centered on the platform but set back toward the north corner, was a large podium temple reported to have been Doric, but most features are unclear. The paucity of architectural terracottas (only antefixes) suggests that the temple decorations were largely in bronze. Other remains found in the vicinity include a colonnaded processional way and numerous enigmatic constructions. Just outside the precinct were a theater and baths (?) of the Imperial period.

Interest in the cult and the *rex nemorensis,* who had to win his priesthood by killing his predecessor in single combat, prompted antiquarian research here as early as the seventeenth century.

The first large-scale excavations were made by the Spanish Cardinal Despuig, 1789–91, whose finds were later taken to the family estate on Mallorca, the principal pieces being acquired for the *Ny Carlsberg Glyptotek in 1898. Others remain in Palma in the town hall. Sir Savile Lumley (later Lord Savile), British ambassador to Rome, excavated in the grove in 1885–86 and divided the finds with Prince Orsini, owner of the land. Lord Savile's share subsequently went to the museum of art of Nottingham. Orsini then undertook further excavations on his own account with the help of the art dealer Eliseo Borghi between December 1886 and May 1887. Orsini's collection as a whole was sold in 1891 to Carl Jacobsen of Copenhagen and went to the Ny Carlsberg. A group of five votive bronzes of the Hellenistic period acquired by the art dealers Spink and Son in 1908 and bequeathed to the *British Museum in 1919 by Viscount Astor is alleged to have come from the vicinity of the sanctuary; there is no reason to doubt this. Other material from subsequent excavations is in the Museo Nazionale delle *Terme in Rome.

From the fifteenth century it was known that under the waters of the lake near its shore lay the remains of two large ships, and several attempts were made to raise these—the first by Leon Battista *Alberti, probably in 1446–48— all futile. Finds from these were brought up by divers and grappling tools from time to time. In 1895 Eliseo Borghi, with the help of a deep-sea diver, brought up seven splendid bronzes, including a lion's head and the famous Medusa, along with quantities of other interesting material. In 1927 it was decided to proceed to the recovery of these wrecks by lowering the surface of the lake through a combination of reopening the ancient emissary of the lake and pumping. This was accomplished between October 1928 and October 1932 (*fascism, archaeology under). The ships were found to have been pleasure barges belonging to Gaius Caligula, 71.30 and 73m long, the hulls made waterproof by a coat of tow smeared with minium, covered with a thick woolen stuff impregnated with waterproofing, covered in turn with sheets of lead held in place by innumerable bronze nails. They provided much information about ancient shipbuilding and design. Unfortunately they were destroyed in World War II, 31 May 1944.

BIBLIOGRAPHY

G. Ucelli, *Le Navi di Nemi* (Rome, 1950, repr. 1983); A. Alföldi, "Diana Nemorensis," *AJA* 64 (1960), 137–44; S. Haynes, "The Bronze Priests and Priestesses from Nemi," *RM* 67 (1960), 34–45; P. J. Riis, "The Cult Image of Diana Nemorensis," *ActaArch* 37 (1966), 67–75.

L. RICHARDSON, JR

NEWELL, EDWARD T. (1886–1941). The greatest of the American numismatists.

Newell first placed the study of Hellenistic coinage on a scientific footing. He made die study a cornerstone of numismatic method, applying it to the massive Demanhur hoard of Alexander the Great's lifetime and posthumous issues, then to the Seleucid coinage. His studies of the mints of Antioch, of Sidon and Ake and of the coinage of Demetrius Poliorcetes (1927) are standard, but his most influential studies were on the eastern and western Seleucid mints. His premature death left much work unpublished; notes, manuscripts and coin tickets, in addition to his personal collections, are preserved at the *American Numismatic Society, which he served as president from 1916 until his death.

BIBLIOGRAPHY

E. T. Newell, *The Coinage of the Eastern Seleucid Mints from Seleucus I to Antiochus III*, Numismatic Studies 1 (New York, 1938); idem, *The Coinage of the Western Seleucid Mints from Seleucus I to Antiochus III*, Numismatic Studies 4 (New York, 1941); *Revue Suisse de Numismatique* (1942), 81–86; P. A. Clement, "A Bibliography of the Writings of Edward T. Newell," *AJP* (1947), 427–32; M. Thompson, "Edward Theodore Newell," *Commission Internationale de Numismatique, Compte-Rendu* 33 (1986), 38–39.

WILLIAM E. METCALF

NEWTON, SIR CHARLES THOMAS (1816–94). English archaeologist and museum curator.

Portrait of *Sir Charles
Newton*, by Sir John
Boehm. London, British
Museum. (Museum.)

A friend and contemporary of John Ruskin, Newton entered the *British Museum in 1840. From 1852, he was able to promote the museum's interests as a consular official in Mytilene and *Rhodes, a watching brief that culminated in the recovery for his country of the principal remains of the *Mausoleum at *Halikarnassos (*History of Discoveries at Halicarnassus, Cnidus and Branchidae*, 1862–63). After a brief period as consul in Rome (1859–61), Newton returned to the British Museum in 1862 as the first keeper of Greek and Roman antiquities, combining his duties from 1880 with the newly created Yates chair of classical archaeology at University College London; his early lectures on Greek art, delivered at the height of the aesthetic movement, were attended by Oscar Wilde. In 1855, Benjamin Jowett had accepted the Regius chair of Greek at Oxford that Newton had declined.

The keynote of Newton's career at the British Museum was acquisition. In the decade following his appointment as keeper, his department spent more than

£100,000 on the *Farnese, Pourtalès, *Blacas and *Castellani collections alone. Meanwhile, the pursuit of knowledge and portable antiquities in the Levant and elsewhere was continued under his direction by a number of scholarly consuls (such as George *Dennis in *Cyrenaica, *Sicily and *Smyrna). Outside the museum, Newton's considerable influence was chiefly responsible for the foundation of the Society for the Promotion of Hellenic Studies (1879) and of the *British School at Athens (1885).

BIBLIOGRAPHY

C. T. Newton, *Essays on Art and Archaeology* (London, 1880); R. C. Jebb, "Sir C. T. Newton," *CR* 9 (1895), 81–85.

DAVID RIDGWAY

NIBBY, ANTONIO (1792–1839). Italian archaeologist.

Born at Rome in 1792, Nibby was employed from 1812 in the Vatican, where he became an interpreting scribe in Greek. After serving as secretary to Louis Napoleon, Comte de Saint-Leu, in 1820 he succeeded his teacher Lorenzo Re as professor of archaeology at the University of Rome. He also taught archaeology at the *French Academy in Rome.

Nibby's first major work was a translation with commentary of Pausanias (1817–18). He collaborated with Sir William *Gell in *Le Mure di Roma* (1820), with text by Nibby and drawings by the English antiquarian. A plan to cooperate on a description of the Roman Campagna did not succeed, and the two published their results separately. Nibby also wrote on the *Basilica of Maxentius, the *Forum Romanum, the Circus of Maxentius, the villa of Horace, the Servilian Gardens, the collection of the Villa Borghese (*Borghese family) and the site of *Ostia. His most important and substantial work is *Roma nel'anno 1838* (4 vols.), a description of Rome ancient and modern.

Nibby excavated in the area of the Roman Forum from 1827. He concentrated on the "eastern" end: the *Basilica of Maxentius and the *Temple of Venus and Roma, but also the *Temple of Concord under the Tabularium. He also excavated in the Piazza Barberini and the Circus of Maxentius on the Via Appia for Giovanni Torlonia (1825), cleared the Cloaca Maxima (1829) and measured the boundaries of the "Servian city," which he calculated at 39,000 feet.

Nibby should not be overvalued as a topographer. His orientation of the Forum followed contemporary ideas and skewed it ninety degrees, running across to the Tiber. He followed the wrong identifications of major monuments (for the *Temple of Saturn: Fortune; for the *Temple of Castor: the "Graecostasis") and placed the Senate house under the Palatine and the Forum of Julius Caesar where the *Basilica Aemilia was. His major triumph was the correct identification, despite abuse by *Fea, of the *Basilica of Maxentius (1819), previously called the Temple of Peace.

In 1809 Nibby founded the Accademia Ellenica, which grew to fifty members and included Tournon and Miollis; it was dissolved by the restored papal government in 1814. He was a member of the Accademia di Archeologia, the Accademia di San Luca, the *Academia Herculanensis and the Akademie der Wissenschaften of Munich and was one of the earliest members of the *Instituto di Corrispondenza Archeologica.

Hampered by a delicate constitution and further weakened by his work in the Campagna, Nibby died at Rome at the tragically young age of forty-seven. He left a large family in dire poverty; the Instituto took up a generous collection for his family and his burial.

BIBLIOGRAPHY

E. Tipaldo, "Nibby, Antonio," *Biografia degli Italiani Illustri* 7 (1834), 137–40; G. Lugli, "Nibby, Antonio," *EI* 24 (1949), 747; R. T. Ridley, "The Monuments of the Roman Forum," *Xenia* 17 (1989), 71–90.

R. T. RIDLEY

NICCOLI, NICOLO DEI (NICCOLÒ NICCOLI; NICOLAUS DE NIC-COLIS; 1363–1437). Italian humanist scholar, collector of manuscripts of classical texts.

Niccoli was the center of a web of book scouts and collectors, ever in search of lost classical texts. His involvement is clear from the correspondence of his friends: *Poggio Bracciolini, Guarino of Verona, Leonardo Bruni Aretino, Ambrogio Traversari and Francesco Barbaro, all scholars of the Early Italian Renaissance, all friends of his and of one another. Niccoli's letters have not survived because he wrote in the vernacular, which was then despised.

The letters portray him as an ardent collector of recently discovered classical texts, as a diligent copyist of them and as a generous and patient lender of his possessions. The earliest-known manuscripts of many classical texts are in Niccoli's beautiful script, believed to be the forerunner of Aldus's Italic type. Several manuscripts in the Laurentian Library in Florence are the original sources of texts sent to him by friends searching in monastic libraries.

Niccoli was eager to receive reports of excavations from his friends and to learn of inscriptions that they copied for him. The *Arch of Augustus at Rimini was described for him by Leonardo Bruni in a letter of 1409, with special attention to the inscriptions. He collected treasures from antiquity; he used ancient vessels at his meals, and he wore antique carved gems. It is reported that Bruni sent Niccoli a jasper intaglio found at *Ostia, representing *Narcissus.* On another occasion, Niccoli by chance encountered a boy playing in the street and purchased from him a stone carved with *Diomedes and the Palladion,* "by Polykleitos." He bought it for a trifle, and resold it with great profit (cf. *collecting [to 1500]).

Poggio Bracciolini in his funeral oration for Niccoli speaks of his learning, generosity, excellent taste and cheerful nature. But he was also notably quarrelsome and easily offended. This is evident in the invectives written against him; in his friends' letters attempting reconciliations; and in some parts he played in dialogues written by his humanist friends. In the end, generosity prevailed. Niccoli left his 800 manuscripts to a distinguished group of Florentine citizens as trustees to set up a public library. Cosimo de' Medici (*Medici family) took charge. The library, beautifully designed by Michelozzo, was established in the monastery of San Marco and opened in 1444.

BIBLIOGRAPHY

G. Zippel, *Nicolo Niccoli* (Florence, 1890); B. L. Ullman, *The Origin and Development of Humanistic Script* (Rome, 1960); V. da Bisticci, *Vite di uomini illustri del secolo XV* (Milan, 1961); B. L. Ullman—P. A. Stadter, *The Public Library of Renaissance Florence* (Padua, 1972).

†PHYLLIS W. G. GORDAN

NICHORIA (RIZOMYLO). Site in Greece, showing occupation from the Late Bronze Age to the Classical period; its acropolis lies 20 km east of *Pylos, overlooking the northwest shore of the Messenian gulf.

The likelihood of a Bronze Age settlement on the Nichoria ridge was first noted in 1957; preliminary excavations were conducted in 1958, bringing to light remains of Late Helladic buildings and tombs.

From 1969 to 1973 the *Minnesota Messenia Expedition (MME) excavated the site as part of its wider interdisciplinary investigation of Messenia (led by W. McDonald and G. Rapp). These excavations—supplemented by work carried out by the *Greek Archaeological Service at a nearby series of Late Helladic and Dark Age cemeteries—revealed evidence of a flourishing Late Bronze Age town, an extensive Dark Age settlement and sporadic occupation thereafter until Classical times; there was also a small settlement of the Byzantine period.

An important aspect of the MME's work at Nichoria was the use of scientific techniques and research strategies that led to the retrieval of valuable information about the settlement, its ancient environment and the changing subsistence patterns of its inhabitants.

BIBLIOGRAPHY

W. McDonald—G. Rapp, *The Minnesota Messenia Expedition: Reconstructing a Bronze Age Regional Environment* (Minneapolis, 1972); G. Rapp—S. Aschenbrenner, eds., *Excavations at Nichoria in Southwest Greece* 1: *Site, Environs and Techniques* (Minneapolis, 1978); W. McDonald—W. Coulson, eds., *Excavations at Nichoria in Southwest Greece* 3: *Dark Age and Byzantine Occupation,* (Minneapolis, 1983); W. A. McDonald—N. C. Wilkie, eds., *Excavations at Nichoria in Southwest Greece* 2, *The Bronze Age Occupation* (Minneapolis, 1992).

S. L. PETRAKIS

NIEMANN, GEORG(E) (1841–1912). German architect and archaeological draftsman.

Born in Hanover, George Niemann studied architecture in Vienna and became professor of perspective and the theory of design at the Academy of Fine Arts in Vienna (1873). As an architect, he played a key role in the first heroic phase of Austrian archaeology. He worked at *Samothrace with A. *Conze and O. *Benndorf (1873, 1875) and again with Benndorf in Karia and Lycia (1881–82). From the latter expedition resulted his much-admired reconstruction drawings of the Heroon at *Trysa. For W. R. von Hartel, Niemann did drawings of the Palace of Diocletian at *Split, and for T. *Wiegand, he drew the temple of Apollo at *Didyma. His drawings of the *Parthenon and the *Erechtheion, Athens, are also highly regarded. Just before his death in 1912, he finished his reconstruction of the Nereid monument from *Xanthos.

BIBLIOGRAPHY

+C. Praschniker, *Sonderausstellung Architekt Georg Niemann aus Anlass seines 100. Geburtstages* (Vienna, 1941); J. Borchhardt, in *Archäologenbildnisse,* 80.

NIKE OF PAIONIOS. Marble statue of the goddess of Victory, Nike, an overlifesize Greek original (height of fig. 1.98m) found in German excavations at Olympia in 1875; "one of the most spectacular originals we possess from the entire Fifth Century" (B. Ridgway).

Though lacking most of its wings and its face, the statue still conveys the dramatic motion of Nike as she soars along with news of victory. The statue is dated to the last quarter of the fifth century B.C. and is an important example of the somewhat mannered style with clinging, transparent drapery that developed at that time. A reconstruction by the Berlin sculptor, Richard Gruttner, in the Olympia Museum suggests the original effect. In recent years, the Nike has been under restoration.

The statue is also significant as an original work by a known Greek sculptor, Paionios of Mende. The inscription with the statue names the artist, and so does a passage in Pausanias (5.26.1). The inscription refers to the Battle of Sphakteria (424 B.C.) and thus has made the statue an important chronological fixed point in the study of Greek sculpture.

BIBLIOGRAPHY

+Richter, *Sculpture and Sculptors,* 186–87; Ridgway, *Fifth Century Styles* 8, 108–11; +Stewart, *Greek Sculpture,* 89, 91, 271.

NILE and TIBER. Two Roman colossal marble statues of reclining river gods.

The *Nile* is probably an Early Imperial (period of Domitian, A.D. 81–96) version of a Hellenistic personification of the Nile. The Tiber seems to be a Roman creation of the same period made as a pendant. The *Nile* has as its attributes a sphinx, a crocodile and sixteen little boys that represent the sixteen cubits the river rises in the rainy season. The *Tiber* has as its attributes a horn of plenty, a rudder and the wolf nursing Romulus and Remus. In the twentieth century, statues of the same two river gods have been found near each other at *Hadrian's Villa.

The fortunes of the two statues were similar. In January 1512, the *Tiber* was found in the general area of the Campus Martius where the sanctuary of Isis and Serapis once stood, when Dominican friars were excavating a foundation near S. Maria sopra Minerva. It was immediately acquired by *Julius II, and by August 1513 it stood in the middle of the statue court of the Belvedere (*Vatican Museums). Its counterpart, the *Nile,* was found in the same area of the Campus

Martius, probably about a year after the Tiber, and was acquired for the Vatican, evidently by *Leo X. It, too, was placed in the middle of the Belvedere court (first recorded there 1523), facing the statue of the Tiber. Each statue had a fountain flowing from it. The two were among the most famous antiquities to be seen in Renaissance Rome and were frequently copied, for example, by Enea *Vico, Hendrick *Goltzius, *Cavalieri, Frans *Floris and others. Many preferred the *Nile* both as a work of art and as a source of curious iconography.

From the time of discovery, both statues were lacking minor parts (e.g., the wolf of the *Tiber* lacked its snout, and both of the twins lacked heads; many of the "cubits" of the *Nile* were severely damaged), but serious restoration was not undertaken until requested by *Clement XIV. Shortly after Clement's death in 1774, the work was completed by Gaspare Sibilla. In this period the statues were placed in the new Museo Pio-Clementino (*Vatican Museums). Both statues were ceded to *Napoleon in 1797 and eventually reached Paris in 1803. The Nile was returned to the Vatican permanently after Napoleon's defeat at Waterloo (1815), but the Tiber remained captive in Paris. Today it may be seen in the *Louvre.

BIBLIOGRAPHY

Helbig, I, 338–39; +H. H. Brummer, *The Statue Court in the Vatican Belvedere* (Stockholm, 1970), 191–204; Haskell—Penny, 272–73, 310–11.

NILSSON, MARTIN PERSSON (1874–1967). Swedish classicist and archaeologist; major authority on Greek religion and mythology.

Born a peasant's son on the ancestral farm at Ballingslöv (Sweden), Nilsson experienced traditional agricultural piety and superstition as no scholar will again. To this he added a superb classical education at Lund, where Sam Wide's influence won him for religion and archaeology. He studied under Wackernagel at Basel, under Diels and *Wilamowitz at Berlin. Then came travel in classical lands. *Griechische Feste von religiöser Bedeutung* (1906) established his method and secured his reputation. He shared in the Danish excavation of Lindos (1905–7; see *Rhodes), from which resulted the pioneer *Timbres amphoriques de Lindos* (1909). He always saw the significant in the insignificant. In 1909 he became professor of archaeology and ancient history at Lund, where he remained until his retirement in 1939. He founded the *Swedish Institute in Rome.

Among his great works are *Primitive Time-Reckoning* (1920); *The Minoan-Mycenaean Religion* (1927); his Sather Lectures, *The Mycenaean Origins of Greek Mythology* (1932); *Homer and Mycenae* (1933); *Greek Popular Religion* (1940); *Geschichte der griechischer Religion,* two volumes in revisions (1941–67); and over 1,000 articles (many in *RE*) and reviews covering Homer to Al Capone, all "crammed with facts and therefore immortal" (*Gjerstad). A practitioner of the *Totalitätsideal,* a confirmed historist, he distrusted theory and abstract thought. Like *Beazley, he created a subject, the scientific study of Greek paganism, for him archaeology, not theology. Unquestionably Scandinavia's greatest classical scholar, he deeply influenced H. J. Rose and A. D. Nock. He has had no successor.

BIBLIOGRAPHY

M. P. Nilsson, "Lebenslauf," *Opuscula Selecta* 3 (Lund, 1960), ix–xi; E. Gjerstad, *Gnomon* 40 (1968), 100–103; idem, "Martin P. Nilsson in Memoriam," and E. J. Knudtzon—C. Callmer, "A Complete Bibliography," *Scripta Minora Regiae Societatis Humaniorum Litterarum Lundensis* (1967–68), 1; J. Meyer, "Martin P. Nilsson," in Briggs—Calder, 335–40; A. Bierl—W. M. Calder III, "Instinct Against Proof: The Correspondence Between Ulrich von Wilamowitz-Moellendorff and Martin P. Nilsson on *Religionsgeschichte* (1920–1930)," *Eranos* 89 (1991), 73–99.

WILLIAM M. CALDER III

NÎMES (NEMAUSUS). Roman colony in southern France, located on the ancient Via Domitia.

Nîmes was originally a Gallic sanctuary centered on a sacred spring and has always been celebrated for its waters. About 20 B.C. Augustus founded there

Cutaway view of the *Amphitheater* at Nîmes, drawing by Fra Giocondo (d. 1515), St. Petersburg, Hermitage, Library. (Deutsches Archäologisches Institut, Rome. Inst. Neg. 1942.236.)

the *Colonia Augusta Nemausus* (Nemausus being a local Gallic water divinity) to accommodate veterans from his Egyptian campaign; this origin is reflected in the municipal badge carried on Roman coins and also the modern city arms, a crocodile in chains by a palm tree bearing a wreath of victory. The chief antiquity is the amphitheater (A.D. 70?), a 131m × 100m structure of two stories and attic. It seated 21,000 and in design is almost a twin of the one at *Arles. Rebuilt by the Visigoths as a fortress in the fifth century A.C. by walling up the arches, it later became a self-contained village of 2,000 inhabitants in hovels built of the plundered Roman masonry and regained its original form only in the excavations of 1866, which cleared from the arena debris 7m deep. Also noteworthy is the *Maison Carrée, a small Corinthian temple dedicated in 16 B.C. to Rome and Augustus and rededicated in A.D. 1 to Lucius and Gaius Caesar. Other lesser antiquities are the ''temple of Diana'' (with an early barrel-vaulted ceiling of cut stone blocks), the Porte d'Auguste, the Tour Magne and the *castellum divisorium* (a distribution tank on the aqueduct). The city of Nîmes received its water supply from the aqueduct of the famous *Pont du Gard. In the archaeological museum, a former Jesuit college, are several inscriptions in Gallic language and Greek script, testifying to the influence of Greek colonization in Provence.

BIBLIOGRAPHY

É. Esperandieu, *L'Amphitheatre de Nîmes* (Paris, 1933, repr. 1967); A. Grenier, *Manuel d'archéologie gallo-romaine, 4 Les Monuments des Eaux* (Paris, 1960), fasc. 2, 493–506; P. MacKendrick, *Roman France* (London, 1971), 74–79; D. Darde—V. Lassale, *Nîmes Antique (Guides archéologiques de la France*, Paris, 1993).

A. TREVOR HODGE

NIOBE GROUP. Marble sculptural group found in Rome, thought to be copied from, or based on, a lost Greek original composition of Niobe and her fourteen children, dating from the fourth century B.C.

In 1583, a group of fourteen or fifteen statues was discovered in the Vigna Tommasini on the Esquiline Hill and was identified immediately as the group of ''Niobe's children dying'' mentioned by Pliny the Elder and attributed to Praxiteles or Skopas (*NH* 36.28). (In Pliny's report, though, the group was set up in the temple of Apollo Sosianus [Medicus], located near the *Theater of Marcellus, some distance from the reported find spot. An additional discrepancy is posed by the fact that Pliny does not refer to the mother's being present.)

The sculptures were promptly purchased by Cardinal Ferdinando de' Medici (*Medici family) and, after restoration, were put on display in the garden of the Villa Medici in Rome (by 1598). They were moved from Rome in 1769, to be transported to Florence, restored once again (by Innocenzo Spinazzi) and set up in the Room of the Niobids in the *Uffizi (by 1781). They remain today in the museum, though temporarily removed from display after the bombing of the Uffizi in 1993.

The original group is thought to have had Niobe herself, her seven sons and seven daughters and an additional figure, a bearded man known as the children's *"Pedagogue."* Other copies of some of the individual figures were known well before the dramatic discovery, for example, the *Dead Niobid Boy* from the *Maffei family collection long known as *Endymion* (now Munich) and the *Pedagogue* now in Copenhagen (thought to have inspired the *David* of Andrea del Castagno, ca. 1450, in the Washington National Gallery). An especially beautiful example was the fleeing *Niobid Girl* discovered at *Tivoli and set up in the *Este gardens on the Quirinal in the sixteenth century, transferred to the Museo Chiaramonti in the Vatican in the nineteenth century.

Critics in the seventeenth and eighteenth centuries noted discrepancies in quality and style among the figures, suggesting even then that the figures were copies rather than originals. Recent studies debate the fact that many of the statues seem to have a flattened, two-dimensional quality and attempt to base the dating of the statues on this observation. The two-dimensional quality may be the result of the work of the restorers on individual pieces. The flatness of the figures was noted by visitors to the Medici collections from time to time, and explanations were proposed for this anomaly. C. R. *Cockerell, fresh from his studies of Greek-style temples, made the appealing hypothesis that the figures were part of a pedimental group, an idea often repeated in modern studies.

BIBLIOGRAPHY
+Haskell—Penny, 274–79; +W. Geominy, *Die Florentiner Niobiden* (Bonn, 1984); Bober—Rubinstein, 138–39; Ridgway, *Hellenistic Sculpture,* I, 82–84.

NOINTEL, CHARLES-FRANÇOIS OLLIER (OLIER), Marquis de (ca. 1625–85). French diplomat and collector of antiquities.

Nointel served Louis XIV as ambassador to the Ottoman court from 1670 to 1679. In December 1674 the flamboyant diplomat entered Athens with great fanfare and was allowed to ascend the *Akropolis, one of the first Westerners to do so since the time of *Ciriaco of Ancona. He had drawings made of the friezes and pedimental sculptures of the "Temple of Minerva," that is, the *Parthenon. The 400 drawings (now in the Bibliothèque Nationale, Paris), the best record of the building before it was blown up in 1687, are usually, but evidently wrongly, attributed to Jacques Carrey of Troyes (1649–1725). Carrey did accompany Nointel, and the drawings were ascribed to him in a sumptuous volume published in 1811 as *Temple de Minerve à Athènes.* But Cornelio Magni, another member of the retinue, specifically stated that the artist who made the drawings was a young Flemish painter; thus, the drawings at this point are regarded by many scholars as anonymous. *Wheler and *Spon were invited to see these drawings when they passed through Constantinople in 1675.

Nointel wanted to carry away some of the marbles for the king; denied permission, he did collect other antiquities, including the elegant stele recording the names of the fallen Athenians from the Erechtheid tribe (ca. 458 B.C.), now in the Musée du *Louvre, Paris. He rolled up enormous debts with his extravagant lifestyle and collecting habits and was finally recalled. He lived on in disgrace and poverty in Paris, dying there of apoplexy in 1685. A painting of Nointel's entry into Athens is now in the National Gallery in Athens.

BIBLIOGRAPHY

A. Vandal, *Les Voyages du Marquis de Nointel* (Paris, 1900); +T. Bowie—D. Thimme, eds., *The Carrey Drawings of the Parthenon Sculptures* (Bloomington, IN, 1971); Tsigakou, *Rediscovery,* 192; D. Constantine, *Early Greek Travellers and the Hellenic Ideal* (Cambridge, 1984), 11–15; Stoneman, *Land of Lost Gods,* 73–75.

MORTIMER CHAMBERS

NOLA. Ancient town of Campania, possibly an Etruscan foundation (Velleius Paterculus 1.7.3) and perhaps on a site already inhabited, on the important inland highway from Etruria to Poseidonia, about halfway between Capua and Nuceria.

Nola lies in the valley between Vesuvius and the first Apennine ridges where a road leads inland to Abellinum and Samnium. It seems to have attained its greatest wealth and power after the collapse of the Etruscan dodecapolis in Campania in the early fifth century but fell to the Samnites at the end of the century, after which it was called Novla. But it continued on friendly terms with Naples. It fell to the Romans in 312 B.C., was loyal to Rome in the Second Punic War, suffered especially severely in the Social War and was overrun by Spartacus's men. It repeatedly received contingents of veteran colonists: under Sulla, Augustus, Vespasian and Nerva. Augustus died here in A.D. 14 at a family property that Tiberius made a temple. In the time of Bishop Paulinus of Nola (409–31), it became a center of monastic life but was plundered by the Goths in 410 and the Vandals in 455. It continues to thrive today.

Due to its continuous inhabitation, little is known about the topography of ancient Nola. Even the course of the walls is unknown, though the ancient center seems to have lain somewhat to the southwest of the modern one. The fame of Nola rests on its necropoleis, especially those to the north, which were plundered beginning in the late eighteenth century for their Greek vases. The Marchese *Mastrilli oversaw excavations on his family estate at Nola, beginning ca. 1740, resulting in the recovery of hundreds of Greek vases and other small-scale antiquities. The brothers Vivenzio dug extensively and have left a manuscript describing their work, dated 1806 and now in the Biblioteca Nazionale in Naples. They were followed by the French Duc de *Blacas, most of whose finds are in the *British Museum, the Polish Stanislav Kostka Potocki and the Austrian Baron von Keller, the majority of whose very large collection, assembled between 1815 and 1826, is in the museums of *Berlin, bought by order of the King of Prussia in 1828. Almost every museum of antiquities of any size has been enriched by the finds at Nola, to such an extent that one sort of Attic neck amphora is called "Nolan." Scientific explorations of the cemeteries have been carried out in more recent times.

The material begins with proto-Corinthian and Corinthian vases and Etruscan *bucchero pesante. Attic black-figure appears in some quantity; Attic red-figure of Severe style is often of the highest quality and the best painters. Attic red-figure of the ripe style is very abundant. Of the Samnite period there are numerous painted tombs and a wealth of South Italian vases.

BIBLIOGRAPHY

E. La Rocca, "Introduzione allo studio di Nola antica," in *Nola, dalle origini al medioevo* (Naples, 1971).

L. RICHARDSON, JR

NORTON, CHARLES ELIOT (1827–1908). American art historian, traveler; founder of the *Archaeological Institute of America.

Born in Cambridge, Massachusetts, son of a Unitarian theologian, Norton took a Harvard A.B. in 1846. Early life as a businessman and journalist boded ill for his later career. He was liberal editor of the *North American Review* (1864–68) and helped found the *Nation* in 1865. Extensive travel in India, Europe and, especially, England (1849–51, 1855–57, 1868–73) turned him to architectural history and adoration of the English, while gaining the friendship of Browning, Carlyle, Dickens, J. S. Mill and Ruskin. In 1874 Charles W. Eliot made Norton first lecturer on fine arts at Harvard, where he taught for twenty-three years. In 1879 he founded the Archaeological Institute of America, organizing the first local society in Boston; soon afterward he sponsored the founding of the *American Academy in Rome.

A dilettante, unashamedly subjective, never a scholar, Norton exerted wide, if sometimes deleterious, influence even outside his discipline. He preferred European travel and study over specialist training. His extensive publications are not read today by scholars.

BIBLIOGRAPHY

C. E. Norton, *Notes of Travel and Study in Italy* (Boston, 1859); S. Norton—M. A. DeWolfe Howe, *Letters of Charles Eliot Norton with Biographical Comment,* 1–2 (Boston, 1913); K. Vanderbilt, *Charles Eliot Norton: Apostle of Culture in a Democracy* (Cambridge, 1959); *The Correspondence of John Ruskin and Charles Eliot Norton,* J. L. Bradley—I. Ousby, eds. (Cambridge, 1987).

WILLIAM M. CALDER III

NUMANTIA. Celtiberian and Roman town, located on the hill of La Muela (Garray), 7km from Soria in northern Spain.

The chief settlement of the Arevaci tribe, it was probably founded, like many Celtiberian towns, in the third century B.C. As a result of Rome's gradual expansion into central Spain, Numantia came into contact with the Romans in 195, 179 and 163 B.C. During the Celtiberian Wars, however, it symbolized native resistance to Rome and, after surviving attacks by several Roman commanders, succumbed to Publius Cornelius Scipio Aemilianus in 133 B.C. The town was sacked, but the site was intensively reoccupied during the Imperial period.

Numantia was excavated by the German archaeologist Adolf *Schulten. It was found to cover twenty-two hectares, containing many simple houses respecting a regular street grid. The town was defended by a substantial wall, but no public buildings were found. Schulten's results were important for Roman military history; he discovered the remains of Scipio's siege works, a circumvallation close to the town, which linked the Roman military camps at Castillejo, Traverseras, Valdevorron, Peña Redonda, Rasa, Dehesilla and Alto Real. Excavations at Castillejo and Peña Redonda provided plans of some of the earliest Roman army camps to survive.

BIBLIOGRAPHY

A. Schulten, *Numantia, Die Ergebnisse der Ausgrabungen 1905–1912,* 1–4 (Munich, 1914–29); B. Taracena, *Carta Arqueologica de Soria* (Madrid, 1941); F. Burillo—J. A. Perez—M. L. de Sus, *Celtiberos* (Zaragoza, 1988).

SIMON KEAY

NUMISMATICS. The study of coins and their relation to history.

Broader historical studies contribute to the more specialized history of coinage, while coinage, properly understood, has its own contribution to make to history. This situation results from the traditional position of coinage as a closely guarded prerogative, usually of state, which has demanded careful control of its form and content.

As a tool for study of the ancient world, numismatics dates from the Renaissance. The first students were humanists—*Fulvio, *Erizzo, Hubert *Goltzius, *Orsini—who appreciated coins for their images of ancient men and monuments. Coins are still studied this way today, though in much more sophisticated ways. Early efforts were devoted to assembling, then cataloging individual collections. The first synthetic study was that of Joseph *Eckhel, an Austrian Jesuit whose *Doctrina Numorum Veterum* was one of the most learned works of any sort produced in his day. Eckhel was a careful scholar who also appreciated the importance of assembling as much evidence as possible, wherever it was located, and his work remains interesting today not only for its erudition but for its citations of contemporary provenances.

Eckhel's work was followed in the nineteenth century by more thorough catalogs, many of which are still used today. In France, Mionnet compiled his *Description* (1806–8; 1819–37) of Greek coins; E. *Babelon brought together the Republican coinage (1885–86) sorted alphabetically by moneyer's family; and H. Cohen produced an alphabetical corpus of imperial coins (2nd ed., 1880–92). In Britain, under the leadership of Barclay Head, the *British Museum began cataloging its massive Greek collection with commentary, and Head himself produced *Historia Numorum,* a large-scale, mint-by-mint treatment of Greek coinage (2nd ed., Oxford, 1911). In Germany, *Mommsen produced a history of Roman coins (1861), but most significant works were monographic in scope.

Attempts to define the corpus of ancient material continue today. The *Sylloge Nummorum Graecorum* is a slow-moving international effort to publish collections of Greek coins; the Roman world, owing mainly to the work of Harold *Mattingly, is better served through both the British Museum catalogs of imperial coins and *Roman Imperial Coinage,* which has now replaced the ahistorical treatment of Cohen; the Dumbarton Oaks catalogs of Byzantine coins have placed study of that series on a scientific footing. Real progress is now made on the basis of individual studies devoted either to particular series or to problems.

Two methods—both known in the nineteenth century but fully exploited only now—are fundamental: die study and analysis of finds. Use of common dies can demonstrate association in space—usually a common mint—or association in time, and usually both. Thus, it is possible, given a sufficient amount of material, to reconstruct the output of whole mints and place them in relative chronological order. The technique is primary; then association of individual issues with historical events can help to give an absolute chronological framework. Hoards—deposits of numbers of coins—can confirm the chronology established by die studies or even (in their absence) suggest chronologies of their own.

The relationship between numismatics and archaeology has always been close: excavations at the *Temple of Artemis in *Ephesos, for example, provide the best evidence for the date of the earliest Greek coins. The Serra Orlando (*Morgantina) excavations proved a particularly dramatic instance of symbiosis of the two disciplines. There ceramic, glass and sculptural remains were at variance with the accepted chronology for the Roman denarius; the Greek coins found at the site suggested a *terminus post quem* of ca. 214 B.C.; the denarii, among the earliest issues, suggested almost immediate deposit and loss. The resulting chronology for the denarius then confirmed the dates of the destruction levels and the identification of the site as ancient Morgantina. In other circumstances coin finds help to date strata or levels, and for the numismatist the huge numbers of coins turned up at sites like Athens and Corinth are invaluable in reconstructing petty currency.

Most twentieth-century advances would have been impossible without the availability of relatively cheap commercial photography, and more modern technology promises still greater advances in our understanding of ancient currency. Analysis of metal content is only in its infancy, but in the last three decades more nondestructive analyses of coins have been performed than in the entire prior history of numismatic study. Though now it is possible to observe only manipulations of fineness, it may eventually be possible to determine the origin of ore used for coinage on the basis of trace elements. Computerized databases will make remote collections more readily accessible, and as videodisc technology advances, it will achieve the fine resolution required for comparison of coin dies. One can also hope that creation of archaeological databases will facilitate statistical analyses.

Great numismatic collections include those in Athens, Berlin, Leningrad, London, Munich, New York (*American Numismatic Society), Paris, Rome, the *Vatican and Vienna.

BIBLIOGRAPHY

T. E. Mionnet, *Description des médailles antiques, greques et romaines,* (1–7 (Paris, 1806–8); suppl. in 9 vols. (Paris, 1819–37); T. Mommsen, *Die Geschichte des römischen Munzwesens* (Berlin, 1861), tr. and rev. by the Duc de Blacas, *Histoire de la monnaie romaine* 1–4 (Paris, 1865–75); H. Cohen, *Description historique des monnaies frappées sous l'empire romain,* 1–7 (Paris, 1859–68); 2nd ed., 1–8 (Paris, 1880–92); T. V. Buttrey, "The Morgantina Excavations and the Date of the Roman Denarius," *Congresso Internazionale di Numismatica Roma 1961, Atti* (Rome, 1965), 261–67. A. R. Bellinger-P. Grierson, eds. *Catalogue of Byzantine Coins in the Dumbarton Oaks Collection and in the Whittemore Collection* (Washington, DC, 1966–); R. Weiss, "The Study of Ancient Numismatics During the Renaissance," *Numismatic Chronicle,* 7th ser., 8 (1968), 177–87; M. H. Crawford, *Roman Republican Coinage* (London, 1974).

WILLIAM E. METCALF

NY CARLSBERG GLYPTOTEK, Copenhagen. Major Danish art museum.

The Ny Carlsberg Glyptotek grew out of the private collections of the Danish brewer Carl Jacobsen (1842–1914), the son of the founder of the Carlsberg Breweries, I. C. Jacobsen. Jacobsen junior was an enthusiastic collector and connoisseur of art who began collecting in Paris in 1878, when he bought a number of contemporary French sculptures. In 1879 he acquired his first piece of classical art, the fine Archaic "Rayet Head" (ca. 520 B.C.). During the next decade Jacobsen continued buying contemporary French and Danish art—still the two main subjects in the modern department. Only after visiting Italy and Greece in 1887 did he begin systematically to buy ancient art. In Rome he met the German archaeologist Wolfgang *Helbig, who became his chief adviser and agent. Jacobsen lived in the right period and had the means to form a collection, but he also had the knowledge and willpower to do so. He bought several collections and finds wholesale, for example, the Tyszkiewiczs in Rome, the Despuig on Majorca.

The modern department of the Glyptotek was opened to the public on its present location in 1897, and the classical collection was added in 1906. In 1902 Jacobsen founded the Ny Carlsberg Foundation, which supports the museum. The majority of the classical collection was bought between 1887–97, but new and important acquisitions have been made recently (e.g., a bronze head of Septimius Severus from ca. A.D. 200 in 1970, an Athenian prize amphora from ca. 430 B.C. in 1977). In addition, the Glyptotek has a fine collection of Egyptian and Near Eastern antiquities.

The classical collection is justly famous for its many sculptures, but it also contains representative specimens of bronzes, vases and Roman coins. The most important pieces are the following: Greek—two Corinthian lions, 600–550 B.C., two Attic sphinxes, 600–570 B.C., Ionic *Siren with Cithara,* ca. 550 B.C., two *Niobids* from a pediment, ca. 430 B.C.; Roman copies of Greek sculpture—fragmentary relief of two figures from the shield of *Athena Parthenos,* a *Hercules,* fourth century B.C., *Hermes Tying His Sandal,* attributed to Lysippos;

Roman copies of Greek portrait busts—*Anakreon,* 450–430 B.C., *Plato* and *Aristotle,* both of the fourth century B.C., and *Homer.* A well-preserved and famous marble statue of *Demosthenes* is thought to be a copy of the bronze statue erected in the Athenian Agora ca. 280 B.C.

The collection of Roman portraits is unequaled outside Italy. Portraits of the Julio-Claudian period include *Augustus, Livia* and *Tiberius,* from the same find in Egypt; *Vergil;* a series of statues from *Nemi (e.g., the actor *Fundilius* and his patroness); and a group of portraits from the Licinian tomb in Rome (*Pompey*). Other noteworthy emperor portraits represent Caligula, Vitellius, Nerva, Septimius Severus, Maximinus Thrax, Gordian III and Valerianus. The outstanding Etruscan collection contains pottery and bronzes from the eighth through sixth centuries B.C. and early Etruscan art from *Chiusi and *Cerveteri, as well as important examples of later Etruscan art.

A series of catalogs in English, edited by A. M. Nielsen and covering all collections, is in the process of being published (1992–96).

BIBLIOGRAPHY

Ny Carlsberg Glyptotek, Billedtavler til Kataloget over Antike Kunstvaerker (Copenhagen, 1907, suppl. 1915, 1941); +V. Poulsen, *Portraits grecs* (Copenhagen, 1954); +V. Poulsen, *Portraits romains* 1–2 (Copenhagen, 1962–74).

J. MEJER

O

OBELISK. Colossal monolithic granite shaft, terminating in a *pyramidion* ("little pyramid").

Originally Egyptian, obelisks were reused or copied by the Romans (cf. Pliny, *NH* 36.14–16) and reerected in modern times, chiefly in the city of Rome. Some forty-eight obelisks (or the material to construct them) were asserted by Michele Mercati (1589) to have been carried from Egypt to Rome on gigantic ships. Today there are thirteen standing in the city and one each in Urbino and Florence. For the Egyptians, the obelisks, often inscribed with hieroglyphics, were "Rays of the Sun" (many were erected at Heliopolis) or had commemorative overtones. The Romans, who took the word *obeliskos* from the Greek (meaning "spear" or "spit"), used them for various purposes, including the gnomon of a sundial, funerary markers and racecourse markers in the circus. In the Renaissance and later, the obelisks—almost all collapsed and buried—were excavated and reerected, especially to provide a visual accent in an urban setting or grand garden.

Augustus was the first to bring Egyptian obelisks to Rome, in 10 B.C. One of these, originally erected by Psammetichos II in the sixth century B.C. to commemorate his conquest of Ethiopia, was used as a gnomon in Augustus's sundial in the *Campus Martius; it was still standing as late as the eighth century, according to the *Einsiedeln Itinerary. Disappearing, it was excavated finally in 1748 (it was drawn by *Stuart) and later reerected in the Piazza di Montecitorio (1792). Another, originally placed on the *spina* of the *Circus Maximus, was discovered in 1587 and erected by Domenico *Fontana in 1589 in the Piazza del Popolo. It was one of four obelisks set up under orders of Pope *Sixtus V, who was the first to realize the possibilities of using the obelisks for urban planning. He was evidently inspired to do so by the Vatican Obelisk, which had remained standing throughout the Middle Ages before the round church of S. Andrea south of St. Peter's. The moving of the obelisk and re-erection of it in front of St. Peter's in 1586 was a spectacular feat, achieved by Fontana with the help of 900 workers, 140 horses and forty-four capstans. *Michelangelo, Antonio da *Sangallo, Ammanati and others had all declared the task impossible.

Five obelisks were found near the site of the temple of Isis in the Campus Martius. One made its way to Urbino, presented by the Cardinal Alessandro Albani (*Albani family) to his native city, in 1739, and yet another, the Medici Obelisk (*Medici family), stood first in the Villa Medici in Rome (acquired 1576) and then was moved to the Boboli Gardens in Florence in 1790. The third obelisk from the Iseum, probably already known in 1374, was set up in front of the *Pantheon (1711), and the fourth, the Dogali Obelisk, was placed near the Rome railway station as a memorial to the 500 Italians who died in the Battle of Dogali (Abyssinia), 1887. Finally, one discovered near S. Maria sopra Minerva in 1665, the smallest of all the ancient obelisks (ca. 5m), was set up anew according to *Bernini's charming design on the back of a sculptured elephant in the Piazza della Minerva near the Pantheon. Other attractive displays of the ancient obelisks were created in front of the church of SS. Trinità dei Monti (1789) and as part of the sculpture group of the *Quirinal *Horse Tamers* (1783–86) as well as at the center of the Fountain of the Four Rivers in Piazza Navona (1649; also designed by Bernini).

The latest obelisk to be raised in Rome in antiquity was the Obelisk of Constantius II, brought to Rome (A.D. 357) by the emperor to fill out the *spina* of the Circus Maximus. It is also the largest of the obelisks (ca. 32m) and now provides a dramatic focus in the Piazza di San Giovanni in Laterano, where it was set up by Fontana in 1588.

The intrinsic meaning of obelisks escaped connoisseurs until the decipherment of their messages in the early nineteenth century by Jean-François Champollion and others. The early Egyptologist, Pierio *Valeriano (*Hieroglyphica,* 1556), noted various interpretations of the obelisk—as the Soul or the Victory of Christ or as a monument to a martyr who died in defense of his country. *Ripa declared that obelisks should be erected in honor of princes, and Achille Bocchi argued in a similar vein that the obelisk was a worthy monument for a great-hearted man (*Symbolicarum quaestionum . . . libri,* 1553). Athanasius *Kircher wrote monographs on both the obelisks used by Bernini (*Obeliscus Pamphilius,* 1650; *Obelisci Aegyptiaci . . . interpretatio,* 1666), noting, among other things, the names of great men—seven Egyptian kings, seven Caesars and four popes—who had erected obelisks. In contrast, *Tischbein's friendship portrait of *Goethe (1786–87), where the great German writer is shown sitting on a broken obelisk (the one from Augustus's sundial), gesturing toward obliterated hierogylphs, seems to refer to the fading of great kingdoms rather in the manner of *Keats's *Ozymandias.*

A remarkable culmination of the idea of the obelisk as a monument to a great man occurs in the monument to George Washington in the U.S. capital, featuring

Moving of the Vatican obelisk from its position beside St. Peter's, engraving from D. Fontana, *Della trasportatione dell'obelisco vaticano et delle fabriche di nostro signore papa Sisto V* (1590).

a marble shaft far taller (ca. 169m) than any of the ancient obelisks, finished in 1884. The idea of placing an obelisk as an accent in a garden or city may be seen in a number of Western cities, for example, in the Place de la Concorde in Paris and in the two "Cleopatra's Needles," shipped from Heliopolis and set up on the Thames Embankment, London (1878), and in Central Park, New York (1880), as gifts of the *khedive* of Egypt, Ismail Pasha.

BIBLIOGRAPHY

W. S. Heckscher, "Bernini's Elephant and Obelisk," *ArtB* 30 (1947), 155–82; J.-J. Gloton, "Les obélisques romains de la Renaissance au Néo-Classicisme," *MEFRA* 73 (1961), 437–69; C. D'Onofrio, *Gli Obelischi di Roma* (Rome, 1965); +Nash, II, 130–62.

OCEANUS. See MARFORIO.

ODESCALCHI FAMILY. Noble Italian family, originating in Como but transferred to Rome when one of their number, BENEDETTO ODESCALCHI (1611–89), was elected to the papacy as INNOCENT XI (1676–89); his nephew LIVIO ODESCALCHI (1652–1713), a distinguished military figure, was invested with the duchy of Ceri and gained control of Bracciano, as well as titles in Hungary, Slavonia and Spain.

In 1692 Don Livio acquired for 123,000 scudi the collection of antiquities that had belonged to *Christina of Sweden; he purchased it from the Marchese Pompeo Azzolini, heir of Cardinal Decio Azzolini (d. 1689), who had, in turn, received it as a bequest from Queen Christina. The collection included some well-known sculptures, such as the *Faun with Kid,* the *Castor and Pollux* and a group of *Apollo* with eight *Muses,* as well as a fine cabinet of coins and gems. The collection was published, with emphasis on the gems, by Nicolao Galeotti in *Museum Odescalchum, sive Thesaurus antiquarum gemmarum* (Rome, 1751/ 52), with illustrations taken from an older set of engravings by P. S. *Bartoli. The most famous piece was the double portrait cameo, now in the Hermitage, St. Petersburg, identified at the time as *Augustus and Livia.* Don Livio also owned for a while the *Dying Trumpeter* (now, *Capitoline Museums), which he took from the *Ludovisi family as a pledge for a debt. From 1694 until his death in 1713, Don Livio dwelled in the Palazzo Chigi (formerly the Palazzo Colonna; it had recently been provided with a new façade by *Bernini), which subsequently came to be called Palazzo Odescalchi; the statues that were in his collection there at the time of his death were inventoried.

Having no children, Don Livio adopted his nephew Baldassare d'Erba, leaving his estate to him at his death. In 1724 the sculpture collection was sold to the king of Spain, Philip V (now at the *Prado; the sculptures in the Palazzo Odescalchi in modern times were acquired after the sale to Spain). Most of the cabinet of coins and gems went to the *Vatican in 1794 for 20,000 scudi.

Portrait of *Livia*, agate cameo from the Odescalchi collection, engraving by P. S. Bartoli, *Museum Odescalchum* (1751–52).

BIBLIOGRAPHY
T. Ashby, "The Palazzo Odescalchi in Rome," *PBSR* 8.3 (1916), 55–90; s.v. "Collezioni archeologiche," *EAA* suppl. (1970), 248; Haskell—Penny, 173, 211—12, 224; Zazoff, *Gemmensammler und Gemmenforscher,* 120.

ODYSSEY LANDSCAPES. Ancient Roman frescoes, now in the *Vatican Museums, illustrating scenes from the *Odyssey* of Homer.

In 1847 the city of Rome acquired a ruined house midway up the Cispian spur of the Esquiline Hill (on modern Via Cavour), to construct public housing on the plot. Under the architect V. Vespignani, excavations for the foundations (7 April 1848) laid bare a subterranean wall of *opus reticulatum* covered with frescoes: four large, figured landscapes set apart by painted pilasters. Construction at the site was suspended until the frescoes could be removed. In 1849, P. Succi was contracted to detach, remount and clean the frescoes. The turbulence of the short-lived Roman Republic intervened before archaeological excavation of the site resumed under L. *Canina; five additional scenes (two incomplete) were brought to light by 22 July 1850. In 1851, the Comune di Roma donated to the pope this "rare, indeed unique collection of paintings"; they were set up in a room adjacent to the Vatican Library, where the *Aldobrandini *Wedding* and other frescoes from Rome and *Ostia were on view. E. Ciuli undertook restoration and a partial repainting (which was largely removed during restorations performed from 1956 to 1959). One fragmentary scene ended up not at the Vatican but at the *Terme Museum.

The structure adorned by these scenes, their placement within that structure, their source and their date all have been subjects of intense scholarly discussion. In the nineteenth century it was suggested that they must have decorated a major public building, such as the *Theater of Pompey, but our current knowledge of Rome's ancient topography places the find spot in a predominantly residential area. Statuary and columns are reported to have been recovered nearby, suggesting to L. Vlad Borelli that the frescoes decorated a ground-level room of a terraced, hillside, Hellenistic-style garden villa, of a type popular in Rome from the Sullan era onward. The preserved portion of the paintings (13.7m × 1.5m) would have covered two—and the original ensemble, entire, probably three— walls of a vaulted room giving onto a porticoed garden. Scholarly opinion first assigned them to the walls' socle, but E. *Petersen suggested that they were seen from below (like the sculptured scenes on the *Ara Pacis Augustae), and A. *Mau placed them high up on the walls, ca. 3.5m above floor level.

It is unclear why the events depicted come only from Books 10–12 of the *Odyssey.* The cycle of paintings evidently derives from a Greek prototype (painted inscriptions in Greek identify individual figures). The exact source is unknown; *Alexandria and Greek South Italy are among the suggestions. Already in 1895, however, F. *Wickhoff noted a number of inherently Roman novelties in these scenes, suggesting that, if their source is indeed Greek, they are adaptations rather than literal replicas. That such scenes may have been common in Late Roman Republican interiors is suggested by the reference in Vitruvius (*De architectura* 7.5.2) to frescoes showing "the wanderings of Odysseus through landscapes" (*Ulixis errationes per topia*). Dating from near, or shortly after, the mid-first century B.C., these paintings are probably too early to be connected with the work of Ludius (or Studius, or S. Tadius), to whom the Elder Pliny attributes the invention of landscape painting in Rome (*NH* 35.116).

BIBLIOGRAPHY

K. Woermann, *Die Antiken Odysseelandschaften von esquilinischen Hügel* (Munich, 1879); P. H. von Blanckenhagen, "The Odyssey Frieze," *RM* 70 (1963), 100–146; +A. Gallina, *Le Pitture con paesaggi dell'Odissea dall'Esquilino* (Rome, 1964); R. Ling, *Roman Painting* (Cambridge, 1991), 108–11.

DAVID L. THOMPSON

OLBIA. Greek city on the Bug-Dnieper estuary, on the north coast of the Black Sea.

Founded by colonists from *Miletos in the early sixth century B.C., the settlement reached its zenith in the fourth century B.C. but suffered from invasions in the second century (Sarmatians and Scythians) and first century B.C. (Getae). The surviving town was small but hosted a Roman garrison in the second century A.C. It, too, was destroyed by the Getae, in the fourth century A.C.

The site of ancient Olbia was determined by Russian scholars nearly 200 years ago, and excavations were begun there in 1801. Much plundering, especially of the cemeteries, occurred, but a new, highly productive phase of excavations took place under B. V. Farmakovskii from 1901 to 1915 and again from 1924 to 1926. These uncovered remains of an upper town and a lower one on the river and an extensive necropolis. Farmakovskii argued that the grid plan of streets excavated belonged to the late sixth century B.C. and thus predated the orthogonal planning of Miletos.

Continuing excavations under Soviet archaeologists stressed the evidence for the life of the indigenous peoples as opposed to the Greeks, who were seen as exploiting the region. The economics of the area have also been emphasized, including an ambitious study of the coinage of Olbia and other Black Sea colonies, prepared by A. N. Zograf before his death in 1942 at the siege of Leningrad. The agora and associated temples (e.g., to Apollo Delphinios, fifth century B.C.) and commercial establishments (granaries, pottery workshops) have also been uncovered. Some of the material from the site is in the Hermitage Museum, St. Petersburg.

BIBLIOGRAPHY

E. H. Minns, *Scythians and Greeks* (Cambridge, 1913), 453–89; A. L. Mongait, *Archaeology in the USSR,* tr. D. Skvirsky (Cambridge, 1959), 189–95; M. L. Bernhard— Z. Szetyllo, s.v. "Olbia," *PECS,* 642–43; J. Boardman, *The Greeks Overseas* (London, 1980), 250–51.

OLIER. See NOINTEL, CHARLES-FRANÇOIS OLLIER.

OLYMPIA, Greece. Site of the world-famous Greek sanctuary of Zeus and Hera and of the original Olympic Games; located in the west Peloponnese at the intersection of the Alphaios and Kladeos rivers and at the foot of the hill of Kronos.

The locality has a rich mythic tradition, with evidence of early worship of Kronos, Ge, Eileithyia and Themis and of the hero Pelops, who won Hippodameia as his bride by defeating her father Oinomaos in a chariot race. Before it was a sanctuary, however, in the Bronze Age Olympia was a settlement with scattered shrines. From the eighth century comes extensive archaeological evidence of religious activities that probably took place in connection with the expansion of the cults and the founding of the Panhellenic Olympic Games in 776 B.C. Numerous bronze votive offerings—figurines, tripods, cauldrons—have been found. The sanctuary embraced a grove, the Altis, whose name is sometimes extended to refer generally to the sanctuary of Zeus.

In the late seventh century B.C. was built the *Temple of Hera, the oldest extant monumental temple in Greece; the Doric structure is historically intriguing because some 800 years later, in the second century A.C., Pausanias could report that one of the original wooden columns was still in place, though all the rest had been replaced in stone. To the east of the temple were built, in the sixth century, a number of treasuries to hold the offerings of Greek states participating in the cults; those of Sikyon, *Selinus, *Metapontion, Megara and *Gela have been identified.

The sanctuary reached its peak with the building of the magnificent Doric *Temple of Zeus (470–456 B.C.), famed for its colossal gold and ivory statue of the *Zeus of Olympia by Pheidias (430 B.C.). The other sculptural decorations—of the metopes (*Labors of Herakles*) and the pediments (*Centauromachy*; race of *Pelops and Oinomaos*)—dating to the time of the building of the temple, are of marble. According to Pausanias, the workshop of Pheidias was adjacent to the Temple of Zeus, and it has been identified with a building to the west. Near the Heraion, Philip II of Macedon began a fine circular building (after 338 B.C.), the Philippeion, completed by Alexander the Great and featuring statues of Alexander with his parents and grandfathers. By this time the entire sanctuary was crowded with honorific and votive statuary, and the site was extremely wealthy.

The original Archaic stadium where many of the games took place stood south (in front) of the treasuries, but in the mid-fourth century a new stadium was built east of this, with stone starting points and earth banks on all four sides, to hold some 45,000 spectators; only a few stone seats for important people were included. To the west of the Altis, around the same time, was built the palaestra, a training ground for wrestling, boxing and jumping; beyond this a gymnasium—for javelin, discus and running—was laid out in the second century B.C.

The first destruction to the otherwise peaceful and prosperous sanctuary came at the hands of Sulla (85 B.C.), who robbed the treasuries and tried to move the games to Rome (80 B.C.). Augustus and Agrippa restored the prestige of Olympia, followed by Nero, who competed in the games. Hadrian sponsored repairs and expansion as was appropriate because the games now attracted competitors from all over the Roman world. The philanthropist Herodes Atticus enriched Olympia with statuary and a grand fountain (A.D. 160).

Upon the threat of invasion by the Herulians (A.D. 267), some monuments were demolished to build a defensive wall (which was not needed, as it turned out, since they did not reach Olympia). Theodosius I ordered the closing of the pagan sanctuaries and the abolition of the Olympic Games in A.D. 393/394; the temples, soon abandoned, were damaged by devastating earthquakes of A.D. 522 and 551, which left columns lying toppled beside the buildings. In the fifth–sixth centuries a small settlement of Christians converted the "workshop of Pheidias" into a basilica. After this, Olympia was deserted and was covered over by landslips from the hill of Kronos and sediments from the Alpheios and Kladeos, in some places as deep as 6m. The site was forgotten.

*Montfaucon called for exploration at Olympia (1713), and *Winckelmann proposed to work there (1768), though he never visited Greece. Richard *Chandler identified the ruins of the Temple of Zeus (1766; published in his *Travels in Greece,* 1776) and stimulated the interest of French and English travelers in the site. *Fauvel (1787) and *Leake (1801) both visited Olympia, and in 1811, L.F.C. Stanhope made a plan of the site.

In 1829 the French *Expédition scientifique de Morée cleared the Temple of Zeus in a six-week campaign; they carried away large parts of three of the temple metopes (now in the *Louvre). In 1853, E. *Curtius in a lecture in Berlin tried to arouse enthusiasm for a German expedition to Olympia, and in 1874 a contract was signed by the Greek and German governments so that work could begin in 1875. The excavation was a *Reichs-grabung,* under royal Prussian sponsorship, for which the government allotted 600,000 marks. The original directors were Curtius and the architect F. *Adler, followed by G. *Hirschfeld and Georg Treu. *Dörpfeld contributed his talents as an architect, and *Furtwängler followed the results of the excavations, especially the sculpture, with interest.

Their work continued until 1881, by which time the whole of the Altis had been uncovered, revealing the state in which the sanctuary had been left by the earthquakes. Besides the two temples, the Germans found the terrace of the treasuries, the Philippeion, the palaestra, the gymnasium and part of the stadium. Hundreds of fragments of sculptures were retrieved, to be assembled by a long and painstaking process into the famous pedimental groups and metopes now on display in the Olympia Museum (casts supply the missing parts from the Louvre). In 1875 was unearthed the shattered *Nike of Paionios, now pieced back together, and in 1877 was found the statue called the *Hermes* of Praxiteles, well preserved by the dissolved clay from the upper walls of the Temple of Hera. Equally important for the history of Greek art were the many votive offerings of clay and bronze figurines of humans and animals, revealing the earliest phases of Greek sculpture.

Reconstruction on the site included the reerection of two columns of the Heraion under G. Kawerau. A small museum was designed by Adler to display the sculptures and architectural fragments. Publication began promptly, with preliminary reports and an authoritative five-volume work edited by Curtius and Adler, *Olympia, Die Ergebnisse* (1890–97).

Three more periods of German investigation at Olympia followed the heroic first campaign. In 1936–42, work was concentrated on the stadium, in response to German nationalist promotion of the Olympic Games in Berlin (1936), under the leadership of E. Kunze. Reports appeared in the *Berichte uber die Ausgrabungen in Olympia* 1–8 (1937–67), edited by Kunze. Work on the site was interrupted by World War II (the Germans evacuated Greece in 1944); meanwhile, Kunze initiated the thorough, scientific reports of the *Olympischen Forschungen* (1944), an ongoing series that has reached twenty volumes. The third phase of work took place from 1952 to 1966, under Kunze, and the fourth began in 1977, under the direction of Alfred Mallwitz. A significant result lay in the

careful examination by W. Schiering of the "workshop of Pheidias" and its unusual finds of statuary molds, tools, ivory and glass (*Zeus of Olympia).
BIBLIOGRAPHY
Michaelis, 124–34; +B. Ashmole—N. Yalouris, *Olympia, The Sculptures of the Temple of Zeus* (London, 1967). A. Mallwitz, *Olympia und seine Bauten* (Darmstadt, 1972); U. Jantzen, *Einhundert Jahre Athener Institut, 1874–1974* (Mainz, 1986).

OLYNTHOS. Well-preserved Greek town of the fifth–fourth centuries B.C., sometimes referred to as "the Greek Pompeii."

Olynthos, located on the peninsula of Chalkidike in northern Greece, was already inhabited in the Iron Age but experienced its greatest expansion from ca. 430 B.C. until its destruction in 348 B.C. by Philip II of Macedon. Except for squatters of the late fourth century B.C., a Byzantine watchtower and a few churches on the outskirts, the site was virtually uninhabited after 348 and thus preserves a vivid cross-section of life at a particular period in ancient Greece.

Four campaigns directed by David M. *Robinson (between 1928 and 1938) revealed a part of the older town, with irregular houses, on the south hill of the site, and a new housing district with a regular grid plan on the east. Altogether, more than one hundred house plans were recovered, providing the most important evidence available for the study of the Hellenic house in the fifth–fourth centuries B.C. The houses yielded the most extensive and finest Greek pebble mosaics known from this period.

Most of the finds (including pottery, figurines, loom weights, door knockers, children's toys and other household objects) are in the archaeological museum of Thessaloniki.
BIBLIOGRAPHY
D. M. Robinson et al., *Excavations at Olynthos,* 16 vols. (Baltimore, 1930–52); J. W. Graham, "Olynthos," *PECS,* 651–52.

OPLONTIS (TORRE ANNUNZIATA). Roman bathing and villa resort area located on the Bay of Naples, buried by the eruption of Vesuvius in A.D. 79.

The existence of Oplontis was once doubted, for it is not mentioned in any classical text. The place-name is known only from medieval itineraries, above all, the *Tabula Peutingeriana,* where Oplontis is marked as being situated three *milia* from *Pompeii and six from *Herculaneum.

Explorations at the site were first undertaken at the direction of the *Bourbon monarchy within the "Mascatelle" zone around which present-day Torre Annunziata has grown up. After a series of initial investigations, Don Michele Rusca, assistant curator at the Royal Museum of Naples, launched a program of deep shaft sampling in this same sector (1839), which revealed the ruins of a villa. No further extensive work was carried out again until 1964, although during this period of a century and a half the remains of baths and aristocratic villas scattered throughout the region were documented.

Systematic excavations since the 1960s have focused on the villa located on the present Via Sepolcri at the center of the modern town—a residence that stands out for its large size and elegant wall paintings. The villa consists of nearly one hundred rooms, along with a garden and a *piscina,* and its mural decoration includes numerous, rich *trompe-l'oeil* architectural views. The paintings are executed in the Second, Third and Fourth Styles, suggesting along with other evidence that building of the villa commenced before the middle of the first century B.C. and that it underwent a number of remodelings, the last of which would have been due to the earthquake of A.D. 62 and interrupted by the eruption of 79. It has been proposed on the basis of an amphora found within the dwelling, stamped *secundo Poppaeae,* that the property at one point may have belonged to the *gens Poppaea,* the family of Nero's second wife. Excavation is ongoing, but the presence of a modern canal, as well as streets and buildings, prevent disclosure of the site to its fullest extent.

On the Peutinger Table, Oplontis is marked with a square surmounted by two towers, a symbol used elsewhere on the map to signify bathing establishments (e.g., at *Baiae) and/or villas (*Stabiae). Discoveries since publication of the map in 1598 have thus confirmed the existence of Oplontis, its exact location and its character, precisely that designated on the itinerary—a leisure resort area. The cumulative evidence indicated that Oplontis was neither a suburb of Pompeii nor a true urban center. Lacking public buildings and presenting no proper city plan, it seems to have been, instead, a locale consisting of baths and private residences that offered to the Roman nobility a comfortable seaside retreat.

BIBLIOGRAPHY

O. Cuntz—J. Schnetz, eds., *Itineraria romana* (1929–40); A. de Franciscis, s.v. "Oplontis," *PECS,* 652–53; J. R. Clarke, *The Houses of Roman Italy, 100 B.C.–A.D. 250: Ritual, Space and Decoration* (Berkeley, 1992), 13, 21–23, 25, 45–47, 113–23, 126–40, 166–70, etc.

CHERYL L. SOWDER

ORANGE (ARAUSIO). Roman city founded ca. 35 B.C. by Octavian as a colony, Colonia Julia Firma Secundanorum Arausio; the colony was strategically placed on the hill of Saint-Eutrope, ca. 5km east of the Rhône River, which had earlier served as a base for the Gallic confederation of the Cavares.

Most impressive of the Roman remains is the monumental *Arch at Orange, now usually dated to the reign of Tiberius, in the 20s A.D. The other structure that has stood through the centuries and has always been admired is the theater, the scene building of which was described by *Louis XIV as "the handsomest wall in my realm." Thought to date from the reign of Augustus, the theater is one of the best-preserved theaters in the Roman world. The auditorium would seat 7,000; the huge stage section, 37m high, was long ago stripped of its marble revetment and most of its columns (there were once seventy-six); it still conveys the grand scale that was possible in a provincial theater. J. Formigé, in charge of excavations at Orange after 1912, excavated a temple and a semicircular structure of uncertain purpose directly to the west of the theater.

Soon after World War II, a singular find was made of fragments of a marble register of the land around Orange, created for tax purposes in A.D. 77 under Vespasian and later. Most of the known pieces of the register were discovered in 1949, during the digging of a cellar to contain the strong room of a local bank. The Abbé Sautel conducted the excavations, inventorying some 1,100 pounds of marble fragments, evidently heaped up ready for the limekiln. Studied by A. Pignaniol, the registers are of the greatest importance for the information they yield about the allotment of land to Roman colonists and to native inhabitants.

Orange was sacked by Visigoths in the fifth century A.C. In the thirteenth century, it became the center of a principality and was later inherited by William the Silent (1544), who then became *stathouder* of Holland. His successor and son, Maurice of Nassau, destroyed most of the Roman remains except the arch and the theater, which he immured within a city wall. When Louis XIV took over the city in 1672, the wall was removed, and the theater was freed.
BIBLIOGRAPHY
A. Grenier, *Manuel d'archéologie gallo-romaine* 3 (1958), 172–93, 398–402, 754–65; C. Goudineau, s.v. "Arausio," *PECS* 83–84; P. Grimal, *Roman Cities,* tr. and ed. M. Woloch (Madison, 1983), 202–5.

ORCHOMENOS. An extremely ancient site in Boeotia, Greece, that rose to prominence in the Bronze Age as capital of the Minyans.

Its inhabitants successfully drained Lake Copais. Homer (*Il.* 9.381) refers to it as proverbially wealthy. It later lost to *Thebes the struggle for regional ascendancy.

Pausanias (9.36) reckoned the "Treasury of Minyas" at Orchomenos no less admirable than the pyramids. Of modern visitors, E. D. *Clarke was the first to identify this "treasury" with the ruined tholos tomb at the site. Lord *Elgin tried to excavate the tomb but was prevented by the massiveness of the stones and a lack of suitable equipment. W. M. *Leake provided the first plan of the site and observed that Pausanias's description suggests that by the second century A.C., the earth that had once covered the roof of the tomb had been washed away.

*Schliemann's excavations in 1880 and 1881 revealed the existence of the side chamber with the magnificently decorated ceiling. When he returned in 1886 with W. *Dörpfeld, proper plans of the whole tomb were drawn. The work of later excavators, such as G. de Ridder, H. Bulle and E. Kunze, on the acropolis behind the tomb and elsewhere uncovered occupation levels at the site from Neolithic to Hellenistic times.
BIBLIOGRAPHY
H. Schliemann, "Exploration of the Boeotian Orchomenus," *JHS* 2 (1882), 122–63; G. de Ridder, "Fouilles d'Orchomène," *BCH* 19 (1895), 137–224; H. Bulle et al., *Orchomenos* 1–3, 5 (Munich, 1907–83); P. Amandry—T. Spyropoulos, "Monuments chorégiques d'Orchomène de Béotie," *BCH* 98 (1974), 171–246, 819.

DAVID A. TRAILL

ORICELLARIUS, BERNARDUS. See RUCELLAI, BERNARDO.

ORLANDOS, ANASTASIOS K. (1888–1979). Greek architectural historian, archaeologist and architectural restorer.

Anastasios Orlandos was educated in Athens at the Polytechnic University, where he studied architecture, and at Athens University, where he pursued a curriculum in philosophy. After additional studies in England, France, Italy and Spain, he became professor of architecture at the Athens Polytechnic (1920) and professor of Byzantine archaeology at the University of Athens (1939).

Orlandos participated in excavations at Sikyon, Lesbos, Nikopolis and elsewhere but is remembered, above all, for his work in architectural restoration on the *Temple of Nike and the *Propylaia on the *Akropolis in Athens, the temple at *Sounion and other monuments. His publications number in the hundreds and include studies on Byzantine architecture as well as classical Greek. His most important publication is his work on Greek architectural techniques and materials, *Les Matériaux et la technique architecturale des anciens grecs* (1969).

Orlandos was appointed or elected to many distinguished posts. From 1917 he was director of reconstruction and ecclesiastical architecture of the Greek Ministry of Education, and from 1956 he served as secretary-general of the Athens Academy. He was honored with membership in numerous foreign archaeological institutes (American, Austrian, German and others) and was a knight of the French Legion of Honor. Orlandos died in Athens at the age of ninety-one.

BIBLIOGRAPHY

Who's Who in Greece (1958–59), 241; J. Heurgon, in *Comptes rendus de l'Académie des inscriptions* (1979), 512–14.

ORSI, PAOLO (1859–1935). Italian archaeologist.

An ascetic and tireless field-worker, Orsi went to *Syracuse in 1888 after a decade of multiperiod excavation and research in his native North Italy and, with F. *Halbherr, in *Crete. In *Sicily, his systematic excavation and detailed publication of innumerable centers ranging in date from Neolithic to Byzantine brought rigorous standards and new order to the interpretation of the island's past, most notably in the period covered by the cultures of the pre-Greek period, in which Stentinello, Thapsos, Plemmyrion, Cozzo Pantano, Pantalica, Cassibile and Finocchito—all discovered by Orsi before 1900—are still the key sites. His chronological classification of them was not changed in its essentials for sixty years, until L. Bernabò Brea incorporated his Lipari findings. Of special significance was Orsi's insistence (e.g., in his 1890 report on Neolithic Stentinello) that prehistoric pottery should not be seen as a precise indicator of either social development or—still less—ethnic affinity and that archaeologists should pay particular attention to environmental and faunal evidence. The Stentinello paper included the first specialist report on animal bones ever appended to the publication of an Italian site, and as early as 1912 Orsi was calling for microscopic analyses to determine the provenance of the numerous obsidian artifacts in Sicily.

Meanwhile, under Orsi's direction, the *Syracuse National Archaeological Museum became one of the great museums of Europe. From 1908, he extended his activity to Calabria, with similar results for the Reggio museum—and for knowledge. Although he taught at Catania in the 1890s, Orsi always regarded teaching as secondary to fieldwork. The chair of prehistoric archaeology (*paletnologia*) at Rome, following the death of L. *Pigorini in 1925, was one of a number of university posts he refused to accept. Today, his massive oeuvre remains indispensable both to his local successors and to the proper appreciation of the Sicilian and South Italian roles in the history of the ancient Mediterranean.

BIBLIOGRAPHY

G. Libertini, "Ricordo di Paolo Orsi," *Archivio Storico per la Sicilia* 1 (1935), 269–73; P. E. Arias, *Quattro archeologi del nostro secolo* (Pisa, 1976), 15–29, with bib. by G. Agnello, 113–26; R. Leighton, "Paolo Orsi (1859–1935) and the Prehistory of Sicily," *Antiquity* 60 (1986), 15–20.

DAVID RIDGWAY

ORSINI, FULVIO (URSINUS, FULVIUS; 1529–1600). Italian antiquarian, collector, Hellenist and bibliophile.

Born and raised in Rome, Fulvio Orsini was the protégé of Gentile Delfini (d. 1559), canon of S. Giovanni in Laterano. In the house of the erudite cleric on the Piazza Capizucchi near the Arco degli Altieri, Orsini found an important library and a collection of antiquities (coins and gems). He also became acquainted with Angelo *Colocci, Bishop of Nocera, and frequently visited the "orti Colotiani" on the Quirinal. Here he also encountered an impressive library and antique monuments. Colocci was especially interested in ancient metrology.

Growing up in this scholarly environment, Orsini became knowledgeable in ancient history and an expert Hellenist. He also developed a passionate interest in bibliography and archaeology and became an ardent collector of manuscripts. He obtained the *Terentius Bembus* and the *Vatican Vergil from the library of Pietro *Bembo, and, after much urging, Claude Dupuy parted with one folio of his *Titus Livius Puteanus* (Paris, Bibliothèque Nationale). Orsini later acquired a portion of Colocci's library and most of Delfini's books.

In 1554 Orsini was appointed canon of S. Giovanni in Laterano and became the church's botanist and keeper of the garden, which contained many rare plants. In this respect Orsini was like many great humanists of the seventeenth and eighteenth centuries (e.g., *Peiresc and *Kircher) in that he was interested in all knowledge, whether in the natural sciences, antiquity or the arts. Through Delfini he had been introduced to the *Farnese family, and in 1558 he was appointed librarian and secretary of Ranuccio Farnese, cardinal of S. Angelo, and accompanied him on his travels. After Ranuccio's death in 1565, Orsini remained in the service of his brother, Alessandro Cardinal Farnese, and was in charge of the family's books, manuscripts and already impressive collection of

Portrait of *Fulvio Orsini*, engraving by N. de Larmessin, from I. Bullart, *Académie des sciences et des arts* 1 (1682). (Westfälisches Landesmuseum für Kunst und Kulturgeschichte, Münster, Porträtarchiv Diepenbroick. Photo: R. Wakonigg.)

antiquities. Orsini advised the cardinal on other purchases, and the collection continued to increase in importance.

Orsini resided in the Palazzo Farnese in a second-floor apartment overlooking the Janiculum; he readily opened his library and "studio" to visitors, such as *Perrenot de Granvelle, who became his intermediary with the Plantin Press in Antwerp, where Orsini published his first books. He was also acquainted with Justus *Lipsius (secretary to Granvelle), who shared his archaeological interests. In addition, Orsini corresponded with many scholars throughout Europe; numismatics he discussed with Carolus Langius; he had glyptic interests in common with Laevinus *Torrentius.

On 2 March 1589, Alessandro passed away, and Orsini continued his task as caretaker of the family collections under Odoardo Farnese, son of the Duke of Parma. Sensing that his life was coming to an end, Orsini drew up his last will on 21 January 1600, bequeathing his library to the Vatican and his own collection of antiquities to Odoardo. (The antiquities remained within the Farnese collection when it was transferred to the *Museo Nazionale, Naples, in the late eighteenth century, and many of his objects are today in this museum.)

While his manuscripts were closest to his heart, he was also an avid collector of gems, coins, inscriptions and portrait busts. His large glyptic collection contained several signed cameos by Aulos, Epitynchanos and Sostratos and quite a few inscribed engraved gems, by Apollonios, Dioskourides, Gnaios, Hyllos, Pharnakes and Solon. A copy of his itemized inventory (Ambrosiana, Milan) lists 404 engraved gemstones (intagli and cameos), 113 portraits (among them images of befriended humanists), thirty-eight inscriptions, fifty-eight portrait busts (now in the Naples Museo Nazionale) and bas-reliefs, seventy gold coins, 1,900 silver and 500 bronze coins, plus sundry objects such as an abacus, a tripod and weights.

Some of the objects in his collection were published in his own books. Thirty-five inscriptions were used for his notes in the work of Antonio *Agustín, *De legibus et senatus consultibus* (Rome, 1583). Thirteen portraits were included in his *Imagines et elogia virorum illustrium et eruditorum* (Rome, 1570), a work in which he used numismatic, glyptic and sculptural monuments to identify the portraits of "Famous Men," mostly Greek, and added a commentary on the life of each, a thing that was novel in iconographical literature. For this kind of work he is often characterized today as the "father of ancient iconography." One of his most influential identifications, however, was later rejected. He was the first to identify the portrait of Seneca, from a bust in the Farnese collection; later he was proved wrong with the discovery of an inscribed portrait bust of Seneca in 1813 (*Pseudo-*Seneca*).

Most of our knowledge about Orsini's collection comes from the work of Dirk Galle (Gallaeus), who visited Rome in 1595 and made drawings of 240 portraits from Roman collections, especially that of Orsini. Galle engraved 151 of these for his own *Illustrium imagines* (published by Plantin, Antwerp, 1598), but Orsini was dissatisfied with the publication because it lacked a scholarly commentary. Orsini prepared notes for such a commentary but was unable to complete the work before he died, and the notes were taken over by Johannes Faber, a German physician and botanist to the pope, who finally issued the commentary for the second edition of the work (Antwerp, 1606). This book, enlarged with seventeen additional reproductions, became the basic reference work on portrait iconography for two centuries.

Fulvio Orsini was a friend to many accomplished artists—Taddeo Zuccari, Daniele da Volterra, Annibale *Carracci. For the latter he devised the program of the "Camerino" in the Palazzo Farnese and very possibly of the famous Galleria as well. The Camerino includes at least six examples of motifs and subject matter drawn from coins, while the Galleria reveals the influence of well-known sculptures such as the *Laocoon* and the *Farnese *Hercules*.

BIBLIOGRAPHY

P. de Nolhac, "Les collections d'antiquités de Fulvio Orsini," *MEFR* 4 (1884), 139–231; idem, *La Bibliothèque de Fulvio Orsini* (Paris, 1887); J. H. Jongkees, *Fulvio Or-

sini's Imagines and the Portrait of Aristotle (Groningen, 1960); J. R. Martin, *The Farnese Gallery* (Princeton, NJ, 1965); M. van der Meulen, *Petrus Paulus Rubens Antiquarius* (Alphen aan den Rijn, 1975); O. Neverov, "Gemme dalle collezioni Medici e Orsini," *Prospettiva* 29 (1982), 2–13; C. Riebesell, *Die Sammlung des Kardinal Alessandro Farnese, Ein "studio" für Kunstler und Gelehrte*, Acta Humaniora (Weinheim, 1989); +C. Gasparri, ed., *Le Gemme Farnese* (Naples, 1994), 85–99.

MARJON VAN DER MEULEN

ORVIETO. Small medieval town in Central Italy, the site of an important Etruscan center.

Orvieto, perched above the middle Tiber valley and known since the sixth century A.C. as *Urbs vetus*, "Old City," conceals an important Etruscan town variously identified as Herbanum (Raffaele da Volterra, *Cluverius; opposed by T. *Dempster), Salpinum (B. G. Niebuhr) and Fanum Voltumnae; modern research confirms K. O. *Müller's hypothesis (1828) that the site is that of *Volsinii veteres* (Etruscan *Velzna*), later transferred by the Romans to the vicinity of Lake Bolsena (*Volsinii novi:* Zonaras 8 7, *Bolsena). As early as the sixteenth century Monaldeschi noted "subterranean roads hewn in the rock in ancient times" and that "many sepulchres [are] found continually, of pagans and Greeks, with vases of black earth . . . and other beautiful things, whereof many are to be seen in the Archivio of the city."

The rich discoveries of the early nineteenth century (Belvedere temple; tombs) were no longer visible to G. *Dennis in 1846; but in 1857 and 1863 the two painted Golini tombs were discovered and were published by Conestabile in 1865; their paintings, detached in 1950 and previously housed in *Florence, are now exhibited in the recently opened National Museum of Orvieto. In 1864 E. Faina began the important collection that has since (1957) passed to the municipality; in 1879 he also resumed excavation of the Belvedere temple—the first example to be recognized of the Tuscan type with three cellae described by Vitruvius; and in 1883 he explored the painted tomb of the Hescanas. Between 1877 and 1890 R. Mancini explored the Cannicella and Crocifisso del Tufo cemeteries, revealing an orthogonal plan of considerable interest to historians of ancient town planning; inscriptions on the tombs demonstrate that Archaic Volsinian society was open to Italic foreigners and even Celts, while among the grave goods are many well-known vases both Attic (Niobid krater in the *Louvre) and Etruscan (Micali Painter; Vanth Group), now in many Italian and foreign museums.

BIBLIOGRAPHY

P. Perali, *Orvieto etrusca* (Rome, 1928); +M. Bizzarri, *La Necropoli di Crocifisso del Tufo* 1, 2 (Orvieto, 1963, 1966); +A. Andrén, *Il Santuario della necropoli di Cannicella* (Orvieto, 1968); B. Klacowicz, *Topografia e storia delle ricerche archeologiche in Orvieto e suo contado* 1–5 (Rome, 1972–78); +A. E. Feruglio, (ed.), *Pittura etrusca a Orvieto* (Rome, 1982).

F. R. SERRA RIDGWAY

OSTIA. The port city of Rome at the mouth of the Tiber River, 25km southwest of the city.

Ostia was founded ca. 338 B.C. as a *colonia maritima* to guard the coast of Latium, collect harbor taxes and discourage smugglers. In the second and first centuries B.C. the city grew rapidly; new circuit walls expanded its territory from two to sixty-four hectares. A new harbor, *Portus, was constructed by Claudius and expanded under Trajan 3km north of the city. This new facility joined Ostia with *Carthage and *Alexandria as one of the empire's major ports. Late in the third century A.C. a slow decline began, but the city was completely abandoned only in the ninth century, when pirate raids and malaria rendered it uninhabitable.

The site had come into the possession of the pope as early as the late seventh century. Pope Gregory IV (827–44) constructed or refurbished a small area as a garrison against Saracen pirates. Martin V (1417–31) built a round tower now known as the "Castello," which became the center of a new town on the edge of the site, which was itself constructed primarily under Cardinal Giuliano delle Rovere (the future *Julius II) from 1483 to 1486. Random excavations seeking works of art and building materials were carried out in the Roman city by Gavin *Hamilton in the eighteenth century and by others until the later nineteenth century; Portus was purchased from the pope in 1856 by the *Torlonia family and remains largely unexcavated. Periodic campaigns of scholarly excavation through the third decade of the twentieth century revealed some of the extent and importance of the site.

An initiative of the Mussolini regime—to prepare Roman Ostia as a central feature for a never-realized international exposition at Rome—led to an intensive campaign of excavation and restoration from 1938 to 1942, directed by G. *Calza. Since World War II, excavation and restoration have continued at a slower pace. Calza's excavations revealed the different periods of growth and decline at Ostia, particularly the earliest plan and its expansion. Restoration on the site has concentrated on reconstruction of the city of the second century A.C. The site must be counted among the finest accomplishments of Italian archaeology, characterized by careful and informative architectural restoration and an excellent site museum. Publication of the excavations, the architecture and the artistic remains has continued regularly; recent publication of Ostia's inscriptions, particularly the brick stamps, has greatly increased scholars' knowledge of the city, its history and its people.

BIBLIOGRAPHY

+G. Calza et al., *Scavi di Ostia,* 1–10 (Rome, 1953–79); +J. Packer, "The Insulae of Imperial Ostia," *MAAR* 31 (1971); R. Meiggs, *Roman Ostia,* 2nd ed. (Oxford, 1973); M. Steinby et al., "Lateres Signati Ostienses," *AIRF* 7 (1977–78).

JAMES C. ANDERSON, JR.

OVERBECK, JOHANNES (1826–95). German archaeologist, specialist in mythology in art, literary sources for ancient art and *Pompeii.

Overbeck's life history is simple. Born at Antwerp, he studied with F. *Welcker at Bonn. Called to Leipzig in 1858 as professor (*Ordinarius*), he remained there until his death in 1895. Known for doing ''useful archaeology,'' Overbeck published a number of comprehensive and systematic studies. His corpus of mythological representations in Greek art (*Griechische Kunstmythologie nebst Atlas . . .*) was issued in five parts, 1871–89. His monograph on *Pompeji,* appearing first in 1856, went through four editions (1884) and was the direct forerunner of August *Mau's authoritative monograph on Pompeii (1899). His collection of literary sources on Greek art, *Die Antiken Schriftquellen zur Geschichte der bildenden Künste bei den Griechen* (Leipzig, 1868; repr. Hildesheim, 1959) remains fundamental and is cited in all good modern bibliographies on this topic.

Overbeck was also well known for his great attention to his students; among his best were P. *Arndt, A. *Furtwängler, G. *Loeschcke, A. *Michaelis, T. *Schreiber.

BIBLIOGRAPHY
W. Miller, ''Overbeck,'' *AJA* 11 (1896), 361–70; H. Döhl, in *Archäologenbildnisse,* 51–52.

P

PAESTUM (POSEIDONIA). Greek colony in Southern Italy, site of three of the best-preserved Greek temples; Roman colony.

Founded ca. 600 B.C. by settlers originally from Troizen, Poseidonia flourished as a Greek settlement until ca. 400 B.C., at which time it was taken over by Lucanian Samnites. Around 335 B.C., the city was attacked by Alexander the Molossian, king of Epirus, and passed briefly under his control. The Lucanians then regained and retained control until 273 B.C., when the Romans founded a colony on the site and changed the name to Paestum. The Roman settlement flourished into the second century A.C.

Of the archaeological remains at Paestum, by far the most significant are the three temples of the Greek period. Given various names by the public or by scholars, they have been most convincingly identified as follows. The temple of Hera I (formerly called the Basilica; ca. 550 B.C.) features a well-preserved peristyle with nine columns on each end and eighteen on each side, as well as a single colonnade down the middle of the cella; the Doric columns are noted for their bulging quality, manifest in the exaggerated entasis. The pediments and the entire roof are lacking on this temple. The temple of Athena (formerly called the temple of Ceres; ca. 500 B.C.), with a formula of 6 × 13 columns, is remarkable for its use of the Ionic order on the front porch, in combination with the Doric exterior colonnade. A portion of the pediments survives along with the peristyle, but the roof is lacking. The temple of Hera II, ca. 450 B.C., is both the latest and largest of the three (ca. 60m × 25m) and preserves not only its Doric colonnades (6 × 14) but also most of its pediments, though the roof is lost.

The temple of Athena was converted into a Christian church in the sixth century A.C., and around it clustered a medieval village built of materials from dismantled classical structures. Due to swampy conditions and the threat of malaria, the site of Paestum became increasingly isolated, and the temples were largely forgotten until the eighteenth century. In 1740 the Neapolitan architect Ferdinando Sanfelice proposed to King Charles of *Bourbon that columns should be taken from the Greek temples at Paestum to adorn the royal buildings at Capodimonte; the proposal was fortunately abandoned. Count Felice Gazzola commissioned drawings of the temples between 1745 and 1750, and soon others arrived to study them—J.-G. Soufflot, Thomas Major, J. J. *Winckelmann, G. B. *Piranesi. Major's publication, *The Ruins at Paestum, Otherwise Poseidonia in Magna Graecia,* appeared in London in 1768.

Land drainage in the early twentieth century facilitated excavations of the principal Roman north-south street and part of the forum by V. Spinazzola. In the 1930s A. Marzullo and A. *Maiuri explored the city walls, gates and main thoroughfares, as well as the area around the temple of Athena, and F. Krauss investigated the other temples. Aerial photographs made before the American landing in 1943 showed the plan of the Roman town with great clarity. Detailed knowledge of the interior of the city resulted from the work of Pellegrino Sestieri in the 1950s. Perhaps the most sensational discovery at Paestum in the twentieth century came in 1968, when Mario Napoli excavated the Tomb of the Diver, a Greek tomb of ca. 480 B.C., painted with scenes of banqueting and of a diver plunging into the water. Napoli also investigated Lucanian painted tombs of the fourth century B.C.

Inside the city, recent research has focused on stratigraphical and topographical surveying, the results of which have been published by E. Greco and D. Theodorescu in *Poseidonia-Paestum* 1–3 (1980–86). Outside the city walls, a joint expedition by the universities of Michigan and Perugia, led by John Pedley and Mario Torelli, investigated a sanctuary of Aphrodite/Venus at the locality of Santa Venera (1981–85).

Some 8km outside Paestum is located the sanctuary of Hera at the mouth of the Sele River (Foce del Sele), a site described by Strabo but searched for in vain until its discovery in 1934 by P. Zancani-Montuoro and U. Zanotti-Bianco. A number of structures have been investigated (new excavations were begun in 1987), most important of which is the treasury building, dating ca. 570–560 B.C. Originally, thirty-three sandstone metopes were found and associated with the building, and, using these as a basis, a reconstruction was done in the Paestum Museum. But excavations in the sanctuary in 1958 unearthed three more metopes and called into question details of the reconstruction. The principal themes in these important Archaic sculptures are the deeds of Herakles and the Trojan War. Nearby was discovered the Doric temple to Hera, dating ca. 500 B.C., with eight columns on each end and seventeen on each flank. Another set of metopes, featuring pairs of dancing maidens, has received fresh examination by Frances Van Keuren (*The Hera I Temple at Foce del Sele: Reinterpretations of the Metopes and a New Reconstruction of the Frieze,* 1991).

BIBLIOGRAPHY
S. Lang, "The Early Publications of the Temples at Paestum," *JWarb* 13 (1950), 48–64; M. Napoli, *La Tomba del Tuffatore, La Scoperta della grande pittura greca* (Bari, 1970); J. Raspi Serra, ed., *Paestum and the Doric Revival 1750–1830* (Florence, 1986); J. G. Pedley, *Paestum, Greeks and Romans in Southern Italy* (London, 1990).

PAETUS AND ARRIA. See LUDOVISI GAUL KILLING HIMSELF AND HIS WIFE.

PALAIKASTRO. Bronze Age Minoan site at the northeast end of *Crete.

Excavations at Palaikastro were first conducted by R. C. Bosanquet for the *British School at Athens (1902–6) in the plain of Roussolakkos. The team unearthed a harbor town that flourished during the Late Minoan (LM) period, featuring dense habitation with houses set in large, irregular blocks on a few main streets. Destroyed by a severe fire in LM I, it was resettled in LM II and III. In Graeco-Roman times a temple of Dictaean Zeus was built in the area of the old town.

The site at Roussolakkos was partly ruined during World War II. Many of the remains were covered with earth for protection, leaving only a part of the town visible. J. A. MacGillivray and L. H. Sackett resumed work at the site in 1986. Their discovery of a gold and ivory statuette with head of serpentine may indicate the presence of a shrine in the LM I town.

On Petsophas, an adjacent hill, J. L. *Myres of the British School excavated a peak sanctuary (1903), and C. Davaras later explored the site. The mountain shrine yielded numerous votive figurines and stone offerings with Linear A inscriptions of Middle Minoan II–LM I (*Linear A and B).

BIBLIOGRAPHY
BSA 9 (1902–3); 10 (1903–4); 11 (1904–5); 12 (1905–6); 40 (1938–40); 60 (1965); 83 (1988); 84 (1989); C. Davaras, *Guide to Cretan Antiquities* (Park Ridge, NJ, 1976), 241–44. J. A. MacGillivray—J. Driessen, "Minoan Settlement at Palaikastro," in *L'Habitat égéen préhistorique, BCH* suppl. 19, ed. P. Darcque—R. Treuil (Athens, 1990), 395–412.

PALATINE HILL, Rome. One of the seven major hills of Rome, location of residences of the Roman aristocracy from the time of Romulus through the Roman Empire.

The mesalike hill of roughly quadrilateral shape overlooks the Tiber and in antiquity was surrounded by watercourses, except for a short stretch toward the east corner. It was the site of an Early Iron Age settlement and traditionally the location of Faustulus's hut and Romulus's city. The original *pomerium* (religious boundary) of Rome ran around its base and was interrupted by three gates, Porta Mugonia at the *Arch of Titus, Porta Ianualis at the north corner on the *Forum Romanum and Porta Romana or Romanula on the Velabrum. The sides of the hill were steep and probably in the early period improved by scarping. The only easy approach was from the Porta Mugonia by the so-called Clivus Palatinus, but the Scalae Caci, a ramped stair cut in the tufa bedrock leading up from the Porta Romana, also gave access.

Although there were various sacred places on the hilltop, such as the Auguratorium, the Curia Saliorum and Roma Quadrata, the only temples down to the time of the introduction of the Magna Mater in 204 B.C. seem to have been that of Victoria, (dedicated in 294 B.C.) and that of Jupiter Victor (vowed in 295 B.C.), probably the one at the east corner (Vigna Barberini). Later, others were introduced, notably Apollo Actiacus Palatinus, whose temple was Augustus's first important building (28 B.C.) and very sumptuous; the Sacrarium Divi Augusti on the site of Augustus's birthplace, later rededicated as the Templum Divi Augusti et Divae Augustae; and the temple of Sol Invictus Elagabalus, probably a splendid rebuilding of the temple of Jupiter Victor in A.D. 221.

On the other hand, around its base were very numerous temples and altars of great age, including the altar of Consus, Romulus's temple of Jupiter Stator and the temple of Vesta. The Lupercal, where the she-wolf had nursed Romulus and Remus, was in its lower slopes on the *Circus Maximus. The spring and pool of Juturna, which must have been the main source of drinking water for the Palatine village, were at its foot on the Forum Romanum.

Although hut foundations of the Iron Age village were excavated in 1948 by P. Romanelli and S. M. Puglisi near the top of the Scalae Caci, and nearby was found a very ancient granary or cistern with a corbeled dome, the layout of the hill in the Regal and Republican periods is very poorly understood. Because of its convenience to the forum, it was a very fashionable place to live in the Late Republic, and we know of numerous prominent Romans who lived there, but almost nothing about their houses. Augustus acquired the house of the orator Hortensius and made it the center of an enclave of his family and friends; his house has been discovered and excavated by G. Carettoni at the head of the Scalae Caci. Probably at least as much as half the house has been lost through erosion of the slope of the hill; what remains is planned around a rectangular court framed with a tufa arcade and preserves important decorations in the Second and Third Pompeian styles. The communication with the temple of Apollo Actiacus to the southeast seems to confirm the identification beyond reasonable doubt.

Tiberius next built a large house occupying much of the western crest of the hill, and this was enlarged by Caligula and then incorporated in the Domus Transitoria of Nero. The main components of the Domus Aurea seem to have been on the Oppian Hill, and, after Nero, Vespasian and Titus lived there. But Domitian returned to the Palatine, and the Domus Augustiana built by Rabirius was from then on the chief imperial residence in Rome. It occupied most of the eastern crest of the hill, except for the temple of Jupiter Victor, and annexes may have extended down the slope in places. From time to time, it was altered and enlarged, notably under Septimius Severus (*Septizodium) and Maxentius, but the main state apartments kept their original character.

Although the Palatine was plundered in the sack of Rome of Alaric in A.D. 410 and subsequently by the forces of Totila and Genseric, it continued to be an imperial residence through the Byzantine period in Rome, and we find that Heraclius received the imperial diadem from the Senate in the Aula Regia in 629 and that Pope John VII in 705 proposed to make the Domus Gaiana overlooking the forum the official residence of the bishops of Rome, although unsuccessfully. Thus, as late as the beginning of the eighth century, it was probably kept in reasonable repair. But a century or so later, we begin to hear of churches and monasteries there, S. Caesarii de Graecis or de Palatio in the ruins of the hippodrome of Domitian and S. Mariae in Pallaria, which is now S. Sebastiano, a strongly fortified place.

By the Early Renaissance the Palatine was no longer inhabited but was covered with vineyards and olives; there were frequent excavations made by those searching for fine marbles for use elsewhere and for material to burn for lime. Between 1540 and 1550, Cardinal Alessandro Farnese (*Farnese family) was able to buy up most of the western half of the hill and to create there the Giardini Farnese with a splendid gateway by *Vignola a little below the *Arch of Titus toward the forum, and a series of terraces embellished with grottoes, statuary and fountains, as well as planting, leading up to a symmetrical pair of aviaries, beyond which stretched the summit of the hill.

The gardens continued to be the prized possession of the family, and from this base F. *Bianchini in 1721–28 conducted excavations at various points in the Domus Augustiana, including the Aula Regia, where the two colossal statues of green basalt that are now in the museum of Parma were recovered; the Aula Isiaca, the decorations of which were carefully copied at this time; and the Casa di Livia (*House of Livia) and "Baths of Livia." Parts of these gardens have been restored and replanted. Much of the rest of the hill, except for the Vigna Barberini, was explored by *Boni in the first two decades of this century; he exposed the Domus Augustiana and precinct of the Magna Mater. Work there continues today, most recently in the Vigna Barberini and on the eastern slope.

BIBLIOGRAPHY

G. Lugli, *Roma antica, il centro monumentale* (Rome, 1946), 389–527; G. W. Cantino, *La Domus Augustana* (Turin, 1966); +G. Carettoni, *Das Haus des Augustus auf dem Palatin* (Mainz, 1983); C. Krause et al., *Domus Tiberiana, nuove ricerche, studi di restauro* (Zürich, 1985).

L. RICHARDSON, JR

PALAZZO MATTEI, Rome. Collection of Roman antiquities.

The Palazzo Mattei di Giove in Via de' Funari, Rome, was built by Carlo *Maderno for Asdrubale Mattei, Duke of Giove, in 1598–1611 (*Mattei family). It is famous for its collection of marble sculpture, much of which was acquired by Asdrubale himself. The collection adorns—at times in great profusion—the entrances, portico, main staircase and courtyards of the palace.

Today the collection contains 212 pieces: statues, reliefs, inscriptions, funerary altars, sarcophagi and architectural fragments. Although the bulk of the collection is Roman, 59 pieces are modern. Some of the latter were commissioned by Asdrubale; others are more recent. Indeed, it is not clear precisely how much of the collection was assembled in the seventeenth century. The inventory made after Asdrubale's death in 1638 is extraordinarily brief, and the first detailed information consists of drawings and a checklist among the papers of Richard Topham (1671–1730), at Eton College. In 1740, Girolamo Mattei commissioned an illustrated catalog, but the project was abandoned, and the first published account of the collection, the *Monumenta Matthaeana,* in three volumes, did not appear until 1776–79. Even this treatment creates problems, for it describes not only the original collection but also antiquities from another Mattei residence in Rome, the Villa della Navicella, and pieces sold to *Clement XIV in 1770.

BIBLIOGRAPHY
G. Panofsky-Sörgel, "Zur Geschichte des Palazzo Mattei di Giove," *Römisches Jahrbuch für Kunstgeschichte* 11 (1967–68), 111–87; L. Guerrini et al., "Sculture di Palazzo Mattei," *Studi Miscellanei* 20 (1971–72) and *Palazzo Mattei di Giove, Le Antichità* (Rome, 1982).

DAVID WHITEHOUSE

PALERMO (PANORMOS). Carthaginian settlement, founded in the mid-seventh century B.C. (Thucydides 6.2.6) on the northwest coast of *Sicily.

The settlement was captured by the Romans in 254 B.C. (Polybius 1.38) and became a Roman colony under Augustus. The ancient name of Panormos was changed to Balarm by the Arabs after A.D. 831, hence the modern name Palermo.

Panormos lies beneath the modern city. Its harbor was examined by Ibn Hawqal in 977, and its topography by *Fazello in 1558 (*De rebus siculis*) and by Moro in 1827 (*Descrizione di Palermo antico*). Since the later nineteenth century, excavation has uncovered aspects of the ancient city, notably tombs from the Punic through the Roman periods.

The Regional Archaeological Museum of Palermo, founded in 1866 as the Museo Nazionale di Palermo, includes material first assembled by the local Jesuit priest Ignazio Salnitro (sculpture, vases, coins, inscriptions) and displayed in his Museo Salnitriano in 1730, as well as Etruscan antiquities from *Chiusi collected by Count Bonci-Casuccini (added in 1865). The Palermo collection is especially important for its antiquities from nineteenth- and twentieth-century excavations at Palermo, *Selinus, Soloeis and other Sicilian cities.

BIBLIOGRAPHY
G. M. Columba, "Per la topografia antica di Palermo," *Centenario della nascità di Michele Amari* (Palermo, 1910), II, 395–426; I. Tamburello, "Palermo: terracotte figurate dalle necropoli," *Kokalos* 25 (1979), 54–63; V. Tusa—E. de Miro, *Sicilia occidentale* (Rome, 1983), 24–27; E. Guralnick, "Regional Archaeological Museum of Palermo," in *Art Museums of the World,* ed. V. Jackson (New York, 1987), 605–13.

SHELLEY C. STONE III

PALESTRINA. See PRAENESTE.

PALLADIO, ANDREA (ANDREA DI PIETRO DA PADOVA, ANDREA DI PIETRO DELLA GONDOLA; 1508–80). Italian Renaissance architect.

Palladio, who marks the successful completion of the Renaissance goal to rediscover and interpret antiquity, was born in Padua, where he began his career as a stonemason. Moving to Vicenza by 1524, he joined the workshop of Giacomo da Porlezza, which was responsible for much of the monumental decorative sculpture in Vicenza. Around 1537 Palladio met the Vicentine humanist Giangiorgio Trissino, who took him into his academy and gave him his first formal architectural training as well as the name Palladio. Contacts with the Padovan circle of Alvise Cornaro and Falconetto, along with the works of Vitruvius and Sebastiano *Serlio, impressed upon the young Palladio the importance of studying and drawing the ancient monuments, particularly those of Rome, where he made five trips in 1541, 1545, 1546–47, 1549 and 1554.

Palladio's contributions to the history of classical archaeology may be divided into three areas: his architecture, with its reinterpretation of classical motifs; his publications; and his drawings of ancient structures, which remained unpublished until long after his death.

In his architecture, Palladio followed Giuliano da *Sangallo (Poggio a Caiano) in applying ancient Roman forms like the temple front to villa façades, but he also used vaulted ceilings and thermal windows borrowed from Roman imperial thermae to elevate the status of private dwellings (Villa Barbaro, Maser; Villa Badoer; Villa Rotonda). Palladio's reinterpretation of antiquity is equally evident in his religious architecture, for example, in the interlocking pediments used for the façades of S. Giorgio Maggiore and the Redentore in Venice, and public buildings like the Teatro Olimpico in Vicenza, which drew inspiration from the stage setting or *scaenae frons* and seating arrangement of a Roman theater.

Palladio's publications reveal his humanist interests as well as his practical bent; the most famous of these, his *Quattro libri dell'architettura* (1570), surveyed building materials and techniques (Book 1), domestic buildings (Book 2), public buildings and town planning (Book 3) and temples (Book 4), illustrating both Palladio's own designs and ancient Rome examples. He published two small guidebooks to Rome in 1554, *Le Antichità di Roma* and *Descritione delle chiese . . . di Roma,* which were intended to replace the medieval *Mirabilia urbis Romae* (*Guidebooks to Rome [from 1550]). The *Antichità,* in particular, provided a succinct description of the topographical sites of ancient Rome, drawing on contemporary scholarship as well as ancient authors; the work was not superseded until the eighteenth century. Palladio also executed the drawings for Daniele Barbaro's 1556 edition of Vitruvius, and himself produced an edition of Julius Caesar's *Commentaries* in 1575 that was illustrated by his sons.

Like other Renaissance architects before him, Palladio spent much time studying and drawing ancient monuments. Of the some 330 sheets of Palladio's drawings that survive, approximately two-thirds represent studies of ancient monuments; most of these are now in the Royal Institute of British Architects in London. Although Palladio had intended to publish these studies organized by type (theaters, amphitheaters, arches, baths, tombs and bridges), it was not until 150 years after his death that the first publication of any of these drawings appeared (Richard Lord Burlington, *Fabbriche antiche disegnate da Andrea Palladio,* London, 1730). Among the first of the drawings to be published were Palladio's studies of imperial thermae, which constitute the most important single group of his studies of antiquities and include site sketches and reconstructed plans as well as elevation and section drawings. It is now recognized that the elevations and sections are not archaeologically accurate, since they represent Palladio's own inventive reconstructions of façades and roofing. The bath plans, however, have been relied upon since their initial publication in 1730 on the grounds that much more of the baths was preserved in the sixteenth century. Recent conservation has facilitated closer study of these plans. Some, such as RIBA XV/11v, a plan of the Baths of Decius in Rome, are demonstrably the product of Palladio's detailed survey of the site, but others appear based on graphic sources, earlier plans of the baths that Palladio studied and copied in the studio. While much work still needs to be done on the evaluation and dating of Palladio's drawings of antiquities, one key element for distinguishing between those plans that document Palladio's own survey and those that reflect surveys by earlier and possibly less reliably accurate draftsmen is the unit of measurement. Palladio generally used the vicentine foot (0.357m) when he himself measured a building; the presence of other units of measurement is often a clue that Palladio has copied an earlier plan.

In assessing the reliability of Palladio's own surveys, it is important to identify the stage in Palladio's working procedure to which the plan belongs. At present three successive stages can be distinguished: a first stage, in which the plan of the building was sketched freehand on the site and liberally annotated with measurements; a second stage, in which the field sketch was transcribed with the aid of straightedge and other equipment back in the studio; and a third stage, in which Palladio added missing elements to produce a reconstructed plan of the complex. While in some cases the reconstructed elements of this final plan were distinguished from those elements Palladio had observed on the site, more often they were not. Although alteration and elaboration to the plan of a Roman building could take place at any of the three stages, on the whole, the freehand site sketches seem to incorporate the least amount of alteration to the remains actually seen by Palladio and should therefore be considered the most archaeologically accurate.

BIBLIOGRAPHY

+G. G. Zorzi, *I Disegni delle Antichità di Andrea Palladio* (Venice, 1959); +H. Burns, *Andrea Palladio 1508–1580: The Portico and the Farmyard* (London, 1975), 268; G. De Angelis D'Ossat, "Invito allo studio dei 'Disegni delle Antichità'," *Bollettino del Centro Internazionale di Studi di Architettura "Andrea Palladio"* 21 (1979), 41–53, esp. 46–47; +D. Lewis, *The Drawings of Andrea Palladio* (Washington, DC, 1981); +C. Constant, *The Palladio Guide* (Princeton, 1985).

LAETITIA LA FOLLETTE

PALMYRA (TADMOR, TADMUR). Ancient Syrian oasis city with important remains of Hellenistic and Roman date.

Located in the north-central Syrian desert, Palmyra (called Tadmor before Greek and Roman times) was ideally placed between Damascus and the middle Euphrates as a strategic entrepôt on trade routes connecting the eastern Mediterranean with inner and southern Asia. The area was occupied from the third millennium; Aramean and Arab groups were present in the first millennium B.C.; then Palmyra came successively under Assyrian, Persian, Macedonian Greek and Roman overlordship, followed by Byzantine and Moslem rule. The city's most significant and wealthiest epoch occupied the first centuries A.C. Semi-independent until made a Roman colony (ca. A.D. 212), it enjoyed a brief emancipation under the famous queen Zenobia (Batzabbai), who conquered most of Anatolia and extended her rule into Egypt. But Rome retook the city, which, after a short-lived revolt (A.D. 273), was sacked by Aurelian's troops; modern Tadmur survived into the twentieth century as a modest village among the highly visible ruins. Most prominent are the well-preserved colonnaded avenues of the orthogonally gridded city, with their Corinthian columns and arches at intersections, and the huge sanctuary of Baal, all of the period of the Roman Empire. Also important are the numerous inscriptions in Aramaic, often with a Greek version added.

Rabbi Benjamin of Tudela was the first European to record his visit (A.D. 1172), followed by seventeenth century travelers—the Italian Pietro Della Valle, the Frenchman Tavernier, English merchants from Aleppo—and the first Palmyrene inscriptions brought back to Europe. Drawings and descriptions of the ruins in *Wood and Dawkins, *Ruins of Palmyra* (1753), made Palmyra a traveler's goal in the nineteenth century. In 1902, digging was inaugurated by German scholars. Henri Seyrig, director of antiquities for Syria under the French Mandate (1920), supervised French, German and Danish archaeological missions, removing (1929) the overlying modern village to a nearby site. After World War II, the Swiss archaeologist P. Collart excavated the great temple of Baal Shamin, and a Polish mission under Kazimierz Michalowski worked primarily on the vast palatial complex known as the Camp of Diocletian.

BIBLIOGRAPHY

+T. Wiegand, *Ergebnisse der Expeditionen von 1902 und 1917,* 1–2. (Berlin, 1932); J. Cantineau et al., eds., *Inventaire des inscriptions de Palmyre,* 1–12. (Damascus, 1930–76); K. Michalowski—M. Gawlikowski—A. Sadurska, *Palmyre,* 1–7. (Warsaw, 1960–84); J. Teixidor, *Un Port romain du désert, Palmyre et son commerce d'Auguste à Caracalla* (Paris, 1984).

                                                                        BERNARD GOLDMAN

PANINI (PANNINI), GIOVANNI PAOLO (1691–1765). The most celebrated painter of views of Rome during the eighteenth century.

Born in Piacenza, Panini arrived in 1711 at the Eternal City, where he studied landscape painting and scenographic design. Initially he worked as a fresco decorator of architectural and landscape views in the great Roman palaces (e.g., Palazzo del Quirinale, 1721–22). He then turned to a type of painting for which he is famous—pictures commemorating recent public events and official celebrations in the capital (e.g., *Festival at the Teatro Argentina for the Wedding of the Dauphin, 1747;* *Louvre, Paris).

Accorded high acclaim by his contemporaries, Panini received membership in the Academy of St. Luke, Rome, and the French Academy of Painting and Sculpture, Paris. His ties to France were numerous, consisting of French patrons as well as artists. His work exerted a profound influence on Hubert *Robert, whose mentor he was. He was probably also the teacher of Giovanni Niccolo Servandoni.

Panini's paintings of ancient Roman monuments were conceived in two complementary manners: the documentary, in which ancient sites and buildings were recorded with the precision of an archaeologist; and the capricious, in which the buildings were depicted accurately but reassembled in an imaginary space. Many of the paintings show a straightforward contemporary view of an ancient structure, such as his best-known work, *The Interior of the *Pantheon* (ca. 1740; National Gallery, Washington D.C.). The most oft-repeated monuments in his paintings were the *Colosseum and the *Arch of Constantine, usually paired in realistic views (e.g., 1735 version; Detroit Institute of Art). He also painted historical narratives either in an invented classical setting (*Alexander Visiting the Tomb of Achilles,* 1719; Galleria dell'Accademia di S. Luca, Rome) or in a recognizable context (*Adoration of the Magi,* taking place in the ruins of the Colosseum! ca. 1710; coll. Antonin-Zambelli, Piacenza). Similarly, throughout his career he painted scenes of either pagan sibyls or Christian apostles preaching in the midst of archaeological fragments of his own invention.

Immensely popular were Panini's caprices of numerous famous classical monuments brought together in a fictitious setting. For example, *The Return of the Veteran* includes the Pantheon, the *Arch of Septimius Severus, the *Obelisk of Augustus, the *Marcus Aurelius* Equestrian Statue, the *Farnese *Hercules* and several ruined Roman temples, seemingly located cheek by jowl (1730; coll. Piero Candiani, Busto Arsizio). In an interesting variation of this idea, Panini created for the Duc de Choiseul, the French ambassador to Rome, a pair of large canvases showing imaginary palatial galleries stocked with pictures of the greatest structures of ancient Rome and modern Rome (1756; Staatsgalerie, Stuttgart). The sources for the capricci may be traced to the architectural *Roman wall paintings of ancient villas and the freely invented perspectival backdrops of Renaissance and Baroque stage performances. In Panini's imagined views, the rustic and togate figures serve principally as staffage, rather than to provide a narrative.

Visitors on the *Grand Tour bought Panini's paintings to take home with them as souvenirs, while ardent antiquarians desired pictorial catalogs of the monuments they had visited. For example, the Englishman Henry *Blundell purchased Panini's *Capriccio of Roman Ruins* to install in the Pantheon-like rotunda he built at Ince Blundell House for the purpose of displaying his trophies of the southern sojourn (1741; Walters Art Gallery, Baltimore). These images of crumbling buildings allowed the viewer to ruminate in a melancholy vein on the waning of civilizations and the unbridgeable gulf between the distant past and the present.

Panini's paintings had a considerable impact on the development of the print-maker Giovanni Battista *Piranesi, although the latter was motivated by a more fanatical archaeological fervor. Panini's views are always evenly lit, sharply focused and thus seemingly objective in nature; in this respect they lack the more sublime effects achieved by both Piranesi and Robert through dramatic juxtapositions of scale and strong contrasts of light and dark. In short, his *vedute* were more the picture postcards of the eighteenth century, albeit on a grand scale.

BIBLIOGRAPHY
+L. Ozzola, *Gian Paolo Pannini pittore; cinquanta tavole* (Turin, 1921); +F. Arisi, *Gian Paolo Panini* (Piacenza, 1961); +idem, *Gian Paolo Panini e i fasti della Roma del '700,* 2nd ed. (Rome, 1986).

ROBERT NEUMAN

PANOFKA, THEODOR (1800–1858). German archaeologist; pioneer in organized archaeology as a member of the *Hyperboreans.

Born in Breslau, Panofka studied classical philology in Berlin from 1819. In the spring of 1823 he set off for Rome, where he joined the union of northerners known as the Hyperboreans, devoted to the study of classical remains; his collaborators were O. M. von *Stackelberg, A. Kestner and E. *Gerhard. Panofka was considered imaginative and stimulating and attracted others, especially Frenchmen, to the group. Becoming friends with the generous collector the Duc de *Blacas, he followed him to Paris; when, in 1828, the Hyperborean union was succeeded by the *Instituto di Corrispondenza Archeologica, Panofka became the secretary for the Paris branch of the new organization.

Soon Panofka visited Naples. Becoming deeply committed to archaeological research as he worked on South Italian vases, he helped catalog the antiquities of the *Museo Nazionale, Naples. (Gerhard did the sculpture, and Panofka did the vases.) In Paris he pursued his interest in ceramics with his *Recherches sur les véritables noms des vases grecs* (1829).

By 1836 Panofka had ceased to work for the Instituto and had returned to *Berlin to become an assistant at the museum. Eventually, in 1856, he was made conservator of the vase collection. In spite of financial problems and increasing deafness, he worked indefatigably. His *Terrakotten des Kgl. Museums zu Berlin* appeared in 1842. In his later years Panofka was much criticized for the arbitrary nature of his opinions and errors in his scholarship. He died in Berlin in 1858.

BIBLIOGRAPHY
Michaelis, 57–58; *Archäologenbildnisse,* 25–26.

PANORMOS. See PALERMO.

PANTHEON, Rome. Roman temple, dedicated to all the gods.

The best preserved of all major classical buildings, the Pantheon was built at the direction of the Emperor Hadrian (reigned A.D. 117–38) and surely reflects his strong architectural and cultural interests. The inscription on the portico, which says that it was erected in 27 B.C. (Marcus Agrippa the Son of Lucius, Three Times Consul, Built This) refers to an earlier building, whose dedicatory words Hadrian later had copied for his own, entirely new construction. The location of the Pantheon in Rome has ensured its ready accessibility and thus its fame, and it has been admired, studied, and analyzed for centuries. Its state of preservation is due to the excellence of its construction—it is made largely of concrete—and to the fact that, once having been made a church (about A.D. 609), it was given at least minimal maintenance and repair before Renaissance and modern engineers and architects came to its aid. The vast dome over the central cylinder, 150 Roman feet in diameter, is probably the largest vault of simple masonry in the world.

Domed rotundas with temple-front porticoes were very rare before the Pantheon; after it was built, the idea caught on quickly and has been a part of the architecture of Western people ever since. But no actual copies of the original seem ever to have been made, nor any versions so large and spacious. In its original setting the building was fronted by an elongated, colonnaded courtyard, stretching to the north, whose paving level was considerably lower than that of the present Piazza della Rotonda, and as a result the building now appears to be less high than it was intended to be. A function of this courtyard was to limit the view presented to the approaching visitor of the traditional forms and symbols of the temple front, the vast bulk of the rotunda behind being obscured. The pediment of the porch may have contained a relief sculpture of a huge, wreathed eagle of a kind common in the Roman world, and the external surface of the dome was covered with gilded bronze tiles. Almost nothing is known of the other features of the exterior decor, but the cylinder proper was probably covered with a thick appliqué of stucco drafted to look like masonry. The bricks one sees today are the weather cover of the concrete core that does the actual work of enclosing the rotunda and supporting the great concrete dome.

In the interior there would have been a good deal of sculpture, whether of Olympian or planetary deities is not known. Seven major and eight minor niches provide ample space for conjecture as to the location and nature of the sculpture; that it was there, however, is certain, and whatever was left of it in the early seventh century, when the building became a church, was ordered removed by the Byzantine emperor when he gave his permission for conversion to Pope Boniface IV. In 663 another Byzantine ruler, visiting Rome, had the roof tiles removed; subsequently he lost them, in Sicilian waters, to Arab corsairs. As Sancta Maria ad Martyres, or, more popularly, Santa Maria Rotonda, the building became a depository for martyrs' relics. It may have been in the eighth

The *Pantheon*, Rome, etching by G. B. Piranesi, 1761.

century that the dome was re-covered with sheets of lead, later repairs to which are recorded by sheets embossed with the coats of arms of various popes. In the late thirteenth century, a bell tower appeared, centered over the portico roof, the eastern corner of which, together with its huge supporting granite columns, had collapsed at some unknown date. Meanwhile, cuts had been made through the rotunda wall, near the south apse, and as time passed the ancient structures surrounding the rotunda gradually disappeared.

Although generalized images of the building appear in medieval art, only in Renaissance times were fairly accurate views of the building made and, in due time, published. A series of *vedute,* or views, dating from the fifteenth century onward gives some account of the building's appearance and condition, and a large number of architects' measured sketches and drawings have survived. The forecourt had begun to fill in, and its colonnades had collapsed, before that time, and some massive ancient sculpture had been parked there. Shops appeared between the portico columns, and at some point a large altar stone, fashioned from a block of marble taken from the audience hall of the Palace of the Caesars on the Palatine, was set before the south apse. In 1520, *Raphael was buried at the base of the southeasternmost small niche, and subsequently several major architects and artists were interred in the building. Early in the seventeenth century, twin towers were erected over the porch, perhaps by *Bernini or perhaps by *Maderno, replacing the single, medieval tower; in the late nineteenth century these were removed in turn. Also in the seventeenth century the eastern end of the portico was repaired by Bernini, who included in his work the heraldry of the popes responsible. The fallen, lost columns were replaced by other great ancient shafts found nearby, new capitals were cut, and the balance and harmony of the façade were restored. Urban VIII Barberini (1623–44) removed tons of ancient bronze from the ancient roof structure of the portico and used the metal to cast cannon for Castel Sant'Angelo; this gave rise to one of the most celebrated of Roman pasquinades (genuine or not): *quod non fecerunt barbari, fecerunt barberini* (What the barbarians didn't do, the little barbarians did).

Meanwhile, appreciation and study of the building had not only increased but had become obligatory for the great Italian masters. They measured it, studied it, and argued and wrote about it. The domed rotunda became one of the essential architectural inspirations of Renaissance and post-Renaissance architecture. The proportions of the interior—equality of height and width—were much admired and, since they were also found in Vitruvius's hallowed treatise, linked such studies directly with the practice of antiquity. It is sometimes difficult to separate genuine from spurious remarks attributed to important persons, but it is worth noting that *Bramante, speaking of his plans for the new Saint Peter's, is said to have wished to ''erect the dome of the Pantheon'' on the arches of the *Basilica of Maxentius and Constantine; *Michelangelo declared that the Pantheon was ''designed not by men but by angels''; and Bernini believed that the ''dome of Saint Peter's has a hundred faults, that of the Pantheon none.''

But no one copied the building; rather, it was a primary source of inspiration, a building whose secrets were to be wrested from it and thus a design as significant in the history of classicizing architecture as the arcades of the Colosseum or the well-preserved temple at Nîmes (*Maison Carrée). Tribute was paid to it in the form of an elaborate fountain placed in the courtyard in the sixteenth century—to which an *Obelisk of Rameses II (1290–24 B.C.) was added in 1711. But in the eighteenth century, a tasteless stucco lining of blank windows was applied to the attic zone of the interior, replacing the original grilled openings and marble decor. In 1878 and 1900, respectively, Umberto I and Victor Emmanuel II were buried in the rotunda. Major structural consolidation and investigation were carried out in 1929–34, and since then there have been shorter campaigns of cleaning and necessary repairs.

Archaeological study of the Pantheon long centered on the question of its date and on the relationship between the portico and the rotunda. Although an Agrippan date for the building has long been disproved, the inscription is still taken literally by some. The correct date of the entire structure has been shown to be Hadrianic, so that it was begun shortly after his accession in 117 and finished in the later 120s. This conclusion is based chiefly on the study of the brickstamps found in the structural fabric of the building and on comparative studies of Hadrianic architectural forms. Still, the idea that the portico is Hadrianic has met with some resistance, partly because its junction with the rotunda is somehat awkwardly managed. An inscription on the portico architrave records a restoration of A.D. 202, and that, too, has been brought into the arguments about dating and homogeneity, but without success. There are remains of Agrippa's smaller, different building beneath and beside the Hadrianic work, and the study of them is in good hands.

The structure of the building and the means by which it was put in place are still being studied. To medieval people, the Pantheon seemed to have been made by demons, being an effort beyond mere mortals. Unable to comprehend how it had come to be, people repeated fanciful stories of its origin, for example, that the great vault was built over an immense mound of earth heaped up inside the cylinder and that in order to encourage the Romans to remove the earth when construction was finished, Hadrian had the mound seeded with gold pieces (the same story was told of other awesome constructions). In fact, the vault was built over a forest of supports and braces that carried the spreading hemispherical wood surface against which the concrete was laid, an impressive performance by any standards. The great load of the dome is discharged by means of huge, radially placed barrel vaults onto what are, in effect, eight enormous piers formed by the solid portions of the cylinder wall between the niches. The foundations of the building extend well down into the blue clay of the Campus Martius, where the aggregate of the concrete is made of heavy marble. As the building rises, the aggregate is of ever lighter stone, with pumice used at the top, in the zone of the thirty-foot oculus.

Another telling aspect of this most imperial of Roman monuments is the use of marbles and other stones from around the empire. Some of the Egyptian granite portico columns are tinted, though dirt and pollution have made them all more or less uniformly gray. The portico walls are finished with white Italian marble and, inside the rotunda, marbles from North Africa, Asia Minor, Greece and Italy, together with granites, porphyries and serpentines from various provinces, appear in the pavement (restored), the niches, and the veneering of the walls. The original bronze doors, somewhat reworked, are still in use, and long ago, it seems, there was a huge, gilded bronze rosette anchored in the center of each of the 140 perspective coffers of the dome. Thus, the building is a museum of structural materials and techniques, its fabric the result of centuries of experience and experiment both Greek and Roman. The Pantheon, however, still keeps many of its secrets, such as the way in which Euclidian propositions were turned into architectural shapes or the fashion in which the necessary, if primitive, calculations were made before construction could begin. Above all, the building resists giving up the mystery of its meaning, of the things it chiefly symbolized to Hadrian and his contemporaries.

BIBLIOGRAPHY

+A. Desgodetz, *Les Édifices antiques de Rome* (1682 and subsequent eds.); +L. Beltrami, *Il Pantheon* (1898); +idem, *Il Pantheon rivendicato ad Adriano* (1919); +F. Cerasoli, "Il restauro del Pantheon dal secolo XV al XVIII," *BullComm* 37 (1909), 280–89; +A. Terenzio, "La restauration du Panthéon de Rome," *Museion* 20 (1932), 52–57; H. Kähler, "Das Pantheon in Rom," *Meilensteine europäischer Kunst* (Munich, 1965), 47–75; +K. de Fine Licht, *The Rotunda in Rome* (Copenhagen, 1968); T. Buddensieg, "Criticism and Praise of the Pantheon in the Middle Ages and the Renaissance," *Classical Influences of European Culture* (Cambridge, 1971), 259–67; +M. E. Blake, *Roman Construction in Italy from Nerva Through the Antonines* (Philadelphia, 1973); +W. L. MacDonald, *The Pantheon—Design, Meaning, and Progeny* (Cambridge, MA, 1981), and *The Architecture of the Roman Empire,* rev. ed. (New Haven, CT, 1982).

WILLIAM L. MacDONALD

PANVINIO (PANVINIUS), ONOFRIO (1530–68). Italian ecclesiastical historian, liturgiologist and antiquarian.

Panvinio, an Augustinian friar from Verona whose precocious bent for scholarship drew him to Rome in 1547, published erudite studies of the Roman consular *Fasti,* of the monuments and institutions of Republican Rome (*Reipublicae romanae commentariorum libri tres*) with new topographical sources (both Venice, 1558); engravings of Roman triumphs based on Roman sculpture and coins (Antwerp, 1556, Rome, 1565); and volumes on Roman names and imperial *comitia.* He died prematurely, leaving manuscripts on the Roman antiquities of *Verona, on aspects of Roman religion, games, theaters and gladiatorial combats, and detailed plans for a vast survey of Roman antiquities to be written in one hundred books distributed in five volumes. In these he hoped to describe accurately the principal monuments of ancient Rome, private and public life, the empire beyond Rome, inscriptions of Rome and the empire and a history of Rome from its foundation to his own day.

BIBLIOGRAPHY
D. A. Perini, *Onofrio Panvinio e le sue opere* (Rome, 1899); Mandowsky—Mitchell, 14, 19, 22, 24, etc.; W. McCuaig, "Andreas Patricius, Carlo Sigonio, Onofrio Panvinio and the Polish Nation of the University of Padua," *History of Universities* 3 (1983), 87–100; K. Gersbach, "The Books and Personal Effects of Young Onofrio Panvinio," *Analecta Augustiniana* 52 (1989), 51–76; idem, "Onofrio Panvinio's 'De comitiis imperatoriis' and Its Successive Revisions," *Analecta Augustiniana* 53 (1990), 409–52.

ROBERT W. GASTON

PAPHOS. Greek city in southwest *Cyprus, the legendary birthplace of Aphrodite.

The region of Paphos, unusually rich in archaeological remains spanning the Chalcolithic through Lusignan periods, was added to the World Heritage List of the United Nations Educational, Scientific, and Cultural Organization (UNESCO) in 1980. In antiquity the site was renowned as the birthplace of Aphrodite and boasted the goddess's most famous sanctuary. While never a great commercial center, Paphos derived substantial wealth from its tourist trade and agricultural resources. Around 320 B.C., the town was moved from its original, slightly inland location near the modern village of Kouklia (Palaeopaphos) to the coast at the modern town of Kato Paphos, about ten miles to the northwest. This new settlement became the capital of Cyprus during the Ptolemaic and Roman periods.

In the Middle Ages the extensive Hellenistic and Roman remains at the site of Saranda Kolonnes (Forty Columns) in Kato Paphos were incorrectly identified as the famous sanctuary of Aphrodite. An inscription found at Kouklia in 1800 provided the first clue that the sanctuary was located at the older settlement. Late nineteenth-century excavations by *Cesnola and the British Cyprus Exploration Fund provided no significant information about the ancient sanctuary, although several Bronze Age tombs were explored.

The modern era of excavation at Palaeopaphos began in 1950, when the British Kouklia Expedition, working until 1955, revealed more Bronze Age tombs and remains of the Archaic, Classical and Roman periods and of the Middle Ages. In 1966 F. G. Maier began a continuing project that has investigated a Bronze Age predecessor to the sanctuary of Aphrodite, a Persian siege mound and a medieval sugarcane refinery.

Systematic explorations of the harbor town of Paphos did not begin until the 1950s, when A.H.S. Megaw, then director of antiquities, began excavating the crusader castle at Saranda Kolonnes. A major discovery was made nearby in 1962, when plowing uncovered the ruins of a Roman villa (the "House of Dionysos") decorated with magnificent floor mosaics. Other lavish villas (e.g., the "House of Theseus" and the "House of Aion") have since been explored. Also, rock-cut tombs of Hellenistic and Roman date have been investigated (popularly called "the Tombs of the Kings"). To the northwest of Paphos, a Late Bronze Age fortified site has been excavated on the coastal promontory of

Maa-Paleokastro. The development of Paphos as a modern tourist resort necessitates almost continuous salvage excavation of archaeological remains.

BIBLIOGRAPHY

K. Nicolaou, s.v. "Paphos or Nea Paphos" and "Paphos or Palaipaphos," *PECS*, 673–75; F. G. Maier—V. Karageorghis, *Paphos: History and Archaeology* (Nicosia, 1984).

PAMELA J. RUSSELL

PAROS. Island located in the central Cyclades of the Aegean Sea.

Originally called Minoa, Paros was renamed for the son of Parision, the Arcadian king, who escaped there during the Dorian invasion. Oddly, no Minoan remains have been discovered. On the neighboring islet of Saliagos, C. Renfrew excavated a Final Neolithic settlement. Early Cycladic cemeteries and settlements were excavated by C. *Tsountas and, more recently, by C. Doumas. O. Rubensohn found Middle Bronze Age and early Mycenaean remains in Paroikia. D. Schilardi excavated a late Mycenaean fortress on Koukounaries Hill, overlooking the Bay of Naoussa, with a Geometric settlement and an Archaic Athena sanctuary on its slopes. By the seventh century B.C., Paroikia was probably the main city. A cemetery of the Orientalizing to Roman periods was excavated near the modern harbor by the *Greek Archaeological Service. During the fifth–fourth centuries B.C., the island became a major source for marble, notably, for the sculpture of the *Temple of Zeus at Olympia. Its Classical buildings were destroyed and reused in later monuments. However, extramural sanctuaries to Pythian and Delian Apollo and Asklepios were excavated by Rubensohn. A Hellenistic sculptor's workshop and Roman burials in marble sarcophagi attest to Paros's continued prosperity.

Although its population decreased during the Byzantine period (395–1204), its most famous church, the Ekatontapyliani, was built between the fourth and sixth centuries on the site of a Roman gymnasium. Paros formed part of the duchy of Naxos in the Latin period (1204–1453), when its Kastro was built over the Classical acropolis, incorporating architectural elements from temples and a theater. It was part of the Ottoman Empire in 1537 until the liberation of Greece in 1829.

Accounts of the island's remains visible to eighteenth- and nineteenth-century travelers may be found in P. de Tournefort, L. *Ross and T. Bent.

BIBLIOGRAPHY

T. Bent, "Researches Among the Cyclades," *JHS* 5 (1885), 42–58, O. Rubensohn, *Das Delion von Paros* (Wiesbaden, 1962); N. Aliprantis, *Paros and Antiparos* (Athens, 1978); G. Moussa, *Paros, The White Island* (Amsterdam, 1980).

ROBERT B. KOEHL

PARS, WILLIAM (1742–82). English painter and draftsman, known especially for his topographical and archaeological views.

Born of a London family of artists, Pars received early training at Shipley's drawing school in the Strand and received prizes from the Society of Arts for his drawings of the head of *Laocoon and other subjects. By 1761 he was assisting his brother Henry in the running of Shipley's school and was occupied with portrait painting. He also began to do history painting and produced a prizewinning version of *Caractacus Before the Emperor Claudius* (1764), a work that may have attracted the attention of the *Society of Dilettanti so that they sought him out for a special commission.

The Dilettanti, on the heels of the success of the first volume of *Antiquities of Athens* by James *Stuart and Nicholas *Revett (1762), resolved to send out a similar expedition to Asia Minor, with Richard *Chandler to prepare the text and Revett and Pars to prepare the illustrations. The team departed in 1764 and worked in Asia Minor through the summer of 1765, continuing to Greece, where they visited *Sounion, *Aigina, Athens and *Corinth. Pars made drawings all along the way, often using his favorite combination of pen and ink and water-color. The resulting materials were accepted with approbation by the Dilettanti, and selected drawings were published in Chandler's *Ionian Antiquities* in 1769. Included were views by Pars of Alexandria Troas, *Ephesos, *Miletos, *Didyma, Mylasa, Teos, *Priene and others. Some of his engravings were later used as illustrations for Robert *Wood's *Essay on the Original Genius and Writings of Homer, with a Comparative View of the Ancient and Present State of the Troade* (1775).

While in Greece, Pars had made numerous drawings of sculpture in Athens, especially of the *Parthenon, and these were taken over for the second volume of *Antiquities of Athens* (1788), as well as the two subsequent volumes (1795, 1816). They constituted the first comprehensive illustrations of these marbles and provided information about their appearance before the Turkish vandalism that allegedly led Lord *Elgin to remove the sculptures from Greece. A great part of the drawings made during the Ionian tour was presented by the Society of Dilettanti to the *British Museum in 1799.

After the successful outcome of the Ionian expedition, Pars was appointed by the Dilettanti to study in Italy (1775); for several years he worked in and around Rome, painting and drawing. At the age of forty he died suddenly from an illness contracted as a result of standing too long in water while he was drawing at *Tivoli.

BIBLIOGRAPHY
+R. Chandler, *Travels in Asia Minor, 1764–1765,* ed. E. Clay, with an appreciation of William Pars by A. Wilton (London, 1971), xxi–xlv.

PARTHENON, Athens. Most famous of all Greek temples, sacred to *Athena Parthenos, erected on the *Akropolis at Athens, 448–432 B.C.

Constructed during the age of Perikles, the temple represents a period that is traditionally viewed as a turning point in human development, when the earliest institutions of modern democracy, together with many of the disciplines and classifications still recognized today as the basis of the Western tradition in arts and sciences, were for the first time defined and given a classical form. Among the monuments of art and architecture that survive from the Periklean Age, the Parthenon with its sculptures is by far the most important and the best preserved and has thus become a major source of our knowledge of Classical Greek art at the time of its greatest achievements.

Ancient literary sources, mainly Plutarch and Vitruvius, provide some basic facts concerning the early history of the Parthenon, and there are fragments of building inscriptions excavated on the Akropolis that provide additional details. Plutarch, in his *Life of Perikles,* informs us that the sculptor Pheidias was placed in a position of overall supervision of the reconstruction of the Akropolis, an undertaking that marked the end of a period of more than thirty years during which the sanctuaries of Athens, destroyed by the Persians in 480 B.C., were allowed to remain in ruins as a reminder of the danger of invasion by eastern armies. The reconstruction of the Akropolis temples signaled the end of the Persian wars and the conscious beginning of a new era in which Athens proposed to take the lead in a great confederation of Greek city-states that would be strong enough to meet the threat of foreign invasion. The political ambitions of Athens at this historic juncture may explain the extraordinary grandeur of the Parthenon, which was built entirely of Pentelic marble on a scale far exceeding that of earlier Doric temples in Greece. Its sculptured adornment was more elaborate than, for example, the *Temple of Zeus at *Olympia, completed about two decades earlier. In addition to the pedimental groups planned for the two façades, the Parthenon received a series of sculptured metopes that continued on all four sides of the exterior Doric entablature, and, in addition, a continuous sculptured frieze, an Ionic feature, ran around the upper walls and porch entablatures of the cella building set within the peristyle. The themes narrated in these sculptures celebrated the birth and victory of Athena, the protector of Athens, and the victories of Greek gods and heroes in mythology. The Parthenon frieze is traditionally interpreted as the depiction of the Panathenaic procession, the parade from the *Agora of Athens to the Akropolis that marked the beginning of the Great Panathenaia, an international celebration of Athena's birth with games and contests that was held at Athens on every fourth year. The suggestion made by Chrysoula Kardara in 1961 that the Panathenaia shown on the Parthenon may refer to the period of the earliest mythological kings of Athens has recently gained new support.

The chief architect of the Parthenon appears to have been Iktinos. Two other names are mentioned in the sources, Kallicrates and Karpion, but scholars still debate the various possibilities regarding their roles and the authorship of the design. The situation is further complicated by the fact that an earlier version of the Parthenon was apparently under construction when the Persian wars began, and some elements of the earlier design may have been taken over in the new project. However, the plan of the earlier structure has been recovered through excavations beneath the floor of the present Parthenon, and enough is now known to make it clear that the Periklean temple rendered the earlier design obsolete. A widened cella permitted a complete reinterpretation of the interior

View of the *Parthenon*, Athens, from J. Stuart–N. Revett, *The Antiquities of Athens* 2 (1787).

space, with an interior colonnade returning across the back to form a continuous ambulatory on three sides of the room, greatly reducing the axial emphasis inherited from Archaic times. The widening of the cella and other changes in the plan made it necessary to rebuild parts of the foundation, but the curvature of the Parthenon floor, a feature of the design that helps to give the temple its unique sense of lightness and grace, was already present in the foundations of the earlier structure, according to *Dinsmoor.

Plutarch, writing some 500 years after the temple was built, states that the results achieved by the architects of the Parthenon gave the traditional forms of the peripteral Doric temple a new interpretation, retaining a sense of being "ancient" while at the same time expressing a spirit of freshness and youth. Plutarch also mentions a mysterious power of regeneration that the building seemed to possess. Speaking of the Periklean Akropolis, he wrote, "[I]t is as if some ever-flowering life and unaging spirit had been infused into the creation of these works." Possibly Plutarch had in mind not only the architectural designs but also the Pheidian sculptures that adorned the Parthenon, which by Plutarch's day had inspired many copies and imitations. Certainly, in these words, written within the period of classical antiquity itself, there seems to be a recognition of the kind of influence the Parthenon was to exert even more strongly on the art and architecture of later periods.

The history of the Parthenon after the close of antiquity may be divided into a number of periods corresponding to the various religious functions served by the building once the worship of Athena came to an end. In outline, the periods are as follows: (1) the Early Christian and Byzantine periods from the fifth century A.C. to 1204, during which the temple was transformed into a Christian basilica dedicated to Saint Sophia; (2) the so-called Frankish period (1204–1458), when Athens was ruled by a succession of French, Catalan and Italian adventurers, and the Parthenon became a cathedral church dedicated to the Virgin Mary; (3) the Turkish period (1458 to the Greek War of Independence, 1821–33), which may be divided in two parts: from 1458 to the explosion of the Parthenon in 1687, during which the building functioned as a Great Mosque; from the explosion of 1687 to Greek Independence, during which the building lay in ruins.

An account of the remaining history of the Parthenon would cover the archaeological studies and reconstructions of the original temple and its sculptural designs. These efforts began immediately after the expulsion of the Turks during the Greek War of Independence and continue to the present day.

While the Parthenon was kept in excellent repair throughout its long history as a temple of Athena, one outrage is recorded during the Greek period itself (Pausanias 1. 25. 7; Athenaios 9. 70). An Athenian general, Lachares, in the early third century B.C., made himself tyrant of Athens and, in seizing power, abolished the democratic tradition of compulsory military service, creating an army of mercenaries. In order to pay these troops, Lachares is supposed to have robbed the gold plating from Pheidias's chryselephantine statue of Athena in the Parthenon. The gold was eventually replaced for the statue and was seen intact by later travelers, including Pausanius himself, but no record is preserved of when or by whom the restoration was accomplished.

The exact moment when the worship of Athena in the Parthenon came to an end in the Early Christian period is also unknown. In A.D. 426 Theodosius II ordered the destruction of pagan temples, but in the years that followed this edict, the Parthenon evidently remained untouched. In 435 a second Theodosian edict called for the closing of all existing pagan shrines to worshipers. Yet according to Zosimos, a Greek historian under Theodosius II, the cult of Athena was still observed in the Parthenon after the edict of 435 (Zosimus 4. 18. 2). Only later in the fifth century, in the writing of Marinos, the pupil and biographer of the neo-Platonist philosopher, Proklos, do we find an indication that Athena had at last been removed from her ancient dwelling place in the Parthenon. This is a passage describing a dream of Proklos in which he is informed that "the lady of Athens," having been dispossessed, would move in with him.

There is little in either the literary evidence or the archaeological remains of the building that provides a means of dating the various structural modifications made to the Parthenon during the period of its service as a Christian basilica and church, yet it seems reasonable to conclude with Dinsmoor and other observers that most of the major changes took place within the late fifth or early sixth centuries A.C. Among these changes, the construction of an apse at the east end of the temple seems to have entailed the removal of major elements of the pedimental sculptures of the east façade. The statues of Zeus and Athena and other central figures in the scene of Athena's birth from Zeus's head (Pausanias 1. 24. 5) were already missing when the earliest preserved drawings of the east pediment were made some years before the explosion of 1687. These statues have never reappeared, except for minor fragments recently identified in the collections of the *National Archaeological Museum at Athens.

The construction of the apse closed the eastern entrance that in antiquity had been the main and only entrance to the cella. In keeping with Christian practice, three doorways were now cut through the middle cross-wall that had separated the cella from opisthodomos, giving access to the cella from the western porch. Also attributable to this first period of reconstruction are the alteration of the interior colonnades and the replacement of the original roof.

Later additions included the construction of a bell tower in the opisthodomos, probably during the period of the Frankish dukes.

The Italian traveler *Ciriaco of Ancona visited Athens during this period, and a number of fifteenth-century drawings of the Parthenon have been attributed to him. One of these was evidently copied by the Florentine architect Giuliano da *Sangallo, together with other sketches by Ciriaco of ancient monuments in Athens. While the extant drawings do little to help us reconstruct the building history of the Parthenon during the Frankish period, they make it clear that the interest of Renaissance artists and architects in the original monuments of classical Athens began as early as the fifteenth century.

After the Turkish conquest in 1458, the bell tower that had been part of the Christian church was heightened to serve as a minaret when the building was transformed into a mosque. This was the only major modification to the structure after the Early Christian period, so that the condition of the building was still relatively good when the explosion of 1687 occurred. The exterior colonnades of the Parthenon were still intact, its precious sculptured frieze, its metopes and pedimental statues still in situ, with the exception of the sculptures on the east façade that had been displaced during the construction of the apse.

The siege of Athens by a Venetian-led expeditionary force that resulted in the explosion of the Parthenon took place as part of a European reaction to the Turkish invasion of Europe, when the armies of the Ottoman Empire crossed the Danube and threatened Vienna. In September 1687, the Venetian fleet under Count *Morosini, after having carried out a series of raids on other Turkish strongholds along the coast of the Peloponnese, arrived at Athens and laid siege to the Akropolis, which had been fortified by the Turkish garrison. A bombardment of the Akropolis ensued and continued for two days, until, on the night of 26 September, a supply of gunpowder stored in the mosque ignited. The explosion that resulted destroyed the center of the building, throwing down fourteen of the forty-six columns of the peristyle and the walls of the cella, together with the sculptured metopes and the Parthenon frieze from much of the north and south sides of the structure.

The most important events in the history of the Parthenon during the period between this explosion and the Greek War of Independence are those surrounding the removal of the sculptures of the Parthenon from the Akropolis by the British ambassador to Turkey, Lord *Elgin. The Turks, having regained control of the Akropolis when Morosini and his fleet withdrew, made no effort to restore the building but, rather, built a much smaller mosque in the midst of the ruins. Throughout the eighteenth century, as interest increased in ancient Greek art on the part of European connoisseurs and travelers, the Turkish administration was under pressure to permit collectors to remove examples of the sculptures. Morosini's followers may already have been responsible for the disappearance and destruction of a number of pieces—apparently the great rearing horses of the west pediment crashed to the ground when a rope parted as they were being lowered from the tympanum by Morosini's crew. Several fragments of the sculptures reached France, either directly or via Venice, and are today to be found in the *Louvre. When Napoleon was driven out of Egypt by English forces, Turkish authorities at Istanbul, anxious to find favor with the British, granted Lord Elgin the permission he had been seeking for several years. Originally, the stated intention of Elgin's agents on the Akropolis had been to make drawings and casts to provide a record of the sculptures and architectural details for purposes of study in British academies and schools, but soon after arriving, they began to report that through bribery of the local officials, the French and other collectors were carrying off important fragments of the sculptures. Perhaps because of these reports of looting on the Akropolis, Elgin resolved to remove as much as he could of the remaining portions of the sculptures. These were crated and shipped off, eventually to arrive in England. The marbles were offered to the British government by Elgin when he returned to England after a period of imprisonment in France during the Napoleonic wars, provoking a controversy over their removal that continues to the present day, some arguing that the sculptures would have been scattered and far less accessible than they are today had not Elgin kept the majority of items together, others that there can be no excuse for the wholesale looting of the sculptures that indeed took place.

During the Greek War of Independence the Akropolis was under siege on two occasions, as control of Athens passed back and forth between Greek and Turkish forces, and some slight additional damages reportedly occurred during these campaigns when Greek and foreign troops allied with the Greeks were at various times encamped in the ruins.

After the war and while a Bavarian garrison still occupied the small Turkish mosque, the first archaeological excavations on the Akropolis took place under K. Pittakis. Pittakis uncovered, among other things, a number of slabs of the Parthenon frieze. Such excavations continued sporadically after the formation of the *Greek Archaeological Society in 1837, but no reports of their activities were published until the excavations of 1885–1900 by P. *Kavvadias and F. Kawerau. The Bavarian architect Leo von *Klenze is credited with formulating a plan, as early as 1834, to demolish all later structures on the Akropolis of Athens and to undertake the reconstruction of the Periklean buildings in their original form. Ludwig *Ross became ephor of antiquities in 1835, and the work of demolition began. By 1836 the pronaos had been cleared by Pittakis, and the first act of restoration took place when Ross reset some floor blocks on the north side of the cella. The mosque within the confines of the peristyle was demolished in 1842–44, and a number of the fallen columns were at that time reerected, while excavations continued to produce new finds of the sculptures.

The east end of the temple was cleared beginning in 1862 by K. Bötticher, who dismantled most of the remaining elements of the apse (photographs published in 1868 and 1870 show elements of the lower courses of the apse still in place). When Bötticher removed the floor of the apse, which was at a higher level than the original stylobate, among the ancient blocks that he found reused in the Early Christian construction was a fragment of the raking sima from the roof of the Parthenon. The presence of the sima in the apse floor supports the theory that the removal of statues from the east pediment, for whatever reason, predates the construction of the apse.

The earthquake of 1894 caused the cracking of several architrave blocks in the restored Parthenon, and this, together with a general dissatisfaction on the part of many experts with the way the restorations had been carried out, led to a complete reevaluation of the project. Detailed plans by J. Durm called for the removal of brick facings that had been used to support weakened sections of the original masonry and for the restoration of the colonnades and other features of the building. An international committee was formed to supervise the restorations with the engineer N. Balanos, in charge of actual construction. Work began in 1898 and continued for over thirty years. When the reerection of the north colonnade actually took place between 1922 and 1930, only six drums and two capitals proved to be missing from the columns themselves, although nineteen triglyph blocks and many other elements of the entablature had to be remade. The restoration of the south colonnade was never completed. A. K. *Orlandos succeeded Balanos (1940) and espoused a philosophy that the building should be made to appear as much as possible as it originally did in antiquity. He removed a Christian spiral staircase and proposed restoring the ceiling of the west colonnade in marble.

Unfortunately, in the restorations of the late nineteenth and early twentieth centuries, many iron clamps and rods were employed to strengthen the structure. Oxidation caused the iron elements to expand, thus damaging and cracking the blocks in which they were embedded, and became a major threat to the building. Damage also resulted from the feet of thousands of tourists climbing on the stylobate every year. Even more threatening is the problem of air pollution at Athens. Sulphur dioxide from industrial chimneys and other sources reacting with the humidity in the atmosphere produces sulphuric acid, which collects on the marble and makes it soluble to water. In heavy rains the surfaces of sculptures, architectural decorations and structural blocks alike thus become subject to serious erosion. In 1968 an article describing the dangers to the building appeared in the *Courrier de l'Unesco,* calling the world's attention to the seriousness of these problems. Since then the Greek government has organized a permanent Committee for the Preservation of the Akropolis Monuments. For the Parthenon, the committee has recommended a major program of restoration, now even more urgently needed since an earthquake in 1981 further weakened the structure. This program of repairs, the most extensive ever undertaken in the history of the Parthenon, involves the dismantling and reerection of much of the structure. The building has been closed to tourists, and three original statues that had remained in the east pediment were moved into the *Akropolis Museum. The east façade has been dismantled and restored using a painstaking system of inventorying and studying every block removed and, where necessary, carving new replacement stones from Pentelic marble. Under the supervision of Manolis Korres, directing architect of the work since 1977, further restoration is envisioned in accordance with the recommendations of the Akropolis committee and with the approval of the Greek Ministry of Culture. The funding for the restoration program is provided by the Greek government and members of the European Economic Community.

The history of modern scholarship on the Parthenon begins over 200 years ago with the studies of *Stuart and *Revett and embraces numerous monographs and special studies on the so-called refinements of the architecture and its rich and complex sculptural program. Among the major achievements of modern research belong the studies of W. B. *Dinsmoor, with his definitive description and measurements of the Parthenon and his study of the building inscriptions;

the excellent photographic record provided by Alison Frantz of the Parthenon and its sculptures and the description of them by Bernard Ashmole; the detailed catologs of the sculptures by Frank Brommer and the reinterpretations of the iconography of the sculptures by E. B. Harrison. The symposium on the Parthenon organized by E. Berger in 1982 at Basel provided the occasion for a review of various aspects of the problems concerning the monument.

BIBLIOGRAPHY

N. Balanos, *Les Monuments de l'Acropole: relevement et conservation* (Paris, 1938); +B. Ashmole, *An Historical Guide to the Sculptures of the Parthenon* (London, 1961); C. Kardara, "Glaukopis, the Archaic Naos and the Theme of the Parthenon Frieze," *ArchEph* 1961 (1964), 115ff.; A. D. Norre, *Studies in the History of the Parthenon,* diss., University of California, Los Angeles, 1966; W. B. Dinsmoor—E. B. Harrison, et al., in *The Parthenon, Norton Critical Studies in Art History,* ed. V. J. Bruno, with photos by A. Frantz (New York, 1974); M. Robertson—A. Frantz, *The Parthenon Frieze* (London, 1975); +F. Brommer, *The Sculptures of the Parthenon* (London, 1979); C. Bouras et al., *Study for the Restoration of the Parthenon* 1 (Athens, 1983); E. Berger, ed., *Parthenon-Kongress Basel* (Mainz, 1984); J. Boardman—D. Finn, *The Parthenon and Its Sculpture* (London, 1985); M. Korres et al., *Study for the Restoration of the Parthenon* 2a (Athens, 1989); +S. P. M. Harrington, "Shoring up the Temple of Athena," *Archaeology* 45 (1992), 30–43; Stewart, *Greek Sculpture,* 150–60.

VINCENT J. BRUNO

PASQUALINO, LELIO (PASQUALINI; LAELIUS PASCHALINUS; 1549–1611). Italian cleric and collector of antiquities.

Lelio Pasqualino, the canon of Sta. Maria Maggiore in Rome, was praised by Giuseppe Castiglione in his biography of Fulvio *Orsini as one of the greatest experts on antiquarian matters, exceeding Orsini himself in knowledge and connoisseurship. *Peiresc visited Pasqualino during his tour of Italy in 1602 and made notes on thirty-three coins and some seven engraved gems and cameos. Baronius discussed and illustrated forty-nine of his coins in the *Annales ecclesiastici* (1–3; Antwerp, 1595–1607). P. P. *Rubens also paid a visit to his museum while he was in Rome; a page in his *Itinerary* mentions six antique cameos and intagli that he saw: a cameo with *Venus Chasing Cupid* (now in Naples), a *Hermaphrodite Supported by Silenus and Pan,* a large onyx with a *Battle of Alexander Against the Indians* (now lost), an amethyst intaglio with *Demosthenes's* bust inscribed "Dioskouridou," a *Diogenes* and an *Empedokles.* A final entry concerned an (ancient?) gold necklace with a snake biting its tail. Peiresc corresponded with Pasqualino until the latter's death and then exchanged letters with his nephew Pompeo, to whom the collection was bequeathed. In 1622 Peiresc contacted him with a request for casts of the *Venus* and *Battle* cameos, which were to be included in the great book on gems that Peiresc and Rubens were planning to publish. Rubens apparently made a drawing of the *Battle* cameo, known only from a nineteenth-century etching. Peiresc's papers reveal that the cabinet of Pasqualino eventually came into the possession of Cardinal Buoncompagno, archbishop of Naples. After Buoncompagno's death in 1644,

the gem collection passed to the hands of the *Ludovisi family. Sixty-seven of the Buoncompagno gems are preserved in plaster casts in the Vatican (Medagliere, Chigi Vol. a III, 67).
BIBLIOGRAPHY
P. de Nolhac, *La Bibliothèque de Fulvio Orsini* (Paris, 1887), 34; C. Rizza, *Peiresc e l'Italia* (Turin, 1965); M. van der Meulen, *P. P. Rubens Antiquarius* (Alphen aan den Rijn, 1975), 10, 24, 56–57 etc.; +A. Herz, "Lelio Pasqualini, A Late Sixteenth-Century Antiquarian," *IL 60, Essays Honoring Irving Lavin on His Sixtieth Birthday,* ed. M. A. Lavin (New York, 1990), 191–206; +D. Jaffe, "Aspects of Gem Collecting in the Early Seventeenth Century, Nicolas-Claude Peiresc and Lelio Pasqualini," *BurlMag* 135 (1993), 102–20.

MARJON VAN DER MEULEN

PASQUINO. Marble sculpture group found in Rome, representing a slain youth being held in the arms of a soldier.

The group is one of many versions that were long thought to be based on an original created at Pergamon in the third or second century B.C.; recent scholarship places it in the first century B.C. The figures have been identified as Hercules and Geryon, the dying Alexander supported by a soldier, Ajax and Patroklos and many others, but the most widely accepted argument is that of *Visconti, who suggested in 1788 that the figures represented Menelaos and the slain Patroklos.

The badly mutilated group was first recorded in the late fifteenth and early sixteenth centuries. It was set up originally by Cardinal Oliviero Caraffa in 1501 and since 1791 has stood at the corner of the Palazzo Braschi in Piazza Pasquino.

In 1509, the *Pasquino,* supposedly so named after the schoolmaster on whose property it had been found (or after a witty barber or a neighborhood tailor), became a feature of the annual St. Mark's festival in Rome. On this day it was decorated with mythological costume (as Janus, Hercules, Mars, Mercury, Orpheus, even Flora and Minerva), and Latin verses were attached to it. The practice of attaching the verses had been initiated in order to encourage the study of the humanities, but the tradition did not continue along these lines. The verses, or "Pasquinades," became increasingly satirical, and the satire was often directed at the papacy. The tradition, by this time no longer restricted to the festival, culminated in a one-year ban on the St. Mark's festival in 1519 by *Leo X, and, later, other popes attempted to halt the tradition as well. In addition to Latin, French and Italian were used for the verses. Sometimes the Pasquinades were dialogues between *Pasquino* and another famous sculpture, *Marforio.*

Although the group alienated the papacy, it scored high marks for its aesthetic value among artists, connoisseurs and critics. Certain admirers of the group in the early seventeenth century praised it as an equal to the *Belvedere Torso, and *Bernini even called it the finest example of ancient sculpture in Rome. The fact that there are no fewer than thirteen ancient versions of this group known also reveals the respect it received from artists and collectors in antiquity.

Although the *Pasquino* at the Palazzo Braschi was never itself restored, the famous version in Florence in the Loggia dei Lanzi was restored after its acquisition by Cosimo de' Medici (*Medici family); Lodovico Salvetti performed the restoration (1677) for the Grand Duke Ferdinand II. Yet another version, also acquired by Cosimo I, was in the courtyard of the Palazzo Pitti in Florence in 1677; it underwent several restorations that left it in poor condition and virtually forgotten. Modern scholarship on the *Pasquino* has focused on debates over the identity of the two figures, including the interesting possibility that the group may have had varying identities in different contexts in antiquity (for example, *Odysseus with the Body of Achilles* at Sperlonga; *Menelaos with Patroklos* at *Hadrian's Villa). The later date in the first century B.C. has been argued on the basis of similar compositions on coins.

BIBLIOGRAPHY

G. Dickinson, *Du Bellay in Rome* (Leiden, 1960), 155–207; G. Bermond Montanari, s.v. "Pasquino," *EAA* 5 (1963), 985; Haskell—Penny, 291–96; Bober—Rubinstein, 187–88; Ridgway, *Hellenistic Sculpture* I, 275–81; N. Himmelmann, "Laokoon," *AntK* 34 (1991), 109.

PAUL II (PIETRO BARBO; 1417–71). Pope and collector of antiquities.

Born in Venice, Pietro Barbo was raised to the college of cardinals in 1440 by Pope Eugenius IV and was given the title of cardinal-priest of San Marco by Pope Nicholas V; he was elected pope in 1464. In Rome he long resided in the Palazzo San Marco (later, Palazzo Venezia), where he maintained his exquisite collection of antiquities.

Accused of being hostile to humanism by members of the *Roman Academy of Pomponio *Leto, Paul II nevertheless reveals himself as interested in the classical world in numerous ways. He surpassed all other popes of the Quattrocento in his involvement in restoration of ancient monuments, such as the *Pantheon, the *Marcus Aurelius* Equestrian Statue, the *Arch of Titus and the *Quirinal *Horse Tamers.* He sought to preserve and call attention to other monuments by moving them to the Piazza San Marco in front of his palace (e.g., the great porphyry sarcophagus of Constantina, now in the Vatican). Above all, he is known as one of the great collectors of the fifteenth century; an inventory made in 1457 reveals that he owned forty-seven ancient bronzes, the handsome Late Antique ivory diptych later possessed by A. M. Querini (the Querinian Diptych, now in Brescia), as well as 227 cameos and many intaglio gems, with portraits identified as Philip of Macedon, Octavian, Caligula, Nero, Vespasian, Titus and Antoninus Pius. Also among the gems was the famous chalcedony intaglio of *Diomedes and the Palladium,* which had come from the collection of Niccolò *Niccoli and later belonged to Lorenzo de' Medici (*Medici family). He also owned the spectacular *Farnese Cup, which went to the Medici and is now in the *Museo Nazionale di Napoli, along with some twenty-two others of the gems of Paul II. He was so passionate, even unscrupulous, in his acquisition of ancient coins that other collectors in Rome complained that scarcely any coins were left on the market. The inventory of 1457 lists ninety-seven gold and nearly 1,000 silver coins, almost all Roman.

BIBLIOGRAPHY

R. Weiss, *Un Umanista veneziano, Papa Paolo II,* Civiltà Veneziana, Saggi 4 (1958); N. Dacos—A. Giuliano—U. Pannuti, *Il Tesoro di Lorenzo il Magnifico,* I, *Le Gemme,* catalog of exhibition (Florence, 1972); Bober—Rubinstein, 123, esp. 471.

PAUL III (FARNESE, CARDINAL ALESSANDRO I; 1468–1549). Italian humanist and collector, pope from 1534 to 1549.

Paul III's early education under the humanist Pomponio *Leto instilled in him a lasting love of antiquity. He spoke Greek well and added many rare classical manuscripts to the Vatican Library. But, besides his patronage of literature and art, his real importance lies in his role as founder of the *Farnese family collection of classical antiquities.

One of Paul's first acts as pope in 1534 was to depute Latino Giovenale Manetti, a distinguished classical scholar, as commissary of Roman antiquities. ''Not without deep sorrow,'' states the bull of appointment, ''are we aware that not merely Goths, Vandals and other barbarians . . . but our own indifference . . . and greed . . . have squandered the venerable adornments of the city.'' The professed concern that ancient monuments were overgrown and decaying and that much of Rome's heritage had been dispersed to foreign collections is impressive and was presumably influential. In practice, however, Paul himself authorized the destruction of a number of antiquities: buildings in the *Forum Romanum were demolished when a path was cleared from the *Arch of Titus to the *Arch of Septimius Severus for Charles V's triumphal entry in 1536; in 1540 a bull licensed the deputies in charge of rebuilding St. Peter's to quarry marble and travertine anywhere within or outside the city. Classical sites at *Tivoli and *Ostia, as well as the Aurelian temple of the Sun, near the Quirinal, also provided stone for the magnificent Palazzo Farnese, which Paul had built.

The justification for this activity was Paul III's program of urban renovation, a major priority after the extensive devastation of the Sack of Rome in 1527. As part of this program Paul commissioned *Michelangelo to redesign the Campidoglio (*Capitoline Hill), and he had the celebrated bronze equestrian statue of *Marcus Aurelius* moved there from the *Lateran. It seems that Paul also planned to erect the *Quirinal *Horse Tamers* on the same site, but this scheme was not eventually carried out.

The licensed demolition of monuments was not entirely without archaeological benefit. A number of important statues were unearthed during the quarrying. Most notable perhaps was the discovery of the *Farnese *Bull* and the *Farnese *Hercules.* These were found in 1545 by workers seeking materials for St. Peter's in the *Baths of Caracalla. The same site yielded other sculpture that entered the Farnese collection during Paul's pontificate, although the excavations were apparently directed by his grandson, Alessandro Farnese. These included the two colossal Floras (*Farnese *Flora*) that stood in the courtyard of the palace, the *Hercules Latinus,* which was erected in the same place as a pendant to the Farnese *Hercules,* and the Farnese *Athena,* as well as numerous reliefs, bronze statuettes, cameos, coins and other sculptures. Guglielmo della Porta restored the *Hercules* and other works. Columns and inscriptions were also preserved and set up in Palazzo Farnese.

Apart from these prizes from excavations, Paul also made purchases of antiquities, notably, the *Farnese *Captives,* and in 1547 the extensive *Grimani collection of gems and medals. He also enriched the papal collections, buying several statues, including the *Belvedere *"Antinous,"* which completed the superb array of classical sculptures in the Belvedere court.

BIBLIOGRAPHY

Lanciani, *Storia degli scavi, passim;* L. von Pastor, *Geschichte der Päpste,* 5 (Freibourg, 1909), 750 ff.; F. de Navenne, *Rome, Le Palais Farnèse et les Farnèse* (Paris, 1914), 311–34; Haskell—Penny, passim.

                                                                          CLARE ROBERTSON

PAYNE, HUMFRY GILBERT GARTH (1902–36). British archaeologist, well known for his work on sculptures from the *Akropolis, Athens, and on Corinthian vase painting.

Payne was educated at Christ Church, Oxford, receiving his degree in 1924. He studied Greek art with *Beazley and Alan Blakeway. Payne was awarded numerous honors, including the Conington Prize for classical learning (1927) and a position at Christ Church as a senior scholar (1926–31). He was appointed director of the *British School at Athens in 1929, though he was but twenty-seven years old.

In 1935 he made the striking discovery that the head of the Rampin *Horseman* in Paris joined with the body found on the Akropolis. Among his chief publications were *Archaic Marble Sculpture from the Acropolis* (1936) and the first volume on his excavations at two sanctuaries of Hera at *Perachora, near Corinth.

Payne died at the age of thirty-four in Athens following an operation. A memoir by his wife, Dilys Powell, records extensively his career in Greece.

BIBLIOGRAPHY

H. Payne, "Early Greek Vases from Knossos," *BSA* 29 (1928), 224–98; idem, *Necrocorinthia, A Study of Corinthian Art in the Archaic Period* (Oxford, 1931); +D. Powell, *The Traveller's Journey Is Done* (London, 1943).

                                                                          SHELLIE WILLIAMS

PEIRAEUS. Greek site, the port of Athens in ancient and modern times.

Peiraeus takes the form of a hilly peninsula with three natural harbors: Kantharos, Zea and Munychia. The largest of these, Kantharos, was the principal harbor and a great commercial center, lined on the east side by a series of great stoas known as the *emborion.* In a nice example of continuity, inscriptions indicate that in antiquity ferryboats left from virtually the same location as today.

In the outer part of the harbor there were 94 ship sheds for triremes. The main war harbor, Zea, lay to the east and had 196 ship sheds. Nearby was a great arsenal for the storage of tackle, built by the architect Philo in the second half of the fourth century B.C., and not far from that lay the agora, laid out by the Milesian city planner Hippodamos, who was also credited with the grid plan of most of the city. The third harbor, Munychia, was the smallest, housing 82 ship sheds and overlooked by the venerable shrine of Artemis Munychia.

The walls of Peiraeus were begun as early as 493/2 B.C. at the behest of Themistokles. Torn down in 404, they were rebuilt by Konon in 394–390 B.C., repaired in the third century and finally destroyed by Sulla in his siege and sack of the city in 87/6 B.C. The original circuit was close to 12k in length, and extensive remains can still be traced along the southwest shoreline of the Akte peninsula, built of good, squared blocks and measuring 3.00–3.60m thick.

In addition to Artemis, Zeus and Athena, Asklepios and especially Aphrodite were worshiped in the Peiraeus. The cosmopolitan nature of the port is reflected in the cults as well, with Cyprian Aphrodite, Egyptian Isis and Thracian Bendis all attested as early as the fourth century B.C.

Little systematic excavation has been carried out, but over the years parts of the walls, a theater and several ship sheds have come to light. Much that was visible late in the nineteenth century has since disappeared. In July 1959 a cache of four large bronze statues and other sculpture was found by chance (*Peiraeus Bronzes) and excavated by J. Papademetriou and E. Mastrokostas just east of the Kantharos, apparently deposited and awaiting shipment when Sulla atacked and destroyed the city. Along with other important finds from Peiraeus, they are now housed in a handsome museum by the ancient theater.

A monumental lion of marble, described by early travelers as standing by the Kantharos, gave the port its medieval name, Porto Leone; it was removed by *Morosini in 1688 and set up at the arsenal in Venice.

BIBLIOGRAPHY

J. G. Frazer, *Pausanias's Description of Greece* 2 (London, 1898), 6–32; H. Angelo-poulou, *Peri Peiraiōs* (Athens, 1898), 1–24; C. Panagos, *Le Pirée* (Athens, 1968); N. Papachatzis, *Pausaniou Hellados Periēgēsis* (Athens, 1974), 96–129; R. Garland, *The Peiraeus* (Ithaca, 1987); K.-V. von Eickstedt, *Beiträge zur Topographie des Antiken Piräus* (Athens, 1991).

JOHN McK. CAMP II

PEIRAEUS BRONZES. A group of lifesize and larger Greek bronze statues discovered in 1959 by workers digging a sewer line in the *Peiraeus, the port of Athens.

The excavation was supervised by J. Papademetriou and E. Mastrokostas. Included in the group are an *Apollo* or *kouros* (height 1.91m; cf. *korai* and *kouroi*), two statues of *Artemis* (height 1.94m and 1.55m), an over-lifesize *Athena* (height 2.35m) and a tragic mask (height 0.45m), now in the Peiraeus Museum. Evidently, the statues had been brought to a warehouse in the Peiraeus in the first century B.C., where they were stored when the building was destroyed by fire, perhaps during Sulla's sack of 86 B.C. When found, they were stacked neatly side by side or on top of one another. Three marble sculptures were also found. C. Houser has argued that the whole cache of Greek bronzes, the largest on record, may have been removed from a single sanctuary and brought to the port of Athens to await shipment overseas.

The *Apollo* has the right foot forward, a feature not common on *kouroi,* and also has an uncanonical treatment of the arms, which are extended forward from the elbow. The right hand probably once held a phiale, the left a bow. On stylistic and technical grounds the statue is usually dated late sixth or early fifth century B.C.

The helmeted *Athena* wears peplos and aegis, her right hand outstretched and a spear originally in the left. The statue has been attributed by G. Dontas to Euphranor; it is similar to the marble Mattei *Athena* in the *Louvre. Both statues of *Artemis* wear the peplos, with a quiver strapped across the right shoulder; each held a phiale in the right hand and bow in the left. These statues are usually dated to the later fourth century B.C. or the Hellenistic period.

BIBLIOGRAPHY

M. Paraskevaidis, *Ein wiederentdecker Kunstraub der Antike? Lebendiges Altertum* 17 (1966); G. Dontas, ''La grande Artemis du Pirée: Une oeuvre d'Euphranor,'' *AntK* 25 (1982), 15–33; C. Houser, *Greek Monumental Bronze Sculpture* (New York, 1983), 50–69; G. Dontas, ''Ho Chalkinos Apollon tou Peiraia,'' *Archaische und Klassische Griechische Plastik* (Mainz, 1986), 181–92.

CAROL MATTUSCH

PEIRESC, NICOLAS-CLAUDE FABRI DE (PEIRESKIUS; 1580–1637). French humanist, botanist, astronomer, antiquarian, epigrapher, numismatist, collector, bibliophile, linguist.

Born in Belgentier (Provence), Peiresc attended Jesuit College in Avignon and studied philosophy in Aix. He traveled to Italy in 1599, visiting Padua, Venice, Florence, Rome and Mantua and meeting along the way G. Pinelli, P. Gualdo, *Pasqualino, *Orsini and *Aldrovandi. He returned to France in 1602 and obtained his legal degree at Montpellier in 1604; the following year he became a senator in the parliament of Aix. Soon afterward he left for Paris with Du Vair.

In 1606 Peiresc traveled to England and the Low Countries, where he visited many humanists and their collections of books, antiquities and other objects. Appointed secretary to Du Vair in 1616, he settled in Paris and remained there until 1623. He became acquainted with leading humanists and bibliophiles, such as de Thou, Malherbe and the brothers Claude and Pierre Dupuy. In 1622, he met Peter Paul *Rubens during the latter's visit to Maria de' Medici. Returning to Provence, he received the Cardinal Barberini (*Barberini family) and his retinue on their way back from Paris in 1626; Peiresc graciously gave the cardinal his late antique ivory with the *Emperor Heraclius on Horseback* (now in the *Louvre, Paris).

Portrait of *Nicolas-Claude Fabri de Peiresc*, engraving by A. van Dyck, ca. 1625. (N. T. de Grummond.)

His library contained 5,000 volumes and 200 manuscripts. He kept extensive notes on his travels and visits to libraries and cabinets of antiquities. Eighty-three dossiers of notes inventoried at the time of his death bear witness to the many interests of this polymath: the titles refer to French history and genealogy, ecclesiastical matters, legal and government affairs, geography, curious inventions and classical antiquity.

Antiquity held his lifelong interest. He studied several branches of it: ancient weights and measures, inscriptions, coins and gems. He studied it from every angle, in order to "unravel the secrets of antiquity." Numismatics, however, interested him most. His interest started with a coin of Arcadius that his uncle gave to him as a child and developed under the guidance of Rascas de Bagarris. During his peregrinations in Italy, he collected 200 silver, eighty bronze and five or six gold coins. He collected early French, Arabian and "Gothic" coinage, as well as antique specimens. *Rockox and Rubens donated their few "Gothic" coins to him. At his death he had brought together some 18,000 pieces. Peiresc appreciated coins especially for their historical value, since they played an active part in public life.

He also possessed 1,119 "graveures," or engraved gems and cameos. To his glyptic collection belonged a cornelian identified as *Aetion* (Chatsworth, Devonshire Collection), an intaglio with *Scylla* and inscribed cameos with *Hercules* signed by Onesas (Archaeological Museum, *Florence). He owned many precious uncut stones, ancient rings, fibulae and a large number of vases made of precious stones, as well as statues of bronze, several marbles (including a *Lectisternium* and a herm of *Crinas*), inscriptions, sacrificial instruments and miscellaneous objects such as an abacus, a tripod, strigils, seals, fossils and even three paintings after ancient cameo carvings: the *Gemma Tiberiana by Rubens, the *Gemma Augustea by N. dell'Abbate and the vase of the Cardinal Del Monte (i.e., the *Portland Vase, now in London). He was the first to research the figures of the frieze of the Del Monte Vase. He also owned a copy of the mural painting of the *Aldobrandini *Wedding*. One of the objects in his collection that intrigued him most was his tripod (now Paris, Bibliothèque Nationale), found at Frèjus in 1629. He wrote a lengthy treatise on it and dispatched copies to his archaeological friends.

In 1619, Peiresc had discovered in the Ste. Chapelle in Paris the large Roman cameo known today as the Gemma Tiberiana, but at that time identified as the *Triumph of Joseph in Egypt*. His correspondence shows the scientific way Peiresc not only traced back its pedigree but also sought to identify the persons depicted. Using imperial coins, he identified it as the *Apotheosis of Augustus*, matching it to the Gemma Augustea in Vienna, which he called the *Apotheosis of the Living Augustus*. He contacted Rubens about it and with him planned to publish both cameos as well as other major ones known in Europe at the time. His notes, collected for a scholarly commentary, show his careful observations of the stone colorings and his knowledge of ancient iconography.

Throughout his life Peiresc brought together a wealth of material but unfortunately never published anything. Petrus Gassendi used much information for his biography of the great French scholar; his *Vita Peireskii* was published in 1641. Many of Peiresc's files came into the possession of Bishop d'Inguimbert and are now in the library at Carpentras or the Bibliothèque Nationale in Paris. Jacob *Spon was one of the first to publish material from the *schedae Peirescii*, followed by B. de *Montfaucon and the Count de *Caylus.

His country home ("maison de campagne") in Belgentier was the center of Peiresc's studies. Apart from his library, antiquities and an astronomy observatory, he had gardens containing rare plants imported from all over the world, of which he dispatched cuttings to his friends. He introduced to France ginger, jasmine and tulips, and in his orchards he grafted the stems of new kinds of fruit trees. Unfortunately, the property has undergone drastic changes since the days of its famous occupant. Of the antiquities only a Roman milestone remains standing. In the garden a tall, lonely sequoia may date from the time when ships brought back exotic vegetation for Peiresc to the ports of southern France. This garden has now become the "Camping de Peiresc."

BIBLIOGRAPHY
J. Guibert, *Les Dessins du Cabinet de Peiresc au Cabinet des Estampes de la Bibliothèque Nationale* (Paris, 1910); P. Humbert, *Un Amateur Peiresc, 1580–1637* (Paris, 1933); R. Lebègue, *Les Correspondents de Peiresc dans les anciens Pays-Bas* (Brussels, 1943); M. van der Meulen, *P. P. Rubens Antiquarius* (Alphen aan den Rijn, 1975); J. Hellin—A. Willems, *Nicolas-Claude Fabri de Peiresc, 1580–1637* (Brussels, 1981); +D. Jaffe, "Aspects of Gem Collecting in the Early Seventeenth Century, Nicolas-Claude Peiresc and Lelio Pasqualino," *BurlMaq* 135 (1993), 103–20.

MARJON VAN DER MEULEN

PELLA. Macedonian Greek capital from ca. 400 to 167 B.C. and birthplace of Alexander the Great.

Pella is mentioned by Herodotos (7.123) and Thucydides (2.100.4) and located and described by Livy (44.46.4–7) and Strabo (7.fr.20). Built on the site of Bounomos (Stephanos of Byzantium), it replaced Aegae (*Vergina) as capital under Archelaos. Following capture by Aemilius Paullus after the Battle of Pydna in 146 B.C., its portable wealth was paraded in a daylong triumph through Rome. Pella had once been Macedonia's largest city (Xenophon, *Hell.* 5.2.13) until it was replaced in significance by *Thessaloniki under the Romans. It later became a Roman colony.

Travelers and archaeologists of the late eighteenth and nineteenth centuries mistakenly located Pella some distance away (north of Giannitsa). Greek excavations of 1912 placed it correctly. Continuous investigations by Greek archaeologists have taken place since 1954.

Activity is documented from at least the Bronze Age until today. On the acropolis are remains of a palace of fourth-century date with later modifications. Whether the palace of Archelaos (Aelian, *Varia Historia* 14.17) lies below is uncertain. The painter Zeuxis decorated Archelaos's palace, which played host to the poet Timotheos and the dramatist Euripides. Demosthenes's derogatory remarks concerning Pella's insignificance can be understood as hostile rhetoric. In the lower city, ongoing excavations have revealed monuments primarily of the Hellenistic period laid out in orthogonal Hippodamian plan; there are sanctuaries, an extensive agora, pottery workshops and numerous spacious peristyle houses. Some houses have spectacular mosaics and stuccoed walls. Part of the surrounding fortification walls has also been uncovered. Significant portable finds include house furnishings, inscriptions, coins and sculptures of terracotta and marble. In addition, cemeteries of Late Classical through Hellenistic date are rich in grave goods. Numerous finds are housed in a small local museum.

BIBLIOGRAPHY
ArchDelt (1960 ff.); +D. Papaconstantinou-Diamantourou, *Pella* 1 (Athens, 1971); +M. Andronikos et al., "Pella Museum," in *The Greek Museums* (Athens, 1977), 253–64; +*Pella, Protevousa ton archaion Makedonon,* catalog of exhibition (Thessaloniki, 1987); C. Makaronas and E. Giouri, *Oi Oikies Arpagis tis Elenis kai Dionysou tis Pellas* (Athens,

1989); R. Ginouvès, ed., *Macedonia from Philip II to the Roman Conquest* (Athens, 1993), 88–96, 120–35; M. Lilimbaki-Akamati, *Lazevtoi Thalamotoi Taphoi tis Pellas* (Athens, 1994); I. Touratsoglou, *Macedonia. History, Monuments, Museums* (Athens, 1995), 136–59.

STELLA G. MILLER

PENDLEBURY, JOHN DEVITT STRINGFELLOW (1904–41). British archaeologist, a specialist in Minoan studies and in the Amarna period in Egypt.

Son of the eminent surgeon Herbert Stringfellow Pendlebury, he was born in London and educated at Winchester College and at Pembroke College, Cambridge, where he was an outstanding athlete as well as scholar. After further study at the *British School at Athens, he joined excavations in Macedonia (1928, under W. A. Heurtley) and in Egypt (1928–29, at Armant and Tell el-Amarna, both under Henri Frankfort). While in Greece, he visited *Crete, where his promise was recognized immediately by Sir Arthur *Evans. In 1930 he was named both curator of *Knossos (until 1934) and director of the Egypt Exploration Society's excavations at Tell el-Amarna; until the closing of the Amarna expedition in 1936, Pendlebury excavated there every year while continuing fieldwork and study in Crete. In 1930 he published his first book, *Aegyptiaca, A Catalogue of Egyptian Objects in the Aegean Area,* which has remained a standard reference; in 1933 there followed *A Handbook to the Palace of Minos at Knossos* and the second volume of *The City of Akhenaten,* in which he collaborated with Frankfort. In the years 1933–37 he undertook the organization of a stratigraphical museum at Knossos, which George *Mylonas has described as "a model service to scholars interested in prehistoric antiquities." In 1935 came the publication of *Tell el-Amarna,* an authoritative account for the general reader. From 1936 to 1939 he directed excavations at Karphi, on Mt. Dicte (Lassithi) in Crete. His major synthesis of Minoan materials, *The Archaeology of Crete, An Introduction,* was published in 1939, as was *The City of Akhenaten,* III.

Pendlebury was named British vice-consul at Candia, and when war was declared soon after, he became a captain on the general staff. He was killed in action 22 May 1941, during the German invasion of Crete. He left unfinished a work on the archaeology of post-Roman Crete.

BIBLIOGRAPHY
Who's Who 92 (1940), 2494; G. E. M(ylonas), *AJA* 46 (1942), 412; S.R.K. Glanville, *JEA* 28 (1942), 61–63.

W. W. DE GRUMMOND

PENROSE, FRANCIS CRANMER (1817–1903). English archaeologist and architect.

Educated at Winchester and Magdalene College, Cambridge, Penrose studied art and architecture on the Continent from 1842 to 1845 as a "traveling bachelor" of the university. He turned to the monuments of Rome and Greece, which he visited and measured lovingly, at the same time appraising them with a critical eye and making new observations. He objected to the pitch of the pediment of the *Pantheon and was one of the first to record the various refinements of the *Parthenon, such as its use of entasis and its horizontal curvature in the steps and entablature. Penrose's results were given in *Principles of Athenian Architecture* (1851; enlarged ed., 1888). He also participated in the argument over "hypaethral" temples, joining the other scholars who believed that a reference in Vitruvius (*De architectura* 3.2.1) implies that some Greek temples were left unroofed. He did research on the orientation of temples, having a special aptitude for the problem because of his training as an astronomer. (He had made observations of solar eclipses at Jerez and at Denver, Colorado.)

Also a practicing architect, Penrose designed the *British School at Athens (1882–86) and served as first director of the school (1886). He was president of the Royal Institute of British Architects (1894–96) and recipient of honorary degrees from Oxford and Cambridge.

BIBLIOGRAPHY

Sandys, III, 445–46; "Penrose, Francis Cranmer," *Concise DNB* 2 (1982), 527; Stoneman, *Land of Lost Gods*, 187, 253, 279.

PERACHORA (PERAION; PERAIA). District of Greece known for its sanctuaries of Hera; located on the Corinthian gulf.

Research has concentrated on the promontory site, Heraion, noted by Le Bas, *Leake and other early travelers in the Peloponnese. Humfry *Payne excavated two sanctuaries of Hera at this site for the *British School at Athens between 1930 and 1933. The excavations produced a great amount of Archaic votive material and shed light on the local history of the area and on early Greek architecture. Results were published, with the help of T. J. Dunbabin and C. M. Robertson, after Payne's death in 1936. Payne's widow, Dilys Powell, preserves anecdotes about the area and the excavations in *The Traveller's Journey Is Done* (London, 1943).

British School students have continued work at the site, in 1938 (Dunbabin), 1963 (J. J. Coulton, A.H.S. Megaw), 1964–66 (R. A. Tomlinson) and 1982 (Tomlinson with K. Demakopoulou of the *Greek Archaeological Service).

BIBLIOGRAPHY

H. Payne, *Perachora* 1 (Oxford, 1940); T. J. Dunbabin, *Perachora* 2 (Oxford, 1962); R. A. Tomlinson, "Perachora: The Remains Outside the Two Sanctuaries," *BSA* 64 (1969), 155–288; R. A. Tomlinson—K. Demakopoulou, "Excavations of the Circular Building, Perachora," *BSA* 80 (1985), 261–79; H. Waterhouse, *The British School at Athens: The First Hundred Years* (BSA suppl. vol. 19, London, 1986), 31, 44, 62, 110–13.

CHRISTOPHER G. SIMON

PERGAMON (PERGAMUM). City in Mysia (northwestern Asia Minor) located on the Caïcus River at modern Bergama.

The city rose to prominence in the third century B.C. under the Attalid dynasty

(283–133 B.C.), whose kingdom rivaled the realms of the Seleucids and Macedonians in western and southern Asia Minor. In this period Pergamon became an international center of art and learning. In 133 B.C. the extensive Pergamene possessions passed to Rome as part of a bequest of Attalos III (138–133 B.C.). Pergamon retained its importance in Roman Imperial times, when the city received the patronage of Augustus, Hadrian and Caracalla, among others.

Pergamon was visited and described by the Byzantine emperor Theodorus II Lascaris in 1250 and by *Ciriaco of Ancona in 1431 and 1444. From the late seventeenth century through the nineteenth, a number of travelers, including C.F.M. *Texier and C. *Fellows, visited the site and made drawings and descriptions of monuments.

A series of German archaeological expeditions, begun in 1878 under *Conze, *Dörpfeld and *Humann and still in progress, has uncovered and restored large areas of the ancient city. A focus of early investigation was the acropolis, where many public buildings and temples were constructed during Hellenistic times and renovated in the Roman period. In addition to the palaces of the Pergamene kings, the acropolis housed temples to Athena and Dionysos, the library and the *Great Altar. Structures added to the acropolis in Roman times included the temple of Trajan begun under this emperor and completed by Hadrian, recently restored by the German expedition. On the southern slope of the ridge forming the acropolis stood additional major buildings of the Hellenistic city: sanctuaries dedicated to Demeter and Kore, agoras and gymnasia.

Between the ridge and the lower city are structures mostly of Roman date, including a theater, amphitheater, stadium and temple of Serapis. In the lower city are preserved remains of the sanctuary of Asklepios, a center of healing that gained international recognition, especially under the patronage of Hadrian. The main buildings of the sanctuary included a temple to Asklepios, a theater and structures presumably used to house patients during treatment.

BIBLIOGRAPHY

+*Die Altertumer von Pergamon* 1–15 (1885–1986); +*Pergamenische Forschungen* 1–6 (1968–88); E. V. Hansen, *The Attalids of Pergamon,* 2nd ed. (Ithaca, 1972).

ANN C. GUNTER

PERGAMON MUSEUM, Berlin. German museum, the last to be built on the Museum Island (cf. Antikensammlung, *Berlin) and presently home of the Antikensammlung (Collection of Greek and Roman Antiquities), the Vorderasiatisches Museum (Near East Museum), the Ostasiatisches Museum (Islamic Museum) and the Museum für Volkskunde (Museum for Folklore).

The old Pergamon Museum, designed by Fritz Wolff, opened in 1902. It housed antiquities from Prussian excavations at *Pergamon and the Near East Museum. It included very high rooms with skylights for the display of architecture, including the reconstructed *Great Altar of Pergamon. This building was razed in 1908 to make space for a larger Pergamon Museum designed by Alfred Messel. The construction of the new museum was carried out by Ludwig

Hoffmann over a protracted period. The central section of this π-shaped building opened in 1930. The remaining parts were completed in 1936. The central section, composed of tall, windowless rooms, housed architecture and sculpture generally acquired through excavations in Asia Minor. The Near East Museum and the Islamic collection were housed in the south wing, and the Deutsches Museum was housed in the north wing.

Most of the artworks were removed from the museum during World War II, first to safer places within the city and later to the Soviet Union (shortly after the fall of Berlin). One notable exception is the market gate from *Miletos, which remained in the museum building and was badly damaged in an air raid (February 1945). The objects taken to the Soviet Union were returned to East Berlin in 1958–59. Now the Pergamon Museum is one of the most-visited sites in Berlin, its chief attractions being the Pergamon Altar, the Ishtar Gate from Babylon and the market gate from Miletos.

BIBLIOGRAPHY

K. Schifner, ed., *Staatliche Museen zu Berlin* (Leipzig, 1963); S. Schultz, *Staatliche Museen zu Berlin: Gesamtführer,* 2nd ed. (Berlin, 1966); H. Trost, ed., *Hauptstadt Berlin, 1, Die Bau- und Kunstdenkmale in der DDR* (Munich, 1983).

ELIZABETH C. TEVIOTDALE

PERGE. City in Pamphylia (southern Asia Minor), ca. 18km northeast of modern Antalya.

Founded according to tradition after the Trojan War by settlers led by Mopsos and others, Perge entered history in the Athenian tribute lists in 425 B.C. The city was cordial to Alexander on his arrival in 333 B.C. Under Seleucid control until 190 B.C., Perge subsequently passed to Pergamene, then Roman domination.

An Austrian expedition led by K. Lanckoronski visited and recorded monuments at Perge in 1885. Excavations by a Turkish expedition, which began under A. M. Mansel in 1946 and continue under J. Inan, have contributed new finds and information on the surviving monuments of Hellenistic and Roman date. These include a theater and a well-preserved stadium. The lower city with its agora and colonnaded streets is enclosed by towered fortification walls. The acropolis is thought to have sheltered the original settlement at Perge, but the remains preserved there date to the Byzantine period.

BIBLIOGRAPHY

+K. Lanckoronski, *Die Städte Pamphyliens und Pisidiens* (Vienna, 1890), 33–63; +A. M. Mansel—A. Akarca, *Excavations and Researches at Perge* (Ankara, 1949); +A. M. Mansel, ''Bericht über Ausgrabungen und Untersuchungen in Pamphylien in den Jahren 1957–1972,'' *AA* 1975, 57–96; +idem, ''Die Nymphaeen von Perge,'' *IstMitt* 25 (1975), 367–72.

ANN C. GUNTER

PERNICE, ERICH (1864–1945). German archaeologist.

Born in Greifswald and descended from a noble Italian family, Erich Pernice studied classical philology and archaeology at Berlin and Bonn (with H. *Usener, R. *Kekulé and others). In 1889 he worked in Italy for the first time, visiting Rome, *Pompeii and *Sicily. Receiving a travel stipend from the *German Archaeological Institute, he went off to Greece, where he was to take part in the *Kerameikos excavations in Athens.

Returning to Germany, Pernice was hired as an assistant at the *Berlin Museum and published various items in the collection, culminating with the great work on the Hildesheim treasure (*Der Hildesheimer Silberfund,* 1901, with F. Winter). In 1903 he was called to Greifswald, where he rose to become the ranking professor (*Ordinarius*). He spent four months in 1908–9 working with T. *Wiegand at *Miletos, unearthing traces of the Archaic city.

Then followed Pernice's years of work at Pompeii. From 1912 until the start of World War I and from 1925 on, he occupied himself with the publications on Pompeii of the German Archaeological Institute, serving as editor and/or author for the series of *Die Hellenistische Kunst in Pompeji.* He is also remembered for his new edition of *Die Kunst des Altertums,* originally prepared by W. Lübke (16th ed., 1924), still considered worthwhile today.

BIBLIOGRAPHY
R. Lullies—W. Schiering after E. Boehringer, in *Archäologenbildnisse,* 156–57.

PERNIER, LUIGI (1874–1937). Italian archaeologist, one of the first to explore Minoan and Graeco-Roman sites on *Crete.

One of Pernier's first assignments, under the direction of Federico *Halbherr, was to conduct for over a decade the excavations of Minoan *Phaistos, beginning in 1900, as well as to reveal the Archaic temple and its adjacent rooms at Prinias to the north of Phaistos (1906–8). With others he also discovered and interpreted important areas of Roman *Gortyn, in particular, the odeion, the agora and the temple of Pythian Apollo (1911–14).

BIBLIOGRAPHY
L. Pernier, *Il Palazzo minoico di Festos,* 1 (Rome, 1935) and 2, with L. Banti (Rome, 1951); L. Pernier, "New Elements for the Study of the Archaic Temple of Prinias," *AJA* 38 (1934), 171–77; V. La Rosa, "Luigi Pernier a cinquant' anni dalla morte," *Magna Graecia* 21 (1986), 23–24.

JOSEPH W. SHAW AND GIULIANA BIANCO

PERRENOT DE GRANVELLE, ANTOINE (1517–86). Renaissance cardinal and diplomat, collector of art and patron of artists and scholars.

The son of Nicholas Perrenot, who had gathered a collection of antiquities at his palace in Besançon (Franche-Comté), Antoine Perrenot de Granvelle studied at Paris, Padua and Louvain and had a highly successful career as minister to Charles V and Philip II. He was made cardinal in 1561 and turned to duties in the Church. Called to Rome in 1568 to attend the conclave that chose Pius V, he lived an active life there, both politically and intellectually, and was a well-known figure in Rome. He also served as viceroy of Naples (1570–75), and in 1579 Philip appointed him secretary of state (of Spain).

Perrenot de Granvelle carried on an immense correspondence with leading scholars and political figures of the sixteenth century and took a lively interest in the study of classical antiquity. He hired Justus *Lipsius as his Latin secretary and commissioned drawings of antiquities from *Pighius, who published a silver vase belonging to the cardinal in his *Themis dea* (1568). He also owned a marble replica of the "*Bed of Polykleitos,*" the famous Roman relief showing Cupid and Psyche, which had once belonged to *Ghiberti. The architect Jacob van Noyen (1533–1600) built the cardinal's palace in Brussels, complete with garden and porticoes, and Perrenot filled it with a collection of statues, coins and other works of art. He also had palaces at Rome, Madrid and Naples that were magnificently appointed.

Van Noyen dedicated a book to the cardinal, an illustrated study of Roman ruins, *Operum antiquorum romanorum reliquiae et ruinae* (1562). Perrenot also patronized the engraver Hieronymus Cock in his preparation of two archaeological works, *Praecipua aliquot romanae antiquitatis ad veri imitationem affabre designata* and *Thermae Diocletianae imperatoris,* on the *Baths of Diocletian (1550–51).

BIBLIOGRAPHY
L. Lacour, "Perrenot de Granvelle, Antoine de," *NBG* 39 (1865), cols. 638–41; Stark, esp. 105, 120; Bober—Rubinstein, 477–78.

PERSSON, AXEL W. (1888–1951). Swedish archaeologist.

Persson served as professor at Uppsala University from 1924 to 1951. Starting as a philologist (Greek), he became one of the most successful field archaeologists of his generation. His excavations were mainly conducted at prehistoric sites in the Argolid: *Asine, 1922–30; Dendra/Midea, 1926–27, 1937 and 1939; Berbati, 1935–37; he also excavated in Turkey: Milas, 1938; Labraunda, 1948–50. His most spectacular find was the unplundered tholos tomb at Dendra (1926). In addition to scholarly publications of the excavation results, *The Royal Tombs at Dendra* (1931), *Asine* (1938, together with O. Frödin and A. Westholm) and *New Tombs at Dendra* (1942) and much-appreciated popular accounts in Swedish, he also published *Staat und Manufaktur im römischen Reiche* (1923) and his Sather lectures on *The Religion of Greece in Prehistoric Times* (1942). During World War II (1943–45) he was a delegate of the Swedish Red Cross in Greece.

BIBLIOGRAPHY
+L. Hollman, *Svenska män och kvinnor* 6 (Stockholm, 1949), 63–64; E. Gren, *OpAth* 1 (1953), 224–36 (bib.).

ROBIN HÄGG

PERUGIA (PERUSIA). Etruscan town.

The modern regional capital of Umbria (Italy) stands on the same hill, dominating the mid-Tiber valley, that was occupied by its Etruscan predecessor, which flourished especially from the fourth to second centuries B.C.; later a *municipium*, it was destroyed and then restored by Augustus, becoming Colonia Vibia under Trebonianus Gallus (A.D. 251–53). The impressive city walls and arched gates, dating to the third century B.C., have always been visible, and Etruscan antiquities were discovered and described as such in the sixteenth and seventeenth centuries (F. Ciatti, *Delle memorie annali et istoriche delle cose di Perugia,* 1636). Sculpted ash urns and inscriptions were published from the early eighteenth century. G. *Dennis (1883) knew the Perugia Cippus, with one of the longest Etruscan texts (found 1822), the figured bronze urn now in St. Petersburg (1841), the multichambered Tomb of the Volumni (1840) and the vaulted San Manno Tomb (also described by *Gori and Passeri), besides the sixth-century Sperandio Sarcophagus and Castel San Mariano bronzes. Recent finds include the Hellenistic Tomb of the Cutu (1983).

BIBLIOGRAPHY

G. Dennis, *The Cities and Cemeteries of Etruria,* 3rd ed. (London, 1883), II, 412–51; Greenhalgh, *Survival,* 81–82; *Gens antiquissima Italiae:* Vatican (1988); Budapest— Cracow (1989); Leningrad (1990); New York (1991).

F. R. SERRA RIDGWAY

PERUZZI, BALDASSARE (1481–1536). Italian Renaissance architect and painter.

Born in Siena, Peruzzi was active in Rome by ca. 1503. He joined the workshop of *Raphael and moved in the "archaeological circle" of artists who studied the *Column of Trajan (especially Jacopo *Ripanda) and the *grottesche* of the *Domus Aurea. Attributed to him in Raphael's Stanze of the Vatican apartments is the ceiling picture of *Apollo and Marsyas* (Stanza della Segnatura, ca. 1508), with its quotation of the ancient statue of the *Hanging Marsyas* in the della *Valle family collection (now, *Uffizi).

Soon afterward, between 1509 and 1511, Peruzzi designed, built and decorated the villa of the Farnesina for Agostino Chigi. In his paintings for the interior he made a number of references to antiquities visible in Rome. His fresco of *Sol in Sagittarius* (Sala di Galatea) shows a close imitation of the *Apollo Citharoedus* type known in several versions at that time, and in the Sala delle Prospettive he drew from a sarcophagus with the *Forge of Vulcan* (later della Valle family collection), to create his fresco on the same theme. Drawings directly from the antique show his tendency to modify and restore as he copied, for example, in the *Tiber* river god (*Nile* and *Tiber;* drawing in London, *British Museum) and in an image of Trajan from the great Trajanic frieze on the *Arch of Constantine (Paris, *Louvre).

Much of Peruzzi's later career was occupied with architectural commissions, especially at the *Vatican, where he was associate, then chief architect of St. Peter's (1520–27; 1531–36) and was employed to complete and restore the Belvedere court. In 1535 he constructed a palace for the *Savelli family by adding two stories to the top of the *Theater of Marcellus.

With Raphael and Annibale Carracci (*Carracci family), Peruzzi is buried in the *Pantheon.

BIBLIOGRAPHY

J. S. Ackerman, *The Cortile del Belvedere* (Vatican City, 1954); *Baldassare Peruzzi— Pittura, scena e architettura nel cinquecento* (Rome, 1987); E. Gerlini, *Villa Farnesina alla Lungara* (Rome, 1988).

PETERSEN, EUGEN (1836–1919). German archaeologist with wide-ranging interests and publications in Greek and Roman art and mythology.

Eugen Petersen, born in Holstein (under Danish control at the time), was trained in philology at Kiel and then at Bonn, where his teachers were O. *Jahn, F. G. *Welcker and F. Ritschl. He was close friends with A. *Michaelis, whose sister he was to marry in 1865.

Having received a stipend for travel from the Prussian government, Petersen went to Rome, where he was assigned to write up the meetings of the *Instituto di Corrispondenza Archeologica. He left Rome in 1861 and for over ten years earned a living as a teacher while he wrote a number of important studies on Greek sculptures: the *Spearbearer* of Polykleitos; the *Marsyas* of Myron; the sculptures from the *Parthenon and *Olympia associated with Pheidias (*Die Kunst des Phidias am Parthenon und zu Olympia,* 1873).

Then came a period in which Petersen concentrated on philological studies, while he was serving as professor of philology and archaeology at Dorpat. Called to Prague to succeed O. *Benndorf, he resumed his art-historical research and published further studies in Greek sculpture. Also at this time, he was invited by Count Karl Lanckoronski, along with the architect *Niemann, to explore Pamphylia and Pisidia in Asia Minor; the result was a brilliant joint publication, financed by Lanckoronski and illustrated by Niemann (*Städte Pamphiliens und Pisidiens,* 1890–92).

In 1886, Petersen went to Athens to serve for a year as secretary of the *German Archaeological Institute. There followed a long period in Rome, from 1887 to 1905, in which he took on, as first secretary, the direction of the institute in Rome. The period was not a particularly happy one for Petersen and his wife, who were never very comfortable with the Italian way of life. In addition, W. *Helbig, who had hoped to return to the institute as first secretary, regarded Petersen as a rival and formed a faction opposing him.

During this period came Petersen's most significant works on Roman art, on the *Column of Marcus Aurelius; the *Arch of Trajan at Beneventum; and the *Column of Trajan. Above all, at this time he made his brilliant conjecture on the nature of the *Ara Pacis Augustae, a reconstruction that was dramatically confirmed in its essentials when excavation was undertaken on the site of the Ara Pacis.

Photograph of *Eugen Petersen* in his study. (Deutsches Archäologisches Institut, Rome. Inst. Neg. 92.959.)

Petersen returned to Greece in 1907, working for a while on topography, especially of the city of Athens. He then settled in Berlin until his death in 1919.
BIBLIOGRAPHY
H. Sichtermann, "Petersen, Eugenio," *EAA* 6 (1965), 94–95; H. Blanck, in *Archäologenbildnisse,* 63–64.

PETRARCH (PETRARCA), FRANCESCO (1304–74). Italian poet, scholar and antiquarian; leading figure of the Early Italian Renaissance.

Born in Arezzo, Petrarch moved with his father, a lawyer, to Avignon in 1312. Trained in law at Montpellier and Bologna, he developed an ardent love for classical literature and antiquities. He traveled through France, Flanders and the Rhineland (1333), everywhere seeking out learned men and monastic libraries that might possess classical texts.

In 1337 he visited Rome for the first time, touring the city in the company of his good friend Giovanni Colonna. A subsequent letter to Colonna (*Familiarum rerum liber* 6.2) recapitulates their wanderings amid the ruins of Rome, referring to monuments such as the Vatican obelisk (*obelisks) and the two great pyramidal tombs of Rome, known then as the Tomb of Remus (*Pyramid of Cestius) and the Tomb of Romulus (largely demolished in 1500 by Pope Alexander VI). He admired the *Pantheon, which he called the "temple of Cybele," following traditional guidebooks such as the *Mirabilia* and the *Graphia aureae urbis.* (But he later referred to it as the "Pantheon of Agrippa.") He noted the ancient belief that the *Column of Trajan was used as a tomb for this emperor.

Reviving ancient traditions, Petrarch sought and accepted an invitation to be crowned with laurel publicly for his poetry; the event was celebrated on the *Capitoline Hill in 1341. Petrarch also enthusiastically supported the efforts of *Cola di Rienzo, whose passion for antiquity led to an abortive attempt to revive the Roman republic.

Petrarch's archaeological interest embraced inscriptions, which he often copied, studied and imitated, and coins, of which he owned a small collection. He studied the numismatic portraits of emperors and their families, including Faustina Major and Minor, one of the Agrippinas and Vespasian and would comment on the physical characteristics of such Roman historical figures. His own great biographical work, *De viris illustribus,* originally featuring a series of famous Romans—from Romulus to Trajan—gave inspiration for the depiction of Roman heroic deeds in the palace of Francesco da Carrara at Padua. The Sala Virorum Illustrium there, frescoed between 1367 and 1379 (later destroyed), featured the lives of famous Romans, sometimes set against a backdrop of classical Roman buildings. It may have been Petrarch who called for the inclusion of the Vatican obelisk, the Column of Trajan, the Pantheon, *Castel Sant'Angelo.

Petrarch was interested in Roman sculpture as well; he described the *"*Regisole*" of Pavia for his good friend and fellow antiquarian *Boccaccio and also admired the famed *Horses* of San Marco. He mentioned the *Quirinal *Horse Tamers* in the eighth book of the *Africa,* his great epic on the Second Punic War, in which he attempted a reconstruction of Rome as it would have been in the third century B.C.

Withdrawing from activity in political and religious circles, Petrarch spent his later years immersed in his writing and studies, moving about and living in Milan, Padua, Venice and finally Arquà, near Padua. There he died, working into the night in his study, where he was found in the morning with his head resting on a manuscript of Vergil.

BIBLIOGRAPHY
P. de Nolhac, *Petrarch and the Ancient World* (1907); T. E. Mommsen, "Petrarch and the Decoration of the Sala Virorum Illustrium in Padua," *ArtB* 34 (1952), 95–116; Valentini—Zucchetti 4 (1953), 1–10; Weiss, *RDCA,* 30–38.

PEUTINGER, KONRAD (1465–1547). German humanist scholar.

Born in Augsburg, Peutinger came from a distinguished family of the merchant class. In 1482 he departed for Italy, where he studied law and literature at Padua, Bologna and Florence. In Rome itself he attended the lectures of Pomponio *Leto, who inspired in him a love of books and rare manuscripts. Returning to his native Augsburg in 1493, he was made secretary of the city, a position of considerable importance. The emperor Maximilian I favored him and charged him with various missions, and he also was respected by Charles V.

After having represented his city at the Diet of Augsburg (1530), Peutinger resigned from politics to devote himself full-time to his studies. He collected statues, coins and inscriptions and published learned treatises on the antiquities he had seen. Especially significant—and early in date for the history of epigraphy—was his assemblage of twenty-two Roman inscriptions from Augsburg and its territory, published in 1505 as *Romanae vetustatis fragmenta in Augusta vindelicorum et eius diocesi.* In addition, through him Petrus Apianus and Bartholomaeus Amantius were able to publish their corpus of Greek and Latin inscriptions, *Inscriptiones sacrosanctae vetustatis* (Ingolstadt, 1534; cf. *epigraphy, Latin). He is remembered as the founding father of the study of Roman antiquities in Germany.

Peutinger's name is especially associated with the celebrated copy of an ancient map known as the *Tabula Peutingeriana, which was bequeathed to him by Conrad *Celtis (d. 1508) and remained in his own possession until his death in 1547. But Peutinger left little evidence of his interest in the map, which was not published until the end of the sixteenth century.

BIBLIOGRAPHY
Stark, 87, 100, 101, 107; "Peutinger, Conrad," *NBG* 39 (1865), cols. 773–75.

PEUTINGER TABLE. See TABULA PEUTINGERIANA.

PFUHL, ERNST (1876–1940). German archaeologist, expert on Greek sculpture and painting.

Pfuhl, born in Berlin-Charlottenburg and the son of a sculptor, studied with *Kekulé, *Wilamowitz and others in Berlin. Four years of travel took him to Rome, where he studied Hellenistic art with his close friend Richard Delbrueck, and on to Greece, where he was assigned by *Hiller von Gärtringen to excavate the Archaic necropolis at *Thera. The work was scientific and systematic and yielded important information on chronology, social strata and commerce. In Athens, Pfuhl found a Greek wife, Sophia, the daughter of the Greek archaeologist A. Rhousopoulos.

In 1909, he was given a position at the university at Basle, where he was to remain until his death in 1940. There he produced the work that has made him famous, *Malerei und Zeichnung der Griechen*, three volumes (1923), richly illustrated with the Greek paintings and vase paintings he sought to organize. An abbreviated version of this great anthology (published 1924) was translated into English by J. D. *Beazley as *Masterpieces of Greek Drawing and Painting* (1926).

Pfuhl was a prolific writer and has left many shorter studies in journals and in the *Real-Encyclopädie* on a wide variety of topics, including architecture, myth and religion. After his death, H. Möbius brought out the two-volume *Ostgriechische Grabreliefs* (1977–79), a corpus of East Greek grave reliefs that had occupied Pfuhl from an early date in his career.

BIBLIOGRAPHY

K. Schefold, in *Archäologenbildnisse*, 192–93.

PHAISTOS. Site in south-central *Crete, location of an important Bronze Age Minoan palace; in mythology Phaistos was the home of Rhadamanthys, brother of King Minos of *Knossos.

In 1900 Luigi *Pernier began excavations at Phaistos for the Italian Archaeological Mission (*Italian School of Archaeology) and spent nine years uncovering the remains of the second largest Minoan palace known. Doro *Levi directed a second series of campaigns (1950–66, 1969, 1971) for the Italian School. Portions of the palace had eroded on the south and east sides; what remains covers some two acres and features a complex plan with a paved central court running north-south as well as four smaller paved courts. The palace took its characteristic shape in the Middle Minoan (MM) period (Levi dated the "Old Palace" to 1800–1500 B.C.), with the "New Palace" of the Late Minoan period reusing appropriate elements. A remarkable feature of the later palace was a monumental open-air entrance stairway some forty-five feet wide.

Although finds at Phaistos were not rich, some highly significant specimens of ancient writing were found in the earlier palace. An archive of some 7,500 clay sealings in Linear A (*Linear A and B) were found in a MM II level, interpreted by E. Fiandra as the sealings for wooden door handles. Most famous of the artifacts found is the "Phaistos Disc," a clay object (ca. 16cm in diameter; MM III), covered with a script with some 241 signs arranged in a spiral pattern on each side. The disc has never been deciphered.

BIBLIOGRAPHY
+L. Pernier, *Il Palazzo minoico di Festos* 1 (Rome, 1935) and 2, with L. Banti (Rome, 1951); +Y. Duhoux, *Le Disque de Phaestos* (Louvain, 1971); D. Levi, *Festos e la civiltà minoica,* 2 vols. (Rome, 1976–88); +V. La Rosa, in *Aerial Atlas of Crete,* 232–43.

PHYLAKOPI. See MELOS.

PIAZZA ARMERINA. Town in south-central *Sicily, adjacent to the site of a luxurious Roman villa of the fourth century A.C.

The villa near Piazza Armerina presents a very large and opulent building complex, including courtyards, an audience hall, living quarters, baths, latrines and a grand three-apsed room (the *triconchos*) that may have been a dining area. Spread over an area 150m × 100m, the villa was adorned with brightly colored wall paintings and featured columns, pavings and facings of a wide variety of marbles of the Roman Empire. Most important of all are the mosaic floors; the enormous expanse of flooring, an estimated 3,500m², is the greatest amount of mosaic in any single building project in the Roman Empire. The scenes of the *Great Hunt* in the corridor hall and of the *Chariot Race* in the baths are regarded as most spectacular.

The villa was reused in the Middle Ages, as is evident from Byzantine, Arab and Norman activity, and parts of it must have always been visible. But the earliest references to rediscovery of the site belong to the eighteenth century; A. Leanti noted (1761) the presence of "vestiges of an ancient temple adorned with mosaics." The British consul Robert Fagan obtained a permit to dig there (1808), as a result of which two granite columns were sold to the principal church of Piazza Armerina. In 1881 the Comune of Piazza Armerina sponsored excavations under the engineer Pappalardo, uncovering portions of the mosaics in the great three-apsed hall. Paolo *Orsi revealed more of the mosaic in excavations of 1929, and G. Cultrera, superintendent of antiquities at *Syracuse, excavated in 1935, 1938 and 1940–41, uncovering the oval court and the south apse of the *Great Hunt* corridor. The rest of the plan of the villa was recovered by G. V. Gentili in five campaigns (1950–54), though not all the results were published. A program of conservation under the superintendents at Syracuse and *Agrigento included roofing of most of the structures.

A. Carandini attempted to make the chronology of the villa at Piazza Armerina more precise with several trenches in 1970, but the question of the dating has remained vexed because of the general scarcity of information from stratigraphic excavation. There is limited evidence of an early building on the site (second century A.C.) under the sprawling complex, which itself shows signs of repairs. A most important addition occurred in the Hall of the Ten Maidens, perhaps in the middle of the fourth century A.C., where a geometric mosaic pattern was replaced by the celebrated scene of the "bikini girls" in athletic competition.

BIBLIOGRAPHY
+G. V. Gentili, *The Imperial Villa of Piazza Armerina,* 4th ed. (Rome, 1970); C. Ampolo et al., "La Villa del Casale a Piazza Armerina, Problemi, saggi stratigrafici ed altre ricerche," *MEFRA* 73 (1971), 141–281; +R. J. A. Wilson, *Piazza Armerina* (London, 1983).

PICCHERI. See PICHLER.

PICCOLOMINI, AENEAS SYLVIUS. See PIUS II.

PICHLER (PICKLER, PIKLER, PICCHERI) FAMILY. Family of Tyrolean origin, masters of gem engraving in the antique manner.

The head of the family was ANTONIO (JOHANN ANTON; 1697–1779), who was born in Brixen in the Tyrol. He intended to become a merchant under an uncle in Nice but soon took employment with a goldsmith in Naples, where he became expert in engraving on metals and precious stones. Rapidly acquiring an excellent reputation, Antonio settled in Rome in 1743. One may say that he rediscovered the art of antique gem engraving; he then inspired three of his sons to follow in his path. He excelled in the reproduction of antique subjects, to the point that his works were often taken for originals. In his extensive production, Antonio also created cameos and intaglios of his own design.

Of the three sons who took up gem engraving, the eldest was GIOVANNI (JOHANN ANTON; 1734–91), born in Naples and early instructed by his father in modeling and glyptography. From the age of sixteen, he began producing handsome replicas of antique gems and soon outshone his father in the quality of both replicas and original works. In 1769 he did a portrait of the Holy Roman Emperor Joseph II that won him a knighthood and the title of Gem Engraver to His Majesty. Giovanni also made portraits of Popes *Clement XIV and *Pius VI. His intaglios excel in mirroring the antique spirit and in exquisite execution, and they display a vivid imagination. His numerous portraits in cameos and intaglios are at once simple, noble and delicate in style.

His brother, GIUSEPPE (JOHANN JOSEPH; 1760–1829), born in Rome, was also a master gem engraver and portraitist. The youngest brother, LUIGI (LUDWIG, ALOIS; 1773–1854), studied painting, modeling in wax and gem engraving under his brother Giovanni. Toward the end of the eighteenth century he visited Austria, where his mastery in the glyptic art attracted wide foreign patronage. Presented to Emperor Francis I in Vienna (1808), Luigi was named to the Viennese Academy of Fine Arts and to the papal Academy of St. Luke in Rome. Occupying the post of professor of engraving in Vienna, 1818–50, he made glass castings of the emperor's collection of gemstones for an imperial present to the pope (delivered 1821). Luigi was elected a member of the Academy of Fine Arts in Florence (1831) and in Milan (1839) and was awarded papal knighthoods (St. Gregory, 1839; St. Silvester, 1842). He made many intaglio portraits of contemporaries that were much esteemed.

All members of the Pichler family signed their works with variants of the name spelled in Greek letters, following the practice of the day.

BIBLIOGRAPHY

Périès, "Pikler (Jean-Antoine)," *BU* 34 (1823), 440–42; H. Rollett, *Die Drei Meister der Gemmoglyptik, Antonio, Giovanni und Luigi Pichler* (Vienna, 1874); L. Forrer, *Biographical Dictionary of Medallists . . . Ancient and Modern* 4 (London, 1909), 507–30 and 8 (London, 1930), 126–28.

J. S. TASSIE

PICKARD-CAMBRIDGE, Sir ARTHUR WALLACE (1873–1952). English classicist, expert on the Greek theater.

A clergyman's son, born in Dorset, educated at Jowett's Balliol under W. R. Hardie and J. A. Smith, Pickard-Cambridge received a double first that secured for him in 1895 a fellowship at Oriel. In 1897 he became fellow of Balliol, where he remained classical tutor for thirty years, briefly serving as professor of Greek at Edinburgh (1927–30). He translated Demosthenes' public orations (1906) and did a life of the orator (1914); but the center of his interest was the scenic antiquities of the Greeks, to which he devoted three masterpieces: *Dithyramb, Tragedy and Comedy* (1927); *The Theatre of Dionysus in Athens* (1946); and *The Dramatic Festivals of Athens* (1953). They are distinguished by copious learning, sound judgment and scrupulous adherence to evidence.

BIBLIOGRAPHY

C. Bailey, "Sir Arthur Wallace Pickard-Cambridge (1873–1952)," *ProcBrAc* 38 (1952), 303–16.

WILLIAM M. CALDER III

PICKLER. See PICHLER.

PIETRO DA CORTONA (PIETRO BERRETINI; 1590–1669). Italian Baroque painter.

Born at Cortona into a family of artisans, Pietro Berretini, known usually by the name of his native city, was trained early in architecture by his father, a stonemason. He then served as a painter's apprentice in Rome (1612 ff.) and absorbed the lessons of *Raphael and antiquity. In this period Cortona made drawings of a variety of antiquities—sarcophagi, funerary urns, statues, triumphal arches, friezes and reliefs. Slightly later were made his drawings of the *Column of Trajan, now in the Gabinetto delle Stampe, Rome (1620s).

Soon he attracted the attention of the nobleman Marcello Sacchetti and was taken into his household in 1623. In the Palazzo Sacchetti, the artist met the powerful Cardinal Francesco Barberini (nephew of Pope Urban VIII), who became his staunch patron, and, at the same time, Cassiano dal *Pozzo, the cardinal's secretary. Almost at a stroke he made the most important contacts of his life and was swept into a highly successful career. This circle of men with whom he was associated, prominent in religion and politics, valued archaeological studies along with the fine arts. Cassiano dal Pozzo hired Cortona to make drawings for him for his famous "Paper Museum" of the vast array of classical antiquities to be seen in and around Rome. The most significant of Cortona's drawings known to have been made for him is the highly finished copy after the *Aldobrandini *Wedding,* created as a design for an etching by the Sienese artist Bernardino Capitelli (1590–1639). Pietro and his assistants were also hired to make reproductions of Late Antique painted manuscripts in the Vatican Library, including the *Vatican Vergil, the "Roman Vergil" and the Vatican Terence.

For the Cardinal Barberini, Pietro created designs for tapestries of the *Life of Constantine,* to complement others on the subject designed by Peter Paul *Rubens in the 1620s. Among the tapestries, woven between 1630 and 1641, were seven over-door panels, representing monuments or reproducing reliefs related to Constantine the Great. Remarkably archaeological are the woven images of the magnificent porphyry sarcophagus of St. Helena (*Vatican Museums) and of a medal with the *Baths of Constantine. In general, his designs for the series from the history of Constantine reveal solid preparation in the study of armor, costume and battle motifs on reliefs from the *Arch of Constantine, Column of Trajan and other monuments.

In his career as a leading painter of the High Baroque style, Cortona produced many grand interpretations of classical themes. His early frescoes of St. Bibiana (1624–26; S. Bibiana, Rome) depict Early Christianity heroically, with details drawn from reliefs of Trajan and incorporating ancient monumental settings. *The Martryrdom of St. Bibiana* shows the saint in a landscape whirling with action, enhanced by the oval of the upper part of the *Colosseum, which acts as a backdrop. The *Rape of the Sabines* (after 1626; *Capitoline Museums, Rome) is set in a classical context that includes an obelisk (*obelisks). Different rhythms are created in the *Age of Gold* and *Age of Silver,* frescoes done for the Grand Duke of Tuscany, Ferdinand II, to decorate his Sala della Stufa in the Palazzo Pitti, Florence (1637). Here a glowing pagan paradise with Bacchic overtones is set in a lush landscape. The *Age of Copper* and *Age of Iron* (1640) return to military themes, utilizing antique armor and a sterner setting with temples of the Tuscan Doric order. Other ceiling decorations for Ferdinand II in the Pitti display allegories with an antique vocabulary and themes from Hellenistic and Roman history.

Cortona's architectural designs show a knowledge of ancient sites and antique vocabulary. In his design for the Villa del Pigneto built near Rome for the Sacchetti family (late 1620s), he imitated the *Sanctuary of Fortuna, Praeneste, and he also proposed a project for a reconstruction of the sanctuary (1636). His façade for S. Maria della Pace (Rome, 1656–57) utilizes an Ionic entablature above a Tuscan Doric porch. In S. Maria in Via Lata (Rome, 1658–62) he conveys the dignity and solidity of a Roman temple, using the Corinthian order on the ground floor and a Syrian arch breaking through the entablature on the second story. The latter motif may have been derived from the palace of Diocletian at *Split.

BIBLIOGRAPHY
+R. Wittkower, *Art and Architecture in Italy,* 3rd ed. (Harmondsworth, 1973), 152–68; +G. Briganti, *Pietro da Cortona,* 2nd ed. (Florence, 1982); +*The Paper Museum of Cassiano dal Pozzo,* catalog of exhibition, *Quaderni Puteani* 4 (1993), 32–34, 52–53, 92–94.

PIETRO DA PADOVA, ANDREA DI. See PALLADIO, ANDREA.

PIETRO DE' GIANUZZI, GIULIO DI. See GIULIO ROMANO.

PIETRO DELLA GONDOLA, ANDREA DI. See PALLADIO, ANDREA.

PIGHIUS, STEPHANUS WINANDUS (STEVEN WYNKENS PIGGE; 1520–1604). Dutch antiquarian, epigrapher and Latinist.

Born in Kampen, the Netherlands, Pighius assumed the name of his mother's brother, Albert Pigge, who educated the child in Utrecht. In 1540 he went to Louvain, where he matriculated in 1543, and he later studied in Brussels as well. He arrived in Rome in 1548 and entered the service of Cardinal Marcello Cervini and later of Cardinal Sirletus.

During this period antiquarian pursuits in Rome were led by Mario Delfini, Fulvio *Orsini and Pirro *Ligorio, all of whom Pighius undoubtedly knew. Here he also met many northern humanists—Laevinus *Torrentius, Justus *Lipsius, Antonius Morillon, Martinus *Smetius. He was on friendly terms with Cardinal Rodolfo da *Carpi, in whose collection he saw a female herm that he made the subject of his study *Themis seu de lege divina* (Antwerp, 1568). He was very interested in epigraphy and frequently copied inscriptions. In 1554 he collected inscriptions at the request of Cardinal Cervini; the resulting sylloge was his *Inscriptionum antiquarum farrago.* He also visited antiquarian collections in Rome such as the vigna of Pope *Julius III and the della *Valle palazzi. On a trip to *Tivoli, he spotted herms of *Themistokles, Miltiades, Isokrates, Herakleitos, Karneades* and *Aristogeiton,* which Julius III acquired on his advice. They were later published by A. Statius (*Illustrium virorum,* 1569). He collected drawings of antique monuments, mostly reliefs. His manuscript, known as the Codex Pighianus, is a valuable source of information since it often records the whereabouts of the sculptures and illustrates the monuments in their unrestored condition. Drawings of many of the same monuments appear in the *Codex Coburgensis (Veste Coburg, Cod. HZ II; ca. 1550), but it is unclear which codex was copied from the other.

Pighius also published the *Fasti Capitolini,* found in 1546 in Rome and placed in the Capitol by Cardinal Farnese. His *Tabula magistratum romanorum* (1561) was reprinted in volume 1 of his *Annales magistratum romanorum* (Antwerp, 1598). (The two volumes, unpublished at his death, were finished by A. Schottus and published in 1615.)

In 1557 Pighius was appointed secretary and librarian to Cardinal Antoine

*Perrenot de Granvelle, bishop of Arras, and moved to Brussels. There he published an edition of Valerius Maximus in 1567. A silver cup with Bacchic symbols in Granvelle's possession was the subject of his learned mythological publication—the first of its kind—*Mythologia* (Antwerp, 1568), in which his *Themis* was also published.

In 1571 he left for Italy in the retinue of Charles Frederick, son of William of Cleves. Charles died in 1575 on the trip, and Pigge wrote up his itinerary and biography in his *Hercules Prodicius* (Antwerp, 1587). In this, the first Dutch guidebook to Italy, he gives a reliable account of the ancient monuments. The work was used by Franciscus Schottus for his book on Italy of 1600 and formed the basis for many other travel guides printed in the seventeenth century.

When Pighius became canon of Xanten in 1575, he moved to Germany, where he spent the last years of his life.

BIBLIOGRAPHY

O. Jahn, ''Über die Zeichnungen antiker Monumenten im Codex Pighianus,'' *Jahresberichte der königl. Sächs. Gesellschaft der Wissenschaften zu Leipzig, Phil.-Hist. Classe* 20 (1868), 161–235; R. Matz, ''Über eine dem Herzog von Coburg-Gotha gehörige Sammlung alter Handzeichnungen nach Antiken,'' *Monatsberichte Königl. Preuss. Akademie der Wissenschaften zu Berlin* (1871), 445–99; A. Roersch, *L'Humanisme belge* (Brussels, 1910), 137–47; J. H. Jongkees, ''Stephanus Winandus Pighius Campensis,'' *Mededelingen Nederlands Historisch Instituut te Rome*, 3rd. ser., 8 (1954), 119–85; R. Harprath—H. Wrede, eds., *Antikenzeichnung und Antikenstudium in Renaissance und Frühbarock* (1989).

MARJON VAN DER MEULEN

PIGNA. See BELVEDERE PIGNA.

PIGORINI, LUIGI (1842–1925). Italian archaeologist and ethnographer, commonly regarded as the father of Italian prehistory.

Pigorini began his archaeological career by investigating the *terramara* piledwellings of his native North Italy. Their bronze-using culture was hailed in the ''Pigorini hypothesis''—in fact underpinned to a significant extent by the work of W. *Helbig—as evidence for the transalpine, Indo-European origin of the Italic peoples; other southward movements were detected archaeologically in the plan of Romulus's *Roma quadrata* and linguistically in the derivation of *Palatinus* (*Palatine Hill) from *palus*. This idiosyncratic view of the origin of Rome has long been abandoned, and the *terramara* settlements are now seen as a phenomenon limited to a comparatively late stage in the Bronze Age sequence of the Po valley.

In 1870, Pigorini was appointed section head in the newly established Direzione Generale dei Musei e Scavi d'Antichità in Rome, where, with P. Strobel and G. Chierici, he founded the influential *Bullettino di Paletnologia Italiana* in 1875. In 1876, he achieved his great ambition: a museum (adjacent to the Museo Kircheriano) devoted exclusively to the prehistory and ethnography of

Italy. Pigorini was appointed to the chair of prehistoric archaeology (*paletnol-ogia*) at Rome University in the same year, and for the next four decades this forceful personality charted the course of Italian prehistoric research. He was elevated to the rank of senator in 1912. The museum he had founded was renamed "Museo Preistorico-Etnografico Luigi Pigorini" after his death; it was moved in sections to a new site in the EUR quarter of Rome from 1962 onward.

BIBLIOGRAPHY

W. Helbig, *Die Italiker in der Po-ebene* (Leipzig, 1879); L. Pigorini, "Perchè la prima Roma è sorta sul Palatino," *Archivio Storico per la Sicilia Orientale* 16–17 (1920), 248–55; *Un maestro di scienza e d'italianità* (Rome, 1925, with bib.); R. Peroni, in *Le Vie della preistoria,* ed. M. Angle et al. (Rome, 1992), 15–33.

DAVID RIDGWAY

PIKLER. See PICHLER FAMILY.

PINZA, GIOVANNI (1872–1940). Italian archaeologist and prehistorian.

Pinza's first major publication was a book-length article on the early cultures of Latium (*BullCom* 26, 1898), from which it was abundantly clear that he opposed the prevailing *terramaricolismo* of *Pigorini and *Helbig. The possibility of dialogue did not arise: Pinza, an undisciplined near-genius who lacked both tact and private means, was simply denied official facilities in Rome. His researches were assisted from 1906 by Bartolomeo Nogara, director of the Museo Gregoriano Etrusco in the Vatican. There, Pinza discovered—and used—the original documents relating to the *Regolini-Galassi material excavated at *Cerveteri in 1836–37. On a wider front, the first installments of two ambitiously conceived but unfinished projects bear tragic witness to the brilliance of what might have been: *Materiali per l'etnologia antica toscano-laziale* (1915); *Storia della civiltà latina* (1924). There is more in them of lasting value than is generally admitted.

BIBLIOGRAPHY

B. Nogara, "Commemorazione di Giovanni Pinza," *RendPontAcc* 16 (1940), 99–111; A. E. Gordon, *The Inscribed Fibula Praenestina* (Berkeley, 1975), passim.

DAVID RIDGWAY

PIOMBINO APOLLO. Bronze statue of a standing youth, found in either 1812 or 1832 off the west coast of Italy at Piombino; taken to Paris in 1833, it was purchased by the *Louvre for 16,000 francs in 1834 (height 1.15m); when its interior was cleaned in 1842, a lead tablet appeared with the names of two Rhodian artists in letter forms that have been assigned to the first century B.C.

The statue is of the *kouros* type (**korai* and *kouroi*); according to a silver inscription on the left foot, it was dedicated to Athena. Both hands are raised to waist level; the left once clasped a cylindrical object, probably a bow, and the right, with palm up, may have held a libation bowl. The bronze alloy contains 8–10 percent tin, which suggests an Italian origin. The eyes, once inlaid, are missing: eyebrows, lips and nipples retain their copper inlays.

The long-haired bronze youth was traditionally attributed to either a Sikyonian or a South Italian artist and appeared in virtually every publication on Greek art as a representative Late Archaic work of the very early fifth century B.C. Now, however, on both stylistic and epigraphic grounds, B. S. Ridgway has convincingly identified the Piombino *Apollo* as an archaizing work of the first century B.C.; it is perhaps to be understood as an ancient forgery.

BIBLIOGRAPHY

+Lullies—Hirmer, 70; B. S. Ridgway, "The Bronze Apollo from Piombino in the Louvre," *AntP* 7 (1963), 43–75; G. M. A. Richter, with M. Guarducci, *Kouroi,* 3rd ed. (New York, 1970), 144–45, 152–53; V.C. Goodlett, "Rhodian Sculpture Workshops," *AJA* 95 (1991), esp. 677.

CAROL MATTUSCH

PIPPI, GIULIO. See GIULIO ROMANO.

PIRAEUS. See PEIRAEUS.

PIRANESI, GIOVANNI BATTISTA (1720–78). Venetian architect, designer and graphic artist.

Few other artists or scholars have left a more indelible impression of the grandeur of Roman antiquity upon the modern imagination than Piranesi, whether through his etched *vedute* (views) or arcane fantasies such as the *Carceri d'invenzione* (*Imaginary Prisons*). Still not sufficiently realized, however, are the sheer extent and significance of his varied contributions to classical archaeology during some thirty years' sustained activity in recording, interpreting and reconstructing the Roman achievement in over 1,000 plates and a corpus of theoretical writings. Moreover, his governing belief in the creative inspiration of antiquity for modern architects and designers, strengthened by his leading role in the Graeco-Roman controversy, placed Piranesi at the center of that revolutionary change in attitude toward the past, neoclassicism.

Architecture was to prove the controlling discipline of Piranesi's career. Born in 1720 at Mogliano, near Venice, the son of a master builder, he trained under Lucchesi and Scalfurotto, architects and hydraulic engineers in the service of the Republic. Piranesi eventually reached the goal of his aspirations in 1740, when he arrived in Rome as a draftsman in Marco Foscarini's embassy. Frustrated by a lack of professional opportunities, he gained a livelihood by engraving views for visiting Grand Tourists (see *Grand Tour) while sublimating his architectural ideas in elaborate fantasy designs. Shortly after publishing a selection of these in 1743, he visited the newly discovered *Herculaneum, where he was convinced of the critical need for more effective illustrations of the growing material revealed by excavation.

After gathering funds for a print-selling business during a brief trip to Venice

Portrait of *Giovanni Battista Piranesi*, etching by F. Piranesi, after a portrait by J. Cades, 1779. (Westfälisches Landesmuseum für Kunst und Kulturgeschichte, Münster, Porträtarchiv Diepenbroick. Photo: R. Wakonigg.)

around 1744, his final return to Rome was marked by the issue of the fourteen *Carceri* plates—an experimental field of architectural compositions on the theme of the Roman vaulted interior. Meanwhile, he began to transform the conventional *veduta* into a vehicle for combining powerful imagery with a wealth of technical information, exemplified by the 135 plates of the *Vedute di Roma* issued individually from about 1748 onward.

Topography rapidly developed into archaeological inquiry. A modest publication on tomb chambers (ca. 1750) and a folio on the so-called *Trophies of Marius on the Capitol (1753) were followed by a four-volume comprehensive survey of ancient Rome in 1756. *Le Antichità romane* represented a landmark in the history of classical archaeology, not only in terms of its innovative illustrative techniques but also in terms of the application of a mind capable of combining a specialized understanding of architecture and engineering with reconstructive faculties of the highest order. The 250 plates fulfilled a crucial and carefully coordinated role, since the 315 monuments depicted were cross-indexed and related to surviving inscriptions and the fragmentary Severan Marble Plan (*Forma Urbis Romae). Their full significance, however, could be grasped only in the topographical context of a master plan that also showed the integration of the aqueduct and defensive systems. Apart from special attention to funerary monuments, an exaggerated emphasis on feats of engineering reflected Piranesi's initial response to the provocative claims made by philhellenes such as *Le Roy and Laugier in the growing Graeco-Roman debate.

While academic recognition was swift—Piranesi was elected an honorary fellow of the *Society of Antiquaries of London in 1757—these scholarly pursuits were soon transformed into intense polemics. In 1761 appeared his first rejoinder, *Della magnificenza ed architettura de' Romani,* establishing his defense with the Etruscans as the sole founders of Roman civilization (*Etruscheria*). Detailed arguments followed in a series of richly illustrated folios: the *Acqua Giulia,* extending his earlier studies of the public water system, and, also in 1761, the *Lapides Capitolini,* featuring a lengthy historical inscription from the *Forum Romanum. In 1762 appeared a highly technical treatise on the hydraulic mastery of the emissarium, or drainage outlet, to Lake Albano while further publications in 1764 recorded the antiquities of the Albano and Castelgandolfo area, as well as the ancient city of Cori. Most significant of all, however, was the *Campo Marzio* of 1762, issued as a reply to *Winckelmann's attack on the decadence of the Late Empire by tracing the evolution of a densely monumental townscape of unprecedented complexity.

The reissue of the heavily reworked *Carceri* plates in the early 1760s marked a climactic point in Piranesi's career. Through Clement XIII and the Rezzonico family, he finally obtained a series of commissions for decorative schemes as well as two architectural works—a new tribune for the Lateran (unexecuted) and the reconstruction of S. Maria Aventina. These activities were controlled by a novel system of design, incorporating a wide range of antique motifs, set forth in the *Parere su l'architettura* of 1765. By the close of the decade, the

View of the *Arch of Gallienus*, etching by G. B. Piranesi, from *Le Antichità romane* (1756). (Deutsches Archäologisches Institut, Rome, Inst. Neg. 86.1434.)

treatise *Diverse maniere* (1769), his final statement in the Graeco-Roman quarrel, set out to illustrate his new system of design in action. The essay, introducing a collection of chimneypieces and furnishings, reasserted the inventive genius of the Etruscans and also advanced a pioneering formal analysis of Egyptian art (featured, too, in certain designs) in an impassioned defense of imaginative eclecticism.

Following Clement XIII's death in 1769, Piranesi developed a prosperous business in dealing, as well as in restoring classical antiquities. Many of these imposing objects, which found their way into British collections, such as the Warwick Vase and the Newdigate Candelabra, were illustrated in a series of striking plates, first published together as *Vasi, candelabri, cippi, sarcofagi* in 1778. By now Piranesi's collaborators included his son Francesco (1758–1810), who also helped prepare a publication of 1774 meticulously depicting the three great relief columns in Rome and another on the three Doric temples of *Paestum. The latter, which received the papal imprimatur shortly before Piranesi's death in November 1778, was ironically to play a decisive part in promoting the heavyweight aesthetic of the later Greek Revival.

Unfinished archaeological publications completed posthumously by Francesco included detailed maps of *Hadrian's Villa, Tivoli (1781), the emissarium of Lake Fucino (1791) and the excavations at *Pompeii. This last, together with a series of *vedute,* was to illustrate the work *Les Antiquités de la Grande Grèce* (1804–7). When Francesco reissued his father's works in a twenty-seven-volume edition between 1800 and 1807, he included his own archaeological works: *Raccolta de' tempi antichi* (1780), *Il Teatro di Ercolano* (1783), *Monumenti degli Scipioni* (1785) and a pictorial anthology of the major classical statues in Rome (1786).

BIBLIOGRAPHY

K. Lehmann, "Piranesi as Interpreter of Roman Architecture," *Piranesi,* Catalog of exhibition (Northampton, MA, 1960), 88–98; J. Wilton-Ely, *The Mind and Art of Piranesi* (London, 1978); W. L. MacDonald, *Piranesi's Carceri: Sources of Invention* (Northampton MA, 1979); J. Wilton-Ely, "Piranesi and the Role of Archaeological Illustration," in *Piranesi e la cultura antiquaria: gli antecedenti e il contesto, Atti del Convegno, 1979,* ed. A. Lo Bianco (Rome, 1983), 317–38; J. Wilton-Ely, *G. B. Piranesi, The Complete Etchings* (San Francisco, 1994).

JOHN WILTON-ELY

PIRCKHEIMER, WILLIBALD (WILIBALD PIRKHEIMER; BILIBALDUS PIRCHKEYMERUS; 1470–1530). German humanist scholar.

Born at Eichstadt, Pirckheimer had the benefit of study at Padua and Pavia and, in all, a seven-year stay in Italy. Returning in 1495 to Germany, he established himself at Nuremberg, where he took part in public affairs. His house was a meeting place for humanist scholars and artists, including his best friend, Albrecht *Dürer, and he was a member of the Rhine humanist society, Sodalitas Rhenana, founded by Konrad *Celtis.

Pirckheimer made a number of translations of Greek authors into Latin—Plutarch, Lucian, Theophrastos, Ptolemy, as well as the *Hieroglyphica* by Horus Apollo—and was especially interested in geography and archaeology. He prepared a description of the Porta Nigra at *Trier, along with drawings. Pirckheimer owned a significant collection of Greek and Roman coins and wrote a treatise on the buying power of ancient coins.

BIBLIOGRAPHY
Stark, 101; Sandys, II, 259; E. Panofsky, *The Life and Art of Albrecht Dürer,* 4th ed. (Princeton, NJ, 1955), 31, 173, etc.; Pfeiffer, 62.

PISA (PISAE). Ancient city in Tuscany, Italy.

The city's origin is disputed (whether Greek, Ligurian or Etruscan), but it seems to have been an Etruscan port town by the fifth century B.C., a Roman outpost against the Ligurians by 225 B.C. and a Roman colony by the time of Augustus (31 B.C.–A.D. 14). In modern times the locations of a theater, baths, amphitheater and temple of Vesta have been identified, and the roughly rectangular plan of the Roman settlement may be seen in the modern city plan.

Pisa is famous for its reuse of ancient materials, as in the *Roman sarcophagi in the *Campo Santo, appropriated for medieval burials, and in the *spolia* of the cathedral. Ancient marbles identifiable by their mutilated inscriptions may be seen today in the walls of the church, as well as numerous columns and capitals of granite, marble or porphyry that appear to come from originally Roman buildings. A great urn of Pentelic marble similar to the *Borghese Vase, with a Dionysiac theme, was set on a column outside the south transept during the Middle Ages (now in the Campo Santo; replaced outdoors by a copy). A precocious interest in imitating ancient sarcophagi and Etruscan sculpture as well as the marble urn may be discerned in the pre-Renaissance carvings (thirteenth–early fourteenth centuries) of Nicola *Pisano and his son Giovanni *Pisano, visible in the baptistery and cathedral, respectively.

BIBLIOGRAPHY
N. Toscanelli, *Pisa nell'antichità,* 3 vols. (1933–34); s.v. "Pisa," *EAA* 6 (1965), 193–95; D. C. Scavone, s.v. "Pisae," *PECS,* 713–14; +S. Settis, ed., *Camposanto monumentale di Pisa, le antichità* 2 (Pisa, 1984).

PISANO, ANDREA (ANDREA DA PONTADERA; 1290?–1348/50?). Tuscan sculptor of the Italian Gothic period.

Trained as a goldsmith, probably in *Pisa, Andrea went to Florence ca. 1329, where he created his masterpieces, the bronze doors of the Baptistery and the design and partial execution of the Campanile, including much of its sculptural decoration. He left Florence ca. 1343 to direct a workshop in Pisa. By May 1347, he was capomaestro of Orvieto Cathedral.

Pisa, a city rich in classical remains, had fostered the revolutionary revival of classical forms in the work of Nicola *Pisano, the fountainhead of Italian Gothic sculpture. Andrea's early training in Pisa brought him into close contact with ancient monuments and with the work of Nicola, both of which were to have a profound influence on his style.

Andrea's classicizing tendencies developed slowly. The bronze reliefs on the Florentine Baptistery doors (1330) are framed in Gothic quatrefoils and represent one of the most salient reflections of French Gothic influence in Italy. They contain, however, a number of isolated references to antique motifs. The seated Zacharias in the *Naming of the Baptist,* for example, depends on ancient Roman patriarch types seen on sarcophagi, and Christ in the *Baptism of Christ* recalls, in many ways, small Greek and Roman bronzes. As is generally true of medieval classicism, however, there is little integration or consistent use of classical elements.

This situation changes with Andrea's next commission, the hexagonal reliefs for the Campanile of Florence (ca. 1334–ca. 1343). In the *Creation* scenes, not only do the poses and proportions of Adam and Eve recall numerous figures on sarcophagi, but the figures achieve something of the tactile qualities of antique marble nudes. There is also evident a new concern with the representation of landscape. One searches in vain for medieval precedents for the Campanile landscapes, with their naturalistic earth formations and smooth transitions from foreground to background; rather, the sources are probably to be found in ancient Roman landscape reliefs.

Following the Genesis scenes on the west façade, all completed before 1337, the program continues on the other sides of the Campanile with representations of the *Mechanical and Liberal Arts.* Among these, one group of hexagons is astonishingly classicizing both in style and in the conception of the images. Classicizing drapery patterns replace the swinging folds and meandering hemlines (still reminiscent of the drapery on the doors) of the earlier hexagons. The iconography consistently makes references to antique prototypes. For example, the conception of the sculptor in the representation of *Sculpture* is that of an ancient, not a medieval, artisan. His chisel is set against an ''antique'' nude in-the-round. There is, moreover, a clear reference to an ancient theme: *Prometheus Shaping the Body of Man.* The Campanile relief may be compared with one illustrating that theme on a third-century Roman sarcophagus in the *Capitoline Museums in Rome. The *Rider* in the scene of *Horsemanship,* mounted *all'antica* without saddle or spurs, recalls several ancient representations known in the Trecento. The standing figure in *Weaving* probably represents Minerva, one of several pagan benefactors of humankind who appear on the Campanile. The conception here is reminiscent of such images as the Minerva who presides over her weavers on a frieze in the Forum Nervae in Rome. While the Roman relief cannot be regarded as the visual source for the Campanile hexagon, the clear intention in the latter is the representation *all'antica* of weaving, i.e. the textile industry upon which the outstanding economic power of the republic largely depended. Daedalus, too, the *Inventor of the Arts,* is obviously based upon ancient examples. The same holds true for *Navigation,* which repeats a motif seen on a third century tomb of a ship's captain. *Hercules* is comparable to countless antique representations, and *Trade* resembles, among other examples, a scene on the *Column of Marcus Aurelius. Clearly, with these reliefs the iconography of the *Labors of Man* is invested with what can only be described as an overtly protohumanistic character: contemporary economic and cultural concerns are conceived in terms of ancient representatives or models—a mode of reference expected in the fifteenth and sixteenth centuries but rare in the fourteenth.

The members of the upper bourgeoisie who controlled the Campanile project were experiencing a new consciousness of the Roman past of their city during the very years these reliefs were conceived. Andrea's hexagons, embellishing a building that had become as much a civic as a religious monument, reflect the new sense of confidence, patriotism and historical pride. On the Campanile, contemporary activities, not least among them those symbols of Florence's economic and artistic dominance—the representations of *Trade, Weaving* and the *Arts*—are identified with antique exponents in a style and a relief mode that depend directly upon ancient prototypes.

BIBLIOGRAPHY

L. Becherucci—G. Brunetti, *Il Museo dell Opera del Duomo* (Florence, 1969); M. Trachtenberg, *The Campanile of Florence Cathedral* (New York, 1971); A. F. Moskowitz, "Trecento Classicism and the Campanile Hexagons," *Gesta* 22, 1 (1983), 49–65; idem, *The Sculpture of Andrea and Nino Pisano* (Cambridge, 1986).

ANITA F. MOSKOWITZ

PISANO, NICOLA (fl. 1258–78) and GIOVANNI (ca. 1248–after 1314). Italian artists, father and son; both are known as sculptors and architects.

The birth date of Nicola Pisano is not recorded, but he is known to have been active in *Pisa by 1259. The fact that his name appears in documents as "Nichola de Apulia" has led to the conjecture that he was born in Southern Italy and thus may have been trained in the classicizing school of sculpture sponsored by the Hohenstaufen emperor *Frederick II at Capua. Some scholars have objected to the link, citing the labored classicism of Frederick as far removed from the more natural, fluid imitation of antiquity seen in the works of Nicola, arguing that Nicola's achievement should be seen, rather, against the backdrop of the general continuity of the antique tradition at Pisa and the particular wave of classicism there in the later Middle Ages, manifest, for example, in Pisan literary works of the twelfth century.

Numerous quotations from ancient art have been noted in the sculptures of Nicola Pisano, indicating clearly his interest in particular monuments at this early date before the Renaissance. Already in the sixteenth century *Vasari noted a specific work that influenced Nicola: the Roman sarcophagus now in the *Campo Santo at Pisa showing *Meleager and the Kalydonian Boar Hunt* next to *Phaidra and Hippolytos,* a monument that had been embedded in the façade of Pisa cathedral and had once contained the remains of Beatrice (d. 1076), mother of Countess Mathilda of Tuscany. The figure of Phaidra on the sarcophagus is seen as a prototype for the figure of the Virgin in the scene of the

Adoration of the Magi on Nicola's pulpit in the Baptistery at Pisa (1260), and E. Angiola has even argued that the evident postantique recutting of the figure of Phaidra may be attributed to Nicola, thus revealing a surprising and significant glimpse of his approach to antiquity. Another frequently noted example of Nicola's classicism appears in the nude Hercules-like figure from the pulpit (to be identified as *Daniel,* not *Fortitude*), with a graceful contrapposto stance and an astonishingly consistent and vigorous musculature. The famous neo-Attic marble krater with a Bacchic revel that long stood outside the Porta S. Ranieri of Pisa cathedral (now in the Campo Santo) seems to have provided a motif for Nicola's group of a patriarch supported by a boy on the relief of the *Presentation in the Temple* on the Baptistery pulpit.

Nicola's son Giovanni was born in Pisa, perhaps around 1248; he was active in Siena (first in 1265, then from 1284 as cathedral architect) and Perugia (1278), as well as Massa Marittima (1287) and his native Pisa. From 1302 to 1310 he was employed with a commission for the pulpit of the cathedral at Pisa, a work in which he shows his debt to the ambience of Pisan classicism as practiced by his father. A figure of *Prudence* on the base of the pulpit adopts the pose and undress (only partial here) of the statue type of the *Medici Venus.* But, in general, Giovanni Pisano's work is regarded as turning away from the solid, natural forms of the antique and of Nicola in favor of a new Gothic style emphasizing expressive distortion and attenuation of the human form. Within this context he shows another aspect of imitation of antiquity; the torn figure of Pentheus on another sarcophagus in the Campo Santo at Pisa has been seen as a source for his depiction of figures in agony in the *Last Judgment* of his cathedral pulpit.

BIBLIOGRAPHY

H. Graber, *Beiträge zu Nicola Pisano* (Strassburg, 1911), 15–19; +J. Pope-Hennessy, *An Introduction to Italian Sculpture* 1: *Italian Gothic Sculpture,* 2nd ed. (London, 1972), 169–80; +M. Seidel, "Studien zur Antikenrezeption Nicola Pisanos," *MittFlor* 19.3 (1975), 307–92; +E. Angiola, "Nicola Pisano, Federigo Visconti, and the Classical Style in Pisa," *ArtB* 59 (1977), 1–27.

PITHEKOUSSAI. Earliest Greek settlement in the West.

According to Strabo (5.247C), Pithekoussai was founded by Euboians from Eretria and Chalkis; Livy (8. 22.5–6) adds that a contingent from Pithekoussai established the colony of *Cumae. Pithekoussai was identified with modern Lacco Ameno (Ischia island, Bay of Naples) at the end of the eighteenth century, when Francesco De Siano noted ancient potsherds on the promontory (acropolis) of Monte di Vico and "pagan tombs" in the adjacent Valle (necropolis) di San Montano.

Paolo *Orsi recommended investigation in 1913; in 1952 excavation began under the direction of Giorgio Buchner and continues to this day. Around 1,500 tombs, primarily of the eighth and seventh centuries B.C., have been found in ca.10 percent of the necropolis; the Acropolis Dump has yielded several thousand painted sherds, mainly imported and local Late Geometric; and the sub-urban Mazzola metalworking quarter was in use until ca.700. Prior to that date, a metrical vase inscription recalling Nestor's cup, an early potter's signature, the local figured Shipwreck Krater and many other "firsts" combine with epi-graphic evidence for a Levantine presence to define Pithekoussai as a techno-logically advanced center that both prefaced the history of Magna Graecia and stimulated indigenous developments associated with the Orientalizing phenom-enon in Campania, Latium and Etruria.

The Euboians have thus emerged as the first Western Greeks: current under-standing of their vital role in ending the Greek Dark Age owes as much to Pithekoussai as it does to the contemporary discoveries (1964 onward) at *Ere-tria and *Lefkandi in the homeland.

BIBLIOGRAPHY

+J. Boardman, *The Greeks Overseas,* 1st, 2nd and 3rd eds. (Harmondsworth, 1964, 1973, 1980), ch. 5; G. Buchner, "Cuma nell'VIII secolo a.C. osservata dalla prospettiva di Pithecusa," in *I Campi Flegrei nell'archeologia e nella storia, Atti dei Convegni Lincei* 33 (1977), 131–48; D. Ridgway, *The First Western Greeks* (Cambridge, 1992); +G. Buchner—D. Ridgway, *Pithekoussai 1, MonAnt,* n.s. 4 (Rome, 1993).

DAVID RIDGWAY

PITT-RIVERS, AUGUSTUS HENRY LANE FOX (1827–1900). English general; anthropologist and archaeologist, pioneer in techniques of recording and comprehending stratigraphy.

Born in Yorkshire of a Scottish mother and a father in the military who died when the child was four, Augustus Henry Lane Fox was bred in the landed, aristocratic stratum of society. He was called by the name of Fox until he took the surname Pitt-Rivers in 1880, when he inherited the title and property of Cranborne Chase.

Commissioned into the Grenadier Guards as a lieutenant in 1845, Fox was to rise to the rank of general, remaining in the military until his retirement in 1882. His early assignment to the study and teaching of riflery led to an interest in ancient weapons and armor, and his military travels gave him the opportunity to explore sites and to collect objects of antiquarian or ethnographical interest. He began collecting around 1851 and eventually displayed his collection in the Bethnal Green branch of the South Kensington Museum (beginning 1874). It remained on display (Fox continued to add to it) until 1884. At that time it was donated to Oxford University, where it remains until the present, in the Pitt-Rivers Museum. Fox first had offered it to the nation for the South Kensington Museum, but the donation was rejected on the grounds that the collection was ethnographical and thus inappropriate for the permanent collection of the mu-seum.

After the publication of Charles Darwin's *On the Origin of Species by Means of Natural Selection* (1859), Fox was profoundly influenced by the concept of evolution, which he attempted to apply to material culture. In his collection he displayed objects according to type rather than geography (as was usual for ethnographic collections). He intended that the visitor should be able to see the evolution of a type of object from primitive to sophisticated. His method of arranging objects is preserved today in the Pitt-Rivers Museum.

During the 1850s and 1860s, Fox grew interested in the investigation of monuments in the field and in the problems involved in the preservation of monuments. He began to experiment with excavating, for example, at a Roman wharf site in London, where he especially was taken by the abundance of animal bones and the importance of identifying and analyzing them.

In 1880, the general experienced a dramatic reversal of fortune when he inherited Cranborne Chase. He was to use his vast properties (2,762 acres in Wiltshire; 24,942 acres in Dorset) and financial resources for the advancement of knowledge, first of all, through the development of parks and museum space. Now collecting objects from Benin, Etruria, Silesia, Switzerland and elsewhere, he housed them in his museum at Farnham, again arranged typologically to show the evolution of artifact categories. Parklands were developed as pleasure grounds with evocative buildings such as the round, colonnaded "Temple of Vesta" at Rushmore Lodge.

Pitt-Rivers used a large amount of his fortune to conduct excavations in a number of areas on his property. Much of his investigation (1884–90) was centered on Romano-British sites, perhaps villages or farmsteads, but he also excavated prehistoric sites. All that he found was painstakingly illustrated and described in the five-volume classic, *Excavations at Cranborne Chase* (1887–1903), printed at his own expense.

Pitt-Rivers's great contribution to archaeology, seen at Cranborne Chase, lay in the use of stratigraphical analysis, placing great emphasis on the process of excavation as much as on the result. His military discipline helped him to deal with cross-sections and plans systematically, and his earlier experiences with the typology of artifacts led him to register objects carefully. He did detailed studies of faunal remains, setting the tone for many future anthropological and archaeological investigations.

BIBLIOGRAPHY

C. F. C. Hawkes, "Britons, Romans and Saxons Round Salisbury and in Cranborne Chase, Reviewing the Excavations of General Pitt-Rivers, 1881–97," *ArchJ* 104 (1947), 27–81; M. W. Thompson, *General Pitt-Rivers, Evolution and Archaeology in the Nineteenth Century* (Bradford-on-Avon, 1977); B. Trigger, *A History of Archaeological Thought* (Cambridge, 1989), 197, 199.

PIUS II (AENEAS SYLVIUS PICCOLOMINI; 1405–64). Sienese humanist and pope.

Bishop of Trieste from 1447, of Siena from 1450, raised to the cardinalate in 1456, Pius was elected pope in 1458. In his *Commentaries,* written in 1462–64, he describes archaeological excursions through Lazio, inspired by classical authors such as Strabo and guided by *Biondo Flavio and Leon Battista *Alberti.

Like Biondo in his *Italia illustrata,* Pius records the first major attempt at an organized archaeological investigation in the Renaissance: to recover a Roman ship from the Lake of *Nemi; he vividly describes the fragmentary finds. At Albano, where he saw the remains of four antique cisterns (Alberti had reported thirty), Pius graphically writes of Roman monuments, such as the *Tomb of the Horatii and Curiatii: ''a square pile despoiled of its outer wall, on the summit of which rise five lofty pyramids. Three are stripped of the hewn stone with which they were once faced while two still retain their ornament.''

While taking an active interest in the protection of antiquities, such as the paving stones of the *Via Appia that were being broken up to build a house near Nemi, Pius himself could be relentless in using ancient building materials for his own projects. According to his own account, the building of his citadel at *Tivoli in 1461 destroyed all traces of a splendid amphitheater nearby, while the papal ledgers show that the steps leading to St. Peter's were rebuilt with stone from the *Colosseum. The supply of columns from the *Portico of Octavia for the construction of his monumental ''Pulpit'' of Benediction in front of St. Peter's was not curtailed by his bull of 1462, surely urged by Alberti, excommunicating plunderers of marble from Roman ruins. An alternative source of marble for the pulpit was found at *Portus, where Pius describes unused fragments, marked on two sides by numbers, as brought from Ligurian quarries.

Pius adapted the Florentine Renaissance style of architecture in his buildings in Gothic Siena, while Corsignano, his birthplace, was rebuilt as Pienza, following Vitruvius; yet, to admit more light, he introduced Gothic elements in the elevation of its cathedral.

Pius was not, like humanists such as *Poggio or like his successor *Paul II, a collector of antiquities, but his library, mostly preserved in the *Vatican, includes many classical and Early Christian texts. Among the books dedicated to him were Biondo's *Roma triumphans* and Leonardo Dati's *Gesta Porsenae regis,* both of great antiquarian interest.

BIBLIOGRAPHY

Pius II, *Commentarii rerum memorabilium quae temporibus suis contigerunt* (Frankfort, 1614); Eng. tr. from Latin (Vat. Reg. Lat. 1995) by F. A. Gragg, ed. L. C. Gabel in *Smith College Studies in History* 22, 25, 30, 35, 43 (1936–58); E. Muntz, *Les Arts à la cour des Papes* 1 (Paris, 1878); R. O. Rubinstein, ''Pius II's Piazza S. Pietro and St. Andrew's Head,'' in *Enea Silvio Piccolomini Papa Pio II, Atti del Convegno per il quinto centenario della morte,* ed. D. Maffei (Siena, 1968); C. L. Frommel, ''Francesco del Borgo: Architekt Pius' II und Pauls II: I. Der Petersplatz und weitere römische Bauten Pius' II Piccolomini,'' *Römisches Jahrbuch für Kunstgeschichte* 20 (1983), 127–74; R. Rubinstein, ''Pius II and Ruins,'' in *A Tribute to Denys Hay, Renaissance Studies*, no. 2 (1988), 197–203.

RUTH RUBINSTEIN

PIUS VI (GIANNANGELO BRASCHI; 1717–99). Pope, ardent collector of antiquities, who played a key role in creating the Museo Pio-Clementino in the *Vatican.

Born at Cesena, Giannangelo Braschi was trained in law, and he went to Rome, where he served as a secretary to Pope Benedict XIV. In 1773 he became cardinal and was soon thereafter elected pope as Pius VI (1775). He engaged in public works such as draining the swamps near Terracina with some degree of success, but he is remembered, above all, for the brilliant climate in the arts during his tenure, when artists such as *Canova and *David and intellectuals such as *Goethe brought immense creativity to Rome and contributed to the formation of a neoclassical style in art.

Pius VI had a passion for antiquities and sought to expand the Vatican museums. He added to the galleries recently created for the display of ancient works of art at his own urging when he had been treasurer to the previous pope, *Clement XIV, extending portions of the existing Museo Clementino and adding in new rooms, including the Sala a Croce Greca in the form of a Greek cross with four equal arms, and the circular Sala Rotonda. Pius took great pleasure in showing distinguished visitors through the museum; one of the five visits of the Swedish king *Gustavus III (1784) was depicted in a fresco by Domenico De Angelis, adorning the Vatican Library.

Pius VI also sponsored excavations, organized by his stalwart *Commissario delle Antichità G. B. *Visconti. The excavations were made for the sole purpose of acquiring works of art and often were conducted by artists who could also serve as restorers. Among the acquisitions made in these years were the colossal statue of *Nerva* in the Sala Rotonda (found near St. John Lateran), various sculptures from *Hadrian's Villa (herms of *Tragedy* and *Comedy,* the *Satyr* in *antico rosso* marble, the colossal head of *Faustina Major*) and the group of *Apollo Citharoedus* and the *Muses* (placed in the Sala delle Muse), found by Domenico De Angelis in the "Villa of Cassius" at Tivoli (1774–75), along with a number of herms of philosophers.

The appearance of the museum, which now became known as the Museo Pio-Clementino, is recorded in a series of engravings made by V. Feoli. The cataloging of the collection was done through the years by Visconti and his illustrious son Ennio Quirino (*Visconti) and published in a highly influential series, *Il Museo Pio-Clementino* (7 vols., Rome, 1782–1807.)

Sadly, the pope was soon to see his treasures dispersed in the aftermath of *Napoleon's invasion of Italy. In accordance with the Treaty of Tolentino (1797), many of the Vatican's finest pieces were taken as booty to be paraded through Paris and installed in the Musée Napoléon. Pius VI did not live to see the return of great statues like the *Laocoon* and the *Belvedere *Apollo* (1815), for he died at the age of eighty-two as a prisoner of war at Valence in 1799.

BIBLIOGRAPHY

R. Russo, "Pio VI," *EI* 17 (1935), 316–9; C. Pietrangeli, *I Musei Vaticani, cinque secoli di storia* (Rome, 1985), ch. 5, "Una grande stagione per i Musei Vaticani: Il Pontificato di Pio VI (1775–1799)"; +*The Vatican Collections: The Papacy and Art* (New York, 1982), 17–18, 116–19.

Pius VI and Gustavus III visit the Museo Pio-Clementino, Vatican Museums, painting by B. Gagnereux. Stockholm, The National Swedish Art Museums, Nationalmuseum. (Statens Konstmuseer, The National Swedish Art Museums, Nationalmuseum, Stockholm.)

PIUS VII (BARNABA GREGORIO CHIARAMONTI; 1740–1823). Pope (1800–23), patron of archaeology and founder of the *Vatican Museums.

At the end of the eighteenth century Chiaramonti interested himself in the scientific excavations at *Ostia. To this enlightened and enthusiastic pontiff, who appointed Carlo *Fea to supervise the digging at Ostia, are owed the Museo Chiaramonti, Galleria Lapidaria and Braccio Nuovo in the Vatican Museums. Friend and patron of artists, Pius keenly promoted the study of antiquities when he was not being detained away from Rome by the French emperor. Into his new halls of exhibition went not only ancient sculptures but also homely Latin inscriptions. The principal provenances of the antiquities were Ostia itself, *Hadrian's Villa near Tivoli, where activity in excavation quickened, and papal inheritance. For the museum bearing his family name Pius assigned the neoclassical sculptor Antonia *Canova the task of arranging the antiquities. Earlier, Canova had been commissioned to carve the "replacements" for sculptures plundered from the Vatican galleries by *Napoleon. (His statues of *Perseus,* executed in 1800, *Creugas* and *Damoxenus* still stand in the Cortile Belvedere.) In 1815 Pius put Canova in charge of bringing back from Paris the Corsican's booty, and in the following year he honored Canova with the marquisate of Ischia. Much of the French reformation of the Papal States was undone by the restored Pius, but the refoundation of the *Pontificia Accademia Romana di Archeologia in that interval suited the learned pontifical patron, who continued to promote the academy then under Canova's presidency.

Although Pius the pope stood forth as a friend to archaeology and the arts, Chiaramonti the nobleman (he was born a count of Cesena) acted in time-honored fashion and in 1803 bought for his nephew Braschi-Onesti, a new papal duke, the greater part of what is Hadrian's Villa, to the end that this oft-exploited site remained the private property of the Braschi until the unification of Italy.

BIBLIOGRAPHY

Helbig, I, 180–81, 228–352; C. Pietrangeli, *I Musei Vaticani, cinque secoli di storia* (Rome, 1985), ch. 7, "Ricostituzione e incremento da Pio VII a Pio VIII (1800–1831)."

ROBERT E. A. PALMER

PIUS IX (GIOVANNI MARIA MASTAI-FERRETTI; 1792–1878). Pope and king of Rome; restorer of many monuments of Rome.

Born in Senigallia, the future Pius IX rose in the church hierarchy as a moderate. When he became pope in 1846, he was to reign longer than any other pope; he was perceived as a liberal. In November 1848, his moderate prime minister, Pellegrino Rossi, was assassinated, and he was forced to flee to Gaeta. The Roman Republic, under Garibaldi and Mazzini, was proclaimed, soon to be overthrown by French armies that restored Pius IX and allowed him to reign as king of Rome until the fall of Napoleon III in 1870. Pius IX is best known today as a political reactionary.

As king of Rome (*Papa Re*), he devoted much time and effort to maintaining the prosperity of his temporal realm and rebuilding the monuments in his kingdom. Many of Rome's churches display inscriptions telling of restorations effected under Pius IX. Much effort went into restoring the *Colosseum, with an appropriately large inscription to match. Pius IX also conducted excavations at *Ostia and planned for the museum there.

BIBLIOGRAPHY

R. De Cesare, *Roma e lo Stato del Papa* (Milan, 1909); G. Martina, *Pio IX (1846–1850)* (Rome, 1974); G. Spagnesi, *L'Architettura a Roma al tempo di Pio Nono (1830–1870)* (Pomezia, 1976).

E. C. KOPFF

PLATNER, SAMUEL BALL (1863–1921). American professor of Latin, known for his work in Roman topography.

Platner taught for thirty-six years at Western Reserve University, pursuing at the same time studies that led to the publication of *The Topography and Monuments of Ancient Rome* (1904) and the conception of *A Topographical Dictionary of Ancient Rome,* which he left well advanced at his untimely death and which was then completed by Thomas *Ashby. Before World War I, Platner had begun work on the dictionary and had invited Ashby to participate, but the latter declined. Rejected for military service in the war, Platner applied all of his energy to the work. In 1921 he sailed for Europe with his wife to spend a few months in Rome completing the text and polishing it, but he fell ill and died on the voyage. Mrs. Platner turned over the manuscript to Ashby, providing him with enthusiastic support as he agreed to bring the project to completion (he prepared eventually an estimated 25 percent of the publication).

BIBLIOGRAPHY

T. Ashby, ''Preface,'' Platner—Ashby, v–vii.

L. RICHARDSON, JR

PNYX, Athens. Large man-made terrace, meeting place for the Ecclesia, the assembly of the Athenian people.

The assembly place, set into a hill on the west of the *Akropolis, Athens, was shaped like a huge semicircle (198.5m in diameter), held in place by a great stone retaining wall. The bema, or speaker's platform, was located at the center of the semicircle, in front of a vertical escarpment cut into the hillside. Three periods of construction have been identified.

The first recorded archaeological activity at the Pnyx took place in 1803, when George, Earl of Aberdeen, cleared earth away from the bema and below the great scarp. But not until K. Pittakis found a boundary stone near the bema, inscribed with the name of the Pnyx, was the identification of the site final (1839). In 1832, Anton Graf von Prokesch-Osten bought the Pnyx Hill from a Turkish owner, and in 1857 his son presented the Pnyx to the Greek government.

In 1862, Ernst *Curtius, sponsored by the king and queen of Prussia, cleared the curved retaining wall belonging to the third period, the scarps on either side of the bema, the southeast corner of the assembly place and the upper terrace above the western scarp. K. Kourouniotis in 1910–11 excavated the filling behind the third-period retaining wall to determine its date and stated that it was no earlier than the second century B.C. He also found the second-period retaining wall with stairway. Later (1930–31) Kourouniotis and H. A. Thompson conducted excavations of the assembly place, the two retaining walls and the northeast shoulder of the hill. They dated the Pnyx third period to the second century A.C. and proved that the third phase was left unfinished. In 1936–37, Thompson and R. L. Scranton investigated the fortifications on the Pnyx Hill and retrieved much of their history, including damage in 267 A.D., rebuilding in the sixth century and repairs in the twelfth century. Much later (1982), Thompson presented a revised chronology of the Pnyx assembly place phases: Period I: ca. 455 B.C.; II: ca. 400 B.C.; III: 350–325 B.C.

A copy of the *Athena Parthenos* (the Varvakeion copy; now in the *National Archaeological Museum, Athens) was found on the west slope of Pnyx Hill in 1859; it was first properly identified by Charles *Lenormant.
BIBLIOGRAPHY
+Travlos, 466–76; +H. A. Thompson, in *Hesperia*, suppl. 19 (1982), 133–47.
JUDITH BINDER AND NANCY T. DE GRUMMOND

POGGIO (POGGIUS) BRACCIOLINI, GIOVANNI FRANCESCO (1380–1459). Italian humanist scholar and writer, famed for his rediscovery of numerous classical texts.

Poggio was essentially a leisure-time archaeologist. Occasionally, his letters mention his attempts to decipher and copy inscriptions, always of interest to his antiquarian friend Nicolo dei *Niccoli. He has left a moving description of the ruins of ancient Rome in his *De varietate fortunae.* Poggio collected antique sculpture, mostly fragmentary, to decorate his house in the Val d'Arno. Sometimes he was fortunate enough to be on the spot when part of an ancient statue was found in an excavation; at other times he boldly asked a well-known collector for a gift. No specific piece is identified with him.

Poggio was famous in the fifteenth century for his professional life and for his private literary activities. Professionally, he served for fifty years as secretary to a succession of popes and, before 1418, antipopes, too. He was responsible for a vast amount of official correspondence between the popes and secular and ecclesiastical rulers and assembled courts and congregations of both high and low degree. Of his private correspondence, nearly 600 letters to other scholars, statesmen, clerics and friends all over Europe have survived.

Poggio's fame as a scholar was widespread and deserved. Early in life he began copying the most notable works of Latin literature, for example, Catullus, Cicero, Livy. When at leisure during the Council of Constance (1414–18), he searched for manuscripts in monastic libraries. Many classical texts known today were Poggio's discoveries. At Cluny, in 1415, he found two orations of Cicero unread for centuries: *Pro Roscio Amerino* and *Pro Murena.* His most renowned discoveries were made at St. Gall in the summer of 1416: the full text of Quintilian's *Institutiones oratoriae,* Valerius Flaccus's *Argonautica* and Asconius Pedianus's commentaries on five of Cicero's orations. On their second trip to St. Gall, Poggio and his friends discovered Lucretius's *De rerum natura;* Manilius's *Astronomica;* Silius Italicus's *Punica;* and Ammianus Marcellinus's *Res gestae.* During the following year, Poggio, traveling in eastern France and southern Germany, rescued eight more lost Ciceronian orations. His lifelong fame as a searcher for lost texts was established. New discoveries, like Cicero's rhetorical works and most of the comedies of Plautus, were immediately reported to him. He had an uncanny ability to recognize a genuine lost text on sight.

Poggio wrote many short works. Best known are his *Facetiae* or *Jocular Tales.* He was admired for his eloquent and deeply felt funeral orations, as well as for his bitter invectives. He wrote tracts on moral matters, in dialogue form, using his friends as speakers: on avarice, nobility, hypocrisy, as well as historical matters: whether the upper and lower classes in ancient Rome spoke the same kind of Latin; who was greater: Scipio or Caesar. After Poggio returned to Florence from the Curia to serve as chancellor (secretary of state) he continued the history of Florence begun by his friend Leonardo Bruni Aretino. Poggio's history covers 1375–1455, approximately his lifetime, year by year.

BIBLIOGRAPHY

R. Sabbadini, *Le Scoperte dei codici latini e greci ne' secoli XIV e XV,* 1–2 (Florence, 1905–14); rev. E. Garin, repr., 1967); E. Walser, *Poggius Florentinus: Leben und Werke* (Leipzig, 1914); G. Francesco—Poggio Bracciolini, *Opera Omnia,* ed. R. Fubini, 1–4. (Turin, 1964–69); P. W. G. Gordan, *Two Renaissance Book Hunters: The Letters of Poggius Bracciolini to Nicolaus de Niccolis* (New York, 1974).

PHYLLIS W. G. GORDAN

POMPEII. The oldest archaeological site in more or less continuous excavation, a city on the Bay of *Naples, southeast of Mt. Vesuvius at the mouth of the river Sarnus, destroyed in the eruption of A.D. 79.

Settlement on the site goes back to the sixth century B.C., as the Doric capitals of a temple in the Forum Triangulare and votive material here and in the temple of Apollo attest. It may have been of mixed population, since there is both Greek and Etruscan material, and the settlement was linked to the great inland highway from Capua to Poseidonia running behind Vesuvius. It became Samnite probably at the end of the fifth century. In the Samnite Wars it was evidently an inconsequential dependency of Nuceria. Its period of greatest prosperity followed the Second Punic War, when great public buildings were constructed, as well as private mansions. In the Social War it opposed Rome and stood siege by L. Sulla in 89 B.C.; in the subsequent settlement it had to accept, about 80 B.C., a Roman colony and a new municipal government.

The arrival of the colony started a new wave of building, but under Augustus we see a decline in vigor and enterprise. Under Nero, in A.D. 59, Pompeii appears in history because of a riot in the amphitheater between the Pompeians and their neighbors the Nucerians that led to bloodshed and numerous deaths.

Tourists view a "discovery" at *Pompeii*, engraving after a design by F. Mazois, *Les Ruines de Pompeii* (1812). (Deutsches Archäologisches Institut, Rome. Inst. Neg. 84.6484.)

The case was sent to Rome for judgment; as punishment the Pompeians were forbidden to hold amphitheatrical shows for ten years. On 5 February 62 Pompeii was largely destroyed by an earthquake; hardly a building was left in habitable condition. But the Pompeians set about rebuilding with energy and imagination. Public buildings were patched up and shored up for temporary use, while a master scheme envisaged general urban redesign on a magnificent scale to be carried out as time and money permitted. It all came to an end before more than a fraction was completed. Beginning on 23 August 79, a tremendous eruption of Vesuvius overwhelmed the city, first in a hail of pellets of pumice, then the next day with ash and flow.

The urban population never exceeded 20,000. The bases of the city's prosperity were agriculture, especially production of wine, shipping (it was the port for the whole of the southern half of the Bay of Naples and the towns behind Vesuvius), manufacture of mills and olive pitters of a special volcanic stone, production of superior fish sauces and training of gladiators. Otherwise, its economy seems to have been largely self-contained. A number of Romans, including Cicero and the emperor Claudius, owned property in Pompeii, and Nero's second wife, Poppaea, may have been a Pompeian, but it was a provincial place with little contact outside the Bay of Naples. In the last period many important Pompeians still had Oscan names.

The site of Pompeii was tunneled through in 1594–1600 during the construction of an aqueduct, and two inscriptions were recovered at that time, but it was not explored further. It was rediscovered in 1748 during quarrying for gravel for the highway from Naples to Reggio Calabria, ten years after the beginning of systematic work at *Herculaneum. The first excavations were small, disappointing, pursued at various points in haphazard fashion and suspended indefinitely in April 1749, though accurate drawings of the amphitheater had been obtained. In 1755 the accidental discovery of the Praedia Iuliae Felicis during agricultural work led to a campaign of more than two years in which the whole of this insula was explored; it was then reburied. The finds of paintings and furniture were spectacular and of the highest importance, and excellent plans of the complex were drawn. Work was then transferred to the slopes along the edge of the site, first in Region VIII Insula ii, especially in the vicinity of the forum, then in Region VII Insula Occidentalis. Beginning about 9 February 1760, excavations were opened in VII vi, northwest of the forum, and continued until that whole insula had been explored. Work was also, at the same time, pursued sporadically at various other points in the neighborhood. All these excavations were refilled with earth. By 18 December 1762, excavation was in progress on the Via dei Sepolcri and its adjacencies, notably, the so-called Villa di Cicerone, and though the part of the villa explored was filled in again, the Via dei Sepolcri was not and was the first part of the city to be maintained as a thing of intrinsic interest.

With the growth of interest in the architectural remains, spectacular buildings became of prime importance. Excavation of the Large Theater began 29 July

1764 and led to the discovery of the adjacent temples of Isis and Zeus Meili-chios, the Ludus Gladiatorius and the Theatrum Tectum. A royal visit to the excavations to show them to Joseph II, emperor of Austria, on 6 April 1769 was the first of what were to become regular occasions. On 29 July 1769 all work was transferred back to the area of the Porta di Ercolano and concentrated on clearing a substantial area.

The director of excavations from 1748 to 1780 was Roque Joaquin de Al-cubierre, an army engineer who owed his position to the necessity of exploring Herculaneum by tunnels. From 1750 to 1764 he was assisted by Karl Weber, a young Swiss engineer who had a keen interest in antiquity and made admirable maps and plans of the excavations. He was succeeded by Francesco La Vega, who eventually took over from Alcubierre and directed excavations from 1780 to 1804. The number of workers employed was always small, thirty at the time of the royal visit, but increased for that occasion, and often was as few as a dozen. The original object was simply to enrich the royal collection of antiq-uities, and pavements and decorations were ruthlessly cut from the buildings and destroyed when they were not sent to the museum at Resina. Work depended on Giovanni Fogliani d' Aragona, prime minister to Charles III, and he put Ottavio Bayardi in charge of the cataloging and publication, a task that pro-ceeded slowly in his hands, the first volume appearing in 1754. In 1755 he was replaced by the Real Accademia Ercolanese (*Academia Herculanensis), fifteen scholars who produced the enormously influential *Antichità di Ercolano* in eight large volumes, 1757–92.

From the beginning, systematic excavations at Herculaneum had been visited by interested travelers, including Charles de Brosse in 1739 and Horace Walpole in 1740. The four visits of *Winckelmann, 1758–66, were particularly influen-tial, because he published descriptions of what he saw and attacked the conduct of the excavations and the competence of those in charge, quite unjustly, in fact. His reports, however, were widely read and translated and propelled Pompeii and Herculaneum into the front ranks of international interest. Sir William *Hamilton, British consul in Naples from 1764 to 1800, an eager student and collector of antiquities and important at court, did much to intensify that interest. The sale of his first collection, mainly vases and small objects, to the *British Museum in 1772, following its publication in English and French in four vol-umes, 1766–67, helped stimulate the neoclassical taste. G. B. *Piranesi visited Pompeii and made a number of drawings just before his death in 1778; after his death his son and collaborator, Francesco, reworked these as engravings and later brought them out in Paris as a volume (1804, 1807). Pompeii was mined for motifs by such taste makers as *Wedgwood and Robert Adam (*Adam family), and beginning in the late eighteenth century, ''Pompeian'' rooms be-came fashionable in interior decoration. In 1787 *Goethe spent a week in the neighborhood under the guidance of *Tischbein and was enthusiastic about everything he saw. He did much to popularize the buried cities in Germany.

In the time of the Repubblica Parthenopea and under the Bonapartes, 1799–

1815 (*Napoleon), part of the work of excavation was shifted to the area south-west of the forum, the Casa di Championnet and the Basilica, but soon was suspended. Thereafter, attention concentrated on extending excavations around the Strada Consolare. On 8 July 1813, however, we find a return to the Basilica and the amphitheater, which were then completely cleared. The forum had emerged by the summer of 1818, and the buildings along its east side by 1823. The excavators then again turned their attention to the northwest quarter of the city, beginning with the Via di Mercurio and the buildings just north of the forum and continuing the full length of the street. Splendid houses amply re-warded them, and work on the whole quarter was completed by September 1844. The western third of the city had now been explored and was accessible to visitors, except for parts that had early been reburied. Royal and otherwise important visitors had now become very numerous; even *Pius IX visited the excavations, in October 1849. In 1859, Garibaldi appointed Alexandre *Dumas, père, as honorary director of the excavations, a post that he exercised only briefly.

With the liberation of a substantial part of the ancient city, enough to give a clear picture of the size and character of its public buildings and the variety and refinements of its houses, one finds a change in the interests of the scholars who tried to explain the life of the city scientifically and in the approach of imagi-native visitors and creative artists, now in the full tide of romanticism. E. *Bul-wer-Lytton's *The Last Days of Pompeii* (1834) exploited the familiar houses, peopling them with fictional inhabitants. Théophile Gautier's *Arria Marcella* followed in 1852. Many poets, including *Shelley and Leopardi, wrote reflec-tions prompted by visits, chiefly on the fragility of life. Plays and operas that ended with the eruption were numerous, as well as pictures that evoked the destruction of this or that building. At the same time, serious students of an-tiquity, such as F. Mazois (*Les Ruines de Pompéi,* 4 vols., 1824–38), Sir William *Gell (*Pompeiana,* with John Gandy, 1817–19; *The Result of Excavations Since 1819,* 1832), and W. Zahn (*Die Schönsten Ornamente und merkwürdigsten Ge-mälde aus Pompeji, Herkulanum und Stabiae,* 3 vols., 1827–59), were attempt-ing to provide accurate and detailed information about every aspect of ancient architecture, decoration and furniture.

In 1860 the brilliant archaeologist Giuseppe *Fiorelli became inspector at Pompeii and was associated with the excavations until 1875. He introduced many reforms: a code for locating all the various parts of the excavations, a rigorous record of the daily progress of excavation and catalog of the finds, an archaeological school at Pompeii and the systematic consolidation of what had already been accomplished, together with a rational program for future work. He also published the old daybooks still available (*Pompeianarum antiquitatum historia,* 3 vols., 1860–64) and a concise but complete description of the site (*Descrizione di Pompei,* 1875). He is credited with putting the excavations on a firm scientific footing and with turning interest from hunting for treasure to recovery of information about ancient life. Decorations and furniture were now, as far as possible, kept in context, and interest in the history of the city in antiquity awakened. Four brilliant German scholars appeared about the same time whose keen interest in Pompeii did much to advance historical understanding of the ruins. J. *Overbeck focused on the reconstruction of the city's life and art (*Pompeji in seinen Gebäuden Alterthümern und Kunstwerken*, 1st ed., 1856, 4th ed., with A. *Mau, 1884); W. *Helbig studied especially the paintings and compiled an authoritative catalog of these (1868); H. Nissen was interested in architectural history (*Pompejanische Studien*, 1877, based in part on work of R. Schoene, going back to 1866–68); and August Mau began by studying and classifying the successive styles of wall decoration (*Geschichte der dekorativen Wandmalerei in Pompeji*, 1882) and went on to take all of Pompeii for his field and to dominate Pompeian studies from then until his death in 1909. His handbook, *Pompeji in Leben und Kunst* (1900, 1908, tr. by F. *Kelsey as *Pompeii: Its Life and Art*, 1902), is still the best introduction to the site.

The discovery of the Casa delle Nozze d'Argento, with magnificent Second Style decorations, in 1892, the Casa dei Vettii with rooms painted in the Fourth Style, remarkably complete and beautifully preserved, in 1894, and the Third-Style Casa di M. Lucrezio Frontone in 1900 led, after some hesitation, to extension of the policy of reconstruction. Roofs were now reconstructed according to the original lines of the architecture over houses with well-preserved decorations, so these could be left in situ, and visitors could form some idea of the total effect of a Pompeian house. Gardens were replanted and fountains occasionally put back in working order. This led eventually to greatly improved methods of recovering evidence about the ruined upper parts of buildings.

In this century the important excavations at Pompeii fall into two groups, those conducted by V. *Spinazzola from 1910 to 1923, especially those along the Via dell'Abbondanza known as the Scavi Nuovi, where meticulous digging has permitted the recovery and reconstruction of a thoroughfare lined with shops and small industries, a bustling, populous street with colorfully painted shop façades, a wealth of electoral programmata and notices painted in rustic capitals and an infinity of graffiti of every sort; and those conducted by A. *Maiuri (1924–63): the *Villa dei Misteri, the Casa del Menandro, the so-called Palestra Grande near the amphitheater and, beginning in 1950, the clearance of the southeast quarter of the city. The Villa dei Misteri, begun as a private excavation, which brought to light the great Bacchic frieze, produced the finest sequence of Second-Style decorations yet known, and the Casa del Menandro contained a treasure of table silver of excellent quality, though no rival of the *Boscoreale treasure. The southeast quarter of the city produced, for the most part, small houses of undistinguished decorations and market gardens, even a vineyard. However, in the same campaign the fascinating Praedia Iuliae Felicis returned to the light, and an important new cemetery was found outside the Porta di Nocera. Maiuri also conducted a series of excavations under the floors of the buildings around the forum of Pompeii, searching for evidence of earlier phases of this civic center. Because of the limited area with which he was working, this was only partially successful, though he was able to date the basilica to 125 B.C. and to prove that the forum colonnades are a comparatively late feature, none being older than the first century B.C. In recent years the official excavations have concentrated on the Casa di Giulio Polibio, IX xiii 1–3, a house of the highest interest for its age and architecture, which has been excavated with maximum care.

BIBLIOGRAPHY

+V. Spinazzola, *Pompei alla luce degli scavi nuovi di Via dell'Abbondanza (anni 1910–1923)*, 1–3 (Rome, 1953); +T. Kraus—L. von Matt, *Lebendiges Pompeji* (Cologne, 1973), tr. into English as *Pompeii and Herculaneum, The Living Cities of the Dead* (New York, 1975); +E. La Rocca—M. de Vos—A. de Vos, *Guida archeologica di Pompei* (Milan, 1976); +H. Eschebach, *Pompeji: Erlebte antike Welt* (Leipzig, 1978).

L. RICHARDSON, JR

PONS MILVIUS. See MILVIAN BRIDGE.

PONS MULVIUS. See MILVIAN BRIDGE.

PONT DU GARD, Gard, France. Monumental Roman bridge carrying the aqueduct serving *Nimes across the river Gard.

Built entirely of cut stone without mortar or clamps and composed of three superimposed tiers of arches, the Pont du Gard is the highest Roman bridge existing, rising to 48.77m above the river. In length it is 275m and consists of six arches in the bottom tier (the largest, over the river, spans 24.52m), eleven in the middle one and thirty-five smaller ones on top. The water conduit, 1.85m high by 1.20, probably delivered 20,000m³ daily but is now largely obstructed by incrustation. It probably ceased to function in the sixth century A.C.

The bridge could be crossed only by animals and pedestrians, and to provide a road crossing, in the Middle Ages the piers of the middle tier were hacked away to half their width; amazingly, the entire monument did not collapse. In 1702 the piers were restored, and soon after, in 1747, the present road bridge opened alongside. In 1842–47 at Roquefavour (Aix-en-Provence) a full-size reproduction of the Pont du Gard was built to carry the water supply of Marseilles and is still in use.

The Pont du Gard was long thought to be a construction of ca. 19 B.C., when Agrippa was governor in Gaul, as argued by É. Esperandieu. A recent investigation by an interdisciplinary team from the Centre National de la Recherche Scientifique led to the argument, on the basis of pottery in the building layers of the bridge, that the Pont du Gard now should be dated between A.D. 40 and 80.

BIBLIOGRAPHY

É. Esperandieu, *Le Pont du Gard* (Paris, 1926; repr. 1968); A. Blanchet—M. Louis, *Forma orbis romani* 8 (Paris, 1941); A. Grenier, *Manuel d'archéologie gallo-romaine, 4, Les Monuments des eaux*, fasc. 1 (Paris, 1960), 88–95; G. Hauck, *The Aqueduct of*

Nemausus (Jefferson, NC, 1988); G. Fabre—J.-L. Fiches—J.-L. Paillet, ''Interdiscipli-nary Research on the Aqueduct of Nimes and the Pont du Gard,'' *JRA* 4 (1991), 63–88.

A. TREVOR HODGE

PONTIFICIA ACCADEMIA ROMANA DI ARCHEOLOGIA (PONTIFI-CAL ROMAN ACADEMY OF ARCHAEOLOGY). Academy for the study of classical antiquity and related subjects, founded by Pope Benedict XIV, orig-inally for the purpose of studying newly excavated material.

In 1738 the first major discoveries occurred at the site of *Herculaneum. For their study, from Rome was summoned an expert who proved insufficient to the task. Two years later, to remedy this kind of situation, the scholarly Pope Ben-edict XIV Lambertini (1740–58) founded the Pontifical Roman Academy of Archaeology. More antiquities began to appear in 1748, at *Pompeii, but, per-haps because the two ancient towns lay within the Kingdom of Naples, the Pontifical Academy was not resorted to, and it apparently ceased to function in 1756. At the end of the century, however, scientific excavations began at *Ostia, guided by the prelate who became *Pius VII, and these gave new impetus to the study of excavated antiquities and the refounding of the academy in 1810. (The pope, however, was away from Rome at the time, a prisoner of Napoleon.) The new president was the Bonapartist philosopher Joseph-Marie de Gérando; the statutes of the academy were issued in 1813, still under French administra-tion. Antonio *Canova succeeded Gérando (1816) and led the academy in its rebirth. The papal chamberlain originally served as the academy's cardinal pro-tector. (Although this dual assignment long continued, today the papal secretary of state is normally the cardinal protector.)

The academy began its history of learned publication in 1821, with the first series of its *Atti,* embracing the reports of the business meetings and the learned *dissertazioni.* In volume 1 are membership lists going back to 1818, as well as an account of the academy's beginning and revival. This first series, which was subject to ecclesiastical censors, ceased publication in 1864 under *Pius IX. The second series was begun in 1881 under Leo XIII and published without eccle-siastical review of the censors. This series continued until 1921, when it was superseded by the third series (the current one), which publishes *Memorie*—monographs, normally long and irregularly published—and *Rendiconti*—the records of business meetings and the papers delivered to academy sessions of fellows.

Fellows of the academy were, and are, elected by the incumbent fellows. The full name of the academy may mislead the unwary modern, for the breadth of interest of the fellows extended, and extends, well beyond the designated name. Learned papers addressed to the fellows include both Greek and Roman art and archaeology, antiquarian research, epigraphy, topography and related subjects, as well as Early Christian and medieval matters. Learned papers are delivered at the regular monthly sessions of the academy (November through June) by the fellows and by scholars invited to address them in their stated meeting place,

the gorgeous Sala dei Cento Giorni in the Palazzo della Cancelleria Apostolica, where the academy's secretariat is lodged. While all oral presentations are made in Italian, the published works normally appear in the author's own language.
BIBLIOGRAPHY
RendPontAcc 1 (1921–23), 217–54; F. Magi, "Per la storia della Pontificia Accademia Romana di Archeologia," *RendPontAcc* 16 (1940), 113–30; A. Busiri Vici, "Intorno alla rinascita dell'Accademia Romana di Archeologia (4 Ottobre 1810)," *RendPontAcc* 44 (1971–72), 329–41.

ROBERT E. A. PALMER

POPULONIA (PUPLUNA; FUFLUNA). Major Etruscan city, the only one known to be situated directly on the edge of the Tyrrhenian Sea.

The town remained continuously prosperous from the eighth century B.C. to Roman times, due to its access to mineral resources of the nearby Monti Metalliferi (copper, zinc, lead, silver) and the island of Elba (iron). Though little remains of the ancient town or port, the cemeteries of Populonia are among the most important in Etruria, providing a history of tomb types from the Villanovan, Archaic, "Classical," Hellenistic and Roman periods. In 540 B.C., the battle of a combined Etruscan/Carthaginian fleet against Phokaian Greek colonists near their settlement of Alalia (Corsica) led to increased influence for Populonia. The continued prosperity of the town is testified by its contribution of iron for the expedition of Scipio (205 B.C.; Livy 28.45). Like *Fiesole and other cities of north Etruria, Populonia was devastated by Sulla in the Social War (80 B.C.); thereafter it became a little town known mainly as an observation point for tuna fishermen. By the fifth century A.C. (Rutilius Namatianus 1.401 ff.) there were only ruins there, and in 842 a bishop's seat attached to Populonia was finally transferred to nearby Massa Marittima.

Populonia was described by geographer-antiquarians such as L. *Alberti (1550) and *Cluverius (1624), and the city coinage of gold, silver and bronze—the most ambitious and longest lasting of all Etruscan series—was studied by *Eckhel and other numismatists. A. *Francois first excavated tombs at Populonia in 1840, but when *Dennis passed through, there was still very little to be seen. Thorough knowledge of the necropoleis became possible only in the early twentieth century with the beginning of commercial exploitation of the heaps of imperfectly processed iron slag (sometimes 7m deep) that had been deposited over the cemeteries in antiquity. The work of Antonio Minto was of the first importance during this period. Most recently, an industrial quarter near the cemeteries has been investigated by M. Cristofani and M. Martelli (beginning 1977), and on the acropolis, A. Romualdi has been excavating a temple complex and restoring the circuit wall.
BIBLIOGRAPHY
A. Minto, *Populonia* (Florence, 1943); F. Fedeli, *Populonia, Storia e territorio* (Florence, n.d. [1981?]); S. Steingräber, *Città e necropoli dell'Etruria* (Rome, 1983), 117–31; G. Camporeale, ed., *L'Etruria mineraria* (Milan, 1985); F. Fedeli—A. Galiberti—A. Romualdi, *Populonia e il suo territorio* (Florence, 1993).

PORCARI FAMILY. Family in Rome during the Renaissance noted for its collections and interest in classical antiquity; it traced itself back to the ancient Porcius family, counting among its ancestors the Roman Republican censor M. Porcius Cato.

STEFANO PORCARI (d. 1453), famous as an orator and for his vast knowledge of classical antiquity, was a passionate collector of antiquities; he was executed by Nicholas V for a conspiracy against the pope that attempted to revive the government of Republican Rome. FRANCESCO (d. 1489/90) had a collection of some 140 epigraphic monuments, and in the sixteenth century, GIULIO maintained the family collections in a house near S. Maria sopra Minerva, visited by *Aldrovandi as well as by Girolamo da *Carpi and *Dosio. Over the entrance portal was a Roman sarcophagus relief showing *Meleager and the Boar,* the latter obviously prized as a punning reference to the family name. The collection was dispersed in 1610, with many pieces going to the Doria-Pamphili. METELLO VARO DE' PORCARI (d. before 1567), from another branch of the family, formed a second collection, also visited by Aldrovandi, that contained a number of portrait busts.

BIBLIOGRAPHY

Lanciani, *Storia degli scavi* 1 (1902), 115–20; P. G. Hübner, *Le Statue di Roma* 1 *Quellen und Sammlungen* (Leipzig, 1912), 110–11; N. W. Canedy, *The Roman Sketchbook of Girolamo da Carpi* (London, 1976), 40, 70; Bober—Rubinstein, 478.

MARJON VAN DER MEULEN

PORTA MAGGIORE (PORTA PRAENESTINA), Rome. Monumental Roman gate and aqueduct bridge, built in the first century A.C.

Porta Maggiore ("The Greater Gate") is the name commonly given to this monumental double arch of travertine carrying the conduits of the Aqua Claudia and Aqua Anio Novus over the Viae Labicana and Praenestina, in the northeast area of the Caelian Hill in Rome known in antiquity as Spes Vetus. It consists of two arches 14m high over the roadways, two smaller outside archways and a third in the central pier framed by engaged columns with composite capitals, entablature and tympanum, never completely finished, in rusticated style. The attic above is divided by strip courses into three panels, the upper two of which front the aqueduct conduits, that of the Anio Novus riding atop the Claudia. Each panel bears inscriptions recording the original construction of both lines by Claudius in A.D. 52 (*CIL* VI 1256) and repairs of the Aqua Claudia undertaken by Vespasian in A.D. 71 and Titus in 81 (*CIL* VI 1257, 1258).

Aurelian incorporated the arches into a major gate of his third century defensive wall, later rebuilt in A.D. 403 by Honorius, who added two rectangular towers in front of the arches, a round tower between the two openings and an interior vantage court (*CIL* VI 1189, reassembled at the west side of the gateway). This gate received the name Porta Praenestina, was later called Porta Maior Sessoriana and by the tenth century became known as the Porta Maggiore, perhaps through popular association with a route to the church of S. Maria

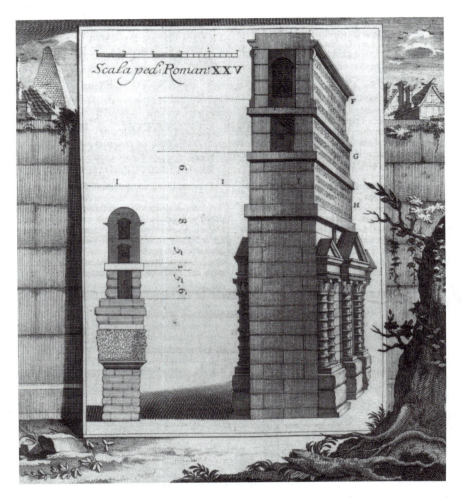

Porta Maggiore, engraving from J. G. Graevius, *Thesaurus antiquitatum romanorum* 4 (1694–99). (The Warburg Institute, University of London.)

Maggiore. In the fifteenth century it was also known as the Porta Dominae or della Donna, probably from a representation of the Virgin on the gate.

Numerous Renaissance views (e.g., by *Du Pérac, G. da *Sangallo) show the gate with its defensive works, which were removed by order of Pope Gregory XVI in 1838, revealing the aqueduct arches themselves and the Augustan tomb of Eurysaces directly to the east between the two roads, which had been incorporated into Honorius's round tower. The most recent excavations in 1956 disclosed the ancient street levels and remains of Honorius's vantage court.

BIBLIOGRAPHY
I. Richmond, *The City Wall of Imperial Rome* (Oxford, 1930), 205–17; T. Ashby, *The Aqueducts of Ancient Rome* (Oxford, 1935), 242–43; Nash, II, 225–28.

HARRY B. EVANS

PORTICO (PORTICUS) OF OCTAVIA, Rome. A large precinct in the southern Campus Martius, adjacent to the *Theater of Marcellus, that, after Marcellus's death in 23 B.C., was rebuilt by his mother, Augustus's sister, as a memorial to him.

The precinct was also to serve as a theater portico, where the audience could stroll or take refuge in the event of a shower. It was a large rectangle, 119m × 132m, within which were two temples, that of Jupiter Stator, probably founded between 221 B.C. and 187 B.C., to the east, that of Juno Regina, founded by Aemilius Lepidus and dedicated in 179 B.C., to the west.

The portico was originally the work of Q. Caecilius Metellus Macedonicus following his triumph in 146 B.C. and was probably the first quadrilateral *porticus* in Rome. As rebuilt it had a single colonnade on the front and double on the sides; the façade was closed but broken by a gateway of six Corinthian columns with a deep tympanum. Included in the complex were a library and a curia, as well as very numerous works of art. It burned in the fire of Titus in A.D. 80, and the loss of the library is mentioned particularly. The Portico of Octavia was restored by Domitian but burned again in A.D. 203, and what we see is what remains of the Severan restoration. At this time the portico was open along part of the façade with columns of gray granite, with white marble bases and capitals.

The portico appears on the Marble Plan of Rome (*Forma Urbis Romae), and its remains have always been known. Here the church of S. Angelo in Pescheria was founded in A.D. 770, and the fish market of Rome found a place in recent centuries. In the fifteenth century, *Pius II plundered columns for reuse in his Pulpit of Benediction at St. Peter's. Among the more picturesque ruins of ancient Rome, the portico has often been painted, but the temples remain encased in later buildings. Part of the southeast wing and south corner of the portico were freed in 1928 in connection with work on the Theater of Marcellus.

BIBLIOGRAPHY
+P. Fidenzoni, *Il Teatro di Marcello* (Rome, 1970), 145–58; H. Lauter, in *BullCom* (1980–81), 37–55.

L. RICHARDSON, JR

PORTLAND VASE (DEL MONTE VASE; BARBERINI VASE). Roman vase made of cameo glass, probably in the early first century A.C.

The ''blank'' for the vase was blown in two layers, white over dark blue, and the white layer was carved in the same way as a cameo. The relief scene going around the vase is mythological and shows seven figures, including an ideally handsome youth who seems to be guided toward a seminude female figure reclining and holding a torch downward. The iconography has been debated, almost desperately, with more than forty different interpretations proposed in the four centuries since the vase appeared. Recent rival theories of note identify the main figures as Peleus and Thetis; Achilles and Deidamia; Achilles and Helen; Apollo and Atia; or Augustus (with his mother) and Hecuba (with her son). The disc (formerly) on the base of the vase seems to show a Trojan theme as well—Paris, at the famous Judgment, but the piece is evidently alien to the original vase, which was repaired either in antiquity or after its discovery. The original vessel may have had an amphora shape, tapering to a pointed or knobbed base, which was broken off or removed at some time. The repair created the squatly proportioned piece with flat base known today (24.5cm high and 17.7cm in diameter).

The rare vase is one of only thirteen cameo glass vessels known and is regarded as one of the greatest treasures of the *British Museum. Its colorful history began in the late sixteenth or early seventeenth century. One tradition states that the vase was excavated in 1582 in a marble sarcophagus buried in the Monte del Grano on the outskirts of Rome. But that provenance is not recorded until over one hundred years later, while a contemporary account of the Monte del Grano find, by Flaminio *Vacca, does not mention the object at all.

It is certain that by 1601 the vase was in Rome in the possession of the Cardinal Francesco Del Monte, who kept it until his death in 1626. The vase was known to *Peiresc and P. P. *Rubens, who have left in their correspondence the earliest written reference to it, as the "Vase of the Cardinal Del Monte." Rubens described the vessel in 1635 as already having the disc with Paris attached to the bottom.

The vase passed from the Cardinal del Monte to the *Barberini family in 1626 and was described by G. Teti (*Aedes Barberinae*, 1642) as a dazzling attraction in the library of Palazzo Barberini. It was drawn for the Museum Chartaceum of Cassiano dal *Pozzo (drawings in Windsor Castle and the British Museum) and reportedly also by *Pietro da Cortona (drawing now lost). De la *Chausse published it in 1690, P. S. *Bartoli in 1697 (he is the first to report the Monte del Grano find) and *Montfaucon in 1722. The Barberini family was forced to sell the piece ca. 1780, evidently to settle the gambling debts of Donna Cornelia Barberini-Colonna. James *Byres bought the vase, planning to resell it, but not before commissioning a mold of it from *Pichler. James *Tassie made sixty plaster copies from the mold (one is now in the British Museum) and then destroyed it. Soon afterward, Sir William *Hamilton saw the vase and was seized with a passion to own it; he purchased it from Byres but was unable to make good on the credit extended him by Byres and was forced to sell the object (1784). It was bought by the Dowager Duchess of Portland and remained in the Portland family after her death in 1785. The fourth Duke of Portland placed the vase on loan at the British Museum, a status that it kept until 1945,

Portland Vase, drawing from the Museo Cartaceo of Cassiano dal Pozzo. Windsor, Royal Library 8318. (Courtesy of Her Majesty the Queen.)

when it was purchased for the museum with funds bequeathed by James Rose Vallentine.

The most dramatic moment in the history of the Portland Vase came in 1845, when it was smashed in its case in the British Museum by a delirious student who had been on a weeklong drinking binge. "William Lloyd," as he called himself (probably falsely) to the police, seized a basalt sculpture from an adjoining display and heaved it at the vase, breaking it into more than 200 fragments. The vase was miraculously reassembled by a museum craftsman, John Doubleday, and put back on display immediately; another restoration was made after the official acquisition in 1945 by request of keeper Bernard Ashmole. It was realized at the time (1948–49) that the disc should be displayed separately from the vase. In the ensuing decades the adhesive grew yellow and brittle, and the vase was restored once again in 1988–89, by Nigel Williams.

The vase had much influence on neoclassical taste, inspiring the famous imitations by *Wedgwood in jasperware; later, daring reproductions were made in actual cameo glass by John Northwood I in 1876 and Joseph Locke in 1878 (collection of Dr. and Mrs. Leonard S. Rakow). Their success touched off a rage for cameo glass that lasted into the twentieth century, influencing, among others, Louis Comfort Tiffany.

BIBLIOGRAPHY

E. Simon, Die *Portlandvase* (Mainz, 1953); D.E.L. Haynes, *The Portland Vase* (London, 1964); N. T. de Grummond, "Rubens, Peiresc, and the Portland Vase," *Southeastern College Art Conference Review* 7 (1974), 6–11; S. M. Goldstein—L. S. Rakow—J. K. Rakow, *Cameo Glass, Masterpieces from 2000 Years of Glassmaking* (Corning, 1982); N. Williams, *The Breaking and Remaking of the Portland Vase* (London, 1989); +D. Whitehouse—K. Painter et al., "The Portland Vase," *Journal of Glass Studies* 32 (1990), 12–188.

PORTRAIT ICONOGRAPHY. The study and identification of portraits of figures from classical antiquity, including rulers and their families, nobles, poets, philosophers and other illustrious persons, as well as private individuals.

In antiquity the Roman scholar Varro (116–27 B.C.) established the tradition of assembling albums of portraits of famous Greeks and Romans, which he published in his *Hebdomades vel de imaginibus,* containing 700 images. *Petrarch revived this practice, with his collection of Roman coins in a series illustrating portraits of emperors and their wives and in his treatise *De viris illustribus,* manuscripts of which were illustrated with Roman portraits. The Petrarchan tradition was continued in many a series of painted portraits of famous men or of the Twelve Caesars used to decorate palaces or libraries, such as those by *Mantegna, *Giulio Romano, *Titian and *Rubens.

By the beginning of the sixteenth century, a certain consistency in images of the emperor may be observed in the classic study that stands at the beginning of iconographical scholarship, the *Illustrium imagines* of Andrea *Fulvio, published at Rome in 1517. It contained 207 woodcut medallions of famous men

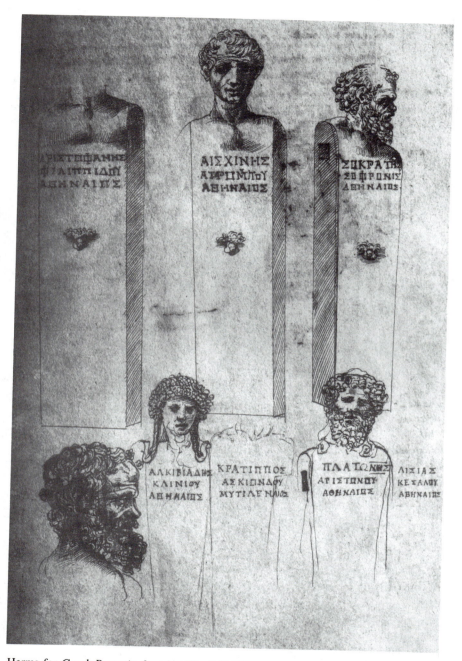

Herms for *Greek Portraits* found at Tivoli (1488), drawing by Pirro Ligorio, with heads contrived by the artist, Naples, Biblioteca Nazionale. (Deutsches Archäologisches Institut, Rome. Inst. Neg. 1824. With permission of the Ministero per i Beni Culturali e Ambientali.)

and women, mainly Roman. (Only one Greek portrait was included, of Alexander the Great.) Though the emperors were based on coin images, the empresses were often fanciful, looking rather like princesses of the Renaissance. Within this tradition is the compendium of Roman iconography created by the Northern European artist and numismatist Hubert *Goltzius, *Icones imperatorum romanorum* (1557), an immensely popular work that included, unfortunately, forged coins and altered inscriptions.

Interest in Greek iconography was stimulated by the discovery at *Tivoli in 1488 of a group of herms, headless but inscribed with the names of a number of famous Greeks, including Isokrates, Karneades, Miltiades and Aischines. The herms aroused considerable interest in the sixteenth century, when they came into the collection of *Julius III at Rome and were drawn by Pirro *Ligorio, who supplied them with alien heads. Some dubious versions were also published by the Portuguese Achilles Statius (Estaco; 1524–81), in his collection of fifty-two plates issued by *Lafréry and dedicated to Cardinal *Perrenot de Granvelle, *Inlustrium viror. ut exstant in urbe expressi vultus* (1569).

Fulvio *Orsini, the "father of iconography," created a new methodology for the study of ancient portraits in his *Imagines et elogia virorum illustrium et eruditorum* (1570; expanded with engravings by Theodore Galle, 1598, and commentary by J. Faber, 1606). His range of portraits was wide, including both Greek and Roman figures—not only rulers and leaders but also poets, philosophers, historians. He rigorously used coins, gems and inscriptions in his search for authoritative images, though he did not succeed in weeding out all forgeries. The authoritative corpus by Orsini was followed in the seventeenth century by *Bellori's *Veterum illustrium philosophorum, poetarum, rhetorum ac oratorum imagines* (1685), which included, for the first time, fourteen physicians, drawn from the illustrated manuscript of Dioskourides in Vienna, and by the volume dedicated to portrait iconography in the *Thesaurus graecarum antiquitatum* of Jacob Gronovius (*Gronovius family).

Iconographic studies in the eighteenth century were especially associated with the study and publication of gems, by such scholars as De la *Chausse, *Winckelmann, *Gori (*glyptics). But the *Illustrium imagines* of Orsini continued to be the fundamental text, until it was supplanted by the great compendia of E. Q. *Visconti. His *Iconographie grecque* appeared in three volumes in 1808, and one volume of the *Iconographie romaine* was published in 1817 before his death; A. Mongez later issued three more volumes. Visconti and Mongez created a systematic and comprehensive corpus of Greek and Roman portraits, based on research in the older standard works of Orsini and others, but with many newly discovered items and new illustrations. Visconti had the benefit of the vastly improved museology of the eighteenth century and the fact that many collections were better organized and the unimportant pieces sifted out. The counterpart in collecting to Visconti's iconographical publication may be seen in the large assemblages of plaster casts of canonical images, such as the collection sold by F. *Albacini to the Trustees Academy in Edinburgh (154 portraits out of the original 255 survive). Whereas earlier study collections were built of the easily portable coins and gems, with their two-dimensional images, now the science of portrait iconography took full account of the three-dimensional busts and statues, which gave a much fuller idea of the subject.

At the end of the nineteenth century and the beginning of the twentieth, J. J. Bernoulli prepared his two great corpora, *Römische Ikonographie* (1882–94) and *Griechische Ikonographie* (1901), scientifically modern publications that are regularly consulted in iconographical studies even today. The Greek material was further sifted and cataloged, with profuse illustrations and copious bibliography, by Gisela M. A. *Richter in the three volumes of *The Portraits of the Greeks* (1965; abridged version by R.R.R. Smith, 1984). Roman portrait iconography has been an enormously popular subject in twentieth-century archaeology, but no counterpart to Richter's catalog has been produced. Numerous systematic treatments of particular groups of portraits, whether by subject, type or present location, make the material available, for example, A. N. Zadoks Josephus—Jitta, *Ancestral Portraiture in Rome and the Art of the Last Century of the Republic* (1932); J.M.C. Toynbee, *Roman Historical Portraits* (1978); P. Zanker, *Studien zu den Augustus-Porträts 1 Der Actium Typus* (1973); D.E.E. Kleiner, *Roman Group Portraiture: The Funerary Reliefs of the Late Republic and Early Empire* (1977); P. Zanker—K. Fittschen, *Katalog der römischen Porträts in den Capitolinischen Museen und den anderen kommunalen Sammlungen der Stadt Rom* (1984–85). The series of Roman ruler portraits *(Herrscherbildnisse)*, founded in 1939 by Max Wegner for the *German Archaeological Institute, continues today.

BIBLIOGRAPHY

G.M.A. Richter, *The Portraits of the Greeks* 1 (1965), 21–24; E. Dwyer, "The Origins of the Modern Tradition in Classical Portrait Iconography: From Fulvio Orsini to Ennio Quirino Visconti," *AJA* 95 (1991), 301; N. T. de Grummond, "Portraits of Augustus and His Family in the Albacini Collection," *Journal of the History of Collections* 3 (1991), 167–81; Kleiner, *Roman Sculpture*, 13–14, 18–19.

PORTUS. The monumental harbor of Rome, two miles north of *Ostia.

Claudius's harbor, a roughly circular enclosure (diameter ca. 1,000m), was completed in A.D. 64. Its most dramatic feature was a lighthouse set on a foundation made from the giant barge, sunken and filled with concrete, that had once transported the Vatican *Obelisk to Rome. Trajan's hexagonal basin (358m on a side), was added ca. A.D. 112. The harbor facilities functioned until the sixth century. The harbors silted up, and the town that had developed south of the hexagon was abandoned by the eighth century.

Portus's later history parallels that of Ostia, until the acquisition of the property by the Prince Alessandro Torlonia in 1856. From 1864 to 1867, sculptures were removed from the site to enrich the *Torlonia family collection. In the 1930s, G. *Lugli was allowed to investigate Trajan's basin when it was restored as a lake for the Torlonia estate. He produced the volume on the site that is still standard. Salvage excavations were conducted at Portus in 1957–60 during the construction of Rome's international Leonardo da Vinci Airport. They revealed details of mole construction and located Claudius's lighthouse.

In 1976, the Torlonia opened the area as a zoo and park, to the dismay of many. The Italian Archaeological Service gained control of the site in 1987.

BIBLIOGRAPHY

G. Lugli—G. Filibeck, *Il Porto di Roma imperiale e l'agro portuense* (Rome, 1935); O. Testaguzza, *Portus* (Rome, 1970); R. Meiggs, *Roman Ostia* (Oxford, 1973); L. Casson, "From Ancient Port to Modern Zoo," *Archaeology* 31.3 (1978), 44–51.

JOHN L. KISSINGER

PORTUS COSANUS. Commercial harbor and fishery serving *Cosa, the oldest-known Roman harbor yet discovered (in use by 273 B.C.), with the earliest-dated hydraulic concrete (late second–early first centuries B.C.).

The facilities continued in a limited capacity as part of an imperial estate from the first to third centuries A.C. During the late sixteenth century, the Medici built a tower nearby, now called the Torre Puccini after the composer, who purchased it in 1919. A modern villa and restaurant, La Strega, are over the Roman villa.

The site was described by G. Santi (1798) and by G. *Dennis, who visited the area in the 1840s. They both referred to the intriguing channel and cavern in the cliffs, known as the Tagliata and the Spacco della Regina, respectively. The first detailed study of these features was made by Raffaele Del Rosso, who noted their likely association with the ancient fishing industry. Excavations in the port and adjacent lagoon areas were carried out between 1968 and 1978 under Anna Marguerite McCann, employing archaeological, geological and engineering analysis. The final report describes the port and its place in the history of ancient harbors, the fishing industry, shipping and trade.

BIBLIOGRAPHY

A. M. McCann et al., *The Roman Port and Fishery of Cosa* (Princeton, NJ, 1987).

JOHN L. KISSINGER

POSEIDONIA. See PAESTUM.

POULSEN, POUL FREDERIK SIGFRED (1876–1950). Danish archaeologist, specialist in portrait iconography.

Born in Dalsgaard, Poulsen studied in 1896–97 at Göttingen, where he won the admiration of *Wilamowitz, and at Munich, where *Furtwängler took an interest in him. He spent 1905–7 in Greece, affiliated with the *French School in Athens, studying Geometric pottery from the Dipylon.

Returning to Sweden, Poulsen soon became an assistant at the *Ny Carlsberg Glyptotek, Copenhagen (1910), and by 1926 had risen to become director. Keeping up his interest in Greek archaeology, he excavated at *Delphi and published works in Danish on the Archaic sculpture and the oracle at Delphi. In 1926 and

1928 he collaborated with Konstantinos Rhomaios at Kalydon, from which resulted his publication in German on the Kalydonian heroon (*Das Heroon von Kalydon,* 1934).

Poulsen is especially remembered for his publications on Greek and Roman portrait iconography, taking inspiration from the splendid collection at the Glyptotek (e.g., in English, *Iconographic Studies in the Ny Carlsberg Glyptotek,* 1931), as well as from collections he visited in his wide-ranging travels (e.g., *Greek and Roman Portraits in English Country Houses,* 1923). Working from the colored drawings of Etruscan tomb paintings ordered by Carl Jacobsen in the 1890s, Poulsen wrote his *Etruscan Tomb Paintings, Their Subjects and Significance* (Oxford, 1922), still worth consulting. Perhaps of most enduring value is his *Katalog over antike Skulpturer der Ny Carlsberg Glyptotek* (1940).

BIBLIOGRAPHY

H. C. Broholm, s.v., "Poulsen, Poul Frederik Sigfred," *Dansk Biografisk Leksikon* 18 (1940), 519–23; L. Curtius, "Frederic Poulsen," *Gnomon* 23 (1951), 115–16.

POUSSIN, NICOLAS (1594–1665). Greatest French painter of the classical style, known for his ardent study of Greek and Roman antiquity.

Born in Les Andelys in Normandy, Nicolas Poussin trained in Paris (from 1612) and arrived in Rome in 1624. There, introduced by his friend, the poet Marino, he was patronized by Cardinal Francesco Barberini (*Barberini family) and began his enduring friendship with the cardinal's secretary, Cassiano dal *Pozzo. Poussin was to spend the rest of his working life in Rome, with only a brief sojourn in Paris in 1642.

Poussin's close friend and biographer *Bellori depicts him as well read and fond of serious discourse. Within the circle of Cassiano and the Barberini, he found sympathetic friends—scholars, collectors and artists who took a passionate interest in the arts and natural science and gave especial attention to antiquity. From around 1620 Cassiano was absorbed in a project to make drawings of all the antiquities of Rome—a "Paper Museum" (Museo Cartaceo) that could serve as a first-class study collection for archaeologists. He hired a number of artists for the purpose, and it is often suggested that Poussin was among them.

It is a paradox that Poussin, an artist famed for his archaeological and intellectual interest in the ancient world, should have contributed so little to the formal study of classical archaeology. In vain have scholars sought to reach agreement on the attribution to Poussin of a single drawing in the surviving corpus of Cassiano's Museo Cartaceo. The strongest candidate, a view of the *Arch of the Argentarii (Royal Library, Windsor), is not very detailed and, in fact, not as accurate as many of the other Cassiano drawings. It features the broad swaths of wash creating strong contrasts of light and shade over the lines of the pen seen in many autograph drawings of Poussin and in a group of drawings after antiquities in the Musée Conde (Chantilly) that have been attributed to him.

A number of well-known antiquities appear in the Chantilly collection. The drawing of *Castor and Pollux, a sculpture group at that time in the *Ludovisi family collection, is of the highest quality. There are also drawings of the two major reliefs of the *Arch of Titus, of the *Marcus Aurelius Equestrian Figure, of one of the processions on the *Ara Pacis and of the *Farnese Flora. Also attributed to Poussin is the fine drawing of a Bacchante from the *Borghese Vase in the British Museum. These drawings are sometimes lacking in detail and serve to capture an impression of the sculptures, as if they are for study by an artist rather than a scholar.

Poussin may have made a copy of the *Aldobrandini Wedding, a rare Roman wall painting discovered in Rome in 1604/5. For over 200 years, an oil reproduction in the Doria-Pamphili Gallery, Rome, was said to be a copy made by him for Cassiano dal Pozzo, but the attribution has been widely rejected by Poussin specialists of the twentieth century. In addition, a small wax model of the celebrated marble *"Cleopatra" from the Belvedere is attributed to him (*Louvre, Paris).

The evidence of the artist's contribution to archaeology is meager, but it may be asserted conversely that the evidence of archaeology's contribution to the art of Poussin is abundant. The debt goes far beyond the quotations from famous sculptures normally occurring in painting of the Renaissance and Baroque, for example, the *Ludovisi Gaul Killing Himself and His Wife in Poussin's Rape of the Sabines (1634, Metropolitan Museum of Art, New York) or the Borghese Vase Bacchante in the Massacre of Innocents (ca. 1628; Musée Conde, Chantilly). It may be seen in his meticulous attention to ancient dress and objects and customs of daily life, as in the depiction of Roman sandals and the magistrate's bundle of rods (fasces) in the Rape of the Sabines; the authentic reconstruction of a triclinium dining room in the scene of Penance from the Seven Sacraments series (1647; on loan to the National Gallery of Scotland, Edinburgh); the ancient musical instruments in the Triumph of David (begun 1620s; Dulwich College Picture Gallery); and the Etruscan-style bronze mirror in Achilles Among the Daughters of Lycomedes (1656; Virginia Museum of Fine Arts, Richmond). We get a strong sense of Poussin's ability to absorb antiquity in his letter to Chantelou referring to tiny, unusual details of representation he had noted in the Egyptianizing *Barberini Mosaic (priests with shaven heads, tambourines, an ibis head), which he had incorporated into his Holy Family in Egypt, along with an obelisk (1655–57; Hermitage, St. Petersburg).

He also had a scholar's knowledge and a profound feeling for the way in which architecture, both as a whole and in detail, could be used to re-create an ancient setting. A telling example is his usage of the Tuscan Doric order in the Rape of the Sabines in the Louvre (1630s). The temple that is depicted features wide intercolumniations and heavy columns, of a type that really was used in the primitive monumental architecture of Etruria and Rome. The preclassical tone is ideal for the story drawn from the early history of Rome.

Poussin's imitation of the antique springs from a total immersion in the ambience of ancient art, architecture, literature and even music. It is well known that he employed in his paintings a theory of modes of expression based on the five Greek musical modes, the Dorian, Ionian, Lydian, Hypolydian and Phrygian. That is, he consciously varied the mood of his scenes to conform to Greek music he had never heard. It has been asserted that Poussin understood Greek antiquity more thoroughly than any other artist of the period and that he had so great a natural affinity with the Greeks that he understood and embodied the purity of Greek art of the Classical period in the fifth century without seeing many original works of Greek art. (Few were accessible in seventeenth century Rome.) His merry *Bacchanal* in the London National Gallery (1630s), on the one hand, and his somber *Funeral of Phocion,* on the other (1648; collection of the Earl of Plymouth, Oakly Park), show his sensitive reading of Greek moods. But he was also capable of an emotionally intense burst of Roman elegy (*Et in Arcadia Ego;* ca. 1627, Chatsworth) and the most dramatic rendering of Roman heroism (*Death of Germanicus;* 1627, Minneapolis Institute of Arts). Examples of his intimate understanding of ancient Roman themes, buildings, sculptures and objects could be multiplied. Clearly, to overemphasize his relationship to Greek models is to belie the significance of the totality of Poussin's understanding of Greek and Roman antiquity.

BIBLIOGRAPHY

+A. Blunt, *Nicholas Poussin 1–2* (Washington, DC, 1967); +K. Oberhuber, *Poussin, The Early Years in Rome* (New York, 1988); +J. Thompson, *Nicolas Poussin, The Metropolitan Museum of Art Bulletin* 50.3 (1992–93); *The Paper Museum of Cassiano dal Pozzo, Quaderni Puteani* 4 (1993).

POZZO, CASSIANO DAL (ca. 1588–1657). Italian scholar, scientist, antiquarian, patron of artists; famed for his unique project to create a Museo Cartaceo (''Paper Museum'') of antiquities known in his time.

Born in Turin, at an early age Cassiano moved with his family to Pisa, where he was educated under the guidance of his uncle, Carlo Antonio dal Pozzo, archbishop of Pisa and a politically powerful figure. In the climate of Pisa, the city of Galileo, he probably developed early some of his scientific interests, especially in botany. In 1612 Cassiano took up residence in Rome near the Piazza di Spagna, and in 1620 he was joined by his younger brother, Carlo Antonio. During these early years, Cassiano moved in the intellectual circle of the nobleman Federico *Cesi, founder of the *Accademia dei Lincei, and was himself elected into the academy in 1622. The organization's emphasis on careful observation (manifest in its choice of the sharp-eyed lynx as its symbol) was consistent with Cassiano's own ideals; this attitude was to manifest itself especially in his collections of drawings of antiquity and the natural sciences. Cassiano took a profound interest in the scientific discoveries of Galileo (who had joined the Lincei in 1610) and served as one of the editors for Galileo's great treatise, the *Assayer* (1623).

A turning point in the life of Cassiano came around the time of the election of Maffeo Barberini (*Barberini family) as Pope Urban VIII (1623–44). Soon afterward, the pope's nephew, Cardinal Francesco Barberini, invited Cassiano to join his retinue. The now mature but still relatively young scholar thus received fresh stimulus from the cultivated atmosphere of the Palazzo Barberini and was provided with an adequate income that gave him ample time to pursue his interests in antiquity and the sciences. There were also significant opportunities for travel, when Cassiano accompanied Cardinal Barberini on diplomatic missions to Paris (1625) and Madrid (1626). He twice visited *Peiresc at Aix-en-Provence and also met Peter Paul *Rubens in Paris. With both of these ardent scholars of antiquity he could discuss their project to publish a book on all the most famous ancient cameos of Europe (the *Gemma Tiberiana, the *Gemma Augustea, the *Portland Vase and others), and he agreed to help with the undertaking. Unfortunately the book never saw the light.

In 1627, Carlo Antonio married, and the dal Pozzo brothers sought new lodging in a palazzo near the church of S. Andrea della Valle. Here Cassiano was able to develop fully his interest in collecting contemporary works of art (above all, by *Poussin; also included were portraits of illustrious men—Peiresc, Galileo, Poussin) and antiquities, such as coins, statues and casts of the *Column of Trajan.

Cassiano's collections also revealed his abiding interest in the natural sciences, as he kept specimens of fossils, shells and animals. In his courtyard he had particularly exotic creatures, including a bearded vulture and flamingos.

His museum and library were significantly augmented in 1638, when he was able to purchase a number of manuscripts and a great corpus of scientific drawings from the collection of Cesi, who had died in 1630. In his library, which contained some 5,000 volumes, Cassiano stored his Museo Cartaceo. This was the name he gave to his collection of drawings in a letter of 1654 to the Jesuit Reinhold Dehnig. The library was organized by subject matter, and his drawings were accordingly disposed, with the segment of antiquities in a section of "Historia." This huge archive of drawings was itself divided according to subject matter, but there is some disagreement in sources over the precise arrangement. Carlo Dati, Cassiano's biographer, stated in 1664 that the corpus was broadly divided into *res divinae* (images of gods, temples, sacrifices) and *res humanae,* which, in turn, were divided according to pursuits of peace (magistrates, theaters, clothing, baths and many other categories) and war (soldiers, weapons, trophies and so on). He also declared that there were twenty-three volumes of drawings, and modern scholarship has been much occupied with trying to locate and identify the scattered parts of the archive. The greatest part of it is today in the Royal Library at Windsor Castle (thirteen volumes), and a number of drawings are in the *British Museum and the British Library, London.

Cassiano seems to have begun collecting his archive by about 1620. In some cases he acquired drawings and sketchbooks of antiquities that had been made in the sixteenth century and that he then arranged according to his own principles. He also had a practice of commissioning drawings of particular monuments and objects from young artists; more than thirty artists worked for him, most prominent of whom were *Pietro da Cortona, Pietro *Testa and the Sienese painter and printmaker Bernardino Capitelli (1590–1639), who made hundreds of drawings for the project. *Poussin was patronized by dal Pozzo for many years, but thus far it has not been possible to make convincing attributions to him from the archives of the Paper Museum.

Cassiano seems to have preferred that the drawings for his collection be in pen and wash. There are also extant colored drawings of such works as the well-known *Barberini Mosaic and the miniatures of the *Vatican Vergil codex as well as the Vatican manuscript of the plays of Terence. The range of material is enormous, including major monuments such as the *Pantheon and the *Temple of Fortuna at Praeneste, paintings such as the *Aldobrandini *Wedding,* reliefs such as those on the *Ara Pacis Augustae, important smaller pieces such as the *Portland Vase, as well as minor antiquities from Etruscan mirrors to *Campana Reliefs and Italic fibulas.

In recent years much attention has been focused on the achievements of Cassiano dal Pozzo, with the formation of an international committee that publishes its findings in *Quaderni Puteani* (1989–   ) and with a major exhibition, "The Paper Museum of Cassiano dal Pozzo," at the British Museum (1993). His place in the history of scholarship has been clarified, so that he is seen as a continuator of the encyclopedic antiquarian practices of Pirro *Ligorio, and as a versatile scholar with wide-ranging interests in science, art and archaeology, in the tradition of *Aldrovandi, *Orsini and Peiresc.

BIBLIOGRAPHY

G. Lumbroso, "Notizie sulla vita di Cassiano dal Pozzo," *Miscellanea di Storia Italiana* 15 (1874), 131–388; +*Cassiano dal Pozzo's Paper Museum, Quaderni Puteani* 2–3 (1992); +*The Paper Museum of Cassiano dal Pozzo,* catalog of exhibition, *Quaderni Puteani* 4 (1993).

PRADO MUSEUM, Madrid. Spain's greatest art museum, originally called the Real Museo de Pintura y Escultura; the most numerous and important examples of classical sculpture in Spain belong to the Prado.

Like the paintings for which the museum is chiefly famous, most of the antiques come from the royal collection and were exhibited in 1839, twenty years after the opening of the picture gallery. With a few exceptions they came from Italy in the period from the sixteenth to the eighteenth centuries, brought as gifts or purchases for the Spanish monarchs. The nucleus of the collection was a group of portrait busts, including two series of emperors, sent from Rome to Philip II (*Hapsburg family), who also owned some statues, among them two marble Venuses from Sagunto.

The first serious attempt to enrich the royal collection and decorate the Alcázar, the Hapsburg palace in Madrid, with antique sculptures as well as paintings was made by Philip IV, prompted apparently by his court painter *Velázquez, who was sent to Italy in 1649 for this purpose. The result of his mission is not fully known, but it seems probable that for lack of available antiques the only originals he acquired were portrait busts, and for the rest he made do with copies and casts in plaster and bronze of many of the most celebrated statues in Rome. Of these only some bronzes, highly prized in their time (e.g., the *Borghese *Hermaphrodite*), are known to survive, in the Prado and in the royal palace. The only notable antique sculpture recorded in Philip IV's possession is the so-called *Apotheosis of Claudius,* presented to him soon after it was excavated in 1654.

The largest major contribution ever made to the Spanish collection was that of the Bourbon king Philip V and his Italian queen Isabel Farnese. This transaction consisted of the purchase in 1724 from the *Odescalchi family of the greater part of the famous collection of antiquities made in Rome by Queen *Christina of Sweden; with papal permission no fewer than 173 cases were shipped to Spain. They contained some celebrated marbles such as the *Castor and Pollux,* the *Faun with Kid* and the much-restored seated *Muses,* some no longer highly esteemed and some even of doubtful origin. The last important addition to the collection came later in the century, a gift to Charles IV from José Nicolás Azara (1731–1804), antiquary, friend of *Mengs and ambassador in Rome. This collection consisted mostly of portraits, many of which Azara himself had excavated in Tivoli in 1779 and restored (cf. *Alexander Azara). Some of these have remained in the palace at Aranjuez.

A few gifts and other acquisitions made in modern times complete the Prado's collection of classical sculpture. It contains more than 200 works considered original and over 140 cataloged today as Renaissance or later copies and imitations. Due to many losses and incomplete records, the history and origin of many of these are still uncertain.

BIBLIOGRAPHY
E. Hübner, *Die Antiken Bildwerke in Madrid* (Berlin, 1862); E. Barrón, *Museo Nacional de Pintura e Escultura, Catálogo de la Escultura* (Madrid, 1908); X. de Salas, "Compra para España de la colección de antigüedades de Cristina de Suecia," *ArchEspArt* 14 (1940–41), 242–46; +A. Blanco, *Museo del Prado, Catálogo de la Escultura* (Madrid, 1957); E. Harris, "La Misión de Velázquez en Italia," *ArchEspArt* 33 (1960), 109–36; S. F. Schröder, *Katalog der antiken skulpturen des Museo del Prado in Madrid, Die Porträts* (Mainz am Rhein, 1993).

ENRIQUETA HARRIS FRANKFORT

PRAENESTE (PALESTRINA). An important Latin town in a strong location at the head of the Hernican valley opposite the Alban hills and in control of a vital throat on the inland highway between southern Etruria and Poseidonia.

The town quickly grew rich on the traffic. It was an early ally of Rome but jealous of its independence until the Social War. It was early famous for its *Temple of Fortuna Primigenia and the *sortes praenestinae* ("Praenestine lots"), by which pilgrims had their fortunes told; the shrine prospered until late antiquity. Praeneste had the misfortune to shelter the younger Marius and the remains of his army in 82 B.C., in retribution for which the citizenry was butchered, the town plundered and a veteran colony settled there by Sulla. In the Late Republican period it became a favorite summer resort for rich Romans (*frigidum Praeneste,* "chill Praeneste"). Hadrian is known to have had a villa there. It fades into obscurity in the late empire but seems to have been continuously occupied.

The antiquities of Praeneste first began to draw attention in the Renaissance, when artists, architects and scholars came to study the remains of the Temple of Fortuna Primigenia. During this period, Praeneste came under the control of the *Barberini family. Palazzo Barberini is built into the top of the remains of the shrine of Fortuna. The impressive *Barberini Mosaic was discovered during the late sixteenth or early seventeenth century. Praeneste next appears in the annals of archaeology in 1738, with the discovery there of the *Ficoroni *Cista.* In 1769–71 substantial fragments of a calendar on marble were brought to light there. These, known as the Fasti Praenestini, are believed to be the calendar compiled by the learned Augustan Verrius Flaccus and set up by him in the forum of Praeneste. They rank as the most important of all ancient calendar fragments. In 1795 Gavin *Hamilton extracted the beautiful Braschi *Antinous* now in the Sala Rotonda of the Museo Pio-Clementino (*Vatican Museums) from the ruins of Villa Adriana near the modern cemetery.

Another wave of discoveries at Praeneste came just after the middle of the nineteenth century and was more orderly. In the necropolis of La Columbella south of the city was discovered a series of *fossa* ("trench") tombs with extraordinarily rich furnishings. The most famous of these are the *Barberini and *Bernardini tombs of the seventh century B.C. The contents of both are now in the *Villa Giulia in Rome. Another discovery reported to have taken place during this period, of the so-called *Praenestine Fibula, has now been widely discredited, along with the fibula itself.

Also during the nineteenth century came the discovery of numerous burials of a later date (beginning in the fourth century). These were usually in stone sarcophagi and marked with the characteristic cippus of Praeneste, a sharply pointed egg shape mounted on a base of acanthus leaves. In these tombs were found a great many bronze *cistae* or toilet boxes, the older ones oval, broader than deep, the later ones round or rectangular. These are normally decorated with engraving (sometimes embossing) with the addition of cast mounts for feet and handles and decorative chains.

Many of the antiquities discovered at Praeneste, including the Barberini mosaic, are displayed today in the Barberini palace.

BIBLIOGRAPHY

F. Fasolo—G. Gullini, *Il Santuario della Fortuna Primigenia a Palestrina,* 1–2. (Rome, 1953); +P. Romanelli, *Palestrina* (Cava dei Tirreni, 1967); L. Richardson, jr, s.v. "Praeneste," *PECS,* 735–36; F. Coarelli, *I Santuari del Lazio in età repubblicana* (Rome, 1987).

L. RICHARDSON, JR

PRAENESTINE FIBULA. Gold brooch, ca. 4⁵/₁₆ inches long, purportedly found at Palestrina in 1871 and featuring an inscription (*CIL* 1²: 2: 1.3) claimed (and accepted by Dessau, *Mommsen, *Wilamowitz et al.) to be the earliest Latin known; proved by Margherita Guarducci (University of Rome), with the aid of a team of scientists/technicians, to be a nineteenth-century forgery, probably of 1886.

Guarducci also demonstrated that the perpetrators were Francesco Martinetti (1833–95), Roman art dealer, antiquarian and skilled craftsman, who was responsible for making the fibula, and Wolfgang *Helbig (1839–1915), who, while second secretary (i.e., assistant director), from 1865, of the *German Archaeological Institute in Rome, concocted the inscription and, the evidence indicates, cut it himself. The arguments for their collusion are circumstantial, but any classical jury, aware of their well-documented collaboration from 1871 to Martinetti's death (and of Helbig's continuation in his nefarious commercial activities thereafter) would certainly bring in a verdict of "guilty." The Fibula's fraudulence has been accepted by the director of the Museo Preistorico in Rome, where the fibula has now been removed from display. Martinetti's motive was greed; Helbig's was the desire to succeed Wilhelm Henzen as first secretary.

BIBLIOGRAPHY
+C. D. Curtis, *The Bernardini Tomb MAAR* 3 (1919), 21 f., no. 2B; A. E. Gordon, *The Inscribed Fibula Praenestina, Problems of Authenticity Univ. Calif. Publ.: Class. Stud.* 16 (Berkeley, 1975); D. Ridgway, "Manios Faked?" *BICS* 24 (1977), 17–30; +M. Guarducci, "La cosiddetta Fibula Prenestina: Antiquari, eruditi e falsari nella Roma dell'ottocento," *MemLinc*, ser. 8, 24 (1980), 413–574.

†ARTHUR E. GORDON

PRAYING BOY. Lifesize (1.28m) Hellenistic bronze statue of a youth, said to have been found at *Rhodes; one of the best-known and most-admired ancient statues known in Venice during the Renaissance.

The statue arrived in Venice by 1503, as reported by Lorenzo da Pavia to Isabella d'*Este. Sometime during the sixteenth century a bronze copy of it was made (now in the Museo Archeologico, Venice), preserving its condition at the time the piece first became known. The boy is represented gently stepping forward, with his head turned upward and his shoulders lifted. The arms, missing from the upper arm to the fingertips, were subsequently restored to show the figure with hands upraised in prayer. He was thus equated with a "praying figure" (*adorans*) mentioned by Pliny (*NH* 34.73) as a work of Boedas, one of the sons of Lysippos, or another mentioned by Dionysios of Byzantion as being in the sanctuary of Zeus Ourios on the shores of the Bosporus. In the Renaissance the statue was admired as *Ganymede* by Pietro Aretino (who glibly attributed the statue to Pheidias) and others. *Bembo was told about the sculpture and, upon hearing that it lacked the front half of one foot, was able to supply a bronze forefoot excavated at Padua that fitted the statue perfectly.

The first owner of the statue was Andrea di Martini, a knight of Rhodes, as was confirmed by another knight, Fra Sabba da *Castiglione. By 1589, the sculpture was in the Bevilacqua collection in Verona, and in the early seventeenth century it passed to the *Gonzaga in Mantua. Its stellar list of subsequent owners includes Charles I of England, Nicholas Foucquet, Prince Eugene of Savoy, Prince Wenzel of Lichtenstein and Frederick the Great. In Berlin from 1747, the piece was carried off to Paris in 1808 but was returned in 1812; it resides today in the Staatliche Museen, Berlin.

BIBLIOGRAPHY

L. Franzoni, *Verona, La Galleria Bevilacqua* (Milan, 1970), 111–23; +M. Perry, "A Greek Bronze in Renaissance Venice," *BurlMag* 117 (1975), 204–11; Ridgway, *Hellenistic Sculpture,* I, 227–28.

PRIENE. Greek city in Turkey, known as one of the best-preserved towns of the Hellenistic period.

The site of Priene, on a rocky promontory overlooking the Maeander River and the Aegean Sea, was chosen around the middle of the fourth century B.C. (The city had previously been located in an unknown spot nearby.) It was laid out with a grid plan, with north-south streets running perpendicular to east-west ones and with large, standardized blocks for the houses. Preserved at Priene are substantial remains of the city walls, agora, temple of Athena, council house, theater, two gymanasia and private houses, dating from the fourth to the second centuries B.C. Alexander the Great was in Priene in 334 B.C. and made the dedication of the temple of Athena. In the first century, Priene came under Roman control.

Priene was visited by *Wheler and *Spon in the seventeenth century and by Robert *Wood, returning from his visit to *Palmyra, in the early eighteenth century. Soon afterward, Priene became one of the sites in Asia Minor that were of passionate concern for the *Society of Dilettanti. Richard *Chandler led a mission to record the topography, inscriptions and the architecture of the temple of Athena, attended by the artist William *Pars and the architect Nicholas *Revett. Their results were published in the first volume of *Antiquities of Ionia* (1769). A second expedition was led by Sir William *Gell (1811–12), with part of the new findings published in subsequent volumes of *Antiquities of Ionia.* In 1868–69 came the third Dilettanti mission, in which the architect Richard Popplewell Pullan conducted excavations, using a two-dimensional grid. J. C. Carter has observed that this is perhaps the earliest use of the grid for recording in archaeology, predating the well-known efforts of *Pitt-Rivers and *Dörpfeld. Pullan also made some three dozen photographs of the site, another pioneer technique. Only part of Pullan's documentation was published in *Antiquities of Ionia,* volume 4.

T. *Wiegand and H. Schrader uncovered much of the rest of the city of Priene in campaigns from 1895 to 1898 for the *German Archaeological Institute. A. von *Gerkan later published the theater. Carter has recently published the sculptures from the temple of Athena and surveyed the history of excavation at the site.

BIBLIOGRAPHY

T. Wiegand—H. Schrader, *Priene* (1904); G. E. Bean, s.v. "Priene," *PECS*, 737–39; J. C. Carter, *The Sculpture of the Sanctuary of Athena Polias at Priene,* Reports of the Research Committee of the Society of Antiquaries of London, no. 42 (London, 1983).

PRIMATICCIO, FRANCESCO (1504–70). Italian painter, sculptor and architect.

Born in Bologna, Primaticcio was trained as an assistant to *Giulio Romano, with whom he worked in creating paintings and stuccos for the Palazzo del Te in Mantua. Called in 1532 to serve the French king Francis I in adorning his lodge at Fontainebleau, Primaticcio collaborated with a number of Italian artists in creating the architecture, sculpture and painting desired.

Primaticcio played a key role in the study of classical antiquities in France and abroad when he secured for Francis copies of some of the best ancient statuary visible in Rome. Around 1540 he was sent to Rome for the first of two trips to make drawings of antiquities and to advise on the purchase of available pieces. He acquired 125 statues, mostly of no great significance, but, in addition, he ordered molds of some of the most important sculptures, especially from the Belvedere court of the *Vatican—*Laocoon, *Belvedere *Apollo, *"Cleopatra," *Commodus as Hercules, *Nile and *Tiber* and *Venus* (*Knidian *Aphrodite). By 1543 bronze casts were made for Fontainebleau of these as well as ornamental figures of sphinxes from the *Vatican; the foundry near Fontainebleau was under the direction of Primaticcio and *Vignola. These works stood in the gardens at Fontainebleau until the French Revolution. In addition, replicas of the *Satyrs* from the della *Valle family collection were set as chimney supports in the *Salle de Bal.*

Primaticcio served three French kings as superintendent of buildings and was influential in spreading his own Italian Mannerist approach to the antique. Much of his work at Fontainebleau was destroyed during the revolution, but the surviving stuccos from the bedchamber of the Duchesse d'Étampes (1541–45) reveal the kind of elongated, small-breasted female nudes he favored. A number of drawings on antique themes indicate how he planned cycles of Ulysses, Hercules and Alexander the Great, as well as stories from Ovid's *Metamorphoses.*

BIBLIOGRAPHY

+S. Pressouyre, "Les fontes de Primatice a Fontainebleau," *BMon* (1969), 223–39; Haskell—Penny, 1–6; +S. Béguin—J. Guillaume—A. Roy, *La Galerie d'Ulysse à Fontainebleau,* with intro. by A. Chastel (Paris, 1985).

PROPYLAIA, Athens. Greek Classical structure, monumental entrance to the *Akropolis and complement to the *Parthenon, built 437–432 B.C.

Designed by Mnesikles, the Propylaia was to include the gate building, two western wings (for purposes unknown) and two other wings on the eastern side (never built). It boasts many unique features: Ionic and Doric columns and entablatures, two-level central building and roof, dark stone accents, structural iron and elaborate decoration. The Propylaia combined the functions of its predecessors: a gate and courtyard.

Pausanias described the building and paintings he saw in the northwest wing.

Many changes were made to the Propylaia. In medieval times the southwest wing was made a church; later, a high tower was built there. The northwest wing was converted into a residence, and the façade intercolumniations were filled in. Finally, in 1687, additional fortification was added, for which the *Temple of Athena Nike was dismantled. A gunpowder explosion seriously damaged the central building.

The fortification of 1687 was removed by 1836. Demolition of the tower began in 1875 but was completed only after World War II. Beginning in 1909, work to rebuild the Propylaia was carried on first by N. Balanos and later by A. *Orlandos. Work by T. Tanoulas under the direction of the Committee for the Preservation of the Akropolis Monuments remains ongoing.

*Stuart and *Revett made excellent drawings of the Propylaia. Systematic excavation by R. Bohn began in 1880, and his publication contains the most thorough drawings. In 1903 C. Weller first fully excavated the remains of the Propylaia's predecessor. Reexcavation in 1975 by H. Eiteljorg, II, brought more information to light about the older propylon and its complex history. W. B. *Dinsmoor and W. B. Dinsmoor, Jr., worked extensively in the area. Volume 1 of their study (on the predecessors) was published in 1980, and their study of the Propylaia itself should supplant Bohn's.

BIBLIOGRAPHY

+R. Bohn, *Die Propyläen der Akropolis zu Athen* (Berlin 1882); C. H. Weller, "The Pre-Periclean Propylon," *AJA* 8 (1904), 35–70; J. A. Bundgaard, *Mnesicles, A Greek Architect at Work* (Copenhagen, 1957); +W. B. Dinsmoor, Jr., *The Propylaia to the Athenian Akropolis,* 1: *The Predecessors* (Princeton, NJ, 1980); T. Tanoulas, "The Propylaea of the Acropolis at Athens Since the 17th Century: Their Decay and Destruction," *JdI* 102 (1987), 413–83.

HARRISON EITELJORG II

PSEIRA. Small offshore island at the east end of the Gulf of Mirabello, in eastern *Crete, supporting a Minoan settlement from Final Neolithic/Early Minoan I until Late Minoan (LM) IB.

Pseira was first excavated in 1906 and 1907 by an American team led by Richard *Seager. About fifty buildings and thirty-three tombs were completely or partly exposed. Fieldwork was renewed in 1985 by P. Betancourt and C. Davaras. The new excavations discovered the Minoan town square and uncovered additional houses. A reoccupation period, from LM III, was also identified. After the Bronze Age, Pseira was not permanently inhabited again until the Byzantine period, when a monastery and two farmsteads were founded on the island.

BIBLIOGRAPHY
R. B. Seager, *Excavations on the Island of Pseira* (1910); P. P. Betancourt—C. Davaras, "Excavations at Pseira, 1985 and 1986," *Hesperia* 57 (1988), 207–25; "Excavations at Pseira," *Cretan Studies* 1 (1988), 35–37.

PHILIP P. BETANCOURT

PSEUDO-SENECA (SENECA; HESIOD). Portrait of an unidentified old man who is recognized in over forty Roman copies thought to derive from the same Hellenistic original (second century B.C.).

The best-preserved copy, a bronze head in the *Museo Nazionale, Naples, discovered in 1754, displays the characteristic features: head turned slightly upward and to the side; long, disheveled hair; short, straggly beard and mustache; nose with decided protrusion below the bridge; small, deep-set eyes; and sagging, furrowed flesh. Other important copies are one with an ivy wreath (*Terme Museum, Rome), one in a double herm with *Menander (Villa Albani, Casino) and one in a double herm with Vergil (?) in the *Ny Carlsberg Glyptotek.

The type was first identified as Seneca in Fulvio *Orsini's *Illustrium imagines* (1598) because of its resemblance to an inscribed portrait on a now-lost contorniate belonging to Cardinal Bernardino Maffei. As Seneca, the portrait won renown during the seventeenth and eighteenth centuries in Netherlandish neo-Stoic circles, prominent in which was P. P. *Rubens, who owned a replica and who reproduced it in drawings and paintings, such as the *Death of Seneca* (Alte Pinakothek, Munich) and the *Four Philosophers* (Pitti Palace, Florence). Other Netherlandish artists, for example, J. van *Sandrart, included the portrait in their paintings, using the Rubens bust as a model.

In 1764 the identification as Seneca was questioned by *Winckelmann, and in 1813 it was abandoned by all, when an unrelated, inscribed portrait of Seneca was excavated at the Villa Mattei, Rome (now in *Berlin). The immensely popular portrait has since been known by the disconcerting name of *"Pseudo-Seneca."*

Archaeologists have proposed numerous identifications based on all or some of the following assumptions: (1) the subject must have been popular in both Hellenistic and Roman times because of the great number of copies; (2) he must have been a poet or dramatist because of the ivy wreath present in one copy; (3) he must be reasonably collocated in a double herm with Menander and with Vergil; (4) he must have lived to an advanced age; (5) his character must conform to his rustic physiognomy; and (6) he may be associated with Epicureanism because several of the copies were found in Epicurean contexts. Consequently, many Hellenistic poets and dramatists have been suggested as possible identifications, including Philetas of Kos, Kallimachos of Kyrene, Theokritos, Aratos of Soloi, Apollonios of Rhodes, Philiskos of Korkyra, Philemon of Cilicia and Syracuse, Eratosthenes of Kyrene, Ennius and Karneades. Writers and philosophers of the first century B.C. who have some connection with Epicureanism have also been suggested, including Philodemos of Gadara, Phaidros, Philistion and Lucretius. These suppositions have not gained acceptance because they do not fulfill all the assumptions in a satisfactory manner. In addition, many scholars have hypothesized that the *Pseudo-Seneca* is an invented portrait representing a person who lived in an earlier age. The following possibilities have been envisaged: Mousaios, Homer, Hesiod, Aesop, Thespis, Epicharmos of Kos, Archilochos of Paros, Hipponax, Euripides, Aristophanes, Xenophanes, Empedokles and Sophron of Syracuse.

Hesiod is the most persuasive identification (J. F. Crome, E. *Buschor, G. M. A. *Richter, H. von Heintze, J. J. Pollitt). He was a poet who lived to an advanced age and who was popular in both Hellenistic and Roman times; what is known of his character corresponds to the physiognomy of the Pseudo-Seneca; and he can be reasonably paired with Vergil (two epic poets who sang of husbandry) and with Menander (two Greek writers popular in Roman times).

BIBLIOGRAPHY

B. Strandman, "The Pseudo-Seneca Problem," *Konsthistorisk Tidskrift* 19 (1950), 53–93; +G. M. A. Richter, *Portraits of the Greeks* 1 (London, 1965), 56–66; W. Prinz, "The *Four Philosophers* by Rubens and the Pseudo-Seneca in Seventeenth-Century Painting," *ArtB* 55 (1973), 410–28; H. von Heintze, "Pseudo-Seneca-Hesiod oder Ennius?" *RM* 82 (1975), 143–63.

ANN M. NICGORSKI

PUNISHMENT OF DIRCE. See FARNESE BULL.

PUPLUNA. See POPULONIA.

PYLOS, Messenia. Site in southern Greece identified as the Mycenaean "Palace of Nestor," dating to the Late Bronze Age.

While Pausanias reported seeing a House of Nestor in the northwest of the Bay of Navarino at Koryphasion, (4.36.2), Strabo recorded three towns that claimed to be Homer's Pylos (8.336), although he believed Nestor lived in "Triphylian" Pylos (8.344, 345). W. *Dörpfeld's 1907 excavations of tholoi and prehistoric remains at Kakovatos in Triphylia seemed to vindicate Strabo. But, by 1939, after digging several tholoi north of the Bay of Navarino, K. Kourouniotis invited C. W. *Blegen to join him to search for an alternative site for Nestor's palace; a joint project of the *Greek Archaeological Service and the University of Cincinnati was formed, with Blegen as field director. After surveying and discovering several Mycenaean sites, Ano (Epano) Englianos was chosen for excavation, from its large size, quantities of Mycenaean sherds on its surface and commanding position.

From the first day of excavation, 4 April 1939, Blegen found remains of a large building destroyed by fire from the end of the Late Bronze Age containing Linear B archives (*Linear A and B), frescoes and stucco floors. By the first season's end, Blegen confidently identified this building as Nestor's palace.

Work was interrupted with the outbreak of World War II, until 1952. Kourouniotis died in 1945 and was succeeded by S. *Marinatos, who continued excavating tombs in the region. His work is now continued by G. Korres. Work concluded at the palace in 1966, and a regional survey was undertaken by the University of Minnesota during the 1960s (*Minnesota Messenia Expedition). A new regional survey is under way, as well as investigations at the palace itself.

The palace comprises a central unit, 50m × 32m, with a propylon, archives, a courtyard and well-preserved megaron. Two wine magazines are behind the megaron; to the north is an oil magazine, and along the sides are pantries. An elaborate suite of rooms in the southeast is identified as the queen's quarters. On the northeast is a separate wine magazine. The Southwest Building, with columned rooms and frescoed walls, may belong to an earlier palace. The Northeast Building contained seal impressions and tablets, the latter attesting to its use as a workshop.

BIBLIOGRAPHY
C. W. Blegen—K. Kourouniotis, "Excavations at Pylos, 1939," *AJA* 43 (1939), 557–76; C. W. Blegen et al., *The Palace of Nestor at Pylos in Western Messenia* 1–3 (Princeton, NJ, 1966–73).

ROBERT B. KOEHL

PYRAMID OF CESTIUS (TOMB OF REMUS), Rome. Roman tomb of C. Cestius, praetor, tribune of the plebs and *septemvir epulonum.*

The pyramid is 22m square at the base with a height of 27m, built in the Augustan period outside Rome on the Via Ostiensis. It was later incorporated into the defensive Aurelian wall, and its position today is close to the sixth-century Porta San Paolo, overlooking the Protestant cemetery.

The pyramid has always been an outstanding landmark and appears on medieval plans of Rome as the tomb of Remus or *Meta Remi.* Another pyramid that stood near the Vatican (demolished ca. 1500) was thought to be the corresponding tomb of Romulus. This identification of the tomb was accepted by *Petrarch in the mid-fourteenth century, although the inscriptions on the east and west faces of the pyramid naming Cestius as its occupant were fairly legible. At the very end of the fourteenth century, Pier Paolo *Vergerio showed that the popular name for the tomb was wrong, and in the early fifteenth century *Poggio expressed surprise that a man as learned as Petrarch should make such a mistake.

Views of the pyramid drawn before the 1660s (e.g., by *Du Pérac, published 1575) show it with its base covered and with trees growing from it, gradually destroying the structure. Alexander VII (1662–63) saw to the partial excavation of the base, the opening of the tomb (creating a new entrance to the burial chamber) and the tomb's restoration. These excavations unearthed two statue bases with inscriptions that name Cestius's heirs, including Agrippa, thus dating the tomb prior to Agrippa's death in 12 B.C. Detailed plans, sections and views of the tomb were published by P. S. *Bartoli in 1697, including drawings of the wall paintings inside the burial chamber. (The paintings had been known at least since 1620 and were first published with a description of the pyramid by O. Falconieri in an appendix to the *Roma antica* of F. *Nardini, 1665.)

The Protestant cemetery was laid out to the northwest of the pyramid in the second half of the eighteenth century. The beauty and solemnity of the site were commented on by *Shelley when he visited Rome in 1818, but his description of the pyramid in *Adonais* is better known: "one keen pyramid with wedge sublime . . . like flame transformed into marble."

BIBLIOGRAPHY

+P. S. Bartoli, *Gli Antichi sepolcri romani* (1697), pl. 60–70; +M. S. Scherer, *Marvels of Ancient Rome* (New York, 1956), 122–24, pl. 23, 196–99; +Nash, II, 321–23; H. Joyce, "Grasping at Shadows: Ancient Paintings in Renaissance and Baroque Rome," *ArtB* 74 (1992), 237–38.

GLENYS DAVIES

PYRGI. The principal port of Etruscan Caere (modern *Cerveteri), on the Tyrrhenian coast thirty miles north of Rome (Greek *Pyrgoi;* Etruscan name unknown), famous in antiquity for the fabulously rich sanctuary sacked by the Syracusans in 384 B.C. (Diodorus Siculus 15, 14. 3; Strabo 5, 225–26; etc).

Excavations started in 1957 by Rome University revealed, first, the foundations of a large Tuscan temple (Temple A: ca. 460 B.C.), possibly dedicated to Thesan-Leukothea, accompanied by extensive terracotta decorations, including the fine relief plaque with episodes of the Theban Cycle. In 1962, thanks to R. *Linington's epoch-making geophysical prospection, the remains of Temple B were found, only a few yards to the south, built on a Greek plan and dating to ca. 500 B.C. From the sacred Area C between the temples, on 8 July 1964, the skillful trowel of the foreman Oreste Brandolini extracted three inscribed gold tablets, carefully rolled up within a chest of tufa blocks and terracotta simas— only a few inches below ground level; they carry the dedication (presumably of Temple B) to Uni-Astarte by the "king" of Caere, Thefarie Velianas, written in Etruscan and Phoenician. Recent campaigns have revealed, farther to the south, a long building where priestesses may have engaged in sacred prostitution (cf. Lucilius's *scorta Pyrgensia:* fr. 1271 M) and another sacred area rich in pottery, containing a dedication to Suri (equivalent to Greek Apollo), dated to the sixth century B.C. A Roman maritime colony, with polygonal walls, was founded on the semideserted site in 273 B.C. The finds are displayed in the *Villa Giulia, Rome, and in the Antiquarium Pyrgense at the site.

BIBLIOGRAPHY

M. Pallottino—G. Colonna, in *ArchCl* (1958–); *Le Lamine di Pyrgi, Quaderni Lincei* 147 (Rome, 1970); *NSc* (1970, pub. 1973), suppl. 2 and *NSc* (1988–89, pub. 1992), suppl. 2.

F. R. SERRA RIDGWAY

Q

QUATREMÈRE DE QUINCY, ANTOINE-CHRYSOSTÔME (1755–1849).
French politician and writer on aesthetics and classical archaeology.

Against the will of his parents, who wanted him to be a jurist, Quatremère de Quincy took up the study of painting and architecture. He made his first trip to Italy in 1776 and his second from 1782 to 1785, during which time he became friends with *Canova. Returning to Paris, he moved in the artistic ambient of *David. Quatremère won the essay prize of the Académie des inscriptions et belles lettres in 1785, with a piece on Egyptian architecture, but the Revolution interrupted his incipient career. With membership in the Académie (1803) and his editorship of the arts section of the *Journal des Savants* came prominence. His appointment as Intendant des arts et monuments publics in 1815 foreshadows, as do some of his writings, the Commission des monuments historiques. He became secretary of the Académie des beaux-arts and professor of archaeology and was a member of the new *Instituto di Corrispondenza Archeologica (1829). Internationally esteemed as an expert on the art of Pheidias, he visited London in 1818 and offered a highly favorable opinion of the *Elgin marbles.

Quatremère played an influential role in the ''official'' art world of early nineteenth-century France. In terms of archaeology, he was not an excavator, and his books and papers provide one of the last examples of the exclusively armchair approach to the elucidation of the past that had characterized French studies in the eighteenth century, in the works of *Montfaucon and the Comte de *Caylus. If neoclassicism has (at least in France) overtones of establishment approval as a suitable style for public art, then Quatremère's range of interests and his attitudes declare him an establishment figure—although occasionally a vociferous one, as his protests against *Napoleon's pillage of artworks from Rome and other cities (in letters to Gerneral Miranda, 1796) make clear.

But his writings are his chief claim to fame—writings that, as Raoul-Rochette

accurately observed in 1830, dwell on reconstructing lost monuments rather than interpreting existing or rediscovered ones, for example, in books like *Le Jupiter olympien*, 1815, in which he enabled archaeologists to understand the largely lost art form of the chryselephantine statue as it appeared in Pheidias's *Zeus of Olympia, or his *Monuments . . . restitués*, 1829. Although he did pioneering work in introducing neglected topics to the educated public (such as the use of polychromy in antiquity or the disadvantages of removing material from its setting in order to form museums), his concern with the Greek ideal was antiquarian rather than historical. If his reconstructions show preoccupations with atmosphere and local color that are incipiently Romantic, his classical interest ensured that he did not devote his energies to national antiquities, which were to be the main preoccupation of research efforts in nineteenth-century France.
BIBLIOGRAPHY

R. Schneider, *Quatremère de Quincy et son intervention dans les arts* (Paris, 1910); A. Momigliano, ''Ancient History and the Antiquarian,'' *JWarb* 13 (1950), 285–315; M. Greenhalgh, ''Quatremère de Quincy as a Popular Archaeologist,'' *GBA* 71 (1968), 249–56; *Porträtarchiv*, no. 132.

MICHAEL GREENHALGH AND NANCY T. DE GRUMMOND

QUEEN OF SWEDEN'S FAUN. See FAUN WITH KID.

QUIRINAL HORSE TAMERS (ALEXANDER AND BUCEPHALUS; DIOSCURI). Colossal marble sculpture group (over eighteen feet high) of two nude male figures reining in two horses, perhaps dating ca. A.D. 200–225.

In antiquity the group may have adorned the *Baths of Constantine on the Quirinal Hill in Rome; they remained on the hill throughout the Middle Ages and stand today, erected anew with an ancient *obelisk and a Renaissance fountain, in the middle of the Piazza del Quirinale. Although they have been traditionally identified by their inscriptions as the works of Pheidias and Praxiteles, they are undoubtedly not Greek originals, but date to the Imperial era. The present inscriptions are later additions dating to the time of *Sixtus V, perhaps based on Late Antique inscriptions.

There have been various interpretations of the two figures and their horses. A typically medieval explanation occurs in the *Mirabilia urbis Romae:* two naked philosophers named Pheidias and Praxiteles appeared in Rome during the reign of Tiberius. The statues were erected to these wise men, for whom all worldly knowledge is ''naked'' and ''open.'' In the Renaissance a popular identification for a single pair of horse and man was *Alexander and Bucephalus* (proposed by *Panvinio); in the seventeenth century the interpretation was expanded to include Philip of Macedon with his horse beside Alexander and Bucephalus. Others argued that the two horsemen were the Dioscuri, Castor and Pollux, and compared or confused them with the sculptures of the Capitoline *Dioscuri*, discovered ca. 1560. The interpretation as the Dioscuri was to become the most popular—indeed, the only—identification from ca. 1800 on.

Between 1589 and 1591 Sixtus V had the statues restored, setting them on pedestals with the fountain between them. Under *Pius VI the statues were rearranged (1783–86), and the obelisk, which formerly stood near the *Mausoleum of Augustus, was set up with them.

Since the *Horse Tamers* were among the monuments of ancient Rome never buried, their influence was immense. They are mentioned in nearly all medieval descriptions of Rome, for example, the *Einsiedeln Itinerary, and were used as a guide for the location of other monuments. They even gave their name to the hill on which they stand, Monte Cavallo. During the tenth century they provided a sobriquet for one of the Crescenzi family, known as Crescentius Caballi Marmorei. They are depicted in the manuscript of Fazio degli Uberti's poem *Dittamondo* (1350 to 1367) and act as a point of reference in the *Circular View of Rome* by Taddeo di Bartolo in the Palazzo Pubblico, Siena, as well as in Antonio *Lafréry's *Speculum romanae magnificentiae* (1546–50). They were drawn and painted by Marten van *Heemskerck, and *Raphael introduced the horse head from the "Pheidias" pair into his *Galatea*. *Michelangelo, after measuring the statues, probably used them as prototypes for the *David*. They also reappear in the seventeenth century in the horses of Marly by Coustou in the Place de la Concorde. *Shelley described them in a letter to Thomas Peacock in March 1819.

BIBLIOGRAPHY

M. Santangelo, "Il Quirinale nell'antichità classica," *MemPontAcc* 5, 2 (1941), 203–8; +M. R. Scherer, *Marvels of Ancient Rome* (New York, 1955), 137–38; Haskell—Penny, 136–41; Sheard, nos. 47–48; +L. Nista, ed., *Castores, L'Immagine dei Dioscuri a Roma*, catalog of exhibition (Rome, 1994), 193–214.

ELIZABETH R. MEANEY

R

RAFFAELLO SANZIO. See RAPHAEL SANZIO.

RAIMONDI, MARCANTONIO (1475/80–1527/34). Italian artist, known for his engravings after *Raphael and the antique.

Little is known of the life of Marcantonio Raimondi. Born near Bologna, he is believed to have visited Venice in 1506 and then proceeded via Florence to Rome. By 1511, he was making engravings from drawings by Raphael and members of his workshop; after Raphael's death, he worked chiefly for *Giulio Romano. Among his assistants was Marco *Dente, also noted for his engravings of antiquities. Raimondi survived the Sack of Rome in 1527, but by 1534 he was dead.

The artist reveals a vigorous output of drawings and engravings of antiquities and antique themes. An early engraving of *Mars, Venus and Cupid* (1508) shows a remarkable understanding of the construction and dynamics of the turning male body, perhaps under the influence of *Michelangelo and the *Belvedere Torso. The *Dido* of ca. 1510 and the *Lucretia* of ca. 1511 show a similar fascination with torsion, this time of the female figure. The *Lucretia* has been linked with a statue evidently of similar pose, discovered ca. 1500 and identified as Lucretia by Giovanni de' Medici (later, *Leo X). On both the *Dido* and the *Lucretia,* he displayed his learning by including Greek inscriptions.

Raimondi made various engravings of famous antiquities, such as the *Belvedere *Apollo,* the *Spinario* and the *Marcus Aurelius* Equestrian Statue. He produced an archaeologically precise drawing of the great Trajanic frieze from the *Arch of Constantine (1520s), with only subtle differences from the original, such as making the gestures more emphatic and increasing the volume and power of the figures; such modest variations are common in the copies of Raimondi.

Showing more of a departure from the original antiquities are several engravings of sarcophagi. One of these, based on a Raphael drawing, shows the blending of two different sarcophagi having the theme of the *Judgment of Paris* (Villa Medici and Villa Pamphili, Rome), setting the whole within a well-developed landscape. One of the first prints made in Rome by Raimondi, it was immensely popular, its influence extending down to the composition of the *Dejeuner sur l'herbe* of Manet (1863). Raphael may have done the preliminary drawings for an engraving by Marcantonio of a *Marriage* sarcophagus in the church of San Lorenzo fuori le Mura; here, selected figures were removed from the composition and depicted standing in a niche. Another print, reproducing a sarcophagus with a *Lion Hunt,* which stood in the forecourt of the old church of St. Peter, has the addition of trees and the changing of details in the animals. His creativity with a theme from ancient architecture is seen in Raimondi's amusing rendering of a two-story façade with female figures as the supports (Caryatids) on the upper story and male figures (Telamones) on the lower.

BIBLIOGRAPHY

G. Becatti, "Raphael and Antiquity," in *The Complete Works of Raphael* (New York, 1969), 491–568; Sheard, esp. 102; I. H. Shoemaker et al., *The Engravings of Marcantonio Raimondi,* catalog of exhibition (Lawrence, KS, 1981); Bober—Rubinstein, esp. 466.

RANDALL-MacIVER, DAVID (1873–1945). English archaeologist, specialist in later Italian prehistory.

Randall-MacIver is best known for two influential syntheses: *Villanovans and Early Etruscans* (1924) and *The Iron Age in Italy* (1927). They introduced a generation of English and American readers to contemporary research in a still unfamiliar field. Slighter treatments of related themes are *The Etruscans* (1927), *Italy Before the Romans* (1928) and *Greek Cities in Italy and Sicily* (1931). The positive value of Randall-MacIver's approach to Italian archaeology is certainly not outweighed by occasional oversimplification and may best be summarized in his own words: "[I]f there are still scholars who protest that such things are not worth knowing, they can no longer have any excuse for asserting them to be unknowable." It is, however, unfortunate that the very title of Randall-MacIver's first Italian study gave wide currency to "the Villanovans" and to the illegitimate juxtaposition of this modern ethnic construct with the *Tyrsenoi* of ancient writers. Randall-MacIver adhered firmly to a Lydian theory of Etruscan origins in his last published statement (*American Journal of Archaeology,* 1943).

By the time he reached Italy in 1921, Randall-MacIver had acquired a wide (and prolifically published) variety of archaeological experience. In 1905, his investigations at Zimbabwe effectively disposed of alleged Phoenician connections—his report was entitled *Medieval Rhodesia* (1906). Between 1907 and 1911, his excavations in Nubia were the first to reveal the existence of the Meroitic culture. From 1911 until the outbreak of World War I, he was librarian of the American Geographical Society in New York, where he died in 1945.

BIBLIOGRAPHY

H. Hencken, "David Randall-MacIver," *AJA* 49 (1945), 359–60; D. Ridgway, "David Randall-MacIver 1873–1945," *ProcBrAc* 69 (1983), 559–77.

DAVID RIDGWAY

RAPHAEL (RAFFAELLO) SANZIO (1483–1520). Italian painter, designer and architect.

Raphael, born in Umbria and trained as a painter in Florence, reached his full development as an artist in papal Rome, under the pontificates of *Julius II (1503–13) and *Leo X (1513–21). A painter of marvelous facility and synthetic power, he quickly became the most popular artist in the Rome of Julius II, his reputation established by two frescoes for a room in the papal suite, the Stanza della Segnatura. These paintings, the *Disputa del Sacramento* (1508–9) and the *School of Athens* (1509–10), present the Renaissance Church as the culmination of biblical and classical prophecy, history, religion and philosophy. Their powerful evocation of the ancient classical world reflects Raphael's close attention, from the beginning of his stay in Rome, to the city's standing ruins, an attention that would become increasingly sophisticated and increasingly critical as the artist reached maturity.

If the spirit of Raphael's classicism was forged under the papacy of Julius II, it is Julius's successor, Leo X Medici, who fostered the development of the artist's archaeological studies. For Raphael himself, the greatest stimulus was probably his appointment, in 1514, as architect of St. Peter's basilica. Most of his work on the ruins of ancient Rome has the ulterior purpose of devising a new architectural style for this highly symbolic project, one that will create a seamless harmony between the formal elegance of the ancients and the content of Christian revelation. In addition, however, Leo commissioned a thorough study of Rome's extant ancient remains that would lead to reconstruction drawings for these monuments; from this enterprise a few drawings survive in the hand of Raphael's sometime collaborator, Antonio da *Sangallo the Younger, as well as a general description of the project couched in the form of a letter from Raphael to the pope (in which, however, neither the pope nor the writer of the letter is explicitly named). The original nucleus of the letter was drafted with the help of the Mantuan humanist Baldassare Castiglione; it was subsequently revised with the help of another humanist, Angelo *Colocci. In addition to valuable information about the state of archaeological monuments in early sixteenth-century Rome, it stands as a significant monument in the development of critical method for the study of art and archaeology, as it introduces two concepts that have been wholly integrated into modern analysis of art: period style and the classical orders.

The beginning of the letter laments the destruction of ancient ruins at the hands of not only barbarian attackers and humble lime burners but also the popes themselves, who had systematically mined the ruins for stone since the Middle Ages. It then proceeds to describe the differences in architectural style from ancient times to the sixteenth-century present. The greatest achievements, in terms of both visual splendor and sumptuous materials, had belonged to the ancient Romans; the barbarian invasions heralding the Middle Ages led to an architecture as miserable as the standard of living of the people who built it (Raphael uses the term "Gothic" to describe this early medieval style). Ultimately, however, medieval builders devised an attractive style that Raphael terms "German" (to which modern art historians apply the term "Gothic"); although building "in the German manner" falls short of the ancients' standards, it resembles ancient architecture in deriving its ornamentation from the imitation of nature, for the pointed arch mimics the intertwining branches of trees. Only the recent work of architects like Donato *Bramante begins to equal the quality of ancient buildings, and these fall short of the ancients in the value of their materials. Noting the consistency of classical style throughout the many vicissitudes of ancient Rome, Raphael cites the *Arch of Constantine as an example of how architecture preserved its integrity long after sculptural technique had lost what he terms its *maniera*—a word whose meaning falls somewhere between "style" and "elegance." The reconstruction of ancient Rome on paper, he argues, will allow the pope to revive good *maniera* in the present day; and, the letter continues, good classical *maniera* derives, in turn, from the five orders of architecture: Doric, Ionic, Corinthian, Tuscan and Attic. (By the latter Raphael means square piers, which are to be seen sustaining the arches of the *Colosseum and every other arcuated concrete structure in the Eternal City.) The influence of this short document on the systematic study of art and architecture has been immense, despite the fact that it was never combined with the book of reconstruction drawings it had been intended to preface. Within a generation, the terminology of classical architecture would be irrevocably changed to include the Five Orders in place of the indeterminate number of loose *genera,* or "families," described by Vitruvius and Early Renaissance writers. The idea that style shifts with time would be applied with increasing precision to the study of art, and eventually art historians would associate Raphael's term "Gothic" with buildings designed in what he himself calls the "German manner."

Of less significant import to intellectual history are various curial posts, nominally involving inspection of antiquities, that Raphael held under Leo X: *maestro delle strade* and *soprintendente;* these were probably lucrative sinecures as much as real responsibilities, especially for a man as overextended as Raphael had become by 1514.

*Vasari's biography of Raphael, written a generation after the artist's premature death in 1520, supplies a vivid account of Raphael as an entrepreneurial *maestro* whose relentless curiosity about antiquities propelled members of his workshop as far away as Greece to seek them out and report back to the great artist. The account may be somewhat exaggerated in factual detail, but in its sense of the energy emanating from the Raphael workshop, Vasari's report, drawn from interviews with Raphael's former pupils and contemporaries, is probably entirely accurate. In one documented and probably representative instance, Raphael took a trip to *Tivoli with the humanists *Bembo, Navagero and Beazzano to study the antiquities in *Hadrian's Villa and the other ruined Roman villas dotting the countryside nearby. In this journey, as in the letter to Pope Leo X, the artist can be seen keeping company with the most acute intellects of his day, his skill with hand and eye apparently a good match for the refinement of their Latin.

Surprisingly few drawings of actual monuments by the hand of Raphael survive (only of the *Pantheon; Uffizi, Florence, and Royal Institute of British Architects, London); a few quite precise renderings of monuments appear in his paintings and tapestry designs—the Colosseum in the *Meeting of Leo X and Attila* in the Stanza di Eliodoro, Vatican; the tomb of Annia Regilla in the *Stoning of St. Stephen* in the Vatican tapestries; and the *"Temple of Minerva Medica" in a fresco in the Stanza della Segnatura. Nonetheless, it is clear that the most powerful expression of Raphael's response to antiquity is left to his art, in which he continued to combine the *maniera* of the ancients, understood in ever-increasing depth, with the content of a Christian present. The simultaneous challenge to his capacities for visual organization and invention represented by the "grotesque" style of ancient Roman painting (*grottesche*), revealed in all its complexity by the opening of Nero's *Domus Aurea (Golden House) to exploration in the 1470s, resulted in Raphael's mastery both of grotesque decoration and of the recipe for ancient stucco in the Logge Vaticane executed for Pope Leo in 1518. Yet a significant part of this decorative scheme is called, for its narration of the Old and New Testaments, "Raphael's Bible." It is a Bible enclosed in a classical framework, symbolic of Rome's past as the center of an ancient empire and the Vatican's significance within Christendom. Raphael's marble-clad funeral chapel for the wealthy merchant Agostino Chigi, first designed in 1513, revised ca. 1519 and never finished, creates a miniature Pantheon for a Christian Augustus. Raphael's greatest achievement was to make classical style accessible to a new generation of artists and patrons, expressive to new ends, and thereby to validate the study of the ancient world in the refreshed creativity of the modern.

BIBLIOGRAPHY

F. A. Gruyer, *Raphaël et l'antiquité* (Paris, 1864); +G. Becatti, "Raphael and Antiquity" and F. Castagnoli, "Raphael and Ancient Rome," in *The Complete Work of Raphael* (New York, 1969), 491–568, 569–84; H. Burns—A. Nesselrath, "Raffaello e l'antico," in *Raffaello architetto* (Milan, 1984), 379–452; C. Thoenes, "La 'lettera' a Leone X," in *Raffaello a Roma: il Convegno del 1983* (Rome, 1986), 373–81; I. D. Rowland, "Raphael, Angelo Colocci and the Genesis of the Architectural Orders," *ArtB,* 76 (1994), 81–104.

INGRID ROWLAND

RASPE, RUDOLF ERICH (1737–94). German mineralogist, art historian, translator and antiquarian.

Born in Hanover, Raspe studied at the universities in Göttingen and Leipzig and was named professor of archaeology in Cassel (1767) and keeper of the antique gems and medals collected by the Landgrave of Hesse. Ostensibly going to Italy for the Landgrave, he absconded with part of his lord's collection and fled to England (1775), where he did mining engineering as well as research in art history.

He is most famous as the presumed author of *Baron Munchausen's Narrative of His Travels & Campaigns in Russia* (1785). At the time he was then already employed by James *Tassie to catalog his large collection of antique and modern gemstone reproductions. In 1788 Raspe went mineral prospecting in northern Scotland, during which excursion it became clear he was making strikes he had himself planted; he fled to Ireland, where he died.

Raspe had a brilliant mind to match his shabby morals. Among his many publications are the *Account of the Present State and Arrangement of Mr. James Tassie's Collection of... Ancient and Modern Gems* (London, 1786) and the *Descriptive Catalogue of a General Collection of Ancient and Modern Engraved Gems... by James Tassie Modeller* (London, 1791).

BIBLIOGRAPHY
Depping, "Raspe (Rudolphe-Eric)," *BU* 37 (1824), 119–20; R. Hallo, *Rudolf Erich Raspe, ein Wegbereiter von deutscher Art und Kunst* (Stuttgart, 1934); L. Stephen—S. Lee, "Raspe, Rudolf Erich," *DNB* 16 (1973), 744–46.

J. S. TASSIE

REALE ACCADEMIA ERCOLANESE. See ACADEMIA HERCULANEN-SIS.

"REGISOLE." Over-lifesize Roman equestrian statue, made of gilded bronze, destroyed in 1796.

The statue takes its name *"Regisole"* from the quarter of Ravenna where it evidently originally stood. (The quarter was called by this name in the tenth and eleventh centuries.) It was removed from Ravenna and transferred to Pavia, where it stood in the courtyard of the Palazzo Reale before 1024. At the beginning of the twelfth century, it was set up in front of the cathedral at Pavia on a column, as recorded in a drawing by Opicino de *Canistris (early fourteenth century) and described in the *Chronicon* of *Benzo d'Alessandria (ca. 1320). The statue was regarded by the citizens of Pavia as a symbol of the city's glory, and they objected bitterly when it was briefly transferred to Milan (1315–35). *Petrarch admired the work (1365) and observed that the masters of painting and sculpture regarded the *Regisole* as second to no other work.

In 1527 a youth from Ravenna attempted to steal the statue and ship it to Ravenna, but it never arrived; it was seized at Cremona and there the piece remained until 1552. Then it was returned to Pavia, underwent restoration and was put back on its pedestal before the cathedral. It was on display there until it was brutally destroyed by the French during their invasion of Italy in 1796.

The original appearance of the lost statue is known from various reproductions, most important of which is a silver seal made in 1532 in Pavia. It shows a figure very similar to the *Marcus Aurelius* Equestrian statue in Rome, with the rider represented in military tunic and cloak and with the right hand raised in a gesture of greeting. The left front hoof of the horse was raised and rested lightly, but artificially, on the image of a puppy standing on its hind legs, probably a medieval addition. Spurs on the rider's heels and long pants may also have been added later.

Various identities have been proposed for the emperor portrayed, who wore a short beard and had curly hair. These are seen mostly on emperors of the second and third centuries A.C. (Antoninus Pius, Marcus Aurelius, Lucius Verus, Septimius Severus, Aurelian). Later dating has also been proposed in connection with an identification of Odoacer (fifth century), Theodoric (sixth century) and Justinian (sixth century), though the beard would be inappropriate for the latter two.

BIBLIOGRAPHY

G. Bovini, "Le Vicende del 'Regisole,' statua equestre ravennate," *Felix Ravenna,* ser. 3, fasc. 36 (1963), 138–54.

REGOLINI-GALASSI TOMB, Cerveteri. Spectacular unplundered Etruscan tomb of the Orientalizing period (seventh century B.C.).

Father Alessandro Regolini and General Vincenzo Galassi were drawn together by their common interest in antiquities and entered into a partnership to explore for Etruscan remains in the countryside surrounding Cerveteri. Regolini was the local priest; Galassi was a general in the pontifical army who had served in Lazio. Their explorations at Cerveteri (ancient Caere) led to one of the most remarkable discoveries in the history of Etruscan archaeology. The famous Regolini-Galassi Tomb, named after the two amateur archaeologists, was the first in a series of important *Etruscan tombs discovered and excavated during the nineteenth century.

On 22 April 1836, Regolini and Galassi discovered and opened an unplundered tomb, with finds of unbelievable wealth, beneath an imposing tumulus in the Sorbo necropolis. The tomb was one of six that lay beneath the large mound and the only one that had not been plundered by the time of Regolini and Galassi's explorations. The tomb, which is dated to around 650–625 B.C., contained three burials, two males and one female, along with extremely rich grave goods, including superb gold jewelry worked in repoussé and decorated with granulation, silver cups, bronze cauldrons, bronze shields and a remarkable bed with a latticework of strips of bronze to support a mattress. Objects made of ivory, gold and amber, some obviously of non-Italian manufacture, and locally produced items made of imported materials provided evidence for Near Eastern and eastern Mediterranean influences in Etruria.

The contents of the tomb were transferred to the Museo Gregoriano Etrusco (*Vatican Museums), where they were to be displayed with wooden items completely reconstructed. (The bed, e.g., was set in a new wooden wagon, for which

some metal parts of the wheels had survived.) Recently, the finds from the
Regolini-Galassi Tomb have received special attention as the Etruscan museum
at the Vatican was rearranged. Many pieces have been cleaned and/or separated
from the earlier reconstructions. Some of the finds from the Regolini-Galassi
Tomb were sent to the United States to be displayed for the first time, in an
exhibition in Memphis, Dallas and other venues.

BIBLIOGRAPHY

+L. Pareti, *La Tomba Regolini-Galassi del Museo Gregoriano Etrusco e la civiltà
dell'Italia centrale nel secolo VII A.C.* (Rome, 1947); P. Dalla Torre, "Galassi, Vincenzo," *Enciclopedia Cattolica* 5 (1950), 1855–56; +D. J. Hamblin, *The Etruscans* (New
York, 1976), 17–18, 47–55; +F. Buranelli, *The Etruscans: Legacy of a Lost Civilization,*
tr. and ed. N. T. de Grummond, catalog of exhibition (Memphis, 1992), 55, 130–33, 189.

CHERYL L. SOWDER

REVETT, NICHOLAS (1720–1804). English painter, architect and draftsman;
important for his study and illustration of Greek architecture.

Nicholas Revett first visited classical lands when he traveled to Rome in 1742.
There he studied with the Italian painter Cavaliere Benefiale. It has been suggested
that while in Rome, Revett probably acted as cicerone to visiting Englishmen. The
explorer James Dawkins noted in 1815 that "Mr. Revett was considered a very
good judge of the hands of different schools of Italian painting."

In 1748 during a visit to Naples, Revett and his companion James *Stuart
discussed plans of forming an expedition to Greece to conduct an accurate survey of the ancient remains in Athens. The plan was publicly announced that
same year. If not for the support of the *Society of Dilettanti, a group to which
they were eventually elected, the expedition could not have been realized. The
Earl of Malton, the Earl of Charlemont, James Dawkins and Robert *Wood—
all members of the society—aided in financing the project. Another Dilettante,
Sir James Porter, the English ambassador to Constantinople, provided support
and protection for Revett and Stuart while they were in Greece.

In the spring of 1751 Revett and Stuart arrived in Athens. Their research
progressed with a comparatively small amount of difficulty. Revett was responsible for all the architectural measurement, while Stuart produced general topographical views of the city in gouache. By 1755 they had returned to England
in order to initiate the publication of their findings. Support for this final stage
of the project was once again provided by the Dilettanti. Three volumes, entitled
*The Antiquities of Athens Measured and Delineated by James Stuart, F.R.S. and
F.S.A., and Nicholas Revett, Painters and Architects,* were published in 1762,
1789 and 1795. However, prior to the publication of the first volume, Revett's
interest had been bought out by Stuart, who therefore received all of the profits
and most of the credit for the project.

Through his association with the Dilettanti, Revett was involved in a second,
more elaborate expedition. The goal of this project was to record the ancient re-

mains along the coast of Asia Minor. Revett was placed in charge of producing all measured drawings, while topographical drawing was the responsibility of the artist William *Pars, and documentation and description were conducted by Richard *Chandler. The group departed from England in the summer of 1764, and by the fall of 1766 they had conducted their research and returned. The results of the expedition were published by the society in two volumes entitled *The Antiquities of Ionia.* The first volume appeared in 1769, and the second in 1797.

Revett's work made accurate knowledge of Greek architecture available to European scholars and architects. This knowledge not only influenced Revett's style as a practicing architect but also played a major role in ushering in the *Gusto Greco* during the early nineteenth century.

BIBLIOGRAPHY

L. Lawrence, "Stuart and Revett: Their Literary and Architectural Careers," *JWarb* 2 (1938–39), 128–46; D. Wiebenson, *Sources of Greek Revival Architecture* (University Park, PA, 1969); J. N. Crook, *The Greek Revival, Neo-Classical Attitudes in British Architecture 1760–1870* (London, 1972); H. Colvin, *A Biographical Dictionary of British Architects, 1600–1840* (London, 1978), 683–85.

PATRICK ROWE

RHAMNOUS. Greek deme-site and sanctuary of Nemesis.

A fortified hill by the sea served as the northeastern limits of the border of Attika, garrisoned in antiquity. Within have been found traces of a gymnasium and theater; on the hillside opposite lies a small Hellenistic sanctuary of Amphiaraos. A sacred way leads up from the fort, lined on both sides by impressive family grave plots of both Classical and Hellenistic date. Above lies the sanctuary of Nemesis, with its handsome Doric temple of the second half of the fifth century B.C. It measures 21.40m × 10.15m and had a peristyle of 6 × 12 columns, with a pronaos, cella and opisthodomos. From the tooling on steps and columns, it is clear that the building was never finished, and, except for the acroteria, the temple carried no sculptural decoration. Within stood the cult statue done by Agorakritos, pieces of which have been recovered and mended, together with the sculpted base. In 45/6 A.D. the temple was rededicated to the deified Livia. To the south lay a small *oikos* generally identified as a Late Archaic temple of Themis.

The temple site was first published by the *Society of the Dilettanti in 1822, and further work was carried out for the *Greek Archaeological Society under Philios (1880), Stais (1890–94) and *Orlandos (1922/3). In 1954 Pouilloux studied the fortress, and since 1975 the temple site and sacred way have been meticulously studied by a team under the direction of B. Petrakos.

BIBLIOGRAPHY

Society of Dilettanti, *The Unedited Antiquities of Attica* (London, 1817); J. Pouilloux, *La Fortresse de Rhamnoute* (Paris, 1954); B. Petrakos, *Rhamnous, A Concise Guide* (Athens, 1983); idem, "Oi Anaskaphes tou Rhamnountos," *ArchEph* (1987), 267, 298;

idem, *To Nemesion tou Rhamnountos* 2 (Athens, 1987); M. Miles, "A Reconstruction of the Temple of Nemesis at Rhamnous," *Hesperia* 58 (1989), 133–249.

JOHN McK. CAMP II

RHODES. Large island in the eastern Aegean Sea.

Rhodes lies on important ancient trade routes from Egypt to Asia Minor and from *Cyprus to Greece. Originally occupied by Carians and Phoenicians, it was colonized by *Argos and became a rich center during Mycenaean times. In Archaic times the island supported three major cities: Lindos, Ialysos and Kamiros, which seem to have lived in uncharacteristic harmony. The island became a rich and major sea power and trading center, founded several colonies and produced a handsome local pottery ("Fikellura"). In the sixth century the island fell under Persian control and, in the fifth century, under Athenian, becoming fully independent only in the fourth century. In 408 B.C. the three cities combined to found a fourth city, Rhodes, at the northeast tip of the island, which soon eclipsed the other three, becoming one of the great and powerful cities of antiquity, as well as a center of learning and the arts.

Caught in the wars of Alexander's successors and allied with Ptolemy, the city was the object of a long and eventually unsuccessful siege (304 B.C.) by Demetrios Poliorcetes. From the spoils of this siege the famous *Colossos was built. It and the city were overthrown by a massive earthquake in 227/6 B.C. (Polybios 5.88). The city was soon rebuilt, and trade flourished in Hellenistic times. Rhodian wine jars have been found by the thousands at Athens and *Alexandria. An early ally of Rome, Rhodes was besieged by Mithridates in 88 B.C., and in 42 B.C., during the Roman civil war, it was seized and plundered by Cassius, who sent some 3,000 statues back to Rome. Thereafter, it was absorbed into the Roman Empire, later drawing a series of invaders through the ages: Isaurians (A.D. 470), Persians (620), Saracens (654), Venetians (1099, 1125), Genoese (1240), and, finally, the knights of St. John, who occupied the island from 1309 until driven out by Suleiman the Magnificent in 1522.

Archaeological work has been carried out in several places on the island. Lindos, the most significant city before the foundation of Rhodes, was the site of the temple of Athena Lindia, and the people of Lindos were said to be the first to worship Athena, thereby earning themselves a shower of gold from Zeus. The sanctuary stands on a spectacular crag overlooking the sea and was excavated from 1902 to 1914 and in 1952 by Danish scholars (Blinkenberg and Dyggve; cf. *National Museum, Copenhagen). Some 3,250 small votives, dozens of statues and over 700 inscriptions were found. The Early Archaic votives came from Sicily, South Italy, Egypt, Persia and Cyprus. The earliest temple, dated to the seventh century, had a cult statue that was an unworked plank of wood. The second, dated to the time of the tyrant Kleoboulos (ca. 570–530 B.C.), had a seated cult statue of green stone from Egypt. The temple was burned in the 340s B.C. and replaced almost immediately by a third, Doric and amphiprostyle in plan. The temple was approached through a long Doric stoa with projecting wings, dated ca. 200 B.C., that led up a monumental stairway to the propylaia with five doors, dating ca. 300 B.C. Stoa and temple were heavily restored by the Italians early in the twentieth century. Of the city, little is preserved except the rock-cut steps of a theater, a large square building of unknown function and numerous parapet blocks from a fountainhouse. Outside, there is a Hellenistic cemetery with rock-cut tombs.

Kamiros, lying on the west coast, was first excavated by Salzman and Biliotti in 1859 and then by Italian archaeologists under *Maiuri and Jacopi from 1929 on. The excavations have revealed the cemetery and much of the town site, including several blocks of houses, a sanctuary with monolithic altars of various gods, a large Archaic cistern and a Doric stoa (third century B.C.) over 200m long, making it among the largest known.

Ialysos was also excavated by the Italians, who uncovered extensive cemeteries, a fourth-century Doric temple of Athena and Zeus Polieus and a very well preserved small Doric fountain. Not far away were the Doric *naiskos* of Apollo Erethimios (ca. 400 B.C.) and a theater of the fourth century.

The ancient city of Rhodes itself lies under the modern town and is less well known, though rescue excavations by the members of the *Greek Archaeological Service have confirmed the regular "Hippodamian" grid plan of the city. On the acropolis above are the remains (heavily restored by the Italians) of the Doric temple of Apollo Pythias, a small theater and a stadium.

BIBLIOGRAPHY

C. Torr, *Rhodes in Ancient Times* (Cambridge, 1885); C. Blinkenberg—E. Dyggve, *Lindos* 1–3 (Berlin, 1931–60); G. Jacopi et al., *Clara Rhodos* 1–9 (Bergamo, 1928–49); J. Currie, *Rhodes and the Dodecanese* (London, 1972).

JOHN McK. CAMP II

RIACE WARRIORS. Two nude, over-lifesize bronze statues of warriors (each is nearly 2m tall), believed by many to be rare examples of Greek originals of the fifth century B.C.

The two stand in similar relaxed poses, their shields and spears now lost. Warrior "A," a younger man, wears a fillet that also once had a wreath attached; Warrior "B" wore a helmet, now missing. Analysis of the bronze alloy shows that a similar formula was used for the two statues, but the arms of "B" were restored using an alloy with added lead.

The two sculptures were discovered in 1972 in waters twenty-five feet deep, off the coast of Riace Marina in Southern Italy, by a skindiver who was on vacation from his job in Rome. The heavily encrusted bronzes underwent expert restoration at the center for archaeological restoration in Florence, under the direction of F. Nicosia, before going on display to astonished crowds in Florence and Rome in 1981. The statues have now been returned to Southern Italy, to be displayed in the National Museum of Reggio Calabria.

Modern scholars have reached few final conclusions about the statues. B. Ridgway has argued that the statues are no earlier than the first century B.C., and are merely classicizing, but most believe they are the work of a major master of the fifth century B.C. (Pheidias, Myron, Onatas and Alkamenes have all been proposed). It is generally thought that the statues represent heroes (from the Trojan War or the Eponymous Heroes of Attica; one argument is that they are *hoplitodromoi*—runners in the armed race). Their original location is not known, though Athens, Delphi, Olympia and Lokroi have all been proposed.

BIBLIOGRAPHY

C. Houser, "The Riace Marina Bronze Statues, Classical or Classicizing?" *Source* I.3 (Spring 1982), 5–11; +L. Vlad Borrelli—P. Pelagatti, eds., *Due bronzi da Riace, rinvenimento, restauro, analisi ed ipotesi d'interpretazione, BdA,* ser. speciale 3 (Rome, 1984); J. Marcadé, "Rapports techniques et publications archéologiques: A propos des bronzes de Riace," *RA* (1986), 89–100.

RICCI, CORRADO (1858–1934). Italian archaeologist and administrator.

Born at Ravenna, Ricci studied painting but graduated in law at Bologna (1882). After working in libraries, he had an illustrious career as art curator: director of the galleries of Parma (1893) and Modena (1894–97); superintendent of monuments at Ravenna (1897–98); director of the Brera at Milan (1898–1903); and, finally, director of the galleries and museum in Florence (1903–6). He ended his career as director-general of antiquities and fine arts in Italy (1906–19). In the same month that he "retired," he was elected the first president of the Institute of Archaeology in Rome, established in the Palazzo Venezia in 1922.

Ricci's term as director-general coincided with most of the time that Giacomo *Boni was in charge of excavations in the *Forum Romanum and on the *Palatine (1898–1925). Other major undertakings were the clearing of the *Baths of Diocletian and systematization of the *Baths of Caracalla. Ricci's own major contribution to Roman archaeology, however, was the spectacular mapping of the *Imperial Fora (1911), the genius of which was revealed by the excavations from 1924, which included also the Forum of Caesar. Ricci was vice president of the excavation committee. He also served as president of the committee for the recovery of the ships of *Nemi.

His main archaeological publications—apart from *Il Mercato di Traiano* (1929) and *Via dell'Impero* (1933)—are his reports in *Capitolium,* 1 (1925) and following.

BIBLIOGRAPHY

In memoria di Corrado Ricci, Istituto Nazionale di Archeologia e Storia d'Arte (1935); R. T. Ridley, *"Augusti manes volitant per auras:* The Archaeology of Rome under the Fascists," *Xenia* 11 (1986), 19–46.

R. T. RIDLEY

RICHARDSON, JONATHAN (1665–1745). English portrait painter and art critic; he collaborated with his son JONATHAN RICHARDSON the Younger (1694–1771), also an artist, in his writings on art.

Active in London as a portrait painter of good reputation, Richardson was also highly esteemed as a writer and art critic. Though most of his writing is on painting—its theory, history and practitioners—he published one important work relevant for the history of classical archaeology. His son Jonathan compiled information during a tour on the Continent, to be edited by the father, for a treatise called *An Account of the Statues and Bas-Reliefs, Drawings and Pictures in Italy, France &c, with Remarks* (1722; 2nd ed., 1754). The treatise appeared with other works by the Richardsons in a French translation, with expanded comments, in volume 3 of *Traité de la peinture et de la sculpture* (Amsterdam, 1728). Its influence and prestige were considerable; *Winckelmann remarked (1764) that the *Account* was the best book to be had on the subject.

The Richardsons are noted for their commonsense approach to antique sculpture. They read what ancient authors said, looked closely at the statuary and the extant artists' signatures and concluded correctly, but contrary to received opinion, that no major works by major sculptors (such as Pheidias, Polykleitos, Lysippos, Praxiteles) were to be seen in their time. In addition, they astutely determined the significance of multiple versions of a statue—not that one was the original, and the others were copies, but that all were probably copies of one lost original.

The Richardsons also had the good idea to look for copies of lost originals on ancient coins and gems; they were the first to note that the *Knidian *Aphrodite* from the Belvedere resembled an image of the famous statue by Praxiteles as shown on a coin of Caracalla. They made wide-ranging comments on iconography (the "*Seated Agrippina*" in the *Capitoline was identified as Poppaea Sabina), style (the Giustiniani *Minerva* had a stiff nature) and technical questions (the inlaid eyes of the *Capitoline *Brutus* produced a disagreeable effect). The younger Richardson was ardent in pursuit of viewing opportunities, spending ten hours looking at the *Medici *Venus* and scaling a wall to look at a version of *"*Cleopatra*" in the Villa Medici. Careful observation led to far-reaching conclusions about discrepancies in quality (e.g., of the *Niobe* Group and the *Farnese *Bull*) and the likelihood of copyism.

BIBLIOGRAPHY

L. H. Cust, "Richardson, Jonathan," *DNB* 16 (1896; repr. 1949–50), 1122–24; Haskell—Penny, esp. 99–100.

RICHMOND, Sir IAN ARCHIBALD (1902–65). English archaeologist, specialist in Roman provincial studies.

The subject of Richmond's postgraduate research at the *British School at Rome was *The City Wall of Imperial Rome* (1930). This brought him into fruitful contact with Thomas *Ashby, whom he succeeded as the school's director and whose posthumous *Aqueducts of Ancient Rome* (1935) he completed. Based in Newcastle upon Tyne (Pons Aelius) from 1935, Richmond's skillful investigations of Romano-British sites molded a brilliant school of military studies. His status as the heir of F. J. Haverfield and R. G. Collingwood was confirmed by his translation in 1956 to a new chair at Oxford, where his later interests included Masada, North Africa, *Palmyra, Scotland and Spain.

BIBLIOGRAPHY

H. von Petrikovits, obituary tribute to IAR's 1955 "Roman Britain and Roman Military Antiquities," *Germania* 43 (1965), 425–28; E. Birley, "Sir Ian Archibald Richmond 1902–1965," *ProcBrAc* 52 (1966), 293–302; I. A. Richmond, collected essays, *Roman Archaeology and Art,* ed. P. Salway (London, 1969).

DAVID RIDGWAY

RICHTER, GISELA M. A. (1882–1972). German-American archaeologist and art historian.

Born in a German and English tradition of literary and art-historical scholarship, Gisela Richter was encouraged at an early age to pursue a career in classical archaeology. Well prepared through her training at Girton College (Cambridge) and at the *British School in Athens, she became one of the first women to join the staff of the *Metropolitan Museum in New York, where she was to become chief curator of Greek and Roman art (1925–48). She considered herself a "museum archaeologist" whose responsibility was to assess the existing collections and to make judicious acquisitions of Greek, Roman and Etruscan objects. Her concern with making ancient art come alive to scholars and to the public was manifested in museum catalogs and in comprehensive works on Greek art, sculpture in particular.

Gisela Richter's approach to ancient art focused on the theory of a gradual development from a stylized to a naturalistic rendering of the human body as a means of establishing a relative and absolute chronology. Her *Handbook of Greek Art* and *Sculpture and Sculptors of the Greeks* exemplify the clarity and analytical overview that characterized her scholarship, carried out in her long and fruitful career at the Metropolitan Museum and, after her retirement, at the *American Academy in Rome.

BIBLIOGRAPHY

+G.M.A. Richter, *My Memoirs: Recollections of an Archaeologist's Life* (Rome, 1972); B. Conticello, "Gisela M. A. Richter," *Colloqui del sodalizio: Sodalizio tra studiosi dell'arte,* 2nd ser. 4 (1973–74), 21–31, +I.E.M. Edlund—A. M. McCann—C. R. Sherman, "Gisela Maria Augusta Richter (1882–1972): Scholar of Classical Art and Museum Archaeologist," *Women as Interpreters of the Visual Arts, 1820–1979,* ed. C. R. Sherman with A. M. Holcomb (Westport, CT, 1981), 275–300.

INGRID E. M. EDLUND

RIEGL, ALOIS (1858–1905). Austrian art historian, formulator of a powerful and influential theory on the nature of late Roman art and the cycles of style in art; in his relatively short life he studied a remarkable variety of art-historical phenomena, including Oriental carpets, Late Antique metalwork and seventeenth-century Dutch group portraiture.

Riegl began as a student of law and history at Vienna University, turning to art history and theory after he became a member of the Institut für Geschichtsforschungen (Institute for Historical Research). Following graduation, he was appointed curator of textiles at the Österreichisches Museum, the Vienna Museum of Arts and Crafts. In 1897 he became professor at Vienna University, having *Wickhoff—another great theorist of Roman art—as his colleague.

Riegl's major contribution to the study of classical antiquity, *Spätrömische Kunstindustrie* ("Late Roman Arts and Crafts"), appeared in 1901 (repr. Vienna, 1926). Here he discussed the development and changing aesthetics of the "Late Roman" period, introducing his controversial theory on the continuity of art; for him Late Antique art was not an aberration from earlier developments but a natural consequence of them. It was the end product of an evolution from "tactile" to "optical" values. While his opponents condemned this period as a debasement due to barbarian influence, Riegl viewed it as representative of an evolved aesthetic. Especially novel and difficult to understand was his concept of *Kunstwollen* (translated variously as "artistic will," "will-to-form" and "that which wills art"), which implies, however it may be translated, that each work of art is embedded in the culture from which it comes.

Riegl's theories, disputed in his own time and still today, have had great influence. His German prose is difficult to translate into other languages and has been a barrier to knowledge of his theories outside German-speaking countries. His ideas have become more accessible with the recent translation of *Spätrömische Kunstindustrie* into English by Rolf Winkes as *Late Roman Art Industry* (Rome, 1985).

BIBLIOGRAPHY
M. Dvořák, "Alois Riegl," in *Gesammelte Aufsätze* (Munich, 1929), 279; M. Schapiro, "Style," in *Anthropology Today* (Chicago, 1953), 301–3; O. Pächt, "Art Historians and Art Critics, VI: Alois Riegl," *BurlMag* 105 (1963), 188–93; H. Zerner, "Alois Riegl: Art, Value and Historicism," *Daedalus* 105 (Winter 1976), 177–78.

SHELLIE WILLIAMS

RIJKSMUSEUM VAN OUDHEDEN (NATIONAL MUSEUM OF ANTIQUITIES), Leiden. Important collection of antiquities in the Netherlands, including Greek and Roman material from early Dutch collections.

The Rijksmuseum van Oudheden contains archaeological finds from the ancient civilizations of Egypt and the Near East and of Greece, Etruria and Rome, as well as local prehistorical and Roman material found in the Netherlands. The museum was founded in 1818 by King William I with a core of material from the Rijksuniversiteit of Leiden, including the collection of Greek and Roman sculpture of G. van Papenbroek (d. 1743). This assemblage, which, in turn, contained material from the earlier Vendramin and van Reynst collections, had been on display at the university since 1745.

The first director of the museum was C.J.C. Reuvens (1793–1835), who also held the first chair of archaeology at the university. During his tenure, the museum made significant acquisitions of vases and sculpture from Greece through the travels and purchases of Colonel Rottiers (1819–25/6) and of antiquities from

North Africa and Italy through the agency of Colonel Humbert. These collections were augmented by a selection of Greek vases donated by William I,
acquired from the collection of Lucien Bonaparte, Prince of *Canino (1839).
Local antiquities were added through excavations undertaken by Reuvens. Many
of the antiquities were first cataloged by L.J.F. Jansen in the mid-nineteenth
century. Recently the Royal Coin Cabinet (formerly at the Hague) has been
transferred to this museum.

BIBLIOGRAPHY

+J. H. Holwerda, *De Ceramiek van Griekenland en Italie in het Leidsche Museum van
Oudheden,* in *Elsevier's Maandschrift* 31 (1921), nr. 1–2; +J.P.J. Brants, *Description of
the Classical Collection of the Museum of Archaeology of Leiden,* pts. 1–2 (The Hague,
1927, 1930); L. Byvanck-Quarles van Ufford, s.v. "Leida," *EAA* 4 (1961), 537–38; W.
Braat—A. Klasens, *Artefact, 150 jaar Rijksmuseum van Oudheden 1818–1975* (Leiden,
1968); *Mozaiek der antieken, Oog in oog met Grieken, Etrusken en Romeinen. Ancient
art: Greece, Etruria and Rome* (Leiden, 1990).

J. FEIJE

RIPA, CESARE (ca. 1560–before 1625). Italian author of the *Iconologia,* an
iconographic manual that regularly cites classical sources.

Ripa's fame derives solely from this work, which was used for, and now
explains, a great deal of Baroque allegory. Ripa did not present programs—
although the *Elements* and *Seasons,* for example, are conveniently grouped together—but simply cataloged and prescribed the form of a great number of
"necessary" and "useful" personifications—nearly 700 concepts and a thousand images, from *Abundance* to *Zeal,* in the edition of 1603. First published
in Rome in 1593, the *Iconologia* went through many editions and translations;
the text was revised and expanded both by Ripa himself and still further by
friends and publishers. Significantly, it was when illustrations were added in
1603 that the book made a real impact.

In his preface Ripa sets down principles for the proper personification of
abstract ideas, using Aristotelian terms: "accidental" manifestations, such as
someone's hanging himself for *Despair,* are to be avoided, while attributes
should serve only to define essential qualities. In practice, however, the images
in the *Iconologia* are not particularly consistent with these criteria. Most were
not invented by the author but taken over from previous publications—mythological manuals, archaeological compendia, emblem books and descriptions of
festivals. The most important source was Pierio *Valeriano's *Hieroglyphica*
(1556), a virtual encyclopedia of symbolism, conveniently indexed. Valeriano
supplied not only figures and attributes but erudite references and explanations
for images that Ripa had found elsewhere.

The title page to the first edition describes the personifications as "derived from
antiquity" as well as "other places." Certainly, Ripa included available precedents in ancient literature (e.g., descriptions from Pausanias already included in
*Cartari's *Imagini,* 1556). Several figures he relates to reverses of classical coins,

and a few to statues visible in Rome. He was presumably familiar with some of the latter, but his information even here is secondhand, from books. Ripa was not a professional scholar; he tells us that he composed the *Iconologia* in spare moments while working as majordomo to Cardinal Antonio Maria Salviati. If he sometimes consulted the learned dissertations on coins by Sebastiano *Erizzo (1559) and Antonio *Agustín (1587), his aim was not to document the personifications represented in antiquity; the classical repertory he both modified and enormously expanded. The *Iconologia* was intended to appeal to, and satisfy the needs of, contemporary artists, whose interest in allegory was rarely archaeological.

BIBLIOGRAPHY

E. Mâle, *L'Art réligieux après le concile de Trente* (Paris, 1932), 383–428; E. Mandowsky, *Ricerche intorno all'Iconologia di Cesare Ripa* (Florence, 1939); G. Werner, *Ripa's Iconologia: Quellen, Methode, Ziele* (Utrecht, 1977); E. McGrath, "Personifying Ideals," in *Art History* 6 (1983), 363–68; C. Stefani, "Cesare Ripa: New Biographical Evidence," *JWarb* 53 (1990), 307–10; C. Witcombe, "Cesare Ripa and the Sala Clementina," *JWarb* 4 (1992), 277–82.

ELIZABETH McGRATH

RIPANDA (RIMPACTA), JACOPO (fl. 1490–1530). Bolognese painter, leading figure in the copying of monuments of ancient Rome around the beginning of the sixteenth century.

Born in Bologna, Jacopo Ripanda went to Rome at an unknown date. For the palace of the Conservators—the Palazzo dei Conservatori—Ripanda painted a series of frescoes depicting the history of the seven kings of Rome and the early centuries of the Republic (ca. 1503–1508). His authorship of this important commission was regularly ignored by commentators and many of the frescoes were later destroyed.

Ripanda was an early visitor to the *Domus Aurea, among those who descended into the "grottoes" and examined the frescoes by torchlight. A considerably more perilous undertaking was his project to copy the sculptures on the *Column of Trajan. Some time before 1506, Ripanda performed the incredible feat of making drawings of all the reliefs on the column, using a mechanical device that would allow him to go around the column as he ascended (*circum machinis scandendo*). The original drawings are lost, but are known in an early copy now in the Palazzo Venezia, Rome (Biblioteca dell'Istituto Nazionale di Archeologia e Storia dell'Arte, ms. 254) and in other copies. Undoubtedly the originals and the various copies had an immense influence on the later publications on the Column of Trajan, such as those by Muziano and Chacon, and by *Bartoli and *Bellori.

A sketchbook assembled ca. 1510–1520 by a follower of Ripanda (Oxford, Ashmolean Museum) reveals his interest in a variety of monuments in Rome— sarcophagi, historical reliefs, urns, altars, capitals, trophies. The sketchbook contains a series of drawings of the *Arch of Constantine, suggesting that Ripanda may have attempted the systematic recording of this monument, too.

BIBLIOGRAPHY
+*EAA, Atlante* (1973), pl. 75–107; +M.G. Pasqualitti, *Colonna Traiana e disegni ri-nascimentali della Biblioteca dell'Istituto Nazionale di Archeologie e Storia dell'Arte* (Rome, 1978); +V. Farinella, *Archeologia e pittura a Roma tra Quattrocento e Cinque-cento, Il Caso di Jacopo Ripanda* (Turin, 1992).

RIZOMYLO. See NICHORIA.

ROBERT, CARL (1850–1922). German archaeologist, best known for his cor-pus of *Roman sarcophagi.

Born into an illustrious academic family of French origin at Marburg, Robert studied at Bonn under *Jahn, *Kekulé and Anton Springer and at Berlin under T. *Mommsen and Kirchhoff. He called himself *Wilamowitz's eldest student. After travel in Italy and Greece, he became associate professor (*Extraordinarius*) for archaeology in Berlin (1877), full professor (1880–90), and then taught at Halle. A friendly and gifted teacher, of highest intelligence and widest interests, he was enormously productive and became certainly the most outstanding prac-titioner of Jahn's *monumental philology. His greatest achievements remain the corpus of Roman sarcophagi (1890–1919), which involved fourteen trips to Italy and was modeled on Mommsen's *Corpus Inscriptionum Latinarum;* the re-vision of Preller's *Mythologie;* and his forty-year editorship of *Hermes*. His publications (1873–1922), with range as wide as Wilamowitz's, number over 300 items and include numerous *RE* articles. The Robertinum at Halle perpet-uates his name.

BIBLIOGRAPHY
G. Karo, ed., *Carl Robert zum Gedächtnis* (Halle, 1922); O. Kern, *Hermann Diels und Carl Robert: Ein biographischer Versuch* (Leipzig, 1927); H. Meyer, *Archäologenbild-nisse*, 96–97.

WILLIAM M. CALDER III

ROBERT, HUBERT (1733–1808). French painter famed for his representa-tions of ancient ruins.

Robert was one of the first French artists of the eighteenth century to adopt as his principal subject views of classical structures in a ruined state as a means of suggesting the ephemeral quality of the great works of humankind. Despite the va-riety of subjects he depicted, ranging from garden scenes to genre, his fame as a painter of ancient buildings led to his being nicknamed ''Robert des Ruines.''

Robert's formative years took place in Rome, to which he traveled in 1754 in the entourage of the French ambassador to the *Vatican, the future Duc de Choi-seul. In many ways Robert was an artistic descendant of such sixteenth-century Romanists as van *Heemskerck, who had journeyed south to record the survival of the ancient past within the fabric of modern Rome. Robert remained in Italy un-til 1765, becoming familiar with the topographical view paintings and ruin scenes of *Panini, who was well known among the residents at the *French Academy in

Rome. While adopting many of the stylistic traits of Panini, Robert never sought the degree of literalism or accuracy that characterizes the work of the Italian, preferring a more poetic and lighthearted approach to the representation of classical buildings. Robert was also influenced by *Piranesi, with whom he visited the ancient city of Cora and from whom he learned the dramatic effects of exaggerated perspective and artificial illumination. In addition, with his compatriot and close friend Jean-Honoré Fragonard, he sojourned in Naples and *Paestum.

The large-scale paintings of Roman monuments created by Robert on his return to Paris were inevitably commissioned as decorative adjuncts to interiors (e.g., the *Pont du Gard, one of a suite of four ancient monuments of Provence painted for the Château de Fontainebleau, 1787; now *Louvre, Paris). On his first Parisian showing at the Salon of 1767, Robert found a champion in the art critic Diderot, who responded to the painter's poignant visions of time and nature triumphant over man-made edifices with the words, "All comes to nothing, all perishes, all passes." More often than not, Robert transposed famous buildings to a new setting, as in the capriccio representing the *Pantheon looming over the Porta di Ripetta (1782; Galleria Nazionale, Rome). Just as frequently, he invented picturesque ruins for a work, perhaps combining a towering colonnade with the irregular silhouette of a tree and a splashing fountain surrounded by small-scale figures in contemporary dress (Garden Scene with Fountain, 1775; Coll. F. Huget, Belgium). Thus, Robert's images frequently lacked the historical or archaeological fervor of Piranesi and Panini.

In Paris, Robert broadened his interest in ruin painting by documenting recent demolitions of buildings and bridges in the capital city. One of his patrons, Catherine the Great, remarked that the French Revolution provided the painter with "the most beautiful and freshest ruins on earth." He even painted imaginary scenes of actual monuments as they might appear with the passing of time, such as The Grand Galerie du Louvre in Ruins (1796; Tsarskoe Selo, St. Petersburg). A contemporary, Charles Lecarpentier, summed up the artist's appeal as follows: "If Robert's paintings delight the eye by the elegance of his compositions and the lightness of his touch, they also fill the soul with a sort of melancholy by taking it through the scattered remnants of a long succession of centuries."

BIBLIOGRAPHY

+P. de Nolhac, Hubert Robert, 1733–1808 (Paris, 1910); +T. J. McCormick, Hubert Robert, 1733–1808; Paintings and Drawings, catalog of exhibition (Poughkeepsie, NY, 1962); +H. Burda, Die Ruine in den Bilder Hubert Roberts (Munich, 1967); V. Carlson, Hubert Robert, Drawings and Watercolors (Washington, DC, 1978).

ROBERT NEUMAN

ROBINSON, DAVID MOORE (1880–1958). American classicist and archaeologist; excavator of *Olynthos.

Born in Auburn, New York, the precocious Robinson had his A.B. from the University of Chicago at the age of eighteen, having read Xenophon, Homer, Vergil, Ovid and Horace in the originals. He studied abroad (*American School of Classical Studies, Athens, 1901–3; Halle, 1902; Berlin, 1903–4) and returned to Chicago for his Ph.D. in 1904.

For many years Robinson taught at Johns Hopkins University, rising to the rank of professor of Greek archaeology and epigraphy (1905–47), all the while accepting numerous visiting professorships and lectureships at other institutions. After retiring from Johns Hopkins, he accepted a post as professor of classics and archaeology at the University of Mississippi (Oxford).

Robinson was a member of dozens of learned societies; he served the *Archaeological Institute of America in a variety of capacities (including Charles Eliot Norton Lecturer, 1924–25, 1928–29) and was president three times of the American Philological Association. He was editor of *Art and Archaeology* (1914–18) and the *Art Bulletin* (1919–21), as well as of forty volumes of *Johns Hopkins Studies in Archaeology*.

A prolific writer, Robinson published some thirty books and more than 400 articles. Much of his publication was related to his excavations at *Olynthos, carried out between 1928 and 1938. He was author or coauthor of thirteen volumes on Olynthos, embracing the architecture, sculpture, coins and vases. Robinson also excavated at *Corinth, *Sardis and Pisidian Antioch.

An eager collector of antiquities, Robinson secured many items for the collection at Johns Hopkins and amassed a personal collection, including many Greek vases. Most of his collection is no longer in Baltimore but may be found today at the University of Mississippi and in the Fogg Museum, Cambridge.

BIBLIOGRAPHY

D. M. Robinson, with M. W. McGehee, *The Robinson Collection, Baltimore, Md., CVA*, fasc. 4, 6–7, Robinson collection, fasc. 1–3 (Cambridge, MA, 1934–38); *Who Was Who in America* 3 (1960), 734–35; L. Turnbull, "The Museum of Classical Archaeology, University of Mississippi," *ArchNews* 2 (1973), 33–41; E. R. Williams, *The Archaeological Collection of the Johns Hopkins University* (Baltimore, 1984), 7–8.

ROCKOX, NICOLAAS (ROCKOXIUS; 1560–1640). Flemish magistrate and collector of antiquities.

Rockox studied law in Louvain, Paris and Tournai, where he obtained his doctor's degree in 1584. He returned to Antwerp, where he became burgomaster and alderman of the city (1588). He hosted the visits to Antwerp of Vincenzo Gonzaga, Duke of Mantua (*Gonzaga family), in 1608, Maria de' Medici in 1631, the Duke of Orleans in 1632 and the Archduke Ferdinand in 1635. For the entry of the latter, decorations were designed by P. P. *Rubens, to whom Rockox had been patron and friend for many years.

Andreas Schott described Rockox in 1617 as "most expert in antiquities and Roman coins" and referred to his cabinet of gold, silver and bronze coins and engraved gems. Nothing is known about his glyptic collection, but on his numismatic cabinet more information is preserved. An itemized manuscript catalog is extant, listing all his coins. The reputation of the collection led to a visit from *Peiresc on his way through the Netherlands in 1606. His letters of 1609 mention a much-admired gold coin of Faustina with the Puellae Faustinianae on the reverse (illustrated in Philip *Rubens, *Electorum libri II* 87) and a Hercules Gaditanus issued by Hadrian. Rockox and Peiresc exchanged coins and casts, and Peiresc also sent Rockox a box of rare plants. When Peiresc inquired after his medieval coins, Rockox reciprocated with nine specimens. After Rockox's death, much of his coin collection (1,129 coins; 744 silver and 385 bronze) was sold in 1641.

The reverse of the title page to Rockox's inventory provides information on his collection of antiquities, for the largest part, portrait busts and herms but including one grave urn of which he copied the inscription. The sculptures standing in his "Museum" are pictured in F. Francken II, *A Banquet in the House of Nicolaas Rockox* (Munich), where six portrait busts, a *Sleeping Cupid* and the urn can be seen. His herm with *Demosthenes* is also known from an engraving by Hans Witdoeck. It has recently been traced to the National Museum, Stockholm, together with heads of *Zeus, Jupiter Ammon, Jupiter Serapis* and an unknown figure, which were sold via Leblon to *Christina of Sweden.

Rockox was involved in various publishing ventures. He assisted in promoting and financing the publication of the coins of the Duke of Aerschot, with engravings made by Jacob de Bie (gold coins, 1615; silver and bronze, 1617) and in 1618 sponsored a new edition of *Goltzius's books. He was also invited to participate in the Rubens-Peiresc project to do a book on gems, but it was never completed.

BIBLIOGRAPHY
C. Ruelens, "Les amis de Rubens: Nicolaas Rockox," *Rubens-Bulletijn,* 2 (1885), 24–47, 89–124; R. W. Scheller, *Nicolaas Rockox als oudheidkundige* (Antwerp, 1978).

MARJON VAN DER MEULEN

RODENWALDT, GERHART (1886–1945). German archaeologist and art historian.

Rodenwaldt studied at Berlin under *Kekulé, Eduard *Meyer and *Wilamowitz and at Heidelberg under von *Duhn; and in 1908 he wrote his dissertation on Pompeian wall painting under Carl *Robert at Halle. Revealingly, he studied as well under Goldschmidt, Thode and Wölfflin and later introduced into ancient art criticism, especially Roman, ideas formed from other periods. His famous distinction between "popular" and "great" art at Rome, because of his contributions to the *Cambridge Ancient History,* 12, became widely known to English-speaking scholars. Painting, relief and (after Robert) Roman sarcophagi remained the center of his interest, but contributions range from *Mycenae to late antiquity.

In 1917 he became professor of archaeology at Giessen. From 1922 to 1932 he was a vigorous president of the *German Archaeological Institute. In 1932 he succeeded Noack at Berlin. In April 1945, his lifework unfinished, he died by his own hand.

BIBLIOGRAPHY
G. Rodenwaldt, *Qua ratione pictores pompeiani in componendis parietibus usi sint* (Halle, 1908) 43; C. Weickert, "Gerhart Rodenwaldt," *Gnomon* 21 (1949), 82–87; O.

J. Brendel, *Prolegomena to the Study of Roman Art* (New Haven, CT, 1979), 101–21; A. Borbein, "Klassische Archäologie in Berlin vom 18. zum 20. Jahrhundert," *Berlin und die Antike: Aufsätze,* ed. W. Arenhövel—C. Schreiber (West Berlin, 1979), 99–150, esp. 143–45; W. Schindler, ed., "Gerhardt Rodenwaldts Beitrag zur Klassischen Archäologie," *Wissenschaftliche Zeitschrift der Humboldt-Universität zu Berlin, Gesellschaftwissenschaftliche Reihe* 35 (1986), 627–705; U. Hausmann, in *Archhäologenbildnisse,* 236–37.

WILLIAM M. CALDER III

ROE, Sir THOMAS (ca. 1581–1644). English diplomat, author and traveler; his assignments often were connected with England's mercantile interests in Asia.

Roe was ambassador to the Sublime Porte, the Ottoman Turk government, at Constantinople (*Byzantium) from 1621 to 1628 and while in this role did his best to help secure Greek antiquities for the Earl of *Arundel and the Duke of *Buckingham. Originally having distaste for the commission from these powerful nobles, Roe grew interested in the task and sought to become knowledgeable about the antiquities trade. He especially profited from his acquaintance with the Reverend William Petty, an agent sent out by Arundel (1624), much trusted because he had been tutor to Arundel's sons and had a discerning taste in antiquities acquired during travels in Italy.

Roe endured staggering difficulties in his diplomatic negotiations with the unstable Turkish government (in the space of fifteen months he witnessed the lightning change of three emperors, seven Great Viziers, and five Agas of the Janissaries) and also suffered from dysentery and paralysis. Nevertheless, he showed an astonishing pursuit of his objectives. He helped Petty make a thorough investigation of ancient marbles in Constantinople and went to incredible lengths in an effort to obtain a series of marble reliefs from the Porta Aurea, built by Constantine in the fourth century A.C. The subjects of these twelve reliefs, never secured by Roe and now vanished, were described as including a sleeping *Endymion,* a *Pegasus* with nymphs or Muses and a *Satyr with Hercules.*

Petty, himself indefatigable, went off to collect marbles in the islands and was shipwrecked off the coast of Asia Minor with a load of statuary, which sank along with the ship. After a stretch of imprisonment by Turkish authorities, the loyal agent of Arundel salvaged most of the marbles and proceeded to Smyrna, where he managed to add to his haul a collection amassed for *Peiresc that had been sequestered by the Turks. In 1626 Petty reached Athens, and from there he shipped the pieces he had gathered, some 200 in all, back to the earl.

Petty's single-minded attachment to Arundel alienated Roe, so that the latter now concentrated on trying to satisfy Buckingham. He bought urns from *Corinth as well as antiquities from *Sparta and Andros, sending off a cargo to Buckingham in June 1628. But some two months later, Buckingham was assassinated and never got to enjoy these treasures.

Turning more now to collecting for himself, Roe acquired a large cabinet of coins, which he was to take back to England with him in 1628. At his death his wife donated his collection (242 items) to the Bodleian Library, Oxford.

BIBLIOGRAPHY
Stoneman, *Land of Lost Gods*, 45–49; M. Strachan, *Sir Thomas Roe, 1581–1644: A Life* (Salisbury, 1989), 167–70.

ROHDE, ERWIN (1845–98). German classicist.

Born a doctor's son in Hamburg and educated at Bonn, Leipzig and Kiel under Ritschl and Ribbeck, Rohde became professor of classical philology at Jena, Tübingen, Leipzig and Heidelberg. He was granted the doctorate for his book on the sources of Pollux for *scenic antiquities (1870). His chief interests were the ancient novel, literary history in antiquity and Greek religion. His masterpiece, *Psyche: The Cult of Souls and Belief in Immortality Among the Greeks* (2nd ed., 1897; English translation, 1925), exploited papyrological, epigraphical, archaeological and literary evidence in order to understand popular piety, and so he methodologically anticipated the school of *Nilsson. His loyal but unwise defense of his friend Nietzsche against *Wilamowitz in 1872 permanently damaged his career. He never acknowledges the influence of Nietzsche in *Psyche.*

BIBLIOGRAPHY
O. Crusius, *Erwin Rohde: ein biographischer Versuch* (Tübingen, 1902); H. Däuble, "Friedrich Nietzsche und Erwin Rohde," *Nietzsche-Studien* 5 (1976), 321–54; C. P. Janz, *Friedrich Nietzsche Biographie* 1 (Munich, 1978), 208–10; W. M. Calder III, "Also sprach Wilamowitz: The Wilamowitz-Nietzsche Struggle, New Documents and a Reappraisal," *Nietzsche-Studien* 12 (1983); H. Cancik, "Erwin Rohde—ein Philologe der Bismarckzeit," *Semper Apertus, Sechshundert Jahre Ruprecht-Karls-Universität Heidelberg 1386–1983: Festschrift in sechs Bande* 2, ed. G. Freiherr zu Pulitz—W. Doerr (Berlin, 1985), 435–505.

WILLIAM M. CALDER III

ROMAN ACADEMY (ACCADEMIA ROMANA). Informal professional organization for the humanists of the city of Rome during the Renaissance.

The Roman Academy began as the brainchild of a Southern Italian humanist, Giulio Pomponio *Leto, who began hosting informal meetings in his own home on the Quirinal Hill in the 1460s, first as a student and then as a professor of rhetoric in the university at Rome. Academy members took classical names, referring to Leto as their Pontifex Maximus, and seem to have spent their time together perfecting their Latin style and exploring the antiquities of Rome. Their graffiti are still to be seen in the Roman catacombs. In 1468, suspicious of the academy's possible republican sympathies and under direct attack by academy members for his attempts to reform the curial bureaucracy, Pope *Paul II attempted to suppress the group, imprisoning many of its members and subjecting them to torture on charges of sodomy, republicanism, irreligion, neopaganism and heresy.

Eventually, the charges were dropped, and the academicians were freed, and under the subsequent papacy of *Sixtus IV the academy reorganized as a religious sodality, whose patron saints Victor, Fortunatus and Genesius happened to have a feast day on the ancient birthday of Rome, the Palilia. This second Roman Academy continued, under Leto's leadership, in the same vein as the first, emphasizing the refinement of its members' neo-Latin style and proceeding with archaeological investigations, notably in the collection of ancient inscriptions. While Leto himself wrote on ancient Roman history, other members of the academy pursued various other lines of antiquarian research, commenting on ancient authors and reviving ancient theater with ardent enthusiasm; Bartolommeo Sacchi (d. 1481), known to the academy as Platina, became head of the Vatican Library and from this vantage composed his famous history of the popes (in which Paul II is vilified for his actions of 1468). The *Domus Aurea (Golden House) of Nero was opened sometime in the 1470s to the exploratory scrutiny of academicians and artists alike (who thought, however, that they had entered the *Baths of Titus); here, as with the catacombs, graffiti provide clear evidence of their presence. Occasional published collections of neo-Latin verse display the enthusiasm of the academicians for re-creating ancient celebrations with antiquarian punctilio. On the whole, however, because of the organization's informality, much of what we know about the Roman Academy is only indirect.

With Leto's death in 1498, the energies of the Roman humanists turned to garden gatherings in the houses of men like the curialist Paolo Cortesi, the wealthy merchant Johann Göritz of Luxembourg and eventually Leto's successor to the leadership of the Roman Academy proper, Angelo *Colocci. In the days of *Julius II and *Leo X, the academy flourished, counting among its members the future cardinals *Bembo and Sadoleto, along with Paolo Giovio and Castiglione. It then disappeared in the general chaos in Rome created by the sack of the city in 1527.

Appropriately enough, one of the great academies, that of the Lincei (*Accademia dei Lincei), still holds its meetings on the site of two Renaissance gardens (those of the Riario and of Agostino Chigi) where the Roman academics held sway in the time of Leto.

BIBLIOGRAPHY

Sandys, II, 92–93; R. J. Palermino, "The Roman Academy, the Catacombs and the Conspiracy of 1468," *Archivum Historiae Pontificiae* 18 (1980), 117–55; J. D'Amico, *Renaissance Humanism in Papal Rome: Humanists and Churchmen on the Eve of the Reformation* (Baltimore, 1983), esp. 89–112.

INGRID ROWLAND

ROMAN AGORA, Athens. Marketplace constructed in Athens under Roman patronage.

The Agora of Athens in the Roman period lay some 150m east of the old Greek Agora (*Agora, Athens). According to the dedicatory inscription on the west gate (*IG* II² 3175), it was the gift of Julius Caesar and Augustus, dedicated to Athena Archegetis ca. 10 B.C. From that time on, it must have served as the commercial center of the city. It takes the form of a large peristyle court, oriented east-west and measuring ca. 98m × 111m. The principal entrance was

from the west, through a large propylon of four Doric columns. A second propylon of four unfluted Ionic columns gave access from the east. Behind the east
colonnade there was a row of shops; along the south side there was a double
colonnade (Ionic outside, Doric inside), broken near the middle by a fountain
and stairway leading up to the south. The original arrangement of the west and
north sides is not clear. The walls were of poros limestone; the colonnades, of
both Hymettian and Pentelic marble.

The building has been the subject of sporadic study and excavation for over
a century, by Boetticher (1862), Koumanoudes (1890), Kastriotis and Philadel-
pheus (1910), Kourouniotis and Stavropoullos (1930–31) and Platon (1965);
even so, the entire north half of the structure lies hidden under a mosque, the
church of the Taxiarchs and modern houses. A section of the Ionic entablature
of the southern colonnade was reerected in 1942 under the direction of the
*Italian School and the *Greek Archaeological Service. The marble paving of
the court was apparently a later addition; two of the slabs were sawed from
stelai bearing imperial letters of the second half of the second century A.C. There
is little reported concerning either the earlier use of the area or the later history
of the building. The Doric propylon at the west has always stood as a landmark
near the heart of old Athens and appears regularly in early drawings and watercolors of the city. The earliest architectural study is that undertaken by *Stuart
and *Revett in 1762.

BIBLIOGRAPHY

H. S. Robinson, "The Tower of the Winds and the Roman Market-Place," *AJA* 47
(1943), 291–305; Travlos, 28–36; T. L. Shear, Jr., "Athens: From City-State to Provincial Town," *Hesperia* 50 (1981), 356–77; M. Hoff, *The Roman Agora at Athens,* diss.,
Boston University, 1988.

JOHN McK. CAMP II

ROMAN HYPERBOREANS. See HYPERBOREANS.

ROMAN SARCOPHAGI. Carved stone coffins produced during the period of
the Roman Empire, from the first century A.C. to the fifth century A.C.

About 9,000 stone sarcophagi have survived from most provinces of the Roman Empire. Most are made of marble: the main sources were the quarries of
Carrara (Italy), Pentelikon (Achaia), Thasos (Macedonia), Prokonnesos (Asia)
and Dokimeion (Phrygia). The most important quarries supplying craftsmen at
Rome were Carrara and, especially in the later empire, Prokonnesos and Thasos.

The earliest Roman marble sarcophagi were similar in shape to the later figured examples but were plain or very limited in decoration. When figured sarcophagi decorated in relief became fashionable in the early second century A.C.,
they were mostly adorned with garlands, like the cinerary urns that had commonly preceded them. Such decoration emphasized the sacred nature of the
burial chest.

The choice of interment in a marble sarcophagus indicated Roman interest in traditional Greek culture and abandonment of cremation, the rite most favored in Early Imperial Rome. By the mid-second century A.C., the decoration of sarcophagus chests strongly reflected cultural interests, with scenes from Greek myth and drama and Dionysiac cult enjoying popularity. By the third century, the "man of culture," often shown with one or more Muses, was a recurrent theme. The fashion for sarcophagi had by then spread to people of humble status, and the individual was sometimes represented on the chest, even playing a role in a mythological scene.

There were few explicit references to "official" Roman religion on pagan sarcophagi, which therefore enjoyed a high rate of survival in the Christian era. Christian sarcophagi were made in large numbers, some adapting pagan motifs. Emperors continued to be buried in sarcophagi, and recent studies of the reuse of pagan sarcophagi for burial in medieval Italy suggest that the chests had not lost their association with high social status and refined culture. *Charlemagne, for example, and the Countess Beatrice of Tuscany were buried in ancient Roman sarcophagi. The relief with the "resurrection of the flesh" on the façade of Orvieto Cathedral (ca. 1330) depicts the dead as rising from Roman sarcophagi. Many more chests were reused as fountains or were dismembered to form decorative panels for the walls of medieval houses. The ornament of Roman sarcophagi, widely used throughout the empire, became a prime influence upon Byzantine and medieval art.

The Western type of sarcophagus, a long, low box designed to fit within an alcove, with decoration confined to the front and short sides, engaged the attention of Renaissance artists and later scholars. Artists were particularly attracted by the outstanding quality of the figured sarcophagi of Antonine Rome. The predominance of sarcophagi from Rome in early drawings and written records was to direct the path of nineteenth- and twentieth-century scholarship, in which overwhelming emphasis was placed on the decoration of sarcophagi and not upon their use as burial chests. The early modern bias to Western decorative relief may be contrasted with the medieval perception of sarcophagi, in which recognition was given to the high status accorded in pagan antiquity to Asiatic columnar sarcophagi and their Western derivatives.

The earliest surviving description of ancient Roman sarcophagus reliefs occurs in a letter written from Rome in 1411 by the Late Byzantine scholar Manuel Chrysoloras, who commented on the Greek myths represented on reliefs set into the walls of private houses. In 1435, the humanist Leon Battista *Alberti recommended the study of sarcophagus reliefs "to learn how to express the movements of the mind by those of the body." Indeed, fifteenth-century artists tended to select individual figures and gestures and copied or adapted them into contemporary works of art.

Following the publication of classical texts and mythological handbooks, artists of the sixteenth century began to record entire reliefs. The Neapolitan antiquarian Pirro *Ligorio accurately identified the subjects of many reliefs and provided written descriptions of the scenes.

Recent research has suggested that the earliest attempt at a corpus of reliefs on Roman sarcophagi was more systematic than has been thought. The *Opera de' Pili*, a record of surviving antiquities compiled in the mid-sixteenth century by members of the Accademia della Vertù in Rome, was to include a volume devoted to a survey of all sarcophagi from Rome and the surrounding area. Drawings of the sarcophagi were to be accompanied by a commentary offering identifications of the figures and interpretations of the scenes. Some treatment of funerary and sacrificial rites, artistic form and development was also proposed. Dating was to be assessed by formal criteria.

The *Opera de' Pili* has not survived, but two contemporary volumes of drawings, the codices Pighianus (*Pighius) and Coburgensis (*Codex Coburgensis), certainly arose in a similar scholarly environment and may even comprise sectors of the *Opera de' Pili*, though it is not possible to prove a direct connection. The codices have served as primary records of surviving sarcophagus reliefs since the beginnings of systematic modern scholarship in the mid-nineteenth century. Ignorant of earlier commentaries, the seventeenth-century papal antiquarian Giovanni Pietro *Bellori wrote the captions for the plates of sarcophagus reliefs, first engraved in reverse in 1545 by Francois *Perrier, then accurately copied with additions by Pietro Santi *Bartoli in 1693.

Many of the drawings collected in the early seventeenth century by the antiquarian Cassiano dal *Pozzo included representations of reliefs on sarcophagi. It is likely that this corpus was originally better ordered than the surviving parts suggest. The drawings were rebound following purchase by George III in 1762.

*Montfaucon included various engravings of sarcophagus reliefs, most correctly identified, in *L'Antiquité expliquée et representée en figures* (1722). This is the first work surviving to modern times to include a chapter on the funerary customs of the Romans. Montfaucon identified the distinctive rectangular and oval chests so typical of Rome. In 1743 was published A. F. *Gori's *Inscriptiones antiquae in Etruriae urbibus exstantes* (vol. 3). Gori provided an excellent account of sarcophagi, including observations on their iconography.

Though J. J. *Winckelmann had some scholarly interest in Roman sarcophagi, in his innovative work on style (1770), he relegated them with all Roman art as products of "the last age of art." The succeeding years saw a growth of interest in the symbolic meaning of sarcophagus reliefs and, with the development of modern Rome and Athens, a large rise in archaeological finds of all types. Various journals were established to report and comment on the latter. Otto *Jahn, a colleague of the great scholar Theodor *Mommsen, who was responsible for compiling the *Corpus Inscriptionum Latinarum,* proposed an equivalent corpus of sarcophagi in 1848. The project was not to be realized until the year of Jahn's death, 1869. The corpus, limited to mythological reliefs, was to be based on the surviving codices of Renaissance drawings, which provided the structure of the first volumes. Jahn's pupil, the elder Friedrich Matz, was entrusted with its preparation. Six volumes were proposed, comprising (1) scenes from daily life, (2) mythological cycles, (3) individual myths, (4) the Bacchic cycle, (5) Muses, Nereids, Erotes, (6) decorative ornament.

Four fascicules of the corpus, prepared by Carl *Robert, appeared by 1919. The text was limited to antiquarian descriptions of an account of iconographical development, illustrated by excellent but expensive photogravures.

In 1921 Gerhard *Rodenwaldt was appointed editor in chief and directed the project until his death in 1945. Only one fascicule appeared in this period, but Rodenwaldt himself prepared numerous articles on Roman and provincial sarcophagi, which remain models of clarity of observation and sensitivity of interpretation. Rodenwaldt changed the direction of the corpus, dividing the material along regional and art-historical lines. This orientation was formally approved on the centenary of the foundation of the corpus in 1969. New volumes are devoted to (7) Late Etruscan sarcophagi, (8) sarcophagi of the Western empire, (9) sarcophagi of Greece and the Danube provinces, (10) sarcophagi of Asia Minor, (11) sarcophagi of Syria, Palestine and Alexandria. Volume 12 is a reworking of the original volumes 1–3.

Since World War II, there has been a considerable rise in interest in Roman sarcophagi, and many provincial areas of production and marketing have been explored. German scholars continue to dominate the field. Five fascicules and two entire volumes of the corpus have appeared, including the younger Friedrich *Matz's publication of the entire Bacchic cycle (vol. 4, 1968–74). G.M.A. *Hanfmann contributed a far-ranging iconographical study of representations of the Seasons on sarcophagi (1951). Other notable postwar achievements include the exploration of the workshops in Asia Minor, where considerable advances in our understanding have been made. A principal focus of interest, particularly among British and Italian scholars, has been on sarcophagi as objects of trade. Exploration of quarries and shipwrecks and scientific advances in the identification of white marbles have made major contributions to knowledge. In 1982, Guntrum Koch, the leading expert on provincial sarcophagi, and Helmut Sichtermann, a distinguished interpreter of iconography, published a comprehensive handbook of Roman sarcophagi, which admirably reflects the expanding interest in this field. Symposia are regularly organized by the *German Archaeological Institute, in which specialists report and discuss the latest advances in knowledge. At the meeting held in Pisa in 1982, a group of Italian scholars presented their findings of pagan sarcophagi reused in early medieval Italy, a formerly ill-explored field. A special study has been made by A. M. McCann of the sarcophagi in the *Metropolitan Museum of Art, and recently catalogs have appeared of sarcophagi in two major collections: the Musée du *Louvre (1985) and the *British Museum (1990).

BIBLIOGRAPHY

G.M.A. Hanfmann, *The Season Sarcophagus at Dumbarton Oaks* (Cambridge, MA, 1951); A. M. McCann, *Roman Sarcophagi in the Metropolitan Museum of Art* (New York, 1978); G. Koch—H. Sichtermann, *Römische Sarkophage* (Munich, 1982); Bober—Rubinstein; H. Wrede, ''Die Opera de' Pili von 1542 und das Berliner Sarkophagcorpus,

Zur geschichte von Sarkophagforschung, Hermeneutik und klassischer Archäologie," *JdI* 104 (1989), 373–414; G. Koch, *Sarkophage der römischen Kaiserzeit* (Darmstadt 1993).

SUSAN WALKER

ROMAN WALL PAINTING. Real interest in Roman wall painting in modern times dates from the discovery of rooms in the *Domus Aurea of Nero on the Oppian Hill about 1480, although ancient frescoes and mosaics survived in churches (e.g., Santa Costanza, Rome), and painted tombs and catacombs must have occasionally come to light earlier.

These rooms were visited and studied by numerous artists and amateurs of the next two centuries and freely plundered for motifs for the various decorations known as *grottesche, especially by *Raphael, his pupil *Giovanni da Udine and the Zuccari brothers, but whole wall schemes were seldom copied. The existence of now lost paintings in and around Rome has been inferred from Renaissance works that show a remarkable similarity to scene types discovered later at *Pompeii or *Herculaneum (e.g., Filippino *Lippi's drawing of the *Death of Laocoon* in the Uffizi, after 1488; G. Bonasone's engraving of the *Toilette of Psyche,* ca. 1560). In the seventeenth century the *Pyramid of Cestius and the tomb of the Nasonii (*Tomb of Ovid) also yielded paintings, but these had little influence. On the other hand, the *Aldobrandini *Wedding* was regarded as of the highest quality and was often copied, studied and imitated. As for scholarship on the subject, the most important early treatise, the *De pictura veterum* of Franciscus *Junius (1637), was based heavily on ancient literary sources about ancient painters and painting, rather than on actually excavated examples. Great devotion to the recording of known works was shown by Cardinal Camillo Massimi, who assembled a famed collection of drawings after ancient paintings, mostly by P. S. *Bartoli; G. P. *Bellori wrote commentaries for the publication of Bartoli's illustrations.

With F. *Bianchini's excavations for the *Farnese family on the *Palatine Hill in 1721–24 and the discovery of the Aula Isiaca, a small part of the *House of Livia and the suite under the Domus Augustiana believed to be part of the Domus Transitoria of Nero, interest was renewed, and careful copies of these decorations were made immediately. But these exerted minor influence on contemporary decoration, probably due to the rediscovery of *Herculaneum in 1738 and *Pompeii in 1748. The wealth of wall painting brought to light there, especially the monumental subject pictures from the "Basilica" of Herculaneum discovered in 1739, eclipsed other remains of ancient painting in interest.

In these excavations pictures were cut from the walls and removed to the Museo Ercolanese at Portici, and the excavation tunnels were backfilled without copying of the wall schemes. Beginning in 1757, the *Academia Herculanensis, a group of fifteen scholars, initiated publication of *Le Antichità di Ercolano,* large volumes richly illustrated with engravings of objects in the royal museum. Eventually, by 1792, five volumes devoted to paintings were published and distributed as royal presents; their effect throughout Europe was tremendous.

The practice of backfilling the excavations after they had been plundered of treasure continued to the discovery of the Porta di Ercolano and Via dei Sepolcri at Pompeii in 1763, when the intrinsic interest of the gate dictated leaving things exposed. Thereafter, the excavation of the temple of Isis, beginning in 1764, and the Villa di Diomede, beginning in 1771, in both of which the wall paintings were especially well preserved, aroused new interest in Roman wall painting as decoration. Early drawings of the walls of the temple of Isis were discovered in the archives of the *Museo Nazionale at Naples by O. Elia and were published in 1942 (*Monumenti della pittura antica scoperti in Italia* 3, Pompei 3–4). Drawings of the Villa di Diomede with much other material were published in an anonymous series issued in Naples from 1796 to 1808, *Gli ornati ed i pavimenti delle stanze dell'antica Pompei.* But already earlier, the taste for ''Pompeian'' decorations had spread through much of Europe, spearheaded in England by Angelica *Kauffmann and her reinterpretations of the classical based on the teachings of *Winckelmann. ''Pompeian'' ceilings were especially popular in the late eighteenth century, and in the country houses decorated by the Adams (*Adam family) in England and by Prud'hon in France, ''Pompeian'' rooms and motifs abound. In La Favorita at Palermo, built for Ferdinand and Maria Carolina of Naples during their years in Sicily (1806–15), one finds an interesting combination of the Pompeian style with the Chinese.

More serious study of Pompeian wall paintings was undertaken by Wilhelm Zahn in 1824 in a series of drawings of individual figures, borders, compositions and whole walls, most in line but many in full color, issued in large folios in Berlin from 1828 to 1852. This was followed by works by Fausto and Felice Niccolini (four large folio volumes issued from 1854 to 1896) and E. Presuhn (1878, 1882). All these endeavored to make the variety, the proportions and especially the colors of Pompeian painting familiar. In the same period appeared W. *Helbig's comprehensive catalog of subject pictures, *Wandgemälde der vom Vesuv verschütteten Städte Campaniens* (1868) and A. *Mau's magisterial division of Pompeian decoration into four styles, *Geschichte der decorativen Wandmalerei in Pompeji* (1882). Helbig's catalog was supplemented by A. Sogliano in 1879 and then by K. Schefold's *Die Wände Pompejis* (1957), still the best catalog available, though abbreviated and with sometimes questionable dating.

With the development of photography, accurate reproduction of ancient painting became the concern of P. Herrmann and the publisher F. Bruckmann; beginning in 1904 and continuing to 1950 were published more than 200 large photogravures of the most important subject pictures in the Museo Nazionale, most in monochrome. G. E. Rizzo (1929) and L. *Curtius (1929) issued profusely illustrated studies of Roman wall painting, the latter attempting especially to understand and define the aesthetics of the various decorations, their development and the place of the subject pictures within these and in their own right; his work, *Die Wandmalerei Pompejis,* remains valuable today.

Since World War II, advances in the techniques of color photography have produced a spate of excellent publications, beginning with A. *Maiuri's *Roman*

Painting (1953). Among the best are T. Kraus and L. von Matt, *Pompeii and Herculaneum, The Living Cities of the Dead* (1975), J. and M. Guillaud, *Frescoes in the Time of Pompeii* (1990) and A. De Franciscis et al., *La Pittura di Pompei* (1991).

Two questions have always beset the study of ancient wall painting: the development and dating of the various styles and the relation of Roman wall painting to Greek painting. The four Pompeian styles identified by Mau have been studied carefully, and attempts have been made to ascertain their chronological limits. The First Style, known mainly from examples found at *Delos and Pompeii and beginning perhaps as early as the fourth century B.C., features imitation masonry in stucco relief; it has recently been analyzed and cataloged by A. Laidlaw (1985). The Second Style probably came to Pompeii with the Roman colony of about 80 B.C., having been invented elsewhere. A few examples of it have been found in southern France, Macedonia, Greece and the eastern Mediterranean. Strongly architectural and illusionistic, it owes much to stage architecture but occasionally features friezes of figures on a large scale. It was studied most comprehensively by H. G. Beyen (1938, 1960), but his theory of its development and dating has not been accepted. It has most recently been investigated by R. A. Tybout (1989). The Third Style, known only in Italy, is characterized by large, flat panels, usually with a single dominant color for each room, and depictions of architecture of exaggerated delicacy. Figures are small, even in large subject pictures, and sometimes float freely in side panels. The style was first definitively described by A. Ippel (1910) and has recently been investigated by F. L. Bastet and M. de Vos (1979) and by W. Ehrhardt (1987). The transitions between the Second and Third styles and Third and Fourth styles are especially thorny problems. The Third Style seems to have begun in the Augustan period and to have extended through the first half of the first century A.C. The Fourth Style, which made its appearance in Pompeii before the earthquake of A.D. 62, seems very likely the creation of Neronian decorators for the Domus Transitoria. It is characterized by a strong architectural framework, often layered and complex and richly ornamented. Subject pictures are large and important, and theatrical ornamentation is ubiquitous. This was especially the style of the last period of Pompeii, from A.D. 62 to the eruption of 79, and in Rome of the Domus Aurea. The Fourth Style is so multifarious that it defies comprehensive treatment; the latest good general study may be that of A. Barbet (1985).

The relationship of Roman subject paintings to putative Greek originals has proved a fertile field for scholarship and speculation but, in the absence of all such originals and with reliance only on written descriptions, cannot be demonstrated. The Aldobrandini *Wedding* and the *Odyssey Landscapes* are examples for which there has been great controversy over the Greek or Roman origin. In general, the repetition of figural compositions at Pompeii shows that painters were sometimes heavily dependent on detailed models, possibly available in pattern books. The settings, on the other hand, seem always to be free inventions, and sometimes in the illustration of a Greek subject buildings are introduced that have purely Italic architecture.

Landscape painting was largely ignored down to the early years of the twentieth century, when M. I. *Rostovtzeff called attention to it (1911). While it has since been the object of several studies (C. M. Dawson, 1944, and, most recently, E. W. Leach, 1988), much remains to be done. So also with still life, H. G. Beyen made a start (1928), and there have been several significant contributions, most recently by N. Bryson (1990), but a comprehensive treatment has yet to appear. Work at present seems focused especially on the documentation of the decorations in neglected and inadequately published buildings and on the questions of social and economic history involved, as well as on the individual painters and organization of workshops.

BIBLIOGRAPHY

+H. G. Beyen, *Die Pompejanische Wanddekoration vom zweiten bis zum vierten Stil* 1 (The Hague, 1938), 2 (The Hague, 1960); +A. Barbet, *La Peinture murale romaine* (Paris, 1985); +A. Laidlaw, *The First Style in Pompeii: Painting and Architecture* (Rome, 1985); +M. de Vos, "La ricezione della pittura antica fino alla scoperta di Ercolano e Pompei," *Memoria dell'antico nell'arte italiana,* ed. S. Settis, 2 (Turin, 1985), 353–80; +W. Ehrhardt, *Stilgeschichtliche Untersuchungen an römischen Wandmalereien von der späten Republik bis zur Zeit Neros* (Mainz, 1987); N. Bryson, *Looking at the Overlooked* (London, 1990), 16–59; +A. De Franciscis et al., *La Pittura pompeiana* (Milan, 1991), 319–26; +H. Joyce, "Grasping at Shadows: Ancient Paintings in Renaissance and Baroque Rome," *ArtB* 74 (1992), 219–46.

L. RICHARDSON, JR

ROME. Greatest city of ancient Italy and the Roman Empire, continuously inhabited from the second millennium B.C. to the present; Rome has been at the center of the study of classical archaeology, both as a subject in itself and as a place that fostered research.

The archaeological history of Rome may be taken to date from the destruction of the classical city. There has been, since the Renaissance, a debate over what portion of the blame is to be assigned to natural causes and what portion to human causes. The city has always been prone to natural disasters: floods (until the great embankment works on the Tiber beginning in 1876), fires and earthquakes. But human ravages have been, it must be admitted, much more destructive; as early as ca. 500 A.C. Cassiodorus complained of the damages inflicted by lime burners.

The obvious starting point is the Visigothic sack of 410, followed by that of the Vandals in 455, though these barbarians were, it seems, much more interested in booty than destruction. The conversion of the empire to Christianity in the fourth century began the wholesale destruction of pagan buildings. On the other hand, Theodoric (493–526) repaired the *Colosseum and the *Theater of Pompey and cared for aqueducts and baths, and the preservation of the *Pantheon must be attributed to its conversion to a church in 609 (the first such); that did not stop Constans from removing its roof tiles in 663, just as Honorius removed the roof of the *Temple of Venus and Roma in 629. Other temples and buildings to be consecrated included the Senate House (S. Adriano, ca. 630), the *Temple of Antoninus and Faustina (S. Lorenzo, ca. 800) and the Temple of Venus and Roma (S. Maria Nova, ca. 840). Perhaps the allocation of the *Column of Marcus Aurelius to a nearby church in 996 and of the *Column of Trajan to S. Nicola by the twelfth century helped to preserve them.

The *Einsiedeln Itinerary notes a number of buildings that could still be seen ca. 800: the *Temple of Saturn, the *Temple of Vespasian, the temple of Concord and the Pantheon, as well as the Theater of Pompey, the *Theater of Marcellus, the Colosseum, the *Circus Maximus, the Amphitheatrum Castrense and the Circus Flaminius; also visible were a number of bath complexes (*Baths of Diocletian, *Baths of Caracalla, *Baths of Trajan, *Baths of Constantine, Baths of Sallust, Baths of Commodus, i.e., Agrippa) and a host of smaller monuments such as arches and columns. Inscriptions on many of them survived and were copied. A major period of ecclesiastical building in the ninth century must have caused great damage to these classical remains, and appalling devastation was wrought in the sack of Rome by Guiscard in 1082, when as much as two-thirds of the city was damaged.

By the Middle Ages, the leading aristocratic families had taken over many classical buildings as palaces and forts: the Orsini, the Mausoleum of Hadrian (*Castel Sant'Angelo) and the Theater of Pompey; the Colonna, the *Mausoleum of Augustus and the Baths of Constantine; the *Savelli, the Theater of Marcellus and the *Tomb of Caecilia Metella; and the Frangipani, the Colosseum and the *Arch of Titus.

The medieval pilgrims' guides (the *Mirabilia urbis Romae and other editions) show that many monuments had by then lost their classical names, and although they are mentioned, there is no information about their condition. One of the most celebrated texts of the Early Renaissance, *Petrarch's account of walks in Rome (Familiarium rerum libri. 6.2) similarly vouchsafes little real evidence for the state of the monuments. The account of the terrible earthquake in 1349 (Fam. 11.7) identifies none of the "ancient buildings" that were damaged. *Lanciani suggests the main sufferers were the south side of the Colosseum and the right aisle of the *Basilica of Maxentius.

In the 1430s *Poggio Bracciolini described the state of the classical remains in his De varietate fortunae. By his time the Tabularium was a salt store, the *Temple of Minerva in the Forum of Nerva had lime works in the portico and the *Temple of Castor and the Temple of Vespasian each had only three columns remaining, but there were still "extensive, fine" ruins of the Baths of Alexander Severus near the Pantheon. The *Capitoline Hill was deserted, the *Palatine Hill was a rubbish heap and the *Forum Romanum was the haunt of animals.

As early as 1462, the government had issued prohibitions (said to go back to the twelfth century) against damaging ancient buildings, but from the beginning the main offenders against such laws were the popes themselves, driven by their insatiable thirst for building materials. Nicholas V (1447–55) caused tremendous destruction to the Colosseum, Basilica of Maxentius and the Temple of Venus and Roma. *Paul II (1464–71) plundered especially the Colosseum to build the church of S. Marco. *Sixtus IV (1471–84) demolished half a dozen temples and arches, for example, the temple of Hercules in the *Forum Boarium and an arch near the Palazzo Colonna. The same pope, however, founded the *Capitoline Museum (1471). Alexander VI (1492–1503) plundered the Mausoleum of Hadrian, the Baths of Diocletian and the Forum Transitorium (*Imperial Fora). In the late fifteenth century the *Basilica Julia was ravaged for the Palazzo Torlonia; the Colosseum and the Arch of Gallienus, for the Palazzo della Cancelleria. It was, however, the construction of the new basilica of St. Peter (1506–1626) that caused the most damage. The Fabbrica di S. Pietro, the department of works for the new church, was given in 1540 the right to take away stone anywhere inside and outside the city.

In the early sixteenth century the destroyers were hard at work in the Forum, the *Basilica Aemilia and Basilica Julia and the *Temple of Vesta, Temple of Saturn and Temple of Vespasian. The city suffered eight days of pillaging at the hands of Charles of Bourbon in 1527, although as usual it was looting rather than destruction of buildings. *Paul III's Palazzo Farnese (begun 1540) came from the temple of the Sun on the Quirinal and the Baths of Caracalla. The Forum of Trajan (*Imperial Fora) was plundered on behalf of the Vatican. It has been calculated that the decade 1540–50 was one of the most destructive for the classical monuments. The center of the Forum especially suffered: the Regia was destroyed, and the lists of consuls (*Fasti*) from the nearby Arch of Augustus were preserved only through the personal intervention of Cardinal Alessandro Farnese (*Farnese family). In the 1560s, the Via Alessandrina and Via Bonella were cut across the Forum. Gregory XIII plundered the Mausoleum of Hadrian and the grove of the Arvals for his chapel in St. Peter's (1572). In the 1580s, *Sixtus V demolished the Severan *Septizodium on the Palatine and much of the Claudian aqueduct and the Baths of Diocletian.

In the same century, many classical buildings were transformed. The Theater of Marcellus was remade, ca. 1520, into the Savelli palace by *Peruzzi. The shell of the Mausoleum of Augustus was partially transformed into the garden of the Soderini (ca. 1550), while the Baths of Diocletian were partially transformed into the church of S. Maria degli Angeli by *Michelangelo in the 1560s. The remains of the Temple of Jupiter Optimus Maximus on the Capitol formed the foundation of the Caffarelli palace (1570s). The founding of the Collegio Romano in 1582 made enormous changes in the southern *Campus Martius.

Against all this destruction and change, the interest in classical antiquities reached new heights. At the end of the fifteenth century, the first attention was given to the *Domus Aurea; *Raphael made his celebrated visit shortly after he came to Rome, in 1509. The *Laocoon* was discovered there or nearby in 1506. Fra *Gioconda da Verona (d. 1515) wrote with great emotion of the continual destruction of classical remains and quoted the boast of some that their houses were founded completely with fragments of statues. Raphael (or Castiglione) wrote to *Leo X at the same time, protesting the way buildings were undermined by digging for *pozzolana* for concrete and the massive destruction of marble for lime in the infamous kilns. Paul III established the office of papal antiquarian (*Commissario delle Antichità) in 1534 to protect the monuments and supervise excavations. By the 1530s, the first fragments of the *Ara Pacis were found, under the Palazzo Peretti Fiano. In 1538 the *Marcus Aurelius* Equestrian Statue was removed from near the *Lateran to the Capitol. In 1545 major art treasures, the *Farnese *Bull* and the *Farnese *Hercules,* were found in the Baths of Caracalla. By the middle of the sixteenth century, indeed, leading antiquarians thronged Rome, studying and drawing the monuments: *Marliani, Sigonio, *Fulvio, *Ligorio, Fauno, *Pighius, *Smetius, *Panvinio. *Lafréry initiated a major engraving business, and artists such as *Cock, *Du Pérac and van *Heemskerck were at work.

The first Christian catacombs were discovered in 1578 on the Via Salaria. In the 1580s *Sixtus V, otherwise the great destroyer, thanks to the genius of Domenico *Fontana, not only moved the Vatican obelisk (*obelisks) but also raised one at S. Maria Maggiore, excavated another in the Circus Maximus and raised it at S. Giovanni Laterano and erected yet a fourth (also from the Circus Maximus) in the Piazza del Popolo. Sixtus also cleared around the Colosseum and restored the Column of Marcus Aurelius and set up the *Quirinal *Horse Tamers* on that hill.

The Temple of Antoninus and Faustina was converted into a Baroque church by Torriani in 1602. In 1612 the church of S. Maria Nova in the Temple of Venus and Roma was rebuilt as S. Francesca Romana. The Baths of Constantine on the Quirinal were demolished for the Rospigliosi palace, begun in 1611. The Temple of Minerva in the Forum of Nerva was plundered by Paul V (1605–21) for the Borghese chapel in S. Maria Maggiore and the Aqua Paola; he also removed the last of the eight marble columns from the Basilica of Maxentius and set it up in the Piazza S. Maria Maggiore. Urban VIII (1623–44) most notoriously removed the bronze beams from the porch of the Pantheon but also restored the missing column on the left-hand corner. On the Capitol in the 1640s, the Palazzo Nuovo was constructed, and the decoration of the contemporary Villa Pamphilii required frenzied excavation. The obelisk of Domitian excavated in the Circus of Maxentius was raised by *Bernini in Piazza Navona in 1651. The *Arco di Portogallo in the Corso was demolished by Alexander VII in 1662, and the bronze doors were removed from the Senate House to S. Giovanni Laterano, but the *Pyramid of Cestius was also extensively restored.

In the late sixteenth and early seventeenth centuries, systematic study of Roman antiquities was promoted by Fulvio *Orsini and Cassiano dal *Pozzo in Rome and by foreigners who visited the city, such as *Peiresc and *Rubens. Discoveries continued apace; work on Castel Sant'Angelo in the 1620s unearthed much ancient sculpture, including the *Barberini *Faun.* One of the most famous collections of classical sculpture, that of the *Ludovisi family, was formed. *Christina of Sweden arrived in Rome in 1655, became the center of a group of antiquarians and made a famous collection of antiquities (sold to the *Odescalchi family in 1692). Important collections of antiquities were lost to the city: the Massimi family collection to Spain in 1677 and the *Mattei family to France in 1682. During this period the publications of *Bartoli and *Bellori presented newly excavated material as well as long-familiar monuments.

Another major earthquake struck in 1703; it brought down a section of the Colosseum, which was promptly reused to build the Porto di Ripetta. Clement XII reorganized the Capitoline collections; the new museum was opened in 1734 and included the *Albani family collection (which cost 60,000 scudi). Clement also carried out extensive restorations to the *Arch of Constantine in 1733. *Clement XIV founded the Museo Clementino in 1771 and bought much of the *Barberini family collection and some of the best of the Mattei. *Pius VI (1775–99) restored and erected an obelisk from the Mausoleum of Augustus on the Quirinal, another of Augustus at Montecitorio and a third from the *Gardens of Sallust at Trinità dei Monti.

The eighteenth century also saw important but mostly destructive excavations: Francesco *Bianchini in the Domus Flaviorum on the Palatine in the 1720s and the columbarium of the freedmen of Livia near S. Sebastiano in 1726 (*Columbaria); Gavin *Hamilton and the Abbé Rancoureuil on the Palatine in the 1770s; Cardinal Palotta near the Basilica of Maxentius; Ludovico Mirri in the Domus Aurea, 1774; von Fredenheim in the area of the Basilica Julia in 1788. The *Tomb of the Scipios was rediscovered and vandalized in 1780. In 1786 Giuseppe *Guattani founded the first journal to report new discoveries, *Monumenti Antichi Inediti,* but only three volumes were published.

The century was, above all, the time when foreign collectors, notably the English, descended on Rome. Their acquisitions were abetted by the greed of the aristocratic owners, willing to dispose of any collection at the right price, the result often of centuries of excavation and assembling: the Giustiniani collection (Vincenzo *Giustiniani) went to the Earl of Pembroke in 1720; the *Odescalchi to Spain in 1724; much of the collection of the *Albani family and of the Chigi to Poland in 1728. The *Medici family removed their collection to Florence in 1769, and the Farnese transferred theirs to Naples in 1787. G. B. *Piranesi arrived in 1740—excavator, collector and, most famously, engraver, whose *Vedute di Roma* were not only essential for any serious visitor but also important beyond all other views in making the classical remains famous throughout the world. From the 1770s, a leading exporter was Gavin *Hamilton; major English collections were thus formed: the Lansdowne (Shelburne), *Townley, *Blundell and Hope.

The nineteenth century was ushered in appropriately by the appointment of the longest-serving papal antiquarian, Carlo *Fea (1800–36). He was also the most important; being a lawyer, he fought relentlessly to establish state ownership of the cultural patrimony and formulated the edicts protecting the antiquities of 1802 and 1820 (the Pacca Edict). Fea was also probably responsible for the impressive program of clearing and investigation by Pius VII, around the *Arch of Septimius Severus (1802–3); in the construction of the Pantheon (1804); around the Arch of Constantine (1805); and in the Colosseum (1805–7), for which the "Stern buttress" was constructed.

Under the treaty made with the Papal States at Tolentino in 1797, *Napoleon carried away to Paris some of the most important sculptures in Rome, from the *Laocoon* to the *Belvedere *Apollo* and many others. Most of these were to be returned to Rome by around 1815, but in these same years the *Borghese family collection was sold to France (1807), and most of it was never returned. The French occupied Rome from 1808 to 1814. During that short period the first comprehensive program of clearing and restoring virtually every major classical monument was undertaken: the Arch of Janus, Basilica of Maxentius, the slope of the Capitol, the Colosseum, the Column of Phocas, the Domus Aurea, the Temple of Fortuna Virilis, much of the Forum of Trajan, the Tabularium, the Temple of Antoninus and Faustina, the Temple of Castor, the Temple of Saturn, the Temple of Vespasian and the "Temple of Vesta" in the *Forum Boarium. The chief architects were *Valadier and *Camporese. The French administration also reestablished the Accademia Romana di Archeologia (*Pontificia Accademia) and appointed the foundation professor of archaeology at the University of Rome, Lorenzo Re. In the middle of the work, in March 1812, a very strong earthquake struck Rome; of the monuments, the Colosseum suffered more than any other.

The three temples in the Forum Holitorium were investigated by Valadier from 1806 to 1816; the Temple of Castor was fully mapped and identified in 1816 by Fea, who also discovered the Temple of Concord in 1817. This led to the correct identification of the Temple of Saturn and the Temple of Vespasian by *Canina. The Basilica of Maxentius was more completely excavated by *Nibby (1818–19, 1828) and conclusively identified (it was previously called the Temple of Peace). Nibby also excavated in the Temple of Venus and Roma (1827–29).

The Arch of Titus was completely dismantled and carefully restored by Valadier (1820–24). The same architect constructed for the Colosseum the second great buttress, on the Forum side (1824–26). A new era was marked by Leo XII's approval for the clearing of the whole Forum down to the classical level in 1827, and a proper scientific underpinning for such work was created by the establishment in 1829 of the *Instituto di Corrispondenza Archeologica, later the *German Archaeological Institute.

The rest of the period of the papal government at Rome (until 1870) saw feverish excavation on all sides: that of the Temple of Mars Ultor (*Imperial Fora) began in 1842; the Basilica Julia was excavated and finally identified by Canina in 1848, establishing once and for all the limits of the Forum on that side; in 1849 in Trastevere the *Apoxyomenos* was found along with a hoard of bronze.

In the 1860s, J. H. Parker excavated the Forum of Caesar, and Guidi investigated the underground areas of the Baths of Caracalla. The *Villa of Livia at Prima Porta was discovered in 1863. Pietro Rosa excavated the Palatine for Napoleon III, discovering the temple of Jupiter and the *House of Livia (1869). The grove of the Arval Brethren on the Via Campagna (known since ca. 1575) was excavated by W. Henzen in 1868.

In 1870, the office of Commissario delle Antichità was replaced by the Soprintendenza, the first incumbent of which was Rosa. He now carried on the work on the Palatine for the state, clearing the stadium (1872–93). The two streets cutting across the Forum were removed in 1882, and the Via Sacra was cleared. *Lanciani excavated the house of the Vestals (1883–84), and H. Jordan and *Hülsen cleared and identified the Regia. Lanciani finally identified the Senate House in S. Adriano in 1882, and Hülsen, following Jordan, correctly identified the Basilica Aemilia in 1884; it was excavated in 1889. In the Baths of Constantine on the Quirinal, the bronze figures of a seated boxer and a *Hellenistic *"Ruler"* were found in 1885. The Museo Nazionale delle *Terme was established in 1889, but the construction of the monument of Vittorio Emmanuele II beside the Capitol (1885–1911) blotted out forever a major part of classical Rome. The true Hadrianic date of the Pantheon was proven by G. Chedanne in 1892.

Another new era was marked in Roman archaeology by the appointment in 1898 of Giacomo *Boni as director of excavations in the Forum and then also the Palatine (until 1925). He discovered most notably the *Lapis Niger, the Archaic cemetery on the Via Sacra (pushing back the archaeology of Rome into the prehistoric period), the Equus Domitiani and the Lacus Curtius. An unsuccessful attempt was made in 1903 to free the Ara Pacis. Major clearings of the Baths of Diocletian were conducted by *Ricci (1908–11), and the underground Pythagorean basilica at Porta Maggiore was discovered in 1917.

Archaeology under *Fascism (1922–43) embraced a vast program of clearing the Senate House, the Basilica Aemilia and the Domus Augustiana on the Palatine by A. Bartoli (director of excavations 1925–45), the *Largo Argentina by A.M. Colini, the Theater of Marcellus by P. Fidenzoni, the Mausoleum of Augustus by G.Q. *Giglioli, the Circus Maximus and the Forum Boarium by A. Muñoz, and the Forums of Caesar and Augustus by Ricci. The most brilliant accomplishment of all was the recovery of the Ara Pacis by Giuseppe Moretti, using the most daring and sophisticated modern techniques. At the same time, however, the whole area on the west side of the Capitol extending to the Theater of Marcellus was wiped out, and the Velian Hill was destroyed in the very center of classical Rome, with remains from prehistoric to imperial.

Following World War II, work has been devoted, as almost everywhere in archaeology, to consolidation and recording; less attention has been given to costly new work. Under P. Romanelli, Bartoli's successor as director of excavations (1946–60) in the Forum, work was carried out on the Arch of Augustus, the Rostra, the temple of Julius Caesar and the Basilica Aemilia. The Iron Age huts on the Palatine and the temple of Magna Mater were uncovered. Since then, the sacred area of *Sant' Omobono has revealed the temples of Fortune and Mater Matuta, and Frank *Brown carried out exemplary investigation of the Regia. Recently, the *American Academy in Rome has conducted investigations in the Atrium Vestae and on the slopes of the Palatine.

The main problem, however, has been increasingly to preserve the already known monuments from degradation caused by atmospheric pollution. An almost unceasing cycle of "interventions" has been necessary. Some success has been achieved in closing to cars most vital areas around the Colosseum, and the road across the Forum under the Tabularium has been removed.

BIBLIOGRAPHY

E. Muntz, *Les Antiquités de la ville de Rome aux 14–16 siècles* (Paris, 1886); R. Lanciani, *The Destruction of Ancient Rome* (London, 1897); idem, *Storia degli scavi,* 1–4 (1902–12; reissued with illus. 1989–1992); C. Pietrangeli, *Scavi e scoperti di antichità sotto il pontificato di Pio VI* (Rome, 1958); R. Ridley, *"Augusti manes volitant per auras:* The Archaeology of Rome under the Fascists," *Xenia* 11 (1986), 19–46; +idem, *The Eagle and the Spade.*

R. T. RIDLEY

ROSELLE. See RUSELLAE.

ROSS, LUDWIG (1806–59). German archaeologist and traveler.

Born in Holstein, son of a peasant of Scottish origin, Ross began medicine at Kiel but turned to classics, which he studied there under Twesten, Dahlmann and Nitzsch. He first met O. *Jahn at Kiel. While privately tutoring at Copenhagen, he was awarded by the King of Denmark the first traveling scholarship; in 1832, after studying at Leipzig under Gottfried Hermann, he sailed to Greece. In 1833 he was appointed ephor of the antiquities of the Peloponnese, and in 1834 general ephor of Greece. He began to direct excavations on the *Akropolis at Athens in 1835. Preservation of the Attic monuments and, in particular, his restoration of the *Temple of Nike in collaboration with the architects Schaubert and Hansen remain his great contribution to archaeology (*Der Tempel der Nike Apteros,* 1839). When appointed professor of archaeology at the University of Athens (1837–43), Ross taught in modern Greek, into which he translated for his lectures K. O. *Müller's *Handbuch der Archaeologie der Kunst.* In 1845 he became professor of archaeology and mythology at Halle.

Endowed with the best qualities of a "learned" traveler, Ross traveled broadly in the Peloponnese, through the Aegean Islands and in Asia Minor. He studied the topography, described with precision the archaeological monuments and carefully copied inscriptions, which he promptly published. A pioneer in the area of the Greek *Altertumswissenschaft,* Ross was no less interested in the contemporary culture and history of the Greeks in whose language and folklore he saw the continuity of ancient Greek civilization.

BIBLIOGRAPHY

L. Ross, *Reisen auf den griechischen Inseln des Ägäischen Meeres* 1–3 (Stuttgart, 1840–45; 2nd ed. of pt. II, Halle, 1912–13, ed. F. Hiller von Gaertringen et al.); idem, *Reisen und Reiserouten durch Griechenland* (Berlin, 1841); idem, *Reisen nach Kos, Halikar-nassos, Rhodos und der Insel Cypern* (Halle, 1852); idem, *Erinnerungen und Mitteilun-gen aus Griechenland* (Berlin, 1863; repr. as *Subsidia Byzantina* 20, (Leipzig, 1982).

ANGELIKI PETROPOULOU

ROSSELLINO, BERNARDO (GAMBERELLI, BERNARDO DI MATTEO DEL BORRA; 1409–64). Italian Renaissance sculptor and architect.

Bernardo Rossellino was born in Settignano near Florence. He became the head of a large Florentine workshop that was instrumental in disseminating the classicizing manner of the Early Renaissance. His first project, the Misericordia Palace in Arezzo (1433–35) with its classical niches, pilasters and entablatures, took little directly from antiquity but appropriated motifs from the work of his progressive contemporaries, *Donatello, Michelozzo, *Ghiberti and *Brunelle-schi. By the 1440s, however, Rossellino was displaying a greater independence. His marble door frame inside the Public Palace of Siena (1446) was one of the finest expressions of the Roman revival to date, and his celebrated tomb for the humanist Leonardo Bruni at the church of Santa Croce in Florence (1446–48) established a whole genre of classically conceived funeral sculpture. The dec-orative language used in the triumphal arch framework of this tomb was a tour de force in antique devices and the Renaissance interpretation of classical ar-chitectural decoration. Rossellino's Spinelli Cloister (1448–52) at the same church displays his knowledge (via Brunelleschi) of Euclidean geometric prin-ciples.

An extended stay in Rome during the early 1450s brought Rossellino into direct contact with the antiquities of that city and exposed him to the influential architectural theories of L. B. *Alberti (and, through him, of Vitruvius). The impact of these new experiences may be seen at the town of Pienza, which Rossellino rebuilt between 1459 and 1464 for Pope *Pius II Piccolomini. At Pienza, Rossellino was responsible for the town square, the cathedral, the Pic-colomini Palace and a number of civic and private buildings. The front of the cathedral reflects the best in humanist architecture, while the exterior of the palace, with its three tiers of pilasters, shows the direct influence of the Roman *Colosseum (a scheme he was to use again on the Rucellai Palace in Florence). Rossellino's greatest accomplishment at Pienza, however, was in thinking of the entire project as a totality and in producing a concept of "city" not seen in Italy since the days of ancient Rome.

BIBLIOGRAPHY
+L. Planiscig, *Bernardo und Antonio Rossellino* (Vienna, 1942); +E. Carli, *Pienza, la città di Pio II* (Rome, 1966); +C. R. Mack, "The Rucellai Palace: Some New Propos-als," *ArtB* 56 (1974), 517–29; A. Schulz, *The Sculpture of Bernardo Rossellino and His Workshop* (Princeton, NJ, 1976); C. R. Mack, *Pienza: The Creation of a Renaissance City* (Ithaca, NY, 1987).

CHARLES RANDALL MACK

ROSTOVTZEFF, MICHAEL IVANOVITCH (ROSTOVZEV, MICHAIL IVANOVICH; 1870–1952).
Russian-born historian, archaeologist and art historian; distinguished authority on economic and social aspects of the ancient world.

Rostovtzeff was born near Kiev (Ukraine) and learned philology from his father, a teacher of Latin and Greek. He entered the university at St. Petersburg in 1890, where he was especially influenced by the Byzantine art historian P. N. Kondakov. He received his degree in 1892, with a thesis on recent work at *Pompeii. On a three-year tour of Europe and the Near East (1895–98), he was able to work at the *British Museum in London, the Cabinet des Médailles in Paris and the *German Archaeological Institute in Rome, as well as to travel extensively to actual sites. Studying at Vienna, Rostovtzeff did epigraphy with E. Bormann and archaeology with O. *Benndorf.

Returning to Russia, he taught Latin at the University of St. Petersburg and ancient history at the Women's College there, until 1918. At that time, a dissenter from the Bolshevik revolution, he immigrated to England and then to the United States. He taught at Oxford briefly, then at the University of Wisconsin, Madison (1920–25), and finally at Yale University (1925–44). His devoted wife, Sophia, accompanied him throughout his life, ever a dedicated secretary and compiler of indexes.

The historical writings of Rostovtzeff were shaped by his ability to assemble details meticulously and comprehensively from a variety of sources—epigraphic, papyrological, cultural, literary and archaeological—to create a masterly synthesis. His best-known works are *The Social and Economic History of the Roman Empire* (1926; 2nd ed., rev. by P. M. Fraser, 1957) and *The Social and Economic History of the Hellenistic World,* three volumes. (1941; 2nd ed., with additions by P. M. Fraser, 1953). These established his place as one of the most original and profound classical scholars of the first half of the twentieth century.

Rostovtzeff wrote one of the enduring classics on the intercultural zone of the Black Sea in antiquity, *Iranians and Greeks in South Russia* (1922), dealing with the Scythians and their relations with the Greeks. His principal fieldwork was in Syria at the Hellenistic/Roman site of *Dura-Europos, where he directed Yale's campaigns from 1928 to 1937. Ten volumes of preliminary reports and six of the final reports on Dura appeared before Rostovtzeff's death, as well as the general work, *Dura-Europos and Its Art* (Oxford, 1938). His immense bibliography, embracing East and West and the art, religion, history, economy and society of ancient Italy and the Hellenistic world, was produced throughout a period of active scholarship lasting over fifty years. The heroic effort involved in finishing *The Social and Economic History of the Hellenistic World* (1941) left Rostovtzeff exhausted and depressed, and his intense preoccupation with the events of World War II led to further deterioration of his mental state. A lobotomy was performed, leaving him unable to pursue his research for some years prior to his death in 1952. During his lifetime, Rostovtzeff was accorded

the highest status and was frequently recognized for his achievements, with numerous honorary degrees (from Oxford, Cambridge, Athens, Harvard, Chicago, Wisconsin) and with membership in almost every European learned academy.
BIBLIOGRAPHY
C. Bradford Welles, "Bibliography—M. Rostovtzeff," *Historia* 5 (1956), 351–88; "Rostovcev, Michael," *EAA* 6 (1965), 1031; J. Rufus Fears, "M. Rostovtzeff," in Briggs—Calder, 405–18.

ROUND TEMPLE BY THE TIBER. See TEMPLE OF VESTA.

ROVERE, FRANCESCO DELLA. See SIXTUS IV.

ROYAL ONTARIO MUSEUM, Toronto. Museum with the largest collection of Greek, Etruscan and Roman artifacts in Canada.

The museum's predecessors were established when Bill 138 of the Ontario Legislature (26 February, 1912) received assent from the English king, George VI, on 16 April 1912. When the museum opened its doors in 1914, one of the five original sections was the Royal Ontario Museum of Archaeology, associated with the University of Toronto and containing a classical section. In 1920, the Classical Collection was the first part of the museum to be designated as a department, under Cornelia Harcum, the first keeper. The Classical Collection was renamed the Greek and Roman Department in 1951 under J. Walter Graham, who now took the official title of curator. In 1968, the University of Toronto gave up control of the museum when it became a cultural agency of the province of Ontario.

The department's collection was started in the early twentieth century, when, in 1902, Charles Trick Currelly (1876–1955) purchased Greek and Roman lamps and pottery in Abydos, Egypt. Currelly, as the official collector of the University of Toronto, also purchased Minoan terracotta figurines, European Bronze Age weapons and Etruscan weapons and jewelry in Europe in 1906. The Etruscan material of this purchase came from G. Pacini of Florence, the first major source for Etruscan artifacts.

While the Western world was realizing that Syro-Palestine was an untapped resource for classical antiquities, Currelly purchased Greek and Roman lamps, Roman pottery and Roman glass from J. Vestor & Co. in the American colony of Jerusalem in 1910. As director of the museum, he purchased in 1919 the Sturges collection, which was assembled by William Allen Sturges of Icklingham Hall, Mildenhall, Suffolk, during the 1880s and 1890s in Italy. This collection also had pieces from older English collections, including the Dodd, Bateman and Forman.

Currelly bought a large collection of Etruscan antiquities in 1923 from G. Petroncini of Rome, the second major source for Etruscan artifacts. The Etruscan collection was added to again in the 1920s, when Sigmund Samuel donated over 240 specimens of ceramics from Etruscan and other cultures.

In the years 1927–30, the Romano-British collection, unique in North America, was started from purchases of Samian ware from G. Lawrence, who acquired his pieces from construction sites in London. J. Iliffe donated a large number of Romano-British artifacts from his excavation of Alchester, Oxfordshire, during the 1930s. This collection was increased in 1939 by a gift of 185 pieces from the city of London. Other artifacts from the 1930s were eight large sculptures, including a Roman copy of an *Athletic Figure* after Polykleitos, purchased by the Reuben Wells Leonard bequest, and seven of the sixteen Roman mummy portraits from Egypt. The eight sculptures constitute the majority of sculptures in the museum because it was established after the great period of collecting classical marbles and sculptures.

There was a gift of 300 pieces of ancient glass from Helen Norton in the 1950s and 216 antiquities came from the collection of Ludwig *Curtius, including a Roman portrait of the third century A.C. But the growth of the Cypriot collection dominated this decade. This collection, the second largest in North America, includes 351 Cypriot antiquities, left to the museum by Colonel G. Flakland, who collected them in 1885. In 1959, Dowager Lady Loch of London donated over 300 more Cypriot items that had been collected in Cyprus by Lord Loch in the years 1900–25.

The department opened the Athenian Public Life Gallery, which included a model of the *Akropolis of Athens, in 1962. Along with this model, there is a reconstruction of the *Athena Parthenos, considered one of the best. In the 1970s, the department decided to concentrate on publishing its collection, a project in which John Hayes has played a large role. In recent years, acquisitions have been mainly donations from the public. Some examples are a miniature marble head of a Ptolemaic king, two Etruscan bronze mirrors and a collection of 300 Greek and Roman coins.

BIBLIOGRAPHY

+J. W. Hayes, *Greek and Italian Black-Gloss Ware and Related Wares in the Royal Ontario Museum* (Toronto, 1984); +idem, *Greek, Roman, and Related Metalware in the Royal Ontario Museum* (Toronto, 1984); +L. Dickson, *The Museum Makers: The Story of the Royal Ontario Museum* (Toronto, 1986); *History of the Classical Department and Its Current Status, Royal Ontario Museum* (Toronto, 1992).

PHILIP J. TRAINA

RUBENIUS, ALBERT. See RUBENS, ALBERT.

RUBENIUS, PHILIPPUS. See RUBENS, PHILIP.

RUBENS, ALBERT (ALBERTUS RUBENIUS; 1614–57). Flemish classical scholar, specializing in ancient clothing and coins and gems; eldest son and second child of P. P. *Rubens.

Encouraged by his father, Albert showed an aptitude for classical studies at an early age. In 1627 the precocious child wrote a Latin poem on the gold coins in the collection of Charles de Croy, published anonymously by J. Hemelaers in *Imperatorum romanorum numismata aurea.* While Rubens was traveling in England and Spain (1629–30), he entrusted the education of Albert to his close friend, the humanist scholar *Gevaerts.

Albert wrote several treatises on Roman antiquities, including studies of the *Gemma Augustea and *Gemma Tiberiana. Undoubtedly in his research he used his father's library, papers and collection, which he inherited at Rubens's death. Albert relied heavily on his father's correspondence with *Peiresc for the interpretation of the Gemma Tiberiana and also used some of the engravings the artist had prepared for an unfinished book on ancient gems. At his death, Albert left a number of manuscripts, some finished and others not. Gevaerts published the treatises on the two great Gemmae and several other short studies, along with a study on clothing (*De lato clavo libri II*) that was finished by *Graevius; the whole collection was brought forth under the title *De re vestiaria veterum* (Antwerp, 1665).

Of the engraved gems and cameos left behind at Albert's death, an inventory was drawn up in duplicate by the canon of Tournai, J. *Chifflet (one copy exists, in Besançon). His gems included a cameo with *Luna* (now in London), a cameo with *Joseph* (now in St. Petersburg) and a stone with *Aqua Virgo,* published by Chifflet (location unknown). The coin collection comprised silver and bronze specimens and was probably rather modest. The early death of Albert Rubens was deplored by his humanist friends, J. F. Gronovius (*Gronovius family), Heinsius and Gevaerts.

BIBLIOGRAPHY

M. van der Meulen, *Petrus Paulus Rubens Antiquarius* (Alphen aan den Rijn, 1975); O. Neverov, "Gems in the Collection of Rubens," *BurlMag* 121 (1979), 424–32; N. T. de Grummond, "The Study of Classical Costume by Philip, Albert, and Peter Paul Rubens," *Journal of the Ringling Museum of Art* (1983), 78–93; M. van der Meulen, "Observations on Rubens' Drawings After the Antique," *Journal of the Ringling Museum of Art* (1983), 36–51.

MARJON VAN DER MEULEN

RUBENS, Sir PETER PAUL (PETRUS PAULUS RUBENIUS; 1577–1640). Flemish artist, collector and scholar of classical antiquity; distinguished political figure at the courts of France, England and Spain in the early seventeenth century.

Rubens was very well known in his time for his knowledge of classical art and archaeology. "In matters of antiquity, especially, he has the most universal and most refined knowledge I have ever encountered," wrote *Peiresc, the famous French scholar, after he had met Rubens in Paris in 1621. Rubens had studied Greek and Latin literature as a boy at the Jesuit school in Antwerp and had received full exposure to the ancient world during his years in Italy, 1600–8.

He studied and made drawings of sculptures in famous private collections in Rome, for example, the *Farnese *Hercules* and *Farnese *Bull;* the *Belvedere Torso, *Laocoon* and *Capitoline *Wolf;* the Chigi *Silenus;* the *Borghese *Fisherman,* the *Borghese *Hermaphrodite, Mars and Venus, Centaur and Amor;* and the Cesi *Roma* and *Togatus.* A surviving fragment of a treatise by Rubens on the imitation of statues, *De imitatione statuarum,* advises artists to avoid the effect of stone when making such copies; Rubens's own drawings are consistent with this practice. His history paintings show his knowledge of the reliefs of the *Column of Trajan and *Arch of Constantine. The cabinet of Fulvio *Orsini, housed in the Palazzo Farnese, interested him, and he had copies made after the drawings of Dirk Galle picturing Orsini's portrait busts and Greek coins.

Rubens also began to collect antiquities while he was in Italy, and he continued to acquire objects throughout his life. His portrait head of the so-called Seneca (*Pseudo-Seneca*), which he used as a model in engravings and paintings (e.g., the *Four Philosophers* in the Pitti Palace, Florence), was obtained in Italy and carried back with him to grace his new house in Antwerp. There he displayed other antique busts and statues that he had acquired (he also owned heads identified as *Cicero* and *Chrysippos*), as well as his cabinet of ancient coins and gems. In 1618, he traded a group of paintings and tapestries to Sir Dudley Carleton, English ambassador to The Hague, for a reputedly fine collection of marbles, including portrait busts, herms, funerary urns and a Christian sarcophagus; however, he was willing to sell this entire collection to the Duke of *Buckingham some ten years later.

Rubens had a special love for, and understanding of, Greek and Roman carved gems and had a superb personal collection of these items. The jewel of his collection was a large agate vase (the *Rubens Vase, now in the Walters Art Gallery, Baltimore), which was purchased for 2,000 gold scudi when it appeared at the Foire St. Germain in Paris in 1619. He also owned a number of large cameos with Roman imperial portraits, which he had bought from an agent in Brussels. Many of these and other items from his collection are today in the Cabinet des Médailles in Paris.

The artist was also interested in publishing books on classical antiquity and assisted his brother Philip Rubens by supplying a number of drawings after antique sculptures as illustrations for a book by the latter on Roman customs and Latin texts, *Electorum libri II* (Antwerp, 1608). His most ambitious publishing scheme was never realized; the artist himself intended to publish a book on "all the most famous cameos of Europe." Peiresc, the Italian archaeologist Cassiano dal *Pozzo and other scholars were invited to collaborate on the project, but the group was never able to coordinate its efforts. Notes and portions of the unpublished text survive, as well as a number of drawings and engravings of gems by Rubens, and these reveal that the book would have included such famous works as the *Portland Vase, the Gonzaga Cameo, the *Gemma Augustea, the *Gemma Tiberiana and the *Great Cameo of the Hague. Also to be included were a number of the finest pieces from Rubens's own cabinet, as well as those belonging to Lelio *Pasqualino.

At his death, Rubens left his collection to his two eldest sons. Albert Rubens took a great interest in this subject, which had been so dear to his father, and succeeded in publishing his scholarship on some of the gems studied earlier by Rubens and Peiresc. At Albert's death in 1657, an inventory was made of 212 gems in his possession; probably many of these originally belonged to his father.

Besides his interest in major works of sculpture and in carved gems, Rubens's study of antiquity embraced a wide range of subject matter: numismatics, ancient landscape painting, Roman armor, ancient dishes, spoons, tripods, weights and measures and the Egyptian calendar. He evidently owned and kept in his studio along with his classical antiquities an Egyptian mummy.

BIBLIOGRAPHY

F. Goeler von Ravensburg, *Rubens und die Antike* (Jena, 1882); W. Stechow, *Rubens and the Classical Tradition* (Cambridge, MA, 1968); +M. van der Meulen, *Petrus Paulus Rubens Antiquarius,* (Alphen aan den Rijn, 1975); +N.T. de Grummond, "A Seventeenth Century Book of Classical Gems," *Archaeology* 30 (1977), 14–25; J. M. Muller, "Rubens's Museum of Antique Sculpture: An Introduction," *ArtB* 59 (1977), 571–82; +idem, *Rubens: The Artist as Collector* (Princeton, NJ, 1989), 150–52; F. Bastet, "Oudheden uit Rubens' verzamling in Leiden," *Nederlands Kunsthistorische Jaarboek* 31 (1980), 72–85; D. Jaffe, "Peiresc, Rubens, dal Pozzo and the 'Portland' Vase," *BurlMag* 131 (1989), 554–59; +M. van der Meulen, *Rubens after the Antique*, Corpus Rubenianum Ludwig Burchard, 23 (London, 1994).

MARJON VAN DER MEULEN AND NANCY T. de GRUMMOND

RUBENS, PHILIP (PHILIPPUS RUBENIUS; 1574–1611). Flemish classical philologist and humanist; brother of Peter Paul *Rubens.

Philip Rubens received his most important classical training as a pupil of Justus *Lipsius in Louvain. In 1601, he went to Italy as secretary to Jean Richardot and as tutor to Richardot's two sons; he obtained his legal degree in Rome (1604) before he departed for Antwerp. Appointed then as secretary to Cardinal Ascanio Colonna in 1605, he returned to Rome, where he prepared a book, *Electorum libri II,* in collaboration with his brother. Philip returned to Antwerp in 1607 and was appointed secretary of the city (1609). His book was published in Antwerp in 1608; it is a volume of emendations and commentaries on passages from classical writers. He acknowledges the contribution of his brother, Peter Paul, who provided drawings for the illustrations, including a togate statue, possibly the *Consul* in the *Cesi family collection; a relief with Circus Games, now in the storage of the Vatican Museums; the Cesi *Roma;* the *Farnese *Flora*; details from a relief on the *Arch of the Argentarii and from a relief with the *Sacrifice of Marcus Aurelius* (Capitoline Museums); and sacrificial paraphernalia depicted on a relief from the *Temple of Vespasian in Rome. Various passages on classical clothing in the book are probably due to the influence of Peter Paul.

BIBLIOGRAPHY
C. Ruelens, *Correspondance de P.P. Rubens* 1 (Antwerp, 1887), 9–17; M. van der Meulen, *Petrus Paulus Rubens Antiquarius* (Alphen aan den Rijn, 1975), 81–82; N. T. de Grummond, "The Study of Classical Costume by Philip, Albert, and Peter Paul Rubens," *Journal of the Ringling Museum of Art* (1983), 78–93; +M. van der Meulen, *Rubens after the Antique*, Corpus Rubenianum Ludwig Burchard, 23 (London, 1994), 97–113.
MARJON VAN DER MEULEN

RUBENS VASE. Vase carved out of a large, rare piece of honey-colored agate (19cm high).

Decorated in relief with heads of Pan, grapevines and acanthus leaves, the vase has been dated to the fourth century A.C. Of the illustrious names on the list of owners of the piece, that of the painter P. P. *Rubens has been attached permanently to it. He owned the vase from 1619 (it was purchased at the Fair of St. Germain in Paris for 2,000 gold scudi) until he sold it to his brother-in-law Daniel Fourment between 1626 and 1628. A spirited engraving of the vase was executed by Paulus Pontius, after a design by Rubens himself.

The earliest record of the vase belongs to the year 1360, when it was inventoried in the collection of the Duke of Anjou. In the sixteenth century it belonged to the royal collection at Fontainebleau and, according to one tradition, was stolen when the palace was ransacked by the Huguenots in 1590. After Rubens owned the vase, it was sent to be sold in the East Indies but was confiscated by the Dutch East India Company. Its later owners include William Beckford, who kept it at Fonthill Abbey from 1823; the Duke of Hamilton, who acquired it in 1845; S. Wertheimer (acquired 1882); Alfred Morrison; and Frances Cook. In 1925 the American collector Henry *Walters purchased it, and soon after, in 1941, the treasure passed into the Walters Art Gallery, Baltimore, where it remains today.

BIBLIOGRAPHY
+M. C. Ross, "The Rubens Vase, Its History and Date," *JWAG* 6 (1943), 9–39; M. van der Meulen, *Petrus Paulus Rubens Antiquarius* (Alphen aan den Rijn, 1975), 164–66; +N. T. de Grummond, "A Seventeenth-Century Book on Classical Gems," *Archaeology* 30 (1977), 22.

RUCELLAI, BERNARDO (BERNARDUS ORICELLARIUS; 1448–1514). Florentine humanist; author of a description of the city of Rome.

Born of a wealthy family in Florence, Bernardo Rucellai was married into the *Medici family, to the daughter of Cosimo il Vecchio, and participated in the climate of ardent humanism in Florence in the second half of the fifteenth century. He was the donor of the famous Orti Oricellari, where the Florentine Platonic Academy met and where various antiquities were brought from Greece and Rome.

Like his father, Giovanni, who had toured Rome and made notes on what he had seen (in the jubilee year of 1450), Bernardo visited the city on more than one occasion; he had the advantage of the guidance of L. B. *Alberti, whom

The *Rubens Vase*, engraving attributed to P. Pontius after P. P. Rubens, 1620s. Vienna, Graphische Sammlung *Albertina*. (Museum.)

he esteemed as the greatest of all students of antiquity. His description of the city of Rome (*De urbe Roma*), written in 1495, set a new, high standard for archaeological scholarship. Rucellai had a passion for inscriptions and copied them carefully, comparing his results with those of other scholars, such as Fra *Giocondo. He had read worthwhile contemporary authors—Pomponio *Leto, *Poggio Bracciolini, Ermolao Barbaro—and had a thorough knowledge of ancient Greek and Latin texts.

His treatise follows the *Notice on the Regions of the City of Rome,* attributed to Publius Victor. After beginning with a discussion of the foundation of Rome and its general layout, including walls and gates, he gives a monument-by-monument description, with a commentary comparable to the explications of classical texts made by humanists. Rucellai took a special interest in aqueducts and even contemplated a monograph study of them.

BIBLIOGRAPHY

F. Gilbert, ''Bernardo Rucellai and the Orti Oricellari: A Study on the Origin of Modern Political Thought,'' *JWarb* 12 (1949), 101–31; Valentini—Zucchetti, IV, 437–56; Weiss, *RDCA,* 77–81.

RUSELLAE (ROSELLE). Etruscan city, ranked by some among the ''Twelve Peoples'' of Etruria (cf. Dion. Hal. 3.51).

Rusellae is known especially for its massive walls, over 3km long, of the sixth century B.C. but also provides important information about Etruscan habitation of both the Archaic and Hellenistic periods. It is one of the rare Etruscan sites for which there is information about both the habitation areas and the cemeteries (outside the walls). Rusellae was captured by the Romans in 294 B.C. but had recovered by 205 B.C. when it was able to furnish grain and wood for the fleet of Scipio. It became a Roman *colonia* at an unknown date. The site today displays many remains from the early Roman Empire, including the forum, a basilica, baths and an amphitheater. Finds from the site may be seen in the museums of nearby Grosseto and *Florence.

The city was described by Rutilius Namatianus as largely abandoned in the fifth century A.C., but it remained the seat of a bishop until 1138, when the bishopric was transferred to Grosseto. The identity of the city as ancient Rusellae was forgotten until the middle of the eighteenth century.

The amphitheater was discovered by J. Boldrini in 1774 and was published by P. Ximenes, along with the results of his own explorations and measurements, in 1775 (*Esame dell'esame di un libro sopra la Maremma senese*). *Dennis visited the area in the 1840s, passing first the ancient site of the Lacus Prilius (Lake Prile), which had been navigable in the great days of Rusellae but now fully deserved the description given by Dennis of its ''putrescent fens.'' (The malaria caused by the swamp was a major cause of depopulation of the area until the marshes were drained in the twentieth century.) The tombs of Rusellae were explored by A. *François in the mid-nineteenth century. Modern explo-

Portrait of *Carlo Ruspi,*
from C. Ruspi, *Metodo*
per disteccare gli
affreschi (1864).
(Deutsches Archäolo-
gisches Institut, Rome.
Inst. Neg. 86.379.)

ration of Rusellae has been undertaken since 1959 by C. Laviosa and P. Bocci
for the Soprintendenza Archeologica della Toscana.

BIBLIOGRAPHY

C. Laviosa, s.v. "Rusellae," *PECS,* 775–76; *Roselle, gli scavi e la mostra* (Pisa, 1977);
+V. Melani—M. Vergari, *Profilo di una città etrusca, Roselle* (Pistoia, 1982); S. Steingräber, *Città e necropoli dell'Etruria* (Rome, 1983), 148–63.

RUSPI, CARLO FILIPPO BALDASSARRE (1786–1863). Italian painter and
restorer.

Little is known of the early life and training of this Roman artist. He assumes
significance for classical archaeology in 1831, when, at the request of Eduard
*Gerhard, he made a series of accurate tracings of the frescoes in the Tomba
Querciola at *Tarquinia. In 1833, when Johann Martin von *Wagner visited
Ruspi's studio, he was so impressed by the quality of the artist's facsimiles of
the Tomba del Triclinio that he helped to obtain a commission for Ruspi from
*Ludwig I of Bavaria.

Although also known as an illustrator and a restorer (his *Metodo per distac-*
care gli affreschi dai muri e riportarli sulle tele was published posthumously

in 1864), the major contribution of this self-styled ''artist-archaeologist'' is his corpus of meticulous color tracings of several Etruscan frescoes he executed between 1831 and 1836. These tracings, now in the *German Archaeological Institute in Rome, are irreplaceable documents preserving much that is now faded or lost on the original frescoes.

BIBLIOGRAPHY

Pittura etrusca; disegni e documenti del XIX secolo dall'archivio dell'Istituto Archeologico Germanico (Rome, 1986); *Malerei der Etrusker in Zeichnungen des 19. Jahrhunderts* (Mainz, 1987); *Die Welt der Etrusker* (Berlin, 1988), 404–6 and items L 5–8, 15–22, 27–30; *Les Étrusques et l'Europe* (Paris, 1992) 362–65, 403, 418–23, 470–71.

RICHARD DANIEL DE PUMA

S

SABRATHA. Punic and Roman city of North Africa, located in the region of Tripolitania, Libya, on the narrow, cultivable coast.

Founded as a Phoenician trading station, Sabratha was under control of *Carthage by the fifth century B.C. After the destruction of Carthage in 146 B.C., it passed to Masinissa of Numidia, finally being added to the Roman province of Africa in 106 B.C. Subject to a series of earthquakes in the first century B.C. and first century A.C., it then experienced enormous expansion in the second half of the second century A.C. The city suffered a major earthquake in A.D. 365 and declined under the Vandal kingdom of the fifth century. The Byzantine invasion and fortification of the city were directed by Belisarius in 533, and there are a few signs of an Arab presence after the Moslem conquest of 643; thereafter the site was abandoned and became covered with sand.

After Italy occupied Libya in 1911, it developed a far-reaching program of research into the antiquities of North Africa, promoted by the energetic governor-general Italo Balbo. At Sabratha the Italians cleared and restored some twenty acres between 1925 and 1942, under successive superintendents of antiquities for Libya, R. Bartoccini, G. Guidi and G. Caputo. Little was recorded and published before the outbreak of World War II, and excavations by the superintendency were suspended at this time.

The theater at Sabratha, arguably the most striking monument of Roman Africa, was restored by Guidi to have a three-storied scene building with ninety-six columns varying in color and in the decoration of the shafts. The sandstone seats of the cavea (seating capacity 5,000) were restored with stone from the same quarries originally used for the building of the theater. The structure is dated to the second century A.C. Among other buildings, the Italians also recovered a nearby bath complex as well as two others—the Seaward Baths and the Oceanus Baths, with a fine polychrome mosaic of the head of *Oceanus.*

Between 1948 and 1951, the *British School at Rome undertook a series of controlled stratigraphic excavations under J. B. *Ward-Perkins and Kathleen Kenyon, many results of which were finally published through the devoted efforts of P. M. Kenrick in 1986. The British team sought to secure evidence about the chronology and development of the town, the forum and some of the more important buildings.

BIBLIOGRAPHY

D.E.L. Haynes, *An Archaeological and Historical Guide to the Pre-Islamic Antiquities of Tripolitania* (Tripoli, 1955), 107–34; G. Caputo, *Il Teatro di Sabratha e l'architettura teatrale africana* (Rome, 1959); J. B. Ward-Perkins, s.v. "Sabratha," *PECS,* 779–80; P. M. Kenrick, *Excavations at Sabratha, 1948–1951* (London, 1986).

SAGUNTUM (ARSE, SAGUNTO). Iberian fortress (known originally as Arse) and city of Roman Spain (modern Sagunto) located 23km north of Valencia, 6km from the coast, on a plateau 1,000m long beside the modern Palancia River (perhaps the ancient Udiba).

Saguntum's capture in 219 B.C. by Hannibal was the immediate cause of the Second Punic War. Retaken by the Romans in 212 and eventually rebuilt, its walls and temples still showed evidence of the Punic sack as late as the 70s B.C. Its role in the Sertorian War is not clear.

A *municipium civium romanorum* under Augustus, Saguntum enjoyed the agricultural and commercial prosperity of the area, and its wealth or that of its citizens was sufficient to provide it all the formal monumental amenities of Roman urban life: forum, theater (in use today for an annual choral competition and other performances) and a circus with a seating capacity of 10,000.

Epigraphical and numismatic remains are abundant. The acropolis offers a mélange of Iberian, Punic and Roman ruins plus a modern museum.

Saguntum declined in the later empire and was virtually destroyed in the course of the fifth century A.C. From the Arab conquest until 1868, when it assumed the modern name of Sagunto, the site was known simply as "murviedro" or other corruptions of *murus vetus,* "old wall." The discovery in 1745 of a mosaic in *opus tesselatum (Bacchus,* on a panther, now lost) is recorded, but most investigations of the site date from the late eighteenth and the nineteenth centuries.

BIBLIOGRAPHY

D. Fletcher, "El teatro romano de Sagunto," *BIM* 55 (1967), 26–43; E. Pla, "Los museos de Sagunto," *BIM* 55 (1967), 44–59; P. Rouillard, *Investigaciones sobre la muralla ibérica de Sagunto* (Valencia, 1979); L. F. Beltrán, *Inscripciones romanas de Sagunto* (Madrid, 1980).

PHILIP O. SPANN

SAINT-RÉMY. See GLANON; ARCH OF SAINT-RÉMY.

SALUTATI, COLUCCIO (COLUCCIUS SALUTATUS; 1331–1406). Florentine chancellor and humanist, described by Roberto Weiss as "the teacher of fifteenth-century humanism."

The archaeological curiosity of Coluccio Salutati more clearly reflects his lifelong devotion to philology than it does any interest in the subject per se. The first recorded evidence of archaeological inquiry on Salutati's part dates from late in the scholar's life: a letter to the physician Domenico Bandini of Arezzo in 1403. During that year Bandini had written to Salutati to ask him for the original Latin name of the Umbrian city Città di Castello. After finding no solution in the ancient geographers Ptolemy, Mela, Pliny and Solinus, the chancellor finally discovered the solution in the *Dialogi* of Gregory the Great. Salutati's search, however, did not end there. His curiosity was so piqued by orthographical discrepancies between the first two manuscripts of the work he had found that he went on to compare the spelling of the city's name in eighteen more. By applying the principles of textual criticism—in the development of which he was a pioneer—Salutati finally arrived at "Tifernum." He attributed the variations to a gender change from neuter to feminine, concurrent with the elevation of the city's status from *oppidum* (town) to *civitas* (episcopal see).

Only at this final stage in Salutati's quest for the ancient name of Città di Castello did he turn to epigraphical evidence for help. On the basis of inscriptions that had survived within Tifernum itself, he determined that the first vowel in the city's name should be *i* and not *y*.

One further indication of Salutati's interest in epigraphy occurs in a subsequent letter, this time to the younger humanist Poggio Bracciolini, written later the same year. On the occasion of his departure for Rome, the aging chancellor asked Poggio to send back copies of whatever inscriptions he found. The request was answered with no fewer than twenty, copied by Poggio's own hand.

These isolated examples, drawn from the life of an influential figure so well known for his interest in ancient texts, underscore the essentially literary, as opposed to archaeological, cast of Salutati's mind. They are more indicative, in other words, of what his recent biographer Ronald Witt calls his "intense concern for accurate manuscripts" than they are of his inquisitiveness regarding classical remains.

BIBLIOGRAPHY

F. Novati, ed., *Epistolario di Coluccio Salutati,* 1–4 (Rome, 1891–1941); B. L. Ullman, *The Humanism of Coluccio Salutati* (Padua, 1963); Weiss, *RDCA* 54–55; R. G. Witt, *Hercules at the Crossroads: The Life, Works and Thought of Coluccio Salutati* (Durham, NC, 1983).

ANDREW P. McCORMICK

SAMOS. Greek island in the eastern Aegean (Sporades) ca. 2.5km from the Mykale peninsula of Asia Minor.

Ancient occupation concentrated at a natural harbor on the southeast coast, near passage to Anatolia and east of a fertile plain enclosed by mountains. Prehistoric settlement began in the Neolithic period and included Early Bronze Age "megaron" houses and fortifications succeeded by Middle and Late Bronze Age occupation. Colonized by Ionian Greeks in the early first millennium B.C.,

Samos flourished as a powerful Archaic city-state with extensive commercial and diplomatic contacts, especially under the tyrant Polykrates (538–522 B.C.). His buildings were praised by Herodotos (3.60), his navy included special warships (Thucydides 1.13.3) and the island sponsored artists, poets and philosophers. Subject to Persians after the assassination of Polykrates, Samos joined the Ionian revolt (499 B.C.) and the Delian League but revolted from Athens (441–39) and eventually suffered an Athenian cleruchy (365 B.C.). Hellenistic Samos experienced Antigonid, Ptolemaic, Seleucid, Pergamene and Rhodian rule before becoming a Roman province of Asia. After the Herulians (267 A.D.), a Byzantine community existed until driven out by the Turks in the fifteenth century but resettled the present capital on the north coast in the sixteenth century. The island played a major role resisting the Turks in the War of Independence, when many ancient harbor blocks went into fortifications.

The ancient renown of Samian monuments, especially the temple of Hera, largest in the Greek world, attracted European travelers on their way to or from Anatolia. The earliest systematic investigation was by Joseph Pitton de Tournefort, French physician and botanist, on an expedition to Anatolia sponsored by Louis XV of France in 1702. De Tournefort identified the Heraion, drew its standing columns and ruins, uncovered a capital and explored the platform. Other early visitors included Pococke (1741), *Choiseul-Gouffier (1776), Dallaway (before 1797) and *Gell, who produced the first scaled drawings of the temple's architectural elements for the *Society of Dilettanti (1811). Naval charts prepared for the British Admiralty in 1835 and 1844 included the first accurate plans of the city walls. Ludwig *Ross was limited by quarantine to two days on Samos in 1841 and reported on areas other than the Heraion and antiquities now disappeared. French interest in the ruins continued with Victor Guerin (1853), who identified the Archaic aqueduct attributed to Eupalinos of Megara (Herodotos 3.60), later explored, with the city wall, by Ernst Fabricius. The *Louvre acquired an Archaic marble kore found near the temple and identified as *Hera, but the swampy site discouraged major expeditions, including the *Greek Archaeological Society in 1902–3. Since 1910, Heraion and city have been explored by Germans: *Wiegand and Schede for the Berlin Museum (1910–14), *Buschor from 1925 to 1939, continued by the *German Archaeological Institute since 1952. Spectacular recent Heraion finds include colossal marble statues, Oriental imports and wooden artifacts preserved below the water table.

BIBLIOGRAPHY

J. Pitton de Tournefort, *Relation d'un voyage du Levant fait par ordre du Roy* (Paris, 1717), I, 420; +W. Gell—E. Bedford, *The Antiquities of Ionia* (London, 1812), I, 59–68; V. Guerin, *Description des iles de Patmos et de Samos* (Paris, 1856); +E. Homann-Wedeking, ed., *Samos* 1–18 (1961–94); R. Tölle, *Die Antike Stadt Samos* (Mainz, 1969).

SARAH P. MORRIS

SAMOTHRACE. Mountainous island in the northeast Aegean famous in antiquity for its Sanctuary of the Great Gods.

Sporadic finds indicate that Samothrace was inhabited in the Neolithic Age, and pottery dating from the Bronze Age has been found to the east of the later Greek city, and at Mikro Vouni, southwest of the modern village of Chora. The island was settled ca. 700 B.C. by Greek-speaking colonists whose Aeolic dialect suggests that they came from northwest Anatolia or Lesbos. They mingled with the local population, whose Thracian tongue is documented as the ritual language of the cult as late as the Augustan age. The city, as yet little explored, was protected by an impressive city wall. A naval power owning territory on the Thracian coast, it became part of the Attic Empire in the fifth century B.C. As its power waned, the fame of the sanctuary outside its walls grew, culminating in the Hellenistic and Early Imperial ages. Under the patronage of the royal Macedonian house and the Diadochs, the venerable sanctuary was embellished with splendid buildings that remained in use until the cult ceased in the late fourth century A.C. An earthquake damaged a number of buildings in the Early Imperial period; finally, in the sixth century, the sanctuary was totally destroyed by a catastrophic earthquake. But small Christian churches dot the island and, like the tenth-century fortification built in the sanctuary of spoils from its destroyed buildings, attest its continuing habitation.

The Great Gods of the Samothracian mysteries included a central divinity of pre-Greek origin, a Great Mother (called Axieros in the native tongue, Demeter in Greek), her spouse (Kadmilos, Hermes) and attendant demons (the Kabeiroi, Dioskouroi), as well as the Greek Hades and Persephone (locally known as Axiokersos and Axiokersa). Their nocturnal initiation rites were available to men and women, freemen and slaves, unlike the related rites at Eleusis. Initiation took place in two degrees, the *myesis* and the *epopteia*, the latter not required, but if taken, preceded by an obligatory rite of confession. It was not restricted to the annual festival but was obtainable at any time. The Great Gods were special patrons of those at sea. Through their mysteries the initiate gained protection, moral improvement, and probably the hope of immortality. The initiation halls were accessible only to initiates; otherwise the sanctuary was open to all visitors.

The sanctuary lies to the west of Palaiopolis, the ancient city, is framed by two streams at its east and west and is cut at its center by a third.

The present Anaktoron, built for the *myesis,* the first degree of initiation, in the Early Imperial period, succeeded earlier forebears. A small building abutting it at its south served as a sacristy. The Doric Hieron, a building for congregational worship, was erected ca. 325 B.C. for the *epopteia,* the second degree of initiation, replacing earlier Archaic and early Classical buildings. Its hexastyle porch was not completed until 150–125 B.C., when sculptures were added to both it and the rear pediment. Toward A.D. 200, the cella was remodeled when the Kriobolia and Taurobolia of the Great Mother were added to the cult.

To its north, ca. 340 B.C., an area previously occupied by *escharai* and *bothroi* where, still earlier, quantities of seventh-century pottery reflecting the debris of sacrificial meals had been found, was enclosed within a temenos or precinct preceded by a terrace. At the northeastern corner, where the processional road descended the eastern hill and led into the sanctuary, a small Ionic propylon was erected. Skopas of Paros was the designing architect-sculptor of this Propylon, which, together with its temenos, was seemingly a donation of Philip II of Macedon.

This first marble building was followed by a series of splendid marble structures. The Doric Altar Court, dedicated ca. 340–330 B.C. by Arrhidaios, half-brother and successor of Alexander the Great, succeeded an Archaic rock altar. Adjacent to it was an Archaic Hall of Votive Gifts.

Between 323 and 317 B.C., another Doric building was erected over a Classical predecessor. Standing on the eastern hill, near the entrance to the sanctuary, it was a gift of Philip III Arrhidaios and Alexander IV. Below its façade lay a paved circular area of Classical date, where an introductory rite was performed at the entrance to the sanctuary.

About 275 B.C., Queen Arsinoe dedicated to the Great Gods the largest rotunda known in Greek architecture. Doric on the exterior, it was Corinthian on the interior and, seemingly, was built for sacrificial purposes. At its periphery, there were altars and shafts for libation. On the hillside to the east of the rotunda, a tiny Doric rotunda was built somewhat earlier, in the last quarter of the fourth century B.C. It may have served as a cenotaph.

The Propylon of Ptolemy II, also erected ca. 275 B.C., gave access to the sanctuary from the city. Ionic on the outer city side, it was Corinthian on the inner sanctuary side. This is the first documented use of the latter order as an exterior structural member in Greek architecture. A ramp led down to the circular area on the eastern hill. The river bounding the sanctuary on the east originally passed through the barrel vault running diagonally through the propylon's foundation. In the wake of an earthquake, it assumed its present course to the west of the building. A wooden bridge now led across the river from the propylon to the higher barren area above the buried Classical circular structure.

A stuccoed limestone Doric Stoa, built on the western hill overlooking the sanctuary in the first half of the third century B.C., provided shelter for visitors. Its painted stuccoed walls were incised with lists of initiates. A line of monuments stood to the east of the columnar façade above the terraced hillside, where structures, probably for ritual dining, were successively built from the fourth century B.C. to late Roman times. A Hellenistic niche of pseudo-Mycenaean style may have represented the tomb of the Samothracian hero Aëtion. To the south, the outline of the theater built ca. 200 B.C. appears. Its *cavea* faced the Altar Court, which served as its *skene*. Above the theater stood the *Victory* of Samothrace, part of a ship-fountain erected at the same period.

North of the stoa, the western hill is largely occupied by a tenth-century Byzantine fortification built of spoils from the sanctuary. Beneath it lie the foundations of a large unfinished building of the Early Hellenistic age; to its west a row of three treasury-like late Hellenistic buildings once stood; to its east, a marble building with an Ionic porch served for ritual dining; it was dedicated by a Milesian lady in the second half of the third century B.C. Yet another building for dining dating from the first half of that century is located on a higher terrace south of the Milesian dedication. To its west and north of the stoa is a rectangular building divided longitudinally by a colonnade and grille and lighted by large windows that contained a warship on one side of the grille. Dedicated in the first half of the third century B.C., both the building and the ship may have been a gift of Antigonos Gonatas of Macedon. West of this *neorion* and over its western end was a Byzantine building used for industrial purposes. These structures on the western hill are still under investigation.

Beyond the southern limits of the sanctuary lies the south necropolis, the most extensive of the several burial grounds hitherto explored. Its tombs range from the Archaic period to the second century A.C. and reveal the use of both cremation and inhumation.

After the tenth century, the island's history becomes shrouded in obscurity. But in 1419, it was visited by the mapmaker Cristoforo *Buondelmonti, who charted it in his *Liber insularum archipelagi* of 1422. Part of the Byzantine Empire, Samothrace was handed over by Johannes VIII Palaeologus to the Italian overlord of Ainos, Palamede Gattilusio, who ruled it via a Greek prefect, John Laskaris. Laskaris guided *Ciriaco of Ancona to the ancient sanctuary and city when he visited Samothrace in October 1444. Merchant, diplomat, humanist-scholar, Ciriaco first revived interest in ancient Samothrace, noting what later proved to be the ruins of the Hieron, the Rotunda or the Propylon of Ptolemy II, and recorded inscriptions and sculptures, some reused in the Gattilusi citadel of Palaiopolis. Self-taught, he interpreted them on the basis of his knowledge of ancient history and literature. After 1453, Mehmet the Conqueror drew on the population of Samothrace to repeople the depleted capital of Constantinople. Once again, until the nineteenth century, the island sank into oblivion.

Then a series of visitors explored the city and sanctuary, in particular, the Germans O. F. von Richter and Blau and Schlottmann, who were followed by Alexander *Conze in 1858. He not only explored the island but, for two weeks, described, measured and recorded monuments in the ancient city and sanctuary. The results of this survey determined Conze's decision that full-scale excavation of the sanctuary was desirable. But before he could undertake this task, two members of the *French School at Athens, Gustave Deville and E. Coquart, inaugurated excavation there in the summer of 1866. Their work had been stimulated by the discovery of the *Victory* of Samothrace in 1863 by the French consul to Adrianople, Charles Champoiseau, who had transported the *Victory* and other marbles found in the Gattilusi citadel to the Louvre. Deville and Coquart made *sondages* and traced the outline of certain buildings, especially in the heart of the sanctuary (what later proved to be the Hieron, the Temenos, the Rotunda and the western hill, where they mistook the stoa for the "main sanctuary"). Ultimately, they abandoned excavation of the site as of no interest.

The campaigns led by Conze in 1873 and 1875 were notable archaeological achievements. Excavating the areas of the Hieron, the Temenos, the Rotunda, the Propylon of Ptolemy II, the stoa and what later proved to be the Byzantine fort, Conze and his architects Alois Hauser and Georg *Niemann explored the surface of buildings, examined selected building blocks and drew up architectural restorations of these edifices, which, although incomplete and faulty by today's standards, were models of precision and thoroughness at the time, and their speedily published volumes (1875, 1880) were the first to be illustrated by photographs as well as line drawings. By agreement with the Turkish government (Samothrace was Turkish until 1912), the Austrians partitioned their finds. Numerous building blocks and sculptures were taken to the *Kunsthistorisches Museum in Vienna. Others, destined for the Ottoman Museum in Constantinople, were shipped to Gallipoli, but only a few, chiefly the frieze blocks of the Propylon of Ptolemy II, reached it.

In 1891, Champoiseau returned to Samothrace and took fragments of the ship on which the *Victory* had stood to Paris. On that occasion, he discovered the theater, later excavated by Fernand Chapouthier.

In 1909, the basic collection of inscriptions recorded in Samothrace was published by C. Frederich (*CIG* [*IG*], XII, 8).

A second time, between 1923 and 1927, two members of the French School, Fernand Chapouthier and Antoine Salač, excavated in the sanctuary. A trench in the Hieron to ascertain the nature of the plan and work in the Byzantine fort were briefly reported.

Under the direction of Karl *Lehmann, founder of the Archaeological Research Fund of New York University, American excavations were inaugurated in the sanctuary in 1938. In 1939 and from 1948 to 1960, until his death, he directed annual summer campaigns. They have been continued, since the mid-1960s under the direction of James R. McCredie, and the site is still under investigation.

Finds made since 1938, as well as the restored entablatures of several buildings, may be seen in the five galleries and courtyard of the Samothrace Museum. Objects found by earlier expeditions, especially sculpture and architectural members, were taken to the Louvre in Paris, the Ephesos-Museum in Vienna, the Archaeological Museums of Istanbul and the Archaeological Seminar of the Charles University, Prague.

BIBLIOGRAPHY
K. Lehmann—P. W. Lehmann, eds., *Samothrace, Excavations Conducted by the Institute of Fine Arts, New York University* (Bollingen Series, 60) in progress: 1. *The Literary Sources,* ed. and tr. N. Lewis (New York, 1958); 2, I: *The Inscriptions on Stone,* by P. M. Fraser (New York, 1960); 2, II, *The Inscriptions on Ceramics and Minor Objects,* by K. Lehmann (New York, 1960); 3. *The Hieron,* by P. W. Lehmann (Princeton, NJ, 1969); 4, I, *The Hall of Votive Gifts,* by K. Lehmann (New York, 1962); 4, II, *The Altar Court,* by K. Lehmann—D. Spittle (New York, 1964); 5, *The Temenos,* by P. W. Lehmann—D. Spittle (Princeton, NJ, 1982); 7, *The Rotunda of Arsinoe,* by J. R. McCredie et al. (Princeton, NJ, 1992); 10, *The Propylon of Ptolemy II,* by A. Frazer (Princeton, NJ, 1990); 11, II, *The Nekropoleis,* by E. B. Dusenberry (in press); +P. W. Lehmann—K. Lehmann, *Samothracian Reflections, Aspects of the Revival of Antiquity* (Bollingen

Series 92, Princeton, NJ, 1983); +K. Lehmann, *Samothrace, A Guide to the Excavations and the Museum,* 5th ed. (Locust Valley, NY, 1983).

PHYLLIS WILLIAMS LEHMANN

SANCTO GALLO, FRANCISCUS IULIANI DE. See SANGALLO, FRANCESCO DA.

SANDRART, JOACHIM VON (1606–88). German painter, scholar and writer on art.

A native of Frankfurt, Sandrart visited numerous cities of Europe, including London, Utrecht, Amsterdam, Munich, Vienna, Venice, Bologna, Naples. He lived at Rome for some seven years (1628–35), where he moved in lively company with leading artists of the Baroque period (*Domenichino, *Pietro da Cortona, *Bernini, *Poussin, *Claude). In later life he settled in Nuremberg.

His work as a painter is not remembered, but Sandrart's treatises on the arts are significant sources for biographies of the artists, museography and publication of antiquities. Appearing at Nuremberg in two volumes was his *L'Accademia todesca della architectura, scultura e pittura, oder Teutsche Academie der Edlen Bau-Bild und Mahlerley Kunste* (1675–79), a general work with an introduction to the three arts of architecture, sculpture and painting, lives of the artists and descriptions of various collections he had visited himself or had report of from the French doctor and numismatist Charles Patin (1633–93). A later work, *Sculpturae veteris admiranda* (Nuremberg, 1680), deals specifically with ancient sculpture, giving special attention to pieces in the *Giustiniani collection. In the *Teutsche Academie* his treatment of architecture includes descriptions, measurements and inscriptions on ancient buildings, while the section of biographies includes numerous ancient artists whose lives were known through Pliny, Pausanias and other writers, complete with invented portraits. In his section on sculpture, he places an iconographical compendium of ancient portraits, based on coins and medallions but drawn largely from *Orsini's *Illustrium imagines.* There is also an album of engravings of famous sculptures, intended to introduce to northern connoisseurs such works as the **Laocoon* (without his sons), the *Belvedere *"Antinous,"* one of the *Quirinal *Horse Tamers,* the **Pasquino,* the *Farnese *Hercules,* the *Belvedere *Apollo,* the Giustiniani *Minerva* and many others.

Other publications relevant for antiquarian and archaeological studies are his *Iconologia deorum* (1680), with illustrations of the ancient gods, and his treatise on Roman topography, *Romae antiquae et novae theatrum* (1684).

BIBLIOGRAPHY

Stark, 154–55; H. Vollmer, "Sandrart, Joachim von," Thieme—Becker 29 (1935), 397–98; J. Schlosser Magnino, *La Letteratura artistica,* 2nd ed., tr. F. Rossi, with notes by O. Kurz (Florence, 1956), 478–79; *Porträtarchiv,* no. 36.

SANDYS, Sir JOHN EDWIN (1844–1922). English classicist.

Born at Leicester, a clergyman's son, Sandys was educated at St John's College, Cambridge, where he was fellow and lecturer, 1867–1907. Public orator of the university, 1876–1919, he early wrote standard commentaries to Demosthenes. His commentary to Euripides, *Bacchae* (2nd. ed., 1885), was remarkable for its use of archaeological evidence. His *History of Classical Scholarship,* three volumes (1903–8), essentially a series of biographies, is an important source of information on the lives of archaeologists. His comprehensive commentary on Aristotle's *Athenaion Politeia* (2nd ed., 1912) remains fundamental. In 1918 he published his introductory *Latin Epigraphy.* He was an industrious compiler of useful works.

BIBLIOGRAPHY

N.G.L. Hammond, *Sir John Edwin Sandys 1844–1922* (Cambridge, 1933); E. E. Sikes, "Sandys, John Edwin," *DNB 1922–1930* (1937), 740–71; T. R. Glover, *Cambridge Retrospect* (Cambridge, 1943), 46–51.

WILLIAM M. CALDER III

SANGALLO, ANTONIO DA, The Younger (1484–1546). Italian Renaissance architect.

A native of Florence, Antonio da Sangallo the Younger was taken to Rome in 1503 by his uncle Giuliano da *Sangallo for the election of Pope *Julius II; he remained there most of the rest of his life. Antonio was a leading figure as architect and confidant of popes (including *Leo X and Clement VII, both of the *Medici family), and his many assignments included that of master of works at St. Peter's (from 1520) and architect of the Palazzo Farnese (left unfinished at his death).

The courtyard of the Palazzo Farnese shows his devotion to antique forms in his usage of the systems of superimposed arches derived from the *Theater of Marcellus and the *Colosseum. Such inventions are based on a thorough study of monuments in Rome and elsewhere in Italy, as is evident from the great body of drawings of antiquities made or collected by Antonio, many of them today in the *Uffizi.

His desire to obtain records of ancient monuments related directly to his fascination with the Roman treatise by Vitruvius, *Ten Books on Architecture.* He studied Vitruvius as a member of the Congregazione of the Virtuosi, a group that included Antonio's brother Battista, Perino del Vaga and others and that gathered in the portico of the *Pantheon to display and discuss their architectural drawings. Antonio's procedure for securing drawings of antiquities often called for assistance from Battista and other artists, who might actually visit a site and make a record, which Antonio would then later annotate and modify. The number of monuments they recorded in this way in the first half of the sixteenth century is truly remarkable and all the more significant because Antonio wanted antiquities outside the city as well. The Sangallo collection included monuments of Ancona (*Arch of Trajan), *Benevento (*Arch of Trajan), Cori (temple of Hercules), Narni (Roman bridge), *Perugia (city gates), Tuscolo (theater), Terracina (temple of Jupiter), *Tivoli (temple of Hercules), *Verona (amphitheater and other buildings).

Within Rome, Antonio and his followers recorded a wide range of material, from smaller antiquities to major monuments. Sangallo has left drawings of a candelabrum with Bacchic dancers (then in Tivoli); a *Boy with Goose* and a sarcophagus with the *Labors of Herakles,* both in the *Savelli family collection; the *Quirinal *Horse Tamers;* and the reliefs of the *Column of Trajan. Architectural drawings include the markets of Trajan; the Theater of Marcellus; the Pantheon; the *Theater of Pompey; and an especially valuable record of the vaults of the *Colosseum with some of the original stucco work indicated.

Yet another type of drawing in the Sangallo corpus is represented by the reconstructions of ancient monuments. A series of drawings of the *Mausoleum of Halikarnassos is based on the description in Pliny (*NH* 36.30–31), as is the reconstruction of the tomb of Porsenna (*NH* 26.91).

BIBLIOGRAPHY

+A. Bartoli, *I Monumenti antichi di Roma nei disegni degli Uffizi di Firenze* 1–5 (Rome, 1914–22); +G. Giovannoni, *Antonio da Sangallo il Giovane* 1–2 (Rome, 1959); Bober—Rubinstein, esp. 467.

SANGALLO, FRANCESCO DA (FRANCESCO DI GIULIANO DA SANGALLO; IL MARGOTTA; FRANCISCUS IULIANI DE SANCTO GALLO; 1494–1576). Florentine sculptor and architect.

Francesco da Sangallo, whose father was the distinguished classicizing architect Giuliano da *Sangallo, had his first dramatic contact with classical art at age twelve, when, during a two-year stay in Rome, he was present with his father and *Michelangelo at the first critical examination of the newly discovered *Laocoon* in 1506. His will, written near the end of his life in 1575, lists ''antique stones and figures'' among his possessions, attesting to his enduring admiration for classical sculpture.

Although Francesco's works display classical influence, they do not conform to widely accepted norms of antique beauty. His inspiration came from the less classical aspects of Greek and Roman art, Etruscan art and the expressive interpretation of ancient art in Donatello's sculpture.

In his first major commission in Florence, the marble *Virgin and Child with S. Anne* in Or San Michele (1522–26), Francesco adopts the motif of intertwined legs found in Leonardo da Vinci's cartoon of the same subject but rejects the classically harmonious rhythms of the overall composition. However, the Virgin's head is idealized *all'antica,* and the drapery recalls the classicizing robes of the Virgin in Donatello's S. Croce *Annunciation.* Francesco's marble bust of Giovanni delle Bande Nere (d. 1526; Bargello, Florence), because of its explicit reference to antique honorific statues, plays a significant role in the Renaissance revival of the classical portrait bust. His bronze medallions and his marble self-portrait in S. Maria Primerana in Fiesole (1542) are modeled on profile portraits from antique coins.

Among Francesco's mature works, the shocking realism of the dead man's face in the marble funerary monument of Bishop Leonardo Bonafede in the Certosa del Galluzzo (ca. 1539–45), with every line and imperfection shown, recalls Roman Republican portraiture. In the marble tomb of Bishop Angelo Marzi in SS. Annunziata in Florence (1546), the reclining effigy derives from those on the lids of Etruscan sarcophagi and funerary urns, while the decorative architectural motifs on the sarcophagus are borrowed directly from Roman sepulchral monuments.

Francesco's only extant architecture, the altar tabernacles in S. Croce in Florence (1568), is overtly classicizing in its simple lines and bold articulation, in contrast to the Mannerist architectural style of many of his Florentine contemporaries.

BIBLIOGRAPHY

U. Middeldorf, "Portraits by Francesco da Sangallo," *Art Quarterly* 1 (1938), 109–38; J. Pope-Hennessy, *Italian Renaissance and Baroque Sculpture* (London, 1970); D. Heikamp, "Der Werkvertrag für die S. Anna Selbdritt des Francesco da Sangallo," *Kaleidoskop, Festschrift für F. Baumgart* (Berlin, 1977), 77–86; A. P. Darr—R. Roisman, "Francesco da Sangallo: A Rediscovered Early Donatellesque 'Magdalen' and Two Wills from 1574 and 1576," *BurlMag* 129 (1987), 784–93; R. Roisman, "Francesco da Sangallo's Tomb of Leonardo Bonafede in the Certosa del Galluzzo," *Rutgers Art Review* 9–10 (1988–89), 17–41.

RONA ROISMAN

SANGALLO, GIULIANO DA (GIULIANO DI FRANCESCO GIAMBERTI; ca. 1443–1516). Florentine architect, originally trained as a woodworker.

With his younger brother, Antonio, Giuliano da Sangallo founded an architectural dynasty that was to play a dominant role in the Roman building industry for over a century. As a young man, Giuliano first traveled to Rome with his master, Francione. His imagination was immediately captured by the splendors of ancient Rome, and he embarked on a passionate study of its glorious remains.

Giuliano's love of the antique was not a passing fancy. He was to devote a lifetime to it. According to the title page of his Vatican sketchbook (*Codex Vaticanus Barberinus latinus 4424*), he began to measure and draw antique monuments in 1465. This sketchbook and his smaller *taccuino* in the Biblioteca Comunale of Siena (S.IV.8) contain a variety of drawings after the antique as well as a number of his own designs. The majority of Giuliano's drawings record antiquities in and around Rome, among them, the market and *Column of Trajan, the *Baths of Diocletian, the *Arch of Constantine, the *Forum Boarium, the *Colosseum, and the *Temple of Fortuna at Praeneste. There are also studies of classical monuments known to Giuliano from his trips to the Bay of Naples (*Baiae, the temple of Mercury and the baths; Tripergole, the baths; Pozzuoli, the temple of Augustus) and the south of France (*Orange, the *Arch and the amphitheater; *Arles, the amphitheater; Cimiez, the baths). On some pages Giuliano copied monuments that were not personally known to him, from the drawings of other artists. Four pages in his Vatican sketchbook are based on the notebooks of *Ciriaco d'Ancona and show monuments in Constantinople (*Byzantium) and Athens, including the *Parthenon, the *Monument of Philopappos and the *Tower of the Winds.

In a sense, the word "sketchbook" is a misnomer, because Giuliano's drawings are not spontaneous, on-the-spot sketches. While there is no doubt that Giuliano did make studies of this kind, what is preserved are carefully perfected copies, almost all of which were drawn with the aid of a stylus, straightedge and compass. In the process of recopying his own sketches or those of someone else, Giuliano often changed his model: proportions were altered, missing parts of ruins supplied, intercolumniations modified, and vertical and horizontal axes shifted. All of these changes seem to have been made in order to bring the monuments closer to Giuliano's own notion of "good" architecture—a notion based upon the theories of Vitruvius and *Alberti and embodying the principles of symmetry, balance and harmonic proportions.

In short, Giuliano's approach was not that of a modern archaeologist, and consequently his record of antiquity often bears a closer resemblance to his own architecture than it does to the classical monuments themselves. The correlation between the antique and his own work is a direct result of having followed Alberti's advice. Alberti drew a parallel between the humanist, who kept a notebook filled with quotations from reputable authors, and the architect, who diligently studied all buildings so that he could ultimately make use of what he learned in his own work. Alberti further counseled architects to study bad buildings with an eye toward improving their obvious defects. Giuliano's sketchbooks are compiled as a compendium of ideas to be reused in his own work. The windows, doors, pilasters and capitals throughout the sketchbooks are closely related to those in his own buildings, such as S. Maria delle Carceri in Prato (ca. 1485), the sacristy of SS. Spirito in Florence (ca. 1493) or the villa at Poggio a Caiano (ca. 1485).

Giuliano's interest in Alberti's theories may have been fostered by his most famous patron, Lorenzo de' Medici (*Medici family). Lorenzo, an amateur architect himself, commissioned Giuliano to design his villa at Poggio a Caiano. It was based on the idea of a classical villa, where one could cultivate the land and one's mind at the same time. Its direct sources, Alberti, Vitruvius and the letters of Pliny the Younger, were more literary than visual. The villa, set on a hill, has a cryptoporticus, a temple front complete with pediment and a barrel-vaulted *salone*—all features that were inspired by antique sources and that had never been used before in contemporary villa architecture.

Giuliano da Sangallo also had a keen interest in classical sculpture. A large number of designs in his sketchbooks record Roman reliefs. He and his brother had a collection of antique sculpture in the garden of their house in Florence. When the *Laocoon* was exhumed in 1506, reportedly Giuliano first recognized the group as one referred to by Pliny as an ornament from the palace of Titus.

Giuliano's own sculpture, such as the tombs of Filippo and Nera Sassetti in S. Trinità in Florence (ca. 1485) or the fireplace in the Palazzo Gondi in Florence (ca. 1490), are filled with quotations from antique coins, sarcophagi and reliefs.

BIBLIOGRAPHY

+R. Falb, *Il Taccuino senese di Giuliano da Sangallo* (Siena, 1902); +C. Huelsen, *Il Libro di Giuliano da Sangallo Codice Vaticano Barberiniano Latino 4424, 1–2.* (Leipzig, 1910); G. Marchini, *Giuliano da Sangallo* (Florence, 1942); B. Brown—D. Kleiner, "Giuliano da Sangallo's Drawings After Ciriaco d'Ancona: Transformations of Greek and Roman Antiquities in Athens," *JSAH* 42, (1983), 321–35; S. Borsi, *Giuliano da Sangallo: I Disegni di architettura e dell'antico* (Rome, 1985); B. L. Brown, "An Enthusiastic Amateur: Lorenzo de' Medici as Architect," *Renaissance Quarterly* 46 (1993), 1–20.

BEVERLY LOUISE BROWN

SANSOVINO, JACOPO TATTI (1486–1570). Italian sculptor and architect, active in his native Florence, Rome and Venice.

After an apprenticeship with the sculptor Andrea Sansovino, whose name he adopted, Jacopo gained his first significant exposure to antiquity when he went to Rome with Giuliano da *Sangallo around 1506. There he studied classical sculptures, like the *Belvedere *Apollo,* the *Spinario* and the *Column of Trajan; he first attracted attention by winning the competition, organized by *Bramante and judged by *Raphael, for the best copy of the recently discovered *Laocoon.* Sansovino's study of the *Laocoon* influenced his treatment of pathos in sculpture while the Belvedere *Apollo* gave him a concept of stylized physique and beauty. His own *Bacchus* and *Madonna del Parto* reflect a profound understanding of antique models, which earned a semiclassical status for the *Bacchus.*

During his youth, Sansovino developed an expertise in architecture that gradually overshadowed his fame as a sculptor. His early work was in the style of the Sangallo family and showed a fondness for piers with engaged columns, a motif whose ultimate sanction was the *Theater of Marcellus.

Sansovino settled in Venice after the Sack of Rome in 1527. There he found employment as architect of the procurators of San Marco, with responsibility for their buildings. His major commissions included a new mint, the Loggetta and the Library of San Marco, as well as several palaces and churches. The mint was a splendid essay in rustication like that of the *Porta Maggiore in Rome, while the Loggetta introduced the composite order and pulvinated frieze of the Late Antique Santa Costanza to Venetian architecture. The library, however, was Jacopo's most brilliant creation: a two-story structure of twenty-one bays, Doric on the ground floor and Ionic above. The library synthesized the classical language of architecture with a type of public palace peculiar to the Veneto, and the ingenious use of a split metope on its corner represented Sansovino's solution to a problem posed by Vitruvius (4.3). *Palladio called the library "the richest and most ornate building since antiquity," and its influence on his own public architecture was profound.

Though well versed in classical sculpture and architecture, Sansovino could not be called an archaeologically correct artist. His vision of antiquity was filtered through the more immediate example of fifteenth– and early sixteenth-century Italian art, and he employed classical motifs in a sophisticated manner to create works, "ancient in the modern style and modern in the ancient style."

BIBLIOGRAPHY

W. Lotz, "The Roman Legacy in Sansovino's Venetian Buildings," *JSAH* 22 (1963), 3–12; M. Tafuri, *Jacopo Sansovino e l'architettura del '500 a Venezia* (Padua, 1969); M. Garrard, "Jacopo Sansovino's *Madonna* in Sant'Agostino: An Antique Source Rediscovered," *JWarb* 38 (1975), 333–38; D. Howard, *Jacopo Sansovino: Architecture and Patronage in Renaissance Venice* (New Haven, CT, 1975); B. Boucher, *The Sculpture of Jacopo Sansovino* 1–2 (New Haven, CT, 1991).

BRUCE BOUCHER

SANTIPONCE. See ITALICA.

SANT'OMOBONO, AREA SACRA, Rome. Sacred precinct containing twin temples of Fortuna and Mater Matuta just inside Porta Carmentalis, later absorbed into the *Forum Boarium; one temple lies under, and the other beside, the little church dedicated to Sant'Omobono (an earlier version of which may have been on the site in Early Christian times).

The area has a long and very complicated history. The temples were believed to be foundations of Servius Tullius (sixth century B.C.), but their final form was a rebuilding after they were destroyed in the great fire of 213 B.C. They were discovered in 1937 during building operations, and excavations were conducted by A. M. Colini; investigations have continued there intermittently ever since. Deep stratigraphic excavations show six major periods, going back to a pretemple phase of the Early Archaic period.

Even in their latest form, the temples were architecturally odd, with a deep pronaos enclosed by walls with two columns in antis and a second pair of columns behind those of the façade. Early altars of Archaic form stood before the temples, on axis but turned ninety degrees to face east.

The finds in the area are of the highest interest and include, besides temple revetments, a Late Archaic terracotta group of Minerva and Hercules (published by A. Sommella Mura) and a fine circular base of peperino with an inscription showing that it held a dedication of M. Fulvius Flaccus from the spoils of Volsinii in 264 B.C. Another dramatic find, made in 1978, was a small ivory plaque in the form of a lion, bearing an Etruscan inscription, the oldest known from the city of Rome (mid-sixth century B.C.).

BIBLIOGRAPHY

A. M. Colini et al., "Ambiente e storia dei tempi più antichi (dell'area sacra di Sant'Omobono)," *PP* 32 (1977), 9–126; F. Coarelli, *Il Foro boario* (Rome, 1988), 205–301; +G. Pisani Sartorio et al., *La Grande Roma dei Tarquini* (Rome, 1990), 111–30.

L. RICHARDSON, JR

SANTORINI. See THERA.

SARDIS. City in Lydia (western Asia Minor) on the Paktolos River, ca. 100km east of modern Izmir.

Herodotos held that Sardis was occupied by the Herakleidai following the Trojan War. The city rose to prominence in the seventh and sixth centuries B.C. as capital of the Lydian kingdom ruled by the Mermnad dynasty. In 546 B.C., during the reign of Croesus, Sardis was conquered by the Persian king Cyrus. The city functioned as the principal satrapal capital in western Asia Minor until its liberation from Persian rule in 334 B.C. by Alexander. Sardis subsequently came under Pergamene, then Roman control. It was destroyed in the early seventh century A.C., probably by Persian forces under Chosroes II.

The ruins at Sardis were first investigated by *Ciriaco of Ancona in 1446. Systematic excavations have been conducted by American expeditions, first led by H. C. Butler (1910–14, 1922), then by George *Hanfmann (1958–76) and presently by Crawford Greenewalt, Jr. These excavations have revealed evidence of pre-Lydian occupation beginning ca. 1400 B.C. Dominating the site is the acropolis, initially fortified in the Lydian period. Additional remains of this date, including houses and gold refineries, have been recovered from the area west of the acropolis, near the modern highway. The principal structures of Hellenistic date are the great temple of Artemis, the theater and stadium. Extensive rebuilding after the earthquake of A.D. 17 included a marble colonnaded thoroughfare and a gymnasium-bath complex, part of which has been restored by the modern excavators. Adjacent to the complex is a basilica structure, also partly restored, used as a synagogue from the early third to seventh centuries A.C. An area known as Bin Tepe, ''Thousand Mounds,'' located ca. 6.5km north of Sardis, formed the Lydian royal necropolis.

BIBLIOGRAPHY
Archaeological Exploration of Sardis, Reports 1–2 (Cambridge, MA, 1975–78); *Monographs* 1–7 (Cambridge, MA, 1971–81); G. M. A. Hanfmann, *Sardis from Prehistoric to Roman Times, Results of the Archaeological Exploration of Sardis 1958–1975* (Cambridge, MA, 1983); F. K. Yegül, *The Bath-Gymnasium Complex at Sardis, Sardis Report* 3 (Cambridge, MA, 1986); P. Gauthier, *Nouvelles inscriptions de Sardes* 2 (Geneva, 1989).

ANN C. GUNTER

SASSI FAMILY. Family in Rome that assembled a small but significant collection of antiquities during the Renaissance.

The collection was first brought together at the end of the fifteenth century by BENEDETTO and IPPOLITO SASSI. Marten van *Heemskerck documented its appearance in the early sixteenth century, when it had been tastefully installed for DICIDIO and FABIO SASSI in the courtyard of their house near S. Tommaso (Via del Governo Vecchio, 48). The stone sculptures were sold to the *Farnese family in 1546, and a list of sculptures documenting the sale may be matched with pieces represented in the Heemskerck drawing. Included are an *Apollo*, made of black basalt, a *citharoedus* type known in the sixteenth century as *Hermaphroditus;* the Farnese *Hermes* (identified at the time as a *Marcus Aurelius;* it is of the same type as the *Belvedere *"Antinous"*); a *Sabina* of the *Venus Genetrix* type; a seated colossal porphyry figure identified as *Roma Triumphant* (later called *Apollo;* *Sassi-Farnese *"Roma"*); and a relief of the type in which Dionysos pays a visit to the poet Ikarios. The *Hermes* is displayed today in the National Gallery, London, while the other sculptures are now in the *Museo Nazionale, Naples, along with the bulk of the Farnese collections.

The painter Jan *Gossaert did a drawing of the *Apollo,* a head of *Pompey* and some inscriptions; *Aspertini and Girolamo da *Carpi also drew several of the statues.

BIBLIOGRAPHY
+A. Michaelis, "Römische Skizzenbucher Marten van Heemskercks," *JdI* 6 (1891), 170–72; Lanciani, *Storia degli scavi* I (1902), 177–78; +C. Hülsen—H. Egger, *Die Römischen Skizzenbucher von Marten van Heemskerck* (Berlin, 1913–16), I, 42–45; +N. W. Canedy, *The Roman Sketchbook of Girolamo da Carpi* (London, 1976), 54–55, 62–63; +Bober—Rubinstein, 479.

MARJON VAN DER MEULEN

SASSI-FARNESE "ROMA" (APOLLO). Colossal Roman statue of a seated figure in a high-belted, flowing gown carved from porphyry, created in the second century A.C.

The piece is depicted in the engraving of the *Sassi family collections (Rome) made by van *Heemskerck in the early sixteenth century and was described by *Aldrovandi in the mid-sixteenth century as having head, feet, hands and part of the arms made of bronze (evidently the work of a restorer). He identified the work as a *Roma Triumphant;* it was also called *Vesta* in the sixteenth century and *Cleopatra* or a *Muse* in the eighteenth century. Restored by Carlo *Albacini in 1790 with marble head, hands and feet as well as lyre and wreath, the figure was interpreted as *Apollo Citharoedus,* an identification that stands today.

The *"Roma"* was sold with the Sassi collection to the *Farnese family in 1546; the statue remained in the Palazzo Farnese, Rome, until its restoration by Albacini and transfer to Naples with other Farnese treasures. It remains there today in the *Museo Nazionale.

The piece was popular with artists of the sixteenth century especially. It was drawn by *Aspertini, Girolamo da *Carpi and Lambert *Lombard and was imitated by Jacopo *Sansovino in his *Madonna and Child,* S. Agostino, Rome. *Cavalieri included it in his album of familiar statuary in Rome in the sixteenth century.

BIBLIOGRAPHY
M. D. Garrard, "Jacopo Sansovino's *Madonna* in Sant'Agostino: An Antique Source Rediscovered," *JWarb* 38 (1975), 333–38; +Bober—Rubinstein, 77–78.

SATRICUM (CONCA). Small Latin, later Volscian, town in the coastal plain of Latium on the edge of the Pontine marshes between Antium and Velitrae.

Satricum figures repeatedly in the Latin wars but disappears from history with the conclusion of these in 338 B.C. The temple of Mater Matuta, its greatest ornament, continued thereafter to be a pilgrimage shrine, and habitation on the site persisted at least through the third century.

The temple was discovered by H. Graillot of the University of Bordeaux in an excavation made early in 1896; he almost immediately happened upon an enormous votive deposit. Thereupon the Italian authorities intervened, and intense excavation of the acropolis was carried out under F. Barnabei, A. Cozza and R. Mengarelli in 1896–98. The site was very thoroughly explored, as was part of the northwest necropolis with Archaic graves of the ninth to sixth centuries, but especially of the eighth and seventh. Small campaigns of work at the site were conducted in 1909–10 and 1934. Although vast quantities of material of the most precious archaeological value were recovered, none of these excavations was ever fully published. In 1977, work on the site was reopened under the auspices of the Dutch Institute in Rome and has continued down to the present. The old excavations have been cleared and cleaned, new excavations have been undertaken of lower strata and the belt of habitation around the temple and part of a new necropolis uncovered by heavy agricultural machinery—the southwest necropolis of the fifth-century Volscian period—has been investigated.

The temple shows a remarkable sequence of transformations: (1) a large hut (*capanna*) of oval shape of 800–650 B.C.; (2) a rectangular *sacellum* or shrine with stone foundations of 650–550 B.C.; (3) a large temple of Etruscan form, peripteral *sine postico,* with four columns on the principal façade and eight down each flank, 550–500 B.C.; and (4) a second large temple, peripteral, with four columns on the principal façade and eight on the sides, 500–200 B.C. The magnificent temple terracottas are probably the richest such find ever made for a single temple.

The habitations on the acropolis begin with a village of *capanne* of various shapes that is succeeded by rectangular buildings with cut-stone foundations. Before the end of the Archaic period there is evidence for buildings with colonnaded courts, but none for orderly planning of these. Pottery of Apenninic type from the Middle Bronze Age has been found in small fragments, and the sequence then descends regularly to Late Republican times.

BIBLIOGRAPHY
C. M. Stibbe et al., *Satricum, una città latina* (Florence, 1982); +P. Chiarucci et al., *Area sacra di Satricum,* catalog of exhibition at Albano (Rome, 1985).

L. RICHARDSON, JR

SAVELLI FAMILY. Family in Rome noted for its collection of antiquities.

The Palazzo Savelli, located in the *Theater of Marcellus on the Piazza Montanara, housed the family's collection of antiquities, mainly reliefs. *Aldrovandi's detailed descriptions of sarcophagi standing in the courtyard match drawings in the dal *Pozzo albums at Windsor and in the *British Museum. Included are a *Hunt,* a triumphal relief, a sarcophagus with a *Liontrainer* and a famous sarcophagus with the *Labors of Hercules,* of which many drawings exist (by Antonio da *Sangallo the Younger, Lambert *Lombard, *Dosio, Pierre *Jacques and others). The collection contained few statues, according to Aldrovandi, who mentions two headless *Dacian Captives* (cf. *Farnese *Captives*). Ten statues are illustrated by Franzini in his *Icones statuarum* (1599).

After the death of GIULIO SAVELLI in 1712, the family died out, and the palazzo was acquired by Domenico Orsini, Duke of Gravina. The greatest part of the sculptures came into possession of Prince Alessandro Torlonia (*Torlonia family), and they are kept in the Villa Torlonia on Via Nomentana.

BIBLIOGRAPHY

C. C. Vermeule, "The Dal Pozzo-Albani Drawings of Classical Antiquities," *ArtB* 38 (1956), 31–46; idem, "The Dal Pozzo-Albani Drawings of Classical Antiquities in the British Museum," *TAPS* 50.5 (1960) and 56.2 (1966); Bober—Rubinstein, 479.

MARJON VAN DER MEULEN

SCALIGER, JOSEPH JUSTUS (1540–1609). French classical scholar.

Scaliger was the son of the doctor and natural philosopher Julius Caesar Scaliger. Educated at the Collège de Guyenne, by his father and by the *lecteurs royaux* Jean Dorat, Adrien Turnèbe and Denys Lambin, he established himself by the early 1560s as a brilliant textual critic of Latin and Greek and a clever Latin and Greek poet in his own right. For thirty years he traveled and wrote at leisure, under the patronage of a noble family; from 1593 to his death in 1609 he served as research professor at Leiden, where his unofficial pupils (he had no teaching duties) included Hugo Grotius and Daniel Heinsius.

His first books dealt with the textual criticism of Latin prose and poetry. But a meeting with the Orientalist Guillaume Postel, two years of work with the great Roman lawyer Jacques Cujas (1570–72) and contact with classical scientific works by Hippokrates and Manilius gradually enlarged his interests. He studied Eastern languages as avidly as Western, nonliterary sources as carefully as poetic texts. In 1583 his *De emendatione temporum*—the first systematic effort to reconstruct all ancient and medieval calendar systems as well as to date all significant events in history—established the discipline of historical chronology as an independent subject.

In 1602–3 he supervised Janus *Gruter's work on the great corpus of ancient inscriptions, which was not replaced until the nineteenth century. Scaliger provided the twenty-four vast systematic indexes that made this the first really orderly and usable corpus, though he derived the idea of doing so not from his mother wit but from his predecessor Martinus *Smetius, whose unpublished indexes to his own corpus formed the foundation on which Scaliger built. In 1606, finally, Scaliger published the *Thesaurus temporum,* in which he reconstructed the lost Greek text of Eusebius's *Chronographia* and attacked thousands of the historical, antiquarian and chronological problems that it and its sources and derivatives posed. Scaliger's work applied a technical method to dry subjects; it found few readers who were not professional scholars. But he was recognized as the greatest polymath in Europe's great age of polymaths, one of the last men in European history, perhaps, to control all areas of learning at a high level. Though not a specialist in antiquities like *Lipsius or Smetius, he filled notebooks with crude, loving reproductions of inscriptions and objects. He saw as clearly as anyone in his time the unique richness of epigraphical materials as historical sources.

BIBLIOGRAPHY

J. Bernays, *Joseph Justus Scaliger* (Berlin, 1855); G. W. Robinson, *Autobiography of Joseph Scaliger* (Cambridge, MA, 1927); A. T. Grafton—H. J. de Jonge, *Joseph Scaliger, A Bibliography 1850–1993* (Leiden, 1993); A. Grafton, *Joseph Scaliger* (Oxford, 1983–93).

ANTHONY GRAFTON

SCENIC ANTIQUITIES. The remains of ancient theaters, especially the *Theater of Dionysos at Athens, and of artifacts, especially vases and terracottas, illustrating accoutrements of the Greek (rarely Roman) stage, for example, masks, costumes, footwear.

K. O. *Müller in his edition of Aischylos, *Eumenides* (1835), founded the discipline. A. Müller, *Lehrbuch der griechischen Bühnenalterthümer* (Freiburg im Bresgau, 1886), was the first, and remains the most comprehensive, collection of the literary testimonia. Dörpfeld-Reisch, *Das Griechische Theater* (Athens, 1896) demolished the Vitruvian stage for Athens. The books of *Bieber, *Pickard-Cambridge and *Webster continue the tradition in English. The discipline has profoundly influenced modern criticism of Greek drama and continues the most flourishing branch of *Jahn's *monumental philology.

BIBLIOGRAPHY

A. W. Pickard-Cambridge, *The Theatre of Dionysus in Athens* (Oxford, 1946); idem, *The Dramatic Festivals of Athens* (Oxford, 1953); C. W. Dearden, *The Stage of Aristophanes* (London, 1976); H.-D. Blume, *Einführung in das Antike Theaterwesen*, 3rd ed. (Darmstadt, 1991).

WILLIAM M. CALDER III

SCHINKEL, KARL FRIEDRICH VON (1781–1841). German neoclassical architect.

Born at Neuruppin in Brandenburg, Schinkel became a follower of Friedrich Gilly in Berlin (1797 ff.) and studied there at the Bauakademie (1800–1802). He made his first tour of Italy from 1803 to 1805 and the second in 1824, followed by travels in France, England and Scotland (1826). A skilled painter of architectural landscapes, he attracted the attention and friendship of the art historian Gustav Friedrich Waagen, first director of the painting gallery of the Berlin Altes Museum. Schinkel called these paintings "historical landscapes," since they were reconstructions of the conditions of life and art, rendered with archaeological precision, of previous times and places. Best known was his *View of Greece in Its Prime* (1825; surviving in copies only), showing a Greek city with artists and builders happily at work.

In his early years, Schinkel showed admiration for buildings of classical and Renaissance style, but also of medieval and Mannerist character. Hired in 1815 by Frederick William III, King of Prussia, he began to think more and more in terms of classical architecture, especially that of Greece. His major works executed in the neoclassical manner had a profound influence on the appearance of Berlin. His guardhouse, the Neue Wache (1817–18), features a Doric portico in front of a Roman-style military *castrum,* while the theater of the Schauspielhaus (1818–21) is accented by an Ionic porch reached by a broad, high flight of steps. The latter reveals study of the *Erechtheion in Athens and the temple of Athena at *Priene. The building he considered his masterpiece, the museum for the Lustgarten (Pleasure Garden) in Berlin, now called the Altes Museum, was built between 1822 and 1830. The façade shows a grand stoalike row of eighteen Ionic columns above a flight of steps, behind which is the domed interior room inspired by the *Pantheon.

After the liberation of Greece, Schinkel created a grandiose design for a royal palace (1834) for the new king of Greece, the Bavarian Otho, intended to be constructed on the *Akropolis in Athens. Schinkel himself had never visited Greece and had no way of knowing how the ambitious scheme, luckily never realized, would have wreaked havoc to the site. Another remarkable project that was never executed was his design of 1838 for a palace at Orianda in the Crimea, for the Tsarina, sister of Crown Prince Frederick William. The façade had a porch of Erechtheion caryatids overlooking the Black Sea, and the interior featured a subbasement with a Musée de la Crimée, vaulted with a stepped roof in the Scythian manner known from monumental tombs of the Crimea.

BIBLIOGRAPHY

R. Carter, ''K. F. Schinkel's Project for a Royal Palace on the Acropolis,'' *JSAH* 38 (1979), 34–46; Tsigakou, *Rediscovery,* 197; M. Snodin, ed., *Karl Friedrich Schinkel: A Universal Man,* catalog of exhibition (London, 1991).

SCHLIEMANN, HEINRICH (1822–1890). German archaeologist, one of the founding fathers of modern archaeology; the excavator of *Troy, *Mycenae, *Orchomenos and *Tiryns; a wealthy, influential, colorful and controversial man.

Born 6 January 1822 in Neu Buckow, a small town in Mecklenburg, Schliemann was the son of a Protestant clergyman, whose career ended in scandal and sorrow. For over five years, 1836–41, Heinrich earned his living as a grocery clerk; then he decided to go to America to seek his fortune. Shipwrecked in the North Sea, he got no farther than Amsterdam, where he was taken on by a commercial house. Schliemann loved languages and had studied French, English and Latin in school. He quickly added Dutch and (sensing its commercial possibilities) Russian. In 1846 his Dutch employers sent him to St. Petersburg as

Photograph of *Heinrich Schliemann*. (Deutsches Archäologisches Institut, Rome. Inst. Neg. 73.1406.)

their representative; he also entered the indigo trade independently and in 1847 was admitted to the merchants' guild of St. Petersburg. Despite unceasing travel (to Paris, London, New York and California, among other places), Schliemann continued to reside in Russia and in 1852 married a Russian woman, who bore him three children. The marriage, never a happy one, subsisted until 1869, when Schliemann obtained an American divorce. He had meanwhile grown rich on profits made from the Crimean War and the American Civil War, while further travels had taken him to the Near East and to Greece. He invested heavily in railroads in Cuba and the United States and in real estate in Paris; in 1863 he liquidated his business in Russia, severed his ties with his Dutch employers and retired from an active role in commerce.

Thereafter he traveled constantly, until in 1866 he returned to Paris, where he intended to settle. For years Schliemann had wanted to become a writer and a scholar, and while crossing the Pacific from Asia to America, he wrote his first book, *Le Chine et le Japon au temps présent* (Paris, 1867). He also gained entry to the Sorbonne, following courses in several languages and literatures, including Greek. His travels in 1868 took him to the Mediterranean and his first systematic tour of Homeric localities, a fact reflected in the title of his second book, *Ithâque, le Péloponnèse, et Troie, recherches archéologiques* (Paris, 1869), in which, as in all his later work, Schliemann categorically proclaims the literal truth of the Homeric narratives and attacks all scholars who doubt that truth.

Frank *Calvert probably first pointed out to Schliemann the likelihood that Hissarlık was the site of the Homeric Troy, as had been proposed in 1822 by Charles Maclaren, a thesis accepted by Grote, among other scholars. Schliemann now informed Calvert that he had determined to excavate Hissarlık and asked him for advice and guidance concerning the region, which Calvert knew intimately, and also concerning archaeological procedures and tools. Excavation, however, was delayed while Schliemann obtained a doctoral degree from the University of Rostock in Mecklenburg, American citizenship, divorce from his Russian wife and, after an organized search, a young Greek wife, all in 1869.

After much negotiation and some clandestine digging, Schliemann received permission from the Turkish authorities to excavate Hissarlık, and he began work in earnest in October 1871. Despite roughshod methods entailing considerable destruction, Schliemann made spectacular discoveries. Within a year he had found not only a fine Greek relief, but also a much older town wall; the following seasons brought forth further prehistoric structures and the famous hoard of precious objects that Schliemann called "Priam's Treasure," as well as an abundance of pottery and other smaller objects, reported in *Trojanische Altertümer* (1874; translated as *Troy and Its Remains,* 1875). In 1874–76, because of difficulties with the Turkish government, he abandoned Troy and turned to Mycenae, where his most spectacular discovery was the ring of shaft graves now known as Grave Circle A, which revealed the unexpected and astonishing wealth of mainland Greece in the Bronze Age, typified in the gold masks (including Schliemann's "Mask of Agamemnon") buried with the bodies of the dead. Schliemann's lengthy reports to the *Times* of London formed the nucleus of his book *Mycenae,* published in 1878 with a preface by Gladstone. Further excavation at Hissarlık occupied 1878–9, followed by *Ilios: The City and Country of the Trojans* in 1880. Schliemann next cleared the so-called Treasury of Minyas at Orchomenos and, after further work in the Troad, turned in 1884 to Tiryns, where he had dug very briefly in 1876. Now, with the assistance and guidance of Wilhelm *Dörpfeld, he brought to light the well-preserved remains of the important Late Bronze Age palace, described in *Tiryns: The Prehistoric Palace of the Kings of Tiryns* (1885). Schliemann returned to the excavation of

Hissarlık in 1889–1890. Efforts to purchase the site at *Knossos in Crete were unsuccessful. Schliemann died in Naples, 26 December 1890.

Schliemann's discoveries at Troy and Myceanae revealed a whole era and opened a new world for archaeological and scholarly exploration. The critical importance of his contribution is undeniable, whatever the shortcomings of his methods. The assessment of Schliemann's career is rendered very difficult by the unreliability of the records, both personal and scholarly, that he himself left.

BIBLIOGRAPHY

C. Schuchhardt, *Schliemann's Excavations: An Archaeological and Historical Study,* tr. E. Sellers (London, 1891); H. Schliemann, *Briefwechsel,* ed. E. Meyer, 1–2. (Berlin, 1953, 1958); L. Deuel, *Memoirs of Heinrich Schliemann: A Documentary Portrait Drawn from His Autobiographical Writings* (New York, [1977]); W. M. Calder III—D. A. Traill, eds, *Myth, Scandal, and History: The Heinrich Schliemann Controversy and a First Edition of the Mycenaean Diary* (Detroit, 1986); D. A. Traill, *Schliemann of Troy, Treasure and Deceit* (New York, 1995).

W. W. DE GRUMMOND

SCHREIBER, THEODOR (1848–1912). German historian of ancient art, specialist in the Hellenistic period.

Born at Strehla on the Elbe River, Theodor Schreiber studied at the University of Leipzig. He pursued philology with F. Ritschl and archaeology with J. *Overbeck, who had a profound influence on him. In 1874, he held the travel stipend from the *German Archaeological Institute and was able to study at Rome with W. Henzen and W. *Helbig. After a trip to Greece, especially Athens (1876), Schreiber returned to Rome to work on the catalog of the *Ludovisi family collection (published in 1880).

In 1885, Schreiber was made associate professor at Leipzig, and the following year he became director of the state art museum there. During this period he published the art-historical studies on the Hellenistic period that were his chief contribution to classical archaeology. In *Die Hellenistischen Reliefbilder* (1894), Schreiber assembled a group of marble relief representations that contain landscape elements and have a pictorial style, associating them largely through literary evidence with Hellenistic *Alexandria. His theories provoked controversy (e.g., Franz *Wickhoff thought the reliefs Roman) but served to bring into focus the problem of Alexandria, where few archaeological remains were known. In 1898 he initiated the Ernst von Sieglin expedition to the necropolis at Kom-el-Shugafa at Alexandria and collaborated in the publication of the results (1908).

BIBLIOGRAPHY

U. Hausmann, in *Archäologenbildnisse,* 90–91; Bieber, 152.

SCHULTEN, ADOLF (1870–1960). German historian, philologist and archaeologist; as successor to the foremost German Hispanist of the nineteenth century, Emil Hübner, Schulten made a dominant contribution to the study of the history and archaeology of ancient Iberia.

Educated at the universities of Berlin and Göttingen, professor at the university of Erlangen and visiting professor at the universities of Barcelona and Valencia, Schulten dedicated himself early in his career to the study of the antiquities of Spain and Portugal. His excavations of *Numantia and the surrounding Roman camps produced the (still) fundamental study of that Celtiberian city, destroyed in 133 B.C. by Scipio Aemilianus.

During the first half of this century, Schulten's work on the archaeology, geography, ethnography and literary sources of ancient Iberia resulted in numerous publications, ranging from reports on his annual excursions in Spain to basic reference works, histories, formal reports on his archaeological excavations and some 300 articles in the *Real-Encyclopädie* of Pauly-Wissowa on the classical antiquity of the Iberian peninsula.

BIBLIOGRAPHY

A. Schulten, *Numantia,* 1–4. (Munich, 1914–29); idem, *Fontes Hispaniae Antiquae,* 1–6. (Barcelona, 1925–52); idem, *Tartessos,* 2nd ed. (Hamburg, 1950); idem, *Iberische Landeskunde* (Strassburg, 1955).

PHILIP O. SPANN

SCIENTIFIC EXPEDITION TO THE MOREA. See EXPÉDITION SCIENTIFIQUE DE MORÉE.

"SCRAPER." See APOXYOMENOS.

SCYTHIAN SLAVE. See ARROTINO.

SEAGER, RICHARD BERRY (1882–1925). American archaeologist, best known for his excavation of Minoan sites in eastern *Crete.

Born in Lansing, Michigan, Seager attended Harvard for only one semester. In 1903 he joined the archaeological expedition of Harriet Boyd *Hawes at *Gournia. The permit for excavation was transferred to Seager in 1906, and he directed excavations at the Bronze Age sites of Vasilike, *Pseira, *Mochlos, Sphoungaras and Pacheia Ammos, with smaller campaigns at Episkopi, Tourloti and Aghios Theodoros, all in the area of the Gulf of Mirabello. His publications include the two books *Excavations on the Island of Pseira* (1910) and *Explorations on the Island of Mochlos* (1912).

BIBLIOGRAPHY

R. B. Seager, in *Transactions of the Department of Archaeology, Free Museum of Science and Art* 1 (1904–05), 207–21 and 2 (1906–07), 111–32; idem, "Excavations on the Island of Mochlos, Crete, in 1908," *AJA* 13 (1909), 273–303; V. E. G. Kenna, "Richard Berry Seager: American Archaeologist 1882–1925," *Archaeology* 23 (1970), 322–32; H. Georgiou—M. Becker, "An American Archaeologist in Crete: Richard B. Seager," *Amaltheia* 18–19 (1974), 74–114.

PHILIP P. BETANCOURT

SEGESTA. Elymian city in northwest *Sicily, famed for hot springs.

In the late fifth century B.C. Segesta came into conflict with *Selinus and provoked several destructive wars. It was destroyed in 307 B.C. by Agathokles but was rebuilt. During the First Punic War, Segesta allied with Rome. It endured into the first century A.C.

Ancient Segesta was identified by *Fazello (*De rebus siculis,* 1558). Excavation outside the walls has focused on an Archaic sanctuary and a (perhaps unfinished) Doric temple of the later fifth century B.C. The latter was visited by Richard Payne *Knight in 1777 (his artist J. P. Hackert made a beautiful watercolor) and well published in 1835 by Serradifalco (*Antichità della Sicilia,* 1). The walls themselves, as well as a theater of the third century B.C. and the street plan, probably Hippodamian, have been examined.

BIBLIOGRAPHY
V. Tusa, "Il santuario arcaico di Segesta," *Atti del VII Congresso Internazionale di Archeologia Classica* 2 (1961), 31–40; D. Mertens, "Die Herstellung der Kurvatur am Tempel von Segesta," *RM* 81 (1974), 107–14; J. de la Genière, "Segeste et l'Hellenisme," *MEFRA* 90 (1978), 33–48.

SHELLEY C. STONE III

SEGOVIA. Ancient town center (*oppidum*) of the Celtiberian Arevaci (or perhaps of the Vaccaei) located some 90km northwest of Madrid on the site of the modern city of the same name.

Segovia played a role in the Viriathic and Celtiberian revolts of the second century B.C. and supported Sertorius during the 70s. An important town in the imperial province of Tarraconensis, on the military road between Emerita and Caesaraugusta, Segovia was justly proud in antiquity of its aqueduct (already mentioned in the first century A.C.) that channeled water some 18km to its acropolis. One of the best-preserved and most beautiful survivals of Roman engineering, the aqueduct is constructed, without mortar, of robust granite ashlars and proceeds, in its final stage, on two tiers where it reaches a height of 28m and, in spite of its striking solidity, achieves a slender grace, equally striking and celebrated by generations of Segovian poets. While even published accounts vary as to the number of its arches (locals are pleased to believe or assert that the devil, traditional builder of this "Puente del Diablo," confounds those who would count them), a canonical figure of 119 prevails.

Segovia survived and thrived in the Visigothic and Arab periods, achieving its "golden age" after the reconquest, as attested by its fifteenth-century Alcázar. In 1974 the city of Rome bestowed on Segovia a modest monument to commemorate the aqueduct's "bimillennium."

BIBLIOGRAPHY
S. C. Ortiz de Zarate, "Segovia y la sociedad de epoca romana: las fuentes epigráficas," *Durius* 6 (1978), 179–219; Barcelona Univ. Inst. de Arqueol. y Prehist., *Segovia: Symposium de arqueología romana* (Barcelona, 1977); +J. L. Gonzáles Cobielo—M. Serrano, *El Aqueducto de Segovia* (Madrid, 1983).

PHILIP O. SPANN

SELINUS (SELINUNTE). Westernmost outpost of Greek civilization in *Sicily.

Selinus was established in Sikan territory as a subcolony of *Megara Hyblaea (Thucydides 6.4.2). Controversy surrounds the foundation date, 651/0 B.C. according to Diodoros (13.59.4) or 628/7 B.C. following Thucydides. The city expanded culturally and politically to the north and west, founding Herakleia Minoa. It came into conflict with *Segesta, causing that city to promote the fateful Sicilian Expedition of Athens. Despite their earlier friendship, Selinus was conquered by *Carthage in 409 B.C. It remained under Carthaginian control until its final destruction in the mid-third century B.C. Only scattered settlement followed, and even the ancient name was lost.

The site was identified in the sixteenth century by T. *Fazello (*De rebus siculis,* 1558). Archaeological investigation began in the early nineteenth century and has dealt with various parts of the city. The Malophoros sanctuary, somewhat to the west, was first explored in the late nineteenth century by Cavallari (1874), Patricolo (1888) and Salinas (1893). Work was resumed for three seasons from 1902 to 1905 and intensified by Gabrici between 1915 and 1926. Within the city itself, exploration began earlier as a result of interest in the temple remains. In 1823 Angell and Harris, in examining the buildings, discovered several metopes and fragments assignable to Temples C, E and F. This launched a new series of investigations under D. LoFaso Pietrasanta, Duca di Serradifalco, which led to the discovery of three more metopes from Temple E and new measurements of the temples on both the acropolis and the eastern hill. A new temple, B, was identified on the acropolis by *Hittorff and Zanth while studying and drawing plans and elevations of the buildings. Toward the end of the century (between 1865 and 1892) excavation was again resumed and continued intermittently under the leadership of Cavallari and Salinas. Important studies of the architecture were executed in this period and the early twentieth century by *Koldewey and Puchstein and by Hulot and Fougeres.

During the present century, investigation has not ceased and, in fact, has intensified in recent years. Between 1920 and 1925, Gabrici carried out excavations on the eastern side of the acropolis. DiVita conducted more extensive campaigns in the same area during 1953 and 1955. He was followed by Marconi Bovio, who examined, in addition, the environs of Temple E and the Malophoros sanctuary. Subsequent researches have focused on the acropolis as well as the habitation remains on the Manuzza hill to the north, with the principal aim of determining the urbanistic development of the city. Because of their importance for the chronology of both sacred and domestic architecture, these areas have received most attention and exploration in recent years. Interest has also been directed toward the remains of Punic Selinus, most notably by V. Tusa. Except for brief excavations in 1872 by Cavallari, the necropoleis were almost entirely neglected by officials until 1963. Extensive operations there have opened thousands of tombs going back in date to the seventh century B.C. Although much work has been done, certain important parts of Selinus remain unknown.

BIBLIOGRAPHY

O. Benndorf, *Die Metopen von Selinunt* (Berlin, 1873), 16–19; E. Gabrici, "Studi archeologici selinuntini," *MonAnt* 43 (1956), 205–408; D. White, "The Post-Classical Cult of Malophoros at Selinus," *AJA* 71 (1967), 335–52; A. DiVita, "Per l'architecttura e l'urbanistica greca d'età arcaica: la stoà nel temenos del tempio C e lo sviluppo programmato di Selinunte," *Palladio* 17 (1967), 3–60.

BARBARA A. BARLETTA

SEPTIZODIUM ("SEPTIZONIUM"). Entrance to the *Palatine palace, created by Septimius Severus (dedicated A.D. 203) to greet those approaching by the Via Appia.

The structure was nearly 300 feet long at the southwest corner of the hill by the rounded end of the *Circus Maximus and stood three stories high, broken into a series of niches, alternately curved and rectangular. It was Corinthian in all three stories, with both fluted and unfluted columns; presumably it was peopled not only with statues of the imperial family but with a gallery of the foremost magistrates and generals.

In the Middle Ages the remains of the Septizodium were fortified by the monastery of SS. Andrea e Gregorio ad clivum Scauri before 975 and later converted into one of the greatest strongholds of the *Frangipani family, the core of their fortress covering the southern half of the Palatine, although it still belonged to the monastery. Various names were applied to the building, corruptions of the attested ancient designation of Septizodium, which probably referred to the seven planetary deities. It was called the "School of Vergil" (Scuola di Vergilio) by those who thought the name referred to the seven liberal arts. The east end of the building was still standing in the Renaissance and is known from drawings of the fifteenth and sixteenth centuries by Marten van *Heemskerck, J. Brueghels and numerous other artists. It was demolished by *Sixtus V in 1588–89, its stones going to enrich many buildings and several of its columns used in the fountain of Moses on the Quirinal. Its foundations have recently been excavated and studied by P. Chini and D. Mancioli.

BIBLIOGRAPHY

+Nash, II, 302–5; P. Chini—D. Mancioli, "Il Settizodio," *BullCom* 91.2 (1986), 241–62 and "Il Settizodio," *BullCom* 92 (1987–88), 346–53; Richardson, *New Topographical Dictionary,* 350.

L. RICHARDSON, JR

SERLIO, SEBASTIANO (1475–1554). Bolognese architectural theorist and minor architect who studied in Rome and worked in Venice and France.

Serlio was the first writer of architectural treatises in the Renaissance to give prime importance to the illustrative content of his books. Unlike his best-known predecessor in the field of architectural theory, Leon Battista *Alberti, who drew his information on the works of the ancients mainly from literary sources, Serlio provided graphic representations of existing antique buildings. He was thus able to communicate even with the barely literate reader, and his publications had enormous influence, especially in Northern Europe.

Sebastiano Serlio was an exact contemporary of *Michelangelo. He was born in Bologna on 6 September 1475 and trained as a painter specializing in perspective. From about 1514 he was in Rome, studying under the Sienese architect and painter Baldassare *Peruzzi. Although Peruzzi was his junior by six years, the younger artist's inspiration was vital to Serlio's artistic formation. In later years he was to acknowledge his profound debt to Peruzzi.

Serlio was in his native city of Bologna from 1520–23 and again from 1525 to 1527/8. He had arrived in Venice by 1 April 1528, when he made his will there. In the same year he applied to the Venetian Senate for copyright privileges for the publication of a series of engravings of the five orders of architecture. Nine woodcuts of the Doric, Ionic and Corinthian orders were issued in the same year, engraved by Agostino Veneziano from Serlio's designs. According to his copyright request, Serlio also planned to publish illustrations of "various buildings in perspective, and various other attractive ancient things." However, no further engravings were actually issued at this time.

During the next decade a more ambitious project took shape. In 1537 Serlio again requested permission from the Venetian Senate for the publication of "some architectural books of mine." In the same year the first volume of the projected treatise, Book 4 on the orders, appeared under the title of *Regole generali di architettura sopra le cinque maniere degli edifici,* with a dedication to Doge Andrea Gritti. Three years later it was followed by Book 3 on the buildings of antiquity, *Delle antichità,* also published in Venice. The latter was dedicated to Francis I, King of France, from whom Serlio was hoping to obtain employment. The gesture proved effective, for, shortly after its publication in 1540, Serlio moved to France, where he spent the remainder of his life. During his years at the French court he published a further four volumes on architecture, leaving three more books in manuscript form at his death in 1554. These later volumes exhibit more strongly Mannerist traits and show his style gradually becoming infused with French characteristics.

The latter of the two volumes issued in Venice, *Delle antichità* of 1540, provided the fullest information on the architecture of antiquity in Serlio's published work, presented for the first time with a strong visual, rather than theoretical, bias. Most of the illustrations were prepared from drawings that Serlio had brought from Rome, including a corpus of drawings by his master, Peruzzi. Serlio hoped to publish a Latin version of the text, in addition to the Italian original, but this never materialized. More skillful, informative drawings of classical architecture already existed in artists' sketchbooks, such as those of Giuliano da *Sangallo, but, being unpublished, these had a far more restricted influence. Before the publication of Andrea *Palladio's more accurate and sophisticated *Quattro libri dell'architettura* (Venice, 1570), Serlio's treatise was the most widely accessible catalog of the buildings of ancient Rome.

Serlio depicted the monuments of antiquity using a mixture of ground plans, elevations, sections and profiles of details such as cornices, bases and capitals. His use of a combination of perspective and orthogonal projection made accurate scale drawing impossible but rendered the sections and elevations easy to visualize. The selection of antiquities in *Delle antichità* is mainly restricted to buildings in Rome, *Verona and Pola (*Arch of the Sergii) on the Istrian coast. Serlio considered the *Pantheon the most marvelous ancient building of all. He also included a limited number of other temples and a range of civic buildings such as theaters, amphitheaters, bridges, baths and *"triumphal arches." Reference is also made to the monuments of ancient Egypt, of which Serlio had heard from the Venetian noble Marco Grimani. Interestingly, Serlio held the view that the antiquities of Greece must have been superior to those of Rome but believed all their buildings to have disappeared.

Serlio evidently knew Vitruvius's treatise well, but he freely criticized and adapted his recommendations. For Serlio, the architecture of antiquity offered not a model of rigorous theoretical discipline but, rather, a rich source of visual ideas with which to feed the free-ranging imagination of a Mannerist architect.

BIBLIOGRAPHY
+S. Serlio, *Tutte l'opere d'architettura et prospettiva* (Venice, 1619); +W. B. Dinsmoor, "The Literary Remains of Sebastiano Serlio," *ArtB* 24 (1942), 55–91, 115–54; M. Rosci, *Il Trattato di architettura di Sebastiano Serlio* (Milan, 1966); A. Blunt, *Art and Architecture in France 1500–1700* (Harmondsworth, 1973), 72–78; +D. Howard, "Sebastiano Serlio's Venetian Copyrights," *BurlMag* 115 (1973), 512–16; C. Thoenes, ed., *Sebastiano Serlio: Sesto seminario internazionale di storia dell'architettura (Vicenza, 1987)* (Milan, 1989).

DEBORAH HOWARD

"SERVIAN" WALL, Rome. Popular designation for Rome's early monumental city wall, ascribed by tradition to Servius Tullius (Livy 1.44.3; Dionysios of Halikarnassos 4.13.5), the sixth king of Rome.

Sound archaeological work has proven that the so-called Servian Wall cannot possibly belong to the regal period and the postulated date of the sixth century B.C. but should, instead, be identified with the fortification constructed in the decades after 378 B.C., following the Gallic sack of the city. Decisive confirmation of this identification is owed to Tenney Frank's demonstration (1924) that the yellowish-gray tufa blocks used predominantly for the wall came from the Grotta Oscura quarries of *Veii, which would have become available to the Romans only after their conquest of that Etruscan town in 396 B.C.

With a circuit of about eleven kilometers in length and including seventeen gates, this city wall was a monumental achievement of the Roman Republic. Among the numerous portions of it still visible, the most impressive are the considerable stretch (ca. 94m) next to the train terminal in Piazza dei Cinquecento, where its character as an earthen rampart revetted with massive squared tufa blocks is apparent, and well-preserved lengths along the south side of the

Aventine Hill, where the siege craft improvements introduced over the course of time are to be seen, namely, the addition of arched casements for *ballistae.*

Although some traces of the wall were apparently first found on the Quirinal Hill as early as the seventeenth century, the majority of its remnants were brought to light in the fervor of archaeological activity in the late 1800s. The segments on the Viale Aventino were unearthed in 1869, while the length in Piazza dei Cinquecento was laid bare in 1870 as a result of tunneling connected with the building of the original railway station of Rome. Upon discovery, these remains excited the interest of many scholars, particularly *Lanciani, who made drawings of practically every fragment of them. Photographs from the era by J. H. Parker and T. *Ashby are also of importance for their documentation of the appearance of the remnants as they were excavated and in the years shortly afterward.

Once visible, the section in Piazza dei Cinquecento even inspired part of the design of the new train station, Stazione Termini, begun in 1938 and completed after the war in 1950 by Eugenio Montuori and a team of architects. The huge, cantilevered construction, which sweeps upward and outward over the walkway at the front, echoes the lines of the ancient wall, as each alert traveler to Rome senses upon exiting the terminal.

Scholarship on the ''Servian'' Wall in the twentieth century has focused especially on explaining the presence of smaller blocks of another tufa, *cappellaccio,* within various sections of the excavated system. *Lugli registered seventeen such segments; he, S. B. *Platner and F. Castagnoli maintained that the occurrence of this tufa—locally available in Rome—proves the existence of an earlier stone circuit as a corresponding forerunner to the post-Gallic wall of Grotta Oscura. The idea was rejected by von *Gerkan and *Gjerstad and by G. Säflund, who demonstrated that nearly all of the *cappellaccio* blocks belonged to later repairs, particularly those carried through in 87 B.C. during the Social War.

BIBLIOGRAPHY
+Nash, II, 104–16; Coarelli, 18–22 and passim; R. Thomsen, *King Servius Tullius* (Copenhagen, 1980), 218–35; +*Archeologia a Roma nelle fotografie di Thomas Ashby, 1891–1930, British School at Rome Archives* 2 (1989), 138–40; Richardson, *New Topographical Dictionary,* 262–63.

CHERYL L. SOWDER

SEVERAN MARBLE PLAN. See FORMA URBIS ROMAE.

SEXTUS MARIUS AND HIS DAUGHTER. See LUDOVISI GAUL KILLING HIMSELF AND HIS WIFE.

SHEAR, THEODORE LESLIE (1880–1945). American archaeologist; known for his fieldwork at the *Agora, Athens, and at *Corinth.

T. Leslie Shear, a native of New Hampshire, received his Ph.D. from Johns

Hopkins University (1904). Then followed a year at the *American School of Classical Studies in Athens and a year of postdoctoral work at Bonn with G. *Loeschcke. During World War I, he held the rank of first lieutenant in the U.S. Air Service and was consulted for strategic information from his knowledge of the Mediterranean war zone.

By 1921, Shear had become associated with Princeton; he soon rose to professor of classical archaeology, a position he held until his death. In 1925, with his wife, Nora Jenkins Shear, he began a series of excavations at Corinth, operated at private expense. The campaigns uncovered most of the Roman theater and a Roman villa with magnificent floor mosaics. Later, after the death of his wife (1927), Shear also excavated a cemetery at Corinth containing material from the Geometric to the Roman period.

Shear next undertook the direction of excavations at the Agora in Athens from 1930 to 1945. He married again (1931), to Josephine Platner, and their son, T. Leslie Shear, Jr., was later to succeed his father as director at the Athenian Agora (1968–93).

BIBLIOGRAPHY

R. Stillwell, "Theodore Leslie Shear," *AJA* 49 (1945), 582–83.

SHELLEY, PERCY BYSSHE (1792–1822). English Romantic poet.

Shelley's education at Eton included the study of the ancient authors Homer, Plato, Vergil, Horace and Ovid. At Oxford Shelley continued his study of Plato and translated half of Pliny's *Natural History.* In 1818 the poet journeyed to Italy, and his enthusiastic and detailed letters record the many ancient monuments he admired. Passing from Venice to Rome along the Via Aemilia, he described a tunnel in which Roman chisel marks were still discernible. In Rome, Shelley was an ardent sightseer; he visited the *Forum Romanum and the *Colosseum often, and he recorded a visit to the *Pantheon by moonlight. Upon climbing to the top of the *Baths of Caracalla, he described the view as "sublime and lovely." Shelley enjoyed working in the baths, too; the second and third acts of *Prometheus Unbound* (1820) were written in the Baths of Caracalla.

The poet also visited *Pompeii and described the city's theaters, temples and houses. From Pompeii he traveled to *Herculaneum, *Paestum and Pozzuoli. So impressed was he by the ruins that he was moved to read *Winckelmann's *History of Ancient Art* (Rome, 1764). Rome, a city in which the very "stones were sepulchres of fame," most inspired and stimulated his active imagination. He lies buried there in the Protestant cemetery (like *Keats), having died in the sea off Livorno when his boat sank there in 1822.

BIBLIOGRAPHY

N. I. White, *Portrait of Shelley* (New York, 1945); E. Raymond, *Two Gentlemen of Rome: The Story of Keats and Shelley* (London, 1952); F. L. Jones, ed., *Letters of Percy Bysshe Shelley: Shelley in Italy,* 2 (Oxford, 1964).

DEBRA L. MURPHY

SICILY (SICILIA; TRINAKRIA). Largest island in the Mediterranean, directly south of the Italian mainland; separated from Italy by as little as 3km, from Africa by as little as 160km, Sicily is at a natural crossroads in the Mediterranean; called Trinakria by the Greeks and Sicilia by the Romans and famed for its fertility.

By the early first millennium B.C. Sicily was inhabited by three peoples (Thucydides 6.2). The Sikans inhabited much of the west, the northwest was the home of the Elymi, while the remainder of Sicily was inhabited by Sikels. In the seventh century B.C. traders from *Carthage founded three cities in northwest Sicily: Motya, Panormos (*Palermo) and Soloeis. Greek colonization of the east, north and south coasts began ca. 734 B.C. with *Naxos and extended to the foundation of *Akragas (580 B.C.). The sixth and fifth centuries B.C. were the high point of Greek Sicily. Large temples were built at *Syracuse, *Selinus, Akragas, *Gela and *Himera. In 480 B.C. the Greeks defeated the Carthaginians at Himera. Despite an attempt by Duketios to found a Sikel state in the 450s B.C., by the end of the fifth century the material culture of Sicily was predominantly Greek. In the last decade of the fifth century, the Carthaginians destroyed Selinus, Himera, Akragas and Gela, and throughout the fourth century were in constant conflict with the rulers of Syracuse.

The last significant Syracusan ruler was Hieron II (272–215 B.C.), who allied with Rome during the First Punic War (264–241 B.C.) Although western Sicily was devastated and came under Roman rule at that war's end, Hieron's realm flourished, as demonstrated by remains at Syracuse and *Morgantina. After Hieron's death, Syracuse revolted against Rome and was sacked, and its territories were made part of the province of Sicily.

Republican Sicily consisted largely of small communities and plantations (*latifundia*). Its tranquillity was disturbed by two slave revolts (139–132 and 104–100 B.C.) and the rapacious *praetor* Verres (73–71 B.C.). In 44 B.C. Sicily was seized by Sextus Pompey. After Pompey's defeat (36 B.C.), Augustus reorganized the province, and the island became a rural backwater. Occupation by the Arabs in A.D. 827 ended the history of ancient Sicily. The island remained predominantly Greek-speaking until the Norman conquest of the twelfth century.

The rediscovery of ancient Sicily began with *Fazello in 1558 (*De rebus siculis*), followed by Philipp *Cluver in 1619 (*Sicilia antiqua*). Deterred by the climate, bandits and the threat of plague, Englishmen making the *Grand Tour did not visit Sicily until the later eighteenth century. In 1777 Richard Payne *Knight organized an expedition to explore Sicily, taking along the German landscape painter J. P. Hackert and the English architect and collector Charles Gore. They visited Selinus, Segesta, Agrigento and elsewhere. The records of their exploration—Knight's diary (later owned by *Goethe) and the artists' illustrations—were never published. But a four-volume work by the Abbé de Saint-Non, *Voyage pittoresque ou description des royaumes de Naples et de Sicile* (1781–86) made the journey seem appealing to tourists. Thereafter numerous travelers published accounts of Sicilian antiquities. Early tracts on ancient Sicilian architecture were published by *Hittorff and Zanth (*Architecture antique de la Sicile*, Paris, 1826–70) and by Serradifalco (*Le Antichità di Sicilia*, Palermo, 1832–42). In the later nineteenth century, A. Holm published the first modern history of ancient Sicily (*Geschichte des Siziliens im Altertum*, Leipzig, 1870–98), while the Sicilian temples received authoritative study by *Koldewey and Puchstein (*Die Griechische Tempel in Unteritalien und Sizilien*, Berlin, 1899). Modern archaeological investigation began in the same period with the work of Cavallari and *Orsi.

In the twentieth century, three important books have greatly enhanced our understanding of ancient Sicily. B. Pace's *Arte e civiltà della Sicilia antica*, in four volumes (Milan, 1935–49) is a comprehensive analysis of ancient Sicilian civilization and its achievements. T. J. Dunbabin's *The Western Greeks* (Oxford, 1948) is the authoritative early history of the Greek colonies on the island, while L. Bernabò Brea's *Sicily Before the Greeks*, 2nd ed. (New York, 1966) provides a survey of prehistoric Sicily.

The twentieth century has also seen extensive archaeological exploration of the island. The most important Italian scholar active since World War II has been L. Bernabò Brea, who has excavated on Lipari, at Tyndaris, Akrai, Mylai, Pantalica and Syracuse. Other Italians who have clarified our knowledge of specific sites include V. Tusa (Selinus, Soluntum and Segesta), G. V. Gentili (*Piazza Armerina, Syracuse), P. Marconi (Agrigentum), E. Gabrici (Himera, Selinus), P. Orlandini (Gela), A. Adriani and N. Bonacasa (Himera), E. de Miro (Agrigentum, Heraclea Minoa), P. Pelagatti (Naxos, Akrai, Camarina), G. Voza (Thapsos, Syracuse) and G. Fiorentini (Gela, Piazza Armerina). Foreign archaeologists doing important work on Sicily in recent years have included F. Villard and G. Vallet (Megara Hyblaea), H. J. Bloesch and H. P. Isler (Monte Iato) and E. Sjöqvist, R. *Stillwell and M. Bell (Morgantina).

BIBLIOGRAPHY
M. I. Finley, *Ancient Sicily*, 2nd ed. (London, 1979); V. Tusa—E. de Miro, *Sicilia Occidentale* (Rome, 1983); F. Coarelli—M. Torelli, *Sicilia* (Rome, n.d. [ca. 1985]); R.J.A. Wilson, *Sicily Under the Roman Empire* (Warminster, 1990); R. R. Holloway, *The Archaeology of Ancient Sicily* (London, 1991).

SHELLEY C. STONE III

SIDE. Greek city on the south coast of Asia Minor, ca. 60km east of Attaleia (modern Antalya), founded in the seventh century B.C. as a colony of Kyme (Strabo 14.667).

The Greek settlers in Side were strongly influenced by the speech of the native people of Pamphylia (Arrian, *Anab.* 1.26.4). In the third century B.C. Side became a pawn in the struggle between the Seleukids and *Pergamon, but despite this it was an important and prosperous port. In 190 B.C. it was the location of a naval encounter in which the Rhodians defeated a fleet commanded by Hannibal on behalf of Antiochos III. During the first century B.C. Side was a stronghold of Cilician pirates, but under the Roman Empire the city prospered once again. During the late empire, it shrank to a small fraction of its former size but retained its importance as a port. Side later became the seat of a bishopric but was abandoned by A.D. 1000.

Little noted until the nineteenth century, the site of Side was visited and briefly described by Beaufort (1811/12), *Cockerell (1812) and *Fellows (1838). Limited excavation was done by the German Lanckoronski (1882–85) and the Italians Moretti and Paribeni (1914–22), but Side was not carefully studied until the excavations carried out by the Turkish Historical Society and the University of Istanbul in 1947–66 under A. M. Mansel and J. Inan. These have revealed most of the Roman city, including the city walls, an agora, a fine theater and temples of Athena and Apollo, as well as much of the ancient harbor.

BIBLIOGRAPHY

A. M. Mansel, *Die Ruinen von Side* (Berlin, 1963); G. E. Bean, *The Inscriptions of Side* (Ankara, 1965); C. Brixhe, "L'alphabet épichorique de Sidè," *Kadmos* 8 (1969), 54–84.

LYNN E. ROLLER

SIPHNIAN TREASURY, Delphi. Greek storehouse, erected to hold religious offerings at *Delphi made by the people of Siphnos.

The treasury's existence was known from Herodotos (3.57–58), whose discussion indicates a foundation date shortly before 525 B.C. for its construction, and from Pausanias (10.11.2). As a dated building it is usually seen as providing a fixed point for the chronology of the architecture and sculpture of the Archaic period, at least in the islands.

The treasury is the richest and best preserved of those known at Delphi. Constructed of island marbles, even including stone particular to the island of Siphnos itself, it takes the form of a single room fronted by a porch, whose roof, in this case, is supported by two female figures (caryatids) instead of the more usual columns. It is richly decorated in Ionic style, including a huge bead and reel molding at the base of the walls and a continuous frieze, which, with a pediment group, are major monuments of Archaic sculpture. The pediment features the contest between Apollo and Herakles for the tripod, and the friezes include scenes from the Trojan War (east side) and the Gigantomachy (north side).

It appears that the south foundation of the treasury was always visible within the village that overlay the ancient site, and ancient blocks of the building were recognized beginning as early as 1850. The foundations were cleared in the French excavations at the sanctuary in the spring of 1894, together with a great number of architectural and sculptural fragments from other buildings. The finds, especially the sculpture, aroused great interest, and plaster casts of them were already in Paris in December of that year, less than eight months after they had been excavated. Although the excavators initially identified the foundations and the sculpture as belonging to the Siphnian Treasury, there occurred some confusion in the identification because of the speed of excavation, the great number of architectural blocks (including some bearing inscriptions in the Knidian alphabet) and scholarly study of the divergence of styles in the sculptures. A cast of the façade of the treasury that appeared at the Paris Exposition of 1900 was labeled as the Treasury of the Knidians and was composed of parts of that treasury as well as of the Siphnian Treasury and the Massiliot Treasury. In the first decades of the twentieth century, a correct understanding of the relationship of the various pieces developed, but many misconceptions remained for a number of years. The definitive architectural presentation of the building did not appear until 1987.

BIBLIOGRAPHY

+C. Picard—P. de la Coste Messelière, *Art archaïque: Les trésors ioniques, Le Tresor de Siphnos, Fouilles de Delphes,* 4.2 (Paris, 1928), 57–171; E. Bourguet, *Inscriptions de Delphes, Trésor des Siphnians, Fouilles de Delphes,* 3.1 (Paris, 1929), 110–49; +G. Daux—E. Hansen, *Le Trésor de Siphnos, Fouilles de Delphes,* 3 (Paris, 1987); Stewart, *Greek Sculpture,* 128–29.

WILLIAM R. BIERS

SIRACUSA. See SYRACUSE.

SIXTUS IV (FRANCESCO DI SAVONA; FRANCESCO DELLA RO-VERE; 1414–84). Pope (1471–84); sponsored civic projects in Rome and started the first public collection of antiquities on the *Capitoline Hill.

Having served as general of the Franciscan order (1464) and having been made cardinal in 1467, Francesco di Savona was elected Pope Sixtus IV in 1471. He enjoyed an excellent reputation as a scholar and theologian but is also remembered as a politically active figure who increased the temporal power of the papacy.

Perhaps because he was so intent on consolidating his own power, Sixtus IV was much concerned with art and architecture and the image of papal prestige. He continued projects of his predecessors, such as Nicholas V, especially in the arrangements for the Vatican Library, the building of the Sistine Chapel (named for him) and the rebuilding and construction of many churches in Rome. He issued regulations designed to improve public hygiene and safety and to straighten, pave and regularly clean major streets; he restored the ancient aqueduct of the Aqua Virgo, first established under Augustus in 10 B.C., and made it bring good water to the Romans once again; he built bridges and a hospital and fostered the building of new palaces. Sixtus assembled many leading artists (*Botticelli, *Perugino, *Ghirlandaio, Filippo Lippi) to decorate the hospital of S. Spirito and the Sistine Chapel. Sixtus also encouraged use of the newly organized Vatican Library, with some 2,500 volumes, many of them Greek and Latin texts.

Although he was not interested in antiquities for their own intrinsic worth, Sixtus did understand their immense historical importance for the city, which he hoped to make the cultural rival of Florence. He regarded *Paul II's cameos, medals and coins as trifles and dispersed much of the collection, but he kept the larger objects, which formed the nucleus of the *Capitoline Museums collection. A few months after his accession, he donated to the Palazzo dei Conservatori on the Capitoline a number of ancient bronzes that had been displayed, most of them on columns, outside the *Lateran papal palace. These included the *Capitoline *Wolf,* the **Spinario,* the *Capitoline *Camillus* and the colossal head, hand and globe of **Constantius II.* He also donated an over-lifesize bronze statue of *Hercules* excavated during his pontificate. The famous equestrian statue of **Marcus Aurelius* was not removed from the Lateran at this time, but Sixtus had it repaired and placed on a new pedestal at the Lateran. The result of this program was that major antiquities were more easily accessible to tourists and artists and were maintained in better condition. But for Sixtus the purpose of gathering these antiquities on the Capitol was not so much artistic or archaeological as political. He wished to assemble tangible testaments of ancient Roman magnificence at the ancient seat of the city's municipal government.

BIBLIOGRAPHY

M. Creighton, *A History of the Papacy: From the Great Schism to the Sack of Rome,* 4 (New York, 1923); +W. S. Heckscher, *Sixtus IV aeneas insignes romano populo restituendas censuit* (The Hague, 1955); E. Lee, *Sixtus IV and Men of Letters* (Rome, 1978); T. Buddensieg, ''Die Statuenstiftung Sixtus' IV. im Jahr 1471,'' *Römisches Jahrbuch für Kunstgeschichte* 20 (1983), 33–73; C. L. Stinger, *The Renaissance in Rome* (Bloomington, IN, 1985).

                                                                    JUDY WAGNER

SIXTUS V (FELICE PERETTI, 1521–90). Counter-Reformation pope (1585–90), who treated Rome's ancient monuments as trophies of Christianity's triumph.

Under Sixtus V, with Domenico *Fontana as overseer, four *obelisks that had been brought to Rome in antiquity were raised at key points in the urban plan, at Saint Peter's, San Giovanni in Laterano, Santa Maria Maggiore and Santa Maria del Popolo. Each obelisk was exorcised and consecrated to the True Cross, an image of which was installed at the top. The historiated victory columns of the revered emperors Trajan and Marcus Aurelius (the latter extensively restored) provided podia for statues of Saints Peter and Paul. On the Quirinal Hill the colossal statues of the Dioskouroi (*Quirinal *Horse Tamers*) were restored and moved to a position in front of the papal residence. Believed to be the works of Pheidias and Praxiteles and representing *Alexander the Great Taming Bucephalus,* these sculptures were also associated with Constantine, who was credited with having brought them to Rome from Greece.

Sixtus seems to have been quite knowledgeable about antiquity. He owned a copy of B. *Marliani's *Antiquae Romae topographia* (Rome, 1534) and appointed his own commissioner of antiquities. He is reported as having said that he wanted to demolish those antique monuments that were deformed and restore others that required it. He razed what remained of the *Septizodium, the monumental entrance that stood at the foot of the Palatine Hill, and employed its lavish materials in other projects. The pope announced plans to demolish the *Tomb of Cecilia Metella and the so-called Arch of Janus in the *Forum Boarium, but neither project was carried out. He intended to transform the *Baths of Diocletian and the *Colosseum into facilities for the production, respectively, of silk and woolen cloth. Certain works were executed before these projects were cut short at his death.

BIBLIOGRAPHY

R. Lanciani, *Storia degli scavi* 4 (1912), 121–75; E. Iversen, *Obelisks in Exile,* 1–2 (Copenhagen, 1968); P. Fancelli, "Demolizione e 'restauri' di antichità nel Cinquecento romano," *Roma e l'antico nell'arte e nella cultura del Cinquecento*, ed. M. Fagiolo (Rome, 1985), 357–403; A. Cerutti Fusco, "Il progetto di Domenico Fontana 'per ridurre il Coliseo di Roma ad habitatione,' " *Quaderno dell'Istituto di Storia dell'architettura, Università degli Studi Roma 'La Sapienza'* N. S., fasc. 12 (1988), 65–88.

JACK FREIBERG

SLOANE, Sir HANS (1660–1753). English physician, scientist and collector.

After studying in London and France Sloane began medical practice in London in 1684. He went to the West Indies in 1687 as physician to the governor-

Portrait of *Sir Hans Sloane*, engraving by J. Faber, after painting by G. Kneller, 1729. London, British Museum. (Museum.)

general and there began a collection, chiefly of botanical specimens. Returning to London in 1689, Sloane continued both his profession and his collection, which by 1691 included zoological and geological sections. He also collected antiquities, including Roman lamps, coins, gems and inscriptions, as well as Etruscan and Egyptian items. In 1702 Sloane's own collection was augmented by a vast bequest of antiquities and natural history specimens from William Courten. The collection was long housed in Bloomsbury, but in 1742 Sloane retired, taking the collection and his library of some 42,000 books to his country house in Chelsea. He died in 1753 and established by his will a trust to perpetuate his museum on payment of £20,000 to his heirs. Within six months an Act of Parliament was passed providing for the purchase of the Sloane collection and the Harleian manuscripts and their addition to the Cottonian Library to form the *British Museum, to the foundation of which Sloane may be said to have contributed more than any other individual.

BIBLIOGRAPHY

H. Sloane, *Catalogus plantarum quae in insula Jamaica sponte proveniunt* (London, 1696); E. Edwards, *Lives of the Founders of the British Museum* (London, 1870); E. Miller, *That Noble Cabinet: A History of the British Museum* (London, 1973); A. MacGregor, ed., *Sir Hans Sloane* (London, 1994).

B. F. COOK

SMETIUS, MARTINUS (d. ca. 1565). Flemish scholar and epigrapher.

Born in Westwinckler near Bruges, Smetius spent six years in Italy (1545–61), working as a member of the household of Cardinal Rodolfo Pio da *Carpi. During this time he copied inscriptions in Rome and many other parts of Italy, as well as from the collections made by other scholars, such as *Pighius, Morillon and Benedetto Egio. Returning to Flanders with his corpus, he experienced a devastating fire in his house near Bruges in 1558, resulting in the loss of a sizable portion of the corpus. Encouraged by his patron Marcus Laurinus, lord of Watervliet, Smetius painstakingly recovered most of the corpus and by 1565 had written the dedicatory preface. Tragically, before the book was published, Smetius was seized and hanged by ruffian soldiers outside Brussels, and at the same time the manuscript was looted from the house of Laurinus. Some twenty years later, the manuscript was acquired by Leiden University and was published by Plantin Press as *Inscriptionum antiquarum quae passim per Europam liber,* with additions by Justus *Lipsius (Antwerp, 1588). This corpus was the basis of the great comprehensive work subsequently prepared by *Gruter, again with additions by Lipsius.

The work of Smetius is notable for its analysis of the chronological development of lettering in Roman inscriptions, the first such published, and its firm stand against excessive or unscrupulous restoration of damaged inscriptions. Smetius also took great care to organize the inscriptions sensibly according to context (rather than topographically, as in some previous publications, or indiscriminately, as in others), so that related inscriptions would be side by side; this is the practice still followed by the *Corpus Inscriptionum Latinarum* in Berlin.

BIBLIOGRAPHY
CIL VI.I. xlix–1; Mitchell—Mandowsky, 25–27.

SMYRNA (IZMIR). Greek site in present-day Turkey.

The antiquities of the Hellenistic and Roman city of Smyrna (modern Izmir) are mentioned by most of the early travelers in Asia Minor. Much epigraphic material has been noted, now being collected in one publication, and work has been carried out in several parts of the city, particularly in the area of the Roman Agora.

The earlier city of Smyrna, referred to as "Old Smyrna" in antiquity (Strabo 14.1.37 [646]), was on a different site (modern Bayraklı). The remains of this Archaic city were first noted by Louis *Fauvel and Prokesch von Osten (who visited the site together in 1825) and excavated by Franz and Helene Miltner in 1930. Major excavation at Bayraklı was undertaken between 1948 and 1951 by J. M. Cook of the *British School at Athens and Ekrem Akurgal of Ankara University. Akurgal, on behalf of the Turkish Historical Society and the General Directorate of Turkish Antiquities and Museums, has been continuing excavations since 1966. The publications of Cook, R. V. Nicholls, Akurgal and others have added to our knowledge of early Greek fortifications, housing and temple architecture. Important discoveries include strata associated with the sack of Alyattes (ca. 600 B.C.; his siege mound has been identified) and a temple of Athena.

BIBLIOGRAPHY
C. J. Cadoux, *Ancient Smyrna* (Oxford, 1938); R. Naumann—S. Kantar, "Die Agora von Smyrna," *IstForsch* 17 (1950), 69–114; J. M. Cook et al., "Old Smyrna," *BSA* 53–54 (1958–59), 1–181; G. Petzl, ed., *Die Inschriften von Smyrna* 1 (Bonn, 1982); E. Akurgal, *Alt-Smyrna* 1, *Wohnschichten und Athenatempel* (Ankara, 1983); H. Waterhouse, *The British School at Athens: The First Hundred Years* (*BSA* suppl. vol. 19, London, 1986), 38, 114–16; R. V. Nicholls, "Early Monumental Religious Architecture at Old Smyrna" in D. Buitron-Oliver, ed., *New Perspectives in Early Greek Art* (Washington, 1991), 151–71; J. M. Cook–R. V. Nicholls, *Old Smyrna Excavations: The Temples of Athena (BSA* suppl. vol., in press).

CHRISTOPHER G. SIMON

SOANE, Sir JOHN (1753–1837). English neoclassical architect and antiquarian.

Born the son of a bricklayer at Goring, Soane was later apprenticed to George Dance II and Henry Holland. While at the Royal Academy he won the gold medal (1776) for his design of a triumphal bridge, and a royal traveling scholarship to Italy (1778–80). There he met Thomas Pitt, Lord Camelford, the cousin of William Pitt, who later became prime minister and secured for Soane the position of architect to the Bank of England (1788). In 1806 Soane succeeded Dance as professor of architecture at the Royal Academy; he was knighted in 1831.

Soane was a prolific and influential architect whose style distilled classical elements to a crisp elegance. His London home at 13 Lincoln's Inn Fields, now the Soane Museum, is an excellent example of his architectural legacy. As early as 1790 Soane had begun to collect. At his death his house contained an eclectic and highly personal display of valuable antiquities, paintings, books and manuscripts, casts and every sort of objet d'art. Among the important antiquities are the alabaster sarcophagus of Seti I (discovered by Belzoni in 1815), a figural fragment from the *Erechtheion frieze and more than 130 Greek and Roman architectural fragments.

BIBLIOGRAPHY

C. Vermeule, *A Catalogue of the Classical Antiquities in Sir John Soane's Museum,* 2nd ed., 1–2 (Boston, 1973); D. Stroud, *Sir John Soane Architect* (London, 1984); S. F. Millenson, *Sir John Soane's Museum* (Ann Arbor, 1987); P. Thornton—H. Dorey, *Sir John Soane: The Architect as Collector* (New York, 1992).

RICHARD DANIEL DE PUMA

SOCIETY OF ANTIQUARIES OF LONDON. English learned society for the discussion, collection and preservation of antiquities, among the earliest outside Italy to study archaeological subjects.

Officially founded in 1707, the Society of Antiquaries stated that its concern was with antiquity and history in Great Britain previous to the reign of James I (1603–25). It received its charter from George II in 1751. In its early years the members met at the Bear Tavern in the Strand but eventually moved to a house in Chancery Lane. From 1781, meetings were at Somerset House; present quarters are at Burlington House (since 1875).

At the time of the founding of its journal *Archaeologia* in 1770, the society's history and purposes were reviewed; it was observed that in 1572 during the reign of Queen Elizabeth I an academy for the study of antiquity and history had been formed, meeting for some twenty years at the house of Sir Robert Cotton. The society was disbanded by James I, who saw it as a secret group that threatened the government, but the group revived in the seventeenth century, counting as its members John Selden, Archbishop Ussher, Elias *Ashmole, John Aubry, Franciscus *Junius and the Earl of *Arundel. After the official foundation in 1707, among the fellows of the society who were especially celebrated were James *Stuart, Josiah *Wedgwood, Charles *Townley and Richard Payne *Knight, as well as foreign honorary members *Piranesi, *Winckelmann and the Cardinal *Albani. Women were not invited as members until 1921.

An idea of the topics discussed in the early years can be gained from the first volume of *Archaeologia,* which contains sixty-one communications dealing with a wide variety of topics, from Christian shrines to a Danish horn and Welsh castles, from Roman roads and a Roman altar in Britain to the *Column of Trajan and an intaglio with *Antinous;* there are also many notes that have to do with British history and antiquities in the Middle Ages. Articles in *Archaeologia* in the nineteenth and twentieth centuries, as well as in *The Antiquaries Journal* (founded in 1921), are remarkably consistent in subject matter with those of the earliest volumes, although there is slightly less classical material. The reports of the Research Committee, initiated in 1913, have given special attention to Roman archaeology in Britain (at *Bath, *Verulamium, Colchester and other sites). The Society of Antiquaries also provides for the publication of monograph studies and maintains a superb research library at Burlington House of 100,000 volumes. The membership has grown from approximately 100 in the eighteenth century to 1,850 at present.

BIBLIOGRAPHY

M. Noble, *The Lives of the Fellows of the Society of Antiquaries in London* (manuscript at the Getty Center for the History of Art and the Humanities, Santa Monica, CA, 1818); R. Bruce-Mitford, *The Society of Antiquaries of London, Notes on Its History and Possessions* (London, 1951); J. Evans, *A History of the Society of Antiquaries* (London, 1956).

SOCIETY OF DILETTANTI. English association of gentlemen formed for the purpose of ''enjoying'' the arts and life; the Dilettanti played a key role in the study of Greek antiquities and in establishing the neoclassical style in England.

The original members of the Society of Dilettanti, founded in 1733, were young Tory aristocrats, opposed to the Whiggery and pedantry of English cultural life under the political dominance of Sir Robert Walpole. Though the principal bond of the members was a shared knowledge of Italy and the Europe of the *Grand Tour, the society's origins and early meetings were more rowdy than scholarly. Horace Walpole noted that the ''nominal qualification'' for membership was ''having been to Italy, and the real one being drunk.'' By 1736 the Dilettanti had forty-six members; soon after, the list had to be limited to fifty-four. Some of the early Dilettanti were noted collectors—*Townley, Lansdowne, Ainslie and especially Sir William *Hamilton, whose election in 1777 was the grand occasion for the first formal portrait of the society, painted by Sir Joshua Reynolds. There were also serious scholars among the members, such as Joseph *Spence, later a professor at Oxford.

But the most significant impetus to archaeological study came with the election of James *Stuart and Nicholas *Revett, whose trip to Athens to make drawings and measurements of Greek antiquities (1751–54) was sponsored by the Dilettanti, along with the subsequent publication of their results in the first volume of *The Monuments of Athens Measured and Delineated* (1762). ''Greek gusto'' became the fashion, ''Athenian'' Stuart was lionized and the society's transition from a Tory drinking club to a scholarly society was complete. Revett was hurt by the greater attention paid to Stuart, however, and gave up his rights to the later volumes, all of which appeared after the death of Stuart himself (1789, 1795, 1816).

From now on, the society was devoted to sponsoring research and publication. In 1764 it organized its most ambitious project, an expedition to the Greek cities of Asia Minor, with Richard *Chandler to prepare descriptions and Revett and

William *Pars to carry out measurement and topographical drawings. The results appeared in four volumes of *Ionian Antiquities* (1769–1881). Also significant was the work of Robert *Wood, who had been with Stuart and Revett in Athens (he appears in their drawings). His own publications of *The Ruins of Palmyra* (1753) and *The Ruins of Balbec* (1757) are important for an understanding of Roman art. Wood's essay on the originality of Homer, in which he argued that one must read Homer's poems at Troy to understand them, was influential in England and abroad, notably on *Goethe and *Wolf. A controversy broke out in the 1790s, when the French scholar le Chevalier questioned Wood's identification of the site of Troy. The conviction that to understand Homer one must know Troy remained and culminated in the work of *Schliemann.

The society's politics came out in the *History of Greece* (1784–1810) by member William Mitford: Greek history exposes "the dangerous Turbulence of Democracy." Mitford's virtues, according to *Byron, were "labor, learning, research, wrath and partiality." He molded his generation's view of Greece and provoked George Grote into answering him. The Dilettanti also published Richard Payne *Knight's important *Specimens of Antient Sculpture* in 1809. The society had nothing to do with the importation of the *Elgin marbles and helped Payne Knight in his efforts to block their purchase by the nation. Neither his reputation nor that of the society survived the episode. The Society of Dilettanti did continue to publish volumes on Athens and Ionia and to meet and make resolutions, but, as time passed, the two great universities at Oxford and Cambridge and the *British Museum took over as the major sponsors in England of investigations into the art and archaeology of the ancient world.

BIBLIOGRAPHY

L. Cust, *History of the Society of Dilettanti* (London, 1898); 2nd ed., ed. S. Colvin (London, 1914); +J. M. Crook, *The Greek Revival, Neo-Classical Attitudes in British Architecture, 1760–1870* (London, 1972).

E. C. KOPFF

SOKRATES (portraits of). Images of the great Athenian philosopher Sokrates (469–399 B.C.), of which the best known was a posthumous bronze by Lysippos, created ca. 340–330 B.C.

Surviving in about thirty copies, the portrait shows the head of Sokrates resembling a Silenos, with a snub nose and thick lips (as he was described by both Xenophon and Plato). There is a fine example of the head in the *Terme Museum (discovered in 1892 in the foundations of the Vittorio Emanuele monument), and the body has been identified in a seated figure in the *Ny Carlsberg Glyptotek, Copenhagen. This statue was bought for the museum with a head of Trajan on it, but G. *Lippold and F. *Poulsen ascertained from an early engraving by Preisler (1733) that the Trajan head of the Copenhagen statue was alien; the engraving shows the sculpture with its original head of Sokrates.

Many portraits of Sokrates were made throughout the ancient Mediterranean world—sculptures, statuettes, reliefs, paintings, gems and coins. Gisela *Richter

Portrait of *Sokrates*, engraving by T. Galle from F. Orsini, *Illustrium imagines* (1606).

has sorted them out and observed that, besides the Lysippos portrait, there is another distinct type, belonging to Sokrates' lifetime and adhering even more closely to his Silenus-like physical appearance.

Ancient images of Sokrates were quickly identified by iconographers of the Renaissance. During the sixteenth century, there were portraits to be seen in the Cesi Gardens (later, *Farnese family collection, now the *Museo Nazionale, Naples) and in the Villa of Julius III (later, *Vatican; now, Conservatori Museum) and elsewhere. *Raphael showed Sokrates in the *School of Athens* (Stanza della Segnatura, Vatican, 1509–10) with the characteristic snub-nosed face, discoursing with Alkibiades. (Ancient statues of the drunken Silenos with Bacchus, such as a group owned by Angelo *Colocci, were sometimes interpreted as Sokrates and Alkibiades.) Fulvio *Orsini included the familiar face, with identifying caption in his *Imagines et elogia virorum illustrium* of 1570 (e.g., no. 50, based on the Julius III herm); subsequent editions of the *Illustrium imagines* (1598, 1606) also included portraits of Sokrates.

Artists and scholars of the seventeenth century knew the philosopher's image well; P. P. *Rubens designed a handsome head of Sokrates from a carved gem for an engraving by Lucas Vorsterman (Rijksprentenkabinet, Amsterdam). Several Sokratean themes were considered appropriate subjects for paintings, executed with varying degrees of accuracy in the depiction of the philosopher, from the seventeenth to the nineteenth centuries: *Sokrates and the Mirror, Sokrates Doused with Water by Xanthippe* and the *Death of Sokrates*. The most successful rendering of the last theme was that of J.-L. *David (1787; Metropolitan Museum of Art, New York), in which Sokrates is represented as balding and bearded, but with straightened profile and ennobling posture.

BIBLIOGRAPHY

Bieber 39, 45–47; G.M.A. Richter, *Portraits of the Greeks* (Phaidon, 1965), I, 109–19; G. Becatti, "Raphael and the Antique," in *The Complete Works of Raphael* (New York, 1969), 519, 521; A. Pigler, *Barockthemen, Eine Auswahl von Verzeichnissen zur Ikonographie des 17. und 18. Jahrhunderts* (Budapest, 1974), II, 431–33.

CAROL MATTUSCH

SOUNION. Greek site of sanctuaries of Poseidon and Athena, including the cape at the southern tip of Attika as well as the deme site, which lay somewhat to the north and northeast.

The sanctuary of Poseidon occupies the high point of the cape and is crowned by the handsome fifth-century Doric temple made of local marble. It is peripteral, six by thirteen columns, and carried sculpture in the pediments and over the pronaos. The sanctuary was also provided with stoas and a handsome propylon. Evidence for an earlier, pre-Persian sanctuary is clear from traces of the earlier temple as well as the discovery in 1906 of a series of early marble *kouroi* (*korai* and *kouroi*). In 412 B.C. the sanctuary was enclosed in a large fortification wall that was improved in Hellenistic times. At the base of the hill to the north was a ship shed for two ships.

On a lower, separate hill to the northeast stood the sanctuary of Athena with its unusual plan of a colonnade on only the south and east sides. Dating to the mid-fifth century B.C., it was of the Ionic order. A smaller temple lay just to the north. Most of the Athena temple and the sima of the Poseidon temple were carried off and reused in the *Agora of Athens in the late first century B.C. Pieces of the Poseidon columns have been recognized in Italy, England and Germany; what remained in situ has been covered in graffiti, the most notable signature being that of Lord *Byron. Excavations on the site were done by the *Greek Archaeological Society (Stais) in the late nineteenth and early twentieth centuries.

BIBLIOGRAPHY

V. Stais, *ArchEph* (1900), 113–50; (1917), 168–229; V. Stais, *To Sounion* (Athens, 1920); W. B. Dinsmoor, Jr., *Sounion* (Athens, 1974); W. B. Dinsmoor, Jr.—H. A. Thompson, *The Temple of Athena Sounias* (forthcoming).

JOHN McK. CAMP II

SPALATO. See SPLIT.

SPARTA. Major Greek city, famed for its legendary associations with Menelaos and Helen of Troy, and for its great military success.

First inhabited in Mycenean times, Sparta became a military power under its kings by the eighth century B.C., ultimately controlling a large area of the surrounding Peloponnese. In 405 B.C. the Spartans defeated Athens but soon after were conquered, in turn, by the Thebans (371 B.C.). The first city wall was built in the later fourth century B.C., symptomatic of the weakened condition of the Spartan army. The city enjoyed a revival under the Roman Empire and survived the Herulian invasion of A.D. 267. But Sparta was destroyed by Alaric in 395 and then abandoned. Its later history included incursions by the Slavs (ninth century) and the French (1248), as well as government by the Paleologus dynasty in the fourteenth and fifteenth centuries. The Turks took the area in 1460, the Venetians in 1669 and the Turks again in 1715.

The remains of ancient Sparta are few. Thucydides (1.10) warned that future generations, looking at its monuments, would find it difficult to believe the city was once great. But the devastation suffered through the centuries is also responsible for the meagerness of ancient buildings. *Ciriaco of Ancona visited Sparta in 1447–48, staying with his friend Gemisthos Pletho at the nearby castle of Mistra. He despised the modern inhabitants of Sparta but found the ancient site still littered with fragments, including some inscriptions. Before 1732 *Fourmont explored Sparta, noting inscriptions and reliefs but also vandalizing the site. The area was further stripped by nearby villagers seeking building materials. In 1770, a Russian military expedition under Count Orlov, digging trenches to do battle with the Turks, accidentally came upon the ancient theater (dating to the second or first century B.C.). Chateaubriand lamented the sad appearance of Sparta in 1811; Edward *Lear painted the view from the theater (ca. 1849).

In modern times, Sparta has been excavated by the *British School at Athens under *Wace, Dawkins and others (1906–10 and 1924–29), revealing portions of the ancient city wall, the location of the temple of Athena Chalkioikos and the important sanctuary of Artemis Ortheia, with its rich deposits of votive offerings, highly significant for the early centuries of Greek art. Outside the ancient city to the north, the masonry remains of the Menelaion, a shrine of Menelaos and Helen, have recently been identified conclusively on the basis of dedications to both individuals. Nearby a Mycenaean ''Mansion'' (destroyed by fire ca. 1200 B.C.) has been excavated.

BIBLIOGRAPHY

R. M. Dawkins, ed., *Artemis Orthia, JHS* suppl. 5 (1929); P. Cartledge, s.v. ''Sparta,'' *PECS,* 855–56; *Pausanias, Guide to Greece,* tr. and ann. P. Levi, rev. ed. (Harmondsworth, 1979), II, 37–38; Tsigakou, *Rediscovery,* 159; J. B. Carter, ''The Masks of Ortheia,'' *AJA* 91 (1987), 355–83.

SPENCE, JOSEPH (1699–1768). English historian and art critic.

Spence was educated at Eton and at New College, Oxford. Having traveled extensively in Europe, he became professor of history at Oxford. Spence was admitted to the *Society of Dilettanti, one of the few commoners among its early members.

His principal contribution to archaeological studies lay in his lengthy work, *Polymetis, or an Enquiry Between the Works of the Roman Poets and the Re-*

Portrait of *Joseph Spence*, engraving by G. Vertue after a painting by I. Whood, from J. Spence, *Polymetis* (1747). (Westfälisches Landesmuseum für Kunst und Kulturgeschichte, Münster, Porträtarchiv Diepenbroick. Photo: R. Wakonigg.)

mains of the Ancient Artists, Being an Attempt to Illustrate Them Mutually from One Another (London, 1747), a work that was translated into German in 1776. The *Polymetis* is in the form of a dialogue among the characters, Polymetis, Musagetes and Philander, which begins with a discussion of the rise and fall of poetry and art in Rome and then proceeds to treat systematically various gods, heroes and astral forces, as well as the inhabitants of the air, earth and underworld. Spence was fiercely criticized by *Lessing in his *Laocoon* (Book VII) for making the relationship between poetry and art too close and for thinking that the similarities between the two genres were intentional. For Lessing, the *Polymetis* was "obnoxious" and a work "absolutely unbearable to every reader of taste."

Spence also wrote *An Essay on Pope's Odyssey* (London, 1726).

BIBLIOGRAPHY

Stark, esp. 170; Sandys, II, 411; *Porträtarchiv,* no. 69.

SPERLONGA. Village on the west coast of Italy, situated near Terracina, above the Bay of Naples; site of a villa associated with the emperor Tiberius (A.D. 14–37) and a grotto popularly known as the "Cave of Tiberius" (Antro di Tiberio).

The cave was known for many centuries, having been identified as the site of a famous incident described by Tacitus (*Annales* 4.59) in which Sejanus shielded Tiberius from a collapse of stone in the cave. The villa had also been investigated (1898, G. Patroni; 1953–54, F. Fasolo) and, in 1957, Sperlonga yielded its most sensational discoveries—a group of sculptures by the artists of the *Laocoon*—Athenodoros, Polydoros and Hagesandros of Rhodes. During the building of a road along the coast between Terracina and Gaeta, the engineer E. Bellante and, subsequently G. Jacopi directed work clearing massive debris from the cave and the extraction from the pools in the cave of over 7,000 fragments of marble sculpture depicting the adventures of Odysseus and other subjects. The marbles had been systematically smashed, evidently by members of Christian sects (one Christian inscription was dated 1736). Jacopi supervised the prompt reconstruction of the finds.

The local population resisted all attempts to transfer the sculptures to Rome. In 1963 the Museo Nazionale di Sperlonga was opened near the site, with Jacopi as director. His basic monograph, *L'Antro di Tiberio a Sperlonga, I Monumenti Romani* (Rome, 1963) was issued at the same time. The massive bibliography on the site embraces many questions about the sculptures, concerned with the reconstruction, the nature of the subject matter, the date of the sculptures and whether they are originals, copies or free variants of lost originals. The style is generally agreed to show a relationship to the "Baroque" of Pergamon and Rhodes in the second century B.C., but opinion is divided on whether these are Rhodian originals shipped to Italy or whether they show a renewal of that style in the first century A.C.

BIBLIOGRAPHY

G.M.A. Richter, "Sperlonga," *PECS,* 856; +G. Säflund, *The Polyphemus and Scylla Groups at Sperlonga* (Stockholm, 1972); B. Conticello, s.v. "Sperlonga," *EAA* suppl. (1973), 751–54; R. Neudecker, *Die Skulpturenausstattung römischer Villen in Italien* (Mainz, 1988), 220–23; +B. Andreae, *Laokoon und die Grundung Roms* (Mainz am Rhein, 1988).

SPINA. Pre-Roman city built on the lagoons of the ancient delta of the Po River in Northern Italy, inhabited mainly by Etruscans and Greeks.

The nature of Spina was long known only from literary evidence. Dionysios of Halikarnassos (1.18.4) and Strabo (5.1.7; 9.3.8) indicated that the city dominated the Adriatic Sea (in the sixth–fifth centuries B.C.) and noted that it had cause to maintain a treasury at the Greek sanctuary at *Delphi. Spina was linked to *Adria, another lagoon city, by a canal built by the Etruscans. The city went into decline, perhaps as a result of the silting up of the lagoon, and after an invasion by the Gauls (third century B.C.), it shrank to a village in the Roman period.

The location of Spina was unknown until 1922, when a huge necropolis was discovered in the Trebba Valley, ca. 6km west of Comacchio. An even larger cemetery was discovered nearby in the Pega Valley in 1954, altogether yielding over 4,000 tombs. The graves were difficult to dig because of the groundwater, and cofferdams of wood or metal were constructed to facilitate the pumping of water. Enormous amounts of fine Greek pottery were found, especially Attic red-figure wares of the period ca. 480–360 B.C., along with Etruscan jewelry and bronzes and inscriptions in both Etruscan and Greek.

The ancient city of Spina was completely covered over with silt, and the new shoreline extended beyond it into the sea. In 1956, parts of the habitation site were identified in the Pega Valley by means of aerial photography. Excavation revealed a grid plan of canals creating rectangular *insulae* (blocks), on which houses were built on pilings.

Thanks to the research of S. Aurigemma, N. Alfieri and P. Arias, the results of Spina have been well published. The finds are all in nearby Ferrara (Museo Archeologico Nazionale); the collection of Attic red-figure vases there has been described as the most comprehensive collection of Athenian vases of this period.
BIBLIOGRAPHY
+N. Alfieri—P. E. Arias—M. Hirmer, *Spina* (Florence, 1958); S. Aurigemma, *La Necropoli di Spina in Valle Trebba*, 1–2 (Rome, 1960–65); F. Boitani—M. Cataldi—M. Pasquinucci, *Etruscan Cities*, ed. F. Coarelli (New York, 1975), 303–6; Steingräber, 551–56, 597.

SPINARIO (THORN-PULLER; IL FEDELE; ABSALOM; PRIAPUS).

Hellenistic or Roman bronze, perhaps of the mid-first century B.C., of a boy seated on a rock, holding his left foot with his left hand across his right thigh and with the fingers of his right hand attempting to remove something, perhaps a thorn, from the foot.

The piece is believed to be a pastiche with the body created during the Hellenistic period and the head in an earlier style, perhaps copied from a statue of a standing boy of ca. 460 B.C. Some critics speculate that the head may actually have come from another work.

It is not known exactly what the boy is pulling from the sole of his foot. A popular story survived into the nineteenth century of a shepherd boy named Martius who had brought a message to the Roman Senate so faithfully that he removed a thorn from his foot only after his arrival. The tale suggests that the

Senate commissioned the bronze statue in gratitude for his faithfulness, giving rise to the popular Italian name for the statue, *Il Fedele*.

The first specific record of the piece comes from Rabbi Benjamin ben Jonah of Tudela, whose visit to Rome may be dated in 1166. He records this bronze along with three others, all placed on marble pillars, in front of the *Lateran Palace. In his account, he refers to the boy as Absalom, the son of David, probably because of the description in II Sam. XIV. 25: "But in all Israel there was none to be so much praised as Absalom for his beauty: from the sole of his foot even to the crown of his head there was no blemish in him." The passage certainly suggests the beauty and appeal of the piece. Magister *Gregorius, visiting Rome in the late twelfth or early thirteenth century, mentions the statue in connection with the other pieces set on marble pillars in front of the Lateran. He calls it a "Priapus," although this is the only record of the bronze by that name. In general, the *Spinario* seems to have been regarded in the Middle Ages as a leading example of the pagan "idol."

The piece is noted next as part of the collection of bronzes from the Lateran that were donated by *Sixtus IV in 1471 to the newly established Palazzo dei Conservatori (*Capitoline Museums). It remained there until 1798, when it was ceded to the French, by the terms of the Treaty of Tolentino. It was put on display in the *Louvre on 9 November 1800, where it remained until late in 1815. After the Battle of Waterloo, the *Spinario* returned to Rome, arriving there 4 January 1816. The bronze has remained in the Palazzo dei Conservatori since that time.

The *Spinario* was a very popular piece and inspired many imitations and copies during, as well as after, the Renaissance. *Brunelleschi used the motif in his well-known competition piece of the *Sacrifice of Isaac* for the Baptistery doors in Florence. The removal of the *Spinario* to the Conservatori gave it wider exposure to tourists and artists alike, and many copies appeared in Italy within only a few years of the move. One of the most famous is perhaps the larger bronze by Antonello Gagini that was part of a fountain in the Palazzo Alcontres in Messina, dated 1500 (this is probably the statue now in the Metropolitan Museum in New York). In 1540 Benvenuto *Cellini handled a transaction of a copy presented to Francis I by the Cardinal of Ferrara. Anton Francesco Doni mentioned in a letter to a friend in 1547 that the *Spinario* was one of the most worthwhile things in Rome to see. That it was considered beautiful enough for copies to be presented as royal gifts is attested by the fact that a replica was given to Philip II of Spain in 1561, another copy to Philip IV in the seventeenth century and one to Charles I of England in 1634. Many smaller, a few larger, and some marble copies of the piece from the late fifteenth through seventeenth centuries are extant. Some artists chose to render their copies rather freely, especially in relationship to the Archaic style of the head, making the entire piece a more harmonious, naturalistic whole.

BIBLIOGRAPHY
+H. Stuart Jones, *A Catalogue of the Ancient Sculptures Preserved in the Municipal Collections of Rome: The Sculptures of the Palazzo dei Conservatori* (Oxford, 1926), 47; P. Borchardt, "The Sculpture in Front of the Lateran as Described by Benjamin of Tudela and Magister Gregorius," *JRS* 26 (1936), 68–70; Helbig, II, 266–68; +Haskell—Penny, 307–9.

                                                                        JUDY WAGNER

SPLIT (SPALATO; ASPALATHOS). Modern city on the Dalmatian coast, site of the Roman Imperial palace of Diocletian (ruled A.D. 284–305).

Built largely of fine limestone from the island of Brač, the palace of Diocletian is a rectangular fortress, surrounded by a high wall punctuated by towers located at the corners and gates and halfway between these. The slightly irregular plan measures 215.5m on the east and west sides, 175m on the north side and 181m on the south. The south façade, fronting the sea, featured a covered gallery running the length of the wall and articulated by forty-two arched openings and forty-four engaged columns. In the middle and at either end was a heightened loggia with an arch rising above the others, in the motif known as the Syrian gable or *serliana* (after the architect *Serlio). The land façades of the palace had a more grimly functional appearance except at the gates, which featured blind arcades of differently colored stones and other decorative details.

The fortess interior was divided into four quarters by intersecting, colonnaded streets. Within these quarters was a remarkable array of Roman building types and forms, including a residential area with baths, a temple of Jupiter, a basilican audience hall and an octagonal mausoleum for Diocletian. The handsome peristyle courtyard leading from the center of the site toward the palace façade makes use of colonnades with arches springing directly from columns. The Syrian gable motif is used once again on the palace façade.

The site of Spalatum appears on the Late Antique map known as the *Tabula Peutingeriana, though no buildings are indicated. The palace was absorbed into the medieval town of Spalato by the tenth century, with the standing Roman structures often incorporated into the new buildings. The mausoleum of Diocletian was converted into a church by 650; it was subsequently dedicated to the local martyr St. Domnus. The temple of Jupiter was turned into a baptistery. In the late Middle Ages, on the southeast side of the palace, large ashlar stones were robbed heavily from the fortress wall, to be reused in the cathedral's bell tower and other new buildings.

The traveler *Ciriaco of Ancona visited the site in 1436, to copy inscriptions. There exist Italian designs of the sixteenth century with two plans of the mausoleum that have been attributed to *Palladio, though perhaps they were only owned and annotated by him (Royal Institute of British Architects, London). The first reconstructions of the palace, published by the travelers *Spon (1678) and *Wheler (1682), were highly schematic but brought the site to the attention of French and English scholars.

The Austrian Baroque architect J. B. Fischer von Erlach produced an elaborate, imaginative reconstruction based on real measurements of some of the remains (1721). But far more accurate were the drawings generated by Robert *Adam, with much of the actual work done by C. L. Clérisseau, during a five-week campaign in Spalato in 1757. These were published by Adam in a sumptuous folio in 1764 and remained the fullest and most reliable published drawings of the palace of Diocletian for approximately 150 years. Two major studies of the remains appeared early in the twentieth century, by G. *Niemann, *Der Palast Diokletians in Spalato* (Vienna, 1910), and by the French architect E. Hébrard and historian J. Zeiller, *Spalato, le Palais de Diocletien* (Paris, 1912).

The first stratigraphic excavations within the palace began in 1968 with a joint expedition of the University of Minnesota (under S. McNally) and the Town Planning Institute of Dalmatia (under J. Marasović). In recent urban renewal, medieval buildings huddled against the outside wall have been removed, and part of the main east-west street has been restored to its original width. Probably best known of the visible remains of the palace of Diocletian are the arcades of the peristyle court, which provide the scenic backdrop for an outdoor café.

BIBLIOGRAPHY

+S. McNelly, "Diocletian's Palace, Split in the Middle Ages," *Archaeology* 28 (1975), 248–59; +J. Marasović—T. Marasović, *Diocletian's Palace* (Zagreb, 1970); +J. J. Wilkes, *Diocletian's Palace, Split, Residence of a Retired Roman Emperor* (Sheffield, 1986).

SPON, JACOB (JACQUES; 1647–85). French physician and antiquarian scholar, one of the first to write and publish an account of his travels to Greece and to publish on Roman provincial archaeology.

Spon was born in Lyons in 1647, the son of a German immigrant doctor. He studied medicine at Montpellier, then continued his education at Strassburg, where he developed a passion for the study of antiquity under the tutelage of the Parisian doctor Charles Patin. After travels to Basel, Geneva and Paris, he returned to Lyons to practice medicine. All of his free time he devoted to the study of antiquities, especially relating to *Lyons itself. In 1673 he published his *Recherches des antiquités et curiosités de la ville de Lyon,* containing precise copies of local inscriptions and the first publication of the so-called Shield of Scipio, found in the Rhône River near Avignon.

In 1674 Spon departed on a journey that was to take him to Italy, the Dalmatian coast, Greece, the Aegean and Asia Minor. After a five-month stay in Rome, visiting monuments and libraries and studying inscriptions, he went on to Florence and then to Venice, from which he took ship in the company of the Englishman George *Wheler and others. Sailing for Constantinople, they stopped at Pola and *Split, as well as Kythera, Tenos and *Delos and also at Alexandria Troas, believed at the time to be the site of *Troy.

Spon spent three weeks in Constantinople (*Byzantium), using the occasion

Portrait of *Jacob Spon*, engraving by M. Ogier. (Westfälisches Landesmuseum für Kunst und Kulturgeschichte, Münster, Porträtarchiv Diepenbroick. Photo: R. Wakonigg.)

to study drawings of antiquities from Athens that were in the possession of the Marquis de *Nointel, as well as reliefs and coins in his collection. Next, Spon made for *Smyrna and *Ephesos, where he crawled through subterranean chambers believed at that time to be part of the *Temple of Artemis.

Wintering in Athens (1675–76), he studied the *Parthenon; viewing the monument called "The Lantern of Demosthenes," he deduced that it was, in fact, the choregic *Monument of Lysikrates; in *Corinth he noted the great antiquity of the Doric columns there. After stops at *Marathon and *Thebes, he turned homeward, reaching Lyons in 1676, by way of Venice and Padua. He carried home in triumph the records of more than 2,000 new inscriptions, some 600 coins and fifty Greek manuscripts.

He began to publish accounts of his journeys, causing quite a sensation, first in Lyons (*Voyage d'Italie, de Dalmatie, de Grèce et de Levant,* 1678) and then in Amsterdam (1679); translations into English, Dutch and German followed (1681). Spon's unwearying devotion to the visual remains of antiquity led to two other great publications, containing many engraved illustrations: *Miscella-*

nea eruditae antiquitatis (Lyons, 1679–85) and *Recherches curieuses d'antiquité contenues en plusieurs dissertations sur des médailles, bas reliefs, statues, mosaiques et inscr. antiques* (Lyons, 1683). In these works he divided the study of antiquity into eight categories of research: numismatics, epigraphy, architecture, iconography (including both sculptured and painted images), glyptics, relief, manuscripts and vases. He used the word *archaeologia* to refer to the study of antiquity and was one of the first to do so.

After the death of his father (1684), Spon fell upon hard times. Destitute, he hoped to find a new life in Zürich, where his father had held citizenship. But on the way he became gravely ill and died at Vevay, at the tragically early age of thirty-eight.

BIBLIOGRAPHY

Stark, 137–41; *Porträtarchiv,* no. 48.

SQUARCIONE, FRANCESCO (1394–ca. 1468). Italian painter and art dealer, active during the middle decades of the fifteenth century in Padua.

His biographer of 1560, Bernardino Scardeone, wrote that Squarcione was a founder of the Paduan school and had instructed no fewer than 137 pupils, including *Mantegna, Crivelli, Schiavone and Zoppo. Squarcione's contribution lay in the fact that his collection of ancient objects and casts of antique sculptures were open to his many pupils. Some have denied that his collection was very extensive or that he did indeed travel as far as Greece (as was claimed) to acquire such objects, but there is no doubt that he owned certain works that served as models of instruction and inspiration for his students. Consequently, Squarcione was an important catalyst in the renewed interest in ancient art in the Veneto during the Renaissance.

BIBLIOGRAPHY

B. Berenson, *Italian Pictures of the Renaissance* (Oxford, 1932); R. van Marle, *The Development of the Italian School* 18 (1937); Weiss, *RDCA* 181.

CHERYL SUMNER

STABIAE. A site of numerous lavish Roman villas situated on the Bay of Naples on the slopes of Monte Faito above the modern town Castellammare di Stabia.

Stabiae was destroyed in the eruption of Vesuvius in A.D. 79. It had been an Oscan town, presumably a port with its center somewhere under the modern town. Under the Samnites it was closely leagued with Nuceria and probably served as its port. In the Social War it fell to Sulla, 30 April 89 B.C., and was destroyed, after which it ceased to exist as a municipality but continued as a resort for the rich.

The first remains were rediscovered in 1749, the year after the discovery of *Pompeii, the site being at first called Gragnano. Since the villas were situated along the brow of the hill called Varano overlooking the Sarno Valley and Bay of Naples, excavation was comparatively easy, and the finds were very gratifying. Stabiae had apparently suffered comparatively little damage in the earth-quake of A.D. 62. Work on a regular basis was evidently pursued there from 7 June 1749 to 11 December 1762 and then suspended until 2 May 1775, when the poverty of finds at Pompeii prompted reopening of the site. It continued until 14 August 1782. During this time, although the excavations were filled in again soon after they were made, daybooks were kept fairly conscientiously, and surprisingly accurate plans of the buildings were made, together with some drawings of pavements and decorations. These were collected and published by Michele Ruggiero in 1881 and form our best account of what the site was like.

Beginning 9 January 1950, excavations were again undertaken, and large parts of two complexes were brought to light. Both had been, to some extent, explored earlier, but neither was, by any means, exhausted. That known as the Villa di Varano proved to be two or more villas in continuity, the living quarters ar-ranged on terraces along the brow of the hill, with service quarters behind. That known as the Villa di San Marco is a very elaborate and luxurious complex, probably not a private house.

Extensive cemeteries have been discovered along the road from Stabiae to Nuceria, most of the tombs being pre-Roman and dating from the eighth to the second centuries B.C.

BIBLIOGRAPHY

O. Elia, s.v. "Stabiae," *EAA* 7 (1966), 459–63; A. de Vos—M. de Vos, *Pompei Ercolano Stabia* (Rome, 1982), 307–31.

L. RICHARDSON, JR

STACKELBERG, OTTO MAGNUS VON, Baron (1787–1837). Painter and draftsman from Livonia, participant in archaeological circles in Greece and Rome.

After early studies in Halle, Göttingen and Dresden, the wealthy noble Stack-elberg journeyed to Italy (1810), there to make friends with *Haller von Hall-erstein and P. O. *Brøndsted. Together the group went on to Greece, where they met the British architect C. R. *Cockerell. After a brief trip to Asia Minor (1811), Stackelberg studied sites in Attika (*Athens, *Eleusis, *Sounion) and joined the expedition led by Cockerell to the temple of Apollo Epikourios at *Bassai. He is known for the exquisite quality of the drawings he made, espe-cially of the temple at Bassai but also of Greek architecture and landscape in general.

In 1813, Stackelberg was taken prisoner by pirates and was rescued with great difficulty by Haller. Leaving Greece in 1814, he went on to Italy, settling in Rome (1816) and becoming part of a second brotherhood of archaeologists and lovers of antiquity. He developed close friendships with August Kestner, a Han-overian diplomat, and the brilliant organizer Eduard *Gerhard. Joined by Theo-dor *Panofka, the friends formed the circle of classicists with the name of *Hyperboreans. These northerners investigated the antiquities in and around

Rome. When news came in 1827 that painted tombs had been discovered at the Etruscan site of *Tarquinia, Kestner and Stackelberg set off to see them and spent several weeks copying the four sepulchral chambers that had been discovered. Stackelberg's drawings of the Tomba delle Bighe ("Tomb of the Two-Horse Chariots") are so well done and have been so influential that he has become identified with the tomb, so that it is now often called the Tomba Stackelberg. (The "Tomb of the Baron," however, is named for his friend Baron Kestner.)

Among Stackelberg's publications are the following: *Der Apollotempel zu Bassae in Arkadien und die daselbst ausgegraben Bildwerke* (Rome, 1826); *La Grèce, Vues pittoresques et topographiques* (Paris, 1834); *Die Gräber der Hellenen* (Berlin, 1837).

BIBLIOGRAPHY

Stark, 260–62; G. Rodenwaldt, *O. M. von Stackelberg, der Entdecker der griechischen Landschaft* (Munich, 1957); +Tsigakou, *Rediscovery*, 103, 115, 156, 160, 200a.

STADIUM OF DOMITIAN, Campus Martius, Rome. A stadium built between A.D. 92 and 96 by Domitian for athletic contests (Suetonius, *Dom.* 5). The area chosen for the stadium in the *Campus Martius was west of that monumentalized by Agrippa in the reign of Augustus; the area is now occupied by the Piazza Navona, which preserves exactly the shape and proportions of the stadium. Ca. 250m in length and curved at the northern end but straight on the south, the stadium possessed neither central *spina* nor *carceres,* which clearly differentiated it from a circus, was encircled by a *cavea* of two tiers of seats for spectators and was entered from the north through an entrance gate of marble. In A.D. 217, after the *Colosseum was damaged by fire, this stadium was used for gladiatorial contests, and it was restored by Alexander Severus in A.D. 228. The arcades beneath the seats contained notorious brothels. As late as the fourth century A.C. the stadium was one of the buildings in Rome admired by Constantius during his visit to the city.

According to legend, St. Agnes was martyred in the brothels of the stadium; by the ninth century A.C. a church—called in later times either S. Agnese in Agone or de Cryptis Agonis—had been erected in her honor atop the center of the west side of the *cavea.* This church was rebuilt by Borromini, and the "Four Rivers" fountain of *Bernini was placed in front of it. The fountain is crowned by one of the *obelisks transferred from the ancient temple of Isis in the Campus Martius. Beneath the church remain some of the *cavea* seats, travertine pilasters and walls of brick-faced concrete. The stadium was first recognized as Domitian's by Urlichs in 1842. Excavations were conducted of the north side in 1868, of the south in 1869, of the east side in 1933–34 and of the north curve and entrance gate in 1936–37, the last two campaigns under the direction of A. M. Colini. Remains of the north curve and of the gate may be seen beneath the houses west of the modern Via Agonale.

BIBLIOGRAPHY
+A. M. Colini, *Stadium Domitiani* (Rome, 1943); Platner—Ashby, 495–96; M. E. Blake, *Roman Construction in Italy from Tiberius Through the Flavians* (Washington, DC, 1959), 107–8; +Nash, II, 387–90.

JAMES C. ANDERSON, JR.

STADIUM OF DOMITIAN, Palatine Hill, Rome. A large garden in the shape of a stadium, east of the so-called Domus Augustiana on the *Palatine Hill.

Brick stamps show that the structure was one of the last Domitianic projects on the Palatine, dating between A.D. 92 and 96. The "stadium" was surrounded by a two-story portico supported on piers faced by semicolumns. The space between the colonnade and the precinct wall was covered by a barrel vault, thus forming an *ambulacrum* around the central open area (which measured 160 by 50m). The south end was curved, and above it stood the *pulvinar* from which the emperor could watch races in the Circus Maximus. Five rooms on the north end, in the normal location for the *carceres* of a racetrack, were richly decorated, and fountains at the ends of the open area took the place of *metae.* Presumably designed by Rabirius, the "stadium" was an elaborate architectural hoax whose form had little to do with its function, although mild exercise might have been taken there.

Excavation in 1939 revealed extensive restorations to the "stadium" by Septimius Severus and further alteration in late antiquity, probably under Theodoric (A.D. 493–526), who made use of the Palatine palace and whose brick stamps have been found there. Theodoric added the oval enclosure still visible at the south end of the open area, the use of which is disputed. The name "hippodromus Palatii" is applied to this building in the twelfth-century *Acta S. Sebastiani;* since the term "hippodromus" is used as early as the time of the younger Pliny for a garden in the shape of a stadium, it is probable that this is the more correct designation for this structure. The church of S. Cesario in Palatio may have been located in the middle of the "stadium" from the mid-twelfth to the early fifteenth centuries; if so, its associated monastery might be the source of the early Christian frescoes reported beneath the Palatine *Antiquario. Excavations in the "stadium" began in 1552 and are reported sporadically for four centuries; the major campaign conducted in the 1920s and 1930s remains largely unpublished.

BIBLIOGRAPHY
Platner—Ashby, 162–64; P. Grimal, *Les Jardins romains* (Paris, 1943), 265–69; G. Lugli, *Roma antica: il centro monumentale* (Rome, 1946), 514–16; M. E. Blake, *Roman Construction in Italy from Tiberius Through the Flavians* (Washington, DC, 1959), 122–23.

JAMES C. ANDERSON, JR.

STARK, KARL (CARL) BERNARD (1824–79). German archaeologist and art historian.

Photograph of *Karl
Bernard Stark*. (Ar-
chäologisches Institut
der Universität, Heidel-
berg.)

Stark was born in Jena to a family whose members on both his mother's and
his father's side were in the learned professions (medicine and law, respectively).
He was well trained in the classics from an early age and was reading the
Odyssey in Greek at nine years.

He studied philology at Jena and Leipzig (1841–45) and turned toward ancient
art under the influence of August *Böckh and a trip to Italy. By the age of
twenty-six, Stark was associate professor at Jena and assistant director of the
museum there. In 1855, he was chosen to hold the new chair in archaeology at
Heidelberg.

Stark's vision was extremely broad, crossing periods and continents, as in his
study of the history, religion, literature and art of Gaza (1852), a work that dealt
with a point of intersection between Asia and Africa, on one hand, and Greece
and the Orient, on the other, covering a time span from antiquity to the time of
the Arab conquest. He wrote a monograph on the artist Albrecht *Dürer (1851)
and a study of the myth of Niobe (1863). Stark is remembered, above all, for
his masterly study of the history of archaeological studies, contained in his

Systematik und Geschichte der Archäologie der Kunst (Leipzig, 1880). The work was published posthumously and actually was only the first volume of a projected survey of the "archaeology of art." This survey of archaeological scholarship from the fifteenth to the nineteenth centuries remains without parallel today.

BIBLIOGRAPHY

T. Hölscher, in *Archäologenbildnisse*, 49–50.

STEVENS, GORHAM PHILLIPS (1876–1963). American architect and administrator; director of the *American Academy in Rome (1912–13; 1917–32) and of the *American School of Classical Studies (ASCS) in Athens (1939–41).

Trained at Massachusetts Institute of Technology and the Beaux Arts Institute in Paris, Stevens started his career as an architect in the firm of McKim, Mead and White (1902–3) but became increasingly interested in classical archaeology. After a stint as a fellow at the ASCS in Athens, he returned to the McKim firm but was called to Rome to be director of the academy there (1912–13). He also served as acting director during the frequent absences of his colorful successor and rival Jesse Benedict Carter, becoming permanent director again after Carter's death in 1917. A conservative who championed training in traditional classical architecture, he was unable to adjust to the demands and needs of students of modern architecture and was replaced in 1932. He subsequently served briefly as the director of the American School in Athens.

Limited in his scholarly production, Stevens worked on, but never completed, a revision of the handbook *Architecture of Greece and Rome* by W. J. Anderson and R. P. Spiers (1902). In 1956, at the age of eighty, he published an article telling "how an exceedingly beautiful Ionic capital can be quickly drawn."

BIBLIOGRAPHY

G. P. Stevens, *The Setting of the Periclean Parthenon, Hesperia,* suppl. 3 (1940); idem, "The Volute of the Capital of the Temple of Athena at Priene—A Machine for Drawing the Volute for Any Column Between Twenty and Sixty Feet in Height," *MAAR* 24 (1956), 33–46; L. Valentine—A. Valentine, *The American Academy in Rome (1894–1969),* 61–83, 200; F. K. Yegul, *Gentlemen of Instinct and Breeding, Architecture at the American Academy in Rome, 1894–1940* (New York, 1991).

STILLWELL, RICHARD (1899–1982). American archaeologist and architect, specializing in Greek architecture; distinguished editor and administrator.

Born in Niagara Falls, New York, and raised in Lakewood, Connecticut, Richard Stillwell graduated from Princeton University in 1921 and subsequently obtained his M.F.A. there. Under a fellowship in architecture at the *American School of Classical Studies (ASCS) in Athens (1924–26), he first studied the monuments of Greece. Returning to America, he accepted a post as instructor in art and archaeology at Princeton (1926) and rose through the ranks to become Howard Crosby Butler Memorial Professor of architecture, a chair he held until he retired in 1967.

During these years he held positions of increasing responsibility at the ASCS, eventually serving as director of the school (1932–35), director of excavations at *Corinth and supervising architect of excavations in the *Agora, Athens. His activities there were interrupted by World War II and service to his country (1942–45) as a teacher in the School of Air Combat (Quonset, Rhode Island) in the U.S. Navy.

Stillwell was involved with the excavation and publication of five major archaeological sites in the Mediterranean, utilizing his skills as field archaeologist, architect, scholar and editor: Corinth, the Athenian Agora, *Antioch, *Kourion and *Morgantina. He was field director at Corinth and principal author of four volumes of the final publication: 1.1. *Introduction, Topography, Architecture* (1932); 1.2. *Architecture* (1941); 2. *The Theater* (1952); 3.1. *Acrocorinth* (1930). In his later years he devoted himself to the Princeton Expedition to Sicily and the excavation of Morgantina, sharing the directorship with Erik Sjøqvist (1955–66).

Amazingly, Stillwell also found time to serve in these years as editor in chief of the prestigious *American Journal of Archaeology* (1954–73), expanding the journal and raising it to a new level. After his retirement came the other monumental editing task for which he is remembered, the direction and publication of *The Princeton Encyclopedia of Classical Sites* (1976).

BIBLIOGRAPHY
New York Times Biographical Service, 1073 (3 August 1982); T. L. Shear, Jr., "Richard Stillwell (1899–1982)," *AJA* 87 (1983), 432–35.

STOA OF ATTALOS, Athens. Hellenistic Greek market-building in the Athenian *Agora.

The stoa was built in the middle of the second century B.C. during the reign of King Attalos II of Pergamon (159–138 B.C.) along the east side of the Agora square. The identification is certain, based on the discovery in 1861 of the dedicatory inscription carved on the epistyle (*IG* II² 3171 and Agora I 6135). It is a large, two-storied stoa, measuring 116.50m in length and 20.05m in width and standing 13.00m high. It had limestone walls, steps and doorways of Hymettian marble and colonnades of Pentelic marble. The orders of the colonnades were, on the first floor, Doric exterior, unfluted Ionic interior, and on the second floor, double Ionic exterior and Pergamene interior. There were twenty-one shops behind the colonnades on each floor, making a sort of precursor of a modern shopping center with forty-two stores under a single roof. The building stood, with minor alterations, until 267 A.D., at which time the colonnade was destroyed in the Herulian sack of Athens. The back wall was subsequently incorporated into a late Roman fortification wall, which preserved it to its full height at the north end into modern times.

Excavations were carried out by the *Greek Archaeological Society in 1859–62 (K. D. Koumanoudes) and in 1898–1902 (K. D. Mylonas), and further work was done by the *American School of Classical Studies from 1931 to 1953. In the years between 1953 and 1956 the stoa was entirely reconstructed under the direction of H. A. Thompson and J. Travlos, with the support of J. D. Rockefeller and numerous private donors. It serves now as the Agora museum, housing the public display area, storerooms, and the archives and workrooms of the excavations.

BIBLIOGRAPHY

H. A. Thompson—R. E. Wycherley, *The Agora of Athens* (Princeton, NJ, 1972), 103–8; H. A. Thompson, *The Stoa of Attalos II in Athens, Agora Picture Book* 2 (Princeton, NJ, 1979).

JOHN McK. CAMP II

STOBI. Roman and early medieval city located in the area of ancient Macedonia, at the confluence of the Crna (Erigon) and Vardar (Axius) rivers, ca. 150km north of Thessaloniki.

Evidence in context for the habitation of Stobi points to the beginning of the town in the Hellenistic period. Burials as early as the third century B.C. show usage of the site prior to the Roman organization of the province of Macedonia in 146 B.C. The city became a *municipium* by Early Imperial times, experiencing an expansion of population and sufficient prosperity to begin minting its own coins in A.D. 69. Remains of a Roman house ("Casa Romana") with wall decoration of the first century A.C. have been partially excavated, but the most prominent monument of this period is the Roman theater, begun in the early second century A.C. and redesigned in the midcentury. With a capacity of ca. 7,600, it had seats of marble with inscriptions in Greek indicating the owners' names and a two-story scene building of local white marble and a reddish limestone.

The later archaeological record of Stobi reveals a number of synagogues, basilicas and churches rising among and over Roman structures. By 325, the city housed a bishop who attended the Council of Nicaea. Earthquakes in the third and sixth centuries and barbarian incursions reduced the city to an abandoned ruin.

Stobi was visited and identified independently by J. G. von Hahn (1858) and Léon Heuzey (1861). During World War I German soldiers exposed parts of the Christian basilicas; systematic excavations from 1924 to 1931 uncovered the theater and a number of buildings in the west and central parts of the ancient city, under the direction of B. Saria and V. R. Petrović, for the National Museum of Belgrade. A joint American-Yugoslav project was carried out from 1970 to 1981 under the direction of Djordje Mano-Zissi, James Wiseman and Blaga Aleksova. In 1992, rescue operations were conducted in connection with highway construction, under the auspices of the Institute for the Preservation of the Monuments of Culture of the former Yugoslav republic of Macedonia. New information was obtained about the city wall, a cemetery on the west of the site and an Early Christian basilica, the sixth to be discovered at Stobi.

BIBLIOGRAPHY
Studies in the Antiquities of Stobi 1–3 (Titov Veles, 1973–81); J. Wiseman, "Archaeology and History at Stobi, Macedonia," *Rome and the Provinces, Studies in the Transformation of Art and Architecture in the Mediterranean World,* ed. C. B. McClendon
(New Haven, CT, 1986), 37–50; V. R. Anderson-Stojanovic, *Stobi 1, The Hellenistic
and Roman Pottery* (Princeton, 1992); C. S. Snively, "Salvage Excavations at Stobi,"
ArchNews 18 (1993), 24–27.

STOSCH, PHILIPP VON, Baron (1691–1757). German diplomat and antiquarian, known for his splendid collection of ancient gems.

Stosch, a native of Küstrin, instead of studying theology as his father intended,
set out to travel to the principal German cities in search of important collections
of coins (1708), followed by courses in Greek in Amsterdam (1709). A cousin
who served as ambassador of Prussia in The Hague induced him to enter diplomatic service there (1710).

The Dutch government sent Stosch on a first mission, to England, in 1712;
during a second mission, to Paris (1713), he became familiar with important
French collections of antique medals, coins and engraved gems. The following
year in Italy he collected quantities of antique coins, maps and gemstones and
made the acquaintance of the Florentine scholar Filippo *Buonarroti. Later in
Dresden, the King of Poland sent him on a mission to The Hague (1719), where
he engineered the return to France of valuable stolen manuscripts.

The British minister Lord Carteret then sent him on a mission to Rome (1721)
to keep an eye on Prince James Stuart, the Jacobite pretender to the British
throne. Stosch was in his antiquarian element there, but Jacobite threats forced
him to move on to Florence (1731) for the rest of his days.

Throughout his life the Baron von Stosch assiduously sought to increase his
antiquarian knowledge and amassed vast collections of coins, paintings, maps,
manuscripts, engravings and gemstones. His erudition in these fields was much
respected. The most important of his publications is *Gemmae antiquae caelatae,
sculptorum nominibus insignitae* (Amsterdam, 1724). After his death, *Winckelmann prepared a catalog of his collection. Frederick II of Prussia purchased
his 3,444 engraved gemstones, and James *Tassie acquired a set of 2,800 of his
casts of antique gems.

BIBLIOGRAPHY
J. J. Winckelmann, *Description des pierres gravées du feu baron de Stosch* (Florence,
1760); "Stosch (Philippe, baron de)," *NBG* 44 (1865) cols. 524–26; Stark, esp. 179–80;
Porträtarchiv, no. 78; P. Zazoff—H. Zazoff, *Gemmensammler und Gemmenforscher, von
einer noblen Passion zur Wissenschaft* (Munich, 1983), 3–67.

J. S. TASSIE

STRADA, JACOPO (1507–88). Italian scholar, antiquarian and draftsman.

Born in Mantua, Strada traveled extensively, meeting and serving a wide
range of masters, including the humanists in the entourage of Cardinal Alessan-

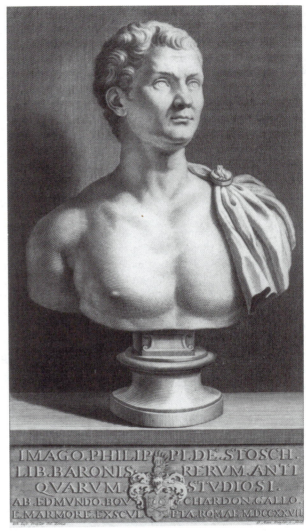

Portrait of *Baron Philipp von Stosch*, engraving by G. M. Preisler after J. J. Preisler, from J. J. Winckelmann, *Description des pierres gravées du feu Baron de Stosch* (1760). (Westfälisches Landesmuseum für Kunst und Kulturgeschichte, Münster, Porträtarchiv Diepenbroick. Photo: R. Wakonigg.)

dro Farnese (*Farnese family), the Archduke Ferdinand, the Duke of Bavaria (*Albrecht V) and, finally (after 1564), the Emperor Maximilian II.

In a letter from Vienna dated 1568, Strada, who signed himself "antiquarian of the Holy Caesarean Majesty of the Emperor" (antiquario de la sacra cesarea maestà del imperatore), spoke of his thirteen manuscripts on medallions, a compendium that he boasted contained no fewer than 12,000 examples. The authorship of the accompanying illustrations and those drawings found in related manuscripts has never been satisfactorily resolved. Strada may have turned this task over to other hands, as he is known to have done as regards the sketches prepared for the Duke of Bavaria, or he may have done the remainder himself. In the same letter, he also mentioned a dictionary he compiled of eleven ancient and modern languages. Strada's *Imperatorum romanorum . . . imagines* appeared in 1559, preceded by the *Epitome thesauri antiquitatum* (1553).

In 1567–68, about the time *Titian executed his portrait (now in Vienna), Strada negotiated for the Duke of Bavaria the purchase of the Loredano collection of antique marbles and provided, at the same time, measured drawings of the main rooms in the Palazzo del Te and the Appartamento di Troia in his native Mantua. Thus, in addition to his more scholarly pursuits (a record of which is found in the archives in Vienna (Codex Vindobonensis 10101), Strada served as a principal agent in the transmission of classical ideas to the major courts of Northern Europe. In fact, the exterior of his own house in Vienna was decorated with copies of antique busts from the Mantuan collection of Cesare *Gonzaga.

BIBLIOGRAPHY

E. Verheyen, "Jacopo Strada's Mantuan Drawings of 1567/68," *ArtB* 49 (1967), 62–69; R. van Bush, *Studien zu deutschen Antikensammlungen des 16. Jahrhundert* (Tübingen, 1973), 193–219; J. Hayward, *Virtuoso Goldsmiths* (London, 1976); D. J. Jansen, "Jacopo Strada's Antiquarian Interest: A Survey of His Musaeum and Its Purpose," *Xenia* 21 (1991), 59–76, with bib; D. J. Jansen, "Antonio Agustín and Jacopo Strada," *Antonio Agustín between Renaissance and Counter-Reform*, ed. M. H. Crawford (London, 1993), 211–46.

CLIFFORD M. BROWN

STRATIGRAPHICAL EXCAVATION. The removal of the layers or strata of an archaeological site with attention to their relationships and sequence, in an effort to interpret the chronology and significance of artifacts, buildings and other man-made materials contained in the strata.

The formulation of the concept of stratigraphy in geology led to the recognition of related principles in archaeology. Scientists of the seventeenth and eighteenth centuries made numerous observations and discoveries about the relative positioning of fossils in geological strata. A similar approach was used by Thomas *Jefferson, who made his well-known observation (1784) of archaeological stratification in native American deposits on his estate in Virginia, noting the presence of artifacts in the various layers.

Charles Lyell articulated concepts of geological stratification in his *Principles of Geology* (1830); most notable and of lasting significance for archaeology was the Law of Superposition, which states that upper units of stratification are younger than those beneath them, if strata are found as originally deposited. Around the same time C. J. *Thomsen proposed his chronology for prehistoric archaeology in the Three Age system of stone, bronze and iron—a scheme that was confirmed stratigraphically by his successor at the Danish National Museum, J.A.A. Worsaae, through excavations in peat bogs (results published in 1843). The observation of stratification played an important role in the archaeological precision of General *Pitt-Rivers (beginning in the 1870s), who utilized cross-section drawings of his trenches though he did not actually excavate strata one by one in sequence. *Schliemann constructed a crude stratigraphy of *Troy, in which he identified seven levels of occupation in the great mound of Hissarlik (later revised to nine by *Dörpfeld). *Evans created his relative chronology of the site of *Knossos, with its Early, Middle and Late Minoan periods, by observing the overlapping of walls and strata and displaying them in plans and cross-sections.

True stratigraphical excavation was developed by Mortimer *Wheeler in the 1930s and was practiced also by his distinguished pupil, Kathleen Kenyon. Their work involved identifying and numbering strata, including pits, ditches and other features, and displaying them in cross-section and plan. The Wheeler school advocated peeling off successive layers of deposits, recording the relevant artifacts in each stratum, a method that stands as one strongly opposed to the widespread system of digging in arbitrary, predetermined spits of earth.

Edward Harris reviewed the spotty history of valid stratigraphical excavation in 1979 in his *Principles of Archaeological Stratigraphy,* noting also the need to separate archaeological stratigraphy from geological stratigraphy, since manmade materials create a different kind of record from fossils. He enunciated a new series of principles to aid in understanding the nature of strata and their interfaces. He introduced a diagrammatic sheet, known as the Harris matrix, which allows for a far more detailed record of stratigraphy than the cross-section drawing. His revolutionary system, adopted on many sites in America and Europe, was advocated for sites in ancient Italy by A. Carandini and D. Manacorda.

BIBLIOGRAPHY

E. Harris, *Principles of Archaeological Stratigraphy,* 2nd ed. (London, 1989); B. Trigger, *A History of Archaeological Thought* (Cambridge, 1989), 196–99; E. Harris—M. R. Brown III—G. J. Brown, eds., *Practices of Archaeological Stratigraphy* (London, 1993).

STRONG, EUGÉNIE SELLERS (1860–1943). English art historian and archaeologist; one of the first women to become a major figure in these areas.

Born in London, part French, educated at Girton College, Cambridge, and under *Furtwängler in Munich, Strong became a pioneer woman art historian. Her first major book was *The Elder Pliny's Chapters on the History of Art* (1896). The next year she married the Orientalist and art historian Sandford Arthur Strong (d. 1904). Her influential translation of Wickhoff's *Die Wiener Genesis* as *Roman Art* (1900) and her *Roman Sculpture from Augustus to Constantine* (1907) first established Roman art as a subject of serious attention for English-speaking peoples. Her American lectures, *Apotheosis and After Life* (1915), based on Roman monuments, remain authoritative. She virtually ran the *British School at Rome from 1909 until her removal in 1925. Her imperial presence and brilliant salon exerted considerable professional influence in Rome.

BIBLIOGRAPHY
G. S. Thomson, *Mrs. Arthur Strong: A Memoir* (London, 1949). J.M.C. Toynbee, "Strong, Eugénie Sellers," *DNB 1941–1950* (1959), 848–49.
                                                            WILLIAM M. CALDER III

STRZYGOWSKI, JOSEF (1872–1941). Polish art historian; proponent of a theory that early medieval art was derived from Oriental cultures rather than from classical antiquity.

Strzygowski was born in Biala in what was then Austrian Silesia and studied art history at Vienna, Berlin and Munich. He was professor of art history at Graz (from 1892) and later at Vienna (1909 and following). Known throughout his career for his polemical disposition, he was a fierce critic of the great art-historical theorists H. Wölfflin, F. *Wickhoff and A. *Riegl. Against the ideas of Wickhoff and Riegl that Roman art gave rise to the most characteristic features of Early Christian art, Strzygowski argued that the chief principles of medieval art were anticipated in cultures of the Orient (in Asia Minor, Syria, Mesopotamia, Armenia, Iran). Among his many publications on the subject, fundamental is his *Orient oder Rom* ("Orient or Rome"), which appeared in 1901 as an answer to *Die Wiener Genesis* of Wickhoff and W. R. von Hartel.

Strzygowski generally regarded southern, Mediterranean art as decadent and opposed to it not only the art of the Orient but also that of Europe in the north,

Photograph of *Josef Strzygowski.* (The Warburg Institute, University of London.)

which he saw as closely related to Eastern art in its formal values and even as having a kind of moral strength. Strzygowski's arguments stimulated an interest in a search for "national" characteristics in Roman art, but the idea that the Orient was more influential than Rome in medieval art has not found general acceptance.

BIBLIOGRAPHY

E. Z. Herzfeld—W.R.W. Koehler—C. R. Morey, "Josef Strzygowski," *Speculum* 17 (1942), 460–61; "Strzygowski, Josef," *EAA* 7 (1966), 522–23; O. Brendel, *Prolegomena to the Study of Roman Art* (New Haven, CT, 1979), 41–47.

STUART, JAMES ("ATHENIAN" STUART; 1713–88). Scottish painter, architect and draftsman; important for his study and illustration of classical architecture.

The son of a Scottish seaman, James Stuart was a competent painter and architect as well as an excellent draftsman and had a self-taught knowledge of Latin and Greek. In 1742 he traveled to Rome in order to pursue his interests in art and classical antiquity. While in Rome he made a number of drawings of the *obelisk discovered in the Campus Martius. These drawings, in addition to his account of the obelisk, were published in Bandini's treatise *De obelisco Caesaris Augusti* (Rome, 1750).

During a visit to *Naples in 1748 Stuart and his colleague Nicholas *Revett conceived the idea of traveling to Greece to record the extant ancient buildings in Athens. In 1748 they publicly put forth this plan in their "Proposals for Publishing an Accurate Description of the Antiquities of Athens." The project was well received by several members of the *Society of Dilettanti, who agreed to finance the expedition. Subsequent to this pledge of support, both men were accepted as members of the society. They left Rome in 1750 and, after a temporary delay in Venice, arrived in Athens in 1751. Their research was conducted with relatively little hindrance, and by 1755 they had returned to England to initiate the publication of their results.

The final product, which included detailed drawings and descriptions of the monuments, was published in three volumes entitled *The Antiquities of Athens Measured and Delineated by James Stuart, F.R.S. and F.S.A., and Nicholas Revett, Painters and Architects*. The first volume appeared in 1762. The authors decided to include in this section the smaller buildings in the town of Athens rather than the major ones of the *Akropolis, as was forecast in their "Proposals." Although Revett was responsible for all the measured drawings of the project, and his name appears on each volume, he had been bought out by Stuart and withdrew from the venture before this first section was issued. The second volume bears the date 1787, but it was not published until 1789, a year after Stuart's death. It includes the major buildings of the Akropolis—the *Parthenon, the *Erechtheion and the *Propylaia. The third volume, edited by Willey Revely and published in 1795, includes the major buildings in the town and a number of smaller ones not covered in the first volume. In addition to these three volumes, a fourth one, edited by Josiah Taylor and consisting of various drawings and papers of Stuart and Revett, was published in 1816, and a fifth, largely edited by C. R. *Cockerell, appeared in 1830. The impact of *The Antiquities of Athens* on the nineteenth century neoclassical movement was significant, and in the history of classical archaeology the work is regarded as a major achievement.

After his return to England, Stuart exhibited a number of watercolor drawings of topographical views of Athens with the Free Society of Artists. As an architect, he made designs that reflect his acquired knowledge of the Greek style. His Doric portico in Hagley Park (1758) and Lanthorn of Demosthenes in Shugborough (1770) are notable examples.

BIBLIOGRAPHY

L. Lawrence, "Stuart and Revett: Their Literary and Architectural Careers," *JWarb* 2 (1938–39), 128–46; D. Wiebenson, *Sources of Greek Revival Architecture* (University Park, PA, 1969); J. M. Crook, *The Greek Revival, Neo-Classical Attitudes in British Architecture 1760–1870* (London, 1972); H. Colvin, *A Biographical Dictionary of British Architects, 1600–1840* (London, 1978), 793–97.

PATRICK ROWE

STUDNICZKA, FRANZ (1860–1929). Austrian art historian and classicist, with wide-ranging interests and publications.

Born at Jaslo in Galatia, son of a Bohemian bureaucrat, Studniczka studied at Prague under Eugen *Petersen and at Vienna under Otto *Benndorf, Otto Hirschfeld, Wilhelm von Hartel and T. Gomperz. In 1888, after two years in Greece and Italy, he became assistant keeper at the Vienna Museum and in 1889, professor at Freiburg, where T. *Wiegand was his greatest student. In 1896 he succeeded Johannes *Overbeck at Leipzig, where, a demanding and revered teacher, he remained until his death, declining calls to Göttingen and Berlin. Deeply influenced by Darwinism, he developed a wide field of interest extending from Archaic Greek to late Roman and the Renaissance, with emphasis on Greek sculpture and Roman art. He was a university man, uninterested in excavation, whose Greek was good enough to emend Euripides. From 1914 to 1928 he served on the Central Committee of the *German Archaeological Institute. Of colossal productivity, he has left a bibliography containing some 170 items.

BIBLIOGRAPHY

H. Koch, "Nachruf auf Franz Studniczka," *Berichte über die Verhandlungen der Sächsischen Akademie der Wissenschaften zu Leipzig: Philologisch-historische Klasse* 82, 2 (1930), 1–20, with bib.; L. Wickert, *Beiträge zur Geschichte des Deutschen Archäologischen Instituts 1879 bis 1929* (Mainz, 1979), 198; W. Pinder, "Gedächtnisrede auf Franz Studniczka," *Gesammelte Aufsätze aus den Jahren 1907–1935* (Leipzig, 1938), 152–60; H. Dohl, in *Archäologenbildnisse*, 138–39.

WILLIAM M. CALDER III

STUKELEY, WILLIAM (1687–1765). English antiquarian and cleric.

The eccentric Stukeley was a typical English antiquarian, enthusiastic in all pursuits whether founded on sound scientific observation or developed to the point of fantasy. His contribution to archaeology was his objective fieldwork done at Stonehenge, Avebury and other sites between 1718 and 1724. Stukeley's surveys, drawings and notes are useful today partly because they reveal the instincts and speculations of the eighteenth century antiquarian and partly because many of his observations were indeed accurate, having since been confirmed by aerial photography.

The Druids and their temples were of primary interest to Stukeley. For his study of Stonehenge he used a scientific approach by first establishing a unit of measurement called "Druid's cubit," which he systematically applied to the Bronze Age site. Although his plan is not accurate by modern standards, it is more scientific than any of his predecessors', and Stukeley's opinion that Stonehenge is the unique prehistoric sanctuary in southern England remains valid today. His precise notes and drawn sections recording the excavations of nearby barrows reveal the archaeologist's desire to understand the sequence of their formation and not simply to sink shafts in order to recover "antient remains" for their curiosity value.

From 1725 or so, Stukeley's archaeological endeavors gave way to more imaginative ones when, as a newly ordained clergyman, he invented a fantastic Druidic cult belonging to the ruins of the magnificent circular sanctuary, and his archaeological fieldwork and notes of the previous years became translated into religious tracts.

Stukeley's interest in Roman remains was just as dedicated as that at Stonehenge, and here, too, his remarks show an odd mixture of accurate observation and careless fantasy. His plan of Silchester was wildly incorrect, although the remains above ground were quite conspicuous and complete, and for this he received strong criticism from fellow antiquarians, who labeled him "fancifull." Many of the roads and earthworks across the country that he thought were Roman have since been established as being of Iron or Bronze age date, but, in a muddled sort of way, he had a considerable grasp of certain basic archaeological principles. Hadrian's Wall made a particular impression upon him. He carefully copied inscriptions and recorded sites of what he called "that amazing scene of Roman grandure." Even more important than these notes were his pleadings for legislation to stop daily pillage and destruction of the wall and other monuments. He blamed the government for its "supine indolence" and neglect of ancient monuments, an accusation perhaps as relevant today as it was in Stukeley's time.

BIBLIOGRAPHY

S. Piggott, *William Stukeley, An Eighteenth-Century Antiquary* (Oxford, 1950).

ELEANOR A. ROBBINS

SWEDISH CYPRUS EXPEDITION. Project to explore systematically, for the first time, the entire early history and culture of *Cyprus, from the Stone Age to the end of the Roman era.

The expedition worked in the island for three and one-half years, September 1927 to March 1931. The four members of the expedition, Einar *Gjerstad, Erik Sjöqvist, Alfred Westholm and the architect John Lindros, excavated settlements, sanctuaries and cemeteries all over Cyprus. Among the important sites are the Stone Age settlements of Petra tou Limniti and Lapithos, the Bronze Age fortress at Nitovikla, the Vouni palace of the Cypro-Classical period, the sanctuaries at Ajios Iakovos, Ajia Irini and Soli, cemeteries at Ajios Iakovos, *Enkomi, Stylli, Idalion, Amathus and others. The full publication, consisting of four volumes in twelve parts, appeared 1934–72; in it the objective descriptions and the archaeological data are strictly separated from the interpretations and conclusions. The finds are mainly in the Cyprus Museum; an important part is in the Medelhavsmuseet, Stockholm.

BIBLIOGRAPHY
+*The Swedish Cyprus Expedition* 1–4 (Stockholm, 1934–72); +E. Gjerstad, *Ages and Days in Cyprus* (Göteborg, 1980).

ROBIN HÄGG

SWEDISH INSTITUTE AT ATHENS. Swedish school founded in Athens for the study of Greek antiquity.

After the successful Swedish excavations in Greece during the 1920s and 1930s (*Asine, Dendra/Midea, Berbati, Asea in Arcadia, Malthi in Messenia), the Swedish Institute was founded in 1946 (inaugurated in 1948) as the seventh foreign archaeological school in Greece. Its first directors were Erik J. Holmberg (1947–48) and Åke Åkerström (1948–56). It has its premises in Mitseon Str. 9 and an annex (guesthouse) in Kavalla. The library comprises some 20,000 volumes, mostly on Greek archaeology, art and history. Since 1952, excavations have been conducted at Asine, Berbati, Dendra/Midea, Chania and Paradeisos (Kavalla). The institute publishes *Skrifter utgivna av Svenska institutet i Athen* (in quarto and octavo), including *Opuscula Atheniensia*. In addition to teaching courses of Greek archaeology and topography to Swedish students, it arranges lectures, seminars and international symposia, especially on topics of Aegean Bronze Age archaeology and Greek religion.

BIBLIOGRAPHY
+C.-G. Styrenius, *Medelhavsmuseet Bulletin* 9 (1974), 75–80; +R. Hägg, *OpAth* 15 (1984), 195–99.

ROBIN HÄGG

SWEDISH INSTITUTE AT ROME. Swedish school founded in Rome for the study of classical antiquity and art history in Italy.

Since its foundation in 1926, the goals of the Swedish Institute have been to conduct courses in Italian archaeology and art history and to provide research opportunities in Italy, including excavations in Rome and at Ardea, San Giovenale, Luni, and *Acquarossa. Beginning with its first director, Axel *Boëthius, the directors of the institute have included Sweden's foremost archaeologists (E.

*Gjerstad, E. Sjøquist, C. E. Östenberg), whose works have appeared in the series of publications (*Acta Instituti Romani Regni Sueciae*) begun in 1932. Since 1940 the institute has been located amid several other foreign institutes on Via Omero in Valle Giulia.

BIBLIOGRAPHY

+C. E. Östenberg, ed., *Svenska Institutet i Rom 1926–1976* (Viterbo, 1976); C. Nylander, "Institutet öppnar igen," *Romhorisont* 16 (1988), 2–3.

INGRID E. M. EDLUND

SWINDLER, MARY HAMILTON (1884–1967). American art historian and archaeologist, professor of classical archaeology at Bryn Mawr College (1912–49).

Swindler participated in the collaborative excavations of Bryn Mawr, Harvard University and the *Archaeological Institute of America (AIA) at Tarsos in Cilicia from 1934 to 1949. She held executive positions for a number of professional organizations—the American Council of Learned Societies, the *American School of Classical Studies, the American Association of University Women and the AIA. In 1932 she became editor in chief of the *American Journal of Archaeology (AJA),* a post that she held until 1946. Under her dynamic leadership, *AJA* enlarged its format and established a high standard of scholarship and integrity. Her book on *Ancient Painting* is considered a classic in the field; she also contributed many articles to *AJA* and served as consulting editor for the *Encyclopedia Britannica.* She is remembered as an inspiring teacher.

BIBLIOGRAPHY

M. H. Swindler, *Cretan Elements in the Cults and Rituals of Apollo* (Bryn Mawr, 1913); idem, *The Beginnings of Greek Art* (New Haven, CT, 1950); D.B.T., "Mary Hamilton Swindler," *AJA* 54 (1950), 292–93; "Mary H. Swindler," *New York Times* (Late City Edition), 18 January 1967.

SHELLIE WILLIAMS

SYBARIS. Site in south Italy, the most celebrated Western Greek colony in ancient times and the least known today.

Sybaris was founded in the late eighth century B.C. by Achaeans on the western arm of the Gulf of Taranto, between the rivers Sybaris and Cratis. The foundation's prosperity derived from its vast and fertile territory and extensive trade with the East Greek and Tyrrhenian coasts. These features made it synonymous with a luxurious lifestyle ("sybaritic") and provoked its annihilation by neighboring Croton (510 B.C.). The site was subsequently (443 B.C.) occupied by the panhellenic colony of Thurii (planned by Hippodamos of *Miletos, and the adoptive home of Herodotos) and later by the Roman colony of Copia.

Archaeological investigation of the marshy and malarial plain was late, sporadic and inconclusive. F. *Lenormant explored the area and unsuccessfully urged the French government to undertake large-scale excavation (1880); but neither he nor later Italian scholars succeeded in defining the extent or the depth of the remains pertaining to the three ancient cities, although they identified structures and cemeteries of various periods mainly on the edges of the plain (F. Cavallari, 1879; L. Viola, 1887–88; E. Galli, 1928–30; U. Zanotti Bianco, 1932).

The extensive land reclamation projects of the 1930s revealed a hydrological situation that required new techniques; these were first applied by D. F. Brown (1949–53). The subsequent joint exploration conducted by the University Museum, Philadelphia, and the *Lerici Foundation, Rome (1960–65), provided a detailed picture of the quantity, nature and depth of the remains beneath the Cratis floodplain. On this basis, coupled with the "well-point" drainage system successfully applied at *Metapontion, the Italian authorities launched an ambitious program of excavation in 1969; the modest results so far achieved concern mainly Thurii and Copia.

BIBLIOGRAPHY

F. Lenormant, *La Grande Grèce* (Paris, 1881); F. Rainey—C. M. Lerici, eds., *The Search for Sybaris* (Rome, 1967); *NSc,* 1970 (pub. 1973), suppl. 1 and *NSc,* 1988–89 (pub. 1992), suppl. 1.

F. R. SERRA RIDGWAY

SYRACUSE (SIRACUSA). Greek colony in *Sicily.

Thucydides (6.3.2) states that Syracuse was founded by Corinthian Greeks following eviction of the native Sikels. This occurred one year after the settlement of *Naxos, thus ca. 733 B.C. Early on, Syracuse began a program of western expansion, resulting in the establishment of subcolonies at Akrai (ca. 664 B.C.), Kasmenai (643) and Kamarina (598) (Thucydides 6.5.2–3). Conflict with *Gela ensued, which led to the eventual fall of the city to Gelon and the transfer of his capital to Syracuse ca. 485 B.C. Under Gelon the city played an important role in the Battle of *Himera (480 B.C.) and under his successor, Hieron I, defeated the Etruscans at *Cumae (474). The city's power and prestige grew throughout the fifth century. In 413 B.C. it successfully repulsed the Athenian expedition and under Dionysios I extended control into South Italy. Despite reverses, Syracuse continued to dominate Sicilian politics until its own conquest by Rome in 212 B.C. The city's importance declined under Roman control. By medieval times it was reduced to the island of Ortygia. A devastating earthquake in 1693 necessitated considerable rebuilding, much of which is still in evidence today.

The city was visited and its remains discussed by travelers since the sixteenth century, including C. M. Arezzo (*Siciliae chorographia,* 1527) and T. *Fazello (*De rebus siculis,* 1558). D. LoFaso Pietrasanta, Duca di Serradifalco (1840), presented extensive descriptions, frequently with dimensions and plans, of the major monuments. His information was based, in part, on observations of visible remains and, in part, on the excavations of F. S. Cavallari in 1839. Another important topography was published by F. S. Cavallari et al. in 1883.

Subsequent investigations have been more limited in scope. The necropoleis were first officially examined in the late nineteenth century. One of the earliest, Fusco, was located in 1874 and explored repeatedly in the following years, especially by *Orsi (1891–1905). Work began in the other major Archaic cemetery, Giardino Spagna, somewhat later (1923). In the meantime, additional cemeteries were discovered and excavated, yielding tomb material datable from the Sikel period onward. Expanding on the several investigations and chance discoveries of architectural remains made during the nineteenth century, Orsi began, at the turn of the century, a continuous series of excavations and publications. Work was carried out in various areas, most important, the environs of Euryalos Fort, the marketplace, theater, altar of Hieron II and the quarries. Operations have continued, although intermittently, to the present, exposing both private and public structures of Greek, Roman and later periods.

Particular attention has been paid to the temples of Syracuse. Visible remains allowed for the early recognition of the Apollo temple. It was examined in detail by Serradifalco, and additional members were discovered in excavations conducted between 1858 and 1865. A full investigation was finally made possible in 1943 through the clearing away of later structures. The Olympieion was first excavated by Cavallari in 1839, with work continuing under Orsi in 1893 and 1902. Only in 1953 was the building fully exposed. A third temple of the sixth century, in the Ionic order, is not yet completely published. Fragments of the superstructure were reported by Orsi in excavations around the Piazza Minerva in 1910–13. Additional elements and cuttings for foundations were located beneath the Palazzo Vermexio in 1960. Large portions of the nearby temple of Athena had long been visible within the cathedral, but details of the building and its temenos came to light only through Orsi's excavations of 1910–17. A series of early revetments and other building remains provides testimony of several structures in this same area. Despite the hampering of excavation by overbuilding, Syracuse is relatively well known throughout its long history (*Syracuse, Museo Nazionale Archeologico).

BIBLIOGRAPHY

F. S. Cavallari—A. Holm, *Topografia archeologica di Siracusa* (Palermo, 1883); P. Orsi, "Gli scavi intorno a l'Athenaion di Siracusa negli anni 1912–1917," *MonAnt* 25 (1918), 353–754; G. Cultrera, "L'Apollonion-Artemision di Ortigia in Siracusa," *MonAnt* 41 (1951), 701–860; L. Bernabò Brea, "Studi sul teatro greco di Siracusa," *Palladio* 17 (1967), 97–154.

                                        BARBARA A. BARLETTA

SYRACUSE, MUSEO ARCHEOLOGICO REGIONALE (formerly NAZIONALE) PAOLO ORSI. Important regional museum in *Sicily.

The collection was initiated with a small group of objects assembled at the end of the eighteenth century in the library of a local seminary. It expanded into a municipal museum in 1811. By 1884 the collection had grown sufficiently in size and importance to demand a new building on the Piazza del Duomo and the designation of national museum. A new facility has recently been opened in the Villa Landolina Park.

The material results from donations and excavations carried out primarily in eastern and central Sicily. It ranges in date from the Upper Paleolithic to Christian and Byzantine periods. The rather large prehistoric collection provides considerable testimony of the pre-Sikel and Sikel cultures of Sicily. Greek civilization is well represented, especially in the sixth and fifth centuries B.C., through architectural remains, sculptures, vases and numismatics. Of particular note are several series of terracotta revetments and large-scale sculptures. Much of this material comes from excavations of the late nineteenth and early twentieth centuries conducted by the Superintendence of Syracuse at sites such as *Megara Hyblaea, Kamarina and *Gela, in addition to *Syracuse. More recent excavations within the region have added to the collection. Of Hellenistic date is an important group of terracottas and vases from Centuripae. The Roman period is attested mainly by inscriptions and sculptures, of which the portraits deserve special mention.

BIBLIOGRAPHY
G. Libertini, *Il Regio Museo Archeologico di Siracusa* (Rome, 1929); M. T. Currò Pisanò, "Siracusa, Museo Archeologico Nazionale," *EAA* 7 (Rome, 1966), 338–39; G. Voza, *Museo Archeologico Regionale Paolo Orsi* (Syracuse, n.d.).

BARBARA A. BARLETTA

T

TABULA ILIACA (ILIAC TABLET). White marble triptych (height 0.25m) in low relief, with the first third lost, representing in miniature the story of the Trojan War; probably dating to the first century A.C.

Found in 1683 at Bovillae near the Torre Messer Paolo on the road to Marino, the Tabula Iliaca passed from the house of Spada to Pope Clement XIII (1758—69), who gave it to the *Capitoline Museum, where it is now on display. The narrative is shown in a series of pictures, with captions in Greek that attribute the scenes to major literary sources: the *Iliad* of Homer, the *Aithiopis* of Arktinos, the *Little Iliad* of Lesches and the *Iluipersis* (*Sack of Troy*) of Stesichoros.

It is one of many Iliac tablets now known; these are dated to the Early Roman Empire and were all found in the vicinity of Rome. Their function may have been didactic, for use by schoolboys or in private libraries. K. Weitzmann noted that they provide important evidence for the use of illustrated books in antiquity. The *tabulae* are part of a series of representations of the epic cycle and Greek tragedy, including the "Homeric Bowls," the cycles of wall painting from *Pompeii and illustrations in papyri of Homer and Vergil.

BIBLIOGRAPHY

K. Weitzmann, *Ancient Book Illumination* (Cambridge, MA, 1959); A. Sadurska, *Les Tables Iliaques* (Warsaw, 1964); N. Horsfall, "Stesichorus at Bovillae?" *JHS* 99 (1979), 26–48; E. C. Kopff, "The Structure of *Amazonia* (*Aethiopis*)," in *The Greek Renaissance in the Eighth Century B.C.* (Stockholm, 1983), 57–62; Pollitt, *Art in the Hellenistic Age,* 202–3.

E. C. KOPFF

TABULA PEUTINGERIANA (PEUTINGER TABLE). Map of the known world, probably created in the third–fourth centuries A.C. and copied at a later date, probably in the thirteenth century; fundamental document for knowledge of geography in the ancient world.

The Tabula Peutingeriana was discovered in 1494 by Conradus *Celtis, librarian of the emperor Maximilian I, in an unspecified library and bequeathed to Konrad *Peutinger in 1508. The map consists of a long, narrow scroll of parchment (6.82m × 0.34m) made up of eleven sections (there were originally twelve). The tabula comprises the world as it was known to the Romans, from Britain to the Ganges River, except that the westernmost part of the empire, which was on the twelfth sheet, is missing. The map is in color, with the sea and rivers green, the mountains yellow or rose-colored and the roads in red and includes vignettes to indicate the presence of major cities, forests, towers, baths, fortifications and so on. Bodies of water, roads and stretches of land are schematically strung out along the horizontal strip of parchment.

Though Peutinger obtained permission in 1511 to publish the map, he never succeeded in doing so. The tabula was copied in its entirety and published at Antwerp in 1598 by his descendant, Marcus Welser. This copy is very valuable, since it was made at a time when the map was far more legible. The work then sank into relative obscurity until the early eighteenth century. In 1737 it was acquired from Prince Eugene of Savoy by the emperor Charles VI and is today in the Austrian National Library (Österreichische Nationalbibliothek), Vienna.

The tabula has received many names; Celtis and Peutinger called it *Itinerarium Antonini,* relating it to the best-known written itinerary from antiquity that has come down to us, dating to the early third century A.C. Some have called it *Tabula Augustana,* identifying it as a version of the map of the world made for Augustus by Agrippa in the first century B.C. Various scholars have proposed various dates. In the early twentieth century, K. Miller convincingly argued that the map was created in A.D. 365–66, on the basis of the emphasis given to the depictions of the cities of Rome, Constantinople and Antioch, the three imperial residences at that time. W. Kubitscheck argued that the original was no later than the time of Caracalla. On paleographic grounds, both scholars thought the tabula itself a copy made in the twelfth–thirteenth centuries A.C. A. Levi and M. Levi recently noted that it was recorded at the monastery of Colmar that a map of the world was made by a monk there in 1265, and this may be identical with the Tabula Peutingeriana.

Among the many editions of the map, perhaps best known and most influential was the facsimile of Franz Cristoph de Scheyb, *Peutingeriana Tabula Itineraria* (Vienna, 1753). A modern color facsimile was published at Graz in 1976, *Tabula Peutingeriana, Codex Vindobonensis 324, Vollstandige Faksimile—Ausgabe in Originalformat.*

BIBLIOGRAPHY

K. Miller, *Itineraria romana* (Stuttgart, 1916); W. Kubitscheck, s.v. "Karten," *RE* 10 (1919), cols. 2126–44; A. C. Levi—B. Trell, "An Ancient Tourist Map," *Archaeology* 17 (1964), 227–36; +L. Bosio, *La Tabula Peutingeriana, una descrizione pittorica del mondo antico* (Rimini, 1983).

TADMOR. See PALMYRA.

TADMUR. See PALMYRA.

TARQUINIA (CORNETO). Small Italian town near the site of ancient Tarquinii (Etruscan Tarch[u]na).

World-famous for its Etruscan painted tombs, Tarquinii was regarded in ancient times as the mother of all the great Etruscan cities: founded by Tarchon, it was the home of Tages and of the Tarquinian dynasty of Rome and the refuge of the Corinthian Demaratos. Tarquinia continued to prosper after the loss of its autonomy in the third century B.C., until the small community remaining in the seventh century A.C. moved to the nearby Monterozzi Hill, site of the ancient necropolis.

Chance discoveries of underground painted chamber tombs inspired *Michelangelo's drawing of the head of Aita (Hades) and poems by humanists unaware of the true identity of the site—although this had been recognized by *Annius of Viterbo; meanwhile, Cardinal Farnese exacted a tax of 6,000 pounds of ancient metal from the tombs to decorate S. Giovanni in Laterano (1546). The "grottoes" of Corneto were drawn by T. *Dempster, Padre G. Forlivesi da Cervia (1736; his work was used by S. *Maffei and A. F. *Gori), F. Piranesi (1760) and J. *Byres and aroused the interest of J. J. *Winckelmann, A.C.P. de *Caylus, L. *Lanzi, F. Inghirami and G. *Micali. The vigorous investigations initiated by the Gonfaloniere, Carlo Avvolta (1823), were continued by Lord Kinnaird (1825), Baron Kestner (1827) and local landowners and culminated in the "donation" of two painted tombs to *Ludwig I of Bavaria.

The vast local collection assembled by the Bruschi family (1864–74) was later added to the municipal collection founded by Luigi Dasti (1875–80) to form the Museo Nazionale (now housed in the Renaissance Vitelleschi Palace); catalogs of its holdings have only recently begun to appear. Government interest began in 1881 (finds in *Florence Archaeological Museum), while the activities of W. *Helbig enriched European and American collections (1888–97). The discovery of Iron Age cemeteries on the surrounding heights ("poggi"; published by L. Pernier, *NSc,* 1907) provided the basis for the chronological classification of the Iron Age in Etruria as a whole. There followed a lengthy break in exploration, apart from soundings in the 1920s and 1930s on the city plateau called La Civita (at the "Ara della Regina" temple and at the town walls and gates: G. Cultrera, P. Romanelli). From the 1950s, over 6,000 tombs were identified on the Monterozzi by aerial photography (J.S.P. *Bradford) and by the *Lerici Foundation's geophysical surveys, ca. 300 of which (60 painted) have been excavated; remains of tumuli were also recovered, superimposed on eighth-century huts. Excavation was resumed in 1982 on the Civita (M. Bonghi Jovino), with already spectacular results, while a prosperous Archaic Greek sanctuary has been revealed in the port of *Gravisca.

BIBLIOGRAPHY
+J. Byres, *Hypogaei, or Sepulchral Caverns of Tarquinia, the Capital of Antient Etruria;* ed. F. Howard (London, 1842); G. Dennis, *The Cities and Cemeteries of Etruria,* 3rd ed. (London, 1883) I, 301–435; M. Pallottino, *Tarquinia, MonAnt* 36 (1937); +M. Moretti, *Nuovi monumenti della pittura etrusca* (Milan, 1966); H. Hencken, *Tarquinia, Villanovans and Early Etruscans* (Cambridge, MA, 1968); M. Bonghi Jovino ed., *Gli Etruschi di Tarquinia* (Modena, 1986); "Materiali del Museo Archeologico Nazionale di Tarquinia" (Rome, 1980–); +S. Steingräber, *Etruscan Painting* (New York, 1987).
                                                                    F. R. SERRA RIDGWAY

TARRACO (TARRAGONA). Roman colony in Spain, capital of Hispania Citerior Tarraconsensis from the late first century B.C.

Tarraco was founded as a military base by Cnaeus Cornelius Scipio in 218 B.C. on the east coast of Spain at the mouth of the river Francoli. It is to be identified with monumental stone walls still encircling medieval Tarragona and overlooking the Iberian settlement (founded in the fifth century B.C.) near the modern port. Tarraco served as a strategic center during the Roman conquest and was the temporary residence of Augustus (27–26 B.C.) during his planning of the Cantabrian Wars. In the Flavian period Tarraco became the focus of the provincial imperial cult and seat of the Concilium Provinciae. These important roles are reflected in the construction of a complex of temple and precinct, circus and forum of the Concilium as terraces cut into the hillside.

Tarraco was sacked by Frankish invaders in the mid-third century A.C. This event had little long-term effect on the fortunes of the town, which persisted as a metropolitan bishopric and capital of Tarraconensis until A.D. 475. It served as an important administrative center during the Visigothic period (A.D. 475–711).

Excavations since the beginning of the twentieth century in the lower town near the port have uncovered traces of the basilica of the municipal forum and theater (both Augustan). Between the town and the river Francoli, traces of large suburban mansions of Early Imperial date were found together with a later Roman cemetery (fourth–seventh centuries A.C.) and church. The amphitheater (first century A.C.) lies between the town and the sea and was later covered by a Visigothic church (seventh century A.C.).

BIBLIOGRAPHY
G. Alföldy, s.v. "Tarraco," *RE* suppl. 14 (1978), 570–614; idem, *Die Römische Inschriften von Tarraco* (Berlin, 1978); M. D. Del Amo, *Estudio crítico de la necrópolis paleocristiana de Tarragona,* 2 vols. (Tarragona, 1979–81); T. Hauschild, *Arquitectura romana de Tarragona* (Tarragona, 1983).
                                                                        SIMON KEAY

TASSIE, JAMES (1735–99). Scottish modeler, specializing in portraiture and gemstone reproductions.

Born at Pollockshaws, Scotland, James Tassie started out as a stonemason. His latent artistic talents were early awakened at an art fair in Glasgow. He enrolled in the Foulis Academy there and within a short time developed considerable skill as a modeler. In 1763 he moved to Dublin, where he became assistant to Dr. Henry Quin, who was reproducing antique gems in a vitreous paste that he and Tassie then perfected.

In 1776 Tassie set up shop in London as a portrait modeler and maker of gemstone reproductions. Since he was a meticulous workman and gifted artist, his stock-in-trade of antique gemstone replicas became very popular in this period of neoclassical revival. As time passed, numerous great private collections of antique and modern gems were put at his disposal for reproduction. His compatriot James *Byres, resident in Rome, provided a most useful connection for Tassie, since he could help secure impressions and could also excite interest in Tassie's work among the many tourists he escorted around Rome. The apogee of Tassie's career was realized after the empress Catherine the Great of Russia ordered a complete set of his gemstones in 1781.

After a small first catalog of available reproductions in 1775, Tassie's large two-volume catalog by the antiquarian *Raspe appeared (1791), containing over 15,000 entries, entitled *Descriptive Catalogue of a General Collection of Ancient and Modern Gems . . . by James Tassie Modeller.* Although it represents much derivative archaeological material, it is still a valuable source on ancient glyptics.

On James's death in London in 1799, his nephew William Tassie (1777–1860) carried on the family trade in the same London studio until 1840. The best collections of Tassie gemstones are found at the Scottish National Portrait Gallery (Edinburgh) and the Hermitage Museum, St. Petersburg.

BIBLIOGRAPHY

J. M. Gray, *James and William Tassie* (Edinburgh, 1894); +J. Holloway, *James Tassie, 1735–1799,* Scottish Masters 1 (Edinburgh, 1986); J. S. Tassie, "Tassie, Raspe and Catherine the Great," *The Antique Collector* (London, February 1989), 46–49.

J. S. TASSIE

TAZZA FARNESE. See FARNESE CUP.

TEGEA. Greek city-state located in the fertile plain of eastern Arcadia on the route from *Sparta to the Argolic Gulf, a position that gave it political and commercial prominence from the Geometric through the Roman periods.

Tegea was famous for its many temples, notably that of Athena Alea, attributed by Pausanias (8.45.4) to Skopas. E. *Dodwell recognized its remains at Piali (Alea) in 1806, and French excavations in 1897 and 1902 brought to light the fourth-century temple and its sculpture (now in Alea and Athens). Sporadic nineteenth-century excavations located an agora, foundations of a Roman theater, a sanctuary of Demeter and a few small stretches of circuit wall, but the city remains largely unexplored, lying beneath deep alluvial deposits.

Recent studies have resulted in a thorough analysis of the Skopaic sculpture (A. Stewart) and a new reconstruction of the temple's cella and altar (N. Norman). Recent Norwegian Institute excavations within the cella of the Alea temple have uncovered remains of two apsidal structures of wattle-and-daub construction of the eighth century B.C. and a metal-smelting installation of similar date.

BIBLIOGRAPHY

V. Bérard, "Tegée et la Tegéatide," *BCH* 16 (1892), 529–49; 17 (1893), 1–24; C. Dugas et al., *Le Sanctuaire d'Aléa Athena* (Paris, 1924); A. Stewart, *Skopas of Paros* (Park Ridge, NJ, 1977); N. Norman, "The Temple of Athena Alea at Tegea," *AJA* 88 (1984), 169–94; E. Ostby et al., "Excavations at the Sanctuary of Athena Alea: First Preliminary Report: 1990–92," *OpAth* 20 (1994), 89–141.

S. L. PETRAKIS

TEMPLE OF ANTONINUS AND FAUSTINA, Rome. Roman Imperial temple, erected in A.D. 141 by the emperor Antoninus in honor of his deceased wife, Faustina; after his death (A.D. 161), the temple was rededicated to the deified couple.

Located on the north side of the *Forum Romanum, the relatively well preserved Temple of Antoninus and Faustina is set on a high podium made of peperino tufa, with cella walls also made of peperino. Once revetted with marble, these walls are preserved up to the entablature, which is decorated with a frieze of griffins, scrolls and candelabra. The deep porch is fronted by six monolithic columns of green cipollino marble, with Corinthian capitals of white marble (height 17m), with two additional columns on either side of the porch.

By the eleventh century, the temple had been converted into the church of San Lorenzo in Miranda. Pope Martin V (1417–31) ceded the church to a confraternity of apothecaries (Universitas Aromatariorum), who set up chapels and kiosks on the front porch; these were cleared away by Pope Paul III for the triumphal procession of Charles V in 1536. The temple was included in 1570 by *Palladio in his *Quattro libri dell'architettura* (IV, pp. 30–35). An anonymous Dutch drawing in pen and ink from the Thomas *Ashby collection in the Vatican Library shows the condition of the building in the late sixteenth century, before the cella was rebuilt and before part of a new façade was erected by Orazio Torriani (1601–14). The façade was completed in the later seventeenth century.

By the beginning of the nineteenth century, the ground level had risen to the height of the porch, at which time the *French Academy in Rome undertook to clear the lofty flight of stairs in front of the temple. *Valadier and *Canova agreed that the clearing would be worthwhile and advised on ways to wall off the deep and dangerous excavated area. The stairs were exposed, but the ground in front of the temple was not removed until 1876. After the discovery of the three lowest steps in 1899, the stairs were reconstructed.

BIBLIOGRAPHY

+Nash, I, 26–27; R. Keaveney, *Views of Rome,* catalog of exhibition (London, 1988), 135–37; Richardson, *New Topographical Dictionary,* 11–12; Ridley, *Eagle and the Spade,* 182–87.

The Temple of Antoninus and Faustina, Rome, engraving by G. B. de' Cavalieri after a design by G. A. Dosio, from *Urbis Romae aedificiorum illustrium quae supersunt reliquiae* (1569).

TEMPLE OF APOLLO, Corinth. Greek Archaic temple.

Seven standing, poros, monolithic Doric columns mark the site of this important Archaic temple on a low hill above the later Roman forum. Generally associated with the Temple of Apollo simply mentioned by Pausanias in the second century A.C., the temple was the second on the site and is generally considered to have been built in the third quarter of the sixth century B.C., although latest research has suggested a slightly earlier date between 560 and 540 B.C.

The building was never wholly destroyed at the end of antiquity, and the standing columns remained a familiar sight to travelers. Its history is, however, one of continued dissolution. When *Ciriaco of Ancona visited *Corinth in 1436, he recorded thirteen standing columns with architraves, while *Spon and *Wheler in 1676 found twelve. *Stuart and *Revett also illustrated twelve columns in 1766 and houses built on the eastern half of the temple. According to *Leake, one column disappeared some time between the visit of *Chandler in 1776 and 1785. By 1795 four more had been removed and used for building material, according to E. D. *Clarke, who wrote in 1818. Several other travelers early in the nineteenth century recorded the remains of the temple, including the *Expédition scientifique de Morée in 1829. *Dörpfeld undertook the first excavations in 1886, soon followed by the excavations of the *American School of Classical Studies that began in 1896 at Corinth. Much of the temple area was cleared in 1898–1901. Further archaeological work was undertaken periodically on the hill in the twentieth century, with the most recent campaign in 1968–72.

BIBLIOGRAPHY
R. Stillwell, *Corinth* 1, Pt. 1: *Introduction, Topography, Architecture* (Cambridge, MA, 1932), 126–34; H. S. Robinson, "Excavations at Corinth: Temple Hill, 1968–1972," *Hesperia* 45 (1976), 203–39.

WILLIAM R. BIERS

TEMPLE OF ARTEMIS (ARTEMISION), Ephesos. Site of two successive monumental Greek temples.

The first temple, built in the mid-sixth century B.C. with sculpted columns from Croesus (Kroisos) of Lydia, burned in 356 B.C. The second temple, under construction during Alexander's visit in 334 B.C., was one of the Seven Wonders of the World. Both temples were in the Ionic order and faced west. The second temple reused the foundations and followed the plan of the first: a dipteral colonnade with twenty-one columns on the flanks, nine columns at the rear and a tripteral front of eight columns surrounded the cella on a stylobate of 51.44m × 111.48m. With eight additional columns in the deep pronaos, the effect was of a dense forest of columns.

The Artemision was sacked by the Gauls in A.D. 262, was partially restored, and was destroyed by Patriarch John Chrysostom in A.D. 401. The ruins, pillaged ruthlessly for building stones, were finally covered entirely by silt.

J. T. Wood, under the auspices of the *British Museum, found the temple on

New Year's Eve 1869, after a six-year search. Wood excavated until 1874, drawing restorations and sending sculpture and architectural members to England; he returned for one season in 1883–84. Austrian archaeologists drew site plans and searched in vain for the Praxitelean altar in 1895. The British Museum sponsored new excavations under D. G. *Hogarth in 1904–5. Hogarth, like Wood, was impeded by groundwater, but he revealed a series of earlier foundations beneath the Kroisos Temple. The earliest, "Temple A," consists of the rectangular central basis (4.34m × 2.86m) abutted by a T-shaped foundation. Hogarth recovered approximately 1,000 early Archaic objects from the central basis and elsewhere below the Kroisos pavement; most important are the coins and the ivory statuettes.

Excavations by A. Bammer (Öesterreichische Archäeologische Institut) began in 1965 with his discovery of the monumental fourth-century B.C. altar at the west end (front) of the temple. A column of the fourth-century temple was reerected in 1971–73. Between the altar and the temple, a foundation from ca. 600 B.C. (the "hekatompedon") has appeared. With low water levels in 1987, Bammer uncovered a structure of the Geometric period below Hogarth's central basis. Bammer's finds include ivory statuettes, gold statuettes and jewelry and electrum Lydian coins. Sculpture and architecture from the two Artemisia have been recovered by Bammer and by excavations at the church of St. John.

BIBLIOGRAPHY

J. T. Wood, *Discoveries at Ephesos* (London, 1877); D. G. Hogarth, *Excavations at Ephesos, The Archaic Artemisia* (London, 1908); A. Bammer, *Die Architektur des jüngeren Artemision von Ephesos* (Wiesbaden, 1972); +idem, *Das Heiligtum der Artemis von Ephesos* (Graz, 1984).

JANE BURR CARTER

TEMPLE OF ATHENA NIKE, Athens. Greek Classical temple built for the cult of Athena as goddess of victory.

About 427–425 B.C., the bastion at the western end of the *Akropolis was sheathed in limestone, and the Temple of Athena Nike was then erected atop the bastion. A surrounding balustrade was added later. The architect may have been Kallikrates, but new studies by J. A. Bundgaard and I. Mark suggest that his work in the sanctuary was earlier.

Other cults are attested on the bastion, the core of which is Mycenaean.

The small, marble, Ionic, amphiprostyle temple (Pausanias's "Temple of Wingless Victory") and its parapet were richly decorated. There were pedimental sculptures, a sculpted frieze and elaborate akroteria on the temple; sculpted figures (including the famous *Nike* fixing her sandal) were on the parapet.

*Spon and *Wheler described some of the sculpture before the temple was demolished, and its stones were used to fortify the Akropolis against *Morosini in 1687. *Stuart and *Revett saw some of the stones in the fortification work, and *Pars also sketched some of them there.

The temple was reconstructed starting in 1835 by *Ross, Schaubert and Hansen. Though *Elgin had taken some of the frieze, most of the building remained, and restoration was possible. From 1935 to 1940, the work was redone by N. Balanos and A. *Orlandos.

BIBLIOGRAPHY

A. Orlandos, "Zum Temple der Athena Nike," *AM* 40 (1915), 27–44; +idem, "Nouvelles observations sur la construction du temple d'Athéna Niké," *BCH* 71–72 (1947–48), 1–38; J. A. Bundgaard, "Le Sujet de IG I² 24," *Mélanges helléniques offerts à Georges Daux* (Paris, 1974); I. Mark, *The Sanctuary of Athena Nike in Athens: Architectural Stages and Chronology* (Princeton, 1993).

HARRISON EITELJORG II

TEMPLE OF CASTOR (TEMPLE OF CASTOR AND POLLUX; TEMPLE OF THE DIOSCURI), Rome. Roman temple; one of the oldest and always one of the finest temples in the city.

The original building commemorated the appearance of the Dioscuri—Castor and Pollux—at the Spring of Juturna to water their horses after the Roman victory at the Battle of Lake Regillus in 493 B.C. The temple stood in the *Forum Romanum at the end of the Vicus Tuscus. It was rebuilt by L. Caecilius Metellus in 117 B.C., and the concrete of its podium remains the earliest securely dated concrete in Rome. It was rebuilt again by Tiberius and dedicated in A.D. 6; the Corinthian capitals of this phase are especially beautiful. It was a single-cella temple with eight columns across the ends and eleven on each side, on a very high platform in which were arranged *loculi,* chambers between the column footings closed with metal doors where the imperial treasury and private individuals could deposit valuables for safekeeping.

By the Early Renaissance, only three columns with a fragment of entablature remained standing; these gave the name Tre Colonne to the neighborhood. The temple was first excavated by the French under *Valadier in 1810, but the full platform was not cleared and mapped (by *Fea) until 1816–18. It has recently been the object of careful investigations by a Danish team.

BIBLIOGRAPHY

T. Frank, "The First and Second Temples of Castor at Rome," *MAAR* 5 (1925), 79–102; +Nash, I, 210–13; I. Nielsen et al., "The Temple of Castor and Pollux on the Roman Forum," *ActaArch* 56 (1985), 1–29.

L. RICHARDSON, JR

TEMPLE OF FORTUNA PRIMIGENIA, Praeneste. Roman sanctuary constructed during the later Roman Republic for the goddess of Fortune, the "first-born."

The temple was renowned for its oracle, where suppliants might find guidance for the future by drawing lots. The date is disputed, the excavators Fasolo and Gullini arguing for a date before the destruction of *Praeneste by Sulla (82 B.C.), while most historians of architecture prefer one just after.

The sanctuary, dramatically positioned on a steep hillside, featured two complexes, a lower and an upper. The lower zone included the structure where the oracular lots were cast; within this zone, too, was found the famous *Barberini mosaic. The upper sanctuary consisted of a sequence of eight levels arranged to accent a central axis; the visitor could ascend for over 700 feet by means of the various stairways and ramps, stopping at terraces along the way and taking in the view, until reaching the culminating point of the complex at the top, the round shrine of Fortuna behind a great hemicycle.

The Temple of Fortuna was in use until the fourth century A.C. During the Middle Ages, the terraces were partially built over by houses and shops. The hemicycle formed the foundations for the late Gothic Palazzo Vitelleschi, rebuilt for the Barberini in the seventeenth century and today housing the Barberini mosaic and other material from the site. The remains of the sanctuary were studied from the sixteenth century on. The earliest drawings are by Giuliano da *Sangallo and Pirro *Ligorio, the latter surviving in a codex owned by Fulvio *Orsini. *Bramante studied the architecture and was influenced by it in his designs for the Cortile del Belvedere (*Vatican Museums).

The culminating point of the Belvedere, featuring a small, circular building reached by convex and concave stairs, was adopted by Ligorio for his own reconstruction of the Temple of Fortuna. Thus, the convex stairway, invented by Bramante and never present in the original sanctuary, became a popular feature in later reconstructions. Remarkably, the concept of the sanctuary that prevailed up until the twentieth century was, in part, a copy of the Belvedere that had copied it.

*Palladio also produced a series of sketches and reconstructions of the plan and elevation; these convey surprisingly well the general impression of the sanctuary, though many parts are invented or erroneous. The sanctuary was published in the seventeenth century by Suaresius in his monograph on Praeneste and was drawn by *Pietro da Cortona and one of the artists of Cassiano dal *Pozzo. In the eighteenth and nineteenth centuries the site was studied by architects from the *French Academy in Rome and by Luigi *Canina, but no one succeeded in producing an accurate plan as long as the houses and shops covered crucial portions of the terraces. During World War II, American bombs destroyed much of the heart of the city and laid bare the terraces, making it possible for Fasolo and Gullini to conduct their investigations and generate authoritative plans and reconstructions of the site.

BIBLIOGRAPHY

F. Fasolo—G. Gullini, *Il Santuario della Fortuna Primigenia a Palestrina,* 1–2 (Rome, 1953); J. Ackerman, *Il Cortile del Belvedere* (Città del Vaticano, 1954); +P. Romanelli, *Palestrina* (Cava dei Tirreni, 1967), 33–55.

L. RICHARDSON, JR

TEMPLE OF HERA (HERAION), Olympia. Greek temple at the panhellenic site of *Olympia, important for the early development of the Doric temple.

Uncovered in 1877, the Temple of Hera was identified as the Heraion when a statue believed to be Praxiteles' *Hermes,* seen by Pausanias (5.17.3), was found within. *Dörpfeld made soundings in and around the temple (1879–80) and published the building in *Olympia* 2 (1892). Pausanias had reported one oak column in the opisthodomos, and Dörpfeld reasoned that stone columns and capitals had gradually replaced wooden originals. No part of the temple's entablature or walls above the stone orthostats was recovered, and Dörpfeld concluded that these elements were built of perishable mud-brick and wood. The Heraion therefore represents a midway phase between mud-brick-and-wood architecture and architecture of stone.

Based on Pausanias (5.16.1), Dörpfeld dated the temple to 1096 B.C. A. *Furtwängler, who published the small finds from the excavation of 1875–81, including bronzes found below the Heraion, believed none of the bronzes were earlier than the eighth century B.C. and that the temple should date ca. 650–600 B.C. Dörpfeld sought to confirm an early date for the temple and the existence of a Bronze Age sanctuary at Olympia with repeated excavations at the Heraion (1906–09, 1922–23, 1927–29). He found evidence for three main building phases (I–III) and maintained a prehistoric date for the first, nonperipteral phase. Dörpfeld's sequence was challenged first by H. Riemann, then by W. B. *Dinsmoor and H. E. Searls, who reduced the building phases to two (A and B). Finally, after new excavations inside the Heraion (1966), A. Mallwitz argued for a single building project of ca. 600 B.C.

A colossal limestone female head, found in 1878 among Byzantine remains near the east wall of the Palaistra, was immediately associated with the seated cult statue of Hera seen by Pausanias (5.17.1). More recent opinion believes the head (and a wing fragment found nearby) to be from a sphinx relief in the Heraion's pediment.

BIBLIOGRAPHY

A. Furtwängler, *Kleine Schriften* (Munich, 1912), I, 339–421, 446–57; +W. Dörpfeld, *Alt-Olympia* 1 (Berlin, 1935); +A. Mallwitz, "Das Heraion von Olympia und sein Vorgänger," *JdI* 81 (1966), 310–76; U. Sinn, "ΕΚΤΥΠΟΝ Der sog. Hera-Kopf aus Olympia," *AM* 99 (1984), 77–87.

JANE BURR CARTER

TEMPLE OF MINERVA, Rome. The temple to Minerva built by Domitian at the northeast end of the Forum Transitorium (Forum of Nerva), thus blocking the street called Argiletum, which had previously connected the *Forum Romanum and the Subura district of the city.

Some reworking of the façade of Vespasian's Templum Pacis (*Imperial fora) was required to accommodate the new temple in the space available, which was severely restricted on the opposite side of the street also by the exterior curve of the south hemicycle of the Forum of Augustus. Von Blanckenhagen proposed that the temple was originally built under Vespasian and altered by Domitian, but the archaeological remains do not support this hypothesis. Rather, Domitian seems to have set his new temple atop the paving slabs of a colonnade that

Vespasian had constructed to line either side of the Argiletum at the time of construction of the Templum Pacis (ca. A.D. 75).

Domitian's temple was of the Italic style faced with marble, frontal with a closed rear wall, set on a high podium and thus dominating the long, narrow forum in front of it. Its cella ended in an apse that served as a niche for the cult statue (most of the temple's plan is preserved on a fragment of the Marble Plan; *Forma Urbis Romae). The façade was hexastyle with either three columns or two columns and an anta on each flank of the pronaos. The order was Corinthian. While only the interior core of the temple survives today, it was well known to artists and architects of the Renaissance: an architectural plan of it, drawn by *Peruzzi before it was dismantled, survives, as do drawings of its façade in the *Codex Escurialensis (ca. 1491), by van *Heemskerck and *Du Pérac (ca. 1635). The temple seems to have been confused with other Domitianic monuments to Minerva, perhaps as early as Cassius Dio, and that confusion persists through the Regionary catalogs into medieval itineraries to the monuments of Rome. The *Mirabilia* of *Gregorius (ca. 1200) describes this temple in some detail, including mention of a headless statue still in place on the temple pediment at that time, which Gregorius identifies as the original cult image.

Contracts for quarrying of building stone in the Forum Transitorium are recorded in 1425, 1504, 1522 and 1527. By 1517 a church, called either S. Maria in Macello or degli Angeli, had been located in the Forum, though apparently not in the ruins of the temple. Dismantling of the temple began in 1592 with the removal of a massive architrave block that was then reworked to provide the new main altar of St. Peter's basilica. The remainder of the temple was dismantled under Pope Paul V in 1606, and the marble was used, in part, to decorate the Acqua Paola on the Janiculum. The podium core was excavated, together with the other remains of the Forum, in campaigns between 1928 and 1936, under the direction of A. Colini, but very little of the temple remained in situ.

BIBLIOGRAPHY

Platner—Ashby, 227–29; +P. Von Blanckenhagen, *Flavische Architektur* (Berlin, 1940), 22–33; +J. Anderson, "Domitian, the Argiletum and the Temple of Peace," *AJA* 86 (1982), 101–10.

JAMES C. ANDERSON, JR.

"TEMPLE OF MINERVA MEDICA" (TERME DI GALLUCCIO; LE GALLUZZE; NYMPHAEUM HORTORUM LICINIANORUM), Rome.

Domed decagonal building, possibly a dining pavilion or fountainhouse (nymphaeum), perhaps belonging to the Horti Liciniani, the gardens of the emperor P. Licinus Gallienus (A.D. 253–68).

The structure, popularly known as the Temple of Minerva Medica (a name that does occur in Regionary catalogs of Rome), received this appellation as a result of the report, evidently erroneous, that the statue of *Minerva* with a serpent from the *Giustiniani collection was found there (so reported by *Ficoroni in

1744). Prior to that, it was known as the Terme di Galluccio or Le Galuzze, names whose origin and meaning are unknown.

The structure of brick-faced concrete is roofed with a dome erected on a skeleton of brick ribs, separating the "rotunda" (diameter 24m) into ten segments, of which nine have semicircular apses, evidently intended to house sculpture. The interior and exterior were faced with marble, and the building was also adorned with mosaics.

The building inspired architects of the Renaissance (*Brunelleschi's S. Maria degli Angeli, Florence, begun 1434; Michelozzo's chapel at the east end of SS. Annuziata, Florence, begun 1444) and was the scene of the discovery of a number of sculptures during the pontificate of *Julius III (1550–55); these were recorded by Pirro *Ligorio. Sixteenth-century drawings (e.g., by Jacob Frankaert the Elder in the Thomas *Ashby collection in the Vatican Library) show the pavilion more or less intact.

In 1828 the vault, which was supported by wooden scaffolding, collapsed, according to the report of A. *Nibby, and the following year the building was hit by lightning. Nibby also notes the names of sculptures discovered earlier there (*Aesculapius, Pomona, Adonis, Venus, Faunus Hercules, Antinous*). Between 1875 and 1878, more sculptures were excavated from the ruins, including two statues of Roman magistrates throwing the *mappa,* the signal cloth to start a race.

Located in Via Giolitti not far from the *Porta Maggiore, the "Temple of Minerva Medica" is today visible from the train for the visitor arriving at Stazione Termini in Rome.

BIBLIOGRAPHY
Nash, II, 127–29; R. Keaveney, *Views of Rome,* catalog of exhibition (London, 1988), 166–69; Richardson, *New Topographical Dictionary,* 269–70.

TEMPLE OF OLYMPIAN ZEUS (OLYMPIEION), Athens. Greek temple, the largest in mainland Greece, dedicated to Zeus, begun in the sixth century B.C. and finished in the second century A.C.

The first version of the Olympieion was begun under Hippias and Hipparchos, the sons of Peisistratos, and was abandoned when Hippias went into exile in 510 B.C. The project was resumed by the Seleucid king Antiochos IV Epiphanes (175–164 B.C.), who hired Cossutius, a Roman citizen, as architect for the new version. Cossutius carried the project to the roof; under Augustus (31 B.C.–A.D. 14) further work was done, but the temple remained incomplete until the time of Hadrian (dedicated A.D. 131/2).

The Peisistratid temple is thought to have been of the Doric order, with two rows of twenty-one columns on each side and three rows of eight across the front and back. The temple of Antiochos, portions of which are visible today, is of the Corinthian order, with a stylobate measuring 41.12m × 107.8m, dimensions almost identical to those of the Peisistratid temple, but with a scheme of 20 × 8 columns (104 total). The temple may have been open to the sky (hypaethral), though this is debated.

Of the forest of columns that graced the temple, only fifteen remain standing today; one lies adjacent to the temple. Plundering of the Olympieion actually began in Roman times, when Sulla sacked Athens and carried some of the capitals and shafts back to Rome (86 B.C.) to be used in the temple of Jupiter Optimus Maximus on the Capitoline. During the Middle Ages, the structure was known as the Palace of Hadrian and was treated as a quarry for its abundant Pentelic marble. Around 1675 the Prussian adventurer/soldier J. G. Transfeldt correctly identified the monument on the basis of the passage in Vitruvius (7. Intro. 15) where it is mentioned.

The structure was admired by architects and travelers of the eighteenth and nineteenth centuries, including *Stuart and *Revett, but its disintegration was noted and lamented, for example, by *Dodwell. In 1858, a cyclone knocked down the single column that now lies in the temple. In 1883, F. C. *Penrose undertook excavations and measurement of the remains, and the *Greek Archaeological Society also conducted excavations, from 1886 to 1901. These investigations, along with those of the *German Archaeological Institute (1922–23), made possible an understanding of the history and plan of the Olympieion.
BIBLIOGRAPHY
G. Welter, ''Das Olympieion in Athen,'' *AM* 47–48 (1922–23); +Dinsmoor, 91, 280–81; Berve—Gruben, *Greek Temples,* 394–97.

TEMPLE OF SATURN, Rome. Roman temple, located at the foot of the Clivus Capitolinus, fronting on the *Forum Romanum; one of the oldest temples of Rome.

There was much confusion in antiquity about the date of the temple's dedication and dedicator, but it was certainly in the first years of the Republic, at the end of the sixth or beginning of the fifth century B.C.

The temple stands on a very high podium in which was arranged the *aerarium* or public treasury of Rome. It was rebuilt by L. Munatius Plancus beginning in 42 B.C. and again after a fire in the late fourth century. What we see today is the last rebuilding, with six unfluted columns of granite across the front, having white marble bases of three types and four-sided Ionic capitals of proto-Byzantine character.

The surviving columns (eight in all) have always been a landmark, but their identity was lost (although in the twelfth century the building was still called the Aerarium). The temple was still well preserved at the beginning of the fifteenth century; by that time Nicola Signorili was identifying it as the temple of Juno Moneta. Its destruction came between 1402 and 1447.

Clearance of the houses in and around the temple was one of the first objectives of De Tournon, beginning in 1810, but the correct identification still had not been made. For *Nibby in 1827 it was still the temple of Fortuna Primigenia, and correct identification came only with Luigi *Canina in 1834. The back parts and area behind the temple have been excavated and cleared only recently.

The remains have always been a favorite subject for artists; the earliest drawing is probably that of the *Codex Escurialensis of ca. 1491, where little more appears than survives today. The most famous representations of it are perhaps the romantic versions of *Piranesi (1756) and *Tischbein (1780–90), complete with modern encumbrances and staffage.

BIBLIOGRAPHY

+P. Pensabene, *Tempio di Saturno, architettura e decorazione* (Rome, 1984); Richardson, *New Topographical Dictionary* 343–44; +Ridley, *Eagle and the Spade* 19, 60, 189, 193–95.

L. RICHARDSON, JR

TEMPLE OF THE DIOSCURI. See TEMPLE OF CASTOR.

TEMPLE OF VENUS AND ROME, Rome. Roman temple, founded by the emperor Hadrian (A.D. 117–38).

Instead of building another imperial forum (*Imperial Fora), Hadrian constructed a huge temple raised on a vaulted platform of concrete, the two cellas back to back, that of Rome looking west down Sacra Via toward the *Forum Romanum, that of Venus looking east toward the *Colosseum. The temple—Corinthian peripteral, with ten columns by twenty raised on a continuous stylobate of five steps—appeared classical in its proportions. The precinct was framed on the long sides with double colonnades. In the interior the cellas were relatively short and broad, probably flanked by files of columns.

The temple seems to have been left unfinished by Hadrian and completed by Antoninus Pius, who may also have decided the statue types. In 307 it burned and was restored by Maxentius, to whom are due the vaulted apsidal cellas with porphyry columns on a high continuous plinth along the sides. In 630 Pope Honorius I was allowed to take the gilt bronze tiles of the roof for the roof of St. Peter's. In the middle of the eighth century, an oratory of SS. Pietro e Paolo was built *iuxta templum Romae,* presumably in the precinct. Around 855 the *cella Romae* was converted into the church of S. Maria Nova, and a community grew up around it. This is now commonly called S. Francesca Romana, from the saint who founded a convent of oblates there in 1421 and is buried there; their beautiful convent adjoining the church on the north is now the *Antiquario Forense.

The clearance of the temple was begun by the French in 1813 and completed by *Nibby in 1827–29, but it remained for Muñoz to systematize the platform in connection with the construction of the Via dei Fori Imperiali in 1934–35. The plan of the temple, almost completely vanished, was re-created on the platform by means of shrubs and flowers.

BIBLIOGRAPHY
M. Manieri Elia, *Quaderni dell'Istituto di Storia dell'Architettura,* n.s. 1–10 (1983–87), 47–54; R. T. Ridley, "The Fate of an Architect, Apollodoros of Damascus," *Athenaeum* 67 (1989), 551–65.

L. RICHARDSON, JR

TEMPLE OF VESPASIAN, Rome. Roman imperial temple dedicated to the deified Vespasian (d. A.D. 79).

The building, located on the Clivus Capitolinus, was begun by Titus and completed by Domitian. It is alluded to only by Statius (*Silv.* 1.1.31). It was Corinthian prostyle hexastyle, 33m × 22m, with its cella built up against the Tabularium. Only three columns (15m high) and their entablature survive. The frieze was finely sculpted with sacrificial paraphernalia of the emperor as Pontifex Maximus. The temple was still whole enough for its inscription to be read in the eighth century (*Einsiedeln Itinerary), but by the 1530s (van *Heemskerk's illustrations) it was reduced to the sad fragment we know today, undoubtedly by the ruthless Renaissance plundering for new churches and palaces. P. P. *Rubens has left an engraving of the frieze, but the lower portions of the temple were rapidly being buried by the debris being tipped down from the Capitol; only the capitals were visible by the time of *Piranesi.

Under the French, Giuseppe *Camporese for the Academy of St. Luke began to clear the columns (1810), only to find that they almost totally lacked foundations and were half a diameter out of line. In the most brilliant of all the archaeological undertakings of the French occupation, Camporese erected huge machinery to raise the fragmented entablature, then excavated 15m to rebuild the foundations, reset the columns and replace the entablature, before clearing the whole slope down to the podium (1812). The temple's plan was thus revealed for the first time.

The remains were known since the Renaissance (e.g., to *Marliani, 1534; *Nardini, 1665) as those of the Temple of Jupiter Tonans. The structure was correctly, but without confidence, identified for the first time by Luigi *Canina (*Foro romano,* 1824, 132), but with sureness in his second edition (1845, 177).

BIBLIOGRAPHY
+C. Hülsen, *Forum and Palatine* (New York, 1928), pl. 11 (reconstruction); Platner—Ashby, 556; +Nash, II, 501; Ridley, *Eagle and the Spade,* esp. 198–205.

R. T. RIDLEY

"TEMPLE OF VESTA" (ROUND TEMPLE BY THE TIBER), Rome. Roman temple.

This shrine is built of marble on a podium of tufa surrounded by three marble steps. It is enclosed by a peristyle of twenty Corinthian columns 8m high (one missing), but the entire entablature is destroyed, and the tiled roof is modern (the original was a cupola). The cella is 10m in diameter.

The temple has been dated between ca. 120 B.C. and the early empire, with

Temple of Vesta (Round Temple by the Tiber), engraving by G. B. Mercati (1600–ca. 1637), Veroli, Biblioteca Giovardiana. (Deutsches Archäologisches Institut, Rome. Inst. Neg. 80.795.)

recent preference for the earlier terminus. The capitals and steps indicate Hellenistic influence. Both the architect and the marble may have come from Greece. By 1140 the temple had been converted into S. Stefano, and by 1800 into S. Maria del Sole.

* The first clearing of the building was carried out by *Valadier under the French occupation (1810), removing the encroaching modern buildings, demolishing the wall between the columns that enclosed the portico and excavating down to reveal the steps. Valadier then saw the possibilities for restoring the temple, relying on the recovered fragments: rebuilding the entablature, completing the walls of the cella and replacing the missing column. The costs appeared prohibitive to the bureaucrats, however, and the plan was vetoed.

The temple was first identified as the Temple of Vesta by Flavio *Biondo (*Roma restaurata,* 1548, bk. 2, 36); Dea (Mater) Matuta was suggested as early as Pomponio *Leto (d. 1498); Nardini favored Volupia (*sic*) (*Roma antica,* 1665, bk. 7, 3); *Piranesi preferred Cybele because of the pine motifs (*Antichità romane,* 1756); *Fea suggested Hercules from inscriptions found nearby (*Nuova descrizione,* 1820, III 609f.), while Jordan favored Portunus (*Topographie,* 1885, I ii 485). These do not exhaust the proposals. All was transformed, however, with the discovery of the temples of Fortuna and Mater Matuta nearby in *Sant' Omobono in 1938. The current consensus is for Hercules.

BIBLIOGRAPHY
Platner—Ashby, 430; +Nash, I, 411–14; F. Coarelli, *Foro Boario* (Rome, 1986); Ridley, *Eagle and the Spade,* esp. 205–16.

R. T. RIDLEY

TEMPLE OF ZEUS, Olympia. Greek temple of the Early Classical period.

Erected between approximately 470 and 456 B.C., this Doric, peripteral temple was the most important building in the sanctuary at *Olympia and one of the biggest ever built on the Greek mainland. Constructed of local limestone by one Libon of Elis, it stands as a paradigm of the Doric style of the first half of the fifth century B.C. with its six columns across the front and thirteen on the sides and its large cella, containing an interior colonnade, pronaos and opisthodomos. The relatively well preserved marble pedimental sculptures (preparations for the chariot race between Oinomaos and Pelops on the east front and the Battle of Lapiths and Centaurs on the west) and metopes (Labors of Herakles in the pronaos and opisthodomos) were found in the excavations of the temple and hold a central place in the history of the Early Classical or Severe Style of Greek sculpture. The building was best-known in antiquity for the colossal, seated, gold and ivory statue of *Zeus placed inside the cella about 430 B.C. by the famous Athenian sculptor Pheidias, whose workshop for the construction of the statue has been found by modern archaeologists. The statue and the sculptures were certainly famous in the second century A.C. when Pausanias visited Olympia and heard about them from a guide.

The ruins of the great building, perhaps destroyed by an earthquake in late antiquity, must have always been visible, and Richard *Chandler, who visited the site in 1766, recorded standing walls and a "massive" Doric capital that probably belonged to the temple. Apart from these remains and traces of Roman brick walls, most of the sanctuary had disappeared under as much as four meters of river sand. In the spring of 1829, the French *Expédition scientifique de Morée worked at Olympia for some six weeks, clearing much of the temple and recovering a number of fragments of the metopes. The results of their work were promptly published in 1834 in volume 1 of their *Expédition scientifique de Morée*. The temple was finally completely cleared and studied in the great German excavations at Olympia (1875–81) and published in the *Ergebnisse* by *Dörpfeld and Treu.

BIBLIOGRAPHY

F. Adler et al., *Die Baudenkmäler (Olympia, Ergebnisse der vom deutschen Reich veranstalteten Ausgrabungen* 2 (Berlin, 1892), 4–27; W. Dörpfeld, *Alt-Olympia* (Berlin, 1935), 222–61; B. Ashmole—N. Yalouris, *The Sculptures of the Temple of Zeus* (London, 1967); A. Mallwitz, *Olympia und seine Bauten* (Munich, 1972), 211–34; Stewart, *Greek Sculpture,* 142–46, 253–54.

WILLIAM R. BIERS

TERME DI GALLUCCIO. See "TEMPLE OF MINERVA MEDICA."

TERME MUSEUM (MUSEO NAZIONALE ROMANO; MUSEO DELLE TERME), Rome. Italian national museum of Roman antiquity, with one of the world's most important collections of Greek and Roman sculpture, painting and other antiquities.

The Museo Nazionale Romano, on the site of the ancient *Baths of Diocletian (Terme di Diocleziano) and popularly known as the Terme Museum, was founded in the wake of the unification of Italy (1870). After several years of temporary arrangements for the relevant antiquities, the state decreed in 1889 the founding of two national museums, the Museo Nazionale di *Villa Giulia, for materials of Italic and Etruscan provenance, and the Museo Nazionale Romano at the Terme for antiquities of the classical Graeco-Roman heritage, especially from Rome itself. The buildings chosen to house the new museum had a rich history, beginning with the enormous baths built by Maximian and Diocletian (dedicated A.D. 305/6); these were partly converted into the church of S. Maria degli Angeli, designed by *Michelangelo (1563–66), and were surrounded by a cloistered monastery of the Carthusians. In these quarters the museum was mainly to be housed.

The new museum contained long-known minor antiquities from the former Museo Kircheriano (Athanasius *Kircher), as well as the powerful bronze sculptures of the *Hellenistic "*Ruler*" and his possible companion piece, the Bronze *Boxer,* both recently found (1885) in or near the ancient *Baths of Constantine. Other new pieces were the *Hermaphrodite* (found in 1880), the *Bacchus* from the Tiber (1885) and the *Apollo* from the Tiber (1891). The highly important

Roman paintings, stuccos and mosaics discovered in 1879 in a villa beside the Tiber, underneath the Renaissance villa of the Farnesina, were brought to the Terme in 1883. The large extraurban villa, with paintings in the second and third Pompeian styles, is thought to have belonged to an important personage, perhaps Agrippa. Found during the construction of the walls of the Lungoteveri, the Farnesina decorations were hastily removed from the moist environment; although many drawings and records were made, some were carelessly lost, and much precious information about the context disappeared.

New purchases and transfers of objects continued to enrich the collection, and enlargement of the space was necessary. In 1901 came the most important single transaction involving the Terme Museum. The state purchased the *Ludovisi family collection from its heir, Don Rodolfo Boncompagni Ludovisi, and at a stroke were added some of the most famous marbles of Europe. Included were the *Ludovisi "Throne," a Greek original of the fifth century B.C., recently unearthed (1887) at the Villa Ludovisi; the *Ludovisi *Ares;* the *Ludovisi *Gaul Killing Himself and His Wife;* as well as the Hellenistic *Boy Strangling a Goose* (from the early *Cesi family collection, like many of the sculptures). In addition, there were splendid Roman sarcophagi (*Ludovisi *Battle* Sarcophagus) and both Greek and Roman portraits.

Pieces from the *Ara Pacis of Augustus (13–9 B.C.) were first brought to the Terme in 1903, followed by another significant work of that period, the *Augustus* from the Via Labicana in 1910. Under successive directors R. Paribeni (1908–28), G. Moretti (1930–42) and S. Aurigemma (1942–52), acquisition continued at a rapid pace, and there were constant changes in the exhibitions. Some works were deaccessioned. Moretti oversaw the reconstruction of the Ara Pacis in the Campus Martius, which required the removal of the appropriate pieces from the Terme. In addition, a group of bronzes from the Lake of *Nemi purchased by the state in 1906 was transferred to the Museum of the Roman Ships at Nemi in 1940. (The bronzes were returned almost immediately because of the danger posed by war, then were sent back to Nemi in 1953.) A major addition was made in 1951–52, when the famed garden paintings from the *Villa of Livia at Prima Porta were removed from that site because of dampness, and their original setting was reconstructed in the Terme.

Administered by the Soprintendenza Archeologica di Roma, the Museo Nazionale delle Terme has had a hectic history of expansion and reorganization as successive directors have tried to cope with problems of insufficient or unsuitable space and conservation; the ongoing process means that items the visitor expects to see are not always on view to the public. The problem is made up for in some measure by the exemplary volumes of the catalog of the collection, *Museo Nazionale Romano,* coordinated by A. Giuliano and initiated with a presentation on Rome's birthday, 21 April 1979, by Adriano La Regina. The sections published include sculpture (I, 1–11); painting (II, 1); terracottas (III, 1); bronzes (IV, 1); and ceramics (VI, 1–2), published between 1979 and 1991. Two recent loan exhibitions to the Emory University Museum of Art and Archaeology

(1988, 1989, Atlanta; now the Michael C. Carlos Museum) brought Roman portraits and colored stone sculptures out of storage for new study and for viewing by the American public.

BIBLIOGRAPHY

+R. Paribeni, Le Terme di Diocleziano e il Museo Nazionale Romano, 2nd ed. (Rome, 1932); +B. M. Felletti Maj, Museo Nazionale Romano, I Ritratti (Rome, 1952); +S. Aurigemma, The Baths of Diocletian and Museo Nazionale Romano, tr. J. Guthrie, rev. A. W. Van Buren, 7th ed. (Rome, 1974); M. L. Anderson—L. Nista, eds., +Radiance in Stone, Sculptures in Colored Marble from the Museo Nazionale Romano (Rome, 1989).

TESTA, PIETRO (1612–50). Italian artist famed for his prints and drawings, employed by Cassiano dal *Pozzo to make drawings of antiquities.

Pietro Testa was born in Lucca, from which he departed for Rome at an early age (ca. 1628). The young artist was befriended by *Sandrart, who encountered Testa passionately making drawings in the *Colosseum and on the *Palatine and *Capitoline hills. Sandrart hired him to make drawings for prints of ancient statuary in the collection of Vincenzo *Giustiniani, for a forthcoming work, Galleria Giustiniani, in two volumes (Rome, 1631). Around this same time, Testa became friends with *Poussin, with whom he may be compared for his intellectual intensity, especially in regard to antiquity. Also within a short time, Testa was employed in the studio of *Domenichino and by Cassiano dal Pozzo to make drawings for his Museo Cartaceo (''Paper Museum''). When Domenichino departed from Rome in 1631, Testa had a brief, disastrous stint in the studio of *Pietro da Cortona, in which he was asked to leave after a quarrel resulting from Testa's lack of knowledge of the art of painting.

Known throughout his life as a draftsman and printmaker, Testa created etchings with classical themes, such as the Sacrifice of Iphigenia, Venus Giving Arms to Aeneas and the unusual theme of the Death of Sinorix (from Plutarch, Moralia 4.257E–258C), in the last of which he was inspired by Roman architectural remains for the setting (the *Pantheon, the *Pyramid of Cestius, the *Arch of Titus) as well as by statuary for the figure composition (*Quirinal Horse Tamers). These themes from ancient history and poetry reveal careful consideration of ancient texts. Testa's deeply intellectual approach is manifest especially in his allegory called Il Liceo della Pittura (The School of Painting, ca. 1638), which displays his use of a classical setting (based on the Forum of Nerva) for the activities of various personifications and deities, with Minerva at the center (based on the Giustiniani Minerva). A collection of Testa's notes and drawings now in the Kunstmuseum, Düsseldorf, provides important clues to the interpretation of the Liceo and information about his readings of ancient literature.

His attraction to Greek antiquity and philosophy may be seen in his invention for an etching of Plato's Symposium, a rare theme (1648), in which the figure of Alkibiades is based on the *Belvedere ''Antinous.'' Around the same time, he planned an ambitious series of etchings of the life of Achilles, not completed at the time of his death.

For a period of time, Testa was probably the principal artist assigned by Cassiano dal Pozzo to draw antiquities. More than 500 drawings in the corpus of the Paper Museum at Windsor Castle and elsewhere have been attributed to Testa on the basis of the elegant, graceful style of pen and brown or gray wash. Among the many drawings attributed to Testa are images of the *"Trophies of Marius"; the "Barberini Landscape," a Roman painting discovered in 1626/7 during the building of Palazzo Barberini; the *Arch of the Argentarii; the miniatures of the *Vatican Vergil; and numerous examples of Roman relief sculpture.

Throughout his life, Testa was known as a difficult and melancholy man. His death by drowning in the Tiber at the age of thirty-six was thought by many to be a suicide.

BIBLIOGRAPHY

E. Cropper, *The Ideal of Painting, Pietro Testa's Düsseldorf Notebook* (Princeton, NJ, 1984); +C. Dempsey, "The Greek Style and the Prehistory of Neoclassicism," in *Pietro Testa, 1612–1650, Prints and Drawings,* ed. E. Cropper, catalog of exhibition (Philadelphia, 1988), xxxvii-1xv; +*The Paper Museum of Cassiano dal Pozzo,* catalog of exhibition, *Quaderni Puteani* 4 (1993), esp. 34–36.

TEXIER, CHARLES-FELIX-MARIE (1802–60). French traveler and archaeologist.

Born at Versailles, Texier was educated at the École des beaux-artes in Paris. Named inspector of public works of Paris in 1827, he was soon put in charge of excavations at Fréjus and *Ostia to determine the cause of lowering of the water level in the Mediterranean. Between 1833 and 1837 he made a series of journeys to the Levant for the French government, visiting such sites as *Assos, *Didyma, *Pergamon, Aizani, the *Monumentum Ancyranum at Ankara and many others. Later he negotiated the transfer to the *Louvre of 70m of the frieze with an Amazonomachy from the temple of Artemis Leukophryene at *Magnesia-on-the-Maeander. His travels were written up as *Description de la Asia Mineure* (Paris, 1838–48).

Texier is repeatedly criticized for the inaccuracy of his elegant drawings but is important in the history of archaeology for stimulating a new interest in the antiquities of Asia Minor. He also traveled to Armenia, Persia and Mesopotamia.

BIBLIOGRAPHY

"Texier, Charles-Felix-Marie," *NBG* 45 (1866), cols. 14–15; Stark, 268, 342, 343, 352; Michaelis, 92, 166, 179, 186, 272.

THEATER OF DIONYSOS, Athens. Greek theater of major importance; site of the first performances of the plays of Aischylos, Sophokles, Euripides and Aristophanes. An early theater (late sixth–fifth centuries B.C.) was cut into the earth on the south slope of the *Akropolis of Athens and fitted with wooden stands from which the spectators watched the performance in the orchestra below, performed against the backdrop of a scene building of canvas and wood.

A permanent stone auditorium and scene building were first built by Lykourgos ca. 330 B.C.; numerous additions and modifications were made in the following centuries during the Hellenistic and Roman periods, creating a site that has often been difficult to interpret.

The site of the theater was first identified in modern times by Richard *Chandler (1765), but not until 1859 were some of the rock-cut benches first cleared. From 1861 to 1867, extensive investigations were conducted by J. H. Strack, A. Rousopoulos, E. Ziller and P. Evstratiades, resulting in the discovery of inscribed marble thrones from the front row; limestone seats; the orchestra and its entrance passages (*parodoi*); and sculpture from the stage front. At this time Ziller created plans and cross-sections of the visible parts. W. *Dörpfeld excavated in the theater in 1886 and 1889, publishing his results in *Das Griechische Theater* (1896), under commission by the *German Archaeological Institute. Further investigations were made in 1923–27 by Dörpfeld, H. Bulle and E. Fiechter, who later published the monograph, *Das Dionysos Theater in Athen* (1950).

In recent years much effort has gone toward consolidation, conservation and documentation. A team under W. Wurster (1977–80) did some consolidation and made new plans of the orchestra, the auditorium and the east retaining wall of the theater and a new topographical plan of the whole. M. Korres followed with conservation work (1980–84) and a close study of bases from the *parodoi*. From 1984, the Committee for the Preservation of the Theater of Dionysos has overseen the monument. A new model (1988) of the theater and its surroundings as they must have looked in the late fourth century B.C. has been placed on display in the Center for Akropolis Studies in Athens.

BIBLIOGRAPHY

W. Larfield, *Handbuch der griechischen Epigraphik* (Leipzig, 1902–7), II, pl. 1; A. W. Pickard-Cambridge, *The Theater of Dionysos in Athens* (Oxford, 1946); +Travlos, 537–52.

JUDITH BINDER

THEATER OF MARCELLUS, Rome. The second permanent theater of Rome (cf. *Theater of Pompey) begun by Julius Caesar, who may not have got beyond acquiring land and clearing it of older buildings; more land seems to have been purchased by Augustus. Construction may not have begun until after the death of Marcellus, nephew of Augustus, in 23 B.C., when the theater was made a memorial to him. Part of the celebration of the Ludi Saeculares of 17 B.C. took place there, but the dedication did not take place until 13 B.C.

The Theater of Marcellus was a freestanding stone structure in the southern Campus Martius between the *Capitoline and the Tiber and was slightly larger in capacity (ca. 13,000 spectators) than the Theater of Pompey. It appears that the theater was intended especially for shows other than plays, but on this point we have no information. While the architecture of the *cavea* has, in large part, been cleared and is well understood, having served as a model for the *Colos-

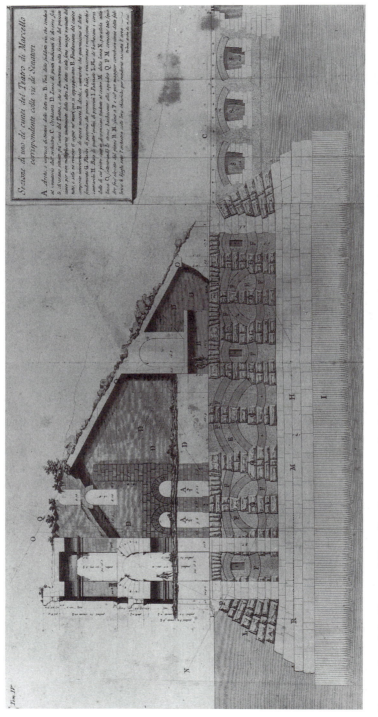

Cross-section of the *Theater of Marcellus*, Rome, engraving by G. B. Piranesi, from *Le Antichità romane* (1756). (Deutsches Archäologisches Institut, Rome. Inst. Neg. 87.415.)

seum, the architecture of the stage building and its adjacencies is not at all clear. The most visible part of the monument lies in the two remaining exterior stories of travertine arcading, with a Tuscan Doric engaged order on the ground floor and Ionic on the second floor. The third story was probably without arcading but was furnished with windows and Corinthian pilasters.

The ruins of the theater are mentioned in the *Einsiedeln Itinerary in the eighth century. Since its mass made an ideal base for a fortress, it was occupied and fortified by the Fabi (or Faffi) in the middle of the twelfth century, perhaps taken over by them from the Pierleoni, who dominated the area a half century earlier. In the thirteenth century it passed to the Savelli and acquired the name Monte Savello, by which it is still sometimes known. It was for the Savelli that Baldassare *Peruzzi in 1523–27 constructed the elegant palace that now crowns it. During the Renaissance, the arcading was an influential model for architects. In 1713, the palace went to the Orsini and then for two centuries was known as Palazzo Orsini. The lower arcades of the Theater of Marcellus had been used as early as the Middle Ages for shops and common dwellings, but these were finally cleared out in restorations of the monument by A. Calza Bini (1926–29). The exterior of the theater has recently been cleaned (1980s).

BIBLIOGRAPHY

+P. Fidenzoni, *Il Teatro di Marcello* (Rome, 1970); P. Ciancio Rossetto, "Le maschere del teatro di Marcello," *BullCom* 88 (1982–83), 7–49; Richardson, *New Topographical Dictionary,* 382–83.

L. RICHARDSON, JR

THEATER OF POMPEY, Rome. The oldest permanent theater in Rome and always the most admired and most important; the curia attached to it was the site of the assassination of Julius Caesar in 44 B.C.

Begun by Pompey as the central element of a vast complex that included porticoes, gardens and a curia, the theater was dedicated in 55 B.C. with lavish games. The stone theater stood entirely free in the southern Campus Martius, almost isolated. It was evidently dedicated unfinished, and the stage building and temple of Venus Victrix were dedicated three years later. It included shrines to five divinities: Venus Victrix, Honos, Virtus, Felicitas and V(ictoria?), probably small affairs arranged at the top of the *cavea*. There were also fourteen figures by Coponius representing the fourteen nations conquered by Pompey, probably set up around the exterior of the *cavea*.

The theater was restored by Augustus at great expense. It burned in A.D. 21, and restoration was begun by Tiberius and completed by Caligula, but Claudius dedicated it. In A.D. 66 Nero had the whole interior gilded and purple awnings installed for the reception of Tiridates of Armenia. The scene building burned in the fire of 80, and Domitian must have restored it. It was restored again by Septimius Severus and in 243 burned again. Other restorations are recorded in the fourth and fifth centuries under Diocletian and Maximian, Honorius and Arcadius, and Symmachus.

The original diameter of the Theater of Pompey is estimated at 150–160m, the capacity at 11,000. In the cellars of various later buildings in the area (e.g., the restaurant Pancrazio) are extensive remains of the vaulted substructures of the theater, made of concrete faced with quasi-reticulate work. The exterior of the *cavea* was arcaded with forty-four arches of peperino; these are no longer visible, but the curvature of the theater is strikingly repeated in the disposition of the modern houses facing on the Via di Grotta Pinta. The scene building has never been explored, and the buildings built over its ruins, especially the seventeenth-century Palazzo Pio-Righetti, have prevented exposure of any remains above the substructures, except for a tantalizing strip much rebuilt in later periods along the edge of the Area Sacra of the *Largo Argentina.

BIBLIOGRAPHY

F. Coarelli, "Il complesso pompeiano di Campo Marzio e la sua decorazione scultorea," *RendPontAcc* 44 (1971–72), 99–122; L. Richardson, "A Note on the Architecture of the *Theatrum Pompei* in Rome," *AJA* 91 (1987), 123–26, G. Sauron, in *L'Urbs, espace urbain et histoire (Ier siècle av. J. C.—IIIe siècle ap. J. C.), Collection de l'École Française de Rome* 98 (Rome, 1987), 457–73.

L. RICHARDSON, JR

THEBES (THEVAI). Major city of ancient Greece, located in Boiotia northwest of Athens; its principal topographical feature is the Kadmeia, the great plateau of the acropolis, some 700m long.

Thebes is rich in mythology, from the story of its founding and the introduction of writing by the Phoenician Kadmos to the tales of King Oedipus and his successors, who carried on the war of the Seven Against Thebes. The earlier history of the city reveals its warlike character and its tendency to covet or rival neighboring states. Theban power reached an acme with Epaminondas commanding its army (370–362 B.C.), but his death left the city to a rapid decline. Thebes then became best known for its misfortunes, including the sacks by Alexander the Great (335 B.C.), the Roman L. Mummius (146 B.C.) and Sulla (80 B.C.).

Sieges and raids of the Middle Ages and earthquakes of the nineteenth century left little to interfere with the building of modern Thebes over the Kadmeia and neighboring areas. The ancient remains of the city are scanty, and it is possible to construct only a general chronology of the city. A. Keramopoullos excavated the most important site of Thebes, the Mycenaean palace known as the "House of Kadmos," in eight campaigns between 1906 and 1929. In 1917, he produced a study of the *Topography of Thebes,* based largely on the analysis of ancient texts, particularly works by Pindar—a native of Thebes (sixth century B.C.)—and Pausanias, who wrote an extensive description of Thebes in the second century A.C.

Many of the excavations carried out in the twentieth century have been salvage operations. The most dramatic of these was the work done by the *Greek Archaeological Service (N. Platon, E. Touloupa) in the winter of 1963–64 on the Kadmeia, where the walls of another Mycenaean palace were found. Numerous fragments of frescoes were recovered, and in a "treasury" area were found hoards of precious stones (onyx and lapis lazuli) and gold; thirty-eight Mesopotamian cylinder seals were found—all but two of lapis—of varying date and origin. Though clearly brought in as the commodity of lapis lazuli, their presence at Thebes was quickly taken as evidence of the eastern connections and innovations of Kadmos.

S. Symeonoglou produced a modern catalog of some 270 archaeological sites in and around Thebes (1985), most of them known through salvage operations. He described finds ranging over a period of 4,500 years, embracing the Bronze Age, Hellenic period and the Christian era. The location of most of the monuments mentioned by Pausanias can only be conjectured; a notable exception is the oracular temple of Apollo Ismenios discovered southeast of the Kadmeia, poorly preserved but firmly identified on the basis of inscriptions found in excavations by Keramopoullos (1910).

BIBLIOGRAPHY
P. Roesch, s.v. "Thebes," *PECS*, 904–6; S. Symeonoglou, *The Topography of Thebes, From the Bronze Age to Modern Times* (Princeton, NJ, 1985).

THERA (SANTORINI). Island in the South Cyclades, Aegean Sea, Greece.

In prehistoric times Thera was of circular form with a volcano in its center; the present, crescent-shaped island and the neighboring islets Therasia and Aspronisi are the remnants of a cataclysmic eruption, perhaps around 1500 B.C., in which the caving in of the volcano formed a large gulf (caldera). Several prehistoric habitation sites are well preserved under the ash and pumice layers formed by this eruption.

The exploration of the island's early history began in the nineteenth century. In 1866–67 excavations conducted in the south part of Therasia by local people together with the French geologist F. Fouqué brought to light Bronze Age buildings with quantities of pottery. Two members of the *French School in Athens, Mamet and Gorceix, dug in 1870 in the neighborhood of the Akrotiri village in the southwest part of Thera and found similar habitation remains, including frescoed walls. Other Bronze Age buildings were excavated in 1899 by the German archaeologist R. Zahn at Potamos near Kamara, east of Akrotiri (finds in the museum at Phira).

The first large-scale work was done by F. *Hiller von Gaertringen's interdisciplinary expedition in 1895–1902; besides exploring the island's history and climate, it excavated the Doric city on the Mesavouno hill and its cemeteries on the Sellada saddle. The city, which flourished especially as a Ptolemaic garrison town in the third century B.C., had a temple of Apollo Karneios, a theater, a stoa of unusual type and barracks. The cemetery yielded important information about the burial customs, especially of the Archaic period.

The most spectacular results have been achieved by the new excavations at Akrotiri, started in 1967 by S. *Marinatos, who had the aim to prove his theory of "the volcanic destruction of Minoan Crete." The well-preserved buildings of palatial quality (although no palace has been identified as yet), as well as the decorated pottery and the numerous wall paintings, show that Thera had a strongly Minoanized culture, contemporary with the Late Minoan IA period, immediately before the catastrophe. The frescoes, which all seem to have had a religious or ideological/political function, are similar to the Knossian ones, but since they are better preserved, they help our understanding also of the Cretan repertory. Since Marinatos's death in 1974, the excavations have continued under the direction of C. Doumas.

BIBLIOGRAPHY

+F. Fouqué, *Santorin et ses éruptions* (Paris, 1879); +F. Hiller von Gaertringen et al., *Thera, Untersuchungen, Vermessungen und Ausgrabungen in den Jahren 1895–1902*, 1–4. (Berlin, 1899–1909); +S. Marinatos, *Excavations at Thera* 1–7 (Athens, 1967–76); +*Thera and the Aegean World* 1–2 (London, 1978–80); +C. Doumas, *Thera, the Pompeii of the Prehistoric Aegean* (London, 1983); +N. Marinatos, *Art and Religion in Thera* (Athens, 1984); C. Doumas, *The Wall Paintings of Thera* (Athens, 1992).

NANNO MARINATOS

THESSALONIKI. City of Greek Macedonia.

Founded ca. 316 B.C. by Cassander as a synoecism of towns on the Thermaic Gulf, the city became an important port. Under Roman rule Thessaloniki flourished as the capital of a Roman province (146 B.C.). It was made a colony by Decius ca. A.D. 250 and in the mid-fifth century became the seat of the prefects of Illyricum. During the Byzantine Empire it was second only to Constantinople. Captured by Saracens in A.D. 904, Thessaloniki fell to Turkey in 1430, and returned to Greece in 1912.

Such eighteenth- and nineteenth-century European travelers as J. *Stuart and N. *Revett, L.-F.-S. *Fauvel, E. D. *Clarke, C. *Cockerell, E. M. Cousinéry, W. M. *Leake, E. *Lear, L. Heuzey and H. Daumet drew and described prominent monuments: the "Incantadas" (whose carved piers were removed to the *Louvre in 1864), the Vardar Gate, the Rotunda and the Arch of Galerius as well as assorted stelai and inscriptions.

Remains of an Ionic temple of 500 B.C. document an earlier, Archaic settlement, probably Therme. Roman remains cover much of the Hellenistic city, which is known from an important Serapeion, a few scattered reliefs and inscriptions and tombs with finds. There was considerable building activity in Antonine and Severan times, including construction of gates, sanctuaries, fortification walls and a remodeling of the agora. A large complex consisting of the tetrarchic palace, the arch of Galerius, the Rotunda and a hippodrome can be dated to around A.D. 300.

The Archaeological Museum houses selected Macedonian and Thracian finds dating from Neolithic through later Roman times. Early Christian through Byzantine remains are in the White Tower and the Museum of Byzantine Civilization. Of special interest in the Archaeological Museum are remains of Archaic

through Roman Thessaloniki (architectural members, sculptures and reliefs, mosaics and grave finds) as well as discoveries from important sites like *Vergina.
BIBLIOGRAPHY
+M. Andronikos—M. Chatzidakis—V. Karageorghis, "Thessalonike Archaeological Museum," in *The Greek Museums* (Athens, 1977), 267–90; +M. B. Sakellariou, ed., *Macedonia. 4000 Years of Greek History and Civilization* (Athens, 1983); *Thessalonikin Philippou Basilissan, Meletes gia tin Archaia Thessaloniki* (Thessaloniki, 1985); I. Touratsoglou, *Macedonia: History, Monuments, Museums* (Athens, 1995).

STELLA G. MILLER

THEVAI. See THEBES.

THOMPSON, MARGARET (1911–92). American archaeologist; administrator and numismatist.

Born in Trenton, New Jersey, Margaret Thompson took her B.A. in English from Radcliffe in 1931. After five years of teaching junior high English at the height of the Depression, she became secretary to T. Leslie *Shear en route to employment at the *Agora in Athens as an assistant in the numismatic finds from the site. Eventually she was to publish a catalog of some 37,000 coins excavated there, dating from the Roman to the Venetian period (1954), as well as a resulting monumental study of *The New Style Silver Coinage of Athens* (1961).

In 1949 Thompson became assistant curator of Greek coins at the *American Numismatic Society (ANS) and eventually curator, a post she held until 1976. She was chief curator of the ANS from 1969 to 1979, and her dedication to administrative tasks extended to the *Archaeological Institute of America, which she served as its first woman president (1964–68) and from which she received the Gold Medal for Distinguished Archaeological Achievement (1984). Not having attended graduate school and obtained a conventional Ph.D., Margaret Thompson received an honorary doctorate from Columbia University in 1985. Among her many services to the discipline of numismatics were her actions as organizer of the International Numismatic Congress at New York/Washington in 1973 and her collaboration with C. Kraay and O. Mørkheim in the publication of the magisterial work *An Inventory of Greek Coin Hoards,* first distributed at the congress of 1973.
BIBLIOGRAPHY
W. E. Metcalf, "Margaret Thompson, 1911–1992," *AJA* 96 (1992), 547–49.

THOMSEN, CHRISTIAN JÜRGENSEN (1788–1865). Danish archaeologist; formulator of the concept of prehistory in the Three Ages of Stone, Bronze and Iron.

Born into a merchant family in Copenhagen, Thomsen showed an early interest in organizing artifacts with his collection of Roman and Scandinavian coins (1804 and following). In 1816, he became secretary of the new Danish royal commission on antiquities and was put in charge of various collections of Danish material, especially at the University of Copenhagen. In arranging the antiquities for the opening of a national museum, Thomsen utilized a system of three phases in the development of human technology. The idea that humans first used weapons of stone, proceeded to bronze and then to iron, already found in Lucretius (*De rerum natura* 5.1280–94) and other ancient authors and disseminated in Danish scholarship in the later eighteenth century (e.g., by L. S. Vedel Simonsen), was articulated by Thomsen as a systematic principle for arranging artifacts. He described his system in a guidebook to the museum, *Ledetraad til Nordisk Oldkyndighed* (Copenhagen, 1836), a work that was immensely influential, as it was translated into other languages (e.g., *A Guide to Northern Antiquities,* tr. Lord Ellesmere, 1848). His concept is a key one in the disciplines of Bronze Age and Iron Age prehistoric archaeology in Greece and Italy, as elsewhere, though his contribution is seldom recognized by classicists.

In later life, Thomsen served in various government posts and continued to dedicate himself to the creation of displays of antiquities. After his death in 1865, his numismatic collection went to the royal coin cabinet in Copenhagen.

BIBLIOGRAPHY

Daniel, *Short History of Archaeology,* 53–59; B. Graslund, "The Background to Thomsen's Three Age System," and J. Rodden, "The Development of the Three Age System: Archaeology's First Paradigm," in *Towards a History of Archaeology,* ed. G. Daniel (London, 1981), 45–50, 51–68; *Porträtarchiv,* no. 174; Trigger, *History of Archaeological Thought,* 73–79.

THORN-PULLER. See SPINARIO.

THORVALDSEN, BERTEL (ALBERT; 1770–1844). Danish sculptor.

Educated at the Academy of Arts in Copenhagen, after winning several awards for his reliefs, mainly in plaster, Thorvaldsen left Denmark in 1796 to go to Rome. Here he lived and worked until 1838, when he returned to Copenhagen. At that time, an arrangement had been made so that he bequeathed his works and collections of art to the city, which, in return, promised to build a museum for him (*Thorvaldsens Museum, Copenhagen).

In Rome Thorvaldsen studied ancient art and learned to sculpture in marble, partly by copying statues from antiquity. (For most of his sculptures, however, Thorvaldsen made a model on a small scale and had his assistants transfer it to a full-scale marble piece, often taking part in the finishing of the stone work.) Thorvaldsen's first large sculpture, *Jason with the Golden Fleece,* 1803, was an immediate success and was considered an embodiment of *Winckelmann's "noble simplicity and quiet grandeur." In time, Thorvaldsen was to be called the "Pheidias of the north." He became one of the leading artists in Rome, and his fame and works spread to most of Europe.

Like other classicistic sculptures, Thorvaldsen's reliefs, portraits and statues may seem cold and remote today, but his sense of composition and his work-

Portrait of *Bertel Thorvaldsen*, Rome, Deutsches Archäologisches Institut (German Archaeological Institute), 1833. (Deutsches Archäologisches Institut, Rome. Inst. Neg. 76.653.)

manship are exquisite. Up to ca. 1820 his main inspiration was classical literature and myths; from then on, Christian motifs became equally important. His statues of Christ and the Twelve Apostles for the cathedral of Copenhagen and his monument for Pope Pius VII in St. Peter's are famous.

Thorvaldsen's main contribution to archaeology—apart from his acquisitions of ancient art—was his restoration of the then newly found pediments from the temple of Aphaia on *Aigina in 1816–17. Though his work was much admired by his contemporaries, his reconstruction was wrong, and it was most unfortunate that he reworked the fractured surfaces of broken parts in order to add the missing pieces in marble.

BIBLIOGRAPHY
J. M. Thiele, *The Life of Thorvaldsen,* collated from the Danish by M. R. Barnard (London, 1865); +*Bertel Thorvaldsen,* 1, *Skulpturen, Modelle, Bozzetti, Handzeichnungen, Gemälde aus Thorvaldsens Sammlungen;* 2, *Untersuchungen zu seiner Werk und zur Kunst seiner Zeit* (Cologne, 1977); +J. B. Hartmann, *Antike Motive bei Thorvaldsen, Studien zur Antikrezeption des Klassicismus* (Tübingen, 1979); +*Kunstlerleben in Rom, Bertel Thorvaldsen (1770–1844), Der danische Bildhauer und seine deutschen Freunde* (Nuremberg, 1991).

J. MEJER

THORVALDSENS MUSEUM, COPENHAGEN. Danish collection of works of art by or once belonging to, the sculptor Bertel *Thorvaldsen.

Located in the center of Copenhagen, the museum is a remarkable piece of architecture, designed by the Danish architect M. G. Bindesböll and built between 1839 and 1848. It was designed to house all the sculptures Thorvaldsen had bequeathed to the city of Copenhagen, as well as his collections of paintings by other artists (some 300) and antiquities. Later, more works by the sculptor and items of importance for the study of Thorvaldsen have been added. The museum has about 1,000 pieces by Thorvaldsen, whether his original models in plaster or his own and others' final representations in marble; there are also casts of those sculptures that are not in the museum.

From an archaeological point of view, Thorvaldsen's collection of Egyptian (mainly late), Greek, Etruscan and Roman antiquities (almost 10,000 items) is especially interesting because it gives an impression of a private collection in the first half of the nineteenth century (including many fakes). The original exhibition cases have been preserved. In the exhibition rooms are also books on archaeology from the library of Thorvaldsen and of the Danish archaeologist P. O. *Brøndsted. In the classical collection, the main items are bronze objects, Etruscan mirrors, gems, coins from the seventh century B.C. to the Byzantine period and more than one hundred Greek (and a few Etruscan *bucchero) vases, in particular, Attic from the sixth and fifth centuries. They have been cleaned recently, and modern additions have been removed. Among the artists are Oltos, Onesimos, the Altamura Painter, Antimenes Painter, Brygos Painter, Foundry Painter, Geras Painter, Harrow Painter, Penthesilea Painter, the Leagros group and the Thorvaldsen group.

BIBLIOGRAPHY
P. Fossing, *The Thorvaldsen Museum, Catalogue of the Antique Engraved Gems and Cameos* (Copenhagen, 1929); +*Thorvaldsens Museum, Katalog* (Copenhagen, 1975); +T. Melander, *Thorvaldsens Graeske Vaser* (Copenhagen, 1984); +idem, *Thorvaldsens antikker* (Copenhagen, 1993).

J. MEJER

THUGGA (DOUGGA). Ancient city in Tunisia, 100km west of Tunis.

Thugga was founded as a Numidian settlement but came under Carthaginian influence. Following the fall of Carthage to Rome (146 B.C.) and the subsequent colonization of Roman Africa, Dougga continued to be administered locally, although a *pagus* of Roman citizens was governed from Rome. Romanization was successful despite the fact that the city did not attain municipal status until A.D. 205. In 261 it became the Colonia Licinia Septima Aurelia Alexandriana Thuggenses.

Spread out on a plateau and steep hillside, Thugga is considered the best preserved of Roman cities in Tunisia. The site is rich in temples, most notable of which is a Corinthian edifice dedicated to the Capitoline Triad in A.D. 166–67 on behalf of Marcus Aurelius and Lucius Verus. Also dating to the second century A.C. are large parts of the forum area and a well-preserved theater cut into a hillside. The Licinian baths (third century A.C.) are quite complete, and a number of fine houses of Imperial date have yielded mosaics (now chiefly at the Bardo Museum, Tunis).

The site was first described for the European audience by Thomas d'Arcos in 1631. The eighteenth century saw an expanded interest in the site, with visits to it by such luminaries as James Bruce, the consul to Algeria, in 1765. In 1882–83 scientific study of the site was undertaken by J. Schmidt, J. Poinssot, H. Saladin and R. Cagnat. Excavation was soon begun under Dr. Carton and continued by L. Poinssot from 1903 until 1938. The outbreak of World War II and its economic aftermath precluded the resumption of excavation until 1954. Work at Thugga in the last half of the twentieth century has been concentrated on the restoration of the principal monuments of the site; the Tunisian government had begun a campaign to preserve Thugga as early as 1883 and had prohibited encroachment on the site in 1913. Inhabitants living in the ancient city were relocated to a new town, southeast of the site.

BIBLIOGRAPHY

A. Ennabli, s.v. "Thugga," *PECS,* 917–19; C. Poinssot, *Les Ruines de Dougga* (Tunis, 1983).

JOANN McDANIEL

TIARA OF SAITAPHERNES. Solid gold crown 18cm high, a notorious forgery purchased by the *Louvre in 1896 for the great sum of 260,000 francs as a major work of the Hellenistic period.

The tiara had been brought to the attention of French experts when it was exhibited in Vienna as part of the collection of a Russian art dealer, Schapselle Hochmann, who claimed that all his antique gold work had been turned up in the site of a former Greek colony, *Olbia, near Odessa on the Black Sea. The mysterious tiara—Persian in function and form but Greek in epigraphy—had two large historiated friezes, containing genre scenes of Scythian life and anecdotes from the *Iliad.* Between the two registers was an identifying inscription in Greek: "The Senate and People of Olbia to the Great Invincible Saitaphernes." The reference to the Scythian chief Saitaphernes suggested a date in the third century B.C. Hochmann's treasure was first offered to the Imperial Museum in Vienna, whose director, Bruno Buchner, noticed the two hallmarks of a modern forgery: anachronistic eclecticism and damage affecting only the irrelevant or nonpictorial parts. For the same reasons, the piece was turned down for purchase by the *British Museum.

The Louvre, however, purchased the questionable object, just as it was to do a year later with the now-suspect *Dama de Elche. As soon as the tiara entered the Louvre, it came under sharp attack. *Furtwängler was among those who condemned it. The forgery was soon acknowledged by its clever creator, Israel Rouchomovski, a Jewish master goldsmith resident in Odessa, who had drawn his inspiration from sources as diverse as a *Bilderatlas zur Weltsgeschicte* (1882) and the *Antiquités de la Russie Méridionale* (1891). The story was first revealed in *Le Figaro* in March 1903; further details emerged when Rouchomovski himself came to Paris a month later to tell all to a fascinated public. An intriguing footnote to the affair is provided by the report that P. T. Barnum later offered to buy the tiara, asking the Louvre to sell him the ''real'' forgery.

BIBLIOGRAPHY
+A. Furtwängler, *Neuere Falschungen van Antiken* (Berlin, 1899), 29–32; ''Roucho-movski (Rachoumowski), Israel,'' in Thieme—Becker, 29 (1935), 109; O. Kurz, *Fakes,* 2nd ed. (New York, 1967), 210–11.

JOHN F. MOFFITT

TIBERIS. See MARFORIO.

TIMGAD (THAMUGADI). Roman colony in North Africa, located in present-day Algeria; one of the best preserved of all Roman cities.

The city of Timgad was founded by the emperor Trajan in A.D. 100 as a colony for veterans of the army, with the name of Colonia Marciana Trajana Thamugadi. Because of its military connection, it was laid out much like a Roman *castrum* with a grid of north-south and east-west streets intersecting, creating city blocks measuring 20m on a side. The original town was surrounded by a wall in a nearly square pattern, 1,076 feet × 1,171 feet. The whole is regarded as the most perfect specimen of the Roman grid plan. The well-preserved site includes a forum, theater and some fourteen bath establishments, as well as numerous blocks of houses, many of them decorated with mosaics.

In the late second century A.C., new areas outside the grid were developed, breaking free from the checkerboard pattern of the original colony. A municipal public library, housing an estimated 23,000 books, was built in the heart of town in the second half of the third century. Christianity was introduced at Thamugadi by the fourth century, and the town was the seat of the heretical Donatist bishop Optatus. Associated with the Donatists is a great Christian basilica located in the newer part of the town. Thamugadi was occupied in the sixth century by the Byzantines, who reused earlier building materials to erect an enormous cit-adel, the best example of Byzantine architecture in North Africa. The town fell to the Arabs in the eighth century, and, with its irrigation system no longer functioning, it was abandoned.

Thamugadi was brought to the attention of modern Europeans by the Scottish diplomat and artist James Bruce (1730–94), who served as British consul in Algiers from 1763. After the French conquest of Algeria in the 1830s, French scholars took an interest in the remains, with full-scale excavation beginning in 1880. E. Boeswillwald, R. Cagnat and A. Ballu collaborated to publish the early results in *Timgad, une cité africaine sous l'empire romain* (1891–1905). Continued exploration in the twentieth century by the French has uncovered most of the city.

BIBLIOGRAPHY

H. Pfeiffer, "The Roman Library at Timgad," *MAAR* 9 (1931), 157–65; J. Lassus, *Visite à Timgad* (Algiers, 1969); P. Grimal, *Roman Cities,* tr. and ed. G. M. Woloch (Madison, WI, 1983), 261–64.

TIRYNS. Major Bronze Age stronghold situated on a low, oval mound between Argos and Nauplion, in Greece.

Mythology tells us that it was for an early king of Tiryns, Eurystheus, that Herakles performed his twelve labors. The citadel walls, which have always been visible, are built of massive stones and have often been considered the finest specimens of Bronze Age fortification architecture on the Greek mainland. The citadel is normally divided into the upper (southern), middle and lower (northern) sections.

The first to excavate at Tiryns were A. Rangabé and F. Thiersch, who dug there for one day in 1831. *Schliemann made more extensive exploratory excavations for a week in 1876 with fifty workers. Full-scale excavations were conducted by Schliemann and *Dörpfeld in April and May 1884. Dörpfeld returned the following spring to conclude the work. These excavations revealed the plan of the impressive Late Helladic III palace complex in the upper citadel, the importance of the megaron as an architectural unit and the existence of Mycenaean wall paintings. Skeptics, notably W. J. Stillman and F. C. *Penrose, argued that the structure revealed by these excavations was, in fact, Byzantine but were soon refuted. Since 1905 excavations have been conducted by the *German Archaeological Institute, Athens, under the leadership of Dörpfeld, G. *Karo and others. These have clarified the various building periods of the different parts of the citadel. More recently, research has focused on the lower citadel and the settlement outside the walls.

The upper citadel was inhabited from the Early Helladic period, and signs of earlier Mycenaean palaces have been found below the Late Helladic (LH) III remains. The imposing gateway in the eastern citadel walls leads through a succession of interior gates and courts to the main hall of the palace with its central hearth and throne. A bathroom is located nearby. Toward the end of the LH IIIB period the fortification walls were extended to enclose the lower citadel, and tunnels were constructed to an underground reservoir. These developments suggest an external threat. The citadel was destroyed by fire at the close of LH

IIIB. The site continued to be inhabited, however, till it was destroyed by Argos in 470 B.C.

BIBLIOGRAPHY

H. Schliemann, *Mycenae* (London, 1878), 1–19; +idem, *Tiryns* (London, 1886); Deutsches Archäologisches Institut, Athens, *Tiryns* 1–9 (Athens, 1912; Mainz, 1980); +U. Jantzen, *Führer durch Tiryns* (Athens, 1975).

DAVID A. TRAILL

TISCHBEIN, JOHANN HEINRICH WILHELM (1751–1829). German neo-classical painter, engraver and connoisseur of antiquities; close friend to *Goethe.

Wilhelm Tischbein began his artistic career as a portrait painter in Berlin. He traveled to Rome in 1779 and again in 1783, when he met Goethe. Soon afterward he created his famous portrait of the poet in the Roman Campagna (1786–87; Städelsches Kunstinstitut, Frankfurt am Main). In 1789 he proceeded to Naples, where he became director of the Royal Academy of Painting under King Ferdinand; the position lasted until the seizure of Naples by the French in 1799. During this period Tischbein made the important engravings recording the ''second collection'' of Greek vases belonging to Sir William *Hamilton (sunk at sea in HMS *Colossus* in 1798; many of the vases have been recovered since 1975).

The portrait of *Goethe in the Campagna,* perhaps conceived largely by the poet, remains Tischbein's most significant creation. It shows Goethe in a land-

Portrait of *J.H.W. Tischbein*, lithograph by W. Unger, 1824. (Westfälisches Landesmuseum für Kunst und Kulturgeschichte, Münster, Porträtarchiv Diepenbroick. Photo: R. Wakonigg.)

scape of the Tusculum plain, Monte Albano, the lakes of Albano and Nemi and the Appian Way. He is seated upon the "Obelisk of Psammetichos" (cf. *obelisk) broken and obliterated, and at his feet is depicted a sculptured relief with the *Recognition of Orestes by Iphigenia,* the climactic moment in the play Goethe was composing, *Iphigenia auf Tauris.* The sculpture may be based on a sarcophagus relief published by *Winckelmann and imitated by Benjamin *West. The painting provides a moving statement about the attitudes of artists and scholars of early neoclassicism, who approached classical antiquity in search of spiritual renewal and cultural rebirth.

BIBLIOGRAPHY

[H.] Vollmer, "Tischbein, Wilhelm," in Thieme—Becker, 33 (1939), 213–15; A. Birchall, "The Story of *Colossus,*" *ILN* 266 (September 1978), 71–77; J. F. Moffitt, "The Poet and the Painter: J.H.W. Tischbein's 'Perfect Portrait' of *Goethe in the Campagna,*" *ArtB* 65 (1983), 440–55.

JOHN F. MOFFITT

TITIAN (TIZIANO VECELLI; ca. 1488/90–1576). Italian Renaissance painter.

Born at Cadore in the Veneto, Titian went to Venice as a child and soon was employed in the workshops of Gentile and Giovanni Bellini (*Bellini family) and associated with the innovative painter Giorgione in various projects. His own first independent commission was in Padua (legends of St. Anthony in the Scuola di San Antonio, 1510). With Venice as his base, Titian received commissions of ever-increasing importance, from Alfonso d'Este at Ferrara (*Este family) and Duke Federico II of Mantua (*Gonzaga family) and then from the Emperor Charles V, Pope Paul III and King Philip II of Spain. His many travels in connection with this patronage included a stay in Rome in 1645–46. Internationally famed and influential for his portraits as well as mythological and religious paintings, Titian lived a long and immensely productive life.

The relationship of Titian to classical antiquity has been much discussed and not totally settled. It is clear that he and others made the comparison of the Venetian artist with antiquity's greatest painter Apelles and of his patron Charles V with Alexander the Great, Apelles's sponsor. In addition, Titian's knowledge of ancient literature on art and his desire to emulate it are evident in his paintings based on descriptions made by the rhetorician Philostratos the Elder, whose *Imagines* describe paintings that were in a picture gallery in the third century A.C.; for Alfonso d'Este he painted the famous scenes of the *Andrians* and the *Worship of Venus* (by 1523; both in the Prado, Madrid), works of immense charm that show an attentive reading of Philostratos's text but are by no means archaeological in tone.

In the total oeuvre of Titian, both paintings and drawings, copies of antiquities are quite rare. In his early fresco of St. Anthony's *Miracle of the Speaking Infant* is depicted a statue of a Roman emperor in armor that is almost identical to a figure in a relief in Ravenna of the period of Claudius (*Apotheosis of*

Augustus; Museo di San Vitale, Ravenna). A drawing in the *Uffizi, probably done soon after his return from Rome, appears to be a fairly close copy of the sleeping male figure in the relief known in the Renaissance as the *Bed of Polykleitos* (present location unknown). For the rest, many references to classical monuments (especially sarcophagi) may be found in his paintings, but these are far more important for understanding the art of Titian than for securing information about actual antiquities. Indeed, Titian was known to create his own fictitious ancient sculptures, such as the sarcophagus depicted in his *"Sacred and Profane Love"* (ca. 1515; Borghese Gallery, Rome). Among the many "borrowings" (or, perhaps a better term is "creative responses" to ancient sculpture), perhaps most compelling is his reference to the well-known statue of the *Falling Gaul,* which could be seen in the *Grimani family collection in Venice from 1523. Titian's *Martyrdom of St. Lawrence* (1548–57; church of the Gesuiti, Venice) shows an ingenious adaptation of the pose for the dying saint, adding limbs that were missing from the statue at the time. His paintings for a series of *Twelve Caesars* (destroyed by fire; known only in copies), created after 1536 for Federico Gonzaga, must have borne a close relation to emperor portraits in ancient marbles, coins and gems, which he could have studied in the Grimani collections or the ducal holdings at Mantua.

Titian's trip to Rome in 1545–46 naturally stimulated his interest in antiquity (not only for the monuments that he saw in Rome but for those visible in and around Venice upon his return). *Vasari reports that the pope gave the artist magnificent quarters in the Belvedere palace at the *Vatican, and he thus would have had ample opportunity to study the important sculptures in the papal collection. No report in Titian's words survives, but he surely would have seen the *Laocoon at this time. (It is possible that he already knew the work in a cast; but the often-repeated remark that Titian owned such a cast was first made in the eighteenth century.) His reaction to the great masterpiece may have been ironic; Titian is thought to have invented the design of an amusing woodcut, attributed to N. Boldrini, that shows a landscape with three apes in the pose of Laocoon and his two sons.

BIBLIOGRAPHY

+O. J. Brendel, "Borrowings from Ancient Art by Titian," *ArtBull* 37 (1955), 113–25; H. Wethey, *The Paintings of Titian* 1 (London, 1969), 18–19, 23–24, 28–30; M. Perry, "On Titian's 'Borrowings' from Ancient Art: A Cautionary Case," *Tiziano e Venezia 1976* (Vicenza, 1980), 187–91; Bober—Rubinstein, esp. 468; D. Rosand, "An Arc of Flame, On the Transmission of Pictorial Knowledge," *Bacchanals of Titian and Rubens* (Stockholm, 1987), 81–92.

TIVOLI (TIBUR), Italy. Italian town, site of an early Latin settlement and later Roman resort area, located on the Anio River, ca. 27km east of Rome; locality of famed quarries producing travertine limestone.

The site of Tivoli was already inhabited in the Bronze Age and has furnished evidence of both habitation and a necropolis (the Rocca Pia cemetery) from the

Iron Age. As a Latin town independent of Rome, Tivoli prospered for centuries, eventually coming under Roman domination in 90 B.C. To the second or first century B.C. belong several important temples of Tivoli, associated with Hercules, Vesta and the Tiburtine Sibyl, Albunea.

The picturesque location in the foothills of the Sabine mountains overlooking Rome provided a pleasant retreat area for wealthy Romans to build their villas. In addition to *Hadrian's Villa (the most famous of these), Tivoli also held the villas of Marius, Julius Caesar, Sallust, Cassius, Catullus, Horace, Maecenas, Quintilius Varus and Trajan. In Renaissance times the height of Tivoli was fortified by Pope *Pius II with a magnificent castle, the Rocca Pia (ca. 1459); following this, Pope *Julius III made Cardinal Ippolito II d'Este governor of Tivoli (*Este family), and in 1550 the architect Pirro *Ligorio was commissioned to build the splendid Villa d'Este, rivaling—and also stealing from—the richly appointed ancient Roman villas.

Tivoli was a magnetic attraction for travelers, tourists and students of antiquity for centuries. *Alberti, Flavio *Biondo and *Bramante were there, and *Raphael led an archaeological excursion to Tivoli for *Bembo, Castiglione and others. Giuliano da *Sangallo has left an early study (Vatican Library) of the ground plan and elevation of the popular round temple, sometimes said to be dedicated to Vesta, sometimes to the Sibyl. Situated on a spectacular height overlooking the cascading waters of the Anio, the travertine temple was encircled by eighteen Corinthian columns, of which only ten remain. It survived as a result of conversion to a church in the Middle Ages, known by 978 as Santa Maria Rotonda. Adjoining the round shrine on the heights is a small rectangular Ionic temple, which may have been dedicated to the Sibyl Albunea (if the round temple was not). It, too, served as a church, dedicated to St. George.

*Palladio did a reconstruction of the great sanctuary of Hercules (ca. 120m × 180m) located on the southwest slope of Tivoli on a terrace supported by vaulted concrete arcades. Long covered over with later buildings that obscured the plan, the site has never been as popular as the two temples overlooking the Anio.

Frequently, visitors toured the Villa d'Este. Building materials from Hadrian's Villa were reused here, and on view was a magnificent collection of ancient statuary gathered from Hadrian's Villa and elsewhere. Further, there were the numerous Renaissance pavilions of the gardens designed by Ligorio that featured antique themes, such as the remarkable "Fountain of Rome," with its miniature *Pantheon, *Colosseum, *Column of Trajan, *Column of Marcus Aurelius, *Arch of Titus and *Arch of Constantine. The *Artemis of Ephesos was the centerpiece of the "Organ Fountain," where she was described as the goddess of nature.

The visit to Tivoli became de riguer for tourists of the eighteenth and nineteenth centuries, and we have the ecstatic descriptions of the place by John Evelyn, Chateaubriand, Ralph Waldo Emerson and Florence Nightingale. By the eighteenth century, however, the Villa d'Este had fallen into decline, and the

Temple of the Sibyl, Tivoli, engraving by G. B. Mercati (1600–ca. 1637), Veroli, Biblioteca Giovardiana. (Deutsches Archäologisches Institut, Rome. Inst. Neg. 80.794.)

marbles were sold off to other collections: to the *Capitoline went the *Satyr* by Praxiteles, *Meleager, Pallas, Diana* and *Pandora;* to Henry *Blundell went *Jupiter, Juno, Mercury, Mars* and others. Further, the temples were less protected in this period, as they ceased to be used for churches—the round temple by 1828 and the rectangular one by 1884.

The series of villas dotting the hills both north and south of Tivoli, higher up than Hadrian's Villa, the better to receive the waters of the Anio, have evocative names. But there is little proof for the ownership of the "Villa of Catullus," "Villa of Quintilus Varus," "Villa of Brutus" or "Villa of Cassius." Marbles were plundered from these, too, and sent to Rome and elsewhere. From a villa perhaps belonging to the Pisones were taken, in 1779, sixteen herms of Greek philosophers and poets (now in the *Prado) as well as the famous head of the *Alexander* Azara (now in the Louvre). In the *Vatican is the group of *Apollo* with the *Muses,* found at the "Villa of Cassius" in 1775 by Domenico de Angelis.

BIBLIOGRAPHY
+N. Neuerburg, "The Other Villas of Tivoli," *Archaeology* 21 (1968), 288–97; W. L. MacDonald, s.v: "Tibur (Tivoli)," *PECS* 921–22; +L. B. Dal Maso, *The Villa of Ippolito II d'Este at Tivoli* (Florence, 1978); R. Keaveney, *Views of Rome,* catalog of exhibition (London, 1988), 249–59.

TIZIO, SIGISMONDO (1458–1528). Italian chronicler, priest and amateur archaeologist.

After taking a degree in civil and canon law from the University of Perugia, Tizio moved to Siena in 1487. Employed as tutor to the sons of Andrea Todeschini Piccolomini, a member of Siena's most prominent family, he was eventually fired for his propensity to gossip. Shortly thereafter, he entered the priesthood and was appointed a canon of Siena Cathedral; in this position he remained for the rest of his long life.

Apart from his priestly duties, Tizio seems to have been a virtual graphomaniac, composing two long chronicles and several shorter works, none of them ever published. Only a book of notes survives from his *Historia barbarica.* His most ambitious project, the *Historia senensium,* or *History of the Sienese,* represents an entire adult lifetime of work. Thousands of folio pages long, the six-volume autograph text, rebound, is now preserved in the Vatican Library.

The *History's* first volume begins with a long account of the Etruscans, tracing not only the Etruscan history of Siena but also that of each of the twelve cities of the Etruscan League. Here Tizio has compiled the first systematic collection of Etruscan inscriptions and the first-known attempt at an Etruscan lexicon. The latter is no more than a curiosity; the former contains information about early collectors and early knowledge of Etruria that is of enduring value. Initially a follower of *Annio da Viterbo, Tizio came to regard the Dominican forger with contempt. He reserved unmitigated scorn for another early Etruscological forgery, the *Gesta Porsemnae regis,* composed ca. 1460 by the Florentine cleric

Leonardo Dati. Despite his idiosyncratic Latin and occasional credulity, Tizio has many admirable qualities as an early antiquarian. His faithful record of archaeological discoveries in his own day provides a useful chronological anchor, and his own trips to *Chiusi and elsewhere provide credible eyewitness reports.

BIBLIOGRAPHY

P. Piccolomini, *La Vita e l'opera di Sigismondo Tizio (1458–1528)* (Rome, 1903); O. A. Danielsson, *Etruskische Inschriften in Handschriftlicher Überlieferung* (Uppsala, 1928); M. Martelli Cristofani, "MS Sloane 3524," in *Siena: Le Origini: Testimonianze e miti archeologici,* ed. M. Cristofani (Florence, 1979), 136–43; M. Cristofani, "Le iscrizioni etrusche," in *Siena: Le Origini: Testimonianze e miti archeologici,* ed. M. Cristofani (Florence, 1979), 125–26.

INGRID ROWLAND

TOMB OF CAECILIA METELLA ("CAPO DI BOVE"). Large Roman tomb on the *Via Appia, just before the third milestone from Rome.

The identity of the people mentioned in the inscription on the tomb (*CIL* VI 1274) has produced a considerable volume of literature, but it is now generally agreed that Caecilia Metella was the daughter of Q. Caecilius Metellus Creticus (consul in 69 B.C.) and was married to a son of Crassus the triumvir, M. Licinius Crassus, who died in 49 B.C. The tomb consists of a circular drum 29.50m in diameter, 11m high, on a square base 7m high. Near the top of the drum is a marble frieze decorated with garlands slung between bucrania, hence the tomb's popular name of "Capo di Bove."

The tomb stands on a rise and commands a good view of the road. It became part of a fortress of the Caetani family in ca. 1300, and it was then that the upper part of the drum was repaired and replaced by medieval merlons. The original conical roof or tumulus of the tomb is last recorded in the eleventh century. The base was plundered of its travertine facing, already gone by the time *Lafréry published a drawing of the tomb in 1549. *Lanciani records that a stonecutter involved in this spoliation, in the pontificate of *Paul III (1534–49), found the entrance to a burial chamber containing a large sarcophagus. It is of much later date than the tomb and cannot have been used for Caecilia Metella herself. The tomb was threatened with destruction by *Sixtus V in 1589 but was saved by popular demand. It seems that in the sixteenth century it was celebrated for its echo as much as for its antiquity.

Careful drawings of the tomb, including a plan and section, were published by *Bartoli in 1697, and *Piranesi produced both a view of the tomb and a speculative illustration of how it was constructed. *Byron described the tomb at some length in Canto IV of *Childe Harold's Pilgrimage* (1812), "a stern round tower of other days," and he speculates about its owner, "the wealthiest Roman's wife; Behold his love or pride!"

BIBLIOGRAPHY
Lanciani, *Destruction of Ancient Rome*, 96, 236–37; A. E. Gordon—J. S. Gordon, *Album of Dated Latin inscriptions*, Pt. 1 (Berkeley, 1958), 30–32; F. Coarelli, *Dintorni di Roma* (Rome, 1981), 47–48.

GLENYS DAVIES

TOMB OF EURYSACES, Rome. Roman tomb of the baker Marcus Vergilius Eurysaces and his wife, Atistia, erected in the late first century B.C. in a prominent position between the Viae Labicana and Praenestina near the later *Porta Maggiore.

Portraits of the deceased in relief appear on the façade, and a frieze depicting baking operations runs around the three other sides of the monument. Under Honorius (A.D. 403), the façade of the tomb was destroyed, and the structure was incorporated into a round defensive tower of the rebuilt Porta Praenestina of Aurelian. Part of the tomb remained visible, however, and one of the inscriptions on the monument was noted already in the mid-fifteenth century, and the exposed part of the edifice was sketched by Sallustio Peruzzi. In 1838, under Pope *Gregory XVI, the later accretions to the Porta Maggiore were removed, and the newly exposed monument was studied and drawn by *Canina and others. Further excavations took place in 1955–57. The portrait relief is now in the Palazzo dei Conservatori (*Capitoline Museums). The tomb and its frieze figure prominently in modern studies of Roman "popular" or "plebeian" art.

BIBLIOGRAPHY
L. Grifi, *Brevi cenni di un monumento scoperto a Porta Maggiore* (Rome, 1838); L. Canina, "Descrizione . . . del sepolcro di Marco Virgilio Eurisace," *AnnInst* 12 (1838), 226–29; +P. Ciancio Rossetto, *Il Sepolcro del fornaio Marco Virgilio Eurisace a Porta Maggiore* (Rome, 1973); D.E.E. Kleiner, *Roman Group Portraiture, The Funerary Reliefs of the Late Republic and Early Empire* (New York, 1977), 11–13, 202–3.

FRED S. KLEINER

TOMB OF OVID. Burial place, much disputed, of the Roman poet Ovid (43 B.C.–A.D. 17).

Ovid is presumed to have died at Tomis (modern Constanţa, Romania). His tomb is not extant, though Ovidian tombs have been imagined at Tomis and elsewhere in the Black Sea area, at Szombathely (Hungary) and at Rome; and one ancient sepulchral chamber near Rome was misidentified as Ovid's (cf. *Tomb of Vergil). Eusebius's *Chronica* says that Ovid was buried at Tomis; Caecilius Minutianus Apuleius (*apud* L. Coelius Rhodiginus, *Antiquae lectiones,* 1516, XIII.1) says that the barbarians put up a tomb before his former house. According to a story told to G. G. Pontano by George of Trebizond (1395–1484), the citizens of Tomis erected, by public subscription, a splendid sepulchre before the city gate. This account succeeded various medieval legends in popularity during the Italian Renaissance. The story most current in the German Renaissance, recorded by Wolfgang Lazius (1551) and by Caspar Brusch (1553),

View of the "Tomb of Ovid," attributed to E. F. Burney. (The Warburg Institute, University of London.)

has Ovid's tomb discovered at Szombathely (ancient Savaria) in 1508. To this story was later added a new epitaph, published by Tobias Fendt in 1574 and included in Lorenz Müller's romance (1585) of the finding and carrying off of Ovid's tomb near the Black Sea about Easter 1581. The tomb was subsequently reported as in Poland and in Russia. A fancy tomb at Rome is engraved in Richard de St. Non, *Voyage pittoresque . . .* , 1781–6, I.160.

The painted tomb chamber of the Nasonii in the suburbs of Rome was, for two centuries after its discovery in 1674, identified as Ovid's. Its paintings were described by G. P. *Bellori and engraved by P. S. *Bartoli (1680ff.); Bartoli, his sons and others made watercolors. Six panels from the tomb are in the *British Museum.

BIBLIOGRAPHY

+J. B. Trapp, "Ovid's Tomb", *JWarb,* 36 (1973), 35–76, repr. w. additions and corrections in idem, *Essays on the Renaissance and the Classical Tradition* (Aldershot, 1990), no. 4; C. Pace, "Pietro Sante Bartoli: Drawings in Glasgow University Library after Roman Paintings and Mosaics," *PBSR,* 47 (1979), 118–38; J. B. Trapp, "Portraits of Ovid in the Middle Ages and the Renaissance," *Die Rezeption der 'Metamorphosen' des Ovid in der Neuzeit: Der Antike Mythos in Text und Bild,* ed. H. Walter—H.-J. Horn—G. Huber-Rebenich (Berlin, 1995).

J. B. TRAPP

"TOMB OF PHILIP II," Vergina. Unplundered Macedonian royal tomb, discovered in 1977 by Manolis *Andronikos.

The tomb is one of three in the Great Tumulus at *Vergina, where the Macedonians are thought to have had their royal burial grounds. The largest known Macedonian tomb, it featured a limestone barrel vault and contained the cremated remains of a male in the main chamber and of a female in the antechamber, each having a wealthy array of associated grave gifts. In the main chamber were a gold larnax (ash chest), gold wreath with oak leaves and acorns, miniature ivory portrait heads, gilded silver diadem and many other items; in the antechamber were a smaller gold larnax, gilded bronze greaves (shin guards), Scythian gold gorytus (bow and arrow case) and numerous other finds. Andronikos identified the owners of the tomb as Philip II (d. 336 B.C.), father of Alexander the Great, and his wife, Kleopatra (in the antechamber), and recognized the images of Philip II and Alexander the Great in the ivory portrait heads.

Considerable dispute ensued, with an opposing school of thought arguing that there were features of the tomb or grave goods that belonged to the fourth quarter of the fourth century B.C., too late for Philip II. P. W. Lehmann and others, arguing that the barrel vault did not develop in the area of mainland Greece until after the conquests of Alexander, countered that the tomb was actually that of Philip III Arrhidaios, half-brother of Alexander, and his warrior wife, Eurydike, both of whom died in 317 B.C. S. Rotroff pointed out that the black-gloss saltcellars found in the tomb are of a type first attested in the last quarter of the fourth century B.C. Supporting Andronikos's claim is the anthropological reconstruction by A.J.N.W. Prag of remains of the male head from the main chamber, which is interpreted to show Philip II with the results of a wound that left him blind in one eye. The discovery of the tomb and the resulting controversy stimulated great interest in the archaeology of Macedonia.

BIBLIOGRAPHY

P. Lehmann, "The So-Called Tomb of Philip II: A Different Interpretation," *AJA* 84 (1980), 527–31; B. Barr-Sharrar—E. N. Borza, eds., *Macedonia and Greece in Late Classical and Early Hellenistic Times, Studies in the History of Art* 10 (Washington, DC, 1982); M. Andronikos, *Vergina, The Royal Tombs and the Ancient City* (Athens, 1984); A.J.N.W. Prag, "Reconstructing King Philip II: The 'Nice' Version," *AJA* 94 (1990), 237–47; articles by J. H. Musgrave, E. D. Carney, et al. in *The Ancient World* 22.2 (1991).

TOMB OF REMUS. See PYRAMID OF CESTIUS.

TOMB OF THE HORATII AND CURIATII. Late Republican Roman tomb located on the Via Appia in Albano, outside Rome.

The unusual form of the tomb consists of five conical elements that rise from the center and corners of a square base. Pope *Pius II recorded (1463) the local tradition associating it with the Roman and Alban triplet brothers (Livy 1.25), of whom only one survived in hand-to-hand combat. Pirro *Ligorio thought it was the tomb Hadrian built for Pompey. A number of artists represented it, including A. da *Sangallo, B. *Peruzzi and *Piranesi, who depicted it four times and recognized its similarity to the tomb of Porsena at *Chiusi described by Pliny the Elder (*NH* 36.91–93). Others suggested it was the tomb of Porsena's son, Arruns, who fell in battle near Albano. At the request of Antonio *Canova, the tomb was extensively restored by Giuseppe *Valadier (1825–37). The base of the tomb as restored measures fifty feet on each side, with a height of twenty-three feet.

BIBLIOGRAPHY

A. Nibby, *Del Monumento sepolcrale detto volgarmente degli Orazii e Curiazii* (Rome, 1854); L. C. Gabel, ed., *Memoirs of a Renaissance Pope: The Commentaries of Pius II,* tr. F. A. Gragg (New York, 1959), 316; L. Corbi et al., "Il sepolcro degli Orazi e Curiazi," *Ricerche di Storia dell'Arte* 31 (1987), 13–14; R. Keaveney, *Views of Rome,* catalog of exhibition (London, 1988), 274–76.

JACK FREIBERG

TOMB OF THE SCIPIOS, Rome. Mausoleum, south of Rome between the Via Appia and Via Latina, belonging to the Cornelii Scipiones, a Roman family prominent especially in the years of the Middle Republic.

The approximate placement of the family's tomb was known from comments by several ancient authors, but its location was pinpointed only in 1614, when there came to light a sarcophagus bearing an inscription (thereafter broken off and sold) identifying its occupant as L. Cornelius Scipio, consul in 259 B.C. The significance of this discovery was not realized, however, until May 1780, when

''Tomb of the Horatii and Curiatii'' at Albano, engraving from B. de Montfaucon, *L'Antiquité expliquée et representée en figures* 5 (1719–24). (The Warburg Institute, University of London.)

the Sassi family—in excavating a section of their vineyard to enlarge a wine cellar—dug anew into the tomb. After an initial discovery of two inscribed sarcophagi, the monument was identified, and a three-year exploration (or better, plundering) was begun. Subterranean galleries were cleared, resulting in the discovery of more inscribed sarcophagi and three sculptured portrait heads, one of which, laureate, has sometimes been thought to represent the early Latin poet Ennius, who evidently was buried in the Scipios' tomb and a statue of whom was located, according to Livy (38.56.4), "in Scipionum monumento." The tomb's contents entered the *Vatican Museums, where they are now displayed together.

The façade was partially cleared in this excavation. Coarelli has reconstructed it in two levels, on the pattern of a Hellenistic stage set, the upper story with engaged half-columns framing three niches for statuary. The lower level, with the central arched entrance to the tomb chambers, today retains poorly preserved traces of wall painting, apparently historical in nature.

On Lanciani's suggestion, the city of Rome bought the land in 1880; the whole complex was restored in 1926.

Lanciani surmised that the tomb was built into a tufa quarry, on land owned by the Scipios, at about the time the Via Appia was opened in 312 B.C. Burials here commenced with the interment of L. Cornelius Scipio Barbatus, consul in 298 B.C. (father of the consul of 259 B.C. and more illustrious than the younger man), and continued well into the second century. The monument evidently was regarded by later ages as historically important, for it was maintained and repaired into the fourth century A.C.

BIBLIOGRAPHY

+F. Piranesi—E. Q. Visconti, *Monumento degli Scipioni* (Rome, 1785); R. Lanciani, *The Ruins and Excavations of Ancient Rome* (Boston, 1897), 321–27; +Nash, II, 352–56; +F. Coarelli, *Il Sepolcro degli Scipioni a Roma* (Rome, 1988); Richardson, *New Topographical Dictionary,* 359–60.

DAVID L. THOMPSON

TOMB OF VERGIL, Naples. Legendary burial place of the Roman poet Vergil (70–19 B.C.).

According to ancient authorities (Suetonius, Donatus), Vergil was buried near *Naples, on the Via Puteolana "before the second milestone." His tomb, no longer extant, was acquired by Silius Italicus (d. ca. 101 A.D.), who kept it as a shrine, and, according to later legend, St. Paul visited it. *Petrarch (1304–74) and *Boccaccio (1313–75) had seen a tomb said to be Vergil's. This was presumably the ancient Roman columbarium (cf. *columbaria) still standing near the Piedigrotta entrance to the so-called Grotta di Virgilio (Grotta Vecchia), the tunnel constructed in Roman Imperial times through the hill of Posilipo to connect Naples and Pozzuoli.

In 1453 Flavio *Biondo reported that he could not find Vergil's tomb. By 1543 at the latest, the columbarium at Posilipo was being shown to tourists as

"Vergil's tomb"; by 1560 it was said to contain a marble urn and an epitaph. This epitaph was said to have been composed by the poet himself. From 1554, other epitaphs were composed and set up near the tomb. In 1591, S. Mazzella refers to a bay tree growing from the tomb's top; later legend said it had been planted by Petrarch. "Vergil's tomb" and the Grotta were on the itinerary of tourists in Southern Italy from the sixteenth to the nineteenth centuries. In Napoleonic times a monument to Vergil was projected nearby. The columbarium is now in the Parco Virgiliano of the Comune of Naples (1930).

The first extant picture of an imaginary tomb of Vergil is a woodcut in S. Brant's Vergil (1502). The columbarium was engraved by Tobias Fendt (1574) and drawn by Jean-Jacques *Boissard at the end of the century. It was often drawn, painted and engraved from the seventeenth to the nineteenth centuries.

BIBLIOGRAPHY

E. Cocchia, La Tomba di Virgilio (Turin, 1889 [cf. idem, Saggi filologici, 3 (Turin, 1902), 135–249], repr. Rome, 1980); M. Capasso, Il Sepolcro di Virgilio (Naples, 1983); +J. B. Trapp, "The Grave of Vergil," JWarb, 47 (1984), 1–31; idem, "Virgil and the Monuments," Transactions of the Virgil Society 18 (1986), 1–17, both repr. with additions and corrections in idem, Essays on the Renaissance and the Classical Tradition (Aldershot, 1990), nos. 5–6.

J. B. TRAPP

TORLONIA FAMILY. Noble Italian family, known for its banking wealth, used to purchase antiquities.

The Torlonia family arrived in Rome from France in the mid-eighteenth century. The head of the family was GIOVANNI (1754–1829), who founded the Banca Torlonia and accumulated a fortune, which was quickly spent on the acquisition of property. In his vertiginous ascent Giovanni—all in one year, 1797—purchased the land for the Villa Torlonia on the Via Nomentana and the Torlonia Palace in Piazza Venezia (later destroyed) and acquired the title of marchese. *Valadier designed the enormous palace of the villa, bringing in cartloads of travertine limestone from the *Baths of Titus on the Esquiline for the construction. Soon it could be said that the Torlonia holdings eclipsed those of the *Borghese family and *Ludovisi family in their best days.

Upon the death of Giovanni, his son ALESSANDRO (1800–86) assumed leadership of the family and the task of promoting its image and prestige. He made many additions to the Villa Torlonia, ever competing with the Borghese, so that it was adorned with false ruins and invented temples, sphinxes and mosaics. In 1842 he erected there two modern obelisks in honor of his parents, before an audience that included Pope *Gregory XVI and *Ludwig I of Bavaria. Inside the palace the adornments included a sculptured frieze by *Thorvaldsen, recalling the *Parthenon and having the flattering theme of the Triumph of Alexander.

In the second half of his life Alessandro changed radically and decided to liquidate the bank, turning to the surprising combination of religion and archaeology. In 1856 he purchased *Portus, the site of Trajan's harbor, and had excavations carried out there as well as at *Cerveteri and *Vulci. He also acquired many antiquities through purchase; in 1866 he bought the Villa Albani (*Albani family) with its rich collection. His later years were sad, as he suffered from many tragic personal problems, including the insanity of his wife.

The family was in decline, and the villa was neglected until Alessandro's grandson, GIOVANNI (1873–1938) sought to recover prestige for the Torlonia name. A friend of Mussolini, Giovanni offered him the use of his villa when he wanted, a privilege the Italian leader retained well after Torlonia's death in 1938. Giovanni was praised for his work in draining the swamps around Portus; for the occasion, he allowed the archaeologist G. *Lugli to study and publish the Torlonia property. At the death of Giovanni, his descendants disputed the inheritance, and the villa was once again left to sink into disrepair.

The collections of art in the Villa Albani have been kept closed to the general public, and for many years Portus was not open to visitors. Over 600 sculptures were placed in the Museo Torlonia on the Via della Lungara, likewise of limited access; they include items from Portus and from various old collections of the city of Rome (*Giustiniani family, *Cesarini family).

BIBLIOGRAPHY
+C. L. Visconti, *Indicazione delle sculture del Museo Torlonia* (Rome, 1884–85); s.v. "Collezioni archeologiche," *EAA,* suppl. (1973), 250; C. Gasparri, "Materiali per servire allo studio del Museo Torlonia di scultura antica," *MemLinc* 377 (1980), ser. 8, 24.2; A. Campitelli, *Villa Torlonia, Storia ed architettura* (Rome, 1989).

TORRENTIUS, LAEVINUS (LIEVEN VAN DER BEKE; 1525–95). Flemish humanist, poet, antiquarian and ecclesiastic.

Born in Ghent, van der Beke went to Louvain to study law and literature (1540–45). He continued his studies in Paris, Padua and Bologna, where he obtained his doctorate in law in 1552. He subsequently resided in Rome; there he became acquainted with Fulvio *Orsini, with whom he remained in contact after his return to Liège in 1557. After a second trip to Rome in 1570, he returned to Belgium for good, settling in Liège, where he helped found the Collegium. He lived in a magnificent residence designed by Lambert *Lombard on the Place St. Pierre, frequently entertaining other humanists. Abraham Ortelius and Jan Vivianus were among those who admired his library and collection. Van der Beke was appointed bishop of Antwerp in 1585 and elected archbishop of Malines in 1594 but did not live to be confirmed.

He owned a large collection of antiquities, including bronze sculpture, gems and vases inscribed with hieroglyphics. His coin cabinet held 556 Roman Republican coins, 1,700 Imperial specimens and 136 Greek coins. But he preferred epigraphy to numismatics; a manuscript in Brussels contains inscriptions he transcribed. In 1573 he purchased the library and coin collection of his friend Carolus de Lange (Langius) when the latter died.

The collection was bequeathed to the Jesuit college at Liège. An early seventeenth-century catalog of van der Beke's coins and gems is preserved. The library was confiscated by Maria Theresa in 1773, and the numismatic collection was surreptitiously acquired by J. H. Ghesquière in Ghent. It was sold off in 1812. *Peiresc apparently visited the collection and made notes on some of van der Beke's coins and gems, but none of the gems have been identified. A silver cup with Bacchic symbols formerly in his possession is drawn in the Codex Pighianus (fol.223; *Pighius).

BIBLIOGRAPHY

V. Tourneur, "La Collection Laevinus Torrentius," *RBN* (1914), 281–332; A. Roersch, *L'Humanisme belge à Liège à l'époque de la Renaissance* (Louvain, 1933), 117–39.

MARJON VAN DER MEULEN

TOTALITÄTSIDEAL. The conviction that literary sources alone cannot provide a comprehensive reconstruction of antiquity but that all material remains (archaeological, architectural, epigraphical, numismatic) must be exploited.

F. A. *Wolf partially anticipated this ideal. Influenced by *Goethe, F. G. *Welcker proposed the view (1824) while reconstructing lost tragedies. K. O. *Müller exemplified its practice. *Wilamowitz, like *Jahn and his *monumental philology, repeatedly urged it, adding, "[O]ne must see the forest and the trees," master generalization based on detail. Growing conviction by philologists that archaeology was indispensable ensured university approval of the new discipline. Decline of classical education since 1914 and the vast accumulation of imperfectly published finds have split archaeology and philology and substituted isolated specialization.

BIBLIOGRAPHY

R. Kekulé, *Das Leben Friedrich Gottlieb Welcker's nach seinen eignen Aufzeichungen und Briefen* (Leipzig, 1880), 359; U. von Wilamowitz-Moellendorff, *Geschichte der Philologie,* 3rd ed. (Leipzig, 1959), 57; H. Patzer, "Wilamowitz und die Klassische Philologie," *Festschrift Franz Dornseiff zum 65. Geburtstag,* ed. Horst Kusch (Leipzig, 1953), 244–57.

WILLIAM M. CALDER III

TOVAR, ANTONIO (1911–85). Spanish linguist and philologist.

Though he was not an archaeologist, Tovar's work (well over 300 books and articles) on the languages, toponymy and ethnography of ancient Iberia is fundamental to the interpretation and identification of archaeological sites and inscriptional finds throughout Spain and Portugal.

Born in Valladolid, educated in Spain, France and Germany, Tovar had an illustrious career as a scholar, educator and administrator, holding important posts at the universities of Madrid, Buenos Aires, Illinois, Tübingen and Salamanca, where he was rector from 1951 to 1956. He also held doctorates honoris causa from the universities of Munich, Buenos Aires and Dublin and was a member of the Real Academia Española.

At the personal request of Adolf *Schulten, Tovar continued the German's work on the geography and ethnography of ancient Iberia, *Iberische Landeskunde.* His three volumes (1, *Baetica,* and 2, *Lusitania,* in German, 3, *Tarraconensis,* in Spanish) complement Schulten's book of the same name and provide the only comprehensive correlation of the literary and epigraphical evidence to the archaeological record of ancient cities, towns and tribes throughout the peninsula.

BIBLIOGRAPHY

A. Tovar, *The Ancient Languages of Spain and Portugal* (New York, 1961); idem, *Iberische Landeskunde,* 1–2 (Baden-Baden, 1974–76); idem, "Las inscripciones de Botorrita y de Peñalba de Villastar y los límites orientales de los celtíberos," *Hispania Antigua* 3 (1973), 367–405; *Geografía de Iberia,* 3 (Baden-Baden, 1989).

PHILIP O. SPANN

TOWER OF THE WINDS (HOROLOGION OF ANDRONIKOS), Athens.
Greek clock tower.

The Tower of the Winds was designed by Andronikos of Kyrrhos, a Macedonian. It is an octagonal tower, built of Pentelic marble, measuring 3.20m on a side and standing with its roof intact to a height of ca. 15.30 m; two distyle porches gave access from the northeast and northwest sides. The building takes its popular name from the sculpted male figures with wings, representing the winds, that adorn the top of each of the eight faces. According to Vitruvius, there was a bronze triton on top of the roof that served as a weathervane, turning to point at the appropriate wind. On each face below the wind there are the incised lines of a sundial; the present gnomons were installed in 1845. The interior of the building housed a large water clock or *klepsydra.* The actual mechanism of the clock has long since disappeared, though cuttings in the floor indicate its position, and a large cylindrical chamber attached to the south face apparently held the water tanks.

The structure is first mentioned and called a horologium by Varro in his *De re rustica* (3.5.17) and is described in some detail by Vitruvius (1.6.4). Traditionally dated in the first century B.C., the building has recently been more plausibly assigned to the middle of the second century B.C. (von Freeden). Since its construction, it has survived, virtually intact, the siege of Sulla (86 B.C.), the Herulian sack (267 A.D.), the attack of Alaric (395), the Slavic invasion (582/3), the Frankish siege (1205) and the siege of the *Akropolis (1826). Standing in the heart of the old city, it was used in the Turkish period as a *teckeh,* associated with the nearby mosque (Fethiye Cami). A *mihrab* was cut in the inner wall toward Mecca, and an early print by *Dodwell (1805) shows Nevlana dervishes at their devotions inside the building.

BIBLIOGRAPHY

+J. Stuart—N. Revett, *The Antiquities of Athens* (London, 1762) I, ch. 2, 13–25; D. J. de Solla Price, "The Tower of the Winds," *National Geographic Magazine* (April 1967), 586–96; J. Noble—D. Price, "The Water Clock in the Tower of the Winds," *AJA* 72 (1968), 345–55; Travlos 281–88; J. von Freeden, *OIKIA KURRĒSTOU* (Rome, 1983).

JOHN McK. CAMP II

View of the *Tower of the Winds*, Athens, from J. Stuart–N. Revett, *The Antiquities of Athens*, 1 (1762).

TOWNLEY, CHARLES (1737–1805). English collector.

As a member of an old Lancashire Catholic family, Charles Townley had to seek his education abroad, at Douai, after which he entered Parisian society under the tutelage of his grandfather's brother. His father having died in 1742, he returned home in 1758 to enter his inheritance.

In 1767 he went to Rome and there in 1768 began his collection of marble sculptures with a fragmentary group of two knucklebone-players (so identified by *Winckelmann), formerly in the Palazzo Barberini. Old Roman collections were a major source of sculptures for young Englishmen on the *Grand Tour, and over the years Townley was also to make acquisitions from the Maccarani, *Giustiniani, *Odescalchi and Burioni collections, from the Villa *Mattei and the Villa Montalto and from Cardinals *Albani and Passionei. Many purchases were made through the banker and dealer Thomas *Jenkins, who, together with Gavin *Hamilton and James *Byres, was also involved in the speculative excavations that were the other main source of ancient sculptures. Townley's collection was enriched by Hamilton's excavations at *Hadrian's Villa, at ''Monte Cagnolo'' near Lanuvium, at *Ostia and elsewhere. For much of 1772 and 1773 Townley was again in Italy, chiefly in Rome and Naples, also traveling as far as Taranto and *Syracuse.

After returning to England, he bought sculptures from many English collections, including those of Topham Beauclerck, Lyde Brown, Thomas Beaumont, Matthew Duane, the Duchess of Portland, the Earl of Bessborough and Lord Cawdor. In 1781 he commissioned Johan Zoffany to paint him with d'*Hancarville and his friends Charles Greville and Thomas Astle in the library of his house in Park Street, surrounded by an imaginary arrangement of sculptures.

He published little but encouraged others to write about his collection, and himself compiled a series of manuscript catalogs for the use of visitors. Together with notebooks of purchases and other documents, they provide a wealth of information about how the collection was acquired and exhibited. He was elected fellow of the *Society of Antiquaries in 1786 and appointed trustee of the *British Museum in 1791.

His last major purchase was a marble copy of Myron's *Diskobolos,* found in Hadrian's Villa in 1791. Following his death in 1805, his marble sculptures were purchased by Act of Parliament for £20,000 and deposited in the British Museum. The rest of his collection, chiefly bronzes, terracottas, coins and sealstones, was purchased from his heirs in 1814. His papers were acquired by the museum in 1992.

BIBLIOGRAPHY

E. Edwards, *Lives of the Founders of the British Museum* (London, 1870); B. F. Cook, ''The Townley Marbles in Westminster and Bloomsbury,'' *British Museum Yearbook* 2 (1977), 34–78; idem, *The Townley Marbles* (London, 1985).

B. F. COOK

Charles Townley in his Gallery, by J. Zoffany, 1781–83. Burnley, Towneley Hall Art Gallery and Museums. (Towneley Hall Art Gallery and Museums, Burnley Borough Council.)

TRADESCANT, JOHN (THE ELDER; d. 1638) and TRADESCANT, JOHN (THE YOUNGER; 1608–62). English gardeners and collectors.

By profession the Tradescants were both gardeners. The elder Tradescant worked successively for the earls of Salisbury, Lord Wotton and the Duke of Buckingham, before being appointed "Keeper of His Majesty's Gardens, Vines and Silkworms" at Oatlands Palace in Surrey, a position inherited by the son on the death of the father. Between them the Tradescants were responsible for the introduction of many exotic plant species to England, notably through visits by the elder to Muscovy, the Low Countries, France and the Mediterranean and by the younger to Virginia. As much as for their contributions to gardening, however, the Tradescants are remembered for the museum—"the Ark"—that they established at their home in Lambeth, then on the outer fringes of London. The Ark was the best-known and most extensive museum in Britain in its day and can also claim the distinction of being the first to open its doors to the public at large: entrance was gained by payment of a small charge instead of by the letters of introduction that were essential for admittance to private collections elsewhere.

In composition the Tradescants' collection was very diverse: it was, indeed, a veritable "cabinet of curiosities." Side by side with hundreds of "natural rarities"—zoological, mineral and botanical specimens—were "artificial rarities," including antiquities. Some of these were no doubt acquired by the Tradescants themselves on their travels; others were given as gifts or may have been purchased. Roman coins and Renaissance medals formed the most numerous category of antiquities, but the catalog of the collection—prepared with help from Elias *Ashmole and Dr. Thomas Wharton and published in 1656—mentions also cameos and intaglios, "Effigies of divers Personages of honor, note and quality," "*Phaëton* with His Chariot and Horses, excellent waxworks," Egyptian idols of Osiris and Anubis and Roman vessels. Visiting the Ark in 1657, John Evelyn particularly admired "the antient Roman, Indian and other Nations Armour, shilds and weapons."

In 1675 the Tradescant collection passed by deed of gift to Elias Ashmole and through him to the University of Oxford. The *Ashmolean Museum was built at Oxford to house the collection, some parts of which may still be seen there.

BIBLIOGRAPHY

J. Tradescant, *Musæum Tradescantianum* (London, 1656); M. Allan, *The Tradescants, Their Plants Gardens and Museum 1570–1662* (London, 1964); A. MacGregor, ed., *Tradescant's Rarities, Essays on the Foundation of the Ashmolean Museum, 1683, with a Catalogue of the Surviving Early Collections* (Oxford, 1983); P. Leith-Ross, *The John Tradescants, Gardeners to the Rose and Lily Queen* (London, 1984).

ARTHUR MacGREGOR

TREASURY OF ATREUS (TOMB OF AGAMEMNON), Mycenae. Mycenaean "beehive" tholos tomb, dating to the thirteenth century B.C., the best preserved of all such tombs.

Portrait of *John Tradescant the Younger* (*l.*) with his friend Zythepsa of Lambeth, attributed to Emanuel de Critz. Oxford, The Ashmolean Museum. (Museum.)

Built of conglomerate ashlar blocks, the tomb is approached by a 36m-long *dromos*. Its 5.40m-high doorway broadens at the base. The chamber's diameter is 14.60m, and height, 13.30m. A doorway inside leads to a rock-cut rectangular chamber. The façade was ornamented with two tiers of columns carved in relief flanking the doorway and the decorated slabs that covered the relieving triangle over the lintel. The capitals may have inspired the Doric order.

Pausanias believed the tomb was the underground treasure house of Atreus (2.16.6). In medieval times, its capstone was removed, and the chamber was used by shepherds, whose fires blackened its walls. The doorway was cleared in 1802 by the Voivode of Nauplia, enabling Lord and Lady *Elgin to enter the chamber that year. The fragments of carved slabs from the façade and pieces of engaged columns they found form part of the Elgin collection in the *British Museum. Pouqueville, *Clarke, Gordon, Mure and E. *Curtius described the tomb; *Leake, *Dodwell and *Gell described and drew its exterior and interior. Veli Pasha excavated the tomb's façade in 1810 and presented column fragments to Lord Sligo; the fragments were later given to the British Museum.

*Schliemann dug two test trenches in the side chamber in 1873 and 1876. Stamatakis cleared the dromos and both chambers for the *Greek Archaeological Society in 1878. In hopes of clarifying the date of the tomb's construction, *Wace conducted a series of soundings whose results spurred an acrimonious debate between Wace and Sir Arthur *Evans.

BIBLIOGRAPHY

A.J.B. Wace, "Excavations at Mycenae," *BSA* 25 (1921–23), 283–87, 338–57; idem, "The Date of the Treasury of Atreus," *JHS* 46 (1926), 110–20; idem, *Mycenae, An Archaeological History and Guide* (Princeton, NJ, 1949); G. E. Mylonas, *Mycenae Rich in Gold* (Athens, 1983).

ROBERT B. KOEHL

TRIER (AUGUSTA TREVERORUM). Roman town (founded ca. 15 B.C.); raised to the status of a colony by Claudius; imperial residence (after A.D. 293).

Trier boasts the most extensive aboveground Roman architectural remains in Germany, including the Porta Nigra (a city gate of controversial date), the imperial baths (fourth century A.C.), the St. Barbara baths (mid-second century), an amphitheater (ca. A.D. 100) and the Aula Palatina (the imperial audience hall, fourth century). The history of the Porta Nigra provides a colorful example of the changing circumstances of the city's Roman remains. In the early eleventh century, a Greek hermit established his cell in the eastern tower. Upon his death, he was venerated as a saint, and the city gate was converted into a monastery church. This occasioned the dismantling of some of the existing structure, various alterations and, eventually, the addition of a Romanesque choir (1160). Thus the building stood until 1804, when Napoleon visited the city. He ordered the municipal government to return it to the state in which it stood "under the Gauls," thereby attempting to accomplish both the secularization of the church and the glorification of a Gallic past. That restoration was continued under the

Prussians but was not completed until after it had been decided to save the Romanesque choir.

The beginning of the modern history of the city's archaeology is marked by the founding of the Société des recherches utiles du département de la Sarre (later, the Gesellschaft für nützliche Forschungen) in 1801. The society sponsored excavations (e.g., at the St. Barbara baths in 1822) and publications. During the Prussian period, government excavations were conducted at the amphitheater and at the imperial baths under the supervision of the imperial architect Carl Friedrich Quednow (d. 1836). He refused to have the government finds housed with those of the Gesellschaft, and not until the foundation of the Rheinisches Landesmuseum Trier in 1877 were the two collections united under one roof. The most spectacular archaeological event of the twentieth century was the discovery in 1946 of fragments of a painted ceiling under the cathedral. The paintings, reassembled and on display in the Bischöfliches Museum, date from the early fourth century and are believed to be portraits of the imperial family. Their discovery seems to provide confirmation of a medieval legend that St. Helena, mother of Constantine, donated her palace at the site to be converted into a church.

BIBLIOGRAPHY
W. Reusch, s.v. "Augusta Treverorum," *PECS* 119–21; J. von Elbe, s.v. "Trier," *Roman Germany,* 2nd ed. (Mainz, 1977), 388–438; E. Zenz, *Geschichte der Stadt Trier im 19. Jahrhundert,* 1 (Trier, 1979).

ELIZABETH C. TEVIOTDALE

TRINAKRIA. See SICILY.

"TRIUMPHAL" ARCHES. Triumphal—or, more accurately, honorary— arches were erected throughout the Roman Empire to commemorate victories in battle and other public acts and occasionally to serve as private, funerary monuments (*Arch of the Sergii, Pola).

As impressive public monuments, arches were already represented in antiquity on coin reverses and in relief sculptures. Originally crowned by statuary groups in most cases, the arches were usually freestanding structures but sometimes served as gates in the walls of a city (*Arch of Augustus, Rimini). The format of the Roman arches ranged from rather austere, relatively unadorned single-bay arches (*Arch of Augustus, Susa) to richly ornamented triple-bay arches (*Arch of Constantine, Rome) or *quadrifrons* arches (i.e., having four similar sides; *Arch of Septimius Severus, Leptis Magna). In the most elaborate examples, the relief decoration could incorporate depictions of triumphal processions, battles, submissions of conquered enemies, distributions of largesse, sacrifices to state gods and important entries into, and exits from, Rome.

Most of the arches that have survived from antiquity have continuously stood above ground, if only in part (*Arch of Septimius Severus, Rome). Always imposing, the Roman arch was often the chief surviving monument of the classical world in a provincial town. Einhard must have been inspired by such examples in creating his remarkable reliquary in the shape of a single-bay arch (*Charlemagne). Otto of Freising included a careful description of an honorary arch in Northern Italy (1158), seen when he participated in a campaign there with his nephew Frederick Barbarossa. The arches inspired later architects and sculptors (Arch of Augustus, Rimini; *Arch of the Gavii, Verona; *Arch of Trajan, Benevento) and were a very popular subject for artists and antiquarians. Hundreds of sketches, prints and paintings of these monuments were made during the Renaissance and later by Giuliano da *Sangallo, *Dosio, van *Heemskerck, *Ligorio, *Serlio, *Bartoli, *Panini, *Piranesi and Hubert *Robert. In some cases these representations are the only pictorial records we possess of monuments that were later torn down (*Arco di Portogallo, Rome).

Restorations and excavations of preserved arches are recorded as early as the Renaissance; in some instances the monuments were completely rebuilt in new locations (Arch of the Gavii, Verona). Modern systematic study of the Roman arches began with the publication of Luigi Rossini's *Gli Antichi archi trionfali onorarii e funebri degli antichi romani* (Rome, 1836), which featured folio-size prints, descriptions and measurements of standing arches (in Italy alone) and even reconstructions of lost monuments known only from coins or earlier drawings. More comprehensive collections and studies of Roman arches were made subsequently by Paul Graef in 1888 for Baumeister's *Denkmäler des Klassischens Altertums;* by A. L. *Frothingham in *AJA* 8 (1904); by C. D. Curtis in the *Supplemental Papers of the American School of Classical Studies at Rome* 2 (1908); and by F. Noack for the 1925–26 volume of the *Vorträge der Bibliothek Warburg.* The compilation made by H. *Kähler in 1939 remains indispensable today.

BIBLIOGRAPHY

H. Kähler, s.v. "Triumphbogen (Ehrenbogen)," *RE,* ser. 2, VII, 1 (1939), 373–493; +G. A. Mansuelli, "El arco honorifico en el desarrollo de la arquitectura romana," *Arch-EspArq* 27 (1954), 93–178; M. Pallottino, s.v. "Arco onorario e trionfale," *EAA* 1 (1958), 588–99; S. De Maria, *Gli Archi onorari di Roma e dell'Italia romana* (Rome, 1988); F. S. Kleiner, "The Study of Roman Triumphal Arches and Honorary Arches 50 Years after Kähler," *JRA* 2 (1989), 195–206.

FRED S. KLEINER

"TROPHIES OF MARIUS." Pair of colossal Roman military trophies, sculptured from marble and featuring armor, helmets, shields and other spoils from a conquered German enemy.

Now usually dated to the first century A.C. and thought to be from a military monument of Domitian, the "Trophies of Marius" were evidently moved in the third century A.C. from an unknown location to the niches of a huge fountain-house (*nymphaeum*) for the aqueduct of the Aqua Julia, on the Esquiline Hill in Rome. The nymphaeum, which dates from the time of Alexander Severus (222–35 A.D.), was identified in the Middle Ages as a temple of Marius, and

One of the *"Trophies of Marius,"* etchings by G. B. Piranesi, from *Opere varie di architettura* (1750). (Deutsches Archäologisches Institut, Rome. Inst. Neg. 86.1375.)

the trophies were thought to be the ones mentioned by Plutarch (*Caesar* 6) and Suetonius (*Caesar* 11) as set up by Marius to commemorate his victories over the Cimbri and others.

An alternate theory espoused in the fifteenth century was that the battered and somewhat misshapen trophies represented geese in armor (!) and that they stood for the geese that had cackled and saved the Capitoline from Gallic invaders (Livy 5.47).

The trophies were drawn or engraved in the nymphaeum by numerous artists (*Aspertini, *Lafréry, *Francisco d' Ollanda, *Du Pérac) before they were removed in 1587 by *Sixtus V and transferred to the balustrade of the *Capitoline Hill by Giacomo della Porta in 1590. Other proposals were made for the identity of the trophies in the seventeenth and eighteenth centuries, and they were associated with Trajan, Octavian and Domitian, but they continued to be called, and are today, the "Trophies of Marius."

BIBLIOGRAPHY
+Nash, II, 125–26; G. Tedeschi Grisanti, *I "Trofei di Mario," Il ninfeo dell'acqua Giulia sull'Esquilino* (Rome, 1977); Haskell—Penny, 46, 88; +Bober—Rubenstein, 205–6.

TROY (ILION). Ancient city located in northwestern Asia Minor, identified with the site of Hissarlık close to the entrance to the Dardanelles near modern Çanakkale.

Visited occasionally by Europeans during the Middle Ages, the region of northwestern Turkey known in antiquity as the Troad was the focus of increasingly intensive exploration by British and European travelers and scholars beginning in the sixteenth century. Attempts to match topography and archaeological ruins with descriptions preserved in classical authors, chiefly Homer and Strabo, resulted in several suggestions for the location of Troy, or Ilion. The site known today as Hissarlık was identified as Ilion in 1801 by Edward Daniel *Clarke, a British scientist. Frank *Calvert, American consul at the Dardanelles, explored the Troad extensively during the 1850s and 1860s. Convinced that the ruins at Hissarlık were those of Troy, Calvert began limited investigations there in 1865 and subsequently encouraged H. *Schliemann to undertake large-scale excavations. The site has generally been recognized as the location of Priam's citadel and scene of the Trojan War described in Homer's *Iliad,* ever since the archaeological investigations conducted there by Schliemann in 1871–73 and 1878–79. These excavations, continued in 1882 and 1890 with W. *Dörpfeld and, following Schliemann's death, from 1893 to 1894 by Dörpfeld alone, recovered evidence for nine major periods of occupation. Further excavation from 1932 to 1938 by an American team led by Carl W. *Blegen has expanded and refined these stratigraphic conclusions. A joint German-American expedition resumed work at the site in 1988.

Levels I through VII, with their subdivisions, represent Bronze Age occupation to ca. 1100 B.C. Some 400 years appear to separate Troy VIIb from Troy

VIII, a settlement founded ca. 700 B.C., perhaps by Aeolic Greeks, which lasted until Hellenistic times. Troy IX represents Hellenistic and Roman occupation.

From its foundation ca. 2600 B.C., Troy was a citadel fortified with impressive stone walls. During the Early Bronze Age (ca. 2600–1900 B.C., Troy I–V), the citadel housed a group of parallel megaron structures, probably the residential and administrative complex of the local rulers. The most striking architecture and finds are from level II, which Schliemann initially identified with Homeric Troy.

After the end of Troy V in ca. 1900 B.C., new cultural elements appear in period VI, representing Middle and Late Bronze Age occupation to ca. 1300 B.C. Again the citadel is protected by massive fortifications. Pottery of Gray Minyan and Mycenaean categories as well as other finds indicate connections with the Middle and Late Helladic cultures of mainland Greece. Troy VI ends in an earthquake, following which the citadel is reoccupied, then violently destroyed (Troy VIIa). The Blegen expedition suggested that the Trojan War known from Homer's epic account, if historical reality, should be correlated archaeologically with the end of VIIa. Troy VIIb1 and b2 represent the final Late Bronze Age occupation of the site.

To Troy VIII and IX belong remains of the Greek and Roman city of Ilion. In classical times it was renowned for its sanctuary of Athena Ilias, where Xerxes made a sacrifice in 480 B.C. The sanctuary also benefited from the visit of Alexander and patronage of Lysimachos. Troy passed from Seleucid to Pergamene control, then, along with the other Pergamene possessions, came under Roman domination in 133 B.C. The city was besieged and destroyed in 86–85 B.C. by G. Flavius Fimbria. Sulla began the process of restoration, which was continued by Caesar and Augustus. The importance of Troy continued in Roman times, when it was celebrated as the home of Aeneas, legendary founder of Rome.

Remains of period VIII are few; these include houses and two altar precincts. The outstanding structure of Hellenistic and Roman Troy is the sanctuary of Athena Ilias. This is preserved archaeologically in the remains of a Doric temple, together with mostly fragmentary carved metopes depicting Helios and his quadriga and scenes from a Gigantomachy, Centauromachy and battle between Greeks and Persians. An early Hellenistic date for the temple is likely, with renovations carried out in Augustan times.

BIBLIOGRAPHY

+H. Schliemann, *Troja* (London, 1884); +W. Dörpfeld, *Troja und Ilion* (Athens, 1904); +C. W. Blegen et al., *Troy,* 1–4 (Princeton, NJ, 1950–58), suppl. monographs 1–4 (Princeton, NJ, 1951–82); +F. W. Goethert—H. Schleif, *Der Athenatempel von Ilion* (Berlin, 1962); +W. Hoepfner, "Zum Entwurf des Athena-Tempels in Ilion," *AM* 84 (1969), 165–81; J. M. Cook, *The Troad* (Oxford, 1973), 14–44, 92–103; M. J. Mellink, ed., *Troy and the Trojan War* (Bryn Mawr, 1986); W. M. Calder III—J. Cobet, eds., *Heinrich Schliemann nach hundert Jahren* (Frankfurt-am-Main, 1990).

ANN C. GUNTER

TRYSA (GÖLBAŞI). Lycian hillside city, located in present-day Turkey, site of a great funerary monument covered with sculptures.

The lofty site (866m above sea level) was discovered by a German schoolmaster, August Schönborn, wandering in the remote region in 1841–42. He described a large monument carved with relief sculptures of "scenes from the Trojan War"; it turned out to be the spectacular Heroon of Trysa, a funerary monument with a rectangular temenos wall (20m × 24m) surrounding it. Relief sculptures covered the upper two courses of the interior wall on all sides and of one exterior wall as well. Included in the Greek mythological scenes are Amazonomachies, Centauromachies, the Seven Against Thebes and the deeds of Theseus, Bellerophon, Meleager, Perseus and others. There are also local Anatolian themes of the hunt, banquet and city siege. Though found in Lycia, the sculptures very probably were created by Greek artists. The monument has been dated to the fourth century B.C.

Schönborn tried to interest the Prussian government in sending an expedition to retrieve the sculptures, but to no avail. Not until 1880 was Otto *Benndorf able to mount an Austrian campaign to search for the site. After the dramatic rediscovery of the place, Benndorf and his colleague G. *Niemann systematically removed some 211m of frieze with about 600 figures. It was necessary to build a road from the site to the coast (an hour and a half's journey) to transport the pieces to the ship. They were then transferred to Vienna, to be set up in the *Kunsthistorisches Museum for viewing in 1883.

Among other finds at Trysa are the citadel proper and a number of funerary monuments—sarcophagi, grave stones and mausoleums, found on terraces adjoining the citadel. During the cutting of the road for the transport of the reliefs, the remains of a temple were discovered southwest of the citadel.

BIBLIOGRAPHY

O. Benndorf—G. Niemann, *Das Heroon von Gjölbaschi-Trysa* (Vienna, 1889); J. Borchhardt, s.v. "Trysa," *PECS* 937–38; Stoneman, *Land of Lost Gods,* 291–96; W.A.P. Childs, *The City Reliefs of Lycia* (Princeton, NJ, 1978), 13–14, 18–21.

TSOUNTAS, CHRISTOS (1857–1934). Greek archaeologist.

Tsountas, born in Stenimachos, Thrace, pioneered research on the Neolithic period and Bronze Age in Greece. He wrote five books and eighty-one articles on excavations and investigations at *Mycenae, *Vapheio, Kampos, the sanctuary of Apollo at Amyklai, Dimini and Sesklo, Syros, Siphnos, Amorgos, Naxos and *Eretria and also on many different aspects of later periods such as literature, inscriptions, pottery and even modern Greek orthography. Tsountas is the finder of the gold repoussé *Vapheio cups, and he found the wonderfully modeled, brilliantly painted plaster head of a goddess or sphinx at Mycenae. According to the opening sentence of *Mycenae and the Mycenaean Age* (1966) by G. E. Mylonas, "In 1893 Tsountas published a book that gave for the first time a clear picture of what came to be known as Mycenaean civilization. . . .

The work became a classic''; Mylonas was referring to the work by Tsountas and J. Irving Manatt, *The Mycenaean Age* (London, 1897).

BIBLIOGRAPHY
E. P. Photiades, *Epitymbion Christou Tsounta* (Athens, 1941), 684–87.

JUDITH BINDER

TULLIOLA. The name assigned to the body of a girl, found preserved intact inside a Roman sarcophagus on the Via Appia in 1485.

The body, alleged to be that of Tulliola, daughter of Cicero, was a sensation, and crowds flocked to see it at the Palazzo dei Conservatori, until Pope Innocent VIII secretly removed it by night. The discovery was described in detail by *Fonzio; in his manuscript (Codex Ashmolensis; Oxford, Bodleian) is also a contemporary drawing of the corpse and the very plain sarcophagus in which it was found.

BIBLIOGRAPHY
F. Saxl, ''The Classical Inscription in Renaissance Art and Politics,'' *JWarb* 4 (1941), 26–27, 44–45; Weiss, *RDCA,* 102.

TZIA. See KEOS.

U

UDINE, GIOVANNI DA (GIOVANNI NANNI; GIOVANNI RECAMA-DOR; 1487–1564). Italian painter, architect and master of stucco decoration.

Born in Udine in the Veneto, Giovanni was in Rome by 1516, employed in the workshop of *Raphael. A visit in the company of Raphael to the "Palace of Titus" (i.e., the *Domus Aurea; Giovanni's signature may be found on the walls) was critical for his development and achievement. *Vasari relates how he was "stupified" by the decoration of the Domus Aurea, especially the stucco reliefs, and how he experimented to find a recipe for stucco that would have the same white color and molding quality of the ancient examples.

Giovanni was to have many commissions to do paintings and stuccos featuring the *grottesche he had seen, for various patrons and their palaces. Best known are his decorations in the Logge of the Vatican palace for Pope *Leo X (completed 1519). Raphael delegated to Giovanni the stucco decoration of the vaults, which was inspired, in a general way, by the ancient stucco schemes in the Domus Aurea and in the *Colosseum but which drew on many ancient sources for particular motifs. He adopted figures from sarcophagi—especially with Bacchic themes and battle scenes—and from "minor objects" such as *Arretine ware, *Campana reliefs, gems and coins. The predilection for ancient erotic art is remarkable in the context.

As Vasari noted, the influence of the inventions of Giovanni da Udine in the Vatican Logge on painted and stuccoed grottesche created in Renaissance Rome and elsewhere in following generations was immense.

BIBLIOGRAPHY

+N. Dacos, La Découverte de la Domus Aurea et la formation des grotesques à la Renaissance (London, 1969); T. Yuen, "Giulio Romano, Giovanni da Udine and Raphael," JWarb 42 (1979), 268; Bober—Rubinstein, esp. 458; +N. Dacos, Le Logge di Raffaello, Maestro e bottega di fronte all'antico, 2nd ed. (Rome, 1986).

UFFIZI GALLERY (GALLERIA DEGLI UFFIZI), Florence. Major European gallery of painting and sculpture; the ancient sculptures were collected by the *Medici family and their successors, the dukes of Lorraine (Lorena).

The Uffizi building, begun in 1560 by *Vasari on commission from Cosimo I de' Medici, Grand Duke of Tuscany, was constructed to be used for administrative offices (*uffizi*). In 1581, Cosimo's son Francesco I decided to convert the top floor of the building to galleries for the display of Medici art treasures; at this time he had Buontalenti create an octagonal room, the Tribuna (1584), which was originally used as a repository of paintings, small sculptures and a large, jeweled walnut cabinet that enhanced the exquisite decor of the room. From 1588, the adjacent "Gallerie delle Statue" displayed Medici sculptures, ancient and modern, such as the famed marble *Porcellino* (*Wild Boar;* on display from 1591) and the *Arringatore,* as well as the splendid frieze from the *Ara Pacis of a goddess in a landscape, called *Air, Water and Earth* (now referred to as *Tellus* or *Pax Augusta;* it had been unearthed in Rome and sold to the Medici in 1569. It remained in the Uffizi until taken to Rome in 1938 for Mussolini). The gallery also included some fifty portrait busts and twenty-nine statues of marble, many of which are still in the Uffizi. Other Medici antiquities were exhibited at this time in the family palaces of Palazzo Vecchio and Palazzo Pitti.

Approximately one hundred years later the Tribuna received the great sculptures for which it is famous—the *Medici *Venus,* the *Arrotino* and the *Wrestlers*—all transferred by Duke Cosimo III in 1677 from the Villa Medici in Rome, surreptitiously but still not without outrage on the part of the Romans. These were joined by the *Dancing Faun,* which was already in the Florentine collections, and by two other *Venus* figures, the whole ensemble being in place by 1688. With the *Venus* de' Medici as its centerpiece, the Tribuna was compared with the Belvedere court in the *Vatican; with its velvet walls and mother-of-pearl cupola and its sumptuous paintings by *Titian, *Raphael and *Rubens on the walls, it qualified as "the most famous room in the world" (Haskell—Penny). The atmosphere of the room is well captured in the painting created by Zoffany for George III in the 1770s, showing a number of gentlemen of the *Grand Tour delighting in the various attractions of the room (Royal Collection of Her Majesty Queen Elizabeth II).

In the eighteenth century, the Uffizi was, for all practical purposes, a major public museum. G. Bianchi published a guide to the antiquities in 1759 (*Raguaglio delle antichità e rarità che si conservano in Galleria*), and a series of detailed inventories record the museum's holdings through the century (1704, 1753, 1769, 1784); a group of drawings made for the Lorena Duke Leopold I records the disposition of the statues in the corridors of the Uffizi.

Under Duke Peter Leopold and with Luigi *Lanzi as *antiquario* of the Uffizi, the collection was considerably enlarged, as many more treasures were transferred from the Villa Medici in Rome, including the *Medici Vase and antiquities that had once belonged to the della *Valle family. The *Niobe* Group of some fifteen statues (discovered in 1583, along with the *Wrestlers*) was brought and installed in its own room. The southern corridor overlooking the Arno housed the great bronzes (the *Chimaera*, transferred from Palazzo Vecchio and newly restored in 1784; the *Minerva* from Arezzo, the *Arringatore* and the *Idolino;* cf. *Florence, Archaeological Museum).

As a result of the Napoleonic invasion of Italy, many of the sculptures of the Uffizi were removed to Palermo in 1779, to be returned in 1802–3, upon which occasion many pieces were in need of restoration. The only important sculpture to be seized by *Napoleon was the Medici *Venus,* taken in 1802 and returned in 1816.

With the unification of Italy and the selection of Florence as its capital, a number of changes were made that resulted in the dispersion of the grandducal collection. Etruscan objects, a source of patriotic pride, were removed to be set up in an archaeological museum (1870), and soon afterward, other antiquities followed (the *Idolino* and Graeco-Roman bronzes in 1890, the coin collection in 1897, the gems in 1898). The loss of the context of the great collection was lamented, and the Greek and Roman marbles that did remain in the Uffizi created a related controversy. Luigi Milani, director of the Florence Archaeological Museum, complained that these pieces were arranged to enhance a Renaissance palace and with an outmoded aesthetic approach fostered by *Winckelmann. He favored a chronological, scientific arrangement of the pieces so that they could be studied properly. In fact, the corridors of the Uffizi are today lined with busts, sarcophagi, altars and mythological statuary that are unrelated in an organic way. Frequently ignored by tourists, they nevertheless preserve something of the decor and flavor of the original Uffizi of the Medici.

The Uffizi also houses a large number of drawings after the monuments and antiquities of Rome, collected by the Medici beginning in the sixteenth century, cataloged by A. Bartoli, *I Monumenti antichi di Roma nei disegni degli Uffizi di Firenze* (5 vols., 1914–22).

BIBLIOGRAPHY

+G. A. Mansuelli, *Galleria degli Uffizi, Le Sculture* 1–2 (Rome, 1958–61); M. Cristofani, "La Collezione di sculture classiche," in *Gli Uffizi, Catalogo generale* (Florence, 1979), 1087–90; *Firenze e la Toscana dei Medici nell'Europa del Cinquecento: Committenza e collezionismo medicei* (Florence, 1980), 19–42.

UNDERWATER ARCHAEOLOGY. The technique of excavating and recovering material from submerged sites; the principal foci for underwater research include ships and shipping, harbors and fisheries and associated commerce and artifacts and works of art recovered (often providing information not normally secured at sites on land).

The history of underwater archaeology is directly linked to the development of marine technology. Ever since Alexander the Great's descent into the sea in 325 B.C. in a submersible device, man's curiosity has led him ever forward to invent new technology to take him onto the seafloor. Leonardo da Vinci made drawings for underwater breathing mechanisms in the fifteenth century; diving bells followed in the sixteenth and seventeenth centuries, enclosed barrels in the eighteenth, submarines and hard-hat diving suits in the nineteenth. The first archaeological exploration with a diving suit, with a wooden and crystal helmet, occurred in 1535, when Francesco Demarchi descended to observe the two Early Roman Imperial pleasure barges lying at the bottom of Lake *Nemi. *Alberti had tried unsuccessfully, in 1446, to raise one of the ships; Mussolini succeeded in raising both in the 1930s.

The first recovery of archaeological artifacts from the sea took place in 1900 off the island of Antikythera at the southern tip of Greece (cf. *Antikythera Youth). Greek sponge divers, wearing hard-hat diving suits, bravely recovered art treasures dating from 80 to 50 B.C. from depths of 60m. Another shipment of Hellenistic artworks was recovered by sponge divers in 1907 off *Mahdia on the Tunisian coast.

The great technological breakthrough came in 1942 with the invention of the ''self-contained underwater breathing apparatus'' (SCUBA) by Jacques-Yves Cousteau and Emile Gagnan. Researchers could now move freely, work and see under the water. The underwater dig was born. But one is limited to shallow working depths with SCUBA. The U.S. Navy's limit for safe working depths with air is no deeper than 130 feet. The first wreck site (now recognized as two superimposed wrecks) to be excavated with SCUBA, carried out by Cousteau and his team, was off the Grand Congloué Island near *Marseilles in 1952. They developed the airlift and some of the other tools still used for underwater excavation.

Scientific method was first brought to the underwater field by Nina Lamboglia. Directing professional divers from a diving bell, in 1958 Lamboglia laid out a system of grid squares over an ancient Roman wreck of the first century B.C. found off the island of Spargi (Sardinia). Since the Spargi wreck, the grid system has been used for all excavations of ancient shipwreck sites by archaeologists.

The archaeologist diver first appeared on the scene in 1960, when George Bass excavated a Late Bronze Age ship at Cape Gelidonya off the southwest coast of Turkey. Since that time, diving archaeologists have excavated over one hundred ships, and many more have been surveyed. In a recent listing of known ancient wrecks in the Mediterranean and Roman provinces, A. J. Parker cites 1,259 (BAR International series 580 [1992]).

From excavations we know that ancient ships were built in a mortise and tenoning construction, first summarized by Fernand Benoît in L'Épave du Grand Congloué à Marseille (1961). That this shell-first technique goes back to at least the early fourteenth century B.C. is now proved by the wreck at Ulu Barun, a project of Bass and his group off the southwest coast of Turkey. That ancient ships could go at a speed of up to twelve knots is known from the reconstruction of the Greek merchant ship dating about 300 B.C. found off Kyrenia, Cyprus, by Michael and Susan Katzev. That ancient ships could carry over 7,000 amphoras and weigh 500 tons has been proved by the Roman wreck (first century B.C.) at La Madrague de Giens excavated by André Tchernia and Patrice Pomey.

But the study of ancient ships is only part of the story of underwater archaeology. Excavations in ancient harbors are revealing a wealth of knowledge about past technology, trade and economic history. Such investigations usually begin with aerial photography, as pioneered in the 1910s by the Jesuit priest A. Poidebard in his studies of the ports of Tyre and Sidon on the coast of Lebanon. In 1965, by combining such coverage with underwater and land excavation, the port of *Cosa (*Portus Cosanus), the earliest Roman harbor thus far known, was uncovered by A. M. McCann along Italy's Tuscan coast. Dating from 273 B.C., the Portus Cosanus served as a center for the export of wine and fish products for more than 200 years. Some of the other major Mediterranean harbor sites that have profited from excavation are Apollonia in *Cyrenaica, Caesarea Maritima, *Carthage, *Kenchreai, *Leptis Magna and the silted ports of Fréjus (Forum Julii), *Marseilles (Massalia) and *Ostia (*Portus).

The most important technical devices now used by underwater archaeologists for locating ships or harbor features that cannot be seen are the side-scan and subbottom profiling sonars developed by Harold Edgerton in the 1960s. Computers also enable underwater archaeologists to map and plot artifacts. The most recent breakthrough is the computer-controlled ''sonic high accuracy ranging and positioning system,'' or SHARPS, developed in 1984 by Martin and Peter Wilcox. With SHARPS, the archaeologist can have instant visual verification on the computer screen of the coordinates of any point.

Deep-sea research has recently become a reality with the emergence of unmanned submersibles or ''remotely operated vehicles'' (ROVs), such as *Jason,* built by Robert D. Ballard and his team of engineers at the Woods Hole Oceanographic Institution. Tethered to a submersible platform by a cable, the 2m-long *Jason* can cruise as fast as one knot and as deep as 6,000m with precise manueverability. It can carry sonar devices, three high-resolution color video cameras, a 35mm still camera and an electronic still camera that transmits digital images to a topside computer. Equipped with a manipulator arm, *Jason* can also lift amphoras and other objects off the seafloor. What used to take camera-carrying SCUBA divers months to accomplish can now be done in safety with much greater accuracy in a matter of days.

The first ancient shipwreck to be found in the deep sea with this new robotic technology is the *Isis,* a late Roman ship dating to about A.D. 400. The *Isis* was discovered by Ballard in 1989 off the coast of Sicily at a depth of ca. 800m. As the archaeologist aboard, A. M. McCann was also able to trace with ROV *Jason* an ancient trade route between Rome and Carthage. Robotic technology opens up the potential for rapid exploration of vast areas of the seafloor never before accessible. The archaeologist can record and learn without excavation and in safety. More than 98% of the world's ocean floors remain unexplored. The future augurs further collaborative efforts among the archaeologist, explorer and engineer; much of the history of underwater archaeology lies ahead.

BIBLIOGRAPHY
G. F. Bass, *Archaeology Under Water* (New York, 1966); D. J. Blackman, "Ancient Harbors in the Mediterranean," pts. 1–2, *IJNA* 11 (1982), 79–104, 185–211; +L. Casson, *Ships and Seamanship in the Ancient World,* rev. ed. (Princeton, NJ, 1986); +A. M. McCann et al., *The Roman Port and Fishery of Cosa: A Center of Ancient Trade* (Princeton, NJ, 1987); +P. Throckmorton, ed., *The Sea Remembers* (New York, 1987); A.M. McCann—J. Freed, *Deep Water Archaeology: A Late-Roman Ship from Carthage and an Ancient Trade Route near Skerki Bank off Northwest Sicily* (*JRA,* Suppl. Ser. no. 13, 1994).

ANNA MARGUERITE McCANN

URSINUS, FULVIUS. See ORSINI, FULVIO.

V

VACCA, FLAMINIO (ca. 1538–1605). Italian sculptor, restorer and antiquarian.

Flaminio Vacca was a favorite of Pope *Sixtus V, who employed him to create sculptures (*Saint Francis of Assisi* in the Sistine Chapel of S. M. Maggiore in Rome, 1587–89), make restorations and procure marbles. For the Villa Medici, Vacca made a marble *Lion* (before 1594), as a pendant to an antique lion dating to the second century A.C. found outside Rome on the Via Prenestina. The pair graced the steps of the garden façade of the villa until 1787, when they were moved to Florence, to be displayed in the Loggia dei Lanzi. Most viewers regarded the lion of Vacca as superior to the antique version.

Throughout his career, Vacca recorded the provenance of the ancient marbles he procured, a rare service, and he left at his death an unpublished manuscript that gives much useful information on antiquities found in Rome during his lifetime. The "Memorie di varie antichità trovate in diverse luoghi della città di Roma," written in 1594, circulated in manuscript form but was not published until 1704 by Falconieri. Various editions were issued in Latin by *Montfaucon (*Diarium italicum*), and in reprint by *Nardini in his *Roma Antica*. It provides clues to the discovery and early study of the *Quirinal *Horse Tamers,* the black marble statue of "Seneca" (*Pseudo-Seneca), the *Borghese *Faun,* the *Pasquino,* the *Portland Vase and the *Borghese Vase, as well as many other antiquities.

Vacca lies buried in the *Pantheon.

BIBLIOGRAPHY

E. Breton, "Vacca (Flaminio)," *NBG* 45 (1866), 825; Stark, 100; W. Granberg, "Vacca, Flaminio," Thieme—Becker 34 (1940), 22–23; Haskell—Penny, esp. 247–50, 296–99.

VALADIER, GIUSEPPE (1762–1839). Italian architect and restorer of monuments, the leading neoclassical architect of his time in Rome.

During the French occupation of Rome (1809–14), along with *Camporese, Valadier was architect-director for the Commission of Monuments (1810) and the Commission of Embellishments (1811). He was especially connected with the Jardin du Grand César, the planned park from the Milvian Bridge to the Pincian Hill. His two most famous archaeological undertakings, however, were the restoration of the *Arch of Titus (1820–24), requiring its complete dismantling and rebuilding, and the construction of the second *Colosseum buttress (1824–26). In both of these he showed remarkable sensitivity and pioneered restoration in materials other than the original stone.

BIBLIOGRAPHY

G. Valadier, "Narrazione artistica sull'arco di Tito," *Dissertazioni dell'Accademia de Archeologia* 1 (1821–23), 275–86; idem, +*Opere di architettura e di ornamento ideate e eseguite da Giuseppe Valadier* (Rome, 1833); +E. Debenedetti, *Valadier, segno e architettura* (Rome, 1985); +Ridley, *Eagle and the Spade.*

R. T. RIDLEY

VALERIANUS BOLZANIUS, PIERIUS (GIOVANNI PIETRO DALLE FOSSE; GIOVANNI PIERIO VALERIANO BOLZANI; 1477–1558). Renaissance humanist, poet and early student of Egyptian hieroglyphics.

The nephew of Fra Urbano Valeriano Bolzanio, Valerianus studied at his native Belluno and Venice in his youth and was writing Latin poetry by the age of fifteen. Later, he was *Vasari's Latin teacher and tutor to Giovanni de' Medici (the future Pope *Leo X; *Medici family). In 1509, as the private secretary of Cardinal Giulio de'Medici, he traveled to Rome, where he studied the city's antiquities.

He is most remembered for three literary works. The *Antiquitatum Bellunensium sermones quattuor* (1522) is an investigation into the origins of Belluno from the literary and epigraphical sources; *De literatorum infelicitate* (1534) was written after the Sack of Rome in 1527 and lamented the sad condition not only of the city but also of the men of letters who survived. His most famous and influential work, the *Hieroglyphica sive de sacris aegyptiorum aliarumque gentium literis* (1556), published in Basel and dedicated to Cosimo I de' Medici, was a vast compilation of all the hieroglyphic knowledge of his time; it drew on Horapollo, the *Physiologus*, the *obelisks he saw in Rome, the Cabala and the Bible as sources. It was so popular that eleven editions were published in the first seventy years. At the time it was believed that hieroglyphs were a purely ideographical form of writing used by ancient Egyptian priests to foreshadow divine ideas and that the Greek philosophers had tapped into "hieroglyphic wisdom." In the dedication of his *Hieroglyphica,* Valeriano writes, "[T]o speak hieroglyphically is nothing else but to disclose the true nature of things divine and human." He contributed no revolutionary ideas to the field, but his compilation was instrumental in changing the study of hieroglyphic symbols from a philosophical to a philological pursuit. The *Hieroglyphica* provided a fountain of emblematic imagery for artists such as Pinturicchio, Leonardo, *Mantegna,

Giovanni Bellini (*Bellini family), *Vasari and others, while the inscriptions in his historical material were used as sources by humanist historians.

BIBLIOGRAPHY

G. Toffanin, "Valeriano Bolzani, Giampietro," *EC* 12 (1954), cols. 986–87; M. Praz, *Studies in Seventeenth Century Imagery,* 2nd ed. (Rome, 1964), 24; R. Wittkower, *Allegory and the Migration of Symbols* (Boulder, CO, 1977), 127–28.

DAVID FUNK

VALLE, DELLA, FAMILY. Distinguished family in Renaissance Rome, ardent collectors of classical antiquities; the della Valle collection was one of the most important of the sixteenth century.

From the fourteenth century, the della Valle family—originally of merchant class, then ennobled—lived in Rome in the Rione S. Eustachio, in several houses built close together. Fra *Giocondo (ca. 1480) noted antiquities, mostly inscriptions, in three collections belonging to different members of the family. In 1484, *Sixtus IV had the houses destroyed, including that of his physician FILIPPO (d. 1494), when the della Valle sided with the imperial party. Filippo's sons ANDREA (1463–1534) and BARTOLOMEO (1468–1526) decided to rebuild the house.

Andrea played a key role in the family, both in building and in collecting. A humanist and lover of antiquities, he was appointed cardinal in 1517 by *Leo X. He constructed the new family palace (later, Palazzo della Valle-Rustici, Palazzo del Bufalo), a three-story building on the Via di Teatro Valle with an inner courtyard designed as a showplace for statuary, with twelve niches containing statues of *Venus, Bacchus, Child Riding a Seamonster* and others. *Aldrovandi described the court in detail, and various artists—*Aspertini, van *Heemskerck, *Francisco d'Ollanda and Pierre *Jacques—made drawings of the statuary. The palazzo, attributed to the architect Lorenzo Lotti (Lorenzetto), also extended over an older house on the Via Papale (Corso Vittorio Emanuele) owned by Andrea's cousin Renzo Stefano. It had a small courtyard with sarcophagi and two famous statues of *Pan,* known as the della Valle *Satyrs.* Now in the *Capitoline and probably dating to the second century A.C., the mirroring images of Pan are in the form of architectural supporting figures. Their immense popularity in the sixteenth century is attested by the large number of drawings made of them. (They occur in numerous sketchbooks: Holkham, Ashburnham, Destailleur, Peruzzi, Codex Pighianus; cf. *Pighius.) The *Satyrs* were displayed in 1513, along with other della Valle antiquities, on a triumphal arch erected by Andrea on the Via Papale, upon the occasion of the solemn elevation of Leo X to the papacy.

After Andrea became cardinal, he started on the construction of another palace with a statue garden, designed by Lorenzetto, on the other side of Via di Teatro Valle. Unfinished at the time of his death (1534), the palazzo was bequeathed to FAUSTINA, the daughter of Bartolomeo, who was married to Camillo Capranica; in 1539 they moved into it. An engraving by Hieronymus *Cock (dated

1553, but possibly made from an earlier drawing by van *Heemskerck), illustrates the statue garden, handsomely decked out with antique sculptures and portrait busts, placed in niches and alternating with reliefs. Enea *Vico engraved several of the draped female statues (1541). Pierre Jacques drew the *Seated Bacchus with Panther,* a cuirassed statue and a number of reliefs, while a dozen reliefs occur in the Codex Pighianus. Engravings by G. B. de *Cavalleriis include a *Marsyas,* a *Bacchant* and the captive barbarian woman, of Trajanic date, known as "*Thusnelda.*"

Andrea's estate was divided between Faustina and QUINZIO, the son of his sister SIGISMONDA, who was married to Francesco de Rustici. The Palazzo della Valle-Rustici was rebuilt in the eighteenth century, when it was owned by the del *Bufalo family. The antiquities in the Palazzo della Valle-Capranica were sold in 1584 by the Capranica sons to Ferdinand de' Medici (*Medici family). An inventory listing all the statues and reliefs with their location was drawn up for the sale.

BIBLIOGRAPHY

Lanciani, *Storia degli scavi* I (1902), 121–24; +(rev. ed., 1989), 165–68; +C. L. Frommel, *Der Römische Palastbau der Hochrenaissance* (Tübingen, 1973), II, 336–53; C. Hülsen—H. Egger, *Die Römischen Skizzenbucher von Marten van Heemskerck* I (Soest, 1975), 56–67; Haskell—Penny, 301–3; +Bober—Rubinstein, 479–80.

MARJON VAN DER MEULEN

VAN DEMAN, ESTHER BOISE (1862–1937). American field archaeologist, specialist in Roman construction techniques.

A native of South Salem, Ohio, Esther Van Deman went to Rome in 1901 as a scholar at the *American Academy after completing graduate study at the University of Chicago and a decade of teaching at Wellesley and Goucher colleges. A participant in major excavations of that period in the *Forum Romanum, she received permission from Giacomo *Boni to study the Atrium Vestae, work that led to what is still the standard publication of the monument (*The Atrium Vestae,* Washington, DC, 1909), as well as other articles on the Forum excavations. As Carnegie Fellow from 1906 to 1910 at the American Academy, where she spent the rest of her life, she studied Roman construction techniques, particularly those of brick-faced concrete, and Roman aqueduct construction. Her work on aqueducts with Thomas *Ashby resulted in *The Building of the Roman Aqueducts* (Washington, DC, 1934), but the fruit of her lifelong research, *Ancient Roman Construction in Italy from the Prehistoric Era to Augustus,* was published only posthumously by her colleague Marion E. Blake (Washington, DC, 1947). Her excavations and travels are documented by an extensive collection of photographs now at the American Academy.

BIBLIOGRAPHY

L. S. Meritt, "Esther Boise van Deman," *Notable American Women* (Cambridge, MA, 1971), III, 205–17; +K. Einaudi, *Fotografia archeologica 1865–1914* (Rome, 1978).

HARRY B. EVANS

VAN DER BEKE, LIEVEN. See TORRENTIUS, LAEVINUS.

VANVITELLI, GASPARE. See WITTEL, GASPAR VAN.

VAPHEIO. Mycenaean Greek Bronze Age site in Laconia.

The tholos tomb at Vapheio, unlike those at Mycenae (which are built into hillsides), is upon the crest of an eminence that, conical by nature, was regularized by piling up the earth removed when the tomb was first dug. Known as early as 1805, when it was found by Gropius and mentioned by *Leake in his travels, the tomb was not excavated until 1888. The remarkable gold cups from the tomb, even before they were published by *Tsountas, their excavator (1889), attracted notice, and W. J. Stillman had already described them in print as "evidently intended as a pair," one "all action and combat," the other "tranquil and peaceful." Even their position in the tomb indicates that they were thought of as pendants.

The tomb is that of the so-called Vapheio Prince, who seems to have controlled the region; grave robbers, when they rifled the contents of the large inner chamber (10.35m in diameter, approached from the east by a dromos 29.80m long), failed to notice the burial proper of the prince, who lay in a pit beneath floor level, surrounded by a heap of finery (rings, jewels, beads, aryballoi and a mirror) and weapons (knives, daggers, spears, axes and a sword). At his right hand lay one cup of gold and one of silver, balanced by a like cup of gold and one of silver at his left hand. The silver cups are ribbed but otherwise undecorated.

The gold cups bear the celebrated scenes of bull catching exquisitely wrought in the repoussé technique. Though very similar in size, they are not identical (the "Violent" Cup is 8.4cm high and ca. 10.3cm in diameter; the "Quiet" Cup is about .5cm lower and .4cm wider), and small discrepancies in technique exist. Although George Perrot in 1894 argued convincingly that the two cups were the work of different hands (giving in the course of his discussion what is still the finest extended description of the cups), scholarly opinion, in general, attributed them to a single source. Their excavator considered them the work of a mainland artist; more often they have been looked upon as Cretan imports. In 1974 Ellen N. Davis brought together compelling evidence that whereas the Quiet Cup is of Minoan manufacture, the Violent Cup, while obviously inspired by the other and intended to balance it, is Mycenaean work. Both cups are usually dated soon after (or shortly before) 1500 B.C.

BIBLIOGRAPHY

C. Tsountas, in *ArchEph* (1889), 129–71; G. Perrot—C. Chipiez, *Histoire de l'art dans l'antiquité: La Grèce primitive: l'art mycénien* (Paris, 1894), 784–93; Ellen N. Davis, "The Vapheio Cups: One Minoan and One Mycenaean?" *ArtB* (1974), 472–87.

W. W. DE GRUMMOND

VASARI, GIORGIO (1511–74). Italian Renaissance architect, painter, scholar and author.

Born at Arezzo, Vasari traveled to Florence in the 1520s and spent much of his life there working for the *Medici family. A practitioner of the Late Renaissance style known as Mannerism, Vasari designed the *Uffizi for Cosimo I (begun 1560) and did a number of paintings for the Palazzo Vecchio in Florence, but on the whole he is not highly regarded for his art.

Vasari's importance is acknowledged to lie in his publication, in chronological order, of the lives of the most eminent Italian architects, painters and sculptors— *Le Vite de' più eccellenti architetti, pittori et scultori italiani* (1550; 2nd ed., 1568). Though he chose to omit classical artists from his biographies, it is clear that Vasari had read the relevant ancient texts of Pliny the Elder's *Natural History,* Vitruvius and other authors and that he was sufficiently familiar with the ancient painters and sculptors to devise a chronological scheme of development. His ideas emerge in the three prefaces he wrote to divide up the biographies. His perception of a cycle in antiquity was probably influenced by his theory on the art of the Renaissance, which he saw as emerging from primitive beginnings and proceeding through three styles, with periodic improvements in quality and in the imitation of nature, until it reached its climax in *Michelangelo. Similarly, Vasari could cite the hard and lifeless early statues by Kanachos, as opposed to the perfection of the sculptures of Polykleitos, or the primitive monochrome paintings of earliest times, as opposed to the richly colored works of Protogenes, Apelles and others.

Vasari also articulated a theory about the decline of art in the Middle Ages that had been expressed in other writers (e.g., *Ghiberti). Dividing history itself into three phases—the ancient (*antico,* i.e., classical antiquity), the old (*vecchio,* i.e., the Middle Ages) and the modern (*moderno,* i.e., the Renaissance)—Vasari argued that there had been a severe decline in art around the time of Constantine. The change of quality in sculpture could be seen in the *Arch of Constantine, with its naturalistic reliefs borrowed from earlier monuments (e.g., of Trajan), contrasting sharply with the sculptural decoration evidently commissioned by Constantine. Like Ghiberti, he believed that the decline was hastened by the combined destructive forces of Christianity and barbarian invasions.

Apart from using the Arch of Constantine to demonstrate his theories, Vasari indicated his intimate familiarity with the great antiquities to be seen in Rome in his day when he proposed that the third style in Renaissance art was strongly influenced by the display of the sculptures in the Belvedere court at the *Vatican—the *Laocoon, the *Belvedere *Apollo, the *Belvedere *Torso, the *Venus Felix, the *"Cleopatra." He argued that the study of the vigor and lifelike flesh of these figures helped artists turn from the harsh, dry style of stage 2 (seen in *Mantegna and others) into the third style, marked by perfection in proportion, design and grace. He also stressed the role of the classical orders—Doric, Tuscan, Ionic and Corinthian—in helping the architect achieve perfection.

Vasari's writings (the *Vite* as well as other treatises, e.g., the *Ragionamenti*) are useful for the information they supply about works discovered in his native Arezzo, such as the many fine examples of *Arretine ware and the famed *Chi-

maera, discovered in 1554 and acquired by the Medici. Vasari was able to identify it as Etruscan on the basis of the inscription and the style. His anecdotes about artists also help to give information about antiquities known at the time, as in the case of the repair of a statue of *Marsyas* by Verrocchio (1435?–88) upon the request of Cosimo de' Medici. The statue, made of red stone, lacked legs and arms, and these were skillfully supplied in the correct proportions by Verrocchio.

BIBLIOGRAPHY

G. Milanesi, ed., *Le Opere di Giorgio Vasari,* 1–9 (1875–85; repr. 1906); P. Barocchi, "Il valore dell'antico nella storiografia vasariana," in *Atti del V Convegno Internazionale di Studi sul Rinascimento* (Florence, 1956), 217–36; G. Vasari, *The Lives of the Painters, Sculptors and Architects,* tr. A. B. Hinds (London, 1963); T.S.R. Boase, *Giorgio Vasari, The Man and the Book* (Princeton, NJ, 1971); G. Zander, "Il Vasari, gli studiosi del suo tempo e l'architettura antica," *Il Vasari, storiografo e artista, Atti del Convegno Internazionale nel IV Centenario della Morte* (Florence, 1976), 333–50.

VATICAN MUSEUMS. One of the world's oldest and greatest museums, with a collection of Greek, Roman and Etruscan antiquities of surpassing significance.

The Vatican Museums began with the desire of Pope *Julius II (1503–13) to display classical sculptures as evidence of the prestige of the papacy. His own sculpture of the *Belvedere *Apollo* was the key piece around which he built the first collection, displaying the antiquities in the Palazzetto of Innocent VIII known as the Belvedere. He had *Bramante create a walled garden adjoining the palace, planted with orange trees and embellished with fountains, and build long corridors connecting the papal apartments of the Vatican with the open *cortile* in which he displayed the antiquities. Thirteen gigantic marble masks, said to come from the *Pantheon, were set into the walls, and in niches were disposed the *Apollo, *Laocoon* (discovered and acquired in 1506), *Venus Felix* and *Commodus as Hercules,* as well as the *Hercules and Antaeus* and the *Tiber* river god (*Nile* and *Tiber*); in addition, the *"Cleopatra" was displayed as a fountain. *Leo X (1513–21) added the *Nile,* and Clement VII (1523–34), the *Belvedere *Torso* and a third river god (*Tigris* or *Arno*); the *Venus ex balneo* (*Knidian *Aphrodite*) was a gift to Paul III (1543–49), who also then purchased the *Belvedere *"Antinous."*

This "Antiquario delle Statue," as it was called, quickly became famous and attracted artists, scholars and visitors to Rome. It was described in its earliest state by Francesco *Albertini in his *Opusculum de mirabilibus novae et veteris urbis Romae* (1510), dedicated to Julius II. Numerous early and well-known drawings and engravings—by Marcantonio *Raimondi, Marten van *Heemskerck, *Francisco d'Ollanda and others—provide evidence of the appearance of these antiquities. *Primaticcio and *Vignola made casts of many of the pieces for Francis I to display at Versailles. The influence of this Antiquario was enormous, affecting the attitudes and ideals of collectors and museums for centuries.

The Belvedere Antiquario was fundamentally altered under Pius IV (1559–

65), when Pirro *Ligorio destroyed the old informal garden and reorganized the other sections to hold a great deal more statuary. At this time Pius gave Duke Cosimo I (*Medici family) the fragmentary group of *Hercules and Antaeus* today at the Palazzo Pitti, Florence; earlier, *Julius III had given him a statue of *Mercury* (1550). These were losses for the Belvedere, but the gravest event was the election of Pope Pius V (1566–72), who regarded the statues—many of them nude—as pagan idols that might distract the faithful from their meditations. With Counter-Reformation zeal, he had the great sculptures of the *cortile* hidden behind wooden shutters, while many other statues were simply given away—to the *Capitoline Museum, to Emperor Maximilian II (*Hapsburg family) and to Grand Duke Francesco I de' Medici.

For approximately a century, the Vatican collections were closed or emptied. Not until the eighteenth century did collecting of antiquities resume in a significant way, when *Clement XIV (1769–74) became alarmed over the accelerated pace at which antiquities were leaving the city of Rome and even Italy. Advised by his treasurer Giovanni Angelo Braschi (the future *Pius VI), he purchased antiquities that were in imminent danger of export (e.g., the *Meleager* attributed to Skopas, the *Mattei family collection) and sought space for all the new antiquities in the old Belvedere palace. It was now completely transformed, according to designs by the architect Alessandro Dori, so that long galleries were created inside the Belvedere, and an entirely new octagonal portico was erected for the *Laocoon,* the *Apollo* and the other traditional favorites. Pius VI (1775–99) continued the expansion and the policies he had himself initiated under Clement XIV to create the magnificent new Museo Pio-Clementino. The various rooms were named after their contents—the Room of the Animal Sculptures (Sala degli Animali), the Room of the Portrait Busts (Sala dei Busti), the Room of the Muses (Sala delle Muse)—or else after the shape of the room—the Round Room (Sala Rotonda), the Greek Cross Room (Sala a Croce Greca), the Octagonal Court (Cortile Ottagonale).

The acquisition of new material through purchase and excavation was a top priority. With the aid of G. B. *Visconti, commissioner of antiquities (1768–84), the popes surveyed Rome's antiquarian market and patronized such dealer/restorers as B. *Cavaceppi, J. Nollekens and G. *Hamilton. Under Pius VI, nearly 600 new marbles were added to the Vatican; many came from excavations (some 130) initiated by the pope. Among the new acquisitions were the eight statues of the *Muses* with *Apollo* discovered near *Tivoli in 1775, the *Boy with Goose* (1789) and numerous animal sculptures. Pius delighted in showing important visitors through the galleries, such as the Swedish king *Gustavus III, whose visit in 1784 was recorded by B. Gagneraux. Visconti began the great catalog of the Pio-Clementino, the bulk of which would be prepared by his more famous son, Ennio Quirino *Visconti, *Il Museo Pio-Clementino,* 1–7 (Rome, 1782–1807).

With the French invasion of Italy and the Treaty of Tolentino (1797), the masterpieces of the Vatican were carried away to Paris for *Napoleon's museum, and Pius himself was put in prison, where he died in 1799. His successor, *Pius VII Chiaramonti (1800–23), with the help of his commissioner of antiquities Carlo *Fea and the new inspector general of the fine arts Antonio *Canova, brought the collection back to life, acquiring new sculptures and building a new section, the Museo Chiaramonti (begun 1805). With the fall of Napoleon, Canova negotiated the return of the majority of the Vatican sculptures (the *Tiber* stayed in Paris), and further expansion was ordered by the pope. The New Wing (Braccio Nuovo) of the Museo Chiaramonti was inaugurated in 1822.

In the ensuing decades major examples of Greek and Roman art were brought into the museum: the *Aldobrandini *Wedding* (discovered 1604/5; acquired 1838), the *Apoxyomenos* attributed to Lysippos, found in Trastevere (1849), the *Odyssey Landscapes* (1851) and the *Augustus* of Primaporta (1863). The Vatican experienced dynamic growth in the pontificate of *Gregory XVI (1831–46), with the opening of the Museo Etrusco Gregoriano in 1837. The immediate impetus was the acquisition of the fine bronze warrior known as *"Mars"* found at Todi (1835) and the discovery of the incomparable *Regolini-Galassi Tomb, an unplundered Etruscan Orientalizing burial from *Cerveteri (1836). Also important were the results of the excavations of Vincenzo *Campanari at *Vulci, undertaken jointly with the pontifical government (from 1834). With the antiquities from these and other excavations in papal territories in Etruria were displayed the Gualtieri collection of vases from *Chiusi and other antiquities that had been acquired in the eighteenth century. Gregory also created the Museo Gregoriano Egizio (inaugurated 1839), which was to include some Roman antiquities, such as the remarkable *Antinous* in Egyptian kilt and headdress found at *Hadrian's Villa at Tivoli (acquired 1742).

In the late nineteenth and twentieth centuries, numerous catalogs, guides and other publications have made the Vatican holdings available to scholars of the world. In 1891 W. *Helbig first published the standard guide to the antiquities as volume 2 of *Führer durch die öffentlichen Sammlungen klassischer Altertümer in Rom;* it was later modernized in its authoritative fourth edition under the editorship of Hermine Speier (1965). W. *Amelung cataloged the sculptures in detail in two volumes of *Die Skulpturen des Vaticanischen Museums* (1903, 1908), with a third volume added by G. *Lippold in 1956. The fortunes of the Vatican collections in the twentieth century have been guided by several strong directors, Bartolomeo Nogara (1920–54), Filippo Magi (1954–61), and Carlo Pietrangeli, who became director in 1978. All have contributed distinguished publications on the collections; those of Pietrangeli on the history of the Vatican Museums are of great utility for the history of archaeology.

Under Nogara was received the Benedetto Guglielmi Collection from Vulci (1935); the Giacinto Gulgielmi Collection, a second portion of the antiquities assembled by this noble family of the nineteenth century, was reunited with the first through the efforts of F. Buranelli, and put on display at the Vatican in 1989. Sensational exchanges of antiquities were effected between the Vatican and entities of the Italian state and the city of Rome, including the donation to the state of a slab of the *Ara Pacis by Pope Pius XII (1954), which was reciprocated by the gift in 1956 of a panel of the reliefs found at the palace of the *Cancelleria. These had been discovered in 1937–39, and the portions found on papal land were already in the Vatican. The donation of the relief found on property of the Comune of Rome made it possible to display all of the remains together in the Vatican. But perhaps the most dramatic event of the era was the long-awaited restoration of the *Laocoon* (1957–60), in which Magi removed the Renaissance restoration of the right arm of *Laocoon* and replaced it with the "Pollak arm," found in 1905 and long agreed to be the real arm of the figure.

In the twentieth century the Vatican has faced the chronic problem of making the vast collections accessible to an enormous public. Entry to the museums was greatly facilitated by the opening in 1932 of a new double-spiral ramp to accommodate traffic going up and coming down. Under Pietrangeli a program of unprecedented exhibitions outside the Vatican included the show sent in 1983 to the United States (New York, Chicago and San Francisco; the Belvedere *Apollo* and the *Augustus* of Prima Porta crossed the ocean) and an Etruscan exhibit, including finds from the Regolini-Galassi Tomb, at Memphis and other venues in 1992 and following.

BIBLIOGRAPHY
Haskell—Penny, 7–15; +*The Vatican Collections, The Papacy and Art,* catalog of exhibition (New York, 1982); +C. Pietrangeli, *I Musei Vaticani, cinque secoli di storia* (Rome, 1985); C. Springer, *The Marble Wilderness, Ruins and Representations in Italian Romanticism, 1775–1850* (Cambridge, 1987); P. Liverani, *Museo Chiaramonti, Sculture* (Rome, 1989); S. Howard, "An Antiquarian Handlist and the Beginnings of the Museo Pio-Clementino," *Antiquity Restored, Essays on the Afterlife of the Antique* (Vienna, 1990), 142–53.

VATICAN VERGIL (VERGILIUS VATICANUS). Ancient illustrated manuscript of the poems of Vergil.

The Vatican Vergil (cod. Vat. lat. 3225) is one of just two illustrated manuscripts of Vergil from late antiquity: it and the Vergilius Romanus (cod. Vat. lat. 3867) are both dated to the fifth century A.C., but parallels with mosaics suggest the Vaticanus be dated earlier, to the first quarter of the century. The text of the Vaticanus, written in rustic capitals of the fourth or fifth centuries (which cannot be more accurately dated), provides no further help with problems of chronology.

The manuscript consists of seventy-six parchment leaves (21.9cm × 19.6cm) and includes some fifty pictures, representing one-fifth of the original codex. The text is badly damaged: we have, with some *lacunae,* books 3 and 4 of the *Georgics* (ten leaves), illustrated by nine miniatures, whose pastoral scenes are considered the best of the series; and the first nine books of the *Aeneid* (sixty-five leaves), illustrated by forty-one miniatures. The pictures depict scenes from Vergil's poems, such as *Dido's Suicide* (folio 26) or *Aeneas Landing in Carthage* (folio 11), but are not an exact translation of the text. The illustrations show the work of at least two different artists, whose individual stylistic idioms are set within one consistent style, generally thought to be that of a *scriptorium* in Rome. Although there is evidence to suggest that the Vatican Vergil reflects earlier illustrated cycles, J. de Wit has demonstrated that its artists did not mechanically copy an earlier cycle. More likely, as H. Buchthal has argued, "they presented traditional pictorial material in more or less original compositions and combinations," drawing from a wide range of classical art and including, as well, elements of Late Antique iconography and style.

In the Renaissance, the Vatican Vergil belonged to two famous collectors, Pietro *Bembo and Fulvio *Orsini. The latter bequeathed it to the Vatican Library in 1600, where it remains today. Scholarly interest in the Vatican Vergil began in 1686. Jean Mabillon, *Bellori and the prefect van Schelstrate examined the manuscript. The opinion of the three scholars was reported in the preface to the influential 1741 edition of the manuscript with engraved plates by *Bartoli. The views of these scholars and the refinements of Bartoli's plates apparently set the scholarly tradition for viewing the miniatures as copies from an earlier manuscript. This view, advanced by de Nolhac, Seroux d'Agincourt and others, was not definitely refuted until the work by de Wit (1964).

BIBLIOGRAPHY

+*Fragmenta et picturae vergiliana cod. Vat.* lat. 3225, 3rd ed., Codices e Vaticanis selecti (Rome, 1945); +J. de Wit, *Die Miniaturen des Vergilius Vaticanus* (Amsterdam, 1959); H. Buchthal, "A Note on the Miniatures of the Vatican Vergil Manuscript," *Mélanges Eugène Tisserant*, 6, *Studi e testi*, 236 (Vatican City, 1964), 167–71; T. Stevenson, *Miniature Decoration in the Vatican Vergil: A Study in Late Antique Iconography* (Tübingen, 1983); D. Wright, *The Vatican Vergil, A Masterpiece of Late Antique Art* (Berkeley, 1993).

MICHELE R. SALZMAN

VATLUNA. See VETULONIA.

VEII. The most southerly of the great Etruscan cities, situated between Caere, Faliscan territory and Rome.

Veii's control of the lower Tiber valley ensured both prosperity in the Orientalizing and Archaic periods and the fatal contest with Republican Rome. The final clash, with Camillus's ten-year siege (396 B.C.; Livy 5.1ff.), was for centuries a central element in the national consciousness of Rome, where, too, the cult statue in the Capitoline temple was attributed to the Veientine artist Vulca (Pliny *NH* 35.157).

Reduced to a modest *municipium* (Propertius 4.10.27), the site of Veii was abandoned from the Late Empire; no structural remains are visible today. From the ruins of the forum, described and drawn by Sir William *Gell (1831) and L. *Canina, came marble columns for churches (S. Paolo) and palaces (Piazza Colonna) in Rome and the Julio-Claudian statues in the *Vatican Museums (1812–17). At this stage, Veii's Etruscan past was represented only by isolated pieces such as the *Chigi Vase (a Corinthian *olpe;* *Villa Giulia) and the Orientalizing painted Campana tomb (cf. *Campana, Giovanni Pietro), already drawn in 1825 but not officially discovered until 1843, with contents exposed by F. Roncalli (1980) as artificially assembled from various sites.

Scientific excavations (G. Q. *Giglioli, 1916) in the extra urban sanctuary of Portonaccio yielded a group of Archaic terracotta statues, including the famous *Apollo,* probably the work of Vulca (in the Villa Giulia, Rome), which revolutionized critical approaches to Etruscan art. In spite of exceptionally favorable conditions, official exploration of the city and cemeteries has since been limited and sporadic, save for topographical surveys conducted by the *British School at Rome in the city and in the Ager to the north and east. The Italo-British excavation and prompt publication in *Notizie degli Scavi* (1961–75) of the Quattro Fontanili Villanovan cemetery provided crucial information for Iron Age chronology.

BIBLIOGRAPHY

+L. Canina, *Descrizione dell'antica città di Veii* (Rome, 1847); G. Dennis, *Cities and Cemeteries of Etruria,* rev. ed. (London, 1883), I, 1–42; +L. Vagnetti, *La Stipe votiva di Campetti a Veio: Scavi 1937–39* (Florence, 1971); M. Pallottino, "Officina veiente," in *Saggi di antichità* (Rome, 1979), III, 1001–91; F. Delpino, *Cronache veientane* 1 (Rome, 1985).

F. R. SERRA RIDGWAY

VELATHRI. See VOLTERRA.

VELÁZQUEZ (VELÁSQUEZ), DIEGO RODRÍGUEZ DE SILVA (1599– 1660). Spanish painter.

Born and trained in Seville, Velázquez became established at the court in Madrid in 1623 and spent the rest of his life in the service of Philip IV. His interest in antiques was stimulated, if not inspired, by a visit to Italy in 1629–31. In Rome, according to his master, father-in-law and biographer, Francisco Pacheco, he wanted to stay in the Villa Medici because there were antique statues for him to copy. No copies of antiques by him are known. But the statue of *"Cleopatra,"* now called Ariadne, is the centerpiece of one of Velázquez's views of the Villa Medici Gardens (Prado) painted during his second visit to Italy. Furthermore, his study and appreciation of classical sculpture is evident in several paintings of mythological subjects, notably, the *Venus* (National Gallery, London), *Mars,* and *Mercury and Argus* (Prado).

Velázquez's second visit to Italy in 1649–51 was made for the purpose of acquiring antique sculpture as well as paintings for the decoration of the Alcázar, allegedly at his suggestion. Because of the difficulty of finding good originals, he followed the example of earlier collectors and had molds or casts made of some of the celebrated statues in Rome. His later biographer, Antonio Palomino, lists twenty-nine statues and a number of portrait busts acquired by Velázquez in Rome. Only a few bronze copies and casts can be identified today, some in the royal palace, others in the *Prado. A few plaster casts are recorded in the

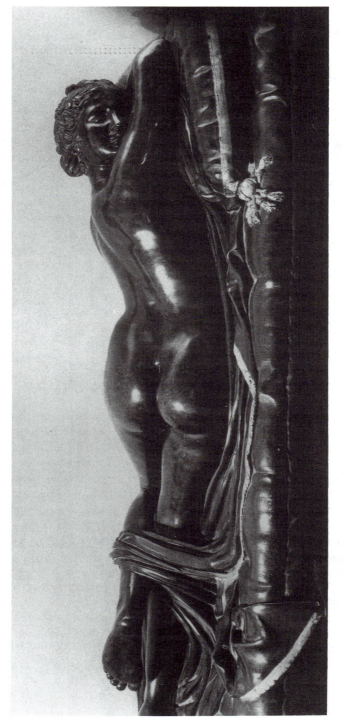

Bronze cast of the Borghese *Hermaphrodite*, by M. Bonarelli, ordered by Velázquez in Rome, 1650–51. Madrid, Prado. (E. Harris.)

inventory of Velázquez's apartments at his death; some twenty volumes of classical literature in his library are further testimony of his interest in antiquity.

BIBLIOGRAPHY

E. Harris, "La Misión de Velázquez en Italia," *ArchEspArt* 33 (1960), 109–36; F. J. Sánchez Cantón, *Velázquez y 'lo Clásico'* (Madrid, 1961); E. Harris, *Velázquez* (Oxford, 1982), 17, 24–29, 85, 132–38, 144, 155–58; M. L. Tárraga Baldó, "Contribución de Velázquez a la enseñanza académica," *Velázquez y el arte de su tiempo, Jornadas de Arte* 5 (1991), 61–79; M. Morán Turina, "Felipe IV, Velázquez y las antigüedades," *Academia, Boletín de la Real Academia de Bellas Artes de San Fernando* 74 (1992), 234–57.

ENRIQUETA HARRIS FRANKFORT

VENTRIS, MICHAEL GEORGE FRANCIS (1922–56). British architect and cryptographer, credited with decipherment of Linear B (*Linear A and B), a script used on *Crete and the Greek mainland during the Late Bronze Age (ca. 1500 to ca. 1200 B.C.).

As a boy, Ventris was fascinated with antiquity and became proficient in Greek and Latin. In 1936, he heard Sir Arthur *Evans lecture on Linear B in London and became determined to decipher the script. Trained as a cryptographer in World War II, Ventris began a full investigation of Linear B in 1949. He set up a cryptographic grid of values for the Linear B signs, aided by the work of Alice Kober, who demonstrated that Linear B was inflected, and by the publication of the Cypriot script, which had many characters in common with Linear B and was used to write Greek as late as the Hellenistic Age. In 1952, he concluded that Linear B was an archaic form of Greek.

Confirmation of the decipherment came when C. *Blegen successfully used Ventris's grid to determine the meaning of a newly excavated tablet from *Pylos with an inventory of tripods. Ventris was joined later by John Chadwick, who had been working on Linear B at Cambridge; together they produced a detailed account of the decipherment, *Documents in Mycenaean Greek* (Cambridge, 1956). For his achievement Ventris was awarded an honorary doctorate from Uppsala University. He died tragically in an auto accident in 1956, shortly before *Documents* went to press.

BIBLIOGRAPHY

London Times, 8 September 1956, 10; J. Chadwick, *The Decipherment of Linear B* (Cambridge, 1967).

MICHAEL L. ROBERTSON

VENUS DE MILO (APHRODITE OF MELOS). Over-lifesize statue (2.03m) of the goddess Venus or Aphrodite, dating to the later second century B.C. In popular culture the *Venus de Milo* is often regarded as the incarnation of feminine beauty, though its reputation has suffered in recent years.

The statue and its base were discovered in 1820 by Colonel Olivier Voutier, and the *Venus* was soon hailed as a great masterpiece. Its instant fame was undoubtedly due to the fact that it was recognized as a Greek original at a time when scholars had become keenly sensitive to the shortcomings of Roman copies and that the statue was known to be without potentially misleading restoration such as had been made on famous statues from the Renaissance on.

One reason the statue remained largely unrestored (it was found in two blocks
that joined together; only the tip of the nose was added) was that there was
considerable disagreement over exactly how the missing arms should be positioned. Various suggestions had her holding an apple (a fragmentary hand with
apple was also found near her), a lyre or a shield. Among modern scholars,
*Bieber noted that the left arm may have rested on a pillar, the existence of
which was implied by a cutting in the statue base, and Robertson observed that
the right hand may have been positioned as if to support the dangerously low
drapery. The absence of the arms in this supposed paragon of beauty has both
intrigued and repelled viewers.

The Comte de Marcellus, an attaché at the French Embassy in Constantinople,
negotiated the purchase of the piece, which was spirited away for the Marquis
de Rivière, French ambassador to the Sublime Porte, who gave the sculpture as
a gift to Louis XVIII. He, in turn, presented it to the *Louvre, where it remains
today. A statue base found with the statue (now lost) had an inscription with
the name of the artist (Ages)andros or (Alex)andros, son of Henidos, from Antioch-on-the-Maeander. The base disappeared after a drawing had been made of
it for Jacques *David; German scholars of the later nineteenth century accused
the French of deliberately losing it because the inscription contradicted the attribution of the statue to a famous master, rather than to the unknown son of
Henidos.

BIBLIOGRAPHY

J. P. Alaux, *La Vénus de Milo et Olivier Voutier* (Paris, 1939); Bieber, 159; Robertson,
I, 553–54; Haskell—Penny, 328–30; +A. Pasquier, *Venus de Milo* (Paris, 1985).

VENUS FELIX. Over-lifesize marble Roman statue (2.14 m) of a Roman lady
in the guise of Venus.

The body, with its nude torso and drapery falling around the hips, reflects the
*Knidian *Aphrodite* of Praxiteles (mid fourth century) and some of its Hellenistic imitations (e.g., the *Venus de Milo*), but the head is a portrait of a Roman
lady with a coiffure of the Antonine period. It may be Faustina Minor (d. A.D.
176), wife of Marcus Aurelius. The statue is labeled *Venus Felix* (i.e., "fruitful"
or "happy" Venus) by an inscription on its base, which also identifies the donor
as a certain Sallustia. A Cupid with (lost) upraised arms shares the base with
her.

The statue was in the papal collection of *Julius II by 1509 and was installed
in the Belvedere court at the *Vatican immediately. There is no solid evidence
to back up the assertion made in the eighteenth century by *Ficoroni that it was
found near S. Croce in Gerusalemme.

During the sixteenth century the piece was highly regarded and was drawn
by *Aspertini, *Dosio, Girolamo da *Carpi and Hendrik *Goltzius, and a fine

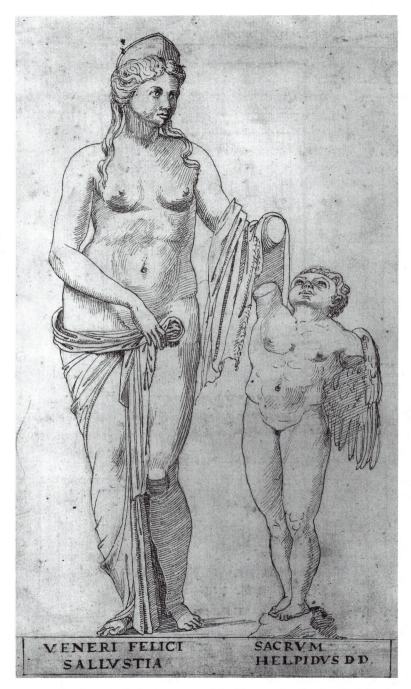

Venus Felix, from the Belvedere court of the Vatican, drawing by. G. A. Dosio, Berlin, Kupferstichkabinett. (© Bildarchiv Preussischer Kulturbesitz, Berlin, 1994. Photo: J. P. Anders, 79 D 1.)

small bronze was made by *Antico, imitating its pose but idealizing the head. In the seventeenth century it was still admired by many (a plaster copy was made for Philip IV of Spain), though there is evidence that it began to lose its appeal. *Louis XIV did not ask to have it copied, and, later, *Napoleon spurned it as war booty. *Winckelmann showed no enthusiasm for the sculpture, and in the nineteenth century it passed into oblivion. Today the *Venus Felix,* ignored by all but specialists, remains in the Belvedere court.

BIBLIOGRAPHY
+H. Brummer, *The Statue Court in the Vatican Belvedere* (Stockholm, 1970), 122–29; Sheard, no. 37; Haskell—Penny, 323–25; Bober—Rubinstein, 61–62.

VERGERIO, PIETRO PAOLO (1370–1444). Italian humanist.

Born at Capodistria, Vergerio studied there and at Padua. In 1386 he was hired to teach dialectic in Florence, and there he became associated with Coluccio *Salutati. From 1388 to 1390 he was lecturer in logic at Bologna, returning to Padua from 1390 to 1397. During those years he edited and published *Petrarch's *Africa* and later composed a biography of Petrarch. He returned to Florence in 1398 to study Greek with Manuel Chrysoloras (1398–99) but otherwise remained in Padua, studying art, medicine and law, until 1405. In 1402 his treatise on pedagogy, *De ingenuis moribus et liberalibus studiis,* appeared. From 1405 to 1409, as part of Salutati's circle, he was at the Curia in Rome. Vergerio's interest in Roman antiquities, aroused by his study of Petrarch, had led him to write of the ruins of Rome in a letter of 1398, and while in Rome he searched for knowledgeable guides to the city's antiquities. Such guides were few, and their competence minimal. In his letters he expressed astonishment at the vast sea of ruins that surrounded the city, and he was one of the first to deplore the destruction of ancient remains, along with Francesco da *Fiano. He became increasingly involved in Church politics, playing a notable role in the Council of Constance (1414–18), and then entered the service of the emperor Sigismund, with whom he left Italy in 1418. He died in Budapest in 1444. His call for preservation of Rome's ruins and his admirable work on Petrarch were widely influential on later humanists.

BIBLIOGRAPHY
K. A. Kopp, *Vergerio der erste humanistische Pädagoge* (Lucerne, 1893); L. Smith, "Note cronologiche vergeriane," *Archivio Veneto,* ser. 5a, 4 (1928), 82–141; L. Smith, ed., *L'Epistolario di Pietro Paolo Vergerio,* with bib. as preface (Rome, 1934); Weiss, *RDCA,* 54–57.

JAMES C. ANDERSON, JR.

VERGINA (AEGAE, AIGAI). Site of the early Macedonian Greek capital known as Aigai, before Archelaus moved to *Pella (ca. 400 B.C.); also royal burial grounds; activity ranges from Iron Age through post-Byzantine times.

Early explorations of 1855 and 1861 by French archaeologist Leon Heuzey revealed a Macedonian chamber tomb and part of the palace. Selected architectural members went to the *Louvre. Since 1938, ongoing excavations have been conducted by Greek archaeologists, notably K. Rhomaios and M. *Andronikos.

The "Cemetery of the Tumuli" revealed more than 300 small mounds containing multiple burials ranging from 1000 B.C. to the second century B.C. Monumental chamber tombs of the fourth and third centuries, presumably royal, have been found in the area. Many have fine paintings and/or spectacular grave goods. Plutarch (*Pyrrhus* 26.6) relates that the royal tombs were sacked in 274 B.C. by Gauls in service to Pyrrhus. One that escaped looting is designated by its discoverer, Andronikos, as the *"Tomb of Philip II."

A late fourth-century palace lies on a plateau below the walled acropolis. Its two-storied façade leads to a colonnaded courtyard surrounded by various chambers. Close by is a theater where the excavator believes Philip to have been assassinated; farther off is a shrine of Eukleia with a dedication by Philip's mother Eurydike.

BIBLIOGRAPHY

+L. Heuzey—H. Daumet, *Mission archéologique in Macédoine* (Paris, 1876); +K. Rhomaios, *O makedonikos Taphos tis Verginas* (Athens, 1951); +M. Andronikos, *Vergina, 1, To Nekrotapheion ton Tymbon* (Athens, 1969); +idem, *Vergina, The Royal Tombs and the Ancient City* (Athens, 1984); idem, *Vergina, 2*, The "Tomb of Persephone" (Athens, 1994); R. Ginouvès, ed., *Macedonia from Philip II to the Roman Conquest* (Athens, 1993), 82–88, 117–19, 145–77, 183–87; S. Drougou, C. Saatsoglou-Paliadeli, et al., *Vergina, The Great Tumulus*, Archaeological Guide (Thessaloniki, 1994); I. Touratsoglou, *Macedonia: History, Monuments, Museums* (Athens, 1995), 210–49.

STELLA G. MILLER

VERONA. Roman city located on the Adige River in the Veneto of Italy.

Called a Latin colony by a native, Catullus (17.1; died 54 B.C.), Verona probably did not have *municipium* status before 49 B.C., but it became one of the most important Roman cities of Venetia. Constantine defeated Maxentius at Verona before their final encounter at the Milvian Bridge in A.D. 312. The city was a vacation haunt of emperors in later antiquity. The Ostrogothic king Theodoric (493–526), who stayed in the city for extended periods, renovated Verona's aqueducts and improved the fortification. "Theodoric of Verona" became Dietrich von Bern in German legend and literature. The city later came under Lombard control.

An anonymous description of the ancient city written between 799 and 805 survives (*Veronae rhythmica descriptio*), transcribed and supplied with a drawing of the city by Raterius, bishop of Verona, made some time before 968 (copy in the Biblioteca Capitolare, Verona).

In the Middle Ages, Verona continued to use the ancient Roman grid plan, which survives in the city to this day. Traces of Roman paving remained, and, in the ninth century at least, the theater seems to have been inhabited. In the fourteenth century, Verona became an early humanist center under Cangrande della Scala, nurturing such scholars as *Mansionario and *Benzo d'Alessandria.

Amphitheater, Verona, etching by G. B. Piranesi, from *Opere varie di architettura* (1750). (Deutsches Archäologisches Institut, Rome. Inst. Neg. 86.1428.)

During this period, in 1368, the "Madonna Verona" was erected atop a fountain in the Piazza Erbe; this antique figure, lacking a head, was appropriately supplied with one.

Among the monuments of Verona, the *Arch of the Gavii was always known. Equally familiar is the great amphitheater, with its exterior arcading of seventy-four entrances; it was investigated in the early fourteenth century by Benzo, who noted that the exterior walls of the *Laberinthum* (or *Harena*) had been damaged by earthquakes, and the stones had been used to build part of the city walls. The traditional story is told that Dante, looking down from the top of the seating area with its concentric arrangement, conceived the plan for the circles of Hell in the *Divine Comedy*. *Ciriaco of Ancona viewed it and assigned it to Augustus with a dating of 3 B.C. Numerous restorations, both medieval and later (the stairways were reconstructed in the sixteenth century; the amphitheater is maintained today for opera and other events), make it difficult to confirm a precise date.

Among the city gates that have survived are the Porta Borsari and the Porta dei Leoni, dating to the mid-first century A.C. Their elegant façades were copied by *Palladio, Antonio da *Sangallo and other Renaissance architects. Inscriptions were studied at Verona from a very early date, with many already discovered in the later Middle Ages. The Veronese architect Fra *Giocondo and Felice *Feliciano noted them in their fifteenth-century sylloges, and in the eighteenth century an epigraphical museum was founded at Verona—the oldest in Italy—by the Veronese scholar F. S. *Maffei. The Museo Lapidario Maffeiano still maintains its original arrangement of Greek and Roman antiquities according to their typology.

BIBLIOGRAPHY

+G. Marchini, *Verona illustrata: Le Antichità* (Verona, 1974); B. Forlati Tamaro, s.v. "Verona," *PECS,* 969; Weiss, *RDCA,* esp. 21–24, 117–18; M. Greenhalgh, *The Survival of Roman Antiquities in the Middle Ages* (London, 1989), esp. 69–70; R. Brigo, *Verona romana* (Verona, 1991).

VERULAMIUM. Pre-Roman and Romano-British town, located near St. Albans, Hertfordshire, England.

The name Verlamio appears on coins of the pre-Roman settlement, which was the chief center of the Catuvellauni. Roman occupation began in A.D. 43–44 and continued into the fifth century. The martyrdom of St. Alban took place at Verulamium, possibly in the early third century. The town had a rectangular street grid, and excavations have revealed shops, a forum, a theater, fortifications and houses (some quite large). The finds from the site are housed in the Verulamium Museum, opened in 1939 near the site.

The chronicle of the abbey of St. Albans reveals that excavations were undertaken at the site in the eleventh century during a search for building materials by the abbot Ealred and his successor, Eadmer. They reported finding streets and subterranean vaults (which subsequently had to be closed, because they were being frequented by thieves and women of ill repute), temples, altars, tiles, columns, statues, coins, amphoras and glass ash urns.

In modern times, excavation was begun in 1930 by R.E.M. (later, Sir Mortimer) *Wheeler and Mrs. T. V. Wheeler, with Kathleen Kenyon directing work at the theater. K. M. Richardson excavated a shopping precinct in 1938. The building of a wide, modern highway in the 1950s was the occasion for the rigorous campaigns directed by S. S. Frere (1955–61), impeccably published so as to provide a clear chronology for the stratification of the site.

BIBLIOGRAPHY

J. Adhémar, *Influences antiques dans l'art du Moyen Age français* (London, 1939), 75–76; S. S. Frere, s.v. "Verulamium," *PECS,* 971–72; idem, *Verulamium Excavations,* 1–3 (Oxford, 1972–84).

VETULONIA (VATLUNA; VETALU). Major Etruscan city, believed by many to have been one of the "Twelve Peoples" of Etruria.

Vetulonia's greatest period was from the late eighth century B.C. to the end of the sixth century B.C., represented by Villanovan ash urns and the spectacular tombs of the Orientalizing period, including the monumental Tomba della Pietrera and Tomba del Diavolino II, which lie in the necropolis below the town. The city experienced decline in the fifth and fourth centuries, perhaps due to the increased power of *Rusellae, which stood across Lake Prile from Vetulonia. During the Hellenistic period a revival occurred, evidenced by roads and buildings in the zones called Costa Murata and Costia dei Lippi. Especially accessible is the Hellenistic part of Vetulonia known as Scavi Città, northeast of the summit of the hill occupied by the modern town. It provides a rare opportunity to study Etruscan town layout and construction methods of this late phase of Etruscan culture. The remains of a Roman villa and other buildings show occupation at Vetulonia into the second century A.C.

Two medieval documents of 1181 and 1204 refer to Vetulonia, but soon afterward the ancient name was replaced by the designation Colonna di Buriano. The location of the ancient city was forgotten until the nineteenth century, when Isidoro Falchi declared that Colonna was actually Vetulonia. He was supported by King Umberto I and by the authority of Theodor *Mommsen. In 1887 the name was officially changed back to Vetulonia. During these same years, Falchi explored the necropolis and discovered the great Orientalizing tombs, as well as the zone called Scavi Città. In the twentieth century, excavations have been conducted for the Soprintendenza Archeologica della Toscana by A. Talocchini and others. Most of the finds are in the Archaeological Museum in *Florence, including the reconstructed Tomba del Diavolino I, moved stone by stone from Vetulonia to the "Garden" at the museum.

BIBLIOGRAPHY

I. Falchi, *Vetulonia e la sua necropoli antichissima* (Florence, 1891); A. Talocchini, "La città e la necropoli di Vetulonia secondo i nuovi scavi, 1959–62," *StEtr* 31 (1963), 435–51; idem, s.v. "Vetulonia," *PECS,* 973–74; V. Cecconi, *Profilo di una città etrusca, Vetulonia* (Pistoia, 1978).

VIA APPIA (APPIAN WAY). The oldest and greatest of the roads linking Rome with the rest of Italy, begun in 312 B.C. by Appius Claudius Caecus and going as far south as Capua in Campania.

The road was extended to Venusia in 291, Tarentum in 281 and Brundisium in 264. It began at Porta Capena of the *"Servian Wall" in Rome and issued from the *Aurelian Wall by the Porta Appia, always one of the main gates of Rome. At first, it was mainly graveled, with the first stretch to the temple of Mars cobbled; ultimately it was paved with stone blocks for its whole length.

The Via Appia was regarded as the "queen of the long roads" (Statius, *Silvae* 2.2.12), and its neighborhood was densely inhabited from an early period, while its borders were soon lined with tombs, including the *Tomb of the Scipios and early imperial *columbaria of the family of Augustus. With the fashion for showy and fanciful tombs following the lead of Augustus, the Appia beyond the temple of Mars soon came to be lined with a rich variety of architectural inventions, of which the *Tomb of Caecilia Metella is only the most familiar. Altar tombs, aedicular tombs, pyramids, tumuli and towers vied with more fantastic forms. Behind this margin stretched suburban villas such as that of the Quintilii, so rich and suggestive in its ruin that it received the name Roma Vecchia, and the summer palace of Maxentius, complete with a circus and pantheon dedicated to his dead son Romulus.

The Via Appia was in use for burials by Christians and Jews from the first century A.C. to as late as the sixth century; the well-known rock-cut underground galleries of the catacombs were created during this period. Churches such as San Sebastiano (originally dedicated to Peter and Paul) were built as centers for pilgrims coming to visit venerated tombs. Medieval watchtowers were often built on the foundations provided by ruined tombs. The highway itself eventually fell into disuse.

The catacombs were rediscovered in the sixteenth century and were studied with great interest by *Bosio and later by G. B. *De Rossi. Portions of the highway were cleared and reopened under a massive program of public works initiated by Pope *Pius VI (1775–99). Although the tombs and villas have been repeatedly plundered for treasure, beginning in antiquity, and individual buildings and complexes have been studied, books dealing with the road itself are appreciative, rather than scientific. A proper study of the geography and engineering has yet to be written.

BIBLIOGRAPHY
+L. Cozza et al., *La Residenza imperiale di Massenzio,* catalog of exhibition (Rome, 1980); F. Coarelli, *Dintorni di Roma* (Rome, 1981), 9–110; +J. J. Rasch, *Das Maxentius Mausoleum an der Via Appia in Rom* (Mainz, 1984).

L. RICHARDSON, JR

VICO, ENEA (ca. 1520–ca. 1570). Italian engraver and numismatist.

Born in Parma, Enea Vico was active in Rome from 1541 to 1567 but is also known to have sought a copyright on his engravings in Venice in 1546. He was

Reconstruction of the Via Appia Antica and the Via Ardeatina, Rome, etching by G. B. Piranesi, from *Opere varie di architettura* (1750). (Deutsches Archäologisches Institut, Rome. Inst. Neg. 86.7362.)

commissioned by Cosimo I (*Medici family) to engrave works of *Michelangelo, and from 1563 he worked for the *Este family in Ferrara. Strongly influenced by Marcantonio *Raimondi and the school of engravers active in Rome in the earlier sixteenth century, he originally worked in a bold style, which later became mannered and calligraphic.

Some 500 prints have been assigned to Enea Vico. His prolific output includes engravings after antiquities and monuments in and around Rome (*Nile river god, the "Thusnelda" of the della *Valle family collection, the *Colosseum, the *Column of Marcus Aurelius, various sarcophagi). His efforts in numismatic reproduction were quite significant, from his Le Imagini de gli imperatori (1548; medals of the first twelve Caesars) to Le Imagini delle donne auguste (1557). The volume on emperors was notable for its inclusion of physical descriptions of the emperors based on Suetonius. The later work presented sixty-three plates of portraits of Roman imperial ladies, many of them convincingly authentic in their derivation from ancient models. The frontispiece to his work was a design closely modeled on the funerary altar of the freedman Amemptus (Paris, *Louvre).

BIBLIOGRAPHY

L. Servolini, "Vico, Enea," Thieme—Becker 34 (1940), 328–29; +The Illustrated Bartsch 30 Italian Masters of the Sixteenth Century, Enea Vico, ed. J. Spike (New York, 1985); Bober—Rubinstein, esp. 469.

VICTORY OF SAMOTHRACE (WINGED VICTORY; NIKE OF SAMOTHRACE).

Over-lifesize marble statue of a goddess of Victory (preserved height 2.45m), key monument of Hellenistic art.

The winged figure of Victory (in Greek, Nike) was discovered on the island of *Samothrace in 1863 by Charles Champoiseau, within the fifteenth-century citadel of the Gattilusi, in an area that later was identified as the ancient sanctuary of the Great Gods. Champoiseau, the French vice-consul at Adrianople, gathered some 200 Parian marble fragments from the work and shipped them off to the *Louvre, where they were pieced together. The resulting figure, armless and headless, depicts the goddess with wings spread out and drapery swirling as if she were in flight. Strangely, at first it was thought of as a mediocre decorative piece of a late period, until Wilhelm Frohner called attention to its real merit in 1869.

Parts of the setting for the Victory were found by the Austrian expedition to Samothrace directed by A. *Conze and O. *Benndorf, including blocks of Rhodian marble used to form the prow of a warship upon which the goddess once stood. Champoiseau, informed of the find, arranged for the new pieces to be shipped to Paris. The base was restored, and in 1884 the whole ensemble was dramatically displayed on the landing of the Escalier Daru in the Louvre. It remains there today, conveying something of the triumphant and uplifting effect it must have had at Samothrace.

Excavations conducted on Samothrace by Karl *Lehmann (1948–60) revealed more of the original setting of the *Victory*. The impression was romantically Baroque, with the ship's prow set amid pools of water and boulders; in addition, parts of the *Victory's* hands were excavated (1950, 1967), and other fragments were rediscovered in the reserve collection of the *Kunsthistorisches Museum in Vienna, where they had been sent by Conze.

First attempts to date the statue compared it with coins of Demetrios Poliorketes showing a Nike on a ship's prow, struck to commemorate his victory at Cyprian Salamis in 306 B.C. Such a dating is inconsistent with the style of the work, however, which is now recognized as very close to the Baroque manner practiced at *Pergamon and *Rhodes in the second century B.C. (first noted by A. S. Murray, 1890). Inscriptional evidence of a complicated nature points in the same direction and suggests that the artist may be Pythokritos, active on Rhodes in the early second century B.C. The victory at sea that is commemorated may be the battle off the coast of *Side in 190 B.C., in which the Rhodians and their allies defeated Antiochos III.

The winged *Victory* has enjoyed enormous popularity ("the most familiar and most reproduced of all Greek statues"—C. M. Havelock, 1971). Its dynamic representation of a figure in motion seems to have been seminal for the Futurist sculpture of Umberto Boccioni, *Unique Forms of Continuity in Space* (1913).
BIBLIOGRAPHY
Michaelis, 118–20; Bieber, 125–26; K. Lehmann, "Samothrace: Fifth Preliminary Report," *Hesperia* 21 (1952), 19–43; Haskell—Penny, 333–335.

VIGNOLA, GIACOMO (JACOPO) BAROZZI, DA (1507–73). Italian architect of the Late Renaissance.

Born at Vignola, near Modena, Giacomo Barozzi began as a painter in Bologna. Arriving in Rome in 1530, he worked for two years as an assistant at the Vatican under *Peruzzi and Antonio da *Sangallo the Younger; he learned architecture from his masters and also became thoroughly familiar with ancient Roman monuments.

His fellow Bolognese *Primaticcio engaged Vignola to work for Francis I, King of France, in preparing molds in plaster and casts in bronze of some of the most famous statuary in Rome. Included were the *Vatican sculptures of the *Laocoon, the *"Cleopatra," the *Commodus as Hercules, the *Belvedere *Apollo*, the *Knidian *Aphrodite* and the *Nile* and *Tiber* river gods. Vignola accompanied Primaticcio to France (1541–43) to supervise the making of casts and to assist in an unspecified way with architectural plans.

Returning to Rome, Vignola became a member of the Vitruvian Academy, a group that had as a major objective the translation of the ancient Latin text of Vitruvius's *Ten Books on Architecture*. Though the manuscript had been rediscovered in Montecassino in 1414 and had been translated from time to time, the academy felt a need to give greater attention to the actual monuments that might clarify the text, and to this end Vignola was employed in measuring various ancient buildings, as reported by *Vasari. His own architectural treatise,

Regola delle cinque ordini d'architettura, was first published in 1562 and was an immediate success. It appeared in a long series of editions, including translations into French and English, that were influential for many years in Europe and in America. In an explication noted for its brevity, he advocates rather rigid rules for the creation of the five classical orders—Doric, Tuscan, Ionic, Corinthian and Composite.

Around the middle of the century, Vignola concentrated increasingly on his many architectural commissions. He was much esteemed as the supervising architect of the *Villa Giulia of Pope *Julius III (1551 and following) and as chief architect for the *Farnese family, for whom he finished the Palazzo Farnese in Rome (1549) and designed the Farnese palace at Caprarola (1558). He also supervised the laying out of the Farnese gardens on the *Palatine Hill (1565 and following). His study of ancient buildings has been seen as fundamentally important for several of his designs, for example, that of the internal curved façade of the Villa Giulia, recalling the hemicycle of the markets of Trajan, and the ramped approach to the façade at Caprarola, inspired by the *Sanctuary of Fortuna at Praeneste.

BIBLIOGRAPHY

+M. W. Casotti, *Il Vignola* 1–2 (Trieste, 1960), esp. I, 25–30; S. Pressouyre, "Les Fontes de Primatice à Fontainebleau," *Bulletin Monumental* (1969), 223–39; H. W. Wurm, s.v: "Vignola, Giacomo [Barozzi] da," *EWA* 14 (1967), cols. 791–99.

VILLA DEI BRONZI. See VILLA OF THE PAPYRI.

VILLA DEI PISONI. See VILLA OF THE PAPYRI.

VILLA GIULIA (MUSEO NAZIONALE DI VILLA GIULIA), Rome. Together with the *Florence Archeological Museum, the Museo Nazionale di Villa Giulia in Rome is the most important collection of Etrusco-Italic material in the world both for quantity and quality; its holdings come mainly from official (as distinct from casual or clandestine) excavations.

Thanks to the efforts of F. Bernabei, the museum was instituted by decree on 7 February 1889 to house antiquities from Lazio; contemporary provision was made in the Museo delle *Terme for material from Rome itself. The actual "villa" was built (1551–55) for Pope *Julius III outside the Porta Flaminia; among Late Renaissance artists engaged were *Michelangelo, *Vasari, Ammanati and *Vignola. Two wings were added in 1909–11; the present internal arrangements date from 1955–60. After initial difficulties, the museum began to function effectively in 1908 under the direction of G. A. Colini; his successors include G. Q. *Giglioli, A. Della Seta, R. Bartoccini and P. Pelagatti. The museum's affairs have been administered since 1939 by the Soprintendenza Archeologica per l'Etruria Meridionale.

With the exception of Tarquinia, all the Etruscan centers in the museum's territory are represented in the collection: *Veii (Villanovan cemeteries; temple of the *Apollo*), Caere (*Cerveteri: Eastern imports, impasto, *bucchero, painted pottery and the Sarcofago degli Sposi from the cemeteries; Manganello votive deposit; inscribed gold tablets and architectural terracottas from *Pyrgi), Bisenzio, *Bolsena and *Vulci (Villanovan and Archaic cemeteries: bronzes, pottery and stone statuary); and also Umbria (Terni, Todi), the Ager Faliscus (early cemeteries at Narce and Capena; cemeteries and sanctuaries at *Falerii) and Latium vetus (Orientalizing "princely" tombs, *Praeneste; *Nemi votive deposit; cemetery, habitation and sanctuary, *Satricum; Alatri temple). Other important features are the antiquarian section (*Chigi Vase, Veii; the *Ficoroni cista, Praeneste; other bronzes—figurines, mirrors and *repoussé* plaques); the *Castellani collection (donated 1919: jewelry, impasto, bucchero, Greek and Etruscan vases); and the Pesciotti collection (acquired 1972: Villanovan bronze ossuaries, incised bucchero, Greek pottery).

BIBLIOGRAPHY

+A. Della Seta, *Museo di Villa Giulia* (Rome, 1918); +P. Mingazzini, *Vasi della Collezione Castellani* (Rome, 1929, 1979); +*Nuove scoperte e acquisizioni nell'Etruria meridionale* (Rome, 1975); L. Proietti, ed., *Il Museo Nazionale etrusco di Villa Giulia*, (Rome, 1980).

F. R. SERRA RIDGWAY

VILLA ITEM. See VILLA OF THE MYSTERIES.

VILLANOVAN CULTURE. Italian Iron Age culture (ninth–eighth centuries B.C.) first discovered at Villanova, near *Bologna, in 1853.

Known especially from cemeteries, Villanovan culture is characterized by the use of the biconical ash urn for cremated remains and by the presence of iron and a rich repertory of artifacts of bronze.

*Gozzadini first discovered such material in the vicinity of his personal estate of Villanova; from the beginning he identified Villanovan as early Etruscan—an opinion much disputed in the nineteenth century (cf. *Brizio) but widely held today. Subsequently, extensive Villanovan remains were found in the area of Bologna in general and at a number of other sites, especially in Etruria, but also in Romagna, the Marche and Campania. Many cemeteries were excavated indifferently and poorly published (at Bologna, *Tarquinia, *Cerveteri), but in recent years several dedicated scholars (R. Pincelli and C. Morigi Govi, H. Hencken, I. Pohl, F. Delpino) have partly remedied the problem by producing definitive publications of material excavated earlier. Modern excavations at the cemetery of Quattro Fontanili at *Veii (1963–76) have been especially useful because of prompt and accurate publication.

Much recent discussion on Villanovan archaeology has been devoted to the problems associated with the term "Proto-Villanovan," often applied to a period of transition from the Italian Bronze Age to the Iron Age.

BIBLIOGRAPHY

M. Zuffa, "La civiltà villanoviana," in *Popoli e civiltà dell' Italia antica* 5 (1976), 197–363; M. A. Fuggazola Delpino, *La Cultura villanoviana* (Rome, 1984); C. Morigi Govi—

G. Sassatelli, eds., *Dalla Stanza delle Antichità al Museo Civico* (Bologna, 1984), passim; D. Ridgway, in *Cambridge Ancient History* 4 (new ed., 1988), 628–33, 640–53.

VILLA OF LIVIA (VILLA OF PRIMA PORTA; AD GALLINAS ALBAS). A Roman villa famous for its breed of white chickens and its laurel grove (Pliny, *NH* 15.136) on the right bank of the Tiber at the ninth mile of the Via Flaminia; owned by the wife of Augustus, Livia Drusilla (d. A.D. 29).

The villa occupied a height with a splendid view down the Tiber valley to Rome, and its lands and pavilions may have eventually extended across the river valley to Fidenae. Remaining today are massive works of terracing and three vaulted subterranean rooms, from the largest of which was removed (1951–52) the famous illusionistic garden painting now in the Museo Nazionale delle *Terme in Rome. There are poor remains of stucco reliefs on the ceiling. Excavations were conducted in various parts of the villa between 1863 and 1894, and various antiquities were recovered, among them the heroic cuirass statue known as the **Augustus* of Prima Porta now in the *Vatican, Braccio Nuovo. The villa, under investigation now by G. Messineo, apparently continued to be an imperial property down to the time of Theodoric.

BIBLIOGRAPHY

+M. M. Gabriel, *Livia's Garden Room at Prima Porta* (New York, 1955); +C. Calci— G. Messineo, *La Villa di Livia a Prima Porta* (Rome, 1984).

L. RICHARDSON, JR

VILLA OF PRIMA PORTA. See VILLA OF LIVIA.

VILLA OF THE MYSTERIES (VILLA ITEM). A suburban Roman villa northwest of *Pompeii on a road branching north off the Via dei Sepolcri.

The villa was excavated first by private initiative of Aurelio Item between 29 April and 16 May 1909, at which time the famous room with megalographic painting came to light. Digging was resumed in October of the same year and continued to January 1910, by which time the west half of the villa had been largely unearthed. The area of the villa was then expropriated by the government, and measures to preserve and protect the excavated parts were carried out. Further excavation was not undertaken until April 1929; it was then continued until June 1930, when the general outline of the building was exposed. Outlying parts, however, still remain buried, notably the fermentation yard for the wine that was the base of the villa's economy, with its dependencies, which may be extensive, and whatever the great south porticus may have led to. The latter is a late addition to the villa but very grand, with the suggestion that it might have led to a second villa or at least a large new wing.

The decorations of the staterooms are the finest sequence of Second Style paintings ever discovered and are justly famous. Less attention has been paid the architecture, due to *Maiuri's early misconception that the villa fell on evil days after the earthquake of A.D. 62 and was being remodeled to serve humble agricultural use. The evidence is, rather, that the remodeling was to be on a sumptuous scale and very elegant.

The interpretation of the megalography of the triclinium at the southwest corner of the house has excited more controversy than any other painting from antiquity, controversy that continues strong today. Maiuri's notion that it represents a ritual of the mystery cult of Bacchus and was a room used especially for weddings is certainly mistaken, but there is no consensus on most other points. The subject is Bacchic, with strong allusion to the mystery cult, but nothing secret or ritual is shown.

A portrait statue of a woman found in the peristyle was identified by Maiuri as Livia, wife of Augustus. In recent years this identification has been questioned.

BIBLIOGRAPHY

+A. Maiuri, *La Villa dei Misteri,* 1–2 (Rome, 1931); A.M.G. Little, *A Roman Bridal Drama at the Villa of the Mysteries* (Kennebunk, ME, 1972); Ling, *Roman Painting,* 101–5, 229, with bib.

L. RICHARDSON, JR

VILLA OF THE PAPYRI (VILLA DEI PISONI, VILLA DEI BRONZI). A large suburban villa at Portici, across the western gully from *Herculaneum, in a position commanding a magnificent view of the Bay of Naples and Capri.

The villa was discovered in June 1750 as a well was driven by a farmer named Ciceri into the circular belvedere at the northwestern extremity of the villa, where a fine marble pavement excited much interest. Regular excavations were begun in August of that year and continued by tunneling until February 1761, when work had to be suspended because of fumes in the tunnels. It was reopened again in February 1764 but abandoned at the end of June without significant discoveries. Much probably still remains buried, since the northeastern quarter of the house close to the library remains to be explored.

The house is a splendid country house entered through a peristyle with the atrium complex beyond opening to a colonnaded front overlooking the sea. The main reception rooms were around this atrium and between the two peristyles. The wing extending northeast of the atrium contained an elaborate bath suite and a library. An enormous colonnaded garden extended to the northwest and was the setting for a collection of statuary of marble and bronze around a long pool. More gardens and pavilions continued beyond.

Throughout, the house was sumptuously appointed and furnished with a wealth of fountains and a magnificent collection of bronze and marble sculptures, both large and small, preponderantly Hellenistic in type but including an Archaic head and several Classical ones and also a number of Roman portraits. Some of the pieces are extremely fine. All these enrich the *Museo Nazionale at Naples.

There were also discovered great numbers of carbonized papyri, mostly rolls, and a few waxed tablets. These were found at various points around the atrium, and their study and deciphering are work that continues today. Very few seem to be Latin; the majority have turned out to be multiple copies of works of Philodemos, the Epicurean philosopher of the first century B.C. Since he is known to have enjoyed the patronage of the Calpurnii Pisones, it has been presumed that this villa must have belonged to them.

BIBLIOGRAPHY

+D. Comparetti—G. De Petra, *La Villa ercolanese dei Pisones, i suoi monumenti e la sua biblioteca* (Turin, 1883, repr. 1972); M. R. Wojcik, *La Villa dei Papiri ad Ercolano* (Rome, 1986).

L. RICHARDSON, JR

VILLARD DE HONNECOURT (WILARS DE HONECORT; ca. 1175–ca. 1233). French Gothic architect.

Villard is the only thirteenth century architect whose sketchbook is preserved (Paris, B.N. ms. fr. 19093, 66 pp., 240mm × 160mm). In his didactic treatise composed between ca. 1215 and 1233, he discussed surveying, proportions, machines, gadgets, seminal examples of Gothic architecture, sculpture past and present, animals and medicine. Educated by the Benedictines in the northern French town of Honnecourt, he was well versed in the rudiments of Pythagorean and Euclidean geometry and wrote faultless French. Like other builders he was an avid traveler. He visited Laon, Chartres, Lausanne and even Hungary. Incessantly, he noted architectural innovations and objects of antiquity. Because of the fundamental nature of his sketches, covering a wide range of fields, he has been compared with Vitruvius, whose books were well known from the ninth century onward.

Villard loved mechanical and hydraulic automata, which were manufactured in the nearby foundry centers of Liège and Dinant (pp. 13, 17, 34, 44). On page 17 he shows and describes a "cantepleure," a chalice from whose cup emerges a bird seated on a turret. The gadget is a gravity syphon. Wine disappears into the hollow foot, and the displaced air escapes through a whistle. The bird, seeing the liquid vanish from its grasp, utters a plaintive cry. The toy corresponds to similar centerpieces described in Heron of Alexandria's *Pneumatica.* The enormous catapult on page 54, with its counterpoise weighing ca. twenty tons, duplicates Vitruvius's interest in military machinery.

Villard drew more directly from classical sources in cityscapes based on Carolingian manuscripts (p. 7) or an ivory representing a circus battle with lions (pp. 52–53). As a humanist architect, he was intensely interested in classical sculpture. He repeatedly stayed at Reims, where he witnessed the work of a neoclassical group of carvers responsible for a series of figures, most notably, the *Visitation* group with its Flavian overtones (pp. 6, 8, 10, 11, 21–24, 43, 49–50, 54–55). Page 11 shows a "Pagan Tomb" with two seminude male Victories holding a wreath above an enthroned emperor or consul. It was inspired by a Gallo-Roman stele or a late classical diptych such as that of Probianus of ca. A.D. 400. The most interesting pseudoclassical figure shows a full-page nude male (p. 22). The figure points heavenward with his left hand and holds a vase with flowers in his right. He has turned away from an altar with an image of a seated medieval king. Washes indicate the musculature and an awkward attempt at a rigid contrapposto. Clearly, Villard had difficulties capturing the classical mode. The figure is probably based on an astronomical manuscript such as the Leiden *Aratus* (Voss lat. 79) or a Carolingian prototype showing the seasons. More successful body images are seen on page 43, with a seated and a standing nude male, the latter in a stiff contrapposto. The bodies are not seen as single entities but remain a collection of parts. Hahnloser compared the figures with small Roman bronzes that may have surfaced in Reims. Pages 10 and 43 display "testes de fuelles," frontal heads from which leaves have sprouted. This motif is found in Roman decorative sculpture and the fifth-century mosaic floor of the imperial palace in Constantinople. In a later drawing (p. 58) showing a gesticulating man in chlamys and skull cap, body motion is resolved with the fluid ease that had already characterized the early twelfth-century work of Renier de Huy. The same curve of the contrapposto was transferred to fully clothed figures based on the sculptures of Reims cathedral of the 1220s (pp. 50, 54–55).

A large number of geometric schemata inscribed in figures prove Villard's attempt at a canon of human proportions that would "facilitate work" (pp. 35–38). His triangles, pentagrams, rectangles and rotational squares provide guidelines for quick sketching. His schema for drawing a face consists of sixteen squares (p. 38). The eyelids bisect the face; the bottom of the nose meets with the third line from the top. The width of the face measures two units, and with the hair it fills four units.

Villard's architectural geometry is based on the quadrature, the principle of rotation of successively inscribed squares at forty-five-degree angles. This method was used in Rome, Asia Minor and North Africa and lies within the general survival of Greek, Roman and Byzantine design theory. The same procedure was used by Villard to halve the volume of two cylindrical vessels. Many other images such as a labyrinth, a nude viola player and "realistic" animals corroborate the general enthusiasm for classical prototypes that characterized the thirteenth-century Renaissance and especially the school of sculptors that spread from Reims to Metz, Strasbourg, Bamberg and, finally, Naumburg. The ideal realism present in Villard's sketchbook surely made a later owner, André Félibien, author of the *Dissertation touchant l'architecture antique et gothique* (Paris, 1707) more receptive to the inventive and classicizing vigor of Gothic art, which had been despised for so long.

BIBLIOGRAPHY

T. Bowie, ed., *The Sketchbook of Villard de Honnecourt* (Bloomington, IN, 1959); +H. R. Hahnloser, *Villard de Honnecourt* (Graz, 1972); +F. Bucher, *Architector, The Lodge Books and Sketch Books of Medieval Architects,* 1 (New York, 1979).

F. BUCHER

VIOLLET-LE-DUC, EUGÈNE EMMANUEL (1814–79). French architect, scholar and restorer of buildings of the Middle Ages.

Viollet-le-Duc was also a designer of stained glass and furniture and a writer. His reputation as a scholar is based on his theoretical writings, the *Dictionnaire raisonné de l'architecture française du XIe au XVIe siècle* and his *Entretiens sur l'architecture.* These works demonstrated his belief in a rational and practical basis for architecture. His preferred style was the Gothic, which he believed was purely functional and had been developed to answer specific needs.

In 1836 and 1837 Viollet-le-Duc spent eighteen months traveling in *Sicily and Italy visiting all the important archaeological sites, including *Pompeii, *Paestum and *Herculaneum and Florence, Venice and Rome. He kept a day-by-day journal, wrote extensive and very interesting letters and made 450 drawings that are fine and detailed. These record both general views and details of classical buildings as well as architectural ornaments and sculpture that he found interesting from museum collections. He admired Greek temples for their fine proportions and for their simplicity and truth and found Roman architecture grand and noble but lacking in character. Just halfway through his Italian journey, le-Duc admitted that buildings of the Middle Ages impressed him more deeply than antique ones because they were more passionate and expressive; from the moment of his return from Italy, he steadfastly adhered to medieval sources for inspiration and Romanesque and Gothic buildings for restoration.

BIBLIOGRAPHY

Viollet-le-Duc, *Lettres d'Italie 1836–1837, adressées à sa famille, annotées par Geneviève Viollet-le-Duc* (Paris, 1971); + *Viollet-le-Duc,* exhibition catalog (Paris, 1980).

ELEANOR A. ROBBINS

VIPSUL. See FIESOLE.

VISCONTI, ENNIO QUIRINO (1751–1818). Italian archaeologist and museum administrator, important for his systematic and thorough approach to antiquities.

Though he cannot be associated with any single innovation comparable to *Winckelmann's "invention" of a new history of Greek art, Visconti deservedly enjoyed almost as wide an international reputation in his day as his illustrious predecessor. Almost all his work took the form of commentary on specific antiquities; here he brought to bear new criteria of relevance and critical rigor that mark his work as the first clear departure from the luxuriant displays of erudition engaged in by previous antiquarians to a modern style of cataloging and analyzing works of ancient art.

Son of the antiquarian Giovanni Battista Antonio *Visconti, who was Winckelmann's successor as commissioner of antiquities to the pope, Visconti was a child prodigy who, at the age of thirteen, had translated Euripides' *Hecuba* into Italian. Though he acquired a doctorate in canonical and Roman law by the age of twenty, he did not accede to his father's wish that he embark on a career at the papal court; instead, he took up a post as librarian to the Chigi family, where he devoted himself to literary and antiquarian pursuits. He collaborated with his father on a monumental catalog of the ancient sculptures in the new *Vatican

Portrait of *E. Q. Visconti*, Rome, Deutsches Archäologisches Institut (German Archaeological Institute). (Deutsches Archäologisches Institut, Rome. Inst. Neg. 76.1845.)

museum set up under *Clement XIV (1769–74) and *Pius VI (1775–99). *Il Museo Pio-Clementino* became his best-known contribution to classical archaeology (7 vols., 1782–1807; even the initial volume published before his father's death was almost entirely Visconti's own work.) In 1784, he was appointed conservator of the *Capitoline Museum, but real public prominence came later, in 1797, after the French had occupied Rome, and he was invited to help form a provisional government in which he served as minister of the interior. When the French were finally driven out of Rome in 1799 by the Neapolitans, Visconti was forced to flee Italy.

On his arrival in France that year, he was appointed administrator and professor of archaeology at the new museum in the *Louvre. Further official recognition from the government of *Napoleon soon followed—in 1803 he was chosen a founding member of the Institut's Classe des beaux-arts, and a year later he also became a member of the Classe d'histoire et de la littérature ancienne. The first of his guides to the antique sculptures on display in the Louvre appeared in 1801, and he subsequently collaborated with Éméric-David on the antiquities section of the luxuriously produced catalog, *Le Musée français,* published in parts between 1803 and 1809. In the introductory ''Discours historique sur la sculpture antique'' (1805–6), the two authors attacked Winckelmann's highly speculative, but by then fashionable, theory that Greek art had gone into irreparable decline after the so-called Classic period, and they argued that the work of later artists producing free imitations of earlier Greek prototypes need not have been inferior, but, on the contrary, might even have been better for being more perfectly refined.

At a time when archaeological opinion was coming round to the view that the best-known antiques were likely to be relatively late Graeco-Roman productions, this new theory served to rescue the reputation of Napoleon's prize booty from Italy—famous statues such as the *Medici *Venus* and the *Belvedere *Apollo*—from any suspicion that they might not be the unsurpassable exemplars of classic excellence they were, until recently, assumed to have been. In the earlier volumes of *Il Museo Pio-Clementino,* Visconti had already taken issue with *Mengs's doubts about the famous Vatican antiques; and in the 1797 volume he commented, with pointed reference to Winckelmann, that the very high quality of the sculptures known to have been produced under the emperor Hadrian destroyed ''the vain systems and periods that have been determined only by the phantasy of those who up until now have written about antiquities.''

Visconti's reflections on the history of Greek sculpture were given a further impulse when, in 1814, he was brought to London by Lord *Elgin in the hope that he might lend his professional authority to certifying the somewhat contested authenticity and artistic quality of the *Parthenon marbles. Visconti had already published an extended commentary on the Parthenon bas-reliefs to accompany the engravings of them in the *Museum Worsleyanum* (vol. 2, probably 1804), where he anticipated some recent speculation that the frieze of the Panatheniac procession might have commemorated the heroes of a particular historical occasion that had special significance for the Athenians. In his *Deux mémoires . . . sur les ouvrages de sculpture dans la collection de Mylord d'Elgin* (1816), which became the standard scholarly text on the subject, he argued that the ''transcendent merit'' of the Parthenon Marbles, equaled by only a very few of the finest traditional masterpieces, demonstrated how Winckelmann was wrong to have supposed that sculpture of the age of Pheidias had been characterized by a residual stiffness of form; Greek sculpture at this point had already ''reached its limits,'' and later artists would not have been able to introduce any significant refinements. While he reaffirmed that careful imitation had kept Greek art at ''almost the same high level'' for six centuries after Pheidias, his suggestion that the ''Ilissos'' showed a ''supple and living'' quality that surpassed anything previously known from antiquity hinted at a more Romantic view of early Greek art.

Among his numerous other publications, the most important were the catalog of the *Borghese family collection, published posthumously in 1821, and a vast iconographical compendium of portraits of famous Greeks and Romans undertaken in 1804 under the auspices of the Napoleonic government (three volumes of the *Iconographie grecque* appeared in 1808, but only one volume of the

Iconographie romaine came out, in 1817, the year before his death). The basis of Visconti's reputation among his contemporaries was explained succinctly by the French antiquarian Millin de Grandmaison: "[F]rom a conjectural science, he made an almost exact science." In addition to the recognizably modern way in which he set out his evidence, with full critical apparatus of citations and comparative illustrations, what mainly distinguishes Visconti's approach is his "method" of systematic comparison between images that are demonstrably replicas of the same motif. Any surviving evidence—an inscription, an extra attribute or the context—relating to one version could then be used to help make sense of the others (the method was one Visconti himself traced back to the seventeenth-century antiquarian Raphael *Fabretti). Visconti, an expert numismatist and palaeographer, made extensive use of coins, recognizing that these often reproduced famous statues; in this way, for example, he identified the copy of the *Tyche of Antioch* in the Vatican. Moreover he (rather than Winckelmann, who had pioneered the chronological classification of antiquities) was the first to bring to bear in a systematic way modern "art-historical" concerns about such matters as date, state of preservation, quality as compared with other known replicas and the identification of the original prototype; earlier antiquarians saw their expertise as confined to seeking out subject matter from ancient texts that might tally convincingly with the image they were discussing.
BIBLIOGRAPHY
T.-B. Eméric-David, "Visconti, Ennio Quirino," *BU* 43 (1854–65), 626–35; +H. Omont, "Inventaire de la Collection Visconti conservée à la Bibliothèque Nationale," *RA,* 3rd. ser. (January–June 1891), 174 ff.; +G. Sforza, *Ennio Quirino Visconti e la sua famiglia* (Genoa, 1923).

ALEX POTTS

VISCONTI, GIOVANNI BATTISTA (1722–84). Roman antiquarian and administrator.

Visconti was born at Vernazza, near La Spezia, on 26 December 1722, son of Marc Antonio, a doctor. His father died early, and he was educated by two uncles; he came to Rome ca. 1736. At the university of the Sapienza he studied botany and medicine but discovered antiquity through numismatics and deepened his understanding while overseeing the education of his sons. He married Orsola de' Filonardi in 1750, by whom he had Ennio Quirino (*Visconti), Filippo Aurelio and Alessandro.

Visconti was the student and assistant of *Winckelmann (commissioner of antiquities, 1763–68) and succeeded him upon his murder; he was appointed commissioner to Clement XIII by Cardinal Rezzonico (papal chamberlain) on 30 June 1768. During his office, Visconti opposed the export of the Barberini candelabra (found at *Hadrian's Villa) and the Verospi *Jupiter* (which went to the *Vatican). The Museo Clementino was founded in 1771, but this was the age of the exploitation of Rome by, in particular, Gavin *Hamilton (digging on the Palatine, at Hadrian's Villa and at *Ostia) and the formation of the major

English collections by Lansdowne, *Townley, *Blundell and Hope. The masterpieces of the *Medici family collection were exported to Florence, the *Mattei family collection was broken up (the best pieces went to the Vatican, but the rest were exported) and Francesco Piranesi was working to build the Swedish royal collection.

Among the most important finds during Visconti's commissariate were Mirri's discovery of painted rooms in the *Domus Aurea (1774), the excavation of the Villa Peretti (1777; the paintings were sold to the Earl of Bristol), the discovery of the Ustrinum Augustorum in the same year, the vandalizing of the *Tomb of the Scipios (1780) and the discovery of the Lancellotti *Diskobolos on the Esquiline (1781; now in the *Terme Museum, Rome).

Visconti published little, mostly "letters," such as one on the Diskobolos (repr. by F. Cancellieri, Dissertazioni epistolari sopra la statua del Discobolo, 1806) and another on the Tomb of the Scipios (in Antologia Romana, 1779). His most important work was the first volume of Il Museo Pio-Clementino illustrato e descritto da Giovanni Battista e Ennio Quirino Visconti (reissue, 1818–22), written with his son. He was also a poet, whose La Susanna (1754) and Il Tobia (1757) were set to music. He was a member of many academies: S. Luca (1774), the Arcadi, Vari (president, 1741), Infecondi, Forti, Aborigini. From 1782 he began to suffer eye trouble, and his son Filippo Aurelio was appointed to assist him (and became his successor). Visconti died on 11 September 1784 and was buried in S. Giovanni dei Fiorentini.

BIBLIOGRAPHY

E. Tipaldo, Biografia degli italiani illustri 2 (1835), 478–81; L. Grillo, Elogi di liguri illustri 3 (1846), 54–58.

R. T. RIDLEY

VITERBO. Italian city, site of a small Etruscan settlement and cemeteries (dating especially to the fourth–second centuries B.C.) and a Roman municipium.

The locale became famous in the fifteenth and sixteenth centuries, when it was patriotically proclaimed a cradle of civilization and wrongly identified with the ancient *Vetulonia by *Annio da Viterbo. In 1494, before the eyes of the papal court of Alexander VI, Annio opened an Etruscan tomb and proclaimed the four "triumphal statues" in it to represent Cybele, Iasius, Armonia and Electra, all "smeared with red" paint. The sculptures, evidently sarcophagi, are now lost. Their nature may have been similar to nine others discovered in a tomb in the same cemetery (Cipollara) 200 years later. These sarcophagi, made of tufa with reclining figures and funerary inscriptions, date to the third century B.C. or later. Finds from the tomb were well described and illustrated by Feliciano Bussi, along with many other antiquities discovered in Viterbo in the seventeenth and eighteenth centuries, in his Veterum etruscorum monumenta in viterbiensi territorio reperta (Rome, 1737–38). The present Museo Civico di Viterbo contains many of these items, as well as the large collection of antiquities amassed by the local archaeologist Luigi Rossi Danieli (d. 1909). Finds from the site of *Acquarossa are on display at the Rocca Albornoz.

BIBLIOGRAPHY
A. Emiliozzi, *La Collezione Rossi Danieli nel Museo Civico di Viterbo* (Rome, 1974); idem, *Il Museo Civico di Viterbo, Storia delle raccolte archeologiche* (Rome, 1986).

VIX KRATER. Huge bronze mixing bowl found in a tumulus burial of a Celtic princess, dating ca. 500 B.C., at Vix (Mont Lassois), near Châtillon-sur-Seine, France; discovered in 1953 by R. Joffroy and deposited at the Musée Municipal at Châtillon-sur-Seine.

Of finest workmanship and firmly dated to the late sixth century B.C., the krater was perhaps made at Sparta (or a colony in Magna Graecia—Taras?) and is the largest vessel known from antiquity (height 1.64m, diameter 1.27m, weight 208kg, capacity 1,100 liters); the bronze is eggshell-thin (1mm). Parts are detachable for transport, but how (or why) it got to Vix at this early date raises problems.

BIBLIOGRAPHY
R. Joffroy, "La Tombe de Vix," *MonPiot* 48 (1954), 1–68.

A. TREVOR HODGE

VOLATERRAE. See VOLTERRA.

VOLSINII. One of the twelve major city-states of Etruria, dominating the middle Tiber valley and considered in antiquity to be the very heart of the Etruscan nation because of the vicinity of the revered federal sanctuary of Fanum Voltumnae (as yet unidentified); renowned for its temple to the goddess Nortia, where nails were ceremonially fixed to mark the passage of years (Livy 7.3.7).

After long controversy, modern research has recognized in the rich remains at *Orvieto the Etruscan city of *Velzna* (Latin *Volsinii Veteres*), virtually deserted by the mid-third century B.C., when, according to ancient authors, the Romans, summoned to assist in quashing a plebeian revolt, moved all the inhabitants to *Volsinii Novi* (265 B.C.); this can be identified in the extensive remains of Late Republican date excavated by the French near *Bolsena on the shores of the lake of the same name in northern Lazio.

BIBLIOGRAPHY
R. Bloch, *Recherches archéologiques en territoire volsinien* (Paris, 1972); G. Colonna, "Considerazioni sull'Etruria interna volsiniese," *StEtr* 41 (1973), 45–72.

F. R. SERRA RIDGWAY

VOLTERRA (VELATHRI; VOLATERRAE). Etruscan and Roman city.

An austere site in the hills of northwestern Tuscany, Volterra is distinguished by the extent (more than 7k) of its fortifications and an arched gate ornamented with three large stone heads, but it is best known today for the hundreds of ash urns found in the ancient city's cemeteries.

These urns were already known in the Middle Ages; one was reused to house the bones of a local saint. In 1466, the humanist Antonio Ivano of Sarzana described the finds of a tomb discovered near Volterra, including ash urns and pottery. Serious exploration of the cemeteries began in 1731 with the discovery of a rock-cut tomb containing "more than 40 urns, some with carved reliefs and inscriptions." Scholars and dilettanti began to dig and to collect; Anton Francesco *Gori published twenty-one of the first tomb's urns and later cataloged the collection of the distinguished Volterran prelate Mario *Guarnacci, who willed his "museum" and library to his city in 1761. This, with earlier donations, became the nucleus of the Museo Etrusco Guarnacci, the first museum of purely Etruscan material.

Excavations continued through the nineteenth century; in 1883 the first Villanovan burial was found, raising interest in the earlier phases of the city. In 1926 Doro *Levi began to excavate the acropolis, the Pian di Castello; excavation was continued there in 1967. Above earlier material were found remains of two Hellenistic temples and, near them, a reservoir of the Augustan period. In 1950 Enrico *Fiumi, director of the Guarnacci Museum and library, began to excavate the Roman theater in Vallebuona, the largest and handsomest architectural complex of the Imperial period in all Tuscany. The fine statuary that ornamented it is among the later additions to the Museo Guarnacci.

BIBLIOGRAPHY

G. Dennis, *Cities and Cemeteries of Etruria,* 2nd ed. (London, 1878), II, 136–93; +E. Fiumi, *Volterra etrusca e romana* (Pisa, 1976); +M. Cristofani, *Urne volterrane 2, Il Museo Guarnacci* (Florence, 1977); +S. Haynes, *Etruscan Bronzes* (London, 1985), 118–22.

EMELINE HILL RICHARDSON

VOS, MARTIN DE (MARTEN; 1532–1603). Flemish painter.

Martin de Vos was educated in Antwerp and traveled to Rome, Florence and Venice, where he worked in Tintoretto's workshop, remaining until 1558.

A sketchbook in the Rijksmuseum, Amsterdam, inscribed on the cover page as "by the great master M. De Vos," contains some 200 drawings of antique and modern subjects in pen and brown ink. Included are statues (e.g., the *Quirinal *Horse Tamers,* the Farnese *Atlas,* the *Farnese *Captives*), relief sculpture (Augustus and Livia from the Altar of the Lares Augusti in the Uffizi) and architecture (*Theater of Marcellus). Netto-Bol argued (1976) that some are copies of drawings made by Marten van *Heemskerck in the 1530s and that the sketchbook was not by Marten de Vos but by an unknown artist in the circle of Frans *Floris.

If the sketchbook is not by Vos, then we have no drawings by him after Greek and Roman statuary. It seems that the study af ancient art, for Vos as for many of his Flemish contemporaries, formed a relatively small part of his Italian studies and that far more important was the influence of *Michelangelo, *Raphael, *Titian and Tintoretto. In early compositions, his uses of draperies, gestures, architecture and decorative elements such as statues or ruins are taken from the antique repertoire (e.g., *Rebecca and Eleazer at the Well,* Mousty, Brussels, Charles van Hove's collection), but the effects of inspiration provided by ancient art disappear in his following works, which are clearly influenced by Tintoretto's painting and Counter-Reformation trends. The Venetian's influence can be seen in Vos's abundant production, meant, in large part, for churches in the Low Countries.

BIBLIOGRAPHY
S. Sulzberger, *Essai de monographie sur Martin de Vos* (Brussels, 1938); M.M.L. Netto-Bol, *The So-Called Marten de Vos Sketchbook of Drawings After the Antique* (The Hague, 1976); +A. Zweite, *Marten de Vose als Maler* (Berlin, 1980).

G. DENHAENE

VULCI. One of the great Etruscan centers, situated on the river Fiora north of *Tarquinia.

Vulci was the home of the brothers Aulus and Caelius Vibenna, active participants in Roman history of the regal period. Already flourishing in the first Villanovan period, Vulci attained a prosperous level in artistic and industrial commerce and production by Late Orientalizing times which increased in the sixth and fifth centuries B.C.; its decline began ca. 450 and (apart from a brief rally in the fourth century) continued after the Roman conquest and the consequent foundation of *Cosa (273 B.C.).

Vulci was deserted after the eighth century A.C.; the ruins on the Pian de' Volci, noted in the fourteenth century, were correctly identified by *Annio da Viterbo (followed by L. Holstenius, F. A. Turiozzi, L. *Canina). Predatory excavations in the cemeteries were conducted by Cardinal Pallotta (1783; *Vatican Museums), F. Prada (1787), Feoli and Candelori (1825) and, especially, L. Bonaparte, prince of *Canino (1828–40: *Prospettiva* 21, 1980, 6–24); European collections were inundated with jewelry, bronzes, ivories, and painted pottery, both Etruscan and—especially—Attic, first recognized as such (and not as Etruscan) thanks to the Vulci material included by E. *Gerhard in his "Rapporto vulcente" (1831). More scientific methods were employed on behalf of the *Torlonia family by A. *François, who discovered in 1857 the painted tomb named after him, and by S. Gsell, who issued the only proper excavation report on Vulci ever published, *Fouilles dans la nécropole de Vulci,* 1892. Two Guglielmi collections later found their way to the *Vatican Museums.

The official excavations of the present century (R. Mengarelli, G. Bendinelli, U. Ferraguti), including those in the city (R. Bartoccini), are largely unpublished. Accordingly, in spite of studies of single monuments (Cuccumella; Tombe di Iside, della Panatenaica) and categories (bronzes, stone sculpture, Etrusco-Corinthian and "Pontic" vases), it is not yet possible to write the history of one of the largest and most affluent centers of the ancient Mediterranean.

BIBLIOGRAPHY
+L. Canina, *L'Antica Etruria marittima* (Rome, 1849), II, 73–108; F. Messerschmidt, *Nekropolen von Vulci* (Berlin, 1930); G. Riccioni, "Vulci: A Topographical and

Historical Survey,'' in *Italy Before the Romans,* ed. D. Ridgway—F. R. Ridgway (London, 1979), 241–76, with historical bib.; F. Buranelli, ed., *La Tomba Francois di Vulci* (Rome, 1987); idem, *Gli Scavi della Società Vincenzo Campanari—Governo Pontifico (1835–1837)* (Rome, 1991).

F. R. SERRA RIDGWAY

W

WACE, ALAN JOHN BAYARD (1879–1957). English archaeologist best known for his excavation at Mycenae and his study of the Late Bronze Age civilization of the site; a specialist also in Near Eastern and Mediterranean embroideries, in particular, those of the Greek Islands.

Wace was educated at Shrewsbury School and at Pembroke College, Cambridge. He excavated widely, in Thessaly, at *Sparta and *Corinth, at *Troy and at *Alexandria, besides *Mycenae, where he began digging in the 1920s and continued at intervals until 1955. In the interim he served as librarian of the *British School at Rome (1905–6), lecturer in ancient history and archaeology, St. Andrews University (1912–14), director of the *British School at Athens (1914–23), deputy keeper in the Department of Textiles, Victoria and Albert Museum (1924–34), Laurence Professor of classical archaeology at Cambridge (1934–44) and, after retirement from Cambridge, professor of classics and archaeology at Farouk I University, Alexandria (until 1952). Wace's publications were extensive and varied: with M. N. Tod, *A Catalogue of the Sparta Museum;* with M. S. Thompson, *Prehistoric Thessaly; Nomads of the Balkans; Mediterranean and Near Eastern Embroideries in the Collection of Mrs. F. H. Cook; Approach to Greek Sculpture;* with Frank H. Stubbings, *A Companion to Homer.* His writings include even poetry and ghost stories; but his most important work centered on Mycenae: *Excavations at Mycenae, 1939–1955; Chamber Tombs at Mycenae* (1932); *Mycenae, An Archaeological History and Guide* (1949). He championed the role of mainland Greece in the Bronze Age, against Sir Arthur *Evans's view, and was vindicated in his belief that Linear B (*Linear A and B) represented an early stage of the Greek language by *Ventris's decipherment of the script in 1952. In collaboration with Carl *Blegen, Wace developed the systematic chronology for mainland Greece in the Bronze Age that is still in use.

BIBLIOGRAPHY
Times, 11–16 November 1957; H. A. Thompson, ''Alan John Bayard Wace,'' *AJA* 62 (1958), 229.

W. W. DE GRUMMOND

WAGNER, JOHANN MARTIN VON (1777–1858). German painter, sculptor, restorer and art dealer.

Born in Würzburg, Wagner studied at the academy of art at Vienna (1797). Upon his return to Würzburg, he was made professor of drawing at the university. He began to travel abroad—to Paris and Rome—and soon was hired (1810) to procure antiquities for (prince and then king) *Ludwig I of Bavaria. In spite of his rather strange personal appearance, he was generally successful in his mission. In Rome, Wagner purchased numerous statues from princes, dukes and cardinals. Traveling to Greece, he underwent hardship and deprivation as he became involved in the delicate negotiations that resulted in the purchase for Ludwig of the impressive sculptures from the temple at *Aigina excavated by *Cockerell and *Haller von Hallerstein. Restored by Wagner and *Thorvaldsen in Rome, the statues were delivered to Munich in 1820.

Portrait of *Johann Martin von Wagner*, etching by C. Kuchler, 1836. (Westfälisches Landesmuseum für Kunst und Kulturgeschichte, Münster, Porträtarchiv Diepenbroick. Photo: R. Wakonigg.)

As the years went by, Wagner acquired various antiquities for himself—pieces of sculpture, including a head of a centaur from a metope of the *Parthenon, and minor antiquities. At his death he bequeathed these to the university in his home city; they became the core of the Martin von Wagner Museum in Würzburg. A highly significant addition to the Wagner museum was made in 1872, when the university bought the Feoli collection, some 480 Greek and Etruscan vases, mostly from *Vulci. These have made the Martin von Wagner Museum famous.

BIBLIOGRAPHY

E. Simon, ed., *Führer durch die Antikenabteilung des Martin von Wagner Museums der Universitat Würzburg* (Mainz, 1975); Stoneman, 192–95; *Porträtarchiv*, no. 137.

WALDSTEIN (changed to WALSTON in 1918), Sir CHARLES (1856–1927). American archaeologist, art historian and political philosopher.

Born in New York, Waldstein studied at Columbia for two years and graduated from Heidelberg University in 1875 with a doctoral degree. In 1880 he accepted a teaching position in classical archaeology at Cambridge University and held various appointments there, including the directorship of the *Fitzwilliam Museum (Cambridge), until 1911. From 1888 to 1892 he was also director of the *American School of Classical Studies in Athens and subsequently professor of ancient art there (1892–97). He directed the American excavations at Plataia, *Eretria and the *Argive Heraion. Energetic, enthusiastic and well liked, Waldstein did much to stimulate interest in ancient art in the English-speaking world. His *Essays on the Art of Pheidias* (1885) was influential in its day. His most lasting work has been *The Argive Heraeum* (1902–5), though his excavation techniques were criticized by G. *Karo as falling below the standards established earlier at *Samothrace and *Olympia. He identified the head of Iris on the *Parthenon frieze.

Some idea of the wide range of his interests can be gathered from a selection of his numerous books: *The Work of John Ruskin* (1893); *The Jewish Question* (1899); *Herculaneum, Past Present and Future* (1908); *The Next War: Wilsonism and Anti-Wilsonism* (1918); *Truth* (1919).

BIBLIOGRAPHY

The Times, 23 March 1927, 14, 19; *Who Was Who 1916–28;* L. E. Lord, *A History of the American School of Classical Studies at Athens* (Cambridge, MA, 1947), 88 and passim.

DAVID A. TRAILL

WALSTON, CHARLES. See WALDSTEIN, CHARLES.

WALTERS, HENRY (1848–1931). American railroad magnate and art collector.

In the course of his studies at Georgetown and Harvard, Henry Walters spent two years in Paris, and there he developed a passion, like that of his father,

William T. Walters, for collecting works of art. On his return from Europe, Walters joined his father in the railroad business, later to become, it was said, "the richest man in the South." On his annual trips abroad, he had the opportunity to renew contacts with artists and sculptors and to develop generally his tastes in art. His interests were wide-ranging; gradually he assembled a remarkable collection of paintings, sculpture, textiles, ceramics, illuminated manuscripts and jewelry from every period of Eastern and Western art.

Often he acquired whole collections. One of these, the Massarenti collection, purchased in 1902, included seven Roman sarcophagi with scenes of Dionysos and one of Persephone and a number of bronze portrait heads of Augustus. Later Walters made single purchases, some Greek and Etruscan bronzes, a very fine Roman copy of a Praxiteles Satyr figure as well as a group of cameo and intaglio rings of the third century B.C. and two small gold Etruscan bullae. Walters's single acquisitions show a keen awareness of quality, something not always true in the larger group purchases. The collection was housed in 1909 at his home in Baltimore, along with the material inherited from his father. On Walters's death, the entire collection was bequeathed to the city of Baltimore as a public museum, the Walters Art Gallery.

BIBLIOGRAPHY

DAB 21 (1936), 399–400; D. Miner, "The Founders of the Collection," *JWalt* 1 (1938), 9–12; D. K. Hill, "The Spectacular in the Classical," *Apollo* 84 (1966), 32–37, and "The Classical Collection and Its Growth," *Apollo* 100 (1974), 6–13; R. H. Randall, Jr., "Jewellery Through the Ages," *Apollo* 84 (1966), 75–79.

ELEANOR A. ROBBINS

WARD-PERKINS, JOHN BRYAN (1912–81). English archaeologist; specialist in Roman architecture.

Qualified by academic achievement (at the London Museum) and war service (in North Africa and Italy), both under the command of Mortimer *Wheeler, John Ward-Perkins was director of the *British School at Rome from 1946 to 1974. The Libyan interests he brought to Rome were joined in the mid-1950s by the school's systematic field survey of South Etruria; these and other programs fueled major studies of architecture, town planning and the marble trade in the Roman world. Ward-Perkins was instrumental in founding the International Association for Classical Archaeology (and its annual bibliographical bulletin, *Fasti Archaeologici*) and the *Tabula Imperii Romani* project.

BIBLIOGRAPHY

D. E. Strong, review of A. Boëthius—J. B. Ward-Perkins, *Etruscan and Roman Architecture* (Harmondsworth, 1970), *AntJ* 51 (1971), 347–49; T. W. Potter, *The Changing Landscape of South Etruria* (London, 1979); J. Reynolds—M. Pallottino, "John Bryan Ward-Perkins, CMG, CBE, FBA 1912–1981," *BSR* 48 (1980), xiii-xviii; J. B. Ward-Perkins, *Roman Imperial Architecture* (Harmondsworth, 1981); H. Dodge—B. Ward-Perkins, eds., *Marble in Antiquity, Collected Papers of J. B. Ward-Perkins,* (London, 1992).

DAVID RIDGWAY

WARREN, EDWARD PERRY (1860–1928). American art collector and connoisseur.

Born in Boston, son of a wealthy paper manufacturer, graduate of Harvard College (1883), Warren early moved to England (Oxford M.A., 1888), where he settled in 1890 at Lewes House, "a monkish establishment where women were not welcomed" (Rothenstein). Platonic homosexuality attracted him to Greece, as it did earlier *Winckelmann. Aided by private income, impeccable taste and his scholarly secretary, John Marshall, he collected Greek vases, marbles, bronzes, terracottas and gems at Lewes. He resold at no profit the great pieces, for example, the Bartlett Head, the Chios Head, the Marotti *Herakles,* to the *Museum of Fine Arts, Boston, and later, others to the *Metropolitan and the Rhode Island School of Design. He donated lavishly to Boston, the *Ashmolean, Bowdoin College and, because of friendship with *Studniczka, Leipzig University. Boston owes the cream of its collection to Warren. *Beazley was a member of his circle. In retrospect, his trust of *Helbig was ill advised. From him he bought for £70,000 the Boston Throne, challenged by some as a forgery (cf. *Ludovisi Throne).

BIBLIOGRAPHY

E. Burnett—E. H. Goddard, *Edward Perry Warren: The Biography of a Connoisseur* (London, 1941); J. D. Beazley, "Warren as Collector," in Burdett-Goddard, 331–63; A. L. Rowse, *Homosexuals in History: A Study of Ambivalence in Society, Literature and the Arts* (London, 1977), 309–13; D. Sox, *Bachelors of Art, Edward Perry Warren and the Lewes House Brotherhood* (London, 1991).

WILLIAM M. CALDER III

WEBSTER, THOMAS BERTRAM LONSDALE (1905–74). British professor of Greek; specialist in Greek art, drama and dramatic monuments.

Influenced at Oxford by J. D. *Beazley and J. L. *Myres, Webster was successively professor at Manchester (1931–48), University College, London (1948–68) and Stanford (1968–70). Between 1939 and 1959, he conducted a brilliant parallel survey of Greek art and literature from Homer to Menander, extending this (after the decipherment of Linear B [*Linear A and Linear B] by his friend M. *Ventris) in a pioneer investigation of the period *From Mycenae to Homer* (1958). The two inseparable elements of his oeuvre were likewise combined in notable studies of Greek dramatists and theater production. An inspiring teacher, Webster was the moving spirit in the development of the unique Institute of Classical Studies in the University of London.

BIBLIOGRAPHY

T.B.L. Webster, *Greek Art and Literature, 700–530 B.C.* (Otago, 1959), xv-xviii; A. D. Trendall, T.B.L. Webster Memorial Lecture (summary), *BICS* 21 (1974), 1–2.

DAVID RIDGWAY

WEDGWOOD, JOSIAH (1730–95). Famous English potter, following family tradition.

Portrait of *Josiah Wedgwood*, engraving by S. W. Reynolds after Sir Joshua Reynolds, 1841. (Westfälisches Landesmuseum für Kunst und Kulturgeschichte, Münster, Porträtarchiv Diepenbroick. Photo: R. Wakonigg.)

Wedgwood's youth coincided with the exploitation of the newly discovered ancient cities of *Herculaneum and *Pompeii; his pottery belongs with the artworks derived from these sources that formed a fountainhead for the whole neoclassical movement.

Born in Burslem, as a child Wedgwood was apprenticed to his older brother Thomas and acquired a consummate skill at the potter's wheel. Unfortunately he was forced by illness to turn to modeling as less strenuous; nevertheless, his fertile imagination then allowed him to expand his capacities endlessly. Over the years he so improved the art and manufacture of pottery that it became a major British industry. His crowning artistic achievement was the invention of the deep-blue jasperware that strikingly sets off his decorative white classic figures in bas-relief.

Starting from modest beginnings, Wedgwood developed substantial potting facilities in his native Staffordshire, finally opening, in 1769, his extensive ceramic works at Etruria, named after the homeland of the Etruscans (*Etruscheria), since they were thought at the time to have created the *Greek vases found in *Etruscan tombs. At that time Wedgwood threw the famous "First Day's Vases" depicting *Hercules in the Garden of the Hesperides.* Showrooms were opened in London as of 1768, and he maintained a studio of modelers in Rome from 1787 to 1795. His first portrait medallions date from 1771 with subjects drawn from antiquity and modern times. During his career, he employed prominent artists as modelers, portraitists and decorators, including John *Flaxman, William Hackwood and George Stubbs, among the best known. He also bought classical casts from other sources such as James *Tassie, and Hoskins & Grant.

On presentation of two sets of creamware vases to Queen Charlotte in 1765, Wedgwood was named Potter to the Queen. In 1774 Catherine the Great of Russia ordered from him a second dinner service, the famous 952-piece "frog service." Thanks to his practical research and public-spirited activities, Wedgwood was named fellow of the Royal Society in 1783 and member of the *Society of Antiquaries in 1786. His practical turn of mind had long since led to the production of a wide range of so-called useful wares, as well as unique decorative creations of classical inspiration. His first catalog of "ornamental wares" was issued in 1773, mainly composed of replicas of antique medals, cameos, intaglios, tablets, statues and so on. A historic achievement took place with the creation in 1790 (and in limited editions since then) of replicas of the famous *Portland (or Barberini) Vase, the original with its enigmatic bas-relief dating from the first century B.C.

Wedgwood died at Etruria in 1795. After his death the firm was taken over by his son and then by successive generations until present times. It still enjoys worldwide respect for the classical elegance of its pottery. Wedgwood Societies in Britain, the United States, Australia and elsewhere pursue active research and publication on the subject of Wedgwood's art.

BIBLIOGRAPHY
F. Rathbone, *Old Wedgwood* (London, 1898); E. Meteyand, *Life of Josiah Wedgwood* (London, 1970); S. Stephen—S. Lee, "Wedgwood, Josiah," *DNB* 20 (1973), 1051–57.

J. S. TASSIE

WEEGE, FRITZ (1880–1945). German philologist, archaeologist and art historian, known for his work on the *Domus Aurea (Golden House) and Etruscan painting.

Born in Frankfort am Main, Fritz Weege studied at Bonn and Berlin with the leading classicists of the turn of the nineteenth century (Usener, *Wilamowitz, *Loeschke, *Kekule et al.). From 1920 he was professor (*Ordinarius*) of classical archaeology at Breslau, a post he held until his death.

Weege published early on the Oscan language and inscriptions and on Oscan tomb painting. Receiving a state travel stipend (1907–8), he was off to Greece to take part in excavations at *Olympia with *Dörpfeld. In Rome he undertook a study of the Golden House of Nero, analyzing the paintings and stucco decoration and recording the signatures of numerous early visitors to the Domus Aurea. Contracting typhus, he refused to give up his studies and, much against the wishes of his nurses, would leave the hospital for excursions to the damp, unhealthy underground site. The ground plans he drew of the rooms became the basis of much subsequent work. At the same time Weege was studying the influence of the *grottesche* of the Domus Aurea in Renaissance art and published a study of their use in the Loggia of *Raphael (1911).

From Weege's pen came the guide to the *Villa Giulia in the third edition of W. Helbig's *Führer durch die Antikensammlungen Roms.* His most influential publication was his book on Etruscan tomb painting, *Etruskische Malerei* (1921), with rich illustrations and commentary on the context of the paintings, as well as a section on the history of the study of *Etruscan tombs and their influence.

BIBLIOGRAPHY
E. von Mercklin, "Fritz Weege," *Gnomon* 23 (1951), 117–18; *Archäologenbildnisse,* 331.

WELCKER, FRIEDRICH GOTTLIEB (1784–1868). German archaeologist and classical philologist.

A clergyman's son, friend of Wilhelm von *Humboldt and correspondent of *Goethe, Welcker was long (1819–68) professor of classical philology at Bonn, where he taught ancient art history along with philology and founded an early museum of casts. He traveled widely in classical lands and was deeply influenced by *Zoëga at Rome (1806–8), whose life he later wrote. He discovered the *Totalitätsideal,* the requirement to command all evidence, philological and archaeological, in order to understand antiquity. This conception molded *Jahn, the *Mommsens, *Wilamowitz and Carl *Robert. His extensive publications stress Greek religion, poetry and art.

BIBLIOGRAPHY
R. Kekulé, *Das Leben Friedrich Gottlieb Welcker's nach seinen eignen Aufzeichnungen und Briefen* (Leipzig, 1880); Sandys, III, 216–17; E. Langlotz, "Friedrich Gottlieb Welcker 1784–1868," *150 Jahre Rheinische Friedrich-Wilhelms-Universität zu Bonn 1818–1968: Bonner Gelehrte Beiträge zur Geschichte der Wissenschaften in Bonn: Philosophie und Altertumswissenschaften* (Bonn, 1968), 215–20; W. M. Calder III, "Ulrich von Wilamowitz-Moellendorff to Kekulé von Stradonitz on Friedrich Gottlieb Welcker," *Studi Italiani di Filologia Classica,* n.s. 3,2 (1984), 116–33; idem et al., eds., *Friedrich Gottlieb Welcker, Werk und Wirkung, Hermes Einzelschriften* 49 (Stuttgart, 1986).

WILLIAM M. CALDER III

WEST, BENJAMIN (1738–1820). American expatriate artist; president of the Royal Academy in London and court painter to England's King George III.

In the summer of 1760, West arrived in Italy, where he was to stay until 1763. His first stop was Rome, at the time in the midst of a great revival of interest in Roman antiquity and excavation. There West, while gazing at the *Belvedere *Apollo,* is said to have remarked that the statue reminded him of a Mohawk warrior in its proportion and form.

In the late summer of 1763, West settled in London, at the time second only to Rome in its passionate interest in, and collecting of, Greek and Roman art. The influence on West can be seen in his *The Choice of Hercules* (1764; Victoria and Albert Museum), where the central figure is modeled after the Vatican

The Temporary Elgin Room at the British Museum, 1819, with Sir Benjamin West in the foreground on the left, by A Archer, London, British Museum. (The Warburg Institute, University of London.)

*Meleager. The *Farnese *Hercules* may also have been influential. Perhaps the best-known borrowing by West from a classical source is in his 1768 painting, *Agrippina Landing at Brundisium with the Ashes of Germanicus* (Yale University Art Gallery). The central group in this work is derived from the processional reliefs of the *Ara Pacis Augustae; West could have seen the reliefs while in Rome or could have been familiar with the engravings of the Ara Pacis in P. S. *Bartoli's *Admiranda romanorum antiquitatum* (Rome, 1693). In 1809, West copied the Elgin marbles (Lord *Elgin) and was a keen supporter of their being brought to England.

Save for a brief retirement in 1805, West was the president of the Royal Academy in London from 1792 until his death in 1820. Throughout his career, he was a strong advocate of classical proportion as found in Greek and Roman art. In his *Discourse* of 1811, he wrote about the use of the classical ideal in painting and praised such works as the Elgin marbles, the Belvedere *Apollo,* the *Medici *Venus,* the *Laocoon* and the *Dying Gaul* (*Dying Trumpeter*) for exhibiting purity of form and proportion.

BIBLIOGRAPHY

+G. Evans, *Benjamin West and the Taste of His Times* (Carbondale, IL, 1959); +*The World of Benjamin West* (Allentown, PA, 1962); +H. Von Erffa—A. Staley, *The Paintings of Benjamin West* (New Haven, CT, 1986).

ROBERT E. JACKSON

WHEELER, Sir (ROBERT ERIC) MORTIMER (1890–1976). English archaeologist.

Born in the year of *Schliemann's death, Wheeler began his archaeological career in 1913, when he embarked on graduate research into the Roman pottery of the Rhineland with the financial assistance of Sir Arthur *Evans. Ceramic typology and European topics were soon abandoned in favor of a more urgent need at home: the extension and employment of the excavation techniques evolved privately by General *Pitt-Rivers in the last decades of the nineteenth century—and subsequently ignored. The essence of the "Wheeler method" (*Archaeology from the Earth,* 1954) resides in its practical application of Pitt-Rivers's fundamental precept of exact, three-dimensional, stratigraphical recording.

On arrival successively in Wales (1920–26), England (1926–44) and India (1944–48), Wheeler identified a number of specific objectives and designed an integrated series of campaigns to attain them as economically as possible by selective excavation. These startlingly innovative procedures were characterized in the field by military discipline and afterward by extensively illustrated and promptly published monographic reports (from *Segontium,* 1923—excavated 1921–22, to *Verulamium,* 1936—excavated 1930–34, and *Charsada,* 1962—excavated 1958) and crisp syntheses (e.g., *Prehistoric and Roman Wales,* 1925; *The Indus Civilization,* 1953; 3rd ed., 1968; *Rome Beyond the Imperial Frontiers,* 1954). Wheeler's additional and deep commitment to haute vulgarisation was recognized by his nomination as British Television Personality of the Year in 1954.

Wheeler's achievements as an excavator were matched by his remarkable administrative ability to revive, if only temporarily, the moribund institutions he was summoned to inherit: the National Museum of Wales; the London Museum, from which in 1937 he secured the foundation of the Institute of Archaeology in the University of London to provide professional training in archaeological retrieval; and the Archaeological Survey of India. Finally, as secretary of the British Academy, Wheeler breathed new life into the British schools of archaeology abroad until 1968.

BIBLIOGRAPHY

R.E.M. Wheeler, *Still Digging* (London, 1955); Idem, *The British Academy 1949–1968* (London, 1970); S. Piggott, "R.E.M. Wheeler, 10 September 1890–22 July 1976," *Biographical Memoirs of Fellows of the Royal Society* 23 (1977), 623–42, with select bib.; +J. Hawkes, *Mortimer Wheeler: Adventurer in Archaeology* (London, 1982).

                                                                        DAVID RIDGWAY

WHELER, GEORGE (1650–1724). English naturalist, early traveler to Greece.

Unexpectedly enriched, Wheler, from Charing in Kent, studied at Lincoln College, Oxford, then traveled abroad. In 1675 and 1676 he and Dr. *Spon of Lyons explored parts of Greece and Turkey. Later each published a memoir, Spon in 1678, Wheler in 1682. The latter's volume owes much to Spon's, yet it is quite different, for Wheler was an amateur botanist and a determined Anglican. Though interested in antiquities, he shed no tears for enslaved Greeks, so unlike his successors in the genre of Greek travel literature. The adventure over, Wheler took Holy Orders and devoted his life and wealth to the ministry.

BIBLIOGRAPHY

R. W. Ramsay, "Sir George Wheler and His Travels in Greece, 1650–1724," *Essays by Diverse Hands,* n.s. 19 (1942), 1–38; D. J. Constantine, "*A Journey into Greece,* by George Wheler Esq. In company with Dr. Spon of Lyons," *Durham University Journal* 72 (1979), 39–45; D. Constantine, *Early Greek Travellers and the Hellenic Ideal* (Cambridge, 1984), 7–33.

                                                                        C.W.J. ELIOT

WICKHOFF, FRANZ (1853–1909). Viennese art historian, known for his reevaluation of Roman art and identification of its positive characteristics.

Born in Steyr in upper Austria, Wickhoff studied with A. *Conze at Vienna. He served as inspector at the Kunstgewerbe-Museum in Vienna (1879–95) and as professor of art history at the University of Vienna from 1882 on.

With W. Ritter von Hartel, he studied the Late Antique/Early Christian illuminated manuscript of the book of Genesis in the library at Vienna. They issued a joint publication, *Die Wiener Genesis* (Vienna, 1895), with a lengthy introduction by Wickhoff in which he discussed the evolution of Roman art from Augustus to Constantine and its invaluable contributions to subsequent generations. He emphasized the development of illusionistic techniques in painting

Portrait of *Franz Wick-hoff*. (The Warburg Institute, University of London.)

and sculpture; achievements in portraiture; and the usage of "continuous narrative." This introductory section of the book, translated into English by Eugenie *Strong as *Roman Art* (London, 1900), has been immensely influential. Like his colleague at Vienna, A. *Riegl, Wickhoff was instrumental in reestablishing the validity of Roman art, originally revered during the Renaissance but regarded as debased by *Winckelmann and his followers. Unlike many of his contemporaries, Wickhoff did not view Roman art as a decadent imitation of Greek art but rather as a manifestation of native genius.

Wickhoff died in 1909 in Venice and was buried on the cemetery island of San Michele.

BIBLIOGRAPHY

R. Bianchi Bandinelli, "Wickhoff, Franz," *EAA* 7 (1966), 1218–19; O. Brendel, *Prolegomena to the Study of Roman Art* (New Haven, CT 1979), esp. 25–41.

SHELLIE WILLIAMS

WIEGAND, THEODOR (1864–1936). German archaeologist, excavator and administrator.

A wealthy doctor's son, Wiegand studied at Munich under Riehl and von

*Brunn, in Athens under *Dörpfeld, to whom he owed lifelong preference for field archaeology and architecture, and at Berlin under Diels, *Robert, *Kekulé and *Kiepert. He completed his dissertation on a Puteoli building inscription under *Studniczka at Freiburg in 1894. In 1900 he made a brilliant marriage with the wealthy heiress Marie Siemens. Financial independence freed him from a confining academic *cursus honorum*. His career became that of excavator, administrator and museum director. He possessed enviable administrative talent, contacts and the ability to get things published.

As director of the Royal Prussian Museum in Constantinople (1899–1911), he undertook excavations at *Miletos, *Didyma and *Samos. He was director (1911–31) of the Antiquities Department of the Berlin Museum, where, against great odds, he created the *Pergamon Museum and arranged remarkable acquisitions. He was inspector general of antiquities for Syria, Palestine and West Arabia (1916–18). He served as president of the *German Archaeological Institute (1932–36), now located in his former Dahlem residence. Among his publications are *Priene* (1904); *Milet* (1906–35); *Sinai* (1920); *Baalbek* (1921–25); *Petra* (1921); *Pergamon* V 1 (1930); *Palmyra* (1932); *Didyma* 1, three volumes (1941). Wiegand combined the restless energy and unscrupulousness of *Schliemann with the scholarly conscience of *Studniczka and so typified the most remarkable of his generation.

BIBLIOGRAPHY

M. Schede, *Gnomon* 13 (1937), 109–11; C. Watzinger, *Theodor Wiegand: Ein deutscher Archäologe 1864–1936* (Munich, 1944); H. A. Stoll, *Götter und Giganten: Der Roman des Pergamons-Altars* (Berlin, 1964), 315–416; T. Wiegand, *Halbmond im Letzen Viertel, Briefe und Reiseberichte,* ed. G. Wiegand (Mainz, 1985); S. Wenk, *Auf den Spuren der Antike: Theodor Wiegand, ein deutscher Archäologe* (Benndorf, 1985).

WILLIAM M. CALDER III

WIGHTMAN, EDITH MARY (1938–83). British historian of the Roman provinces.

After a brilliant undergraduate career in her native Scotland, Edith Wightman studied in Oxford under I. A. *Richmond; in 1969, she emigrated to McMaster University, Canada, becoming a full professor there in 1978. *Roman Trier* (1970), her doctoral thesis, remains fundamental for students of Christian Europe no less than for Romanists; her skillful historical interpretation of archaeological evidence led to penetrating studies of imperial frontier policies; and her posthumously published *Gallia Belgica* (1985), breaks new ground for Celtic specialists. Equally informed and versatile approaches to teaching, excavation at *Carthage and field survey in the Liri valley, Italy, were cut short by her tragic death.

BIBLIOGRAPHY

E. T. Salmon, Words of Tribute, Edith Mary Wightman Memorial Service, McMaster University, Hamilton, Ontario (January 1984).

DAVID RIDGWAY

WILAMOWITZ-MOELLENDORFF, ULRICH VON (1848–1931). German classicist, considered the greatest Hellenist of modern times.

Born at Markowitz (Posen) of Junker parents, Wilamowitz studied at Schulpforte; Bonn under Otto *Jahn and Reinhard *Kekulé; and Berlin. He was professor of classical philology at Greifswald (1876–83), Göttingen (1883–97) and Berlin (1897–1931). His over seventy volumes, dealing with all aspects of Greek literature and philology from Homer through the empire, have exerted incalculable influence on subsequent scholarship. Among his students were E. Fraenkel, Paul Friedländer, Felix Jacoby, Werner Jaeger, Paul Maas and Wolfgang Schadewaldt. His importance for archaeology is far more than the single volume of his *Kleine Schriften* (5.1) devoted to the subject might suggest.

From *Welcker he derived the *Totalitätsideal, the conviction that literary sources alone were insufficient to understand antiquity. This he imbibed through Jahn in the form of *monumental philology, the use of archaeological evidence to elucidate the written word. While in Italy and Greece (1872–74), he first worked with his future father-in-law, Theodor *Mommsen. His lifelong interest in epigraphy and topography dates from this time. Architecture he never learned. Although he recognized *Kekulé's rejection of monumental philology for art history with the assumption that the beauty of an object justifies its study, he never abandoned the view that archaeology, though indispensable, remains the ancilla of philology and that an archaeologist ignorant of the ancient languages was contemptible. He directed *Inscriptiones Graecae* from 1902 to 1931. He did much to reform the Central Committee of the *German Archaeological Institute (1899–1931). He corresponded with the great archaeologists of his time. His creation of a "complex institute" to include archaeology with history and philology realized the dream of F. A. *Wolf. Aged eighty, he wrote: "ab archaeologis discere semper eram cupidus" (From archaeologists I was ever eager to learn).

BIBLIOGRAPHY

W. Schindler, "Die Archäologie im Rahmen von Wilamowitz' Konzeption der Altertumswissenschaft," *Wilamowitz nach 50 Jahren,* ed. W. M. Calder III—H. Flashar—T. Lindken (Darmstadt, 1985), 241–62; M. Armstrong—W. Buchwald—W. M. Calder III, *Ulrich von Wilamowitz-Moellendorff, Bibliography 1867–1990, Revised and Expanded After Friedrich Freiherr Hiller von Gaertringen and Günther Klaffenbach* (Hildesheim, 1991); R. Fowler, "U. von Wilamowitz-Moelendorff," in Briggs—Calder, 489–522.

WILLIAM M. CALDER III

WILLIAM OF MALMESBURY (WILLELMI MALMESBIRIENSIS; ca. 1090–ca. 1143). Anglo-Norman historian, monk and librarian of Malmesbury Abbey.

William showed a great interest in classical literature and defended the study of Roman authors against those who argued that classical learning was not appropriate for the religious man. He collected and compiled manuscripts of Roman historians, including a large number of the philosophical works of Cicero. William took Suetonius as a model for his portraits of the English kings in his *Gesta regum* (ca. 1125).

There are several references to classical remains in William of Malmesbury's writings. The *Gesta pontificum* (ca. 1126), a history of English bishops, includes descriptions of the treasures of English monasteries and cathedrals that William had personally observed. Among these descriptions of church treasures, William recorded an inscription found on a Roman vaulted hall in Carlisle (*Gesta pontificum* 3.99). Although William never left England, he included a topography of Rome in his *Gesta regum* (4.351.), naming all the gates and the church relics found near each. He also copied a poem, which he attributed to *Hildebert of Tours, contrasting the modern city with the glorious ancient Rome, and noted the remarkable "excavation" in Rome (1045) of a gigantic corpse that was identified as Pallas, the friend of Aeneas. An ancient lamp was reported still burning in the tomb.

William records legends that may recall contact with ancient remains in his account of Gerbert of Aurillac (Pope Sylvester II). He portrays the pope as a master of the occult arts and asserts that by following the pointing finger of a statue in the Campus Martius and by magically opening the earth, Gerbert discovered vast golden treasures, including golden soldiers, a king and queen and vessels of high quality (*Gesta regum* 2.169). In order to increase the plausibility of this story, William tells of a similar adventure recounted to him by an Aquitanian monk of his own abbey (*Gesta regum* 2.170). The monk had journeyed into a dark mountain chamber in Italy that was reputed to house the treasures of Octavian and found golden objects similar to those seen by Gerbert. It is possible that underneath the superstition and magic, this story deals with the discovery of an Etruscan tomb.

BIBLIOGRAPHY

W. Stubbs, introd., Willelmi Malmesbiriensis Monachi, *De gestis regum anglorum,* Rolls Series 90 (London, 1889); H. Farmer, "William of Malmesbury's Life and Works," *Journal of Ecclesiastical History* 13 (1962), 39–54; Antonia Gransden, "Realistic Observation in Twelfth-Century England," *Speculum* 47 (1972), 29–51; Weiss, *RDCA* 10.

JOANNE E. SOWELL

WILLIAMS, HUGH WILLIAM (1773–1829). Scottish painter, sometimes called "Grecian" Williams, known for his watercolor views of Greek landscapes.

Born at sea on a voyage to the West Indies, Williams was raised in Edinburgh, where he was encouraged by his grandfather to take up painting. He specialized in views of the Highlands landscape, but after an extensive tour to Italy and Greece, he became famous for his views of these countries. He published *Travels in Italy, Greece and the Ionian Islands, in a Series of Letters,* in two volumes (Edinburgh, 1820), with emphasis on descriptions of the countries and peoples rather than on history or archaeology. In 1822, he held an exhibition in Edinburgh—a great success for the artist—of his watercolors of splendid Greek ruins and famous scenes of Greek history. Scenes of the *Propylaia and of the temple at *Aigina show his typical mellow, golden Grecian landscape. Apart from views of the *Parthenon and of the *Erechtheion in a private collection in Athens, most of Williams's Greek pictures are in the National Gallery of Scotland, Edinburgh.

BIBLIOGRAPHY

J. L. Caw, "Williams, Hugh William," *DNB* 21 (1921), 407–8; +Tsigakou, *Rediscovery*, 23, 30, 108, 116, 122–23, 128, 200.

WILTHEIM, JEAN-GUILLAUME (1594–1636) and ALEXANDRE (1604–84). Members of a family noted for antiquarian and historical studies of the region around Luxembourg.

Having joined the Jesuit Order in 1626, Alexandre became a professor of rhetoric at their college in Luxembourg, following his elder brother, Guillaume, in pursuit of the history and archaeology of the ancient Roman province of Gallia Belgica. His masterwork, *Luciliburgensia, sive Luxemburgum romanum* . . . , did not see publication, however, until edited by Neyen in 1842 from the manuscript in the Bibliothèque de l'Institut Grand-ducal (copy in Bibliothèque Royale, Brussels). Illustrations of this volume reproduce those in Alexandre's separate Atlas, *Delineamenta,* and serve as the record of lost sculptures in volume 5 of Espérandieu's *Recueil.* Unhappily, they are less engaging *ricordi* than those that punctuate the text of Guillaume in his manuscript preserved in the Bibliothèque Royale, Brussels (inv. 7146, cf. also 6745), or in J.-J. *Boissard's *Antiquarum inscriptionum* . . . (Bibliothèque Nationale, Paris, Ms Rés. J 468 bis).

This entire family of learned antiquarians, including a historian, Eustache, contributed to regional scholarship in an exemplary way, inspired by relics of *Orolaunum Vicus* (Arlon), Luxembourg and other Roman sites, including *Trier and Metz. A prosperous region in antiquity, Gallia Belgica was dotted with conspicuous family tomb structures, many of them veritable mausoleums, decorated by reliefs that document daily life and manners. The studies of Guillaume and Alexandre Wiltheim, preserved both in autograph manuscripts and in copies, record vanished monuments of the type, as well as those severely eroded by time (e.g., the *Igel Monument). They also serve to document an outstanding collection of ancient works of art and modern paintings of the Renaissance in the Netherlands, the Palace of Count P. E. *Mansfeld at Clausen.

BIBLIOGRAPHY

C.-A. Neyen, *Luciliburgensia, sive Luxemburgum romanum illustrata a R. P. Alexandro Wilthemio* (Luxembourg, 1842); J.-P. Waltzing, *Orolaunum vicus* (Louvain, 1904–5); E. Espérandieu, *Recueil général des bas-reliefs, statues et bustes de la Gaule romaine* (Paris, 1913), 212–14; M. E. Mariën, *Les Monuments funeraires de l'Arlon romain* (1945).

PHYLLIS PRAY BOBER

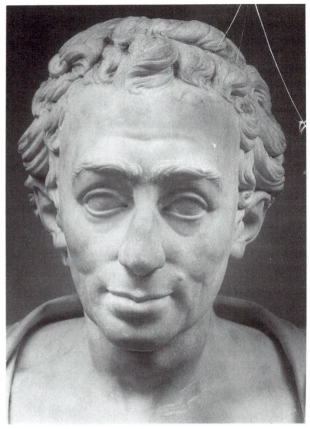

Portrait of *J. J. Winck-elmann*, Rome, Capito-line Museums. (Deut-sches Archäologisches Institut, Rome. Inst. Neg. 1938. 718.)

WINCKELMANN, JOHANN JOACHIM (1717–68). German antiquarian, of-ten, and with some justification, called the father of modern archaeology.

Winckelmann came to the study of ancient art very much as an outsider. Born in the small Prussian town of Stendal, the son of a cobbler, he studied theology, mathematics and medicine, as well as ancient Greek and Latin, at the universities of Halle and Jena. After five years working as a schoolmaster in Prussia, he took up a job in Nöthnitz, just outside Dresden, as librarian to Count Heinrich von Bünau. Access to Bünau's famous library, where he was helping with the compilation of a history of the early German Reich, gave Winckelmann an opportunity to read widely in the most recent Enlightenment literature, including works on history, politics, natural science, classical antiquity and, quite late on, it seems, the visual arts. His entry into the eighteenth-century art world came when he settled in Dresden in 1754. The next year he finally launched his career as a writer with a highly successful polemical essay, *Gedanken über die Nach-*

ahmung der Griechischen Werke in der Malerei und Bildhauerkunst, where he extolled the "noble simplicity and calm grandeur" of celebrated masterpieces of ancient sculpture he had never seen, with all the ardor of a recent convert. Only after he moved to Rome in 1755 did he embark on the scholarly study of ancient art, which his own work was ultimately to transform.

His first important antiquarian publication, the *Description des pierres gravées du feu Baron de Stosch* (1760), was a catalog of antique engraved gems and pastes, miniature antiquities that enjoyed a particular vogue at the time and had been the subject of numerous learned dissertations by such connoisseurs and antiquarians as P.-J. *Mariette and Philipp von *Stosch himself. Winckelmann's major work, the *Geschichte der Kunst des Altertums* ("History of Ancient Art," 1764), was put together at incredible speed in the space of six years (the manuscript was already delivered to the publisher late in 1761). The most comprehensive compendium of information to date on the art of ancient Greece and Rome (the shorter sections on Egyptian, Near Eastern and Etruscan art were not nearly so important) and the first systematic attempt at a chronological classification of antique sculpture, it remained the basic handbook on the subject well into the nineteenth century. K. O. *Müller's thorough recasting of the history of ancient Greek art using the newly excavated finds in Greece and Asia Minor in his *Handbuch der Archäologie der Kunst* (1835) is perhaps the earliest that clearly supersedes Winckelmann's more speculative history derived from the study of Graeco-Roman antiquities. Winckelmann was putting the finishing touches to a new revised edition (integrating material from his 1767 *Anmerkungen über die Geschichte* . . .) at the time of his dramatic murder in Trieste in 1768. A less than satisfactory version of this publication, prepared from Winckelmann's notes (subsequently lost) by a friend, J. F. Riedel, and published in Vienna in 1776, formed the basis for the spate of new editions that appeared over the next few decades in French, German and Italian (but not in English: that came only after the event, with an incomplete American translation published in 1849–56).

Winckelmann's novel idea of trying to classify ancient sculpture according to period, as well as by subject matter, made little impact even in his own illustrated catalog of unpublished monuments, the *Monumenti antichi inediti* (1767), which he produced at his own expense and dedicated to his patron, Cardinal Alessandro Albani (*Albani family). While the introductory discourse made available a summary of his history of Greek art in Italian, the individual catalog entries remained within the bounds of conventional iconographical analysis. Clearly, in this context Winckelmann wished to demonstrate his mastery of traditional antiquarian erudition. He did, however, develop an important general principle already adumbrated in the *Geschichte,* that the subjects depicted in ancient art, with the exception of a few on outdoor Roman public monuments, were almost always mythological rather than historical in content. Previously, it had been common practice to try to identify any slightly mysterious representations with scenes from Roman history. His other antiquarian publications included two short treatises on ancient architecture (1757 and 1762), one on allegory in ancient art (1766), partly designed to encourage the use of antique allegories by modern artists, and two reports on the excavations at *Herculaneum (1762 and 1764).

By his death in 1768, Winckelmann was widely recognized as having had a major impact on antiquarian studies. There were the official rewards, his post as commissioner of antiquities (*Commissario delle Antichità) to the pope, which he had occupied since 1763, and honorary membership of various prestigious learned societies, including the *Society of Antiquaries in London; but more significant was the way in which he was constantly cited as the standard authority in both learned and popular publications on ancient Greek and Roman art. His lyrical descriptions of famous antique sculptures—the *Belvedere Apollo, the *Laocoon, the *Belvedere Torso and the so-called *Belvedere Antinous—became instant anthology pieces, widely reproduced in guidebooks as aids for the visitor to Rome to experience the high beauties of the antique ideal. While he was greatly admired by contemporaries, above all for his ability to combine erudition with a genuine feeling for art (the erudition, though, was often criticized for its inaccuracies), his radically new conception of the history of ancient Greek and Roman art began to be properly assimilated only in the last decade or so of the eighteenth century.

Winckelmann had quite literally invented a history of art where little other than vague generalizations about rise and decline had existed before, one that, whatever its limitations, succeeded in integrating the available literary and visual evidence in a convincing way. Drawing on the standard compendia of ancient texts on art, most notably, Franciscus *Junius's De pictura veterum (1694), and exploiting the new methods of stylistic analysis and classification of antiquities pioneered by the French antiquarian the Comte de *Caylus, he devised a schematic picture of development through a few broadly defined phases—Archaic, austere Early Classic, graceful Late Classic, then Imitation and Decline—whose closest precedent is to be found in the history of modern Italian art set out some 200 years earlier in *Vasari's Lives. The model of a rise and decline through a logical sequence of clearly defined period styles, with chronological limits designed to match the main phases in the political history of ancient Greece, provided a paradigm for describing the evolution of an artistic tradition that has proved very influential in archaeological studies ever since.

BIBLIOGRAPHY

K. Justi, Winckelmann und seine Zeitgenossen, 2nd ed., 1–3 (Leipzig, 1898); +A. Tibal, Inventaire des manuscrits de Winckelmann déposés à la Bibliothèque Nationale (Paris, 1911); +J. J. Winckelmann, Briefe (Berlin, 1952–57), ed. W. Rehm; idem, Kleine Schriften, Vorreden, Entwürfe (Berlin, 1968); A. D. Potts, "Winckelmann's Construction of History," Art History 5 (1982), 377–407, and correction, Art History 6 (June 1983); E. Pommier, ed., Winckelmann: La Naissance de l'histoire de l'art à l'époque des lumières (Paris, 1991); A. Potts, Flesh and the Ideal, Winckelmann and the Origins of Art History (New Haven, CT, 1994).

ALEX POTTS

WITTEL, GASPAR VAN (GASPARE VANVITELLI; 1652/3–1736). Dutch painter and draftsman, specialist in landscape and topography of Italy.

Born at Amersfoort, near Utrecht, Gaspar Van Wittel arrived in Rome around 1674 and never again returned to his homeland. Active in Venice, Naples and Rome, he was known, above all, as a painter of views, *vedute,* of Italian landscapes and cities. He was accepted into the painter's association of the Academy of St. Luke in 1711.

His painted views of Rome often contain or emphasize classical landmarks, as in his *View of the *Colosseum* (1715), *View of the *Arch of Titus* (1685) and his *Piazza del Quirinale,* with the familiar *Quirinal *Horse Tamers.* He has left exquisite drawings of antiquities in Rome such as the colossal head of **Constantine,* the **Pasquino* and the *Demosthenes* of Polyeuktos (probably seen at the Villa Aldobrandini at Frascati). Of special interest is his drawing recording the raising of the *Column of Antoninus Pius, excavated near the Palazzo di Montecitorio under the supervision of Carlo Fontana in 1705.

Gaspar Van Wittel was surpassed in fame by his son, Luigi Vanvitelli, architect of the *Bourbon royal palace at Caserta. His son designed his tomb, in Sta. Maria in Vallicella in Rome.

BIBLIOGRAPHY
+G. Briganti, *Gaspar Van Wittel e l'origine della veduta settecentesca* (Rome, 1966); +W. Vitzthum, *Drawings by Gaspar Van Wittel (1652/53–1736) from Neapolitan Collections* (Ottawa, 1977).

WOLF, FRIEDRICH AUGUST (1759–1824). German classical scholar; a founding father of the great German tradition of scholarship in the nineteenth century; discoverer of the philological seminary, the Homeric Question and the unified "science of antiquity," *Altertumswissenschaft.*

Friedrich August Wolf, born near Nordhausen, Brandenburg, learned Latin, Greek and French as a child. In 1777 he was admitted to the University of Göttingen. There he studied with the philologist Christian Gottlieb Heyne, with whom he never got along. His 1782 edition of Plato's *Symposium* with German notes and careful flattery of the Prussian king won him the professorship at Halle. In his influential seminary there, he presented to students his ideal of a unified science of all antiquity, based on knowledge of the texts, works of art and other physical remains. The vision of uniting philology, art history and archaeology still remains, exemplified by rare scholars such as *Böckh, *Wilamowitz or *Rostovtzeff.

Wolf's *Prolegomena ad Homerum* (1795) posed the Homeric Question, examining the illiteracy of Homer and the history of his text and challenging the idea of the unity of authorship of *Iliad* and *Odyssey.* In 1806 the French victory against Prussia dismantled the university at Halle and sent Wolf to Berlin, where he never again knew the same success.

BIBLIOGRAPHY
A. Grafton, "Prolegomena to Frederick August Wolf," *JWarb* 44 (1981), 101–29; F. A. Wolf, *Prolegomena to Homer, 1795,* tr. with introd. and notes A. Grafton—G. W.

Most—J. E. G. Zetzel (Princeton, NJ, 1985); H. Funke, "F. A. Wolf," in Briggs—Calder, 523–28.

                                                                        E. C. KOPFF

WOLFF, REINIER VAN DER (d. 1679). Wealthy Dutch brewer, collector of Italian Renaissance paintings and Roman antiquities.

Reinier van der Wolff was the master of the Black Lion brewery in Rotterdam and served as a city councilman. His art collection was visited in 1663 by Balthasar de Monconys, who noted that the busts and marbles had been purchased from the Duke of *Buckingham's collection (sold at auction in Antwerp in 1648). Joachim Oudaan (1628–92) drew and transcribed the inscriptions of eight of van der Wolff's marbles during the years 1656–64: a Greek grave stele of Dexandrides and burial urns of Acilia Hygia and P. Aelius Hierax, as well as a large Christian sarcophagus depicting the *Miracles of Christ,* all of which are now in Leiden; the whereabouts of his urns of Aciliae Tertullae Fil. and Claudius Successae are unknown. These antiquities once belonged to P. P. *Rubens, who sold them to the Duke of Buckingham in 1626.

Van der Wolff's collection was dispersed at the sales of 8 April 1677 and 4 April 1693.

BIBLIOGRAPHY

+J. H. Jongkees, "De verzameling oudheden van Reinier van der Wolff," *Mededelingen Nederlands Instituut te Rome,* 31 (1961), 125–45; +J. M. Muller, *Rubens: The Artist as Collector* (Princeton, NJ, 1989), 150–52; +P.P.V. van Moorsel, "De oudchristlijke sarcophag in het Rijksmuseum van Oudheden te Leiden," *Oudheidkundige Mededelingen* 65 (1964–65), 37–46.

                                                            MARJON VAN DER MEULEN

WOOD, ROBERT (1717–71). Irish traveler, statesman and lover of classical literature.

Little is known of the youth of Robert Wood. Born near Trim in County Meath, he was probably educated at Oxford; he then made his living as a traveling tutor. Having been in Greece (1742–43) and France and Italy, he was invited in 1749 by two Oxford graduates, John Bouverie and James Dawkins, to explore the eastern Mediterranean. With the latter he was to enjoy an especially fruitful association, for Dawkins was able to provide generous financial backing to help realize their goals.

After a winter in Rome studying the history and geography of their targeted countries, the well-prepared crew set sail from Naples with an Italian artist, Borra, and with a full research library of Greek authors and the best books on archaeology and travel. Their journey was to include many Greek islands, the Hellespont and Bosporus, Asia Minor, Syria, Phoenicia, Palestine and Egypt.

They investigated the Troad (1750; *Troy) and went on to *Magnesia-on-the-Maeander, where Bouverie died; then they proceeded to *Palmyra and *Baalbek, to encounter the spectacular ruins there, largely unknown in the West. They

Robert Wood and James Dawkins Enter into Palmyra, engraving, 1774, after a painting by G. Hamilton. (The Warburg Institute, University of London.)

continued to Athens, where the party encountered *Stuart and *Revett (whom they had earlier met in Rome) and immediately lent their support (including Dawkins's funds) to their project to publish the antiquities of Athens. The four then banded together to tour *Marathon, Thermopylai, *Delphi, *Thebes and *Corinth, before Wood and Dawkins departed for England.

Back in London, Dawkins was elected to the *Society of Dilettanti (1755) and was a staunch supporter of the project to publish *The Antiquities of Athens.* Unfortunately, he did not live to see even the first volume appear; but at his death in 1758, he left behind £500 for the continued work of the society.

Wood published quickly his sensational account of *The Ruins of Palmyra* (1753) and *The Ruins of Balbec* (1757), and the beautifully produced volumes were an international success. Though his later years were largely devoted to public life (he became undersecretary of state to Pitt in 1756), and he was never able to return to Greece, Wood continued to support the investigation of Greek antiquities. Elected to the Dilettanti in 1763, he became its director of archaeological expeditions and played a key supporting role in Richard *Chandler's voyage to Asia Minor and the subsequent publication of Chandler's *Ionian Antiquities,* volume 1 (1769).

Wood also had a profound influence on the study of Greek literature, because of his novel approach to the poems of Homer. He argued that one could understand and evaluate Homer only by a careful examination of the places and times he described, that is, by a topographical, archaeological approach. He, like many others in the eighteenth century and earlier (*pace,* *Schliemann), believed that Troy was historical and not mythological; but he was the first to make a thorough investigation of the terrain with a view toward showing that Homer had been truthful. Wood was also a pioneer in the use of ethnoarchaeology, examining contemporary Mediterranean and Middle Eastern customs in an attempt to prove that the Homeric code of behavior survived (and thus was real). His ideas were put forth in a work with a complicated publication history, appearing first in English in *A Comparative View of the Antient and Present State of the Troade, to Which Is Prefixed an Essay on the Original Genius of Homer* (1767) and later in an immensely influential posthumous German translation, *Robert Woods Versuch über das Originalgenie des Homers* (Frankfurt am Main, 1773).

BIBLIOGRAPHY

D. Constantine, *Early Greek Travelers and the Hellenic Ideal* (Cambridge, 1984), 66–84; R. Eisner, *Travelers to an Antique Land, The History and Literature of Travel to Greece* (Ann Arbor, 1991), 72–73.

X

XANTHOS. City in Lycia (southwest Asia Minor) on the river Xanthos near modern Kinik.

Homer records that a contingent from Xanthos fought as Trojan allies. Most important of the Lycian cities, Xanthos was besieged by the Persians under Harpagus in 545 B.C. (Herodotos 1.176), surrendered to Alexander and subsequently came under Roman domination.

The Lycian acropolis preserves building remains that include the foundations of a temple and probably a palace. A number of Lycian tombs also survive, mostly of the native pillar-type. Two of the best-known Xanthian funerary monuments, the Harpy Tomb and the Nereid Monument, were studied and excavated by Charles *Fellows, the discoverer of Lycia. In 1838 he made a description of the Harpy Tomb and sketches, which he exhibited in London with great success. Returning in 1840, he took along the draftsman George Scharf, who made fine drawings that were published by Fellows in his landmark book, *An Account of Discoveries in Lycia* (1841) and were presented to the *British Museum. The museum sponsored an expedition to recover the sculptures and bring them to England, an affair that was badly organized but succeeded because Fellows took control of it. With sailors from the British navy, he managed to remove the reliefs from the Harpy Tomb without damaging them and discovered a second tomb, the Nereid Monument (1842). He shipped some eighty-six cases of marbles off to the British Museum, followed by another twenty-seven with material from two additional tombs, the Payava (Horse Tomb) and the Merehi (Chimera Tomb).

The Harpy Tomb, a pillar-type tomb decorated with reliefs of Sirens (originally interpreted as Harpies) dates to 480–470 B.C. The Nereid Monument, a tomb in the form of an Ionic Greek temple with freestanding sculptures of draped females ("Nereids") and relief scenes of battles, the hunt and ceremonial scenes, dates to ca. 380 B.C.

North and east of the Lycian acropolis at Xanthos are remains of the Hellenistic and Roman city, with an agora and a theater. A Byzantine monastery occupies much of the northeast part of the site. Remains of the Letoon, the federal sanctuary of the Lycian League, sacred to Leto, lie 4km to the southwest.

Since 1950 a French expedition has conducted excavations, study and restoration at Xanthos and from 1962 has uncovered at the Letoon Hellenistic temples with Lycian predecessors.

BIBLIOGRAPHY

Michaelis, 93–97; +*Fouilles de Xanthos* 1–8 (Paris, 1958–89); +E. Hansen—C. LeRoy, "Au Letoon de Xanthos: Les deux temples de Leto," *RA* (1976), 317–36; W.A.P. Childs, "Lycian Relations with Persians and Greeks in the Fifth and Fourth Centuries Re-Examined," *AnatSt* 31 (1981), 55–80.

ANN C. GUNTER

XANTHOUDIDES, STEPHANOS (1864–1928). Philologist and archaeologist from *Crete, specializing in Bronze Age Minoan culture.

Born in central Crete, Xanthoudides studied philology at the University of Athens. In 1900 he was named ephor of antiquities on the island of Crete, first at Chania and then at Herakleion, where he became director of the *Herakleion Museum. An extremely versatile scholar, Xanthoudides was interested in the languages, literature and history of Crete from many different periods. He is known as one of the pioneers of Cretan archaeology and of the conservation of its monuments.

His principal fieldwork concerned the prepalatial circular or tholos tombs of the Mesara Plain (published in English as *The Vaulted Tombs of Mesara*, 1924); an oval house at Chamaizi of the Middle Minoan IA period; and the large Minoan villa at Nirou. He also explored the Early Minoan burial cave at Pyrgos, which yielded, for the first time, pottery in the style named after that site, and Late Minoan tholos tombs at Mouliana, Damania and Artsa.

BIBLIOGRAPHY

S. Marinatos, "Stephanos Xanthudidis," *Gnomon* 4 (1928), 406–8.

COSTIS DAVARAS

Y

YOUNG, RODNEY STUART (1907–74). American archaeologist, professor and chairman of classical archaeology at the University of Pennsylvania and curator of the Mediterranean section at the University Museum.

Young was director of the museum's excavations at *Gordion in Turkey, beginning in 1950. In the Phrygian capital, he uncovered a sumptuous palace and royal tombs of the eighth and seventh centuries B.C.

Young had a lifelong interest in Greece and the Near East. His earliest excavations were in the *Agora, Athens, and took place in two campaigns (1933–41; 1946–49). Excavations were halted by World War II, but Young remained in Greece, volunteering as an ambulance driver on the Epiros front. In recognition for wounds received in combat, he was awarded both the Bronze Star of his native country and the Greek Croix de la Guerre.

He served as a very popular president of the *Archaeological Institute of America (1968–72) and was vice president of the American Research Institute in Turkey, as well as an honorary member of the *German Archaeological Institute. Young was killed in an automobile accident in Chester Springs, Pennsylvania, on 25 October 1974.

BIBLIOGRAPHY

R. S. Young, *Late Geometric Graves and a Seventh Century Well in the Agora* (Athens, 1939); "Rodney Stuart Young," *AJA* 79 (1975), 113; *From Athens to Gordion, The Papers of a Memorial Symposium for R. S. Young* (Philadelphia, 1980); R. S. Young, *Three Great Early Tumuli,* the Gordion Excavations Final Reports I (Philadelphia, 1981).

SHELLIE WILLIAMS

Z

ZAKROS. Minoan settlement on *Crete.

Zakros is the modern name for a small, now largely deserted valley and bay on the east shore of Crete, known for its extensive Minoan settlement (Neolithic through Late Minoan [LM] I), first excavated in 1901 by David *Hogarth, who exposed Middle Minoan (MM)/LM I houses but not the palace he sought. The center or palace, chiefly of MM III–LM I date, was to be identified in 1962–63 by Nicolas Platon, who, in a series of ongoing campaigns financed by the Archaeological Society of Athens and the philanthropist Leon Pomerance, revealed the palace as well as many of the surrounding houses. While the MM predecessor of the LM I palace remains to be more clearly defined, the latter has been completely excavated and consists of the usual rectangular central court surrounded by groups of rooms, normally referred to as "wings."

Like so many other Minoan sites, the palace was burned and deserted at the end of the LM I period. The southern and eastern wings were much disturbed by later agricultural work, but the general plan has been recovered, with the residential area on the east with smaller and larger living spaces, a light well and an adyton ("lustral basin") with religious iconography. The better-preserved west wing featured larger ritual rooms, from which much of the cult material, especially vessels, was recovered in a treasury (e.g., rhyta, double axes). Saws and other bronze tools suggested ongoing renovation; copper ingots, trade and manufacture; Linear A tablets, the recording of agricultural and other goods.

BIBLIOGRAPHY

N. Platon, *Zakros* (New York, 1971); idem, in *Praktika* (1961–78).

JOSEPH W. SHAW

ZANNONI, ANTONIO (1883–1910). Italian architect, engineer and archaeologist. Zannoni first became involved with archaeology in *Bologna when he was assigned to trace the city's ancient Roman aqueduct and restore it for modern use, a task that lasted for twenty years (1862–81).

During this same period, Zannoni undertook a number of other projects in Bologna. He was the director of the renovation of the Palazzo Galvani, chosen to be the new seat for the Museo Civico, which opened in 1881. He undertook the excavation of the cemetery of the Certosa, which yielded 421 tombs and included the famous Certosa Situla, a bronze bucket decorated in relief. He subsequently explored five other cemeteries (1871–74) near the Certosa—the existence of which he had predicted from the pattern of tombs in the Certosa itself—excavating thousands of burials of the Villanovan, Etruscan, Gallic and Roman phases of Bologna. He also unearthed a number of Villanovan huts, and in 1877 came his spectacular discovery in one of these of a huge *dolio* or jar containing a hoard of 14,838 pieces of bronze and three pieces of iron, dating to the late Bronze Age and the early Iron Age ("the San Francesco hoard").

Zannoni was known for his rigorous excavation techniques and exceptionally careful recording of the plan of each cemetery and individual tomb. In some cases he transported entire burials to the museum intact. He was criticized by *Helbig especially for his overly romantic and patriotic assertions about the ethnic identity of the inhabitants of the cemeteries.

BIBLIOGRAPHY

A. Zannoni, *Gli Scavi della Certosa di Bologna* (Bologna, 1876–84); idem, *La Fonderia di Bologna* (Bologna, 1888); C. Morigi Govi, "Antonio Zannoni, dagli scavi della Certosa alle 'archaiche abitazioni,' " *Dalla Stanza delle Antichità al Museo Civico* (Bologna, 1984), 243–54.

ZEUS OF OLYMPIA. Colossal gold and ivory statue made by the Greek sculptor Pheidias, probably in the third quarter of the fifth century B.C., for the cella of the *Temple of Zeus, Olympia.

The enthroned god, supporting a Nike figure on one hand and grasping a scepter in the other, filled the entire height of the cella of the temple. Strabo (8. 353–4) observed that if it could have risen, the colossus would have taken the roof off. Of great renown in antiquity, the chryselephantine Zeus was counted among the wonders of the ancient world. It was particularly praised for its size, splendor and majesty. Pausanias (5.11.1–9) gave a detailed eyewitness description of the statue in the second century A.C.

In the first century A.C., the Roman emperor Caligula tried to remove the famous Zeus from Olympia, but the statue is said to have laughed loudly, making the scaffolding collapse (Suetonius, *Caligula* 57). After Theodosius I banned the practice of pagan cults in 391, the statue was removed to Constantinople (*Byzantium); there it was evidently destroyed in a fire in 462. Its appearance is known, however, from numerous copies in other media and from coins of Elis of the first and second centuries A.C.

Pheidias's workshop for the production of the chryselephantine Zeus was built to the same dimensions as the cella of the temple. Within the workshop,

German excavators made the unique discovery of ivory, glass, obsidian, sheet bronze, lead templates, bone tools, a bronze hammerhead and hundreds of clay molds for glass ornaments and glass drapery details. Once thought to be from the production of Zeus's drapery, the molds have now been assigned to the production of a much smaller cult statue for the nearby Metroon (W. Schiering).

BIBLIOGRAPHY

J. Overbeck, *Die Antiken Schriftquellen zur Geschichte der bildenden Kunste bei den Griechen* (Leipzig, 1868), nos. 692–754; A. Mallwitz, *Die Werkstatt des Zeus in Olympia, Olympische Forschungen* 5 (Berlin, 1964); Ridgway, *Fifth Century Styles in Greek Sculpture,* 167–68; W. Schiering, *Die Werkstatt des Pheidias in Olympia, Olympische Forschungen* 18 (Berlin, 1991).

CAROL MATTUSCH

Portrait of *Georg Zoëga*, by C. Stark. Rome, Deutsches Archäologisches Institut (German Archaeological Institute). (Deutsches Archäologisches Institut, Rome. Inst. Neg. 76.663.)

ZOËGA, GEORG (JÖRGEN; 1755–1809). Danish archaeologist.

Born in Denmark and educated in Germany, mainly in Göttingen under Christian Gottlob Heyne, Zoëga lived in Rome from 1783 to his death. He knew the city better than most and acted as guide to many Danish visitors, for example, *Thorvaldsen. At first sight, Zoëga's publications—one book on Roman imperial coins from Alexandria, one on obelisks in Rome, one on ancient Roman bas-reliefs and a catalog of the Coptic manuscripts in the collection of Cardinal Borgia—seem disparate; in fact, his main concern was to make archaeology a discipline as precise and methodical as philology. In his view both disciplines should cooperate to supply information about antiquity *as a whole,* hence, the copious information in all his books. His exact descriptions and learned interpretations in *Li Bassirelievi antichi di Roma* (1808; in 2 vols., though only a part of a larger project) are considered by some to be the first specimen of real archaeological scholarship.

BIBLIOGRAPHY

F. G. Welcker, *Zoëga's Leben,* with Zoëga's *Kleine Schriften* 1–2 (Stuttgart, 1819); K. Friis Johansen, "Georg Zoëga og Rom," *Rom og Danmark gennem Tiderne,* ed. L. Bobé, 1 (Copenhagen, 1935), 223–67; G. Zoëga, *Briefe und Dokumente, 1, 1755–1785; 2, 1785–1790,* ed. O. Andreasen—K. Ascani (Copenhagen, 1967, 1993); J. Mejer, "Welcker and Zoëga," *Friedrich Gottlieb Welcker, Werk und Wirkung,* ed. W. M. Calder III et al., *Hermes Einzelschriften* 49 (1986), 53–78.

J. MEJER

Chronology of the History of Classical Archaeology

In the timeline presented below, emphasis is given to landmark discoveries and publications in classical archaeology, and an attempt has also been made to include events that affected the condition of the sites and monuments and thus the archaeological study of them. Various natural disasters and episodes of human destruction such as wars and invasions have been listed, along with information, when practical, about the removal, conservation and restoration of antiquities. The timeline is of necessity schematic and perhaps gives undue emphasis to easily identifiable moments of discovery, publication and disaster, without fully conveying the processes of excavation, interpretation and conservation that may have taken place at a given site over a number of years. References to the articles of the Encyclopedia, indicated by an asterisk, will help the reader to gain a fuller idea of the historical background for each selected entry in the timeline.

480 B.C.	Sack of *Athens by the Persians
390 B.C.	Sack of *Rome by the Gauls
227/6 B.C.	Earthquake at *Rhodes topples the *Colossus
86 B.C.	Sack of *Athens, *Peiraeus and *Delphi by Sulla
A.D. 79	Eruption of Vesuvius, covering *Pompeii, *Herculaneum, *Oplontis, *Stabiae
267	Sack of *Athens, *Corinth, *Sparta and *Argos by the Herulians
324	Founding of *Constantinople; Constantine moves many antiquities to the new city
379–395	Reign of Theodosius I; orders for the destruction of pagan buildings, shrines, statues and books
410	Sack of *Rome by Alaric
435	Decrees of Theodosius II that all pagan shrines and temples should be closed or converted to Christian churches

ca. 500?	Conversion of the *Parthenon to a church
609	Conversion of the *Pantheon to a church
ca. 800	*Einsiedeln Itinerary
966	Reference to the *Caballus Constantini*, the earliest notice of the *Marcus Aurelius* Equestrian statue
1001	Journey to Rome of *Bernward of Hildesheim
1082	Sack of Rome by Guiscard
11th century	Monks excavate antiquities at St. Albans (*Verulamium)
12th century	*Guibert of Nogent records antiquities excavated by monks at Nogent in southern France
1100–1101	Journey to Rome of *Hildebert of Lavardin
1139–43	Journeys to Rome of *Henry of Blois
ca. 1140	*Mirabilia urbis Romae*
ca. 1155	*Graphia aureae urbis Romae*
1166	Earliest mention of the *Spinario*, at the *Lateran in Rome
1188	Travels through Wales of *Gerald of Wales; recording of Roman ruins
ca. 1200	Magister *Gregorius in Rome
1204	Sack of Constantinople (*Byzantium) by Crusaders
1231	Striking of the Augustalis by *Frederick II of Hohenstaufen
1246	First record of the *Gemma Augustea, at St. Sernin, Toulouse
1335	Memo of O. *Forzetta on the purchase of antiquities
1337	First journey to Rome of *Petrarch
1341	First record of the *Gemma Tiberiana, at the Sainte Chapelle, Paris
ca. 1347	*Cola di Rienzo interprets the bronze tablet of the *Lex de imperio Vespasiani* in St. John *Lateran, Rome
1349	Major earthquake in Rome
1360	First record of the *Rubens Vase, in the collection of the Duke of Anjou
1375	Journey to Rome of G. *Dondi
1412	Beginning of the travels of *Ciriaco of Ancona
1417	C. *Buondelmonti, *Descriptio insulae Candiae*
1420	C. *Buondelmonti, *Liber insularum archipelagi*
1420s or 1430s	Earliest notice regarding the *Belvedere *Torso*
1440s	L.B. *Alberti, *Descriptio urbis Romae*
1444	Discovery at *Gubbio of the Eugubine Tables
1444–46	F. *Biondo, *Roma instaurata*
ca. 1446–48	Attempts by L. B. *Alberti to excavate ships at Lake *Nemi
1448	G.F. *Poggio Bracciolini, *De varietate fortunae*
ca. 1450	John *Capgrave in Rome; writing of *Ye Solace of Pilgrimes*
1452	Journey to Rome of Nicolaus *Muffel
1453	Fall of Constantinople (*Byzantium) to the Turks
1458–64	Papacy of *Pius II; plundering of marbles by the pope from *Tivoli, the *Colosseum and the *Portico of Octavia
1462	Papal Bull of *Pius II excommunicates plunderers of marble from Roman ruins
1464	Expedition to Lake Garda by *Mantegna, *Marcanova, *Felice Feliciano and Samuele da Tradate
1465	G. *Marcanova, *Antiquitates*
1466	Opening of an *Etruscan Tomb at *Volterra
1468	Arrest of Pomponio *Leto and the members of the *Roman Academy

1471   Lorenzo de' Medici acquires the *Farnese Cup (*Sixtus IV; *Medici family)
1471   Pope *Sixtus IV donates bronzes to the *Capitoline Museum in Rome
ca. 1480   First descents into the "Terme di Tito" (*Domus Aurea)
1485   Discovery of the body of *"Tulliola" on the Via Appia, Rome
1490s   Discovery of the *Belvedere *Apollo*
1494   Discovery of the *Tabula Peutingeriana by C. *Celtis
1495   B. *Rucellai, *De urbe Roma*
1499   F. *Colonna, *Hypnerotomachia Poliphili*
1502   Discovery of the Magdalensberg *Youth* (*Kunsthistorisches Museum)
ca. 1503   Arrival in Venice of the *"Praying Boy"*
1503–13   Papacy of *Julius II; founding of the Belvedere sculpture court at the *Vatican
1506   Discovery of the *Laocoon*
1507   Discovery of *Hercules and Telephus (Commodus)*
1510   F. *Albertini, *Opusculum de mirabilibus novae et veteris urbis Romae*
1512   Discovery of the *Nile* River God in Rome, and, one year later, the *Tiber*
1515   *Raphael assigned as overseer of antiquities by *Leo X
1517   A. *Fulvio, *Illustrium imagines*
1519   C. *Ripa, *Iconologia*
1523   *Grimani collection of antiquities bequeathed to the state of Venice
1527   A. *Fulvio, *Antiquitates urbis*
1527   Sack of Rome by Charles V
1530   Discovery of the *"Idolino"*
1532   Journey to Rome of M. van *Heemskerck
1532   Marco Fabio Calvo, *Antiquae urbis Romae cum regionibus simulacrum* (*Leo X)
1533   J. *Leland named King's Antiquary by Henry VIII, King of England
1534   Establishment of the permanent position of *Commissario delle Antichità by Pope *Paul III
1534   B. *Marliani, *Antiquae urbis Romae topographia*
1538   Transfer of the *Marcus Aurelius* Equestrian Statue from the *Lateran to the *Capitoline Hill, Rome
1538   Visit to Rome by *Francisco d'Ollanda
1540   S. *Serlio, *Delle antichità*
ca. 1540   *Primaticcio orders casts of famous sculptures for Francis I
1545   Discovery of the *Farnese *Bull* and the *Farnese *Hercules*
1549–50   Writing of *Delle statue antiche che per tutta Roma in diversi luoghi . . . si veggano* by U. *Aldrovandi (published 1556)
1550   L. *Alberti, *Descrittione di tutta Italia*
1550ff.   Work of P. *Ligorio at Tivoli, including excavation at *Hadrian's Villa
1553   Discovery of the *Chimaera* of *Arezzo
1553   P. *Ligorio, *Delle antichità di Roma*
1554   A. *Palladio, *L'Antichità di Roma*
1555   Discovery of the *Monumentum Ancyranum
1556   V. *Cartari, *Imagini dei Dei degli antichi*
1556   P. *Valerianus, *Hieroglyphica sive de sacris Aegyptiorum aliarumque gentium litteris*

1557   E. *Vico, *Le Imagini delle donne auguste*
1557   H. *Goltzius, *Vitae omnium fere imperatorum a C. Iulio Caesare usque ad Carolum V*
1558   T. *Fazello, *De rebus siculis*
1559   S. *Erizzo, *Discorso sopra le medaglie degli antichi*
1559   J. *Strada, *Imperatorum romanorum . . . imagines*
1560–65   "Libro delle antichità" by G.A. *Dosio
ca. 1561–94   G. B. de' *Cavalieri, *Antiquae statuae urbis Romae*
1562   First discoveries of fragments of the *Forma urbis Romae
1562   G. *Vignola, *Regola delle cinque ordini d'architettura*
1566   The *Arringatore* placed in the collection of the *Medici family
1568   Discovery of the Pax ("Tellus") frieze and processional friezes from the *Ara Pacis Augustae in Rome
1569   G. B. de' *Cavalieri, *Le Antichità di Roma*
1570   A. *Palladio, *Quattro libri dell'architettura*
1570   Rebuilding of the ancient Aqua Virgo to deliver water to the Fountain of Trevi, Rome (*Aqueducts)
1570   F. *Orsini, *Illustrium imagines*
1575   E. *Du Pérac, *Vestigi dell'antichità di Roma*
1580–1583   Discovery of the *Niobe* Group in Rome
1581   Beginning of the usage of the *Uffizi, Florence, as an art gallery
1582   Probable date of discovery of the *Portland Vase
1586   Erection of the Vatican *obelisk by D. *Fontana for Pope *Sixtus V
1587   Placement of the *"Trophies of Marius" on the *Capitoline Hill, Rome
1588   M. *Smetius, *Inscriptionum antiquarum*
1588–89   Restoration of the *Column of Trajan and the *Column of Marcus Aurelius by D. *Fontana for Pope *Sixtus V
1588–89   Demolition of the *Septizodium by *Sixtus V
1593   Map of Rome by A. Tempesta (*Excavations and expeditions)
1594   F. *Vacca, "Memorie di varie antichità trovate in diverse luoghi della città di Roma"
1597–1602   J. J. *Boissard, *Romanae urbis topographia et antiquitates*
1600   *Vatican Vergil bequeathed to the Vatican by F. *Orsini
1603   J. *Gruter, *Inscriptiones antiquae totius orbis romani*
1603   Founding of the *Accademia dei Lincei
ca. 1604   Discovery of the *Aldobrandini *Wedding* in Rome
1606   F. *Orsini, *Illustrium imagines*, 2nd ed., issued by J. Faber
1611   Discovery of the *Borghese *Gladiator* near Anzio
1614   First serious investigation of the *Barberini Mosaic, by F. *Cesi
1619   P. *Cluverius, *Sicilia antiqua*
1619   Rediscovery of the *Gemma Tiberiana in the Sainte Chapelle Paris by *Peiresc
ca. 1620   Cassiano dal *Pozzo begins his Museo Cartaceo
1621   Discovery of the *Ludovisi Battle Sarcophagus
1627   Acquisition of the *Marmor Parium (part A) for *Arundel
1627   Transfer of the *Barberini *Faun*, found at *Castel Sant'Angelo, Rome, to the Palazzo Barberini
1628   John Selden, *Marmora Arundelliana* (*Arundel)

1631   J. von *Sandrart, *Galleria Giustiniani*
1634   A. *Bosio, *Roma sotteranea*
1637   F. *Junius, *De pictura veterum*
1649–51 *Velazquez journeys to Rome to acquire antique sculptures
1655   Arrival in Rome of *Christina of Sweden
1656   J. *Tradescant, *Musaeum Tradescantianum*
1665   G.P. *Bellori and P.S. *Bartoli, *Colonna Traiana*
1665   F. *Nardini, *Roma antica*
1665   A. *Rubens, *De re vestiaria veterum*
1666   Founding of the *French Academy in Rome
1671   A. *Kircher, *Latium, id est nova et parallela Latii tum veteris tum novi descriptio*
1673   J. *Spon, *Recherche des antiquités et curiosités de la ville de Lyon*
1674   Drawings made of the *Parthenon for *Nointel
1674   Discovery of the Tomb of the Nasonii (*''Tomb of Ovid'') in Rome
1675–76 *Spon and *Wheler visit Greece
1675–79 J. von *Sandrart, *Teutsche Academie der Edlen Bau-Bild und Mahlerley Kunste*
1678   J. *Spon, *Voyage d'Italie, de Dalmatie, de Grèce et de Levant*
1680   R. *Fabretti, *De aquis et aquaeductibus veteris Romae*
1683   Discovery of the *Tabula Iliaca at Bovillae
1683   Opening of the *Ashmolean Museum, Oxford
1685   G. P. *Bellori, *Veterum illustrium philosophorum, poetarum, rhetorum ac oratorum imagines*
1687   Bombing of the *Parthenon by the Venetians under F. *Morosini
1688   Completion of the Tribuna gallery at the *Uffizi, Florence
1690   M.-A. de la Chausse, *Museum Romanum*
1694–99 J. G. *Graevius, *Thesaurus antiquitatum romanarum*
1694–1703 J. *Gronovius, *Thesaurus antiquitatum graecarum*
1696–1701 L. *Beger, *Thesaurus Brandenburgicus Selectus*
1700   M.-A. de la *Chausse, *Le Gemme antiche figurate*, with illustrations by P. S. *Bartoli
1702   Investigations and identification of the Temple of Hera at *Samos by J. Pitton de Tournefort
1703   Major earthquake in Rome
1704   P. A. *Maffei, *Raccolta di statue antiche e moderne*, published by D. de Rossi
1707   Founding of the *Society of Antiquaries
1709   Beginning of excavations at *Herculaneum
1709   E. S. Cheron, *Pierres antiques gravées tirées des principaux cabinets de la France*
1718–24 Survey of British antiquities by W. *Stukeley
1719–24 B. de *Montfaucon, *L'Antiquité expliquée et représentée en figures*
1722   J. *Richardson (Senior and Junior), *An Account of the Statues and Bas-Reliefs, Drawings and Pictures in Italy, France &c*
1723–26 T. *Dempster, *De Etruria regali*, with annotations by F. *Buonarroti
1724   Purchase of the *Odescalchi family collection (*Christina of Sweden) for the *Prado, Madrid

1727	Founding of the *Accademia Etrusca
1728	Excavations by F. *Gori of *Etruscan Tombs at *Volterra
1731ff.	F. *Gori, *Museum florentinum*
1732	Discovery of the *Corsini Throne in Rome
1732	*Fourmont at *Sparta
1733	F. S. *Maffei, *Galliae antiquitates selectae*
1733	Founding of the *Society of Dilettanti
1738	Renewal of excavations at *Herculaneum
1738	Discovery of the *Ficoroni Cista at Palestrina (*Praeneste)
1740	Founding of the *Pontificia Accademia Romana di Archeologia
1747	J. *Spence, *Polymetis*
1747–61	G. Vasi, *Delle magnificenze di Roma, antica e moderna*
1748	Beginning of excavations at *Pompeii
1749	Discovery of *Stabiae
1750	P. J. *Mariette, *Traité des pierres gravées*
1750	Discovery of the *Villa of the Papyri at *Herculaneum
1751–53	*Stuart and *Revett in *Athens for the *Society of Dilettanti
1752–67	Comte de *Caylus, *Recueil d'antiquités egyptiennes, etrusques, grècques, romaines et gauloises*
1753	R. *Wood, *The Ruins of Palmyra*
1753	Founding of the *British Museum, London
1755	Founding of the *Academia Herculanensis
1755	J. J. Winckelmann, *Gedanken Über die Nachahmung der griechischen Werke*
1756	G. B. *Piranesi, *Le Antichità romane*
1757	R. *Wood, *The Ruins of Balbec*
1757–96	*Le Antichità di Ercolano* (*Herculaneum)
1758–66	J. J. *Winckelmann visits *Pompeii
1762	A. R. *Mengs, *Gedanken über die Schönheit*
1762	J. *Stuart and N. *Revett, first volume of *The Antiquities of Athens*
1764	R. Adam, *The Ruins of the Emperor Diocletian's Palace at Spalatro in Dalmatia* (*Adam family; *Split)
1764	J. J. *Winckelmann, *Geschichte der Kunst des Altertums*
1765	Discovery of the temple of Apollo Epikourios at *Bassai by J. Bocher
1765	R. *Chandler and W. *Pars in Asia Minor for the *Society of Dilettanti
1766	G. E. *Lessing, *Laokoon: oder über die Grenzen der Malerei und Poesie*
1766[67]–76	P. F. d'*Hancarville, *Collection of Etruscan, Greek and Roman Antiquities from the Cabinet of the Hon. W. Hamilton*
1769	Opening by J. *Wedgwood of his ceramics works, "Etruria"
1769	R. *Chandler, first volume of *Antiquities of Ionia*
1769–71	Excavations at *Hadrian's Villa by G. *Hamilton
1776–88	E. *Gibbon, *The History of the Decline and Fall of the Roman Empire*
1777	R. Payne *Knight in Sicily
1778–87	Marbles moved from the Villa Medici in Rome to Florence (*Medici family)
1779	A. *Desgodets, *Les Edifices antiques de Rome dessinés et mésures très exactement*
1780	Discovery and vandalizing of the *Tomb of the Scipios, Rome

1848   Discovery of the *Odyssey Landscapes

1849   Discovery in Rome of the statue of the *Apoxyomenos, attributed to Lysippos

1851   F. C. *Penrose, Principles of Athenian Architecture

1851   E. W. *Lear, Journal of a Landscape Painter in Greece and Albania

1851   J. I. *Hittorff, L'Architecture polychrome chez les grècs

1853   Discovery of *Villanovan culture by G. *Gozzadini

1853–59   H. von *Brunn, Geschichte der griechische Kunstler

1856   Purchase of *Portus by the *Torlonia family

1857   Discovery of the *Beulé Gate at the *Akropolis, Athens

1857   Discovery of the *Francois Tomb at Vulci by A. *François

1858   Cataloghi del Museo Campana and sale of antiquities from the collection of G. P. *Campana

1860   T. *Mommsen, Geschichte des römischen Munzwesens

1860   G. *Fiorelli becomes director at *Pompeii

1860   N. Hawthorne, The Marble Faun

1862   Publication of the first volume of the Corpus Inscriptionum Latinarum (T. *Mommsen)

1862–63   Excavations at *Marzabotto by *Gozzadini

1862–63   C. T. *Newton, History of Discoveries at Halicarnassus, Cnidus and Branchidae

1863   Discovery of the *Augustus from the *Villa of Livia at Prima Porta

1863   Discovery of the *Victory of *Samothrace

1863–74   Uncovering of the *Kerameikos cemetery in the area of the Dipylon Gate, Athens, by the *Greek Archaeological Society

1865–77   Excavations by General *Cesnola on *Cyprus

1867   Founding of the *Museo Arqueólogico Nacional, Madrid

1868   J. *Overbeck, Die Antiken Schriftquellen zur Geschichte der bildenden Kunste bei den Griechen

1869   Discovery of the *House of Livia, Rome

1869   Discovery of the *Temple of Artemis at *Ephesos by J. T. Wood

1870   Founding of the *Metropolitan Museum of Art, New York

1870   Founding of the *Museum of Fine Arts, Boston

1870   Discovery of a major segment of the *"Servian" Wall in Rome

1871ff.   Excavations by *Schliemann at *Troy, with the help of W. *Dörpfeld from 1882

1871   Alleged appearance of the *Praenestine Fibula at Palestrina

1872   Purchase of the Feoli collection of Greek and Etruscan vases from *Vulci for the Martin von *Wagner Museum

1873   Founding of the *French School in Rome

1874   Founding of the *German Archaeological Institute at Athens

1874–76   Excavations by *Schliemann at *Mycenae; discovery of Grave Circle A

ca. 1875   Discovery of the *Hera of Cheramyes on *Samos

1875ff.   Excavations by the Germans at *Olympia

1875   Discovery of the *Nike of Paionios at *Olympia

1876   Discovery of the *Bernardini Tomb, Palestrina (*Praeneste)

1876   Excavations by *Schliemann at *Tiryns, with the help of W. Dörpfeld, 1884–85

1877   Discovery of the *Hermes* of Praxiteles and identification of the *Temple of Hera at *Olympia

1878–79   Transport of the frieze from the *Great Altar of *Pergamon to Berlin by C. *Humann

1878   H. *Schliemann, *Mycenae*

1879   Founding of the *Archaeological Institute of America

1880   K. B. *Stark, *Systematik und Geschichte der Archäologie der Kunst*

1880   Systematic excavation of the *Propylaia, Athens, by R. Bohn

1880   H. *Schliemann, *Ilios: The City and Country of the Trojans*

1881   Inauguration of the *Florence Archaeological Museum

1882   Founding of the *American School of Classical Studies in Athens

1882   A. *Michaelis, *Ancient Marbles in Great Britain*

1882   Donation to Oxford of the collections of General *Pitt-Rivers, to create the Pitt-Rivers Museum

1882–94   J. J. Bernoulli, *Römische Ikonographie* (*Portrait Iconography)

1883   Transport of the monument from *Trysa to the *Kunsthistorisches Museum, Vienna

1884   Excavations by General *Pitt-Rivers at Cranborne Chase

1884   Discovery of the Law Code of *Gortyn by F. *Halbherr

1885   Discovery of the *Hellenistic "Ruler" and Bronze *Boxer* in Rome

1886   Founding of the *British School at Athens

1886   Beginning of excavations at the *Temple of Apollo at *Corinth, by W. *Dörpfeld

1886–88   Excavation of the palace at *Mycenae by C. *Tsountas

1887   Discovery of the *Ludovisi Throne

1887   Acquisition of *Fayum portraits by T. Graf

1887   Discovery of the *Calfbearer*

1888   H. *Brunn, *Denkmäler griechischer und römischer Skulptur*

1888   Discovery of the *Vapheio Cups

1889   J. *Martha, *L'Art étrusque*

1889   Founding of the *Villa Giulia and *Terme museums

1890   First volume of *Die Antiken Sarkophagreliefs* by C. *Robert

1891ff.   Excavations by P. *Orsi at *Syracuse

1892ff.   "La Grande Fouille," excavations of the *French School at *Delphi under T. *Homolle

1892   Formation of the Danish National Museum in *Copenhagen

1892–95   Excavation of the *Argive Heraion by C. *Waldstein

1893–1901   R. *Lanciani, *Forma urbis Romae*

1894   Appearance in Rome of the Boston Counterpart to the *Ludovisi Throne

1895   Discovery of the *Boscoreale Treasure

1895   Founding of the *American Academy in Rome

1895–1910   O. *Montelius, *La Civilisation primitive en Italy*

1896   Purchase of the forged *Tiara of Saitaphernes by the *Louvre

1896   Beginning of American excavations at *Corinth

1896   Discovery of the *Charioteer* of *Delphi

1896   Discovery of the temple of Mater Matuta at *Satricum

1896   *The Elder Pliny's Chapters on the History of Art*, tr., K. Jex-Blake, with commentary by E. Sellers (*Strong)

1896–1900	C. Cichorius, *Die Reliefs der Trajanssäule* (*Column of Trajan)
1897	Discovery of the *Dama de Elche
1897	R. *Lanciani, *The Ruins and Excavations of Ancient Rome*
1897	E. *Babelon, *Catalogue des camées antiques et modernes de la Bibliothèque Nationale*
1897	Opening of the *Ny Carlsberg Glyptotek, Copenhagen
1898	Commentary on Pausanias by Sir James G. *Frazer
1898ff.	Restoration of the *Parthenon under N. *Balanos
1899	Founding of the *British School at Rome
1899	Discovery of the *Lapis Niger in Rome
1899	A. *Mau, *Pompeii—Its Life and Art*, a translation by F. W. *Kelsey of *Pompeji in Leben und Kunst*, published in 1900
1900	F. *Wickhoff, *Roman Art*, tr. by E. S. *Strong
1900	Beginning of excavations at *Phaistos by L. *Pernier
1900	Beginning of excavations at Kavousi and *Gournia (1901) by Harriet Boyd (*Hawes)
1900	Beginning of excavations at *Knossos by Sir Arthur *Evans
1900	Discovery of the Villa of P. Fannius Synistor at *Boscoreale
1900	A. *Furtwängler, *Die Antiken Gemmen*
1901	A. *Riegl, *Spätrömische Kunstindustrie*
1901	J. J. Bernoulli, *Griechische Ikonographie* (*Portrait Iconography)
1901	J. *Strzygowski, *Orient oder Rom*
1902	Discovery of the Archaic cemetery in the *Forum Romanum, Rome, by G. *Boni
1902	Beginning of excavation at *Hagia Triadha by F. *Halbherr
1902	Beginning of excavation at Lindos under the auspices of the National Museum, *Copenhagen (*Rhodes)
1902	W. J. Anderson and R. P. Spiers, *Architecture of Greece and Rome*
1902–9	Restoration of the *Erechtheion under N. *Balanos
1905	Founding of the *British School in Rome
1906	Founding of the *Budapest Museum of Fine Arts
1906ff.	Reports by the Austrian Archaeological Institute, *Forschungen in Ephesos* (*Ephesos)
1907	Discovery of the shipwreck at *Mahdia
1907	Beginning of German excavations at the *Kerameikos in Athens
1909	Founding of the *Italian School of Archaeology in Athens
1909	Discovery of the Mysteries frescoes in the *Villa of the Mysteries, *Pompeii
1910	Discovery of the pedimental sculptures from the temple of Artemis at *Korkyra
1910–11	H. F. De Cou, assistant at the excavations at *Cyrene, shot to death by Arab assassins
1910	H. A. *Grueber, *Coins of the Roman Republic in the British Museum*
1910	Beginning of excavations at *Leptis Magna by F. *Halbherr
1910–23	''Nuovi Scavi'' at *Pompeii, by V. Spinazzola
1912	Founding of the *Royal Ontario Museum, Toronto
1914–17	World War I

1914–29 A. *Schulten, *Numantia*
1916 Discovery of the *Apollo* of *Veii
1920 Discovery of Roman silver cups at Hoby ("Hoby Cups") in southern Denmark
1922 Discovery of a necropolis at *Spina
1922 M. I. *Rostovtzeff, *Iranians and Greeks in South Russia*
1922–36 Sir Arthur *Evans, *The Palace of Minos*
1922–25 Founding of the *Gennadius Library
1923 E. *Pfuhl, *Malerei und Zeichnung der Griechen*
1923 G. *Lippold, *Kopien und umbildungen griechischer Statuen*
1923–50 H. *Mattingly, *Coins of the Roman Empire in the British Museum*
1924ff. Excavations by A. *Maiuri at *Pompeii
1925ff. Italian excavations and restorations at *Sabratha
1926 Discovery of the *Artemision God, in an ancient shipwreck off the coast of Cape Artemision
1926 Founding of the *Swedish Institute in Rome
1926 Discovery of the Area Sacra of the *Largo Argentina in Rome
1926 M. I. *Rostovtzeff, *The Social and Economic History of the Roman Empire*
1927 Reopening of excavations at *Herculaneum by A. *Maiuri
1927 P. *Ducati, *Storia dell'arte etrusca*
1927–31 *Swedish Cyprus Expedition directed by E. *Gjerstad
1928 L. *Curtius, *Die Wandmalerei Pompejis*
1928–32 Recovery of the Ships of *Nemi
1928–37 Excavations at *Dura-Europos by M. *Rostovtzeff and others for Yale University
1929 S. B. *Platner and T. *Ashby, *A Topographical Dictionary of Ancient Rome*
1929 M. H. *Swindler, *Ancient Painting*
1930 Beginning of excavations by the *American School of Classical Studies in the *Agora, Athens
1931 G. Devoto, *Gli Antichi italici*
1932ff. Final reports on *Corinth, by R. *Stillwell and others
1933 J.D.S. *Pendlebury, *A Handbook to the Palace of Minos at Knossos*
1934 Discovery of the sanctuary of Hera at the Foce del Sele, near *Paestum
1937 Mostra Augustea della Romanità (*Museo della Civiltà Romana)
1937–38 Excavation and reconstruction of the *Ara Pacis Augustae under *Fascism
1937–39 Discovery of the *Cancelleria Reliefs
1938ff. Excavations at *Samothrace by K. *Lehmann
1939 Beginning of excavations at *Pylos, by C. *Blegen
1939–45 World War II
1940 P.F.S. Poulsen, *Katalog over antike Skulpturer der Ny Carlsberg Glyptotek*
1940ff. Restoration of the *Parthenon under A. K. *Orlandos
1941 A. *Furumark, *The Mycenaean Pottery, Analysis and Classification* and *The Chronology of Mycenaean Pottery*
1942 F. *Cumont, *Recherches sur le symbolism funerarire des romains*

1942	G.M.A. *Richter, *Kouroi, Archaic Greek Youths*, 1st ed.
1942	Edith H. *Dohan, *Italic Tomb Groups in the University Museum*
1944	Destruction of the Ships of *Nemi
1945	Discovery of the ''Bee Pendant'' at *Malia
1946	Discovery of the *Cartoceto Bronzes
1946	Founding of the *Swedish Institute at Athens
1947	M. E. Blake, *Ancient Roman Construction in Italy from the Prehistoric Era to Augustus*
1948	A. *Garcia y Bellido, *Hispania graeca*
1948	T. J. *Dunbabin, *The Western Greeks*
1948	Beginning of excavations at *Cosa by Frank *Brown
1950	W. B. *Dinsmoor, *The Architecture of Ancient Greece*
1950–73	Excavations at *Gordion, directed by R. *Young, for the University Museum, Philadelphia
1951ff.	Construction of the *Herakleion Museum
1952	Decipherment of Linear B as Greek by M. *Ventris (*Linear A and Linear B; *Myceneans)
1952	Beginning of excavations at *Pithekoussai by G. Buchner
1952	Use of SCUBA by J. Cousteau, to investigate a shipwreck at Grand Congloué (*Underwater Archaeology)
1952–55	Excavation by G. *Mylonas and J. Papademetriou of Grave Circle B at *Mycenae
1952–58	Excavations at *Lerna by J.L. *Caskey
1953	Discovery of the *Vix Krater
1953–56	Rebuilding of the *Stoa of Attalos, Athens
1954	M. *Wheeler, *Archaeology from the Earth*
1955	Beginning of excavations at *Lavinium by F. Castagnoli and L. Cozza
1956	J. D. *Beazley, *Attic Black-Figure Vase-Painting*
1957	G. *Lugli, *La Tecnica edilizia romana*
1957	Discovery of sculptures in the cave at *Sperlonga
1958ff.	Excavations at *Sardis by G.M.A. *Hanfmann
1959	Discovery of the *Peiraeus Bronzes
1960s	Geophysical prospection in Etruria by the *Lerici Foundation
1960	Discovery of Bronze Age shrine and statuary at *Keos by J. L. *Caskey
1961	M. *Bieber, *The Sculpture of the Hellenistic Age*, rev. ed.
1963	J. D. *Beazley, *Attic Red-Figure Vase-Painting*, 2nd ed.
1963–72	Fourth edition of W. *Helbig, *Fürher durch die öffentlichen Sammlungen klassischer Altertümer in Rom*, ed. H. Speier
1964	*Corpus der minoischen und mykenischen Siegel* initiated by F. *Matz
1964	Discovery of the *Pyrgi tablets
1965	*Underwater excavations at *Portus Cosanus (port of *Cosa)
1965ff.	Excavations by A. Bammer at the *Temple of Artemis at *Ephesos
1966	Flood in Florence, Italy (*Florence, Archaeological Museum)
1966	L. *Bernabò Brea, *Sicily before the Greeks*
1966ff.	Excavations at *Murlo
1967	Discovery of the Bronze Age settlement at *Thera by S. *Marinatos
1968	E. *Nash, *Pictorial Dictionary of Ancient Rome*, rev. ed.
1968	G.M.A. *Richter, *Korai, Archaic Greek Maidens*

1968　Discovery of the Tomb of the Diver, *Paestum

1968　Excavations in the Palace of Diocletian at *Split by a joint American-Yugoslav team

1969　A. K. *Orlandos, *Les Matériaux et la technique architecturale des anciens grecs*

1970　J. B. *Ward-Perkins and A. *Boethius, *Etruscan and Roman Architecture*

1972　Purchase by the *Metropolitan Museum of Art of a vase painted by Euphronios for $1 million

1972　W. A. McDonald and G. R. Rapp, Jr., *The *Minnesota Messenia Expedition, Reconstructing a Bronze Age Regional Environment*

1972　Discovery of the *Riace *Warriors*

1977　Discovery of the *"Tomb of Philip II" at Vergina by M. *Andronikos

1977ff.　Excavations by the Dutch Institute in Rome at *Satricum

1977ff.　Restoration of monuments of the *Akropolis, Athens (*Erechtheion, *Parthenon), under the supervision of M. Korres

1981　Excavation of monumental building and burials at *Lefkandi by M. Popham, L. Sackett and E. Touloupa

1981　Removal of the *Marcus Aurelius* Equestrian Statue from the center of the *Capitoline Hill, Rome

1982ff.　Excavations in the city of *Tarquinia by M. Bonghi Jovino

1989　Discovery of a shipwreck off Sicily by means of a "remotely operated vehicle" (*Underwater Archaeology)

Select Bibliography

Joann McDaniel

[Editor's Note—This bibliography was researched and compiled by Joann McDaniel, with general recommendations from the editor of the volume. As in the bibliographies for each entry, the needs and preparation of students and general readers were an important concern, and thus high priority has been given to works that are in English and readily available. A balance between recent scholarship and older publications has been sought, as well as between general studies and particular ones that have become classics in their own category. The number of sources was limited to one hundred, in an attempt to prepare a concise listing of a starting library for someone who wishes to pursue the history of classical archaeology. Exhaustive and invaluable bibliographies covering the critical period from ca. 1400 to 1900 may be found in Greenhalgh (section 2), Bober—Rubinstein (sec. 4) and Haskell—Penny (sec. 4); the latter two studies deal especially with the rediscovery and evaluation of ancient sculpture, but many of the items in their bibliographies have a wider application.

In recent years, various important handbooks on Greek and Roman art have appeared, for example, two on sculpture from Yale University Press: A. Stewart, *Greek Sculpture, An Exploration* 1–2 (New Haven, CT, 1990) and D.E.E. Kleiner, *Roman Sculpture* (New Haven, CT, 1992). These excellent, well-illustrated handbooks are concerned with the present state of research and were not intended to cover the history of the study of their subject. Stewart stated that the recovery of Greek sculpture was "unfortunately too large a subject for inclusion here" (p. 334). Thus, such handbooks, though important and up-to-date, are not listed in this bibliography, nor are they as frequently cited in this volume as certain older studies that make frequent reference to the history of discovery and scholarship, for example, the works that take account of the long tradition of German scholarship by M. Bieber, O. Brendel and G.M.A. Richter.]

GENERAL TOPICS

1. History of Archaeology

Bracco, V. *L'Archaeologia classica nella cultura occidentale.* Rome, 1979.
Dacos, N. "Sopravvivenza dell'antico." *EAA* Suppl. (1973): 725–46.
Daniel, G. E. *A Hundred and Fifty Years of Archaeology,* 2nd ed. Cambridge, MA, 1976.
————. *A Short History of Archaeology.* London, 1981.
Michaelis, A. *A Century of Archaeological Discoveries,* tr. B. Kahnweiler. London, 1908.
Pallottino, M. *The Meaning of Archaeology.* New York, 1968.
Stark, C. B. *Handbuch der Archäologie der Kunst.* 1: *Systematik und Geschichte der Archäologie der Kunst.* Leipzig, 1880; repr. 1969.
Trigger, B. *A History of Archaeological Thought.* Cambridge, 1989.
Weiss, R. *The Renaissance Discovery of Classical Antiquity,* 2nd ed. Oxford, 1988.
See also Brendel (sec. 4).

2. The Classical Tradition

Fehl, P. *The Classical Monument: Reflections on the Connection Between Morality and Art in Greek and Roman Sculpture.* New York, 1972.
Greenhalgh, M. *The Classical Tradition in Art.* London, 1978.
Howard, S. *Antiquity Restored, Essays on the Afterlife of the Antique,* with preface by E. H. Gombrich. Vienna, 1990.
Panofsky, E. *Renaissance and Renascences in Western Art,* 2nd rev. ed. Stockholm, 1964.
Rowland, B. *The Classical Tradition in Western Art.* Cambridge, MA, 1963.
Vermeule, C. C. *European Art and the Classical Past.* Cambridge, MA, 1964.

3. Biography and History of Scholarship

Briggs, W. W.—Calder, W. M., III, eds. *Classical Scholarship: A Biographical Encyclopedia.* New York, 1990.
Calder, W. M., III—Kramer, D. J. *An Introductory Bibliography to the History of Classical Scholarship in the XIXth and XXth Centuries.* Hildesheim, 1992.
Der Archäologe: Graphische Bildnisse aus dem Porträtarchiv Diepenbroick. Catalog of Exhibition. Münster, 1983.
Lullies, R.—Schiering, W., eds., *Archäologenbildnisse, Porträts und Kurzbiographen von klassischen Archäologen deutscher Sprache.* Mainz am Rhein, 1988.
Sandys, J. E. *A History of Classical Scholarship,* 3rd ed., 1–3. Cambridge, 1958.
von Wilamowitz-Moellendorff, U. *A History of Classical Scholarship,* tr. A. Harris, ed. with introd. and notes by H. Lloyd-Jones. Baltimore, 1982.

SPECIAL TOPICS

4. Ancient Sculpture, Painting and Architecture

Bergstrøm, I. *The Revival of Antique Illusionistic Wall-Painting in Renaissance Art.* Goteborg, 1957.

Bieber, M. *The Sculpture of the Hellenistic Age,* rev. ed. New York, 1961.

Bober, P.—Rubinstein, R. *Renaissance Artists and Antique Sculpture: A Handbook of Sources.* London, 1986.

Brendel, O. J. *Prolegomena to the Study of Roman Art.* New Haven, CT, 1979.

Dacos, N. *La Découverte de la Domus Aurea et la formation des grotesques à la Renaissance.* London, 1969.

Fehl, P. *Franciscus Junius, The Literature of Classical Art.* 1: *The Painting of the Ancients, De pictura veterum;* 2: *A Lexicon of Artists and Their Works.* Berkeley, 1991.

Haskell, F.—Penny, N. *Taste and the Antique: The Lure of Classical Sculpture, 1500–1900.* New Haven, CT, 1981.

Michaelis, A. *Ancient Marbles in Great Britain.* Cambridge, 1882.

Richter, G.M.A. *Portraits of the Greeks,* 1–3. London, 1965; *Supplement,* London, 1972, Revised edition, Ithaca, NY, 1984.

Ridgway, B. *Hellenistic Sculpture.* 1: *The Styles of ca. 331–100 B.C.* Madison, WI, 1990.

———. *Roman Copies of Greek Sculpture: The Problem of the Originals.* Ann Arbor, MI, 1984.

Summerson, J. *The Classical Language of Architecture,* rev. ed. London, 1980.

Swift, E. H. *Roman Sources of Christian Art.* New York, 1951.

See also Nash (sec. 7), Platner—Ashby (sec. 7), Richardson (sec. 7), Travlos (sec. 6).

5. Ancient Glyptics and Numismatics

Clain-Stefanelli, E. E. *Numismatics: An Ancient Science, A Survey of Its History.* Contributions from the Museum of History and Technology, Bull. 229. Washington, DC, 1940.

Furtwängler, A. *Die Antiken Gemmen,* 1–3. Berlin, 1900.

Giuliano, A. *I Cammei della Collezione Medicea nel Museo Archeologico di Firenze.* Rome, 1989.

Meulen, M. van der. *Petrus Paulus Rubens Antiquarius: Collector and Copyist of Antique Gems.* Alphen aan den Rijn, 1975.

Richter, G.M.A. *Engraved Gems of the Greeks, Etruscans and Romans,* 1–2. London, 1968–71.

Zazoff, P. H. *Gemmensammler und Gemmenforscher, Von einer noblen Passion zur Wissenschaft.* Munich, 1983.

6. Greek Topography and Travel

Eisner, R. *Travelers to an Antique Land: The History and Literature of Travel to Greece.* Ann Arbor, MI, 1991.

Stillwell, R., ed. *Princeton Encyclopedia of Classical Sites.* Princeton, NJ, 1976.

Stoneman, R. *Land of Lost Gods: The Search for Classical Greece.* London, 1987.

Travlos, J. *Pictorial Dictionary of Ancient Athens.* New York, 1971.

Tsigakou, F.-M. *The Rediscovery of Greece: Travellers and Painters of the Romantic Era.* New Rochelle, NY, 1981.

7. Roman Topography and Travel

Castagnoli, F. *Topografia di Roma Antica.* Turin, 1980.
Lanciani, R. *The Destruction of Ancient Rome.* London, 1899; repr. 1980.
Nash, E. *A Pictorial Dictionary of Ancient Rome,* rev. ed., 1–2. London, 1968.
Platner, S.—Ashby, T. *A Topographical Dictionary of Ancient Rome.* London, 1929.
Richardson, L., jr. *A New Topographical Dictionary of Ancient Rome.* Baltimore, 1992.
Valentini, R.—Zucchetti, G. *Codice topografico della città di Roma,* 1–4. Rome, 1940–1953.
See also Stillwell (sec. 6), Lanciani (sec. 9).

8. Drawings After the Antique

Ashby, T. "Antiquae statuae urbis Romae." *PBSR* 9 (1920): 107–58.
Bartoli, A. *I Monumenti antichi di Roma nei disegni degli Uffizi di Firenze,* 1–5. Rome, 1914–22.
Bober, P. P. *Amico Aspertini, Drawings After the Antique, Sketchbooks in the British Museum.* London, 1957.
Harprath, R.—Wrede, H., eds. *Antikenzeichnung und Antikenstudium in Renaissance und Frühbarock, Akten des internationalen Symposions 1986 in Coburg.* Mainz, 1989.
Hübner, P. G. *Le Statue di Roma: Grundlagen fur eine Geschichte der antiken Monumente in der Renaissance.* Leipzig, 1912.
Mandowsky, E.—Mitchell, C. *Pirro Ligorio's Roman Antiquities.* London, 1963.
Nesselrath, A. "I libri di disegni di antichità: tentative di una tipologia." In *Memoria dell'antico nell'arte italiana,* ed. S. Settis, vol. 3. Turin, 1986, 87–147.
Piggott, S. *Antiquity Depicted: Aspects of Archaeological Illustration.* New York, 1978.
Vermeule, C. C. "The Dal Pozzo-Albani Drawings of Classical Antiquities in the Royal Library at Windsor Castle." *Transactions of the American Philosophical Society* 56.2 (1966).

9. Collecting and Restoring

Bracken, C. P. *Antiquities Acquired: The Spoliation of Greece.* Newton Abbey, 1975.
de Azevedo, M. Cagiano. *Il Gusto nel restauro delle opere d'arte antiche.* Rome, 1948.
Helbig, W. *Führer durch die öffentlichen Sammlungen klassischer Altertümer in Rom,* 4th ed., ed. H. Speier, 1–4. Tübingen, 1963–72.
Jackson, V., ed. *Art Museums of the World,* 1–2. New York, 1987.
Lanciani, R. *Storia degli scavi di Roma e notizie intorno le collezioni romane di antichità,* 1–4. Rome, 1902–12; "edizione integrale," ed. L. M. Campeggi. Rome, 1989–92.
Michaelis, A. *Ancient Marbles in Great Britain.* Cambridge, 1882.
Pietrangeli, C. *Le Collezione private romane attraverso i tempi.* Rome, 1985.
Salerno, L. s.v. "Collezioni archeologiche (Collezioni dal Rinascimento al sec. XVIII)." *EAA* suppl. (1973): 242–59.
See also Bober—Rubinstein (sec. 4), Haskell—Penny (sec. 4), Weiss (sec. 1), Michaelis (sec. 1), Howard (sec. 2).

10. Etruscan Archaeology

Borsi, F., ed. *Fortuna degli etruschi.* Catalog of Exhibition. Florence, 1985.
Cristofani, M. *La Scoperta degli etruschi: Archeologia e antiquaria nel settecento.* Rome, 1983.
de Grummond, N. T. "Rediscovery." In *Etruscan Life and Afterlife,* ed. L. Bonfante. Detroit, 1986, 18–46.
Les Étrusques e l'Europe: Galeries internationales du Grand Palais. Catalog of Exhibition. Paris, 1992.

11. Bronze Age Archaeology

Calder, W. M., III—Traill, D. A., eds. *Myth, Scandal and History: The Heinrich Schliemann Controversy and a First Edition of the Mycenaean Diary.* Detroit, 1986.
McDonald, W. A. *Progress into the Past: The Rediscovery of Mycenaean Civilization,* 2nd ed. Bloomington, IN, 1990.
Myers, J. W.—Myers, E. E.—Cadogan, G., eds. *The Aerial Atlas of Ancient Crete.* Berkeley, 1992.

PERIODS OF HISTORY

12. Middle Ages

Adhémar, J. *Influences antiques dans l'art du moyen âge français: Recherches sur les sources et les thèmes d'inspiration.* London, 1939.
Benson, R. L.—Constable, G. *Renaissance and Renewal in the Twelfth Century.* Cambridge, 1982.
Bolgar, R. R., ed. *Classical Influences on European Culture,* A.D. 500–1500. Cambridge, 1971.
Greenhalgh, M. *The Survival of Roman Antiquities in the Middle Ages.* London, 1989.
Heckscher, W. S. "Relics of Pagan Antiquity in Mediaeval Settings." *JWarb* 1 (1937–38): 204–20.
Oakeshott, W. *Classical Inspiration in Medieval Art.* London, 1959.
Ross, J. B. "A Study of Twelfth-Century Interest in the Antiquities of Rome." In *Medieval and Historiographical Essays in Honour of James Westfall Thompson,* ed. J. L. Cate—E. N. Anderson. Chicago, 1938; repr. New York, 1966, 302–21.
Schnitzler, H. *Mittelalter und Antike, Über die Wiedergeburt der Antike in der Kunst des Mittelalters.* Munich, 1949.

13. Renaissance and Baroque

Bolgar, R. R., ed. *Classical Influences on European Culture,* A.D. 1500–1700. Cambridge, 1976.
Brummer, H. H. *The Statue Court in the Vatican Belvedere.* Stockholm, 1970.
Lehmann, P. W.—Lehmann, K. *Samothracian Reflections, Aspects of the Revival of the Antique.* Princeton, NJ, 1973.

Mitchell, C. "Archaeology and Romance in Renaissance Italy." In *Italian Renaissance Studies, A Tribute to the Late Cecilia M. Ady*. London, 1960.

The Paper Museum of Cassiano dal Pozzo. [Milan], 1993.

Salis, A. von. *Antike und Renaissance: Über Nachleben und Weitenwirken der alten in der neueren Kunst*. Erlenbach, 1947.

Saxl, F. "The Classical Inscription in Renaissance Art and Politics." *JWarb* 4 (1941): 19–46.

Settis, S. *Memoria dell'antico nell'arte italiana*, 1–3. Turin, 1984–86.

Sheard, W. S. *Antiquity in the Renaissance*. Catalog of Exhibition. Northampton, MA, 1979.

See also Weiss (sec. 1), Bober—Rubinstein (sec. 4), Haskell—Penny (sec. 4), Panofsky (sec. 2).

14. Eighteenth and Nineteenth Centuries

Black, J. *The Grand Tour in the 18th Century*. New York, 1992.

Crook, J. M. *The Greek Revival: Neo-Classical Attitudes in British Architecture, 1760–1870*. London, 1972.

Davies, G., ed. *Plaster and Marble, The Classical and Neo-Classical Portrait Bust (The Edinburgh Albacini Colloquium), Journal of the History of Collections* 3.2 (1991).

Jenkyns, R. *The Victorians and Ancient Greece*. Cambridge, 1980.

Pompeii as Source and Inspiration, Reflections in Eighteenth-and Nineteenth-Century Art. Catalog of Exhibition. Ann Arbor, MI, 1977.

Ridley, R. T. *The Eagle and the Spade: The Archaeology of Rome During the Napoleonic Era, 1809–1814*. Cambridge, 1992.

Skinner, B. C. *Scots in Italy in the Eighteenth Century*. Catalog of Exhibition. Edinburgh, 1966.

Springer, C. *The Marble Wilderness, Ruins and Representation in Italian Romanticism, 1775–1850*. Cambridge, 1987.

See also Greenhalgh (sec. 2), Haskell—Penny (sec. 4).

Index

Page numbers in **bold** indicate main entries.

Aachen, 146, 273
Abbate, N. dell', 870
Aberdeen, George, Earl of, 543, 906
"*Absalom*," 1045
Abydos, **1**, 213
Academia Herculanensis, **1–2**, 186, 416, 586, 804, 911, 973
Académie des beaux-arts, 158, 164, 942
Académie des inscriptions et belles-lettres, 158, 261, 271, 459, 468, 706, 942
Académie royale de peinture et sculpture. *See* Royal Academy of Painting and Sculpture
Academy of Saint Luke. *See* Accademia di San Luca
Accademia d'Italia, 3
Accademia dei Lincei, **2–3**, 36, 120, 256, 361, 600, 657, 929, 968
Accademia della Crusca, 751
Accademia di San Luca (Academy of St. Luke), 19, 142, 231, 233, 631, 793, 804, 845, 885, 1086, 1177, 1201
Accademia Ercolano. *See* Academia Herculanensis
Accademia Ellenica, 803
Accademia Etrusca, **3–5**, 330, 410, 416, 459, 462, 511–512, 527, 706
Accademia Nazionale dei Lincei. *See* Accademia dei Lincei
Accademia Pontificia dei Nuovi Lincei, 3
Accademia Romana. *See* Roman Academy
Accursio, M., 348
Acharnai, 9
Achilles, 700, 920; portrayals of, 174, 496, 695
Achilles Among the Daughters of Lycomedes, by N. Poussin, 928

Achilles and the Centaur Chiron, 186
Achilles Painter, 8
Achilles Sacrificing Trojan Prisoners, 462
Acilia Hygia, 1202
Aciliae Tertullae Fil., 1202
Acquarossa, **5,** 556, 1065, 1177
Acragas. *See* Akragas
Acrobat (Knossos), 583
Acta Triumphorum, 398
Ad Gallinas Albas. See Villa of Livia
Adam, 31
Adam, James, **5,** 20
Adam, John, **5**
Adam, L. S., 449
Adam, R., **5–7,** 20, 28, 410, 487, 532, 911, 1047
Adam, S., 588
Adam, by Michelangelo, 755
Adam, W., 5
Adam and Eve, by A. Dürer, 145, 381
Adam family, **5,** 28, 410, 630, 974
Adam Style, 5–6
Adamesteanu, D., 748
Adamklissi, 475
Adler, Johann Heinrich Friedrich, **7,** 372, 685, 825
Adonis, 264, 695, 1083
Adoration of the Magi: by Botticelli, 185; by Ghirlandaio, 448; by Panini, 845; by Pisano, 899
Adoration of the Shepherds, by Ghirlandaio, 499
Adrastus, 316
Adria, **7–8,** 166, 1044
Adrian VI, Pope, 574
Adriani, A., 35, 612, 1029
Adventus of Marcus Aurelius, 723
Aegae. *See* Vergina

Iasos, 612
IBM, 320
Ibrahim Pasha, 80
Ibycus, 321
Idaean Cave, 335, 337, 560, 583
Idalion (Idalium), 344, 1065
Idolino (Apollo; Bacchus; Ganymede), 527, **602–603,** 740, 1138
Igel Monument, 517, **603,** 714, 1197
Iguvine Tables. *See* Eugubine Tables
Iguvium. *See* Gubbio
Ikarios, 708, 1012
Iktinos, 127, 388, 855
Iliac Tablet. *See* Tabula Iliaca
Iliffe, J., 987
"Ilissos," 1175
Imbros, 288
Imperato, F., 782
Imperial Academy of Science (Russian), 589
Imperial Archaeological Commission (Russian), 183
Imperial Fora, Rome, **603–607**
Inan, J., 875, 1030
Incoronata, 748
Indiges, 665
Infancy of Bacchus, 224
Infant Bacchus, 37
Inghirami, F., 85, 1072
Inghirami, T., 587
Ingot God, 393
Ingres, Jean-Auguste-Dominique, 450, 468, **607–608,** 704; *Envoys to Achilles from Agamemnon,* 607; *Jupiter and Thetis,* 607; *Romulus, Conqueror of Acron,* 607; *Vergil Reading the Aeneid to Augustus,* 607
Innocent II, Pope, 664
Innocent III, Pope, 70
Innocent VI, Pope, 297
Innocent VIII, Pope, 144, 291, 322, 716, 1135
Innocent XI, Pope, 282, 742
inscriptions, study of. *See* epigraphy
Institut de correspondance hellénique, 468
Institut de France, 164
Institute of Archaeology, Moscow. *See* Moscow, Institute of Archaeology
Instituto di Corrispondenza Archeologica, 109, 162, 189, 222, 231, 241, 408, 418, 436, 462, 470, 489, 491, 601, **608–610,** 702, 804, 846, 879, 942, 981
Interior of the Pantheon, by G. Panini, 845
Inventor of the Arts, by A. Pisano, 897
Io, 79
Io and Argos, 598
Io and Jupiter, by Correggio, 540
Iolaus, 440
Ioulis, 634
Iphigenia, 190
Ippel, A., 975

Iris, 1184
Irvine, J. T., 129
Isabella II, Queen of Spain, 774
Isabella of Parma (Elisabetta Farnese), Queen of Spain, 185, 429, 932
Isambert, E., 550
Isaurians, 954
Ischia. *See* Pithekoussai
Ischia di Castro, 224
Isidore of Seville, 533
Isis, 150, 633, 806, 867, 911
Isis, 49, 426
Isis (Roman Ship), 1140
Isler, H. P., 1029
Ismail Pasha, 820
Isokrates, 888, 924
Issos, 34
Istanbul. *See* Byzantium
Isthmia, 45, 199, **610–611;** museum, 634
Istituto di Studi Etruschi, 509
Istituto Nazionale di Archeologia, 658
Italia, 60
Italian School of Archaeology, Athens, 107, 335, 418, 469, 528, 560, **611–613,** 651, 679, 883, 969
Italica (Santiponce), **613**
Item, A., 1169
Ithaka (Ithaki), 195, **613–614,** 787
Itinerarium Antonini, 1071
Ivano, A., 406, 1179
Ivanoff, S. A., 130
Ivanovitch, F., 388
Ixion, 138

Jacobsen, C., 576, 800, 815, 927
Jacobsthal, Paul, **615,** 688, 744
Jacoby, F., 728, 1195
Jacopi, G., 54, 955, 1043
Jacques, Pierre, 66, 207, 247, 267, **615–616,** 1014, 1144, 1145
Jaeger, W., 1195
Jahn, Otto, 150, 164, 223, 538, 576, 610, **616–618,** 752, 767, 879, 962, 971, 983, 1015, 1121, 1189, 1195
Jakovidis, S., 789
James I, King of England, 91, 204, 1036
James, H., 313
James Stuart, Prince, 1057
Jansen, L. J. F., 960
Jantzen, U., 495, 496
Janus, 433, 533, 863
Jason, 564
Jason and Medea, 523
Jason (ROV), 1140
Jason with the Golden Fleece, by B. Thorvaldsen, 1100
Jeanti, G. A., 583
Jebb, R. C., 194

Pikler. *See* Pichler Family
Pilato, L., 166
"Pillar of Pompey." *See* Alexandria, "Pillar of Pompey"
Pillet, M., 378
Pincelli, R., 170, 1168
Pindakos, 278
Pindar, 1096
Pindemonti, F., 72
Pinelli, G., 868
Pinturicchio, 49, 67, 544, 1143
Pinza, Giovanni, **890**
Piombino *Apollo,* 648, 693, **890–891**
Pippi, Giulio. *See* Giulio Romano
Piraeus. *See* Peiraeus
Piranesi, F., 547, 555, 558, 892, 895, 911
Piranesi, Giovanni Battista, 6, 67, 73, 77, 165, 211, 229, 236, 284, 315, 316, 410, 450, 454, 553, 556, 558, 559, 567, 632, 736, 837, 846, 848, **891–895,** 911, 963, 1036, 1085, 1086, 1088, 1094, 1112, 1116, 1130, 1131, 1160, 1164, 1177
Pirckheimer, Willibald, 380, 603, **895–896**
Pisa, 83, 262, **896,** 898, 899; Campo Santo, **227,** 896, 898, 899
Pisano, Andrea, **896–898;** *Baptism of Christ,* 897; *Creation,* 897; *Horsemanship,* 897; *Inventor of the Arts,* 897; *Labors of Man,* 898; *Naming of the Baptist,* 897; *Navigation,* 897; *Prometheus Shaping the Body of Man,* 897; *Sculpture,* 897; *Trade,* 898; *Weaving,* 897, 898
Pisano, Nicola and Giovanni, 83, 227, 466, **898–899;** *Adoration of the Magi,* 899; *Daniel,* 899; *Last Judgment,* 899; *Presentation in the Temple,* 899; *Prudence,* 899
Pisones, Calpurnii, 1111, 1171
Pithekoussai, 269, 338, **899–900**
Pitigliano, 366
Pittakis, K. S., 16, 18, 105, 396, 536, 537, 635, 796, 860, 906
Pitt-Rivers, Augustus Henry Lane Fox, 417, 782, **900–901,** 935, 1060, 1191
Pius II, Pope, 22, 23, 161, 299, 605, **901–902,** 919, 984, 1109, 1116
Pius III, Pope, 727
Pius IV, Pope, 57, 110, 132, 255, 315, 373, 427, 680, 1148–1149
Pius V, Pope, 57, 240, 268, 739, 1149
Pius VI, Pope, 236, 291, 292, 429, 464, 540, 556, 564, 640, 782, 792, 885, **902–904,** 944, 1149, 1150, 1163, 1174
Pius VII, Pope, 71, 231, 233, 234, 792, 794, **905,** 915, 981, 1101
Pius IX, Pope, 3, 57, 109, **905–906,** 912, 915
Pius XII, Pope, 229, 1151
Pizzofalcone, 791

Plancus, L. Munatius, 704, 1084
Plarasa, 54
Plataia, 354, 355, 1184
Platina, 720, 968
Platner, J., 1027
Platner, Samuel Ball, 93, 554, 696, 795, **906,** 1026
Plato, 139, 299, 816
Platon, N., 336, 337, 528, 583, 969, 1096, 1208
Plautianus, 71
Plautilla, 71
Plautius, Aulus, 689
Plemmyrion, 829
Pliny the Younger and His Mother at Misenum, by A. Kauffmann, 630
Plutarch, 857
Pnyx, Athens, 45, 106, **906–907**
Pococke, R., 344, 655, 999
Poe, E. A., 545
Poggio Bracciolini, Giovanni Francesco, 24, 50, 160, 299, 397, 398, 552, 718, 772, 804, 902, **907–908,** 940, 977, 993, 998
Poggio Buco, 224
Poggio Civitate. *See* Murlo
Pohl, I., 1168
Poidebard, A., 1140
Poieessa, 634
Poinssot, J., 1103
Poinssot, L., 710, 1103
Pola, 287, 1047; Arch of the Sergii, **72–74,** 139, 1025, 1129
Pole, R., 689
Poletti, L., 313
Poli collection, 777
Policoro, 493
Polidoro da Caravaggio, 175, 246, 255
Polignac, M. de, 153
Polimartium. *See* Bomarzo
Poliochni, 612
Poliphilus, 306
Poliziano, A., 282, 738, 753
Pollaiuolo, A., 184, 242
Pollak, L., 661, 775
Pollini, J., 60, 251, 426
Pollitt, J. J., 578, 939
Polydeukes, 440
Polydoros, 660, 1043. *See also Laocoon*
Polyeuktos, *Demosthenes,* 1201
Polygnotos, 8, 298, 518
Polyhymnia, 4
Polykleitos (architect), 395
Polykleitos (sculptor), 299, 364, 448, 804, 957, 987; *Amazon,* 693; *Doryphoros (Spearbearer),* 602, 879; *Hera,* 79
Polykles, 179
Polykrates, 999

About the Contributors

ROBERT ACKERMAN is Director of Humanities at the University of the Arts, Philadelphia. He is the author of *J. G. Frazer: His Life and Work* (1987) and *The Myth and Ritual School: J. G. Frazer and the Cambridge Ritualists* (1991). He has also published many articles on J. G. Frazer in such journals as *American Scholar* and *Greek, Roman, and Byzantine Studies*.

JAMES C. ANDERSON, JR. is Professor of Classics at the University of Georgia. He is the author of *Historical Topography of the Imperial Fora* (1984) and *Roman Brick Stamps: The Thomas Ashby Collection* (1991). He has also authored articles on Roman topography and architecture in the *American Journal of Archaeology*, *Bonner Jahrbücher*, and *Historia: Zeitschrift für Alte Geschichte*.

BABETTE E. ARTHUR, an art historian with a special interest in Roman imperial iconography, is Adjunct Instructor and Curator of Collections at the University of Central Florida.

R.L.N. BARBER is Senior Lecturer in Classical Archaeology at the University of Edinburgh. He is the author of *The Cyclades in the Bronze Age* (1987) and the Blue Guide volume on *Greece* (1988, 1995). His articles include a study on the Early Cycladic period in the *American Journal of Archaeology*.

BARBARA A. BARLETTA is Associate Professor of Art History at the University of Florida. She is a specialist in Greek art, particularly that of Southern Italy and Sicily. Her publications include *Ionic Style in Archaic Sicily: The Monumental Art* (1983) as well as articles in the *American Journal of Archaeology* and *Römische Mitteilungen*.

GEORGE CHARLES BAUER is Professor of Art History at the University of California, Irvine. He is the author of *Bernini in Perspective* (1976) and *Paul Fréart de Chantelou, Diary of the Cavaliere Bernini's Visit to Paris (1665) Annotations* (1985), as well as an article on "Experimental Shadow Casting and the Early History of Perspective" in *The Art Bulletin*.

PHILIP P. BETANCOURT is Laura H. Carnell Professor of Art History and Archaeology at Temple University. His many publications on the archaeology of Bronze Age and early Greece include *The Aeolic Style in Architecture: A Survey of Its Development in Palestine, The Halikarnassos Peninsula and Greece, 1000–500 B.C.* (1977) and *The History of Minoan Pottery* (1985). He is also editor with Costis Davaras of the reports on excavations at Pseira.

GIULIANA BIANCO, with an architectural background and an M.A. in Art History, has worked with the University of Toronto since 1976 at the excavations of Kommos, preparing and publishing architectural and survey drawings of the site in *Hesperia*. She has a special interest in the Italian archaeologists who pioneered excavation on Crete.

WILLIAM R. BIERS is Professor of Art History and Archaeology at the University of Missouri, Columbia. He is the author of *The Archaeology of Greece: An Introduction* (1980, rev. ed. 1987) and *Art, Artifacts, and Chronology in Classical Archaeology* (1992). With wide-ranging interests in Greek art and classical archaeology, he has published in *Hesperia*, the *American Journal of Archaeology*, *Antike Kunst*, and other journals.

JUDITH BINDER is Senior Associate Member of the American School of Classical Studies at Athens. She is the author of *The Athenian Agora, 7, Lamps of the Roman Period* (1961) and articles on the sculpture of the Parthenon in *Archaiologikon Deltion* and volumes in honor of Nikolaos Kontoleon and Sterling Dow.

PHYLLIS PRAY BOBER is Leslie Clark Professor Emeritus in the Humanities and also Professor Emeritus in the Department of the History of Art and the Department of Classical and Near Eastern Archaeology at Bryn Mawr College. She is co-author with R. Rubinstein of *Renaissance Artists and Antique Sculpture* (1986). Among her many publications are articles on Roman provincial sculpture, the usage of antiquity during the Renaissance, and the history of food and gastronomy.

E. W. BODNAR is Professor Emeritus of Classics at Georgetown University, Washington, D.C. He is the author of *Cyriacus of Ancona and Athens* (1960) and *Cyriacus of Ancona's Journeys in the Propontis and the Northern Aegean 1444–1445* (1976). He has also published articles on Cyriacus of Ancona in the *American Journal of Archaeology, Archaeology, Hesperia*, and *Mediaevalia*.

ANDREA BOLLAND is Assistant Professor of Art History at the University of Nebraska, Lincoln. She is the author of ''Art and Humanism in Early Renaissance Padua'' in *Renaissance Quarterly*.

GIULIANO BONFANTE, formerly professor of linguistics at Princeton University, the University of Turin, and other institutions, recently celebrated his ninetieth birthday. He has issued hundreds of publications on Roman and Italian literature, Indo-European linguistics, and the Etruscan language; most recent is his *La Lingua parlata in Orazio* (1994).

LARISSA BONFANTE is Professor of Classics at New York University. She is the author of *Etruscan Dress* (1975) and editor and author of *Etruscan Life and Afterlife*, as well as co-author with her father, Giuliano Bonfante, of *The Etruscan Language* (1983). She has published numerous articles and reviews on the archaeology of Italy in the *Journal of Roman Studies, Studi Etruschi, American Journal of Archaeology*, and elsewhere.

BRUCE BOUCHER is Reader in the History of Art at University College, University of London. He is the author of *The Sculpture of Jacopo Sansovino* (1991) and *Andrea Palladio: The Architect in His Time* (1994).

G. W. BOWERSOCK is Professor of Ancient History at the Institute for Advanced Study, Princeton. Among his many books are *Augustus and the Greek World* (1965) and *Hellenism in Late Antiquity* (1990). He has published extensively in scholarly journals, with articles on Greek, Roman, and Near Eastern history and the history of classical traditions.

MARTHA W. BALDWIN BOWSKY is Professor of Classics at the University of the Pacific. She is the author of ''Roman Crete: No Provincial Backwater'' published in the *Proceedings of the Seventh International Cretological Congress* (1991). In addition, she has published many articles on Roman Crete and Greek inscriptions and social history in *Classical Journal, Historia, Hesperia* and other journals.

BEVERLY LOUISE BROWN is Assistant Director at the Kimbell Art Museum, Fort Worth. She is the author of *Jacopo Bassano* (1992) and *Giambattista Tiepolo: Master of the Oil Sketch* (1993). She has published articles on Italian Renaissance architecture and Venetian painting in many journals, including *The Burlington Magazine, Mitteilungen des Kunsthistorischen Instituts im Florenz, The Renaissance Quarterly*, and *Venezia Arti*.

CLIFFORD M. BROWN is Professor of Art History at Carleton University, Ottawa. Among his books are *La Grotta di Isabella d'Este: un simbolo di continuità dinastica per i duchi di Mantova* (1985) and *"Our Accustomed Discourse on the Antique": Cesare Gonzaga and Gerolamo Garimberto—Two Renaissance Collectors of Greco-Roman Art* (1993). He has also published many articles in journals including *The Burlington Magazine*, and *The Art Bulletin*.

VINCENT J. BRUNO is Professor Emeritus at the University of Texas at Arlington. His publications include *Hellenistic Painting Techniques* (1985) and *Cosa, 4, The Houses* (1993) as well as articles on archaeology and the history of art in the *American Journal of Archaeology, Archaeology*, and the *International Journal of Nautical Archaeology*.

FRANÇOIS BUCHER is Professor of Medieval Art and Architecture at Florida State University. He is the founder and editor (1961–70) of *Gesta*, and is the author of many books and articles, including *Architector, The Lodge and Sketchbooks of Medieval Architects* (1979), *A Blazing End* (1984) and *The Traveler's Key to Medieval France* (1986).

WILLIAM M. CALDER III is Wiliam Abbott Oldfather Professor of the Classics at The University of Illinois at Urbana/Champaign. He has published over six hundred books, articles and reviews in the areas of Greek and Latin literature, including *Studies in the Modern History of Classical Scholarship* (1984), *The Prussian and the Poet* (1991), *An Introductory Bibliography to the History of Classical Scholarship Chiefly in the XIXth and XXth Centuries* (1992), and *Further Letters of Ulrich von Wilamowitz-Moellendorff* (1994).

VIRGINIA W. CALLAHAN is Professor of Classical Languages Emerita at Howard University, Washington, D.C. She is the author of *Gregorii Nysseni Opera Ascetica–Vita S. Macrinae* (1952) and *Andreas Alciatus–The Latin Emblems* (1985). Her works also include numerous articles on the relationship between Alciatus and Erasmus.

JOHN McK. CAMP II is Mellon Professor of Classical Studies at the American School of Classical Studies at Athens and Director of the Agora excavations. He is the author of *The Athenian Agora* (1986) and *The Birth of Democracy* (1993). He has contributed numerous articles on Greek archaeology to *Hesperia, American Journal of Archaeology*, and other journals.

JANE BURR CARTER is Associate Professor and Chair of the Department of Classical Studies at Tulane University. She is the author of *Greek Ivory-Carving in the Orientalizing and Archaic Periods* (1985) and the forthcoming *The Beginning of Greek Sculpture*. She has written articles on preclassical Greek art and culture published in the *American Journal of Archaeology*.

MORTIMER CHAMBERS is Professor of History at the University of California, Los Angeles. He is the author of *Georg Busolt: His Career in his Letters* (1990) and *Aristoteles, Staat der Athener* (1990). He is also the author of articles on Greek history and historians in *American Historical Review, Classical Philology*, and other journals.

B. F. COOK, now retired, was Keeper of Greek and Roman Antiquities at the British Museum from 1976 to 1993. He is the author of *Greek and Roman Art in the British Museum* (1976), *The Elgin Marbles* (1984), *The Townley Marbles* (1985), and *Greek Inscriptions* (1987), as well as numerous articles on a wide variety of subjects from Greek, Roman, and Etruscan antiquity and the history of archaeology.

WILLIAM D.E. COULSON is Director of the American School of Classical Studies at Athens. He is the author of *Cities of the Delta*, 1, *Naukratis* (1981), and *Sculpture from Arcadia and Laconia* (1993). He has published many articles on the archaeology of the Greek Dark Ages in *Hesperia, American Journal of Archaeology, Annual of the British School at Athens*, and other journals.

ELIZABETH CROPPER is Professor of Art History at Johns Hopkins University. She is the author of *The Ideal of Painting: Pietro Testa's Düsseldorf Notebook* (1984) and *Pietro Testa, 1612–1650: Prints and Drawings* (1988). She has written articles on Italian art of the sixteenth and seventeenth centuries in *The Burlington Magazine, The Art Bulletin*, and the *Journal of the Warburg and Courtauld Institutes*.

COSTIS DAVARAS is Professor of Minoan Archaeology at the University of Athens. He is the author of *Die Statue von Astritsi und die Anfänge der griechische Plastik* (1972) and *Guide to Cretan Antiquities* (1990). He has written articles on Minoan and Cretan archaeology and Greek epigraphy in *Cretan Studies, Kadmos, Hesperia*, and other journals.

GLENYS DAVIES is Senior Lecturer in the Department of Classics at the University of Edinburgh. She is the editor of *Plaster and Marble: The Classical and Neo-Classical Portrait Bust* (1991). Among her articles are "The Significance of the Handshake Motif in Classical Funerary Art" in the *American Journal of Archaeology* (1985) and "The Albacini Cast Collection: Character and Significance" in the *Journal of the History of Collections* (1991).

JACK L. DAVIS is Carl W. Blegen Professor at the University of Cincinnati. His publications include *Papers in Cycladic Prehistory* (1979) and *Landscape Archaeology as Long-Term History* (1991), as well as articles on Greek prehistory, the Ottoman history of Greece, and surface survey in the *American Journal of Archaeology*, the *Journal of Mediterranean Archaeology*, and *Hesperia*.

JOYCE M. DAVIS is Associate Professor of Art at Valdosta State University in Georgia. She received the Master's degree from the University of North Carolina at Chapel Hill, with a thesis on "Dürer's Animals: A Study of the Drawings" (1969). She has a special interest in the Baroque period in France.

NANCY THOMSON DE GRUMMOND is Professor and Chair of the Department of Classics at Florida State University. She was founder and editor of *Archaeological News* (1973–1985) and served as editor and co-author of *A Guide to Etruscan Mirrors* (1982) and *The Etruscans, Legacy of a Lost Civilization* (1992). She has contributed articles on Etruscan and Roman archaeology and Renaissance and Baroque art to the *American Journal of Archaeology*, *The Art Bulletin*, *Studi Etruschi* and other journals.

W. W. DE GRUMMOND is Professor of Classics at Florida State University. He is the former editor of the *Classical Journal* (1983–1991). Articles he has published include "Aeneas Despairing" in *Hermes* (1977), "Hands and Tails on the Vapheio Cups" in *American Journal of Archaeology* (1980), and "The Animated Implement: A Catullan Source for Vergil's Plough" in *Eranos* (1993).

G. DENHAENE is an art historian specializing in Flemish painting and humanism during the Renaissance. She is the author of *Lambert Lombard, Renaissance et humanisme à Liège* (1990) and articles in the *Bulletin de l'Institut historique belge de Rome*, as well as numerous entries in the forthcoming *Dictionnaire des peintres belges* and *The Dictionary of Art*.

RICHARD DANIEL DE PUMA is Professor of Classical Art and Archaeology at the University of Iowa. Among the books he has written are *Etruscan Tomb Groups* (1986) and two fascicles of the *Corpus Speculorum Etruscorum* (1987, 1993). Recently he served as co-editor (with J. P. Small) of *Murlo and the Etruscans* (1994). He is the author of numerous articles on the Etruscans in the *American Journal of Archaeology*, *Studi Etruschi*, *Archaeology*, and other journals.

B. UNDERWOOD DURETTE is an art historian who earned her Ph.D. from Florida State University, with a dissertation on "The History and Interpretation of the Aldobrandini *Wedding*" (1992). She is also the author of "The Smoking Candle of the Merode Altarpiece," published in *Athanor*.

MARY ANN EAVERLY is Associate Professor of Classics at the University of Florida. She is the author of *Archaic Greek Equestrian Sculpture* (1995).

INGRID E.M. EDLUND is Associate Professor of Classics at The University of Texas at Austin. She is the author of *The Gods and the Place: Location and Function of Sanctuaries in the Countryside of Etruria and Magna Graeca* (1987) and *The Seated and Standing Statue Akroteria from Poggio Civitate (Murlo)*

(1992). She has also published articles on Etruscan archaeology and Roman history in *Archaeological News, American Journal of Archaeology, Eranos*, and other journals.

HARRISON EITELJORG II is Director of the Center for the Study of Architecture. He is the author of *The Entrance to the Acropolis Before Mnesicles* (1994). In addition, he has published many articles on the use of computers in archaeology, in the *CSA Newsletter* and elsewhere.

C.W.J. ELIOT is President of the University of Prince Edward Island. He is the author of *Coastal Demes of Attica, A Study of the Policy of Kleisthenes* (1962) and of numerous articles in *Hesperia* on Greek archaeology, art, and topography. He has a special interest in the activities of travelers to Greece in past centuries.

JOHN A. ELLIOTT is Associate Professor of Art History at the University of South Carolina, Aiken. He is the author of *Study Guide, Art: History of Painting, Sculpture, Architecture by Frederick Hartt* (1993) and of ''The Etruscan Wolfman in Myth and Ritual'' in *Etruscan Studies*.

CHRISTOFFER H. ERICSSON, now retired, was Professor of Art History and Lecturer in Classical Archaeology at Jyväskylä University. He is editor-in-chief of the journal *Helikon* and author of *Roman Architecture Expressed in Sketches by Francesco di Giorgio Martini* (1980). He has also written articles on Roman imperial architecture and maritime history and archaeology for various publications.

HARRY B. EVANS is Professor of Classics at Fordham University. He is the author of *Publica Carmina: Ovid's Books from Exile* (1983) and *Water Distribution in Ancient Rome: The Evidence of Frontinus* (1994). He has also published articles on Roman topography and Latin poetry in the *American Journal of Archaeology*, the *Classical Journal*, and *Hermes*.

DIANE FAVRO is Associate Professor in the Department of Architecture and Urban Design at the University of California, Los Angeles. She is co-editor of and a contributor to *Streets: Critical Perspectives on Public Space* (1994). Her articles include ''*Pater Urbis:* Augustus as City Father of Rome'' in the *Journal of the Society of Architectural Historians* (1992) and ''The Roman Latrine: Urban Technology and Socialization'' in *On Architecture, the City and Technology* (1990).

PHILIPP FEHL is Professor Emeritus of Art History at the University of Illinois, Champaign–Urbana. He is the author of *The Classical Monument: Reflections on the Connection between Morality and Art in Greek and Roman Sculpture* (1972) and, with his wife, Raina Fehl, and K. Aldrich, of *F. Junius, The Lit-*

erature of Classical Art (1991). He has published numerous studies on the history of art and the history of archaeology and on the survival and revival of the classical tradition.

J. FEIJE is Librarian of the Instituut voor Kunst-, Architecturgeschiedenis en Archeologie at the Rijksuniversitet Groningen. He is the editor of the journal *Pharos*.

ENRIQUETA HARRIS FRANKFORT is an Honorary Fellow and former Curator of the photographic collection at the Warburg Institute, University of London. She is the author of *The Prado Museum, Treasure House of the Spanish Royal Collections* (1940) and *Velázquez* (1982). She has also written articles on Velázquez and Spanish painting published in *The Burlington Magazine*, *Archivo Español de Arte*, and *Journal of the Warburg and Courtauld Institutes*.

JACK FREIBERG is Assistant Professor of Art History at Florida State University. He is the author of *The Lateran in 1600: Christian Concord in Counter-Reformation Rome* (1995). He has also published articles on Italian Renaissance and Baroque art and architecture in *The Burlington Magazine* and *Zeitschrift für Kunstgeschichte*.

DAVID FUNK is a candidate for the doctorate in Humanities at Florida State University and a member of the staff at the university excavations at Cetamura del Chianti. He has a special interest in the Romanization of Etruria.

ROBERT W. GASTON is Senior Lecturer in Art History at La Trobe University. He is the editor and co-author of *Pirro Ligorio, Artist and Antiquarian* (1988) and has published numerous articles on Renaissance antiquarian studies and religious paintings, in *Medievalia et Humanistica, Journal of the Warburg and Courtauld Institutes, Mitteilungen des Kunsthistorischen Instituts in Florenz* and elsewhere.

BERNARD GOLDMAN is Professor Emeritus at Wayne State University. He is the author of *The Sacred Portal* (1986) and *The Ancient Arts of Western and Central Asia* (1991). Among his published articles are "Asiatic Ancestry of the Greek Gorgon" in *Berytus* and "A Dura-Europos Dipinto" in *Oriens Antiquus*.

NORMA GOLDMAN is Adjunct Professor at Wayne State University. She is the author of *Latin Via Ovid* (1978, 1983) and *Cosa: The Lamps* (*Memoirs of the American Academy in Rome*, Vol. 39, 1994). She has also written the articles "Ancient Roman Footwear" and "Reconstructing Ancient Roman Costumes" in *The World of Ancient Costume* (1994) and has published an article on "Reconstructing the Colosseum Awning" in *Archaeology*.

ULRICH K. GOLDSMITH is Professor of German and Comparative Literature Emeritus at the University of Colorado at Boulder. He is the author of *Stefan George: A Study of his Early Work* (1959) and various studies on Goethe, Shakespeare, Rilke and Mallarmé. He has written many articles and reviews in *Comparative Literature Studies, German Quarterly, Publications of the Modern Language Association,* and other periodicals.

FERNANDO FERNÁNDEZ GÓMEZ is Director of the Museo Arqueológico Sevilla, and has served as Director of excavations at El Raso de Candeleda since 1970. He is the author of *La Lex Irnitana y su contexto arqueológico* (1990) and "La fuente orientalizante de El Gandul (Sevilla)" in *Archivo Español de Arqueología* (1989), as well as other articles in *Trabajos de Preistoria, Noticiario Arqueológico Hispánico,* and *Revista de Arqueología.*

PHYLLIS W. G. GORDAN, a specialist on early Italian Renaissance humanism, was the author of *Fifteenth-century Books in the Library of Howard Lehman Goodhart* (1955) and *Two Renaissance Book Hunters, the Letters of Poggius Bracciolini to Nicolaus de Niccolis* (1974).

ARTHUR E. GORDON was Professor of Latin Emeritus at the University of California, Berkeley. A leading expert on Latin epigraphy, he was frequently aided by his wife Joyce in his publication of enduring works in this field: *Album of Dated Latin Inscriptions* (1958–1965), *The Inscribed Fibula Praenestina: Problems of Authenticity* (1975), and *Illustrated Introduction to Latin Epigraphy* (1983).

ANTHONY GRAFTON is Professor of History at Princeton University. He is the author of *Defenders of the Text* (1991) and *Joseph Scaliger* (1983–1993).

MICHAEL GREENHALGH is Professor of Art History at the Australian National University, Canberra. He is the author of *The Classical Tradition in Art* (1978) and *The Survival of Roman Antiquities in the Middle Ages* (1989).

ANN C. GUNTER is Associate Curator of Ancient Near Eastern Art at the Arthur M. Sackler Gallery, Smithsonian Institution. She is the author of *Gordion Final Reports, 3, The Bronze Age* (1991) and *Ancient Iranian Metalwork in the Arthur M. Sackler Gallery and the Freer Gallery of Art* (1992). She has also written articles on Near Eastern architecture and sculpture in *Iran, Revue des Études Anciennes,* and *Culture and History.*

ROBIN HÄGG is Professor of Classical Archaeology and Ancient History at Göteborg University. He has edited numerous books, including *Excavations in the Barbouna Area at Asine* (together with I. Hägg, 1973, 1978, 1980) and *Greek Sanctuaries: New Approaches* (together with N. Marinatos, 1993). He is also the author of articles on Minoan and Mycenaean archaeology, iconography, and religion; burial customs and sanctuaries of the Argolid in the Iron Age; and Protogeometric and Geometric pottery.

JEFFERSON C. HARRISON is an art historian specializing in the works of Maerten van Heemskerck.

KIM J. HARTSWICK is Associate Professor of Art History at The George Washington University. He is the author of articles on Greek and Roman sculpture published in the *American Journal of Archaeology, Jahrbüch des Deutschen Archäologischen Instituts*, and *Revue Archéologique*.

PAMELA HEMPHILL is Professor Emeritus of Art History and Archaeology at West Chester University, West Chester, Pennsylvania. An archaeological surveyor who works in South Etruria, Italy, she has most recently published "The Romans and the San Giovenale Area," *Opuscula Romana* (1993).

A. TREVOR HODGE is Professor of Classics at Carleton University, Ottawa. He is the author of *Future Currents in Aqueduct Studies* (1991) and *Roman Aqueducts and Water Supply* (1992). He has published the articles "Barbegal: A Roman Factory" and "Siphons in Roman Aqueducts" in *Scientific American*, as well as many articles on the study of aqueducts in the *American Journal of Archaeology*.

MICHAEL HOFF is Assistant Professor in the Department of Art at the University of Nebraska. His central interest is Roman Athens, and he has published articles in *Hesperia, Museum Helveticum*, and *Archäologische Anzeiger*.

PETER HOLLIDAY is Associate Professor of Art History at California State University at San Bernardino. He is the editor of and a contributor to *Narrative and Event in Ancient Art* (1993). He is the author of "History, Time and Ritual on the Ara Pacis Augustae" published in *The Art Bulletin* as well as many other articles on Etruscan and Roman art in such journals as the *American Journal of Archaeology, Getty Museum Journal*, and *Etruscan Studies*.

ERNST HOMANN-WEDEKING is Professor Emeritus at the Universität München. He is the author of the books *Die Anfänge der Griechische Grossplastik* (1950) and *Archaic Greece* (1968). He has written articles on Greek, Roman and Etruscan archaeology in *Römische Mitteilungen* and *Athenische Mitteilungen*.

DEBORAH HOWARD is Fellow of St. John's College and Librarian of the Faculty of Architecture and History of Art at the University of Cambridge. She is the author of *The Architectural History of Venice* (1980, 1987), *Jacopo Sansovino: Architecture and Patronage in Renaissance Venice* (1975, 1987), and

The Architectural History of Scotland: Scottish Architecture from the Reformation to the Restoration 1560–1660 (forthcoming).

S. HOWARD is Senior Professor Emeritus at the University of California at Davis. His books include *Bartolomeo Cavaceppi: Eighteenth Century Restorer* (1958, 1982) and *Antiquity Restored: Essays on the After Life of the Antique* (1990). He has also written articles on the restoration of ancient sculptures for the *American Journal of Archaeology*, *The Art Bulletin*, and the *Journal of the Warburg and Courtauld Institutes*.

SERENA Q. HUTTON is a tutor and freelance lecturer in the History of Art through the Department of Adult Education at the University of Oxford. She has published an article on Gavin Hamilton, ''A Historical Painter'' in *The Burlington Magazine* as well as various exhibition reviews in *Artwork*.

AMILCARE A. IANNUCCI is a Professor in the Department of Italian Studies at the University of Toronto, and has also been a Visiting Professor at the Università per Stranieri in Siena, the University of Rome and the University of Venice. Professor Iannucci is the author of a book on Dante, *Forma ed evento nella Divina Commedia* (1984) and of numerous articles on various aspects of Medieval and Renaissance Italian literature, which have appeared in *Dante Studies, Forum Italicum, Medioevo Romanzo*, and other journals.

ROBERT E. JACKSON, an art historian with a special interest in American art, received the Master's degree at the University of North Carolina at Chapel Hill, with a thesis on ''The French Influence upon the Art of Winslow Homer, 1836–1881'' (1978).

SIMON KEAY is Senior Lecturer in Archaeology at the University of Southampton. He is the author of *Roman Spain* (1988) and co-editor, with T.F.C. Blagg and R.F.J. Jones, of *Papers in Iberian Archaeology* (1984).

DALE KINNEY is Professor of the History of Art at Bryn Mawr College. She has recently published an article in the *American Journal of Archaeology* on the authenticity of a Late Antique ivory diptych (1994) and is the author of ''Mirabilia urbis Romae'' in the volume *The Classics in the Middle Ages* (1990).

JOHN L. KISSINGER is Assistant Reference Librarian of the Gould Memorial Library at Brunswick College. He has a special interest in Greek and Roman ports and harbor installations.

DIANE E.E. KLEINER is Professor of the History of Art and Classics and Chair of the Department of Classics at Yale University. She is the author of *Roman Imperial Funerary Altars with Portraits* (1987) and *Roman Sculpture*

(1992). Recent articles include 'Social Status, Marriage, and Male Heirs in the Age of Augustus'' in the *North Carolina Museum of Art Bulletin* (1990) and ''Politics and Gender in the Pictorial Propaganda of Antony and Octavian'' in *Classical Views* (1992).

FRED S. KLEINER is Professor of Art History and Archaeology at Boston University and Editor-in-Chief of the *American Journal of Archaeology*. He is the author of *The Arch of Nero in Rome* (1985) and co-author of *Art through the Ages*, 10th ed. (1995). In addition, he has written articles on Greek and Roman art, architecture, and numismatics in leading European and American journals.

E. R. KNAUER is Consulting Scholar at the University Museum of the University of Pennsylvania, Mediterranean Section. She is the author of *Ein Skyphos des Triptolemosmalers* (1973) and *Die Carta Marina des Olaus Magnus von 1534, Ein Kartographisches Meisterwerk und seine Wirkung* (1981). She has published numerous articles on a wide range of subjects, including Greek vase painting, cartography, costume history, and objects from the cult of Isis.

ROBERT B. KOEHL is Associate Professor in the Department of Classical and Oriental Studies at Hunter College, State University of New York. He is the author of the forthcoming *Aegean Bronze Age Rhyta*, as well as articles on Mycenaean pottery, Minoan frescoes, and Minoan initiation rites, published in the *American Journal of Archaeology* and the *Journal of Hellenic Studies*.

GERHARD M. KOEPPEL is Professor of Classical Archaeology at the University of North Carolina at Chapel Hill. Professor Koeppel is the author of a series of articles on Roman historical reliefs of the Imperial period appearing in *Bonner Jahrbücher*. He has also published articles on the Roman pontifical college as shown on the Ara Pacis (in *Archaeological News*), on reliefs from the Arch of Claudius in Rome and a military itinerarium on the Column of Trajan (both in *Römische Mitteilungen*).

E. C. KOPFF is Associate Professor of Classics at the University of Colorado at Boulder. He is the editor of *The Seaborne Commerce of Ancient Rome: Studies in Archaeology and History* (1980), and of the Teubner text of the *Bacchae* of Euripides.

LAETITIA LA FOLLETTE is Associate Professor of Art History at the University of Massachusetts at Amherst. She is the author of a monograph on *The Baths of Trajan Decius on the Aventine* (1994). She has also published ''A Contribution of A. Palladio to the Study of Roman Thermae'' in the *Journal of the American Society of Architectural Historians* (1993) and ''The Costume of the Roman Bride'' in *The World of Roman Costume* (1994).

VICTOR LANGE is Professor Emeritus of German Literature at Princeton University. He is the author of numerous articles on Goethe and his age in various journals, both American and German.

STEPHEN C. LAW is Chair of the Department of Humanities at Central State University, Edmond, Oklahoma. He received the doctorate in Humanities from Florida State University with a dissertation on "In risu veritas: The Dialectics of the Comic Spirit" (1985).

PHYLLIS WILLIAMS LEHMANN is William R. Kenan, Jr. Emerita Professor of Art at Smith College. She is the author of *Roman Wall Paintings from Boscoreale in the Metropolitan Museum of Art* (1953) and *Samothrace, 3, The Hieron* (1969). Professor Lehmann has published many articles on ancient and Renaissance art in *The Art Bulletin*, the *American Journal of Archaeology*, and the *Journal of Architectural Historians*.

ANNE J. LYONS received the Master's degree in Classical Archaeology from Florida State University, with a thesis on "Ring Dance Compositions: A Diachronic Study of the Iconography and Find Spots of Ring Dance Compositions in Crete, Cyprus and Mainland Greece from the 18th to the 6th centuries B.C."

WILLIAM L. MacDONALD, formerly of Yale University and Smith College, is the author of *Architecture of the Roman Empire* (1982, 1986) and *Hadrian's Villa and Its Legacy* (with John Pinto, 1995). He has also written many articles on the history of architecture published in *Studies in the History of Art, Archaeology, Perspecta*, and others.

ARTHUR MacGREGOR is Assistant Keeper of the Ashmolean Museum, Oxford. He is the author of *Tradescant's Rarities* (1983), *The Origins of Museums* (1985), *The Late King's Goods* (1989), and *Sir Hans Sloane* (1994). He has published a number of articles on aspects of the history of collecting.

CHARLES RANDALL MACK is Professor of Art History and William J. Todd Professor of the Italian Renaissance at the University of South Carolina. He is the author of *Pienza: The Creation of a Renaissance City* and *Paper Pleasures: Five Centuries of Drawings and Watercolors* (1992). His publications include "Montaigne in Italy: Of Kidney Stones and Thermal Spas" in *Renaissance Papers* (1993) and "Rediscovered: A Painting of St. Mary Magdalene" in the *Southeastern College Art Conference Review* (1994).

NANNO MARINATOS has taught classics and archaeology at Oberlin College and the University of Colorado at Boulder. She is author and editor of a number of books on Minoan archaeology and religion, including *Art and Religion in Thera: Reconstructing a Bronze Age Society* (1984) and *Minoan Religion: Ritual*

Image and Symbol (1993). Much of her research is centered on the Minoan site of Akrotiri (Thera), discovered by her father, Spyridon Marinatos.

CAROL MATTUSCH is Professor of Classics at George Mason University. She is the author of *Bronzeworkers in the Athenian Agora* (1982), *Greek Bronze Statuary: From the Beginnings through the 5th Century B.C.* (1988) and the forthcoming work *Classical Bronze Statuary: The Limits of Style and Technique.* Her articles and reviews have appeared in the *American Journal of Archaeology, The Art Bulletin, Classical Review*, and elsewhere.

ANNA MARGUERITE McCANN is Archaeological Consultant at Woods Hole Oceanographic Institution. Dr. McCann is the author of *The Roman Port and Fishery of Cosa* (1987) and *Deep Water Archaeology* (1994). She has also written many articles on underwater archaeology for such publications as *National Geographic Magazine, Scientific American*, and the *Journal of Field Archaeology.*

ANDREW P. McCORMICK received the Ph.D. from Duke University in Renaissance History with a dissertation on "The Anatomy of Early Renaissance Propaganda: A Study of Goro Dati's Storia di Firenze" (1980). Parts of his dissertation have appeared in *Bibliothèque d'Humanisme et de Renaissance, Studi Medievali*, and other journals. He co-authored (with H. van Veen) *Tuscany and the Low Countries* (1985).

JOANN McDANIEL is a candidate for the Ph.D. in Classics at the University of North Carolina at Chapel Hill. Her areas of special interest are Roman architecture and topography, Augustan society and literature, and Latin epigraphy. She has been a researcher for *L'Année Philologique* since 1992. Her publications include "Signum, Simulacrum, Statua, Palladium?" in *Archaeological News.*

ELIZABETH McGRATH is Curator of the Photographic Collection at the Warburg Institute, University of London. Her book *Rubens: Subjects from History (Corpus Rubenianum)* is in press. She has also written many articles on Rubens and Renaissance iconography, appearing in the *Journal of the Warburg and Courtauld Institutes* and *The Burlington Magazine.*

ELIZABETH R. MEANEY received the Master's degree in Classical Archaeology from Florida State University, with a thesis on "Ancient Equine Breeds: Their Influences on the Development of Greek Horses" (1979).

J. MEJER is Reader of Classics at the University of Copenhagen. His books include *Diogenes Laertius and his Hellenistic Background* (1978) as well as three Danish works on Presocratic Philosophy and the history of Ancient Greek and Latin translations. Professor Mejer has also published many articles on ancient philosophy and the history of classical scholarship.

WILLIAM E. METCALF is Chief Curator and Curator of Roman and Byzantine Coins at the American Numismatic Society. Among his books are *The Cistophori of Hadrian* (1980) and *The Silver Coinage of Cappadocia, Vespasian-Commodus* (1995). He has authored numerous articles, mostly on Roman coinage, in *American Numismatic Society Museum Notes, Revue Suisse Numismatique* and other journals.

MARJON VAN DER MEULEN is an independent researcher in the field of art history. She is the author of *Petrus Paulus Rubens Antiquarius* (1975), *The Rembrandt Documents* (1979), and *Rubens After the Antique* (1994). Among her articles are "A Note on Rubens's Letter on Tripods" in *The Burlington Magazine* and "A Rubens Drawing Reattributed" in *Essays in Northern European Art.*

STELLA G. MILLER is Professor of Classical and Near Eastern Archaeology at Bryn Mawr College. Professor Miller is the author of *Two Groups of Thessalian Gold* (1979) and *The Tomb of Lyson and Kallikles* (1993). She has also written many articles published in various journals on Greek (particularly Macedonian) subjects, as well as excavation reports on the Athenian Agora, Corinth, Nemea, and Troy.

S. G. MILLER is Professor of Classics at the University of California at Berkeley. Among his books are *Arete: Greek Sports from Ancient Sources* (1991) and *Nemea, 1, Architectural Studies* (1992). He is also the author of the Nemea Excavation reports from 1975–1982 and 1988, as well as an article forthcoming in *Historia*, "Old Bouleuterion or Old Metroon?"

CHARLES MITCHELL is Professor Emeritus of Art History at Bryn Mawr College. He is the author (with Erna Mandowsky) of *Pirro Ligorio's Roman Antiquities* (1963) and co-editor (with Edward W. Bodnar) of *Cyriacus of Ancona's Journeys in the Propontis and the Northern Aegean, 1444–1445* (1976).

JOHN F. MOFFITT is Professor of Art History at New Mexico State University. Among his books are *Spanish Painting* (1973) and *Art Forgery: The Case of the Lady of Elche* (1995). In addition, he has written numerous articles on the history of Spanish art for journals in both Europe and the United States.

JENNIFER MONTAGU is an Honorary Fellow at the Warburg Institute, University of London. She is the author of *Alessandro Algardi* (1985) and *Roman Baroque Sculpture: The Industry of Art* (1989). Professor Montagu has also published articles on Roman Baroque sculpture and French seventeenth-century art and theory in *The Art Bulletin, The Burlington Magazine*, and elsewhere.

SARAH P. MORRIS is Professor of Classics at the University of California, Los Angeles. She is the author of *The Black and White Style* (1984) and *Daidalos and the Origins of Greek Art* (1992). Professor Morris has published articles on the miniature frescoes from Thera, Greek pottery, and early Greek art and the Near East in such journals as the *American Journal of Archaeology, Hesperia*, and *Arethusa*.

ANITA F. MOSKOWITZ is Professor of Art History at the State University of New York at Stony Brook. She has authored *The Sculpture of Andrea and Nino Pisano* (1986) and *Nicola Pisano's Arca di San Domenico and its Legacy* (1994). She has published articles on Italian Gothic and Renaissance sculpture in *The Art Bulletin, Gesta*, and *Antichità Viva*.

DEBRA L. MURPHY is Assistant Professor of Art History at the University of North Florida. She is the author of *Joseph Jeffers Dodge: An American Classicist* (1992).

C. NAUMER is a Humanities instructor at Florida A and M University, and a candidate for the Ph.D. at Florida State University. Her dissertation is in progress, on "The Theme of Antiquity Displayed within Nature in Renaissance and Baroque Painting."

ROBERT NEUMAN is Professor of Art History at Florida State University. He is the author of *Robert de Cotte and the Perfection of Architecture in Eighteenth-Century France* (1994). Professor Neuman has also published articles on Italian Baroque ceiling painting, French Baroque architecture, and French Rococo painting in *Studies in Iconography, Journal of the Society of Architectural Historians*, and *Gazette des Beaux-Arts*.

JONATHAN NELSON is Adjunct Professor of Art History at Syracuse University in Florence. He has published on Filippino Lippi and Agnolo Bronzino in *Rivista d'Arte, Gazette des Beaux-Arts*, and elsewhere.

ANN M. NICGORSKI, who teaches at Willamette University, holds a Ph.D. in art history from the University of North Carolina, Chapel Hill. Her dissertation was a study of the significance of the Herakles Knot in ancient art.

NAOMI NORMAN is Associate Professor of Classics at the University of Georgia at Athens. She has published widely on Roman North Africa, Greek architecture and cult, and excavations at Carthage. Professor Norman is editor of *Archaeological News* and is working on a book on the archaeology of Carthage.

JOHN OSBORNE is Professor of Medieval History in Art at the University of Victoria, and currently Director of the Medieval Studies program. He is the author of *Master Gregorius: The Marvels of Rome* (1987) and articles on the material culture of medieval Rome in *Gesta, Papers of the British School at Rome*, and *Zeitschrift für Kunstgeschichte.*

CLAIRE PACE is Lecturer in the History of Art at the University of Glasgow. She is the author of *Felibien's Life of Poussin* (1981) and of an article on Bellori's drawings after Roman paintings in *Papers of the British School at Rome.*

THOMAS G. PALAIMA is Dickson Centennial Professor of Classics and Director of the Program in Aegean Scripts and Prehistory at the University of Texas at Austin. He is the author of *The Scribes of Pylos* (1988) and the editor of *Aegean Seals, Sealings and Administration* (Aegaeum 5: 1991). In addition, he has authored numerous articles and edited four other books on Aegean scripts, sealing systems, Mycenaean kingship and society, and the history of Linear B scholarship.

ROBERT E.A. PALMER is Professor of Classical Studies at the University of Pennsylvania. Among Professor Palmer's books are *The King and the Comitium* (1969), *The Archaic Community of the Romans* (1970), *Roman Religion and Roman Empire* (1973), and *Studies in the Northern Campus Martius* (1990). He has published extensively in scholarly journals in both the United States and Europe.

S. L. PETRAKIS is Visiting Lecturer in the Department of Classics at the College of William and Mary. She is completing the Ph.D. at the University of Pennsylvania with a dissertation on ''Ayioryitika, a Prehistoric Settlement in Eastern Arcadia.'' Her research interests lie in the topography and prehistory of mainland Greece.

ANGELIKI PETROPOULOU is a Research Fellow at the National Hellenic Research Institute/Center for Greek and Roman Antiquity. She has pursued the study of ancient Greek religion and epigraphy publishing articles in the *American Journal of Philology, Talanta*, and *Greek, Roman and Byzantine Studies.*

ALEX POTTS is Senior Lecturer at Goldsmiths' College, London University. He is the author of *Flesh and the Ideal, Winckelmann and the Origins of Art History* (1994) as well as articles on eighteenth-century visual aesthetics, history, and sculpture in *Art History, Oxford Art Journal*, and elsewhere.

ANTONY RAUBITSCHEK is Professor Emeritus at Stanford University. He is the author of hundreds of articles and reviews in scholarly journals in both the United States and Europe on a wide range of subjects, including Greek epigraphy, social customs, and literature, and the Olympic Games.

EMELINE HILL RICHARDSON, Professor Emerita of Classical Archaeology at the University of North Carolina at Chapel Hill, is the author of *The Etruscans: Their Art and Civilization* (1964) and *Etruscan Votive Bronzes: Geometric, Orientalizing, Archaic* (1982). She has contributed numerous articles on Etruscan sculpture, bronze mirrors, and iconography to the *Memoirs of the American Academy in Rome*, *Archaeological News*, and other journals.

L. RICHARDSON, JR is James B. Duke Professor of Latin Emeritus at Duke University. He is the author of *Pompeii: An Architectural History* (1988) and *A New Topographical Dictionary of Ancient Rome* (1992).

DAVID RIDGWAY is Reader in Classics at Edinburgh University, and was Jerome Lecturer in Michigan and Rome in 1990–1991. He has edited the second English-language edition of M. Pallottino, *The Etruscans* (1975) and, with F. R. Serra Ridgway, *Italy before the Romans* (1979). He is the author of *The First Western Greeks* (1992) and with G. Buchner, *Pithekoussai I*, and has contributed articles and reviews on Etruscan, Western Greek, and Sardinian archaeology to *Archaeological Reports*, *Classical Review*, and *Studi Etruschi*.

FRANCESCA R. SERRA RIDGWAY is Honorary Fellow in the Department of Classics at Edinburgh University. With David Ridgway, she edited *Italy before the Romans* (1979) and the English-language edition of S. Steingräber, *Etruscan Painting* (1988). She is the author, jointly with L. Cavagnaro Vanoni, of *Vasi etruschi a figure rosse dagli scavi della Fondazione Lerici nella necropoli de Monterozzi a Tarquinia* (1989), and of articles on Etruscan archaeology in *Classical Review*, *Journal of Roman Archaeology*, and *Mélanges de l'Ecole Française de Rome*.

RONALD T. RIDLEY is Reader at the University of Melbourne, Australia. Among his books are *The Eagle and the Spade* (1992) and *Jessie Webb, a Memoir* (1994). He has also published many articles, mostly in European journals, on classical history, the history of historical writing, and the history of archaeology.

ELEANOR A. ROBBINS is a freelance art historian in London. She has published book reviews and articles on Anglo-Saxon archaeology and various other subjects in *Archaeological News*, *Scottish Slavonic Review*, and other journals.

CLARE ROBERTSON is Reader in the History of Art at the University of Reading. Professor Robertson is the author of *"Il Gran Cardinale": Alessandro*

Farnese, Patron of the Arts (1992) and *Veronese* (1992). She has also published articles on aspects of Renaissance iconography in *The Burlington Magazine* and the *Journal of the Warburg and Courtauld Institutes.*

MICHAEL L. ROBERTSON is Humanities Instructor at Johnson County Community College. He is the author of an article on Etruscan graffiti from Cetamura del Chianti in *Studi Etruschi.*

RONA ROISMAN is the author of "Francesco de Sangallo: a Rediscovered Early Donatellesque 'Magdalen' and Two Wills from 1574 and 1576" in *The Burlington Magazine* and "Francesco da Sangallo's Tomb of Leonardo Bonafede in the Certosa del Galluzzo" in *Rutgers Art Review.*

LYNN E. ROLLER is Associate Professor of Classics at the University of California, Davis, and the author of *Gordion Special Studies*, 1, *The Non-Verbal Graffiti, Dipinti, and Stamps* (1987). Among the articles Professor Roller has published are "Attis on Greek Votive Monuments" in *Hesperia* and "The Great Mother at Gordion" in *Journal of Hellenic Studies.*

BETSY ROSASCO is Associate Curator of The Art Museum, Princeton University. She is the author of *The Sculptures of the Chateau of Marly during the Reign of Louis XIV* (1966) and of numerous articles on French Baroque art and architecture in American and European journals.

PATRICIA A. ROSE is Associate Professor and Chairman of the Department of Art History at Florida State University. She is the author of *Wolf Huber Studies: Aspects of Renaissance Thought and Practice in Danube School Painting* (1977). Among the articles she has published are "The Iconography of the Raising of the Cross" in *Print Review* (Tribute to Wolfgang Stechow) and "Bears, Baldness and the Double Spirit: Identification of Donatello's Zuccone" in *The Art Bulletin.*

PATRICK ROWE is Associate Professor of Art History at Pensacola Junior College. He is the author of the chapter "The Fabric of Etruscan Mirrors: The Manufacturing Process, The Chemical Composition" in *A Guide to Etruscan Mirrors* (1982). Along with N. T. de Grummond, Rochelle Marrinan, and Glen H. Doran, Professor Rowe published the reports of the excavations at Cetamura del Chianti in *Etruscan Studies.*

INGRID ROWLAND is Assistant Professor of Art at the University of Chicago. She is the author of *The Correspondence of Agostino Chigi* ((1995). Professor Rowland has also published "Raphael, Angelo Colocci and the Genesis of the Architectural Orders" in *The Art Bulletin* and "The Patronage of Agostino Chigi" in *Renaissance Quarterly.*

RUTH RUBINSTEIN is Research Consultant for the Census of Antique Works of Art Known during the Renaissance at the Warburg Institute, University of London. With Phyllis Pray Bober, she is the author of *Renaissance Artists and Antique Sculpture: A Handbook of Sources* (1986) and with E. Casamassima, of *Antiquarian Drawings from Dosio's Roman Workshop* (1993). She has published articles on antiquities known in the fifteenth and sixteenth centuries in Italy in *The Burlington Magazine, Renaissance Studies*, and elsewhere.

PAMELA J. RUSSELL is the author of *Kalavasos-Ayios Dhimitrios, 2, Ceramics, Objects, Tombs, Special Studies* (1989) and *Ceramics and Society: Making and Marketing Ancient Greek Pottery* (1994). In addition, she has published articles on Roman and Cypriot pottery in *Hesperia* and the Report of the *Department of Antiquities, Cyprus*.

MICHELE R. SALZMAN is Associate Professor of Classics at Boston University. She is the author of *On Roman Time: The Codex-Calendar of 354 and the Rhythms of Urban Life in Late Antiquity* (1990) as well as the article ''The Representation of April and the Calendar of 354'' in the *American Journal of Archaeology*. She has published on Latin literature, Roman religion, and the Christianization of the Roman aristocracy in *Historia, Helios*, and other journals.

INGEBORG A. SCHWEIGER received the Master's degree in Classics from the University of Cincinnati.

JOSEPH W. SHAW is Professor in the Department of Fine Art at the University of Toronto. He is the author of *Minoan Architecture: Materials and Techniques* (1973) and editor of the series of publications on Kommos (1990). A specialist on Bronze Age Aegean architecture and archaeology, he is a frequent contributor to *Hesperia* and the *American Journal of Archaeology*.

PHOEBE S. SHEFTEL is a member of the staff of the Center for the Study of Architecture. She is the author of ''The Archaeological Institute of America, 1879–1979: A Centennial Review'' in the *American Journal of Archaeology*.

CHRISTOPHER G. SIMON is Visiting Assistant Professor at the University of California, Berkeley. He has written the article on ''Greek Art and Religion'' for Macmillan's *The Dictionary of Art* and ''The Archaeology of Cult in Geometric Greece: Ionian Altars, Temples and Dedications'' for *From Pasture to Polis: Art in the Age of Homer*.

JEFFREY S. SOLES is Head of the Department of Classical Studies at the University of North Carolina, Greensboro and co-director of the Mochlos Excavations. He is the author of *Prepalatial Cemeteries at Mochlos and Gournia*

(1992) as well as articles on the Gournia Palace and the excavations at Mochlos in the *American Journal of Archaeology* and *Hesperia*.

MARY ELLEN SOLES is Curator of Ancient Art at the North Carolina Museum of Art. She is the author of "Tradition and Innovation: A Statue of Aphrodite" in the *North Carolina Museum of Art Bulletin*.

CHERYL L. SOWDER is Assistant Professor of Art History at Jacksonville University. She is the author of the chapter "Etruscan Mythological Figures" in *A Guide to Etruscan Mirrors* (1982) and editor of *Alexander Brest Museum and Gallery, a Guide to the Collections* (1994). In addition, Professor Sowder has published "Utilitarian Pottery at Cetamura del Chianti" in *Archaeological News*.

JOANNE E. SOWELL is Associate Professor of Art History at the University of Nebraska at Omaha. She is the author of articles on Spanish Cistercian architecture in *Studies in Cistercian Art and Architecture*, and on the teaching of art history in *College Teaching* and *Art Education*.

PHILIP O. SPANN is Associate Professor in the Department of Languages and Literature at the University of Utah. He is the author of *Quintus Sertorius and the Legacy of Sulla* (1987) and contributed "Southeast Hispania" for the forthcoming *Atlas of the Greek and Roman World*. He has also published articles on the Late Roman Republic and on Roman Spain in *Classical Journal*, *Historia*, and *Hispania Antiqua*.

CHRISTINE SPERLING is Associate Professor in the Department of Art at Bloomsburg University. She was a Fellow at Villa I Tatti (the Harvard University Center for Renaissance Studies in Florence), 1989–1990. She has published "Donatello's Bronze *David* and the Demands of Medici Politics" in *The Burlington Magazine* (1992) and an article on Alberti in the *Journal of the Warburg and Courtauld Institutes*.

JEANINE STAGE is Principal at Avondale Elementary School in Birmingham, Alabama. With John James, et al., she is co-author of *A Guide to the Sacred Architecture of Medieval France* (1986). She contributed entries on Boblinger and Ensinger to the *Macmillan Encyclopedia of Architecture* (1982) and published an article on "Extant Etruscan Textiles" in *Studi e Materiali* (1991).

SHELLEY C. STONE III is Associate Professor of Art History at California State University, Bakersfield. He wrote the article "The Toga: From National to Ceremonial Garment" for *The World of Roman Costume* (1994). He is also the author of "Sextus Pompey, Octavian and Sicily" in the *American Journal of Ar-*

chaeology and "The Imperial Sculptural Group in the Metroon at Olympia" in *Athenische Mitteilungen.*

CHERYL SUMNER holds the Ph.D. in Art History from Florida State University; her dissertation (1989) was on "The Artistic Observation of the Copernican Universe (1543–1750)."

JOHN SVARLIEN is Assistant Professor of Classics at Transylvania University, Lexington, Kentucky. His verse translations from Ovid's *Amores* appear in *Latin Lyric and Elegiac Poetry* (eds. D. Rayor and W. Batstone, 1994). He is also the author of "Lucilianus Character" published in the *American Journal of Philology.*

J. S. TASSIE is Adjunct Professor of French at Carleton University, Ottawa. He is the author of a number of articles on French-Canadian language and literature and on eighteenth-century art history. He was also a contributor to the *Collins-Robert French Dictionary*, 2nd edition (1987).

ELIZABETH C. TEVIOTDALE is Assistant Curator of Manuscripts at The J. Paul Getty Museum. She has published articles in *Current Musicology*, *The British Library Journal, Imago musicae*, and *The Rutgers Art Review.*

DAVID L. THOMPSON is Associate Professor of Classics at Howard University. He is the author of *Mummy Portraits in the J. Paul Getty Museum* (1982) as well as various articles on Greek and Roman art and archaeology in the *American Journal of Archaeology, Archaeology, Archeologia Classica*, and *La Parola del Passato.*

DAVID A. TRAILL is Professor of Classics at the University of California, Davis. He is the author of *Myth, Scandal and History: The Heinrich Schliemann Controversy and a First Edition of the Mycenaean Diary* (1986) and of *Schliemann of Troy, Treasure and Deceit* (1995). Professor Traill has also published articles on H. Schliemann, Homer, Catullus, Horace, and Vergil in *Classical Philology*, the *Journal of Hellenic Studies*, and the *American Journal of Philology.*

PHILIP J. TRAINA recently earned the Master's degree in Classical Civilization from Florida State University. His interest lies in Rome under the Julio-Claudians.

J. B. TRAPP is former Director, now Honorary Fellow, at the Warburg Institute, University of London. He is the author of *Essays on the Renaissance and the Classical Tradition* (1990) and *Erasmus, Colet and More: The Early Tudor Humanists and Their Books* (1991). He has published numerous articles on English humanism and the history of archaeology during the Middle Ages and Renaissance.

MICHAEL VICKERS is Senior Assistant Keeper in the Department of Antiquities at the Ashmolean Museum. He is the author (with David Gill) of *Artful Crafts: Ancient Greek Silverware and Pottery* (1994), and articles on archaeology and art history in the *American Journal of Archaeology*, the *Journal of Hellenic Studies*, and *The Art Bulletin*.

JUDY WAGNER is Professor of Humanities and Composition at St. Johns River Community College.

SUSAN WALKER is Assistant Keeper in the Department of Greek and Roman Antiquities at the British Museum. She is the author of *Memorials to the Roman Dead* (1985), *Roman Art* (1991), and articles on Roman Greece in the *Journal of Roman Studies*, *Archäologischer Anzeiger*, and the *Annual of the British School of Athens*.

J. K. WASANO received the Master of Arts in Art History at Florida State University.

CATHERINE MORRIS WESTCOTT is Adjunct Associate Professor of Humanities at Jacksonville University. She is the author of the forthcoming book *The Believer's Art* and of articles on the works of Jean Delville and John Martins in the *Journal of the Fantastic in the Arts* and *Athanor*.

DAVID WHITEHOUSE is Director of The Corning Museum of Glass. He is the author of *Glass: A Pocket Dictionary* (1993) and *English Cameo Glass* (1994) as well as more than three hundred articles and reviews on Islamic and Medieval European archaeology in *Iran, Medieval Archaeology*, and other journals.

SHARON WICHMANN received the Master of Arts in Humanities from Florida State University. She is currently teaching English at the Deutsche Aussenhandles und Verkers Akademie, Bremen.

SHELLIE WILLIAMS is Curator of Education at the Gibbes Museum of Art in Charleston, South Carolina. She received the Master's degree in Art History at Florida State University with a thesis on the representation of the griffin in Etruscan art. She served as an archaeological illustrator for the excavations at Cetamura del Chianti.

JOHN WILTON-ELY is Professor Emeritus in the History of Art at the University of Hull. Among his books are *Piranesi as Architect and Designer* (1993) and *Piranesi: The Complete Etchings* (1994). Professor Wilton-Ely has also published "Piranesi and the role of archaeological illustration" in *Piranesi e La Cultura Antiquaria* (1983) as well as a number of related articles in *Apollo, The*

Burlington Magazine, and elsewhere. He is a Fellow of the Society of Antiquaries of London.

FIKRET K. YEGÜL is Professor of Classical Art and Architecture at the University of California, Santa Barbara. Among his books are *Gentlemen of Instinct and Breeding: Architecture at the American Academy in Rome* (1992) and *Baths and Bathing in Classical Antiquity* (1992). For the latter he was awarded the 1994 *Hitchcock Award* of the Society of Architectural Historians. Professor Yegül is the author of articles on Roman architecture and iconography in the *Journal of Roman Archaeology* and elsewhere.

TOBY YUEN has published articles on the influence of the Graeco-Roman minor arts on Renaissance artists in the *Journal of the Warburg and Courtauld Institutes*, *The Burlington Magazine*, and the *Gazette des Beaux-Arts*.